PC Networking Handbook

Ed Tittel

AP Professional

**Boston San Diego New York
London Sydney Tokyo Toronto**

Copyright © 1996 by Academic Press, Inc.

AP PROFESSIONAL
1300 Boylston St., Chestnut Hill, MA 02167

An Imprint of ACADEMIC PRESS, INC.
A Division of HARCOURT BRACE & COMPANY

United Kingdom Edition published by
ACADEMIC PRESS LIMITED
24–28 Oval Road, London NW1 7DX

Tittel, Ed.
    The PC networking handbook / Ed Tittel
            p. cm.
    Includes bibliographical references and index.
    ISBN 0-12-691398-6
    1. Computer networks. I. Title.
    TK5105.5.T62   1995
    004.6'16--dc20   95-20918
                                                            CIP

Printed in the United States of America
  95   96   97   98   99   CP   9   8   7   6   5   4   3   2   1

CONTENTS

About the Author

Ed Tittel is a 14-year computer industry veteran with an interesting background. A graduate of Princeton University and the University of Texas, Ed started his academic career with undergraduate and graduate degrees in anthropology. Realizing the need for gainful employment, he moved into computer science. Ed spent his first six years in the computer industry writing code, primarily for database-related systems and applications, at companies like Information Research Associates (now known as Scientific and Engineering Software, Inc.), Michael Leesley Consulting, and at Schlumberger's Austin Research Center.

In 1986, Ed switched from staring at a CRT to the softer side of the business and moved into management and marketing. From 1988 through 1994, he was employed in a variety of positions at Novell, initially at Excelan (acquired by Novell in June 1989). Ed's last "real job" was as director of technical marketing for Novell's Corporate Marketing group, where he oversaw technical content for corporate strategies, publications, trade shows, and developer conferences.

At present, Ed's working full-time as a freelance writer and consultant and as a member of the NetWorld + Interop Program Committee, specializing in networking industry topics, training, and issues. A principal of LANWrights, a networking-oriented writing and consulting organization,

Ed tries to keep his team of talented and wild-eyed writers and researchers busy, if not gainfully employed.

From 1987 through 1994, wrote 12 books, ranging from the best-selling *Stupid PC Tricks* and *Stupid Windows Tricks*, written with Bob LeVitus (Addison-Wesley, 1991 and 1992), to *NetWare for Dummies* (coauthored with Deni Connor, IDG Books, 1993), *The Trail Guide to CompuServe* (coauthored with Robert R. Wiggins for Addison-Wesley, 1994), and *Network Design Essentials, Electronic Mail Essentials,* and *Internet Access Essentials* (coauthored with Margaret Robbins, AP PROFESSIONAL, 1994). His most recent publications, in addition to this one, include *HTML for Dummies* (coauthored with Steve James, IDG Books 1995) and *Foundations of WWW Programming, with HTML and CGI* (coauthored with Mark Gaither, Sebastian Hassinger, and Mike Erwin for IDG Books, 1995).

Ed has also written extensively for the trade press, with over 150 articles for publications including *Byte, Infoworld, Iway, LAN Magazine, LAN Times, MACazine, MacWEEK, MAXIMIZE!, NetGuide, PC Magazine,* and *Windows-User* magazine. At present, Ed is a columnist for *MAXIMIZE!*, where he cowrites a regular column with Bob LeVitus that takes a whimsical look at Windows esoterica and problems.

Ed Tittel
CIS: 76376,606 or Internet: etittel@zilker.net
<URL: http://www.io.com/~mcintyre/lanwrghts/lanwrghts.html>

ACKNOWLEDGMENTS

I have an awful lot of people to thank for making this book possible and for contributing so substantially to its contents and direction. First and foremost, I must thank the group of dedicated, talented and persistent individuals who helped me research and write this book's many chapters and parts. These individuals include

- Dawn Rader is the managing editor at *NetWare Solutions* magazine, where she helps keep a close watch on the chaotic and intense activities involved in getting a magazine out the door every month. Somehow, she found the time to do that, get married, handle the copyedits for this manuscript, and research and write the initial drafts of the cabling chapters for this book. All I can say is "Great job! What a champ!"
- Mary Madden is a freelance writer. After a hectic and educational five years at Texaco Chemical and the Huntsman Corporation as a network administrator, Mary decided to make the jump into the freelance writing world early in 1995. I am extraordinarily grateful that she chose to work with me, and to bring her expertise and enthusiasm to bear on the many server-, management-, and protocol-related chapters that she researched and drafted. She is also a great

team player and helped mightily to keep morale up during some of the delays and difficulties we encountered during this project.

- Dave Smith is a man of many more talents than I have been able to figure out how to use. He backed me up as an editor and project manager on this book, as well as contributed substantially to the protocol chapters, proving himself a great hand at writing introductions on just about any topic. I can't say enough good things about his willingness to learn and his writing ability, so I'll stop with a giant: "Thanks, Dave!"

Close to the home front, I'd also like to thank Michael Stewart for pulling the Vendor Database together and handling the photography and artwork for so many of the graphics in this book. In the same vein, I'd like to continue my ongoing paean of thanks to Susan Price and her faithful sidekick Shelley for doing such a good job on pulling a big and ugly manuscript together. Finally, I'd like to thank the technical editor and long-time friend and colleague, Jim Huggans, for picking as many nits and issues as he could find, and generally improving the value and accuracy of the book.

There are also lots of folks at AP PROFESSIONAL who deserve thanks and mention. First and foremost, I'd like to thank my project editor, Jenifer Niles, for sticking with me when one delay seemed to lead inevitably to another. Although I have never had a "dark night of the soul" when writing a book to compare with this one, Jenifer stuck with me and helped this project see the light of day. Thanks also to Jacqui Young, for managing the many logistical details and minutiae of pulling a big book together.

Also, I'd also like to thank the many vendors and networking experts whose hard work and good advice made this book possible. If it wasn't for the work all these people had done before our team, we couldn't have marshaled the facts and figures you'll find in here. The many individuals and companies who provided us information, evaluations, references, and resources are just too numerous to mention by name, but I'd like to wish them all a fervent and well-meant "blanket thank-you" all the same.

Finally, I'd like to thank my family for putting up with me through the course of a difficult, time-consuming, expensive, and all-absorbing project. I've learned that being a "virtual husband" and a "virtual stepfather" is nowhere near as much fun as the real thing. So, Suzy, Austin, Chelsea, and Dusty, please accept my thanks for sticking with me, and my apologies for the many days and nights I was unavailable because of this wonderful, wicked, giant, overwhelming beauty of a book!

NETWORK CABLING AND MEDIA

Just as railroads can't run without rails, networks can't work without media. Be it a piece of wire, a length of light-conducting fiber, a beam of light, or some kind of broadcast spectrum, a network just can't do its thing without a medium to support its signaling and operation.

Here in Part I, you'll learn about the various types of networking media in regular use, beginning with several of the most common wire-based networking media. Then, we'll move on to investigate the marvelous properties of light-conducting fiber, as we investigate fiber-optic networking. After that, we'll take a page out of the phone company's book and show how affordable, convenient and usable twisted-pair wiring can be for networking as well as for your telephone system.

From there, we proceed to a quick investigation of several of the options available for wireless networking in the workplace, both for internal use and for interconnecting multiple buildings or sites. Finally, Part I concludes with an examination of the common cable-testing and diagnostic equipment, followed by a review of the most widely used networking topologies (which, after all, represent ways of connecting the networking media we're looking at here).

The purpose of this part of the book is to lay the foundation for what comes next. Because a working connection is fundamental to a network that's working, you may end up spending far more time mucking around with cables or media-related equipment than you might believe possible. In this part of the book, we want to give you the tools to understand what you're dealing with and where to look for more information.

NETWORK CABLING AND MEDIA TYPES

CABLING CONSIDERATIONS

When it comes to networking, one of the most important decisions to make is what type of media to use. This is more than an investment because no matter how expensive or advanced your network may be, if the cable doesn't work, the network won't work.

Not only is cabling what ties a network together, it is also one of the main sources for networking problems. A properly laid-out cabling system helps to ensure network integrity and keeps you up and running. A poorly planned and designed cabling system can bring it all down. This chapter describes the types of network cable and briefly explains some of the buzzwords associated with cabling. The following chapters go into greater detail on each of the various cable types and their respective pros and cons.

Decisions, Decisions

Smaller networks may seem to have little need for investigation when it comes to cabling. All it takes is a few cables attached to the PCs, and presto, there's your network! Unfortunately, it's not that simple. Keep in mind that as your business grows so does your network. Therefore, an inadequate cabling system implemented in the beginning will not only cause problems, it will cost you more in the long run. It is much easier to pull extra cables during initial installation than it is to go back and pull more cable later.

And, although the best types of cable cost more, it is an investment that you are making in the future success of your network and therefore often worthwhile.

There are many different types of cable to choose from. In this book, we investigate coaxial, fiber-optic, shielded twisted-pair (STP), unshielded twisted-pair (UTP), and wireless media. The prices and characteristics for each vary, but they all have the same function—to connect your users to a network, making it possible for them to communicate with each other or share expensive devices that cost too much to have at each workstation.

Coaxial Cable

Coaxial cable, or coax as it is generally referred to, consists of a central copper conductor surrounded by a layer of insulation (generally plastic or foam), further surrounded by an outer conductor, which consists of a woven copper braid and a layer of outer insulation (see Figure 1.1). Because of the way it's designed, coax isn't as susceptible, but not immune, to radio frequency interference (RFI) or electromagnetic interference (EMI) as some of the other cable options. You probably recognize coax as the wire that connects your television to your VCR or to connect to cable television. The name *coaxial* comes from the fact that the center conductor and the shielding braid share the same axis.

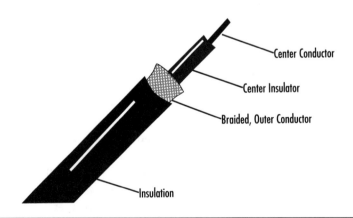

Center Conductor

Center Insulator

Braided, Outer Conductor

Insulation

Figure 1.1   *Inside a coaxial cable.*

Ethernet Coaxial Varieties

For Ethernet networks, coax can take one of two forms. The first, called *thickwire coax*, is easily identified by its bright yellow color. Thick coax is less susceptible to interference and can be run for distances up to 500 meters. Its most common use is for Ethernet network backbones. Its downfalls are that it requires a transceiver for each device attached to the cable, a device that sends and receives signals over the cable, and it is not very flexible, thus it is difficult to use in areas that have tight corners. Thick coax isn't used as frequently as its slimmer counterpart, appropriately called *thin coax* or *thinwire Ethernet*.

Tip:
Thin coax is less expensive than the thick stuff and easier to work with. It attaches directly to network interface cards (NICs) using a T-shaped British Naval Connector (BNC) connector. You can buy preassembled cables with the connectors already attached or you can construct them yourself. Ready-made cables are generally recommended because expensive special tools are required to attach the connectors, and it's easy for a novice to damage the cable if a connection is made improperly.

Ethernet Wiring Standards

Specs:
The organization responsible for network standards and rules is the Institute of Electrical and Electronics Engineers (IEEE). The IEEE has formulated several standards for coaxial cable for Ethernet networks. These standards take the form NBaseM, where N describes the maximum data rate for the network medium, *Base* indicates that the network uses baseband signaling, and M indicates the maximum number of meters per individual cable segment (not counting insertion losses).

Following these standards, thickwire Ethernet is called 10Base5, meaning that it supports maximum throughput of 10 megabits per second, Base to indicate Ethernet's baseband signaling technology, and 5 to indicate that the maximum cable length for a thickwire segment is approximately 500 meters.

In the same vein, for thinwire the standard is 10Base2, which means it uses the same speed and baseband signaling, with a maximum network segment length of approximately 200 meters (in this case, the true value is actually 185 meters, so be careful when measuring out thinwire segments).

Ethernet Topologies

Coaxial cable on an Ethernet network is generally laid out in a bus topology, which means that the network, in effect, functions as if it were composed of one piece of cable. Therefore, transmitted signals travel over all sections of the cable. In order to avoid signal collisions from multiple transmitters, Ethernet employs a carrier sense multiple access with collision detection (CSMA/CD) access method. This means that computers listen to the network before transmitting a signal, and if no other signal is already being transmitted, the computer sends the message. While sending, the computer continues to listen to the signals on the network to make sure that the signal was successfully transmitted (Ethernet network architecture is explained in greater detail in Chapter 9).

Baseband vs. Broadband Signaling

Transmissions over coaxial cable are classified as either baseband or broadband signaling. Networks employing the baseband method transfer data over one frequency using the entire bandwidth of the cable. Because the entire bandwidth is used, only one data signal can be on the network at any time. In order to make up for this use of bandwidth, data is sent in short bursts.

Using the baseband method, multiple devices on the network can share the network, but only one device can transmit signals at a time. Therefore, each node must wait its turn to use the communications channel. Due to the single channel limitation, complex transmissions such as video, voice, and data are not efficient using baseband signaling. However, most networks are implemented with the primary concerns being a combination of transmission speed and cost. With these criteria in mind, baseband cable fits the bill. Also, baseband is significantly less expensive than broadband, and data can be transferred up to millions of bits per second.

Another advantage of baseband is that, as networks grow or change, connecting or disconnecting devices without disturbing network performance remains easy. This is an important aspect because networks have a tendency to change over time, as businesses and their computing needs change.

Broadband transmission uses a different method to send data across the network. Broadband local area networks (LANs) also use a single communications channel, but this channel is subdivided into several different frequency subchannels. Different devices on the network use different frequencies, so multiple streams of data can be transmitted across the network simultaneously without interference from one another.

Broadband's flexibility can be illustrated by using cable television (CATV) as an example. CATV offers multiple channels that are stacked onto the cable and available simultaneously on different frequencies; to access any channel you just "tune in" the proper frequency, and the desired information can then be displayed on your TV screen.

Broadband computer networks transmit signals across the media in the same manner. Broadband's advantages include its ability to transmit voice, data, and video over the same medium, no limitations on the size or number of users, and the ability to support multiple data signals simultaneously in individual channels, thereby eliminating the time that a workstation must wait to transmit data over the network.

Broadband's downfalls include its considerable expense and the great complexity of the equipment involved in splitting and shifting signal frequencies. If the network installation is a large one, signal amplifiers must to be installed to avoid signal losses. Finally, due to its complex layout, broadband networks are difficult to change after being built; because changes are difficult, detailed and painstaking advanced planning is both expensive and crucial.

What Kind of Coaxial Cable Should You Use for Your Network?

In general, both thick and thin coaxial cable types are viable solutions for your network for Ethernet. For ARCnet architectures, a relatively thin coaxial cable called *RG-62* is your only option. Thickwire's inflexibility and greater costs—for both the cable and the required transceivers—means it's usually deployed only for backbones or in areas where this cable's additional resistance to interference is required. In both cases, reliability and greater length are typically more important than matters of cost.

When selecting a medium for new networks, cost considerations, data transmission rates, and ease of installation all combine to make coax a worthy cabling option for your networking needs.

FIBER-OPTIC CABLE

Fiber-optic cable consists of two fibers, each of which carries light in opposite directions and terminates into two separate connectors (sometimes, although not often, each light-conducting fiber might be packaged as an individual cable). Each half is made of a center glass strand, or core, surrounded by a reflective cladding, a plastic coating, a layer of Kevlar, and an outer jacket for protection (see Figure 1.2 on page 9).

Some fiber-optic cables also contain wire or other materials for added protection. Fiber-optic cable is virtually immune to RFI and EMI and is used by numerous long-distance phone carriers because of its high bandwidth, low maintenance, and low error rates. Whereas coaxial cables transmit electrical signals over copper wire, fiber-optic cables use an injection laser diode (ILD) or light-emitting diode (LED) to transmit pulses of light over glass or plastic.

An LED emits light when a current is applied; it costs less, can handle varying temperatures, and has a longer operational life. An ILD works on laser principles in which a tightly focused beam of light of narrow bandwidth stimulated by quantum electronics traverses the fiber. ILDs are more efficient and have greater data transmission rates than LEDs.

For very long cable runs (we're talking miles/kilometers here, folks), optical repeaters may be used to capture and reamplify a signal so that it will be received at its destination at its full strength. Repeaters are usually necessary only for wide-area networks, like long-distance telecommunications links.

At the receiving end of a fiber-optic cable, a photodiode translates the pulses of light back into digital or analog signals. Due to its sensitive components, fiber optic cable is difficult to tap into. Therefore, in environments where network security is a major concern, fiber is the best cabling option.

Because of its immunity to RFI and EMI, fiber is the cable of choice in environments that have heavy machinery, strong electrical fields, or in networks that must use elevator shafts to go between floors. It is also capable

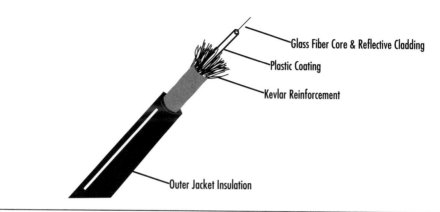

Glass Fiber Core & Reflective Cladding
Plastic Coating
Kevlar Reinforcement
Outer Jacket Insulation

Figure 1.2   *Inside fiber-optic cable.*

of transmitting data for several miles at a time, thus it is a good cable for linking multiple sites together.

Fiber's Not-so-Hidden Costs

If fiber-optic cable has so many advantages, why isn't its use more commonplace? For one, it is the most expensive of all the cable choices. The cable itself is expensive, as are the transceivers at each end of the cable, and because it is extremely difficult to install, well-trained and educated contractors should be used, thus the hourly costs of labor for installation is high.

Because it is made of glass, it can be damaged easily and doesn't lend itself to situations where there is heavy traffic or numerous tight corners, so fiber makes it more difficult to add more workstations after installation. This means that careful advance planning must include extra network extensions, adding further to the cost of the initial installation.

Caution:
Another one of fiber's downfalls derives from its installation requirements. Fiber-optic connectors must mount flush with the cable's ends at precise right angles; this requires a highly polished connection at each end of the cable. When negotiating with a cable installer for a

job that includes fiber installation, make sure to obtain and check references with prior fiber-optic customers. This is not a do-it-yourself technology, nor do we recommend paying an installer to become proficient at this kind of exacting and expensive task. Fortunately, recent developments have found plastic replacements for the glass in fiber-optic cables, so costs are decreasing.

Fiber's Many Talents

Fiber-optic cables can be used to connect copper-based LANs across sites or between wiring closets, where differences in ground potential can sometimes cause problems for electrical connections. Fiber can also be used in Ethernet and token-ring architectures. Because of its immunity to noise and grounding problems, it serves well in environments where copper cable cannot go because of electrical or atmospheric conditions.

Its most common use is in the Fiber Distributed Data Interface (FDDI) or equivalent high-speed network architectures. The IEEE has also defined standards for a variety of fiber networking media. The standards relevant for FDDI include a 100Mbps signaling variety, with cable runs up to 2 kilometers, and a copper distribution scheme, also with 100Mbps signaling, that supports cable run of up to 100 meters.

Other related IEEE specifications include a fiber-optic inter-repeater link (FOIRL) that stipulates how a pair of so-called Ethernet half repeaters can communicate over fiber-optic cable; this uses normal Ethernet 10Mbps signaling but allows the links between the half repeaters to be a maximum of 2 kilometers in length. The IEEE 10BaseF standards that describe normal Ethernet use of fiber include two variations:

1. 10BaseFL, which encompasses connections between LAN nodes and cable hubs, and
2. 10BaseFB, which describes backbone connections between cable hubs.

Both the 10BaseFL and the 10BaseFB standards allow cable runs of up to 2 kilometers. Unlike the link between half repeaters, however, these cables do count toward the "five-segment rule" for Ethernet, which stipulates no two nodes on any single Ethernet network may be separated by more than three intervening cable segments (not counting the segments to which the sender and receiver are attached—hence the term *five-segment*).

Fiber Has Flavors!

Fiber-optic cable can come in two flavors: multimode and singlemode (a.k.a. monomode). What differentiates these two varieties is the light source and the way light moves through the cable.

Monomode fiber carries signals faster and over longer distances—which may be measured in tens of miles—than multimode. Monomode is thinner, making it more difficult to handle and install. For the same reason, monomode requires special expertise and tools when it needs to be spliced.

Monomode fiber consists of a single core fiber and requires an ILD for signaling, which makes its use more expensive. If your needs include sending data over extremely long distances, monomode is the way to go. Because there is a single transmission path in monomode fiber, distortions such as different path lengths and transmission times, which exist in multimode transmissions, do not take place.

Multimode fiber, which consists of multiple core fibers twisted around each other, reflects and propagates rays of light at shallow angles. While some light rays in multimode fiber will be absorbed by the surrounding material, others will bounce at varying rates, causing the differing path lengths to result in variable transmission times for the same data (this is the problem that monomode, with its single path, avoids).

Nevertheless, multimode fiber is still quite useful in a number of circumstances where path length does not get too long. Multimode fiber-optic cables are commonly found in campus-wide or multiple-site networks where the maximum overall distance does not exceed 6 miles. Multimode cable comes in two sizes, 62.5 microns and 100 microns, with 62.5 microns being the most widely used of the two.

Caution: Installation ahead!
Please consider these few cautionary items before installing fiber-optic cabling on your network.

Don't Do It Yourself Unless You Absolutely Have To

First of all, if you intend to install this type of cable yourself, which is not recommended unless you have the time and expertise for such a project, you should definitely attend a fiber-optic training course to learn the specifics of fiber installation. If you are going to hire an outside contractor for the installation, be sure to check the references of that contractor to make sure that the installation was done properly, within the budget, and with little or no problems after installation was complete. If the contractor has no references to provide, find someone else who does.

The Job Isn't Done Until It Passes the Tests

It is also a good idea to state in any cable-installation contract that the job is not complete until it passes standards-based cable testing (covered in detail in Chapter 6). There is plenty of sensitive instrumentation that can tell you if a fiber-optic connection is working within its expected tolerances; don't consider the cable to be operational until those tests are completed satisfactorily.

Don't Look into the Light!

Never look into a live fiber-optic cable. Fiber-optics uses infrared light that is not visible to the human eye but can cause serious injury when it strikes the interior of the eye. The best way to avoid even a remote possibility of such injury is to make sure both ends of any cable are disconnected from their customary attachments before handling them. This may require coordination between two widely separated sites, but it is a precaution well worth taking.

All in all, fiber-optic technology offers some remarkable capabilities and adds tremendous reach to today's networks. It's an important factor in making possible the kinds of far-flung networks that we all take for granted.

Twisted-Pair Cable

Twisted-pair cable consists of at least two insulated copper wires wrapped around each other within a layer of insulation. In its unshielded form, twisted-pair cable is most commonly used for telephone wiring. Telephone wire can be used for networking, but only if it contains at least three pairs of wires, one for telephone connections, one for incoming network signals, and one for outgoing network signals.

Twisted-pair (TP) wiring is alluring because of its availability, and because it is more flexible and therefore easier to work with than other cabling types. Likewise, TP is attractive because of its ease of installation, and its lower costs when compared with other cabling types.

It All Comes Together at the Hub

Especially for networking, twisted-pair cables require wiring hubs—also called *wiring centers* or *concentrators*—for maintenance and regular retransmission of the signals that traverse a network. Twisting the wires around one another reduces, but does not eliminate, RFI and EMI. For TP, more twists per foot means less environmental interference.

Specs:
Twisted-pair cables come in a variety of sizes, based on conductor diameter and numbered by the American Wire Gauge (AWG) numbering system. In AWG notation, the higher the gauge, the smaller the diameter of the wire. The most common gauges for network use are 22 and 24.

Will That Be Shielded or Otherwise?

Twisted-pair cabling comes in two varieties, called *unshielded twisted-pair* (UTP) *cable* and *shielded twisted-pair* (STP) *cable*. UTP, as noted earlier, is commonly used for telephone wiring and is easily accessible as well as inexpensive. UTP consists of a center copper conductor in each set of pairs, surrounded by color-coded plastic insulation and an outer jacket (see Figure 1.3 on page 14).

Each member of a UTP pair is twisted together to reduce the impact of environmental noise. Otherwise, noise becomes part of the transmitted signal and reduces the medium's overall carrying capacity. Even though twisting reduces the impact of environmental noise, it does not completely eliminate it or the crosstalk between the individual wires. While it may seem appealing to use already-installed telephone wire for networking, you should (as with all other cable types) have the wires thoroughly tested to make sure that they are up to networking standards before considering this seriously as an option

The Not-so-Subtle Appeal of UTP

Nevertheless, UTP continues to grow in popularity. Because it can be used in ARCnet, Ethernet, and token-ring networks, UTP has nearly universal applicability. Also, UTP requires less training to install than fiber-optic or coaxial cables, and because of its prevalence in the telephone industry, it is easy to find reliable contractors..

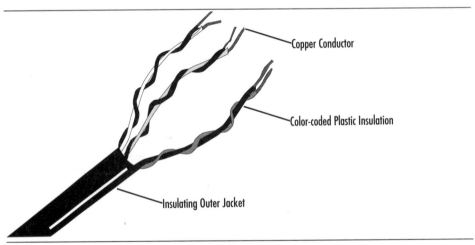

Copper Conductor

Color-coded Plastic Insulation

Insulating Outer Jacket

Figure 1.3   *Inside unshielded twisted-pair cable.*

UTP's costs per foot and cost of materials are lower than any other type of cable. It can be used in architectures with signaling speeds of 10 or 16 megabits per second, and new standards even allow UTP to transmit at 100 megabits per second (but these types of cable schemes call for careful installation and planning and normally won't permit existing phone wiring to be recycled).

Yet another UTP advantage is its size: it is a thinner cable so it doesn't take up as much room as some other cable types. Therefore, in existing buildings, UTP is much easier to pull through the walls. Also, adding more connections as the network grows is much easier.

UTP's downfalls appear somewhat benign but can have profound effects on your network. UTP supports only limited data transmission speeds (the 100Mbps capability for FDDI and related technologies is an exacting applications) and supports runs of limited distances (the 100 meter limitation for FDDI is matched by a nearly equivalent limit for token ring, with not much more for Ethernet, and just over double for ARCnet).

Shielded Twisted-Pair Cable

STP cables provide protection from interference from both their twists and an added layer of protective shielding. STP consists of at least two pairs of wire twisted around each other, each with a center copper conductor surrounded by color-coded plastic. Each pair is wrapped in foil shielding both

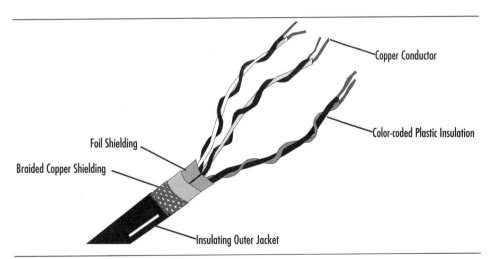

Figure 1.4   *Inside shielded twisted-pair.*

individually and together, then surrounded by a braided copper shielding and an outer layer of insulation (see Figure 1.4 on page 15).

STP's advantages include protection from outside noise and interference and support for higher data transmission speeds than UTP. These qualities also make STP a good choice for cable runs in elevator shafts and in environments where EMI and RFI are prevalent (but not overwhelming; for really noisy environments, coax or fiber will work better still). STP can also be run over longer distances than UTP.

STP's shortcomings include its greater expense, compared to UTP. Because of its thick shielding, UTP is not very flexible and therefore doesn't lend itself well to tight corners. Its greater size also takes up more room in wiring spaces.

Another of STP's disadvantage comes from its built-in shielding, which causes greater signal loss (attenuation). This has numerous implications. For one thing, equipment such as signal amplifiers or repeaters are often required to ensure that transmissions are received at proper signal strength. Proper grounding techniques are essential because, if the wires are not well grounded, the shield becomes an antenna for additional interference.

Despite these shortcomings, STP is commonly used for token-ring and Ethernet network architectures. It is also a good cable choice for network backbones that do not have to cross regions of especially high interference (e.g., across any sizable transformers).

IEEE TP Wiring Standards

Specs:
The IEEE standard for twisted-pair wiring is 10BaseT, which allows for a 10 megabit per second signaling speed and baseband signaling with a maximum distance of 100 meters. According to the 10BaseT standard, all workstations must be connected to a wiring hub that includes built-in diagnostics. This is attractive to network managers because, if the hub recognizes that a workstation is faulty, it can automatically bypass that workstation to avoid disrupting the network.

Twisted-pair cables are classified by categories numbered 1 through 5, where the best is Category 5:

- Category 1—any unrated UTP
- Category 2—non-data application cable, supports up to 1 MHz, used for voice applications
- Category 3—10BaseT cable, supports up to 16 MHz, used for 4Mbps token-ring and 2.5Mbps ARCnet networks
- Category 4—supports up to 20 MHz, used for 16Mbps token-ring networks
- Category 5—supports up to 100 MHz, used for 155Mbps ATM and FDDI on UTP networks.

Although Category 5 cable is the most expensive, it is the best choice because of its superior performance and because it leaves the most room to migrate to higher bandwidth technologies in the future. A staggering 60% of the cost of most new networks is cabling, so this logic may even work on your own management. Give it a try!

WIRELESS MEDIA

In environments where mobile computing is the norm or there is regular relocation of personnel, wireless media offer a solution when conventional networking schemes just can't do the job. Presently, wireless computing is a niche market, but that niche is growing.

Wireless network transmissions take the form of point-to-point or multipoint connections. Multipoint connections are used when it is difficult to install cable or when mobility is required. Point-to-point connections are generally used between buildings.

Recently, a number of developments in the communications market have changed the face of wireless computing. First on the list is the Federal Communications Commission's (FCC) round of auctions of frequencies for personal communications services (PCS). By the time these auctions end, the FCC will have sold 123 megahertz of the PCS spectrum that supports wireless voice and data applications.

Companies have already begun creating hardware and software that combine fax, cellular telephones, digital paging, and electronic mail (e-mail) for use in wireless networking. The various technologies for wireless network communications covered in this book include

- cellular technology
- radio transmission
- laser beams
- infrared signals
- microwave transmissions.

In the sections that follow, we'll examine each of them in turn.

Cellular Technology Is Wireless

The cellular telephone industry has grown very quickly since its introduction, and now, devices such as modems, portable computers, and fax machines are being developed for use in conjunction with cellular technology. Cellular systems transmit data across transceivers in multiple broadcast areas, or cells. As a person travels through the cells, the connection is maintained even though different transceivers are being used. The transmission rates and distances covered are less than with copper or fiber-based networks, but as the technology becomes more advanced, these will increase. Cellular networking products are currently available from Racotek, Inc., of Minneapolis.

Radio-Based Wireless Networking

Radio transmissions are currently capable of data transmission rates from 2 to 10Mbps. The range of most radio-based LANs is limited to a few hundred feet, but some point-to-point connections can extend over a mile. These radio frequencies don't penetrate thick masonry walls or floors, but work extremely well in environments like warehouses containing heavy machinery or between buildings in which there is no way to lay cable underground. Current radio frequency networking solutions are available from Xircom Inc. of Thousand Oaks, Calif., and Wi-LAN Inc. of Calgary, Alberta, Canada.

Lighting up for Wireless!

Laser beam technology works by passing modulated beams for point-to-point connections through open space. Laser beam technology is most commonly used for building-to-building connections for Ethernet networks. The distance limitation of laser beam technology currently stands at a kilometer or less. Currently, laser beam networking products are available from Photonics Corp. and Laser Communications, Inc.

Seeing Red for Wireless

Infrared signals are used in open spaces for point-to-point and multipoint connections. Infrared signals are limited to distances of up to several hundred feet. Ethernet and token-ring network architectures can use infrared signals for networking connections. Today, companies like InfraLAN Wireless communications and Jolt offer wireless infrared-based devices that are compatible with Ethernet, ARCnet, token ring, and FDDI.

Nuke the Net: Microwave Wireless

Microwave signals are sent through the air between microwave antennas, which are generally mounted on towers anywhere from 30 to 50 miles apart. The only requirement is that the antennas be in one another's lines of sight.

A major downfall of microwave transmissions is susceptibility to weather conditions. Heavy fog or rain can cause severe attenuation or distortion of signals which can last several minutes or even hours depending on atmospheric conditions. Microwave transmissions are generally used where long distances need to be traversed or in situations where it is difficult to lay cable (Chapter 5 covers wireless networking as well as vendor-specific wireless products).

CONCLUSION

Faced with all of these cable choices, it is obvious that a deeper investigation is necessary before a decision can be made on what type of cabling would be best suited to your networking needs. Each cable type offers its own unique advantages and disadvantages, and of course cost will play a role in the decision making as well. Whether you are installing the network yourself or intend to use a contractor to do the installation for you, it is important that you educate yourself, not only so that you are aware of your cabling options, but also that you have an idea of what to do if problems occur.

The chapters that follow go into greater detail on coaxial, fiber-optic, twisted-pair, and wireless networking, as well as cable testing and diagnostic equipment, cable topologies, and layouts. Whatever you decide, keep in mind that all of the options discussed here are viable solutions for your cabling needs.

COAXIAL CABLE

WELCOME TO THE WONDERFUL WORLD OF COAX CABLE

As described in Chapter 1, coaxial cable, or "coax," as it is generally called, is most commonly recognized as the cable that runs from the back of your television or VCR to connect to your friendly neighborhood cable television (CATV) provider. Network coax is different from the kind used for CATV, but all kinds of coax works more or less the same way.

Coaxial cable is made up of a center copper conductor surrounded by a layer of insulation, an outer conductor made of a woven copper braid, and a layer of outer insulation. The term *coaxial* is used because the center conductor and the shielding braid share the same common axis.

Coax is not as susceptible to radio frequency interference (RFI) or electromagnetic interference (EMI) like some other electrical cable types, but it is not immune to it either. In environments where interference is prevalent, such as manufacturing warehouses, elevators, or in ceiling spaces near fluorescent lighting, it is a good idea to further shield coax with a special metal pipe called an *electrical conduit*. Or, you can mix and match coax with another cable type that is immune to most forms of interference; such as fiber-optic cable (see Chapter 3 for the run-down on this type of cable). These techniques costs more, but they may save you from catastrophe later on.

Standards

Specs:
The Institute of Electrical and Electronics Engineers (IEEE) is the organization responsible for setting cabling standards. The Ethernet standards for coaxial cable are

- 10Base5. Where *10* indicates a frequency of 10 Mbps, *base* means that the cable employs baseband signaling, and the *5* represents a maximum cable length of 500 meters.
- 10Base2. Where again, *10* stands for 10 Mbps frequency, baseband signaling is used, with a maximum cable distance of 200 meters.

Other coaxial-based networking technologies include ARCnet, and a variety of broadband-based methods like Allen-Bradley's Net/One or the factory automation networking scheme defined by IEEE 802.4, sometimes called MAP/TOP.

Coax Varieties

Coax comes in thick and thin diameters and in baseband and broadband varieties (described further, later in this chapter). Each type of cable, and signaling approach, has its own uses and standards.

Thin coax is less expensive and is easier to work with and uses baseband signaling. Thick coax also uses baseband signaling but provides greater immunity to noise and can be run for longer distances. Both are most commonly used in Ethernet network architectures using a bus topology (see Chapter 7 for more information on topologies).

Depending on the type of data to be sent over the network, each cable type merits consideration. If, for example, you plan to use integrated voice and video transmissions, broadband cable typically offers higher bandwidth and will probably be more suitable for carrying the loads involved. If your primary concerns are low cost and only basic networking services are required, baseband cable would be ideal.

Baseband Coax

Baseband signaling employs a direct-current voltage to transmit signals that represent a one or a zero across the network via a single communications channel. Baseband uses a signal that is between positive 15 and negative 15 volts to distinguish between the ones and zeroes that make up binary data transmission.

Baseband signaling uses the entire cable bandwidth on a single channel and carries transmissions at very high speeds across the network. Only one data signal at a time can be sent because the entire bandwidth is used in transmission, therefore, frequency-division multiplexing (FDM) cannot be employed. Data packets are sent in short bursts to make up for this use of bandwidth. On a multinode network, all devices can use the cable, but only one device can transmit signals at a time; therefore, each node must wait its turn to transmit its signals. Integrated transmissions such as video and voice are not possible over baseband cable due to the single channel limitation.

The maximum distance of a baseband network is limited by the distance that a transmission signal can travel before becoming too weak to distinguish between the voltages signifying ones and zeroes. This signal loss is called *attenuation*. Additional devices, such as repeaters, can be attached to individual network segments to amplify the signals to their original strengths to compensate for attenuation and permit longer cable runs.

The lower the data rate, the longer the cable can be, because lower data rates permit individual signal pulses to last longer and they can be received without much signal loss. The higher the transmission rate, the shorter the distances the signal can travel before becoming unusably weak. Depending on the network, baseband coaxial cable can manage data rates of 10 to 80 megabits per second (Mbps). Although baseband coax is unable to send integrated signals, this may not be a major concern if transmission speeds and cost are the primary criteria for cable selection.

Broadband Coax

Broadband also uses a single communications channel, but that channel is subdivided into several different frequencies for data transmission using the FDM method. Because each device on the network uses a different frequency, data may be simultaneously transmitted across the network without interference from other channels. This is technique similar to that used by cable television. Broadband networks can use a single cable with bidirectional amplifiers or a dual-broadband cable system.

In a single-cable broadband network, the cable is split by frequency so that data can be transmitted in two directions (SeeFigure 2.1 on page 24). The head end is a broadcasting and translating device that serves as a central point for receiving the signals; the data is then retransmitted across the network.

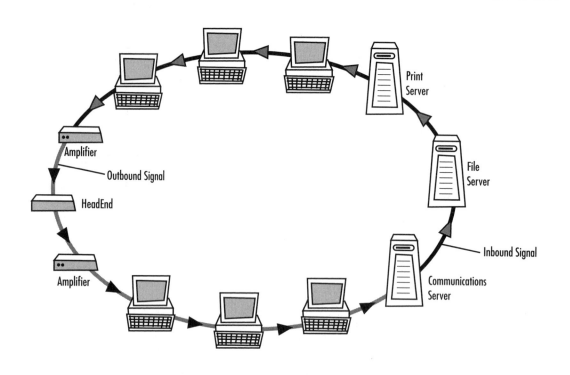

Figure 2.1   *A single broadband network splits the cable by frequency for bidirectional transmission.*

Dual-broadband networks use one cable for all transmissions toward the head end and a separate cable for transmissions in the opposite direction (see Figure 2.2 on page 25). Because broadband signals must be broadcast, amplifiers are needed to prevent signal attenuation. The complexity of multiple channels, which require a tuner to permit each attached node to send and receive on a single frequency and the need for head-end and amplifier units, add significantly to the cost of broadband networking.

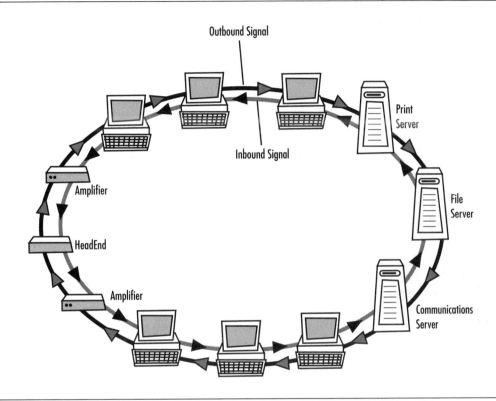

Figure 2.2   *A dual-broadband LAN uses two cables for bidirectional transmission.*

Broadband coax's advantages include the ability to transmit voice, data, and video, as well as other types of integrated signals. There are no limitations to the size or number of users, and multiple data signals can be transmitted simultaneously, thus eliminating the time that a workstation must wait to send data. However, broadband coax is more expensive to install than baseband cable and there is great complexity to the equipment involved in splitting and shifting the signal frequencies. Twice as much cable must be used in dual-broadband networks, and due to the way signals are transmitted, amplifiers must also be used, adding even more to the overall installation costs.

Thick Coax

Thick coaxial cable, or thickwire Ethernet, is roughly $\frac{1}{2}$ inch in diameter and generally coated with a bright yellow outer jacket. It is difficult to work with because of its thickness, but provides a reliable link for Ethernet networks. It is not used very often anymore, except for Ethernet backbones.

Thick coaxial cable is less susceptible to interference, therefore, it is commonly used in "noisy" areas. It can also be run for longer distances (up to 485 meters). It is more expensive to lay out a network using thick coax because the cable itself is expensive and a device called a *transceiver* (short for transmitter/receiver) is required for each network node.

We don't recommend that you install thick coax yourself. You are better off finding a qualified installer to do the job, because once the network is up, it is difficult to go back and make changes to the cable plant. Also, if you install the cable yourself and problems do occur, you have no one to blame but yourself. If you do end up having cable problems, you will generally have to find a contractor to fix the problems anyway.

Make sure the installer you choose uses thick coax that meets IEEE specifications. It should also pass standard cable testing and be a plenum grade cable since it will probably be run in the ceiling. Plenum grade cables are manufactured using fire-resistant, low-smoke materials to decrease the amount of poisonous fumes in the event of a fire.

Thin Coax

Thin coax is about $\frac{1}{5}$ of an inch in diameter, which makes it much easier to work with than thick coax. It is less resistant to EMI and RFI interference, although not as susceptible as unshielded twisted-pair. Although a single segment of thin coax is more limited in distance (to approximately 185 meters), it can be run for longer distances by using repeaters between cable segments. At the end of thin coax cable segments, terminators are required to prevent signal reflections from the cable ends (which would otherwise bounce back and continue traveling over the medium) from interfering with normal transmissions.

Thin coax is used in Ethernet networks. The IEEE specifications for thin coax were originally based on a bus architecture, but now, multiport repeaters that act like wiring hubs can be used to set up thin coax LANs in a star configuration (or a star of buses, at any rate).

Characteristics

The many varieties of coaxial cable share the same basic characteristics. One similarity is the layout of the coaxial cable, where the inner and outer conductors are centered around a common axis. In all types of coaxial cable, the outer braided conductor makes up half of the electrical circuit as well as providing a shield for the inner conductor.

Both conductors in a coaxial cable must make a solid connection at both ends of the cable for best results. Often, poorly connected shields cause hard-to-spot problems on the network, so careful attention to electrical connections is imperative. Other shared qualities include relatively long maximum segment lengths and high transmission rates.

Some common negative characteristics for coax include poor bend-ratios (the maximum angle at which a cable may be bent without introducing potential breakage or signal losses), problems with connectors, and incompatibility between cable types. Coaxial cable used on one network might not be compatible with another due to different electrical grounding and impedance levels.

Nevertheless, coax is moderately priced for the advantages it provides, and the connectors, tools, and the cable itself are widely available from numerous sources. Thinwire Ethernet remains the cable of choice for small, do-it-yourself networks today, primarily because of its availability and ease of installation and use.

Coax Connections

Some kinds of coaxial cable attach directly to network interface cards using a T-shaped BNC connector. Other types of cable require special taps that must connect to external transceivers, requiring a tap in the main medium, and a second cable (called a *transceiver cable*) to run from the medium to the network interface.

For both types, you can buy preassembled cables with the connectors already attached, or you can construct them yourself. Ready-made cables are generally recommended because special tools are required to attach the connectors, and it's easy for a novice to damage the cable if a connection is made improperly.

A common problem with coaxial cable is poor BNC connections. Many less skilled contractors use twist-on connectors. These connectors are less reliable—if they're twisted on, they can also be twisted off fairly easily, causing a faulty connection.

When it comes to attaching connectors to coaxial cables, crimp-on connectors are the best way to go. Crimp-on connectors have their own problems, and special tools such as a cable stripper and a die-based crimping tool are needed for a good connection. It is important not to be fooled by less expensive crimping tools. You may think you are getting a better value, but they make unreliable connections, causing expensive problems down the road. A die-based crimping tool is best because it makes precise creases that fit perfectly into the connector, creating a solid mechanical and electrical connection. Whereas a good connection will last, a poor one can bring down the network and may leave you stumped as to the origin of the failure.

When installing thick coax, connections to workstations are made by using a vampire tap. Vampire taps got their name because they pierce the cable through to the center copper conductor with a metal "fang," or media access unit (MAU). A drop cable is connected to the workstation on one end and attached to the MAU in the ceiling. The maximum distance for the drop cable is 50 meters. This type of connection does necessitate bringing down the network, so once again, it is a good idea to schedule additions during off hours to avoid loss of productivity on the network.

Coax Limitations

As previously mentioned, coaxial cable is not immune to interference. In areas that have large electrical motors —like elevator shafts or manufacturing areas—a more interference-immune cable might be a better choice (for the ultimate in immunity, see Chapter 3 for coverage of fiber-optic cables).

Coax also requires precise grounding. Copper-based media is particularly susceptible to electrical surges that can damage network interface cards and cause signal distortion. Always be sure that your coax LAN is properly grounded.

Caution:
Because coaxial cables are thicker than other cable types, they are easily damaged if bent too far. In tight areas where a lot of twisting and turning is necessary, twisted-pair cable might be better choice. Many networks have been brought down because of poor coax connections,

which is the basis for our recommendation to use die-based crimping tools and the best crimp-on connectors you can afford.

Another coax limitation is cost. Although it is not as expensive as fiber-optic or wireless media, coax is more costly than twisted-pair cable. You'll want to do a thorough cost-benefit analysis between coax and twisted pair before making the coax decision. The only case where it's a hands-down winner is for a small (less than 5 node) network where all nodes are in close proximity; in this case, nothing beats thinwire Ethernet!

Costs

A coax installation is moderately priced when compared to the other types of network cable. It is not as expensive as a fiber-optic cable scheme, but it will be more expensive than a twisted-pair installation. Because of coax distance limitations, extra components like repeaters, transceivers, and media access units may be required, adding further to the overall installation costs.

All things considered, a thin coax installation is cost efficient if you have only 5 to 30 workstations. You are limited to 30 devices for every 185 m of cable, with no repeaters required. Thick coax is considerably more expensive and should be used only as a network backbone or as a site-specific solution for moderate to medium levels of interference.

Troubleshooting

The first issue to cover when troubleshooting a coax LAN is to avoid trouble in the first place. Never run coax through areas with high EMI and RFI. Interference causes signal distortion and is a major concern for coax installations. Also, be sure that your cables meet or exceed IEEE specifications. Make sure that plenum grade cables are used in ceiling areas. It is also a good idea to have your cable installer use a time domain reflectometer (TDR) to test the cables before installation begins, to definitively check cable lengths and transmission characteristics (Chapter 6 goes into more detail on cable testing).

Because coax has a low bend radius, be certain that the cables are not bent too far—this is a sure way to damage coax. Avoid tight corners and use cable hangers as opposed to allowing the cable to support its own weight. It's also a good idea to avoid basement floors because rats can nibble through the waterproof covering and short out the cable.

Thin coax standards allow for no drop cable from the T-connector to workstations on an Ethernet architecture, so attach the connector directly to the computer's NIC. Also, the IEEE length specifications must be strictly followed to avoid problems, so be sure to limit your thin coax runs to stay within specified maximum lengths. Also, be aware that each device attached to a coax cable segment imposes an insertion loss (which should be documented in the device's specifications); when calculating maximum lengths, reduce the theoretical maximum by the combined insertion loss for all devices to determine the actual maximum length for any particular segment.

Remember also that connectors are a known trouble spot for coax networks. If you have problems, checking connections and connectors is generally a good place to start. Let your users know that they should avoid moving cables unnecessarily because connectors can loosen during the process.

If your network is failing intermittently or regularly, ask yourself if any changes have been made to the network. If you have added or moved a workstation, installed a new NIC, or added a cable segment, go back to where these changes were made—most cabling problems are caused by the users themselves.

As an added precaution, it remains a good idea to hire an experienced cable contractor. Most cable problems are caused by poor installation. By using a licensed professional with good credentials (and references—always be sure to get and check those before hiring an installer), you can avoid many problems. Finally, if problems do occur, the contractor's on the hook, not you!

Terminating the Coax Discussion

In this chapter, you've learned about the many varieties of coaxial cable. You have read about the standards that apply to coax, which should be strictly followed. You've also covered the costs, connections, and limitations of coax and have some choice details on how to troubleshoot your coax installation. Coax is a good choice for a moderately priced network. If you follow the guidelines in this chapter, you should be well on your way to a successful coax network.

FIBER-OPTIC CABLE

3

THE POWER OF LIGHT

Of all the cable types available, fiber-optic provides the greatest immunity to interference of any kind. Single segments of fiber-optic cable can also be deployed over greater distances than any other cable. Because fiber-optic cable is difficult to tap, it is suitable for networks requiring high security. All these special features originate with the physics of light conduction, where light-conducting glass (or sometimes plastic) fibers transmit light from an emitter on the sending end of the cable to a photosensitive receiver on the receiving end of the cable. In this chapter, you'll explore the many applications for which fiber-optic cable is suited, as well as its pros and cons.

Fiber-Optic Varieties

Like other types of cable, fiber-optic comes in different varieties. Depending on the bandwidth requirements of your data and the distances a fiber-optic cable must span, you will use either singlemode (sometimes called *monomode*) or multimode cable. The light-conducting fibers in this type of cable may be either plastic or glass, but virtually all of the "serious" applications call for glass. This is the case primarily because the special glass formulations used in glass-based fiber-optic cables are thousands to millions of times more transparent (and, hence, light-conducting) than their plastic equivalents. All applications of plastic-based fiber-optic cable are for short runs, typically only over a few meters.

Multimode cables incorporate large fiber-optic cores with varying degrees of dispersion. Higher degrees of dispersion result in increased "smear" of the signals transmitted by the cable, as varying reflections take varying amounts of time to make it from the sending to receiving ends of the cable. The greater the dispersion, the more the signals "spread out" over time (which equals distance in most cables); what this means in English is that higher dispersion multimode cables are best suited for LAN applications, where cable segments seldom exceed 1 km in length. These are by far the most common type of fiber-optic cables in use. All plastic fiber-optic cables are multimode.

Singlemode cable uses a small core that can provide high bandwidths across long distances. Laser emitters are typically used to generate the light signals for singlemode fiber-optic cables, which can span distances of hundreds of km. Because of the signaling sources and the extreme amount of precision required for this type of cable (in manufacturing, finishing, and installation), singlemode cable is the most expensive and hardest to handle of the various types of fiber-optic cables available. It's commonly used for long-distance telecommunications and in environments where cable segments longer than 2–10 km are necessary.

Although the different types of fiber-optic cable use different signaling methods and may be composed of different substances, they all require two conductors to support two-way communications. Each of these two fibers carries pulses of light in opposite directions and terminates into two connectors (a sender and a receiver are necessary on each end of a fiber-optic connection). Sometimes each fiber is wrapped as an individual cable, although they are generally packaged together. Each half consists of a center light-conducting core (usually glass), where the core is surrounded by a reflective cladding, a plastic coating, a layer of Kevlar (the same material used in bullet-proof vests), and an outer jacket for protection.

Another characteristic shared by fiber-optic cables is a low bend radius. Because data are transmitted over hair-thin conductors, it is important to use care in handling fiber-optic cable. Any bends in a fiber-optic cable can cause light to leak into the protective jacket, so even small bends can cause signal attenuation. This makes fiber-optic installations particularly tricky. Some cable breaks are immediately apparent, but sometimes they won't make themselves known for years and will cause intermittent, hard-to-diagnose problems along the way. Be sure to adhere to all specifications regarding bending, placement, and stress on any fiber-optic cable, both during and after installation.

Singlemode Fiber

Singlemode, also called *monomode fiber*, has a very wide bandwidth and carries signals for distances that can be measured in tens of miles (or kilometers) at greater speeds than multimode fiber. Light is transmitted in a single direct beam through a single precisely engineering glass fiber. Singlemode cable is smaller in diameter, which making it more difficult to install. Monomode is so thin, it requires time, expertise, and special tools to splice; and this is one factor that makes it so secure (another is that any tap will cause an attenuation of the signal, which can easily be detected with measurement equipment). Singlemode is also more expensive, so unless your distance requirements are extreme, multimode fiber may be a more affordable medium for your fiber-optic cabling needs.

Multimode Fiber

Data travels over multimode fiber differently than it does over a singlemode fiber. Light traverses the fiber so that the light waves bounce through the core. Because multiple propagation paths will manifest themselves during the journey from sender to receiver, this results in different path lengths for the same signal. Consequently the signal will arrive over a range of times equal to the difference between the shortest and longest paths traveled. Ultimately, this difference can become large enough to make the signal unintelligible; this proves to define the limit on the distance over which data can be correctly received on a multimode cable. In fact, most manufacturers will recommend a safe maximum distance that stays well inside this theoretical maximum distance, because most reception equipment won't be capable of reading a nearly attenuated signal any better than a completely attenuated one.

Light Sources

Tip:
Singlemode fiber requires an injection laser diode (ILD), a device that produces a superradiant beam of concentrated light of narrow bandwidth for signaling. Because ILD emissions are more intense than those created by the light-emitting diodes (LEDs) used for multimode fiber transmissions, there is also less signal loss on a singlemode fiber than on a multimode equivalent. (See Figure 3.1 on page 36.)

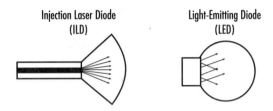

Figure 3.1 *Characteristics of ILDs and LEDs.*

ILDs also transmit 10 times more light energy into a fiber than do LEDs. Both ILDs and LEDs are expensive and contribute to fiber's overall high costs, but the correspondingly higher cost of ILDs compared to LEDs helps to explain singlemode's higher expense compared with multimode cables.

If you need to transmit data over long distances (over 10 km), singlemode is the medium of choice. Singlemode fiber offers a signal path that is both narrow and precisely defined enough to permit only a single transmission path between sender and receiver. This makes it immune to the distortion imposed by multimode's broader diameter, which permits multiple paths between sender and receiver. The only characteristics that ultimately limit singlemode fiber's maximum segment length are the strength of the emitter used and the optical impedance of the fiber itself.

Fiber Connections

At the receiving end of fiber-optic cable, an attached PIN or APD photodiode converts incoming light pulses back into electrical signals. PIN photodiodes are less expensive but also less sensitive than APDs. APD photodiodes are similar in appearance to PINs, but use stronger electrical fields. Both are basically photon counters that translate light pulses into electrical pulses. Many types of connectors for fiber-optic cable will connect to these sensors; here we'll cover those most commonly used:

- The ST connector
- The SC connector
- The MIC connector
- The SMA connector

ST Connectors. ST stands for *straight-tip*, and an ST connector is an optical fiber connector used to join single fibers together at interconnects or to connect them to optical devices. The ST connector is most commonly found in an Ethernet environment that uses fiber-optic cable as a network backbone. The core of the ST connector is a 2.5 mm sleeve glued to the fiber. For the best possible connection, the end of the fiber must be polished until it is free of scratches and is perfectly perpendicular to its length. Like the BNC connector used for coaxial cable, the ST connector is locked onto the jack by twisting it.

SC Connectors. SC stands for straight connection; hence, SC connectors are push-on connectors, which make them easier to install and require less space between them. The SC connector makes a strong connection and can be used in splices. It, too, requires polishing and precise alignment for best performance. It is a one piece connector, with two receptacles for sending and receiving fibers.

MIC Connectors. MIC stands for medium interface connector, and it is used as a connector for the Fiber Distributed Data Interface (FDDI) architecture. This type of connector is keyed to be connected in only one way, thereby preventing the receiving fiber from being plugged into the sending jack, or vice versa. One drawback to this type of connector, as well as the SC connector, is that if one connection is bad and the other is good, the installer must start over anyway because both connections must be removed and replaced, owing to the connector's design.

SMA Connectors. SMA stands for subminiature type A, a former microwave connector modified by Amphenol to become a widely used fiber-optic connector. The 905 version of the SMA uses a straight ferrule design, and the 906 uses a stepped ferrule with a plastic sleeve for more precise alignment. The SMA connector, like the ST connector, uses a single connector for each fiber strand. It is important to make sure that each fiber is plugged in to the correct jack.

Lengths

Fiber-optic cable, when used in a FDDI architecture, can be run for up to 100 km. The FDDI standard is explained in detail later in this chapter. Fiber-optic cable is most commonly used as a network backbone because it can be run for such great distances. Most campuswide networks employ fiber as the backbone of choice due to its immunity to electrical, magnetic, and radio-frequency interference and because it can traverse the kinds of distances typical in a campus environment.

Another typical use for fiber-optic cable is when a network link must stretch between buildings. Not only does fiber-optic cable provide higher data transmission rates over greater distances, it is also called for by the IEEE because it doesn't serve as conductor for differences in ground potential nor will it be affected if lightning should strike in the cable's vicinity.

Standards

The FDDI architecture calls for two rings of fiber-optic cable that transmit signals in opposite directions. It constructed for a limited degree of transmission redundancy, so that if a single segment is broken in the first ring, that ring's signal can be transmitted across the second ring.

The FDDI specification is based on a 100 Mbps signaling rate. Although *fiber* is the first word in FDDI, the National Standards Institute has extended FDDI to include shielded and unshielded twisted-pair and coaxial cable.

Specs:

FOIRL stands for Fiber Optic Interrepeater Link, the specification that describes how Ethernet repeaters communicate over fiber-optic cable. It is the standard that governs how fiber-optic cable can be used as the backbone for an Ethernet network.

The Ethernet 10BaseF standard can be broken down into two parts: 10Base-FB and 10BaseFL. The IEEE 802.3 specification describes these standards as a way to replace copper media with fiber-optic cable. The 10BaseFL gives rules on how connections should be made between network nodes and a cable hub. The 10BaseFB gives specifics on using fiber-optic cable as a backbone between cable hubs. Both standards allow cable lengths up to 2 km.

Costs

Currently, fiber-optic cable is one of the most expensive cabling options available. The cable itself is more expensive than copper media, and the components required for fiber-optic connections are also costly. Unless your networking needs call for high transfer rates over long distances or you need to run cable through areas with high electromagnetic interference or radio-frequency interference, another type of cable choice will probably be more cost efficient.

Advances in plastics technology may enable cable manufacturers to replace glass fibers in fiber-optic cable with plastic ones for a broader range of uses than is the case today (where plastic cables are typically limited to 5 m or less in length). This could drastically reduce the costs of fiber and make it less susceptible to bend damage since plastic is so much more flexible than glass.

Advantages

Using fiber-optic cable for your network has many advantages. The first advantage is immunity to EMI and RFI. It provides a safe link through noisy areas. This is important for companies who have offices in different buildings, or large manufacturing warehouses.

Fiber-optic cable also supports very high bandwidths. If your network requires a large amount of throughput, fiber-optic cable can carry the load. Fiber-optic installations, once completed, tested, and shown to be working, provide high reliability. If properly installed, a fiber-optic LAN should not have many problems.

Another of fiber optic's many advantages is security: If you are transmitting sensitive information, fiber offers the most secure medium. Because it uses light rather than electrical energy, fiber-optic produces no significant emissions that could be captured through passive monitoring technologies (unlike electrical media, which can be monitored without being tapped by sufficiently sensitive signal-detection equipment). Also, fiber-optic cable is difficult enough to tap that any attempts to do so would likely be discovered before any damage could occur. It's reliability and extensive ability to carry large loads for very long distances with little or no interference is what makes this medium so attractive.

Disadvantages

Some of the items that make fiber-optic cabling attractive create disadvantages as well. As mentioned earlier, fiber-optic cable is difficult to tap; this is fine if you don't plan for your network to grow. Since most networks do grow, we recommend that you invest in extra links from the outset.

Another disadvantage is fiber's susceptibility to breaks if not handled properly. Hiring trained fiber-optic installation professionals is not only a good idea, it's absolutely necessary. Fiber installations are never cheap, but you will get what you pay for.

Fiber-optic components and connections are also costly: Not only are the parts themselves expensive, they are also labor intensive, adding even more to installation costs. If you haven't figured it out by now, cost is the main drawback to fiber-optic networking. But many companies are willing to pay the price, because what they get in return for their high investment is a reliable, high-capacity network link. This is especially true for the telecommunications and broadcasting industries, which have invested heavily in fiber-optic infrastructure in the past 15 years to prepare for the oncoming onslaught of ubiquitous high-bandwidth communications and networking.

Troubleshooting Fiber-Optic Cable

Fiber-optic cable installations include indicator lights that can give you good information when troubleshooting your network. This is the best place to start. However, even the most educated network professionals still leave fiber-optic testing to the people who installed it or to other highly trained professionals. This is true not only because fiber-optic troubleshooting is a difficult task, but also because testing this medium requires specialized, expensive tools. Fiber-optic testing requires optical time-domain reflectometry. In English, this means that, because light is scattered through the fibers in the cable, many detailed and sensitive tests must be made to measure a fiber-optic cable's "health" and efficiency.

The best way to avoid fiber-optic problems is to make sure that every cable in the network meets IEEE and EIA/TIA standards before taking your fiber-optic network into production use. It is easier to find problem spots in a testing and compliance-checking phase during and immediately after installation, rather than when your daily business is at stake.

Remember that a fiber-optic LAN must be taken off-line to be investigated, maintained, or expanded. Therefore, the best way to avoid headaches is to make sure from the beginning that future plans are taken into consideration and that the cable segment is working properly and meets industry specifications. This is why final payment and acceptance of a fiber-optic cable installation should always be made contingent on demonstration that the network is in good working order and that it meets or exceeds all industry specifications for signal strength and throughput on the fiber-optic cables themselves.

Fiber's Finale

In this chapter, you're learned about many different aspects of fiber-optic cable for your network. You're now familiar with the differences between singlemode and multimode fiber and how each is best used. You're also acquainted with the standards that cover fiber-optic installations and the related maximum segment lengths and transmission requirements for this medium.

You should also understand the advantages and disadvantages involved in a fiber-optic installation. We hope that we have stressed adequately that fiber-optic cable installation is a difficult undertaking best left to the professional cable installers. To be blunt, it's definitely not a do-it-yourself job. We hope, however, that you have educated yourself enough to know that fiber-optic cable is a superior networking medium.

Twisted-Pair Cable

4

Twist and Shout

Twisted-pair (TP) cable is the most popular type of networking cable in use today. It is small in both diameter and cost, therefore, it is both practical and affordable. It is important to note that existing telephone wire is a form of twisted-pair cabling, but not all telephone wiring is capable of handling networking. The types of telephone cable to avoid in particular include so-called silver satin wiring, as well as quad and key system wiring.

Twisted-pair cable consists of one or more pairs of wires twisted around one another inside a protective jacket. This twisting provides protection against EMI and RFI. Each twist also helps to cancel out crosstalk and noise. Each set of wires in a bundle will have a different number of twists per foot to help reduce noise between individual pairs. Like other types of cabling discussed in this book, twisted-pair cable comes in different varieties, including both unshielded twisted-pair (UTP) and shielded twisted-pair (STP) cables.

Twisted-pair cabling can be used in Ethernet, ARCnet and token-ring environments. It is not uncommon to see fiber-optic or coaxial cable backbones with twisted-pair wiring to the workstations. It is necessary to use repeaters or hubs with twisted-pair cable. These hubs come in especially handy when a bad connection or faulty wire appears on the network: Hubs can bypass a faulty segment, allowing the rest of the network to continue working (where a true bus or ring would fail altogether).

Unshielded TP

Unshielded twisted-pair wiring is growing in popularity. In areas where there is little interference (EMI or RFI) and cost is an important criterion, UTP is a good choice. It can be used for ARCnet, Ethernet, and token-ring networks, and many such network interface cards (NICs) come preconfigured for UTP installation.

Typically, UTP installations require less specialized equipment and training than fiber-optic ones. Due to its ubiquitous use in the telephone industry, experienced TP installers are not hard to find. UTP is also thinner in diameter than other cable types, making it is easier to install and easier to add into an existing building.

UTP uses RJ-45 connectors, which are modular, eight-pin telephone-style connectors. It is important in twisted-pair installations to make sure that the appropriate wires make the proper connections. Otherwise, you'll end up with reversed pairs, crossed pairs, or split pairs. All of these types of connections can cause intermittent problems with UTP installations.

From a central wiring hub, UTP cable can run up to 100 m from the hub to the workstations. Many twisted-pair installations use a coaxial or fiber-optic backbone to interlink hubs, with UTP between individual hubs and the workstations.

The Ethernet standard for UTP is 10BaseT (and the most common form of UTP-based networking in use today). This standard allows for a 10 megabit per sec transmission speed using baseband signaling with a maximum distance of 100 m per cable segment.

TP Cable Classifications

Specs:
Twisted-pair cables are classified into five categories, numbered 1 through 5, where the best is Category 5. These classifications are as follows:

- Category 1—any unrated UTP
- Category 2—non-data application cable, supports up to 1 MHz, used for voice applications

- Category 3—10BaseT cable, supports up to 16 MHz, used for 4 Mbps token-ring and 2.5 Mbps ARCnet networks
- Category 4—supports up to 20 MHz, used for 16 Mbps token-ring networks
- Category 5—supports up to 100 MHz, used for 155 Mbps ATM and FDDI on UTP networks.

An essential point to consider is cabling costs. Category 5 cable is the most expensive, because of its superior performance and because it leaves room to move to higher bandwidth technologies in the future. Category 3 or 4 may be able to handle your networking present needs, but it is best to go ahead and install Category 5 if you can afford to. According to a study in 1994 by AT&T, the average costs associated with installing Category 5 cable are only 1% higher than Category 3, but Category 5 provides a 600 % performance advantage. With numbers like that, it's hard to disagree that Category 5 should be your TP cable of choice.

The obvious advantage to using UTP is its cost: UTP is the least expensive of all the cable options available. It has a smaller diameter than coaxial cable with a less stringent bend ratio. These characteristics make UTP much easier to install both for new installations and for extending existing cable plants. Another advantage to using UTP for network cabling is that it employs widely available standard modular connectors and tools. This makes it easier to add and remove devices when necessary.

One profound disadvantage to using UTP cable is that interference problems are more likely. While the twists in UTP cable help to protect it against interference, they do not prevent it. Another typical UTP problem is reliability, because there are so many different potential problems (e.g., crossed pairs) that can be hard to diagnose. Often, the only clue to network difficulties will be intermittent communications delays or short failures, both of which are notoriously difficult to track down and remedy.

UTP also offers lower bandwidth, so that many more demanding applications like networked video and audio cannot be run successfully over UTP. Even if you do use Category 5 cable, unless you also use Category 5 patch cords, wall plates, and other related equipment, you may not have real Category 5 network. It is important to ensure that all components of your cabling systems belong to the proper category, especially if you aspire to support more bandwidth-intensive technologies or applications over your network at some point in the future.

Shielded TP

For environments with more interference (EMI or RFI), shielded twisted-pair cables may be adequate. STP uses the same twisting methods to cancel out noise as UTP, but also employs an added exterior copper shield to further protect transmissions from interference. There are two types of STP: one type consists of pairs of wires twisted together with a braided copper shield, while the other type uses individual shielding for each pair within the wire, with an outer protective shield. Unfortunately, the protective shielding in STP can sometimes be a catch-22—it protects from interference, but it makes the cable more bulky and expensive, and can even sometimes act as an antenna (see later).

STP uses the same kinds of connectors as UTP. For STP, it is equally important to make sure that connections are properly established to avoid crossed, split, and reversed pairs. It is also important to make sure that STP is properly grounded. Unlike coaxial cabling, where the shield is part of the signal path, the shielding used in STP is grounded at both ends and not a part of the signal path. If the STP cable is not properly grounded, it can become like an antenna, causing unwanted signal distortion.

STP also falls under the 10BaseT wiring standard. Like UTP, it is limited to distances of 100 m or less from hub to workstation. The same categories used for UTP classification are also used to classify STP. Both UTP and STP can be used for 100 megabit per second transmission speeds, but Category 5 cables must be used to achieve these high rates.

The advantages of STP include protection from interference and support for higher transmission speeds than UTP. Because STP is better shielded from interference, STP is a good choice for cable runs in environments where EMI and RFI are prevalent (but not overwhelming; for really noisy environments, coax or fiber will work better). STP can also be run over longer distances than UTP.

STP costs more than UTP. Because of its thick shielding, STP is also more difficult to install than UTP. Because of its thickness, it doesn't bend as well around tight corners, and its greater diameter takes up more room in wiring spaces.

Another STP disadvantage comes from its built-in shielding, which causes greater signal loss (attenuation). Because of this, signal amplifiers or repeaters are required to ensure that transmissions are received at their acceptable signal strengths. This adds to the already higher costs of installation.

Troubleshooting TP

The first thing to look for when troubleshooting a twisted-pair network is for improper wiring. A good way to check for miswiring is by using a handheld cable tester. This type of tool can tell you exactly how a miswire occurred, making it easy to remedy. If no miswires are present, examine the hubs, routers, and switches on your network to help locate the problem. Many hubs come with built-in testing features that can help troubleshoot your network for potential power or connectivity problems.

Another way to locate a TP network fault is by using a cable diagram: Make sure that you have compiled a detailed map of all cable runs and related components during installation and keep it updated thereafter. If a problem affects only a few workstations, look in that area for loose connections or sharp bends in the cabling. Knowledge of your layout is a key ingredient to pinpointing the site for problems, and a key ingredient in fixing them.

A good TP troubleshooting tool is called a time domain reflectometer. This device can calculate cable lengths precisely, by sending a signal down the wire and calculating how long it takes for the signal to return. This can indicate when cable bends may have exceeded tolerances or when cable runs measure out longer or shorter than expected. A TDR also pinpoints the exact location (measure from the point where it is inserted onto the cable) where a bend or short is located.

When troubleshooting (or simply performing routine network maintenance) be certain that all RJ-45 connectors meet 10BaseT requirements. Because this is where physical connections are most often made and broken, one common trouble spot for TP networks occurs at the connector and the wall plate (Chapter 6 goes into greater detail on the tools and diagnostic equipment used to test network cabling).

Twisting the Net Away

In general, twisted-pair wiring is a good choice for networks that don't have to contend with significant interference. In this chapter, you learned about the similarities and differences between shielded and unshielded twisted-pair. Both of these cables fall under the 10BaseT wiring standard, which should be strictly adhered to in order to avoid cable problems.

You also covered the basics of troubleshooting twisted-pair wiring, along with some of the tools used in those procedures. Remember this is the bottom line for choosing the TP technology that's right for your networking needs: when compared to any other cable types, twisted-pair wiring is the least expensive, and UTP is the least expensive of all. For more details, the use of twisted-pair wiring in Ethernet and token-ring architectures will be discussed further in Chapters 9 and 10.

WIRELESS NETWORKING

5

WACKY FOR WIRELESS

Office computing is changing. It is no longer enough to communicate from just the desktop! Many of today's professionals travel extensively and need communication from various locations. Remote LAN access over telephone links has become a standard for home office workers and traveling executives. The LAN can be extended over these links into homes, remote offices, hotels, and conference rooms.

But traditional telephone links aren't always convenient or even possible. Traditionally wired LANs do not provide the mobility required by some corporate nomads or roving individuals. Therefore, an alternative technology for LAN access is beginning to grow in popularity; it is called wireless networking. Technologies like cellular technology, radio transmission, infrared signals, and microwave transmission offer alternatives solutions to conventional cable-based LAN connectivity. Although wireless networks are not as common as some of the other networking schemes, as the mobile work force grows, they too are growing in popularity.

Wireless networks are sometimes required in buildings where it is too difficult to lay traditional cabling. Wireless connections also come into play where building-to-building communications are required but it is impossible to connect them using copper-based or fiber-optic media. Whatever the circumstances, communication is sometimes necessary in situations where traditional networking schemes are too confining or impractical. If wireless transmission will do the trick, a number of options are available.

Wireless network transmissions can be either point-to-point or multipoint connections. Multipoint connections are used when it is difficult to install cable or when mobility is required. Point-to-point connections are used between buildings to replace or provide individual links.

Hardware and software products are already on the market that are used to adapt fax machines, cellular telephones, digital paging equipment, and electronic mail (e-mail) services for use in wireless networking. In this chapter, we'll do our best to explain these alternatives, and to indicate what kinds of uses they'll support.

Cellular Communications

The cellular telephone industry has grown quickly since its introduction. Devices like modems, portable computers, and fax machines are being developed for use in conjunction with cellular technology. Cellular networking systems operate over the same transmission facilities as cellular telephones.

Cellular phone transmissions are switched across transceivers in separate multiple broadcast areas known as cells. While traveling through these cells a mobile user's connection is maintained, even though different transceivers may be used along the way.

The standard adopted by the cellular industry for cellular communications is called Cellular Digital Packet Data (CDPD), a wireless data protocol standard that covers transmission of packets of data. CDPD technology leverages existing cellular services by using spare packets on cellular networks for data transfer. CDPD is the fastest wireless wide area networking technology on the market today and supports speeds up to 19.2 kbps.

The CDPD standard also incorporates the Transmission Control Protocol/Internet Protocol (TCP/IP). With TCP/IP support, mobile users can access Internet services and e-mail remotely.

The body responsible for the CDPD standard is the CDPD Forum, an industry association made up of companies that provide CDPD products and services. The CDPD Forum works to ensure that the products developed for cellular communication are compatible. The Forum's goals include creating interoperability among services, carriers, and mobile computing equipment.

To achieve interoperability within the cellular industry and to avoid users being locked into limited carrier options, an application portability standard has been adopted by CDPD developers. The application portability standard, developed by the Portable Computer Communications Association (PCCA), uses extensions layered on top of current LAN standards, such as the Network Driver Interface Standard (NDIS), and the Open Datalink Interface (ODI). By adding wireless extensions to current LAN standards, applications need no longer interface to the network using proprietary network drivers. Application portability allows users to use other networks if their network of choice lacks coverage in an area and allows different networks to communicate.

A hybrid wireless specification allowing CDPD users to communicate over circuit-switched cellular connections is under consideration by the CDPD Forum. Such a linkup increases the range of cellular data networks for mobile workers. Thus, when users travel outside areas with CDPD service, their connections automatically change to a circuit-switched network. Circuit-switched cellular data links are similar to modem connections and are well-suited for sending large amounts of data.

A major drawback to cellular networking is its cost. Sending data over CDPD can cost as much as 58 cents per kilobyte. Transmission fees, added to service and startup fees, can lead users to pay hundreds of dollars per month for cellular e-mail capability. Development of more efficient e-mail programs is expected to bring the cost of cellular data links into a more acceptable range (ideally, under $100 per month).

Radio Networking

Radio transmissions communicate over radio frequencies that are available for unlicensed use. This technology offers data transmission rates that range from 2 to 10 Mbps. The broadcast coverage for most radio-based LANs is limited to a few hundred feet, but some point-to-point connections can extend over a mile. These radio frequencies don't penetrate thick masonry walls or floors. They do, however, work extremely well in environments like warehouses that contain heavy machinery or between buildings if there is no way to connect them by cable.

Interference can be a problem with radio-based transmissions. This may be caused by transferring signals over radio bands that conflict with other devices also using these bands. This causes intermittent but regular interference. One method for limiting interference for such radio transmissions is called *frequency hopping*.

In this approach, a frequency band will be divided into several 1 megahertz (MHz) channels, called *hops*. Frequency hopping devices can perform well in the presence of interference because transmissions dwell on a specific hop for only a short period of time before moving on to another hop. As specified by a hopping sequence, each hop will be visited in a predefined order. When interference is present, it usually affects only a few hops. Hopping sequences are designed so that hops are several MHz apart. Interference may interrupt a transmission on one hop but will be unlikely to affect the next hop in the sequence.

Another alternative is called *spread-spectrum transmission*. Spread-spectrum systems operate in an area of bandwidth between 902 and 928 MHz. Spread spectrum products typically offer between 1.35 Mbps to 2 Mbps throughput. They spread part of their transmissions across multiple frequencies to avoid the possibility that interference on one particular frequency will stymie reception. This lets multiple devices use the same overall frequency ranges without interfering with one another and promises to become an important form of wireless communication for that reason.

Infrared Information

Infrared signals are used in open spaces for point-to-point and multipoint connection. Infrared light signals are limited to distances of up to several hundred feet. In an infrared LAN, workstation requires a receiver and transmitter to allow a direct line of sight between workstations (or their associated transceivers). Infrared transceivers are immune to interference from incidental radio-frequency (RF) sources. Ethernet and token-ring network architectures can use infrared signals for networking connections.

The Infrared Data Association's (IRDA) standard for infrared data communications allows data to be transmitted at speeds close to 115.2 Kbps using an infrared (IR) serial connector. Today, there are wireless infrared-based devices compatible with Ethernet, ARCnet, token ring, and FDDI network systems.

Point-to-point IR technology offers 10 Mbps throughput and a high level of security. These systems are typically deployed in a hub configuration and can be used in place of cable in a LAN or for a backbone when an intrabuilding link is required. Point-to-point IR can reach distances of up to 1,500 feet with a clear line-of-site and is able to maintain communication even during severe weather conditions.

A major complication to infrared transmission is that line-of-sight pairs must be in near-perfect alignment to maintain their link. Because of this, infrared wireless networking can be used effectively only in an open, unobstructed area. The line of sight limitation makes it impossible to connect different rooms or buildings. On the other hand, the fact that light cannot penetrate walls could be construed as a benefit for applications where security is important.

Microwave

Microwave signals are sent through the air between microwave antennas, which are generally mounted on towers anywhere from 30 to 50 miles apart. The only requirement is that the antennas be in one another's lines of sight. Typically, microwave systems are used in metropolitan areas or to cross rivers, mountains, and deserts where running cable is either impractical or too expensive (or both).

A major downfall of microwave transmissions is its susceptibility to weather conditions. Heavy fog or rain can cause severe attenuation or distortion of signals that can last several minutes or even hours, depending on atmospheric conditions. Microwave transmissions are generally used where long distances need to be traversed or in situations where it is difficult to lay cable. They are also quite expensive and therefore are deployed either by communication companies (like telephone companies or other private organizations that provide long-haul communication systems) or by large companies with multiple campus operations in a metropolitan area.

Conclusion

With wireless LAN technologies just emerging, it will be a matter of time before complete standards are developed and adopted. As with most emerging technologies, wireless LAN networking products are now among the most expensive options for networking. As these systems mature, however, prices will continue to fall and overall performance will increase.

With the mobile work force growing by leaps and bounds, you can assume that these types of network systems will be in increasing demand. For WAN implementations wireless technologies like microwave and even satellite-based communications (VSAT) have been in use for some time, but their complexity and expense makes them impractical for LAN use (which is why we've given them such short shrift in this book).

Top Vendors

InfraLAN Wireless Communications
Products: 10 Mbps Ethernet System;
16/4 and 4 Mbps Token Ring Systems
380 Massachusetts Avenue
Acton, MA 01720
Phone: (800) 266-1505 or (508) 266-1500; Fax: (508) 635-0806

Laser Communications, Inc.
Products: LACE Transceivers, Ethernet, T1, Token Ring,
V.35, and so forth.
PO Box 10066, 1848 Charter Lane, Suite F
Lancaster, PA 17605-0066
Phone: (717) 394-8634; Fax: (717) 396-9831

Proxim, Inc.
Products: RangeLAN 2 family
295 North Bernardo Avenue
Mountain View, CA 94043
Phone: (415) 960-1630; Fax: (415) 964-5181

RAM Mobile Data
Products: RAM Mobile Data family
RAM Mobile Data
10 Woodbridge Center Dr., Suite 950
Woodbridge, NJ 07095
Phone: (908) 602-5500.

Solectek Corporation
Products: AirLAN family
6370 Nancy Ridge Drive, Suite 109
San Diego, CA 92121-3212
Phone: (800) 437-1518; Fax: (619) 457-2681

RESOURCES: BIBLIOGRAPHY & STRATEGIES

Use the search terms *wireless LAN* on any of the Web search engines (Yahoo, Lycos, WWW) and you'll be able to locate most of the wireless companies and a fair number of on-line resources.

CABLE TESTING AND DIAGNOSTIC EQUIPMENT

6

CABLING CATASTROPHES

We've said it before: If your network cabling doesn't do its job you'll be faced with nagging problems that are hard to diagnose and difficult to isolate. You can avoid this headache by simply making sure that your network cabling meets Electronic Industries Association/Telecommunications Industries Association (EIA/TIA) requirements.

A multitude of technical service bulletins (TSBs) have been released by the EIA/TIA, defining proper measurements for testing cabling quality. Testing network cabling is only part of the network diagnosis, though; connectors, patch panels, hubs, and routers are all additional hardware that can have a severe impact on a network's performance and operation.

This chapter covers cable testers, protocol analyzers, and some software tools that help you avoid network problems and downtime by maintaining the physical integrity of the networks hardware and physical links. These tools can also help you isolate, locate, and repair problems if and when they do occur (which they will, from time to time) and are therefore doubly worth including in your LAN administrator's tool kit.

Specs:
Cabling standards address the physical layer in the ISO reference model. The EIA/TIA takes these standards a step further by detailing network cabling specifications. The standard for building wiring is the EIA/TIA 568. This specification establishes standards for:

- Pathways and spaces for cables
- Cable administration for LANs, and
- Physical makeup of network cabling.

All the different standards can be confusing, but they establish the requirements for safe and proper LAN operation. A savvy network administrator can keep the network up and running by making sure these standards are met.

Network Troubleshooting

It has been estimated that 70% of network downtime is caused by faulty cabling systems. For this reason, it is important to follow cabling guidelines strictly when installing your network. One of the most valuable tools to have in your possession is a handheld cable tester.

Cable testers are offered by Datacom Technologies, Unicom Electric, Inc., Fluke, and Microtest, and range from inexpensively simple tools to extravagantly complex ones. These analyzers measure cable integrity and performance, ensuring that your network cables meet Institute of Electrical and Electronics Engineers (IEEE) EIA/TIA standards.

Testing ... Testing ...

Cable testers measure the distance of a cable using time domain reflectometry (TDR), sending a pulse down a cable and timing how long its echo takes to return to the transmitter. This testing can isolate network faults caused by exceeding cable length specifications, as well as shorts or opens (cable breaks).

Both these testing types are important in identifying and isolating cable faults in a network system, and they assure that network punch-down blocks and cross-connect panels also meet standards. They can be invaluable for locating loose or broken cables, bad connections, and a host of other problems typical to cable-based networks.

What's NEXT?

Cable testing equipment also identifies NEXT faults in the network. Near-end crosstalk (NEXT) occurs when the transmitting pair radiates energy that is coupled into the receiving pair and mistakenly interpreted as a transmission signal. Crossed wire pairs are the most common cause of high levels of NEXT in twisted-pair networks. Other possible suspects are cables that are pulled too tightly or pairs that have become untwisted for whatever reason (usually cable stress or motion).

What Plugs Where?

Cable testers sometimes include wire map functions. A wire map can be particularly useful when troubleshooting a twisted-pair installation. This function verifies correct pin-to-pin connectivity. The tester points out reversed pairs, crossed pairs, and split pairs, each of which can cause sporadic network malfunction.

Could You Repeat That?

Attenuation is the decrease of signal strength as it travels down the cable, which is a major cause of problems in networking. Cable testing devices can measure attenuation, which is measured in decibels (dB). An 11.5 dB loss is allowed in the 10-Base-T specification. Anything more than that is bound to cause problems.

Tip:
A number of factors can cause signal attenuation above the allowable level: capacitive and inductive reactance can reduce signal strength and excessive cable length always lead to excessive attenuation. One solution to the attenuation problem is the use of repeaters, which are devices that reduce attenuation by increasing an incoming signals to their original amplitudes before sending further down a wire.

Be Wise—Analyze

Protocol analyzers plug into a network and capture the traffic traveling across the medium. Traffic can be filtered based on the protocols in operation at various layers in the network architecture. Analyzers may even come with a dedicated CPU, typically packaged as one or more special-purpose network interface cards in a portable PC of some kind.

With the right software, protocol analyzers can gather statistics on different types of traffic and identify malformed packets. This type of software is useful for decoding network activity at any of the OSI layers and for displaying the results on the screen for further analysis.

Analyzing network traffic can identify network access problems that may be either network or cable related. The percentage of network utilization, peak traffic loads, and collision rates can all be continually monitored onscreen, giving network administrators graphical information on LAN performance and behavior. Protocol analysis is a faster and far more elegant method for identifying faulty connections than performing a node-by-node survey by hand.

Technobabble: Electrical Elements

Impedance is the opposition to the flow of an alternating current in a circuit. Cables require specific impedances to match the electrical components in the NICs that use them. Distributed inductance, distributed capacitance, and resistance all contribute to the creation of impedance. Because impedance is measured in ohms, many confuse it with resistance, which is also measured in ohms. Resistance is a factor of impedance, but they are not the same thing. If you hire a consultant to troubleshoot your network, make sure he or she knows the difference.

The Softer Side of Network Management

Network administrators shouldn't have to spend all their time reacting to problems that pop up out on the network. As network technology advances, more and more software tools are available to network managers that have been designed for network monitoring, fault diagnosis, and error correction.

Tip:

Some of these products can give you a detailed map of the network as well as list all of the separate network components. It is important to monitor these readings to establish the kinds of readings that are normal for your network (this is called the *network baseline*, in technospeak). This baseline defines the starting point for any diagnosis of what's ailing your network. Network management products by vendors like NHC Communications and Quyen Systems can assist you in providing a baseline statistical network report that can become a valuable troubleshooting tool.

CCC (Choose Consultants Carefully)

If you plan on hiring an outside consultant, you must make sure that he or she can perform cable diagnostics that are up to par. The road to network hell is paved with apparently good analysis reports from bad consultants. On the other hand, a good consultant can be your earthly guide to networking bliss.

The best way to pick any contractor is by obtaining good references from someone whose abilities you know and whose opinions you trust. Even so, always check references. Be sure to ask if the work performed was satisfactorily, whether or not any network related problems have cropped up since the contractor worked on the system, and if the work was performed on time and within budget constraints.

Tip:
One way of assuring contractor reliability is through certification programs. The Registered Communications Distribution Designer (RCDD) program, overseen by the Building Industry Consulting Service International (BISCI), is one worth checking into. To achieve certification, the contractor must demonstrate a knowledge of materials and techniques for the proper design of communications cabling systems. Certification is no guarantee of competence, and lack of certification is even less informative. By asking for credentials, you'll tell your contractors implicitly that you understand how their industry works and what kinds of knowledge really counts.

SUMMARY

This chapter detailed some of the common pitfalls associated with network cabling. We touched on the tools and technology that can help assure cable quality. We also gave you some pointers on how to choose the right contractor for the job.

With all this in mind, keep an eye on those cables! Remember that most network downtime is related to cable failure. If that's not enough to make you look after your network cabling, just wait and see what happens when you don't.

TOP VENDORS

Network General Corporation
Products: Network Sniffer, Distributed Sniffer (protocol analyzers)
4200 Bohannon Street
Menlo Park, CA 94025
Phone: (415) 473-2000

Fluke Corporation
Products: Electronic and cable test equipment and tools
PO Box 9090
Everett, WA 95206
Phone: (800) 44F-LUKE; Fax: (206) 356-5116

Microtest, Incorporated
Products: Cable Testing equipment
4747 North 22nd Street
Phoenix, AZ 85016-4708
Phone: (800) 526-9675; Fax: (602) 952-6401

Novell, Incorporated
Products: LANalyzer for Windows (software protocol analyzer)
122 East 1700 South
Provo, UT 84606
Phone: (800) 453-1267; Fax: (810) 429-5500

Network Communications Corporation
Products: Network LANalyzer (hardware protocol analyzer)
10120 West 76th Street
Eden Prairie, MN 55344-9814
Phone: (612) 944-8559; Fax: (612) 944-9805

Resources:
Bibliography and Strategies

Use the search terms *protocol analyzer* or *cable tester* on any of the Web search engines (Yahoo, Lycos, WWWW, etc.) and you'll be able to locate some of the companies just mentioned, and several on-line resources as well.

Mark A. Miller, *LAN Protocol Handbook,* Redwood City, CA: M&T Publishing Company, 1990. A good overview of all the major networking protocols, along with tips and tricks for performing network troubleshooting and analysis.

CABLE LAYOUTS

TOPOLOGIES

A topology, simply put, is the design that you use to lay out your network cabling. There are three commonly used topologies—bus, ring, and star— where each name describes the physical arrangement of cabling used to create a particular network. Each topology can be used by itself, or different topologies can be used together, but there are certain affinities between network access methods—like Ethernet, ARCnet, token ring, FDDI, etc.— that you'll also discover as you read the sections that follow.

The Bus Topology

The bus topology is the simplest network layout. It requires less cable than any other topology. Workstations are connected to each other in linear fashion along the network cable (see Figure 7.1 on page 66). The linear bus uses a single trunk cable with individual nodes connected to it, where connections are made to each workstation using a tap and a drop cable for some technologies or by inserting a T-shaped connector between two segments of cable to attach a workstation or other device for other technologies.

Traffic on a bus topology—usually referred to as a *bus* for brevity—is bidirectional. This means that any workstation on the network can communicate with any other workstation. It also means that when a workstation

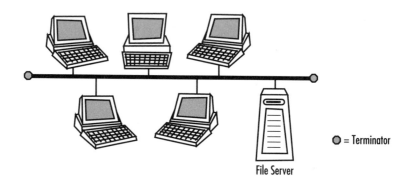

Figure 7.1   A bus topology.

transmits a signal, it is heard by all other workstations. That is why bus-based networks are frequently paired with broadcast-based access methods, like Ethernet. The common, shared medium characteristic of a bus means that all network traffic is available to every device on the network. By definition, a broadcast is a network message delivered to all devices, so every message on a bus is a broadcast message.

Bus topologies are often used in conjunction with the other topologies to create larger, more complex networks, or to combine multiple access methods into a single logical network. For example, it's not uncommon to find a bus used as a method of linking multiple rings or stars together, acting as what's called a *backbone* among multiple physical networks.

Caution:
The biggest disadvantage inherent in a bus topology is imposed by the shared nature of the network medium. Because the signals on the bus must be available to all devices equally, this creates a number of side-effects:

- The physics of transmission and reception over a physical medium requires a minimum distance between devices on the cable, to create a time delay long enough to support collision detection and to avoid signal reflections between adjacent transmitters.

- Because the bus is a shared medium, any break in the cable brings down the entire bus. An uninformed user could easily kill a bus-based network by improperly disconnecting his or her workstation, for instance. Likewise, any cable breaks or shorts will render the network inoperative.

- Because the timing of transmission is critical to detecting and recovering from collisions, the propagation delay imposed by the network medium (the time it takes for a signal to get from Point A to Point B) can never exceed the time it takes to send the smallest allowable network message over the medium. Otherwise, collisions could occur and not be detected. In English, this means that bus cables must be restricted in length to keep this kind of problem from happening—that's why 10Base2 and 10Base5 have maximum cable length restrictions right in their names!

Despite these potential gotchas, bus topologies remain quite popular, especially for smaller networks. That's because the disadvantages are often outweighed by the bus topology's advantages, which include

- Installation and reconfiguration is easy, especially for technologies like 10Base2, which use cable segments and connectors that can be easily assembled and disassembled.

- Because a bus uses only a single cable, cable installation is often simpler (and more appealing to do-it-yourselfers for that reason).

- Bus topologies require less equipment, wiring, and infrastructure than do other topologies, making them cheaper to install and use than the others (here again, this will be a concern in smaller organizations where capital or equipment outlays typically consume a greater portion of the budget).

- With the right combinations of equipment (e.g., multiport transceivers, a.k.a milking machines) even tap-based bus topologies like thickwire Ethernet can be easily reconfigured and devices rearranged, simply by moving transceiver cables around, without having to reroute the bus itself. In fact, it's fair to say that the cable arrangement with a multiport transceiver is exactly the same as that supplied by a hub in a pure star topology.

All in all, the bus is a robust topology whose simplicity and ease of design and use makes it appealing to a broad range of users.

The Star Topology

The star topology is slightly more complex than the bus topology and, if installed correctly, can be more efficient as well. In a star topology, each device on the network is connected to a network server or hub to transmit information across the network (see Figure 7.2 on page 68).

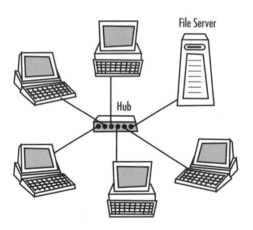

Figure 7.2   *A star topology radiates wires from a hub or concentrator.*

In this formation, computers are connected to a central device rather than to each other. Therefore, if one workstation has a bad link, it will not affect the other computers on the network. A good example of this type of technology is the telephone system. Any telephone can connect with any other telephone, providing it has a working link, through a central switching station.

As with most topics covered in this book, the star topology has advantages as well as disadvantages. One positive aspect derives from the workstations' indirect connections to one another. In this type of topology, a cable that malfunctions on the network, does not affect the entire network; it only affects the link between the hub and the workstation that's out of whack.

In a star topology, it's also easier to maintain centralized control and diagnostics for each computer and device on the network. Centralized management means that some workstations can be given higher priority over others, granting these higher priority workstations immediate access to the network. Combined with built-in premises wiring schemes and punchdown blocks, the star wiring systems that create the links between end nodes and hubs can be easily reconfigured at a single location—the wiring center or punchdown block—without having to move any physical wires at all.

Caution:

As with other topologies, the star has disadvantages that must be weighed against its many positive aspects. These include a shared point of failure—namely, if a hub or concentrator fails, all of the devices attached to it lose their access to the network. This also applies to any other cable segments linked into and out of that hub or concentrator. Because most such devices include bus-type connections to support a common backbone for linking multiple hubs or concentrators together, it's easy to see that loss of a single hub can bring down an entire network, in much the same way that any cable break can bring down a bus.

Because each connection to a hub or concentrator requires its own cable, building a star-wired network requires more cable to link each workstation to the central device, making the overall costs higher. If you add in the cost of the hubs themselves, it's not unusual to find that the cost of a network attachment to a given machine can be twice as high for a star-wired network as for a bus topology.

Nevertheless, star-wired networks represent the fastest growing and most widely used topology today. Apparently, savvy consumers have decided that the flexibility and convenience of the star topology outweigh the impact of its added costs. This is especially true for network installations in new business facilities, which very often include built-in network cabling as a part of their construction these days.

The Ring Topology

In a ring topology, all workstations are hypothetically connected to one another in a circular fashion, as shown in Figure 7.3. In this topology, one workstation in the ring may be designated as the monitoring node for the network, making it responsible for diagnostic functions.

Chief among these functions is the generation of a token that is passed around to each workstation in the ring, by order of connection. When a workstation receives the token, it transmits any data that needs to be sent, and the token is passed to the next workstation in the circle.

There are two ways in which a ring topology can be set up. The first requires running a cable from the back of one workstation directly into another. This is a potentially dangerous way to lay out a ring topology because if one workstation has a bad link, the entire network fails. In fact, this implementation is exactly like a bus except that instead of having two separate and distinct ends, the ends are joined to form a circle. Because of the potential problems with network failure, this literal implementation of a ring is seldom used, except when two cables are employed to create dual rings, so that a single cable failure can result in automatic rerouting that does not cause the network to fail (this method is sometimes used for FDDI, for instance, because it's fiber-based technology supports only point-to-point links anyway).

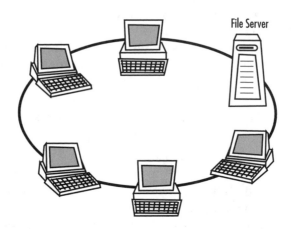

Figure 7.3   *The ring topology.*

Another option for implementing a ring is to connect each workstation to a hub and then connect the hubs in a ring. This is by far the most common method, because if a workstation or individual cable segment fails, the network can bypass it until repairs are made. It is also easier to add new workstations to this configuration because the network can remain up and running, whereas with direct connections between workstations, the network must be brought down to make any necessary changes.

As there is an affinity between broadcast access methods and bus topologies, there's a profound affinity between rings and token-passing methods like ARCnet, token ring, and FDDI. Nevertheless, it's safe to look at ring topologies as a subclass of star-wired topologies because that's how they're most often implemented. In token-passing environments, the hub may be called a *multiple access unit* (MAU) or a *connection arrangement unit* (CAU) but it still fulfills the same role and uses the same kinds of wiring schemes as those used for star-wired topologies.

Caution:

Therefore, the upside and downside for ring topologies is nearly the same as that for star topologies. This includes the same tradeoffs of wiring flexibility, centralized management, and automatic failure handling against added equipment and associated costs. The two topologies also share the ability to fit into premises wiring schemes, which helps to explain their continued growth and popularity.

Conclusion

Each of the topologies discussed in this chapter is in widespread use in the networking community. As noted, each has its benefits and shortcomings. The type of access method you choose to employ—Ethernet, token-ring, etc.—will often determine what topology you'll use.

Keep in mind that it's not necessary to limit your network to a single topology. In many cases, multiple stars will be linked in bus or ring topologies, and multiple stars can even be linked in a hierarchical fashion (often called a *star of stars*). Numerous configurations will occur naturally as you integrate each topology as dictated by your networking needs or as you internetwork existing, but isolated, network installations.

NETWORKING TECHNOLOGIES AND ACCESS METHODS

p a r t

II

Once you've set up your networking medium, the next issue to decide is how and when to use it—or the rules and regulations that determine its access methods.

Here in Part II, you'll learn about the various kinds of networking technologies in regular use, beginning with the ver-popular Ethernet developed in the early 1970s. Then we'll move on to investigate the beauties of token-passing access methods like token-ring and FDDI. Following our excursion into token land, we'll proceed into the digital world of the Integrated Services Digital Network (ISDN) and of Asynchronous Transfer Mode (ATM).

As we make this progression, the network support keeps getting faster and faster, starting with a respectable 10 Mbps for Ethernet and ending with the possibility of 2.4 Gpbs for ATM (or more, if we ever move beyond OC-48). Therefore, we'll also try to explain what this bandwidth can be used for, and why it's important, so that it's not just obscene overkill.

The purpose of this book is to explain the different networking technologies in use today, in terms of both their architecture and operations, and their most appropriate applications. Along the way, we hope you'll understand that they can safely be combined and used in tandem, often with very good results. Here, too, we'll show that your knowledge of how the network operates at a communications level also gives you a valuable understanding of networks can and can't do.

NETWORKING TECHNOLOGIES AND ACCESS METHODS

c h a p t e r

8

A smoothly functioning LAN results from a combination of several factors. LAN designers and administrators must understand the nature of their organizations and the nature of their output requirements. They must be conversant with current technologies and practices in networking, and they also must be sensitive to emerging technologies.

Successful network administrators know their organizations inside and out. The whole point of network technology is to increase the volume and quality of an organization's productivity. A good network administrator must therefore understand the politics of the enterprise, the roles involved in business activity, and the people who fill those roles to deploy and extend the network properly. To get the right results, network technology has to be put into the right hands.

Network administrators themselves know that networking is a combination of technology and sociology. But to the managers and the end users in an organization, the network administrator's foremost responsibility is technological awareness. For the enterprise to function, the network must work. It's as simple as that. The network administrator's job is to make sure the network works by choosing the right technology, implementing that technology properly, and maintaining its integrity and function in the face of day-to-day operations critical to the organization's survival.

Maintaining awareness of state-of-the-art technology is getting harder and harder. Technology is evolving at an incredible pace in the worlds of telecommunications and computing. The network administrator is responsible for keeping up with new technologies, evaluating emerging technologies, and choosing the right ones to enhance, extend, or replace those already in use. All this must happen in the background, while today's network is kept up and running.

In previous chapters we've presented the different physical characteristics of LANs. Now, we're going to look at how the network uses these characteristics. We've explored how network stations and devices are connected; now we'll see how the network uses these physical connections to transmit information. We'll take a look at common access methods, and we'll look at some important emerging networking technologies.

ACCESS METHODS

Network access methods are the ways in which networks decide which station has the right to transmit over the medium. Local area network stations will typically be connected to some sort of wire-based medium. Even so, only one station at a time can transmit data correctly. Therefore, the network needs to apply a set of consistent rules to decide which station gets to transmit, especially when two or more wish to use the medium at the same time The rules governing access to a shared medium are collectively known as the *access method*.

The type of access method used for networking has a lot to do with what functions the network provides and how the network performs. Different access methods have different characteristics; these characteristics must be understood before you can choose which access method is best for your organization. This choice is pivotal, because the access method you choose determines what type of network you'll install, and how that network will operate.

Two types of access methods are in common use: carrier sense and token passing.

Carrier Sense

Two carrier sense access methods are used in networking. Each handles multiple attempts at simultaneous access to the network medium differently, but both are based on contention for the medium. *Contention* means that network nodes jockey for position and fight it out for access to the network.

The nature of the fight for the cable is governed by carrier sense protocols, the Marquis of Queensbury rules for networking.

- *Carrier Sense Multiple Access/Collision Detection (CSMA/CD)*. *Carrier sense* means that network nodes monitor the cable for transmissions. If a node wants to transmit, it first listens for activity on the cable and transmits only when it senses no activity. If two or more nodes detect no transmissions they may begin to transmit simultaneously, which causes a collision. When this happens, each node senses the collision and then waits a random length of time before attempting to retransmit (this is called a *random backoff and retry* approach).
- *Carrier Sense Multiple Access/Collision Avoidance (CSMA/CA)*. Collision avoidance works a lot like collision detection, except that nodes wishing to transmit use logic to guess when collisions are likely to have occurred and retransmit after a time-out period following transmission elapses without receiving an acknowledgment of their transmission.

These two methods are similar. The main difference between them is in the amount of circuitry required for collision detection. CSMA/CD implements considerable circuitry to detect collisions electronically; CSMA/CA doesn't require all that circuitry but imposes greater delays on transmission.

Only two nodes can communicate over the network medium at any one time. If a node makes a request of a server at the same time that the server is transmitting a reply to another node, a collision occurs. The more traffic on the network, therefore, the higher is the likelihood of a collision. During peak load times on the network, like just before quitting time when lots of users are saving and printing files, the volume of collisions rises sharply and network performance suffers.

CSMA/CD is the foundation for the most popular business networking access method—Ethernet. We'll be discussing Ethernet in detail in the next chapter.

Token Passing

The sluggish performance of CSMA/CD and CSMA/CA networks inspired the search for a more trustworthy access method. Contention, and the resulting battles for access, is acceptable on smaller networks and network segments, but really big networks with lots of nodes and traffic sometimes can't perform as well. The limitations of CSMA/CD networks inspired researchers and technicians to search for a better way to share the network medium. One result of this search was the development of token-passing networks.

In a token-passing network, a token circulates around the network. A *token* is really a short network message that announces network availability to the nodes as it passes. A station waiting to transmit must have grabbed and reset token before it can send a message over the wire. Because only one node can possess the token at any given time, only one node can transmit at any given time. This eliminates the possibility of collisions.

Token-passing networks are logically arranged in a circle, or ring, so that the token passes sequentially from one node to the next. A node waiting to transmit *captures* the token as it passes. The node changes one bit of the token, changing the token into a start of frame sequence so that other nodes will know that a transmission is taking place. When the transmission is complete, the token is released back onto the ring. Any type of network application that needs guaranteed delivery of network information runs more effectively on a token-passing network.

Token-passing is the foundation for token ring networking as well as Fiber Distributed Data Interface (FDDI) networking. We'll be looking at both in the next few chapters. Token ring hardware is more expensive than Ethernet, and not as many manufacturers are creating token ring products as are creating hardware and software to support Ethernet networks. FDDI is based primarily on fiber-optic cable as its transmission medium and offers much greater speeds and reliability than either Ethernet or token ring.

Speed

Ethernet networks carry data at a rate of 10 Mbps. Token ring was introduced at 4 Mbps, but later implementations have brought the speed up to 16 Mbps. Today, 100 Mbps implementations of token ring and Ethernet are also available.

Bear in mind that, when computer networking was brand-new, 4 Mbps was absolutely acceptable. Of course, just having a network was a privilege, too. Ethernet's 10 Mbps has provided sufficient bandwidth for satisfactory business networking since the early 1970s. The 16 Mbps token ring provides bandwidth to spare for traditional business and manufacturing applications.

More Speed

The 4, 10, and 16 Mbps networks have proven durable in face of emerging computer technology. Nevertheless, there are some circumstances can require more bandwidth.

Local area networks (LANs) handling traditional business processes perform acceptably at these speeds, but large organizations usually have several LANs up and running in different parts of the enterprise. These LANs are usually connected by *backbones*. The 10 or 16 Mbps bandwidth that might be acceptable on one LAN segment might not be sufficient to handle all the traffic over a backbone. The need for higher performance for backbones has been one of the factors that pushed the development of access methods allowing speeds of 100 Mbps and more.

At the same time, there have been dramatic changes in the types of information carried on the LAN. In the beginning, networks carried mostly data and network messages. Today the LAN is called on for transmission of video, voice, e-mail, real-time data, graphics, and *multimedia* applications that may contain any of the aforementioned in any combination. These sophisticated transmissions and their corresponding bandwidth requirements are also pushing the demand for faster access methods.

NETWORKING TECHNOLOGIES

The push for faster access methods has also driven the development of some new communications technologies. LAN technology has become crucial to business survival, so the changing nature of business has caused changes in the way networks are designed and implemented.

LANs

The first networks to be implemented were LANs. LANs radically changed the way people got their work done. Businesses usually started out with one LAN as a test, and once the technology was proven, they added more

stations to the original LAN and more LANs throughout their enterprises.
Over time, separate LANs were connected by backbones, and soon everybody who was anybody was connected to the corporate network.

Unless they were traveling. Or unless they worked in another building.
Not all businesses fit in one room or on one floor of a building, or even in
one building. It's not uncommon for a big company to have multiple buildings at multiple sites around the country and around the world. Widespread acceptance of LANs, and business's subsequent dependence on the
LAN started the push for more far-reaching types of networking.

WANs

Acceptance of LAN technology for business quickly brought about a new
type of networking, wide area networks (WANs). A wide area network ties
together remote LANs and computer users into one extended network.
There's no particular limit on how widely WAN stations can be separated.
A LAN, or a stand alone PC in your office or home, could be connected
over a wide area link to another LAN hundreds or even thousands of miles
away.

There's no limit on how many LANs and PCs can be linked together over
into a WAN—at least, not in theory. However, a few practical limitations
nag at network administrators trying to keep a WAN up and running. One
limitation is imposed by the distance separating the remote stations on the
WAN. It's a lot harder to coordinate operations on a WAN than to keep
even a large LAN running efficiently. At least you can walk around and
look at every station on your LAN. Inspecting and inventorying every station on a WAN could take weeks and lots of frequent flyer miles.

Another major concern when establishing wide area links is cost. Network administrators have a hard enough time keeping hardware and software costs in line locally. WANs have all of those normal equipment and
maintenance costs, along with the additional cost of the *links* that connect
remote stations.

Getting It Together

The first WAN links used were simple dial-up connections made between
asynchronous modems. A remote computer or a gateway machine on a
LAN initiates and establishes a modem connection allowing the transfer of
information across the established link. Modem connections are a simple

and effective way to tie together a WAN, but they have their limitations. The relatively slow speeds of asynchronous modems make them unwieldy for some types of communications. Modems are great for transferring files of a certain size across the link, but they aren't really capable of carrying some types of information effectively. Full motion video over an asynchronous modem connection would be like watching your grandmother's slide show of her trip to St. Louis.

If you're using a telephone line as a wide area link between your LAN in California and another LAN in Texas, you're also paying the telephone company, or companies, providing the link for a lot of long distance service. Organizations that use a particular WAN link heavily often find it cheaper to lease a 56 Kbps line from the telephone company or to have the telephone service provider set up a T1 link between the remote stations. A T1 line is a digital telephone line that carries the equivalent of 24 regular telephone lines. Really big WANs might have multiple T1 links all tying in to a T3 backbone. A T3 link carries the equivalent of 28 T1 lines.

Public and Private Networks

The WANs we've been talking about have all been private networks. Even though the links may belong to public carriers (i.e., phone companies), the hardware and software used to establish the link are privately owned.

A different type of wide area network is commonly used. *Public data networks* have been established worldwide by communications companies. A private LAN may access the public data network (for a fee, of course) and use the phone companies own links to transfer information. Frame relay networks and the X.25 packet relay network are two examples of public data networks.

Backbones

Traffic between LANs can get pretty heavy. If all the LANs in a wide area network are connected to a single link, that link carries a heavy load of network traffic. That's why network designers like to provide a heavy duty common carrier for all that traffic, called the *backbone*. Because of the heavy load it must carry at peak use times, a backbone requires significantly more bandwidth than the average LAN. The need for higher and higher levels of bandwidth has pushed the development of some high speed transmission standards that are now being used in private and public networks.

Digital WANs

For the past 20 years or so, the communications network carriers (i.e., telephone service providers) have been moving toward creation of an all digital telephone network system called the *IDN*, or *Integrated Digital Network*. Standards call for the IDN to metamorphosize into a structure called the *ISDN*, *Integrated Services Digital Network*. The ISDN provides digital services of many types to its users over high bandwidth pipes running over telephone lines. IDN and ISDN represent years of planning and upgrading of communications network technology. ISDN is an effective carrier for many applications requiring accurate high bandwidth transmission.

Broadband Transmission

ISDN standards define a carrier service, *Broadband ISDN*, which provides extremely high bandwidth for applications that require it. Broadband ISDN (B-ISDN) can provide transport for real time full motion video teleconferencing and multimedia applications that mix up voice, data, graphics and video.

Asynchronous transfer mode (ATM) has been designated as the carrier technology to provide B-ISDN services. ATM is a cell relay technology, based on the transmission of 53-byte cells that carry information over the communications link. ATM is used now to provide high bandwidth transmission over telephone carrier trunk lines (T1 and T3) and as a backbone technology for many large corporate and government organizations.

Fiber-Optics

Fiber-optic technology has also provided high bandwidth transmission capability. Fiber-optic cables carry signals made of frequencies of light. Standards for data communication over fiber-optic networks and backbones have resulted in the creation of very reliable high bandwidth (100 Mbps) transmission links. Fiber-optic links are used as backbones in private and public networks alike. Telephone companies use fiber-optic links for communications and data transfer. Private networks often implement fiber-optic lines as backbones for a WAN.

WAN Applications

In the early days of networking, WAN links were used primarily for file transfers and e-mail services. These applications are relatively straightforward and don't really need lots of bandwidth. Lots of today's WAN and LAN traffic is still of this nature. But advances in technology and application development have put a much heavier load on these links.

Today a WAN might be carrying applications such as digital sound or voice, full motion video, high speed data transfer, complex graphics, and any combinations of the aforementioned. Competition for limited amounts of bandwidth on LAN and WAN links has led to the development of new technologies and protocol sets designed to let more of these types of traffic travel over the links.

SUMMARY

The next few chapters are going to explain all this in a lot more detail. We'll get a look at the most popular ways for moving information around on LANs and WANs. We'll look at some technologies that are already in common use, and we'll take a look ahead and see what's emerging in the way of communications and data transfer technology.

ETHERNET

9

INTRODUCTION

Although Ethernet is a popular current LAN technology, it has been around since the early 1970s, when it was first introduced by Xerox. Although Xerox may lay claim to the original design of Ethernet, it had help from Digital Equipment Corporation and Intel in drafting and formalizing the first Ethernet standard. Based on the three organizations' initials, the standard became known as the DIX standard and is sometimes referred to as *Ethernet II* or *Ethernet 2.0*.

Specs:

The Institute of Electrical and Electronics Engineers (IEEE) adopted a slightly different form of the DIX standard and called it Ethernet 802.3, which was later adopted by the International Standards Organization (ISO) as ISO 8802/3. The IEEE's purpose in formalizing Ethernet as a standard was to promote interoperability between different vendors' products. Because of this, Ethernet technology gained early popularity and today holds over 66% of the current LAN networking market.

Ethernet technology remains popular today because of its high speed, low cost, and the many vendors that support this technology. A multitude of NIC manufacturers, software vendors, and peripherals manufacturers tend to provide support for Ethernet first, and only later provide support for other LAN technologies, like token ring or ARCnet.

Earlier Ethernet

In the early days of networking, LANs spanned only short distances. Consequently, older Ethernet LANs were relatively simple in design. Typically, they consisted of just a few computers connected by a single coaxial cable. Today, Ethernet networks can span campuswide environments and can incorporate a plethora of equipment and cable types, including underground fiber-optic cabling, concentrators, hubs, repeaters, and other system components.

As networking technology continues to grow, Ethernet technology continues to evolve and change apace. The addition of 10BaseT, fiber-optic technologies, and 100 Mbps transmission rates all provide ample evidence that Ethernet has kept pace with new developments, and will continue to remain marketable.

In other chapters of this book, we discuss additional LAN technologies like token ring, ARCnet, FDDI, and LocalTalk. Here, we'll focus primarily on Ethernet and make references to the other technologies for comparison purposes only. Turn to Chapters 10–21 for detailed discussions of other LAN technologies.

Let's begin our discussion with some LAN basics before we move onto the details of Ethernet.

BASIC NETWORKING AND ETHERNET

The basic areas of LAN design are as follows:

- media
- topology
- access method

Let's take a look at each of these as they apply to Ethernet networks.

Media

The media supply the pathways used to transmit data over a LAN. Bounded media are manifested primarily by cabling; unbounded media can be represented by microwave, radio wave, and other types of broadcast transmission technologies. Bounded media, or cabling, are also divided into three categories: twisted pair, coaxial, and fiber. Ethernet supports all three types of bounded media.

Media are important to Ethernet because the type of cabling defines the distances that Ethernet LANs can span. If you do not know your network's media and their capabilities, you could end up with an Ethernet LAN that doesn't work!

Coax, Twisted Pair, and Fiber-Optic Cables

Ethernet was originally developed for thick coaxial cabling—a bulky, expensive cabling technology that is difficult to install and maintain (please consult Chapter 2 for a detailed discussion of coaxial cable). Today, Ethernet has progressed to support all of the following cable types: thin coaxial, unshielded twisted pair (UTP), and fiber optic (Chapter 3 provides the details on fiber-optic cable, while Chapter 4 covers twisted pair).

Ethernet has always been one of the least expensive LAN technologies, primarily because the cost of the cabling and boards was lower than most other options. Now, with the ability to run Ethernet over UTP, the cost of Ethernet technology continues to plummet. UTP is easier to install and support than thick or thin coaxial cable. Even though the initial implementations of Ethernet over UTP cable ran at 10 Mbps, newer implementations of Ethernet are available today that run over fiber and UTP at 100 Mbps.

Ethernet is sometimes referred to by the type cable it uses. Table 9.1 summarizes the different Ethernet IEEE specifications, along with their associated speeds and cable spans. Before we look at this table, let's define some terms that should assist your understanding. That is, when we say *10Base5*, you can break this down into XYZ, where

X: Maximum speed of the medium, measured in Mbps

Y: *Base* for baseband, or *Broad* for broadband

Z: Typically, this refers to the maximum span for a cable, measured in meters, divided by 100

Thus, if we use this approach, the term *10Base5* means that this medium's maximum speed is 10 Mbps, that it is a baseband technology, and it can span a maximum distance of 500 m per individual cable segment.

Unfortunately, more recent medium designations do not always follow this XYZ formula, as in the designation 100VG-AnyLAN. *VG* means voice grade TP wiring, but no distance maximum is included in the name, even though it is limited to 100 m per segment. This confusion appears to indicate that this medium type, developed and marketed by Hewlett-Packard, has not yet become an official IEEE standard. We will discuss all of these specifications in greater detail later on in this chapter.

Specification	Speed (Mbps)	Cable type	Distance in Meters	Topology
10Base5	10	Thick coaxial	500	Linear bus
10Base2	10	Thin coaxial	200	Linear bus
10BaseT	10	UTP-Lev 3–5	100	Star bus
1Base5	1	Twisted pair	500	Star bus
10BaseF	10	Fiber	4000	Star bus
100BaseX	100	Twisted pair	150	Star bus
100VG-AnyLAN	100	Twisted pair	100	Star bus

Table 9.1   *Ethernet Specifications.*

Topology

Topology describes the layout of a network's cabling and can be broken down into two main categories: physical and logical. Physical topology deals with what you can see with your eyes (i.e., how the actual cabling is arranged), while logical topology describes how data traverses the resulting network. For example, you can physically connect your network nodes to a hub in a star format, but logically configure the backplane of the hub so that each node belongs to a single logical bus.

Physical Topology

The main physical topologies used in networks are described by terms that illustrate their arrangements; that is, bus, ring, star, tree, and mesh. Ethernet uses a logical bus topology that can be physically laid out in one of two ways: as a true linear bus or as a star configuration that logically emulates a linear bus. Chapter 7 covers these topological arrangements in more detail and includes depictions of the three most popular topologies—bus, star, and ring.

Linear Bus. For a depiction of a bus topology, please consult Figure 7.1 on page 66. If you're visually adept, think of a cable strung in a straight line, with computers hanging off it here and there along its length. Because of its arrangement, all nodes on a bus can see and talk with one another. The more nodes on a bus, the greater is the traffic on the common wire that interconnects them.

Because signals bounce back when they hit the end of a wire, please note that terminating resistors must be placed at each end of every cable segment arranged in a bus topology. These terminating resistors should match the impedance of the networking medium in use; otherwise, your network may experience sometimes mysterious problems.

Star Bus. For a depiction of a star topology please consult Figure 7.2 on page 68. It's basically an arrangement where a device called a *hub* acts as the center of a set of cables, which radiate out to a matched set of devices (typically, computers) on the peripheral. This resemblance to a starfish or a wagon wheel (sans rim) is what prompted the name for this configuration.

A star topology was made possible when hubs and concentrators for Ethernet were introduced in the 1980s. In this type of arrangement, workstations can be connected via UTP to a centralized hub that creates a star topology. Remember, this physical arrangement of cables describes only the resulting physical topology. For Ethernet, the overlying logical topology still operates as a bus.

Access Method

For networking, the access method operates at the medium access control (MAC) sublayer in the data link layer of the Open Systems Interconnect (OSI) model. It defines the rules for communication between network interfaces over the network media in use. Ethernet typically uses an access methods called *CSMA/CD*, but another recent method introduced for 100VG-AnyLAN Ethernet networks is called *demand priority*. Likewise, some special Ethernet implementations use a high-speed switching technology inside the hubs and concentrators to permit the hub to support multiple simultaneous "conversations" between pairs of devices; this variety of

Ethernet is called *switched Ethernet.* Despite these possible variations, CSMA/CD remains the most common—and popular—Ethernet variety.

Carrier Sense Multiple Access with Collision Detection

Ethernet networks use the carrier sense multiple access with collision detection (CSMA/CD) access method. Given this incredible string of gibberish, you might be better able to appreciate the benefits of a good acronym! CSMA/CD is similar to a telephone party line, where many people are connected together sharing one line. If everyone talks at the same time, no one can hear the conversation. However, if people on the party line listen and wait for a time when no one else is talking, then one person can begin speaking and can usually assume that everyone can hear the conversation clearly. Another way to state this is to say that Ethernet depends on "listening" to the network medium and that no one else may "speak" while the medium is already carrying a message.

Carrier Sense Multiple Access. Ethernet works the same way as the preceeding examples. We can break down CSMA/CD into two steps and look at each one separately. CSMA is where all nodes on a segment listen for the line to be free. When it is free, any node that has something to transmit tries to grab the line. If another node tries to transmit at the same time, a collision occurs when their messages "run into" each other on the medium.

Collision Detection (H4)

Collision detection means that the network interfaces attached to the medium can sense collisions when they occur. This is possible because packets that collide create the electronic equivalent of garbage, which is immediately distinguishable from a valid transmission. Once the interfaces attached to the medium detect a collision, any would-be transmitters cease transmission and use a random back-off timer to wait an indeterminate amount of time to try again. The nodes that wish to transmit are then permitted to try again after their time-out period has expired, provided that the line is free.

CSMA/CD might permit faster PCs to grab the line more frequently than slower ones since faster processors can process and respond more quickly. That's why a random back-off period is used when a collision occurs; this helps to make the actual access to the medium more democratic, since a faster PC has an even chance of taking longer to be allowed to try to transmit again compared to a slower one.

CSMA/CD does have a significant drawback to its design. It cannot really support the full theoretical bandwidth implied by the "speed limit" for the medium. That's because more collisions occur as more traffic traverses the medium; in other words, as the medium gets busy, the chances of a collision increase. Statistical studies of network utilization have shown that Ethernet starts to bog down when utilization exceeds a range of 56–60%. This is apparently the point at which collisions begin to swamp the carrying capacity of the medium. Because this can cause the network to slow down or even halt altogether, when this happens, the LAN administrator's pager will usually start beeping.

Demand Priority

Demand priority is the new kid on the block for Ethernet networks using 100VG-AnyLAN. It is a much more efficient access method than CSMA/CD for several reasons.

1. Demand priority uses a centralized hub that manages how nodes are permitted to utilize the medium, determining when and in what order transmissions can occur. Any workstation wishing to transmit data must first signal a transmission request to the hub. The hub then assigns that request a priority along with other pending requests. If two requests arrive simultaneously, the hub arbitrates the requests based on the order of assignment of priority.

2. Demand priority lets the hub act as a traffic manager, to keep purely local traffic from broadcasting throughout the entire network to each workstation.

3. Demand priority is able to transmit and receive at the same time by using four pairs of twisted pair cabling instead of the more standard two pairs. This two-way communications decreases latency and improves a network's performance.

Demand priority is basically a switched technology that supports high-bandwidth transmissions. Because it can limit extraneous traffic and arbitrate transmission requests explicitly (rather than randomly), it is both more efficient and democratic than CSMA/CD.

ETHERNET FRAMES

Once a node gains access to the network, it must begin the process of transmitting its data. It does this in the form of packets that can also be called frames. Ethernet supports four different frame formats.

Frame Types

- *Ethernet II (DIX)*—This frame format is used for PCs using TCP/IP, AppleTalk Phase I, and networks hooked up to DEC computers.
- *Ethernet 802.2*—This frame type contains both 802.3 and 802.2 fields. NetWare 4.X uses this frame type.
- *Ethernet 802.3 (IEEE)*—Used exclusively by Novell's IPX/SPX protocol in NetWare 3.X and prior versions of NetWare. No other protocols support this frame type.
- *Ethernet Subnetwork Access Protocol (SNAP)*—This frame type is derived from the Ethernet 802.2 frame type. The protocols that can use this frame type include IPX/SPX, TCP/IP and AppleTalk Phase II networks.

Field of Frames

Frames break down a packet into fields that contain bits, where each bit's location within the frame gives some information, such as source or destination address. Figure 9.1 illustrates an 802.3 frame format.

Preamble	SFD	Destination Address	Source Address	Length	Data	FCS
7 bytes	1 byte	6 bytes	6 bytes	2 bytes	46–1500 bytes	4 bytes

Figure 9.1   *802.3 Frame Format.*

Tip:
In the following list, we can get a better idea of what each field is used for in the 802.3 frame:

- *Preamble*—This field flags the beginning of a frame and can be considered similar in use to the start bit in serial operations. According to the original Ethernet design, the preamble is considered to be 8 bytes long, but for 802.3, the final byte of the preamble is called a *start frame delimiter*, so here, the preamble can be only 7 bytes long.

- *Start frame delimiter (SFD)*—This is the final byte of the preamble.

- *Destination address*—This field is similar to an addressee on a memo or an envelope. It marks the node that should receive the packet of data and can be 2-6 bytes in length.

- *Source address*—This 2-6 byte field represents the sender of the packet very much like a return address on an envelope. The source address cannot be the "broadcast address" (FF-FF-FF-FF-FF-FF).

- *Length of data field (LEN)*—The real purpose of any Ethernet packet is to transmit data, often called the *payload* of the packet. Ethernet packets can carry payloads of up to 1500 bytes. This 2 byte field provides the byte count for the data in the payload.

- *Data*—This field contains the payload for the packet, which can be up to 1500 bytes long. Also, if there is less than 64 bytes of data, the PAD field (described next) will have "empty" bytes added to bring it up to the minimum length requirement.

- *PAD*—IEEE standards require that an Ethernet frame be no less than 64 bytes long. If a packet is assembled that is only 50 bytes long, then 14 more bytes will be added to this area to bring the packet size up to the required minimum. That padding actually comes from the buffer area on the NIC card—which could pose a security problem if your workstation passes a lot of sensitive information.

- *Cyclic redundancy checksum (CRC)*—This is a method of error detection while sending packets, based on a calculation that the sender and receiver both use. The receiver calculates its own version and compares it to the one shipped inside the packet; if the two values agree, the assumption is that the information in the packet has been correctly delivered.

Mix and Match

It is possible to run multiple frame types on the same wire if the network operating system supports it. Novell's NetWare 3.X and above supports multiple frame types, however, you must load each frame type on the server. A difference in the frame preamble distinguishes Ethernet II from Ethernet 802.3. Also, Ethernet II does not contain a packet length field but uses the bits in that field to define a packet type. Software is able to distinguish between packet length and packet type because no packet type is defined for values less than hexadecimal 1500.

Addressing

The source and destination addresses have to be unique for the correct packet to get delivered to the right node. Ethernet NICs each contain a unique physical MAC address that is 6 bytes long and burned into an Ethernet board's BIOS. The first 3 bytes of this address are unique to each registered hardware vendor, assigned by the controlling body of IEEE. The last 3 bytes are assigned by the hardware manufacturer. This guarantees that each NIC will always have a unique MAC address. In addition, if your organization purchases the same NIC cards for all of your PCs, it will be easy to spot a "foreign NIC" on your network—its MAC address will stand out in boldly from your local NICs.

Understanding Frame Formats

Understanding frame formats is crucial to network troubleshooting; an ability to investigate and diagnose their contents can uncover as much as 75% of all network-related problems. If it's a network problem, like seeing garbage on the wire, you can usually find its source by examining frames off the wire with some kind of protocol analyzer, like Novell's LANalyzer for Windows or the Network General Sniffer.

Being able to read what's actually going on across the wire can save a network administrator lots of time. If you have no protocol analyzer, start the cost-benefit analysis now so you can get one—a software-based analyzer (like the Novell product) can be purchased for less than $1,000 if you really shop around, so obtaining this kind of assistance may cost less than you think (for more details on protocol analyzers and similar tools, please consult Chapter 22, "Protocol Analyzers and Diagnostic Tools," and Chapter 41 "Wire-Level Management Tools").

ETHERNET CABLING SPECIFICATIONS

Refer back to Table 9.1 for a complete listing of Ethernet specifications. In this section, we will describe each of those specifications in greater detail. Ethernet specifications originally permitted the use of only thick coaxial cable. Thin Ethernet cable followed later, lowering the cost of Ethernet networking. Current specifications call for Ethernet over UTP, coaxial, or fiber-optic cabling (not to mention the various wireless implementations available). Let's begin with the 10 Mbps specifications and work our way up to the 100 Mbps varieties.

10 Mbps Ethernet Technology

Table 9.2 provides a comparison of thick and thin Ethernet coax cables, which were the first two specifications for this technology. When some sources reported different maximum segment lengths and diameters, we chose the most conservative numbers for those cases.

10Base5, Thick Ethernet, Thickwire, or Ethernet?

As you can see from this section title, there are many names for this specification. 10Base5 is sometimes called *Ethernet* because it was the original IEEE specification. However, as later specifications were finalized by IEEE, the term *Ethernet* became more generic. Thickwire Ethernet uses heavy rigid 50-ohm coaxial cable approximately 0.4" in diameter, normally coated with a bright yellow Teflon jacket.

Specification	Cable Type	Diameter (mm)	Distance Segment (m)	Number ofSegments	Number of Nodes/Seg
10Base5	Thick	20	500	5	250
10Base2	Thin	6	185	3	30

Table 9.2   *Thick vs. Thin Ethernet.*

New purchases for this type of Ethernet are waning, nevertheless, an installed base of this technology still remains that requires maintenance and upgrades. As you may know, upgrades involving cabling can be costly and therefore shouldn't be done unless absolutely necessary.

As you can see from Table 9.2 on page 95, IEEE's 10Base5 specification supports longer distances than the later 10Base2 specification. The 10Base5 specification calls for more expensive, bulkier cabling, making it more difficult to handle. Individual taps on thickwire Ethernet must be at least 2.5 m (approximately 8 ft) apart.

Adding a workstation to thick Ethernet cabling involves connecting a transceiver to a tap directly into the cable. Individual taps on thickwire Ethernet must be at least 2.5 m (approximately 8 ft) apart, with a maximum of 100 devices per cable segment. Here are the steps involved in connecting a transceiver to thickwire Ethernet:

1. Attach the tap to the network cable (be sure to follow all the necessary instructions, or better yet, get a cable installer to do it for you). Recall that you must bring an Ethernet network down before you can tap into a cable.

2. Attach the transceiver to the drop cable. Up to a 50 ft long drop cable may be used for this purpose.

3. Attach a cable from the transceiver's attachment unit interface (AUI) to a female DIX-type connector (this cable is called the transceiver cable) on the NIC card in a workstation.

A transceiver (*transmitter / receiver*) is a small device used to electrically isolate the workstation from the network cable. It can connect to the network in two ways: an N-type tap where the cable is physically cut and a T-connection is inserted between the newly created cable ends, or a vampire tap where a probe is inserted through the cable cover and shield directly into the copper wire. Both taps require a transceiver to do the transmission and receiving onto the wire.

10Base2, Thin Ethernet, Cheapernet, Thinnet, or Thinwire?

Nodes on a 10Base2 network are connected differently from a 10Base5 network. 10Base2 nodes are interlinked in a daisy chain, using barrel-shaped BNC connectors on the NIC that connects a workstation to T-shaped connectors that link individual segments of network cabling together. All

NICs that follow the 10Base2 specification are designed with onboard transceivers and cannot use an external transceiver with drop and transceiver cables to connect to the network, unless the AUI port on the NIC is used rather than the BNC connector.

The 10Base2 uses a 50-ohm, RG-58 coaxial cable, which is approximately 0.2 in. in diameter and can be purchased with the connectors already attached to the cable ends. This cable comes in precut, prefabricated lengths or in bulk, should you need to build your own cables.

Although 10Base2 is cheaper and easier to handle than 10Base5, it spans a significantly shorter maximum segment length. Regardless, thinwire coax cable can be an ideal scheme for smaller networks, where all the nodes are situated in close proximity.

Nodes in 10Base2 networks must be located at least 0.5 m apart with a limit of 30 nodes per segment. Figure 9.2 shows a diagram of a 10Base2 connection from the workstation's NIC to the network cable.

10BaseT (Twisted Pair)

The 10BaseT is the most popular variety of Ethernet in use today. It discards the use of coaxial cabling in favor of twisted pair wire. Twisted pair wire is much cheaper than coaxial cabling, far easier to install and maintain, and less sensitive to mishandling. This makes 10BaseT attractive to many organizations.

Figure 9.2   *10 Base 2 diagram.*

The 10BaseT requires the use of a hub to interconnect nodes. This confers the advantage that a broken or disconnected UTP wire need no longer bring down an entire Ethernet segment. If an end user disconnects his or her workstation from the network, there is far less chance of bringing down the entire network.

In a 10BaseT wiring scheme, nodes are connected to a hub using straight through wires. Connecting one hub to another requires a modified cable that crosses the wires (i.e., reverses the order of connectors from one end to the other). Because some hubs have the ability to cross these wires internally, this can forestall the need for two different cable types.

In a 10BaseT environment, each workstation must attach to its hub using a segment of two-pair UTP cable that cannot exceed 100 m in length. Each hub-to-hub connection is also limited to a maximum of 100 m. Since each hub usually has 12 ports, the maximum number of hubs that can be connected to a central hub is 12. To facilitate backbone connections and integration of other Ethernet cabling types, hubs generally incorporate coaxial or fiber-optic cable connections.

10BaseT uses RJ-45 connectors and four wires to conduct its signals. The UTP cable used for 10BaseT can be Category 3, 4, or 5. If you wish to expand your UTP Ethernet network in the future to speeds of 100 Mbps, use Category 5 cable.

10BaseF (Fiber)

The introduction of fiber into the networking community brought even greater distances and more reliable transmissions than previous specifications. Although use of fiber to connect workstations to a network is expensive, constructing a backbone, or connecting two or more buildings together with fiber-optic cable provides reliability and electrical isolation that can easily justify the costs involved.

100 Mbps Ethernet

High-speed Ethernet offers a maximum theoretical throughput of 100 Mbps, where regular Ethernet is limited to 10 Mbps. Two technologies are competing to attain the status of an IEEE 100 Mbps Ethernet standard right now: 100BaseX and 100 VGAnyLAN. Both technologies were originally designed to provide high-speed backbones to link routers, hubs, and other key networking devices, but are beginning to branch out to the desktop as well (defining a whole new category of power users).

100BaseX (Fast Ethernet)

The 100BaseX uses the CSMA/CD access method with some modifications. The 100BaseX runs over two-pair UTP Category 5 cabling. This IEEE 802.3-based draft standard was originally developed by 3Com, Intel, SynOptics, Grand Junction, and other vendors. Their main objective was to increase speed while using CSMA/CD so that current Ethernet networks could be preserved and migrated without requiring a large up-front investment.

In the 100BaseX environment, the throughput between workstations and the hub remains fixed at 10BaseT standards of 10 Mbps, and 100 Mbps links are reserved for a limited number of high-speed connections. This preserves existing investments in end-user NICs and wiring, while providing better throughput over the backbone.

The 100BaseX is similar to the 10BaseT standards because it uses the CSMA/CD access method and also uses a star topology, where all nodes are connected through a centralized hub.

100BaseVG (100VG-AnyLan)

The second contender for the IEEE 100 Mbps Ethernet crown is covered by the IEEE 802.12 draft standard. Also known as *100BaseVG*, this technology is derived from HP's 100VG-AnyLAN and may be finalized as a standard as early as mid-1995.

The IEEE 802.12 method is similar to 100BaseX with two exceptions. First, the current implementation requires four-pair Category 3, not two-pair Category 5 wiring. Because the specification permits the use of Category 3 wiring, the additional two pairs are necessary to ensure reliable transmission at speeds of 100 Mbps. If you're using Category 3 wiring, the distance limitation for 100BaseVG is 100 m, but if you're using Category 5, the limitation is stretched to 150 m.

Second, the access method between workstations and the hub is replaced with a newer method called demand priority (which is covered in the "Access Methods" section earlier in this chapter). *Demand priority* currently utilizes the additional two pairs of wires, but future implementations may allow 100VG-AnyLAN to run over two-pair UTP without requiring an additional pair of wires for out-of-band signaling (i.e., when the workstation talks to the hub to request permission to transmit).

Since both varieties of Ethernet use a similar star topology, the same cable ratings, identical frame types, and the same kinds of connectors, the 100BaseVG standard is quite compatible with the existing 10BaseT standard, despite its use of a different access method.

Table 9.3 summarizes some of the features of the 100BaseX and the 100VG-AnyLan standard.

Specification	Access Method	Pairs of Wiring	Wiring Category/ Grade	Speed (Mbits/sec)	Distance
100BaseX	CSMA/CD	2	5/data	100	150
100VG-AnyLAN	Demand priority	4	3/voice	100	100

Table 9.3   *Summary of 100BaseX/100VG-AnyLAN.*

HARDWARE CONSIDERATIONS

NICs

The NIC is an important interface between a PC and the LAN and is discussed in detail in Chapter 24. As we mentioned earlier, each Ethernet NIC has its own MAC address burned into the card's BIOS for unique addressing purposes.

Housed on the back of Ethernet NICs are the specific connectors used to connect to the network depending on which type of cabling you've laid out for you LAN. As we look at each of the media types in the next section, we'll discuss which type of connector to use.

NIC cards come in a variety of sizes: 8-bit, 16-bit, and 32-bit. The number of bits represents the amount of data the NIC can transfer to and from the LAN at one time. Since all traffic must pass through the NIC, the wider the pipe you put in your PCs, the faster the data will flow.

On the workstation end, you'll probably want to outfit your organization's PCs with at least a 16-bit card for about $99.00. On your server PC, don't consider anything less than a 32-bit card, since the server will be handling a lot of traffic.

Ethernet networks can be segmented to better balance the traffic and improve performance. Network segmentation requires that you put an additional NIC card in the server and that you break your existing cable layout into multiple segments (we're assuming two of nearly equal size and reach here). Furthermore, additional cards allow two or more segments to be bridged together. By segmenting your network, you can take all of the nodes that used to reside and talk on one wire and split their traffic across two wires. The number of collisions will decrease, and both you and your users should see at least a modest boost in performance.

Building Your Network

The selection of your network's topology must be based on your unique needs and circumstances. As you try to decide what Ethernet implementation is right for you, remember that 10Base5 type is falling out of favor because of the cost and difficulty in cabling. Today, 10Base2 and 10BaseT seem to be the most popular Ethernet implementation, but they're limited to the slower speed limit of 10 Mbps for the original IEEE Ethernet specification. If you foresee a need for high-speed or high-volume applications in your future, you'll want to consider at least a limited introduction of one of the 100 Mbps Ethernet varieties, probably for backbone use at first.

When it comes to laying out a network, the basic building block is the individual cable segment. It is not unusual for the network to consist of segments with different wiring types. You can interconnect 10BaseT segments to 10Base2 or 10BaseF segments with little problem. You can also buy adapters that will allow you to connect DIX devices to 10Base2, 10BaseF, or 10BaseT.

IEEE standards set the maximum for an Ethernet network to be five segments, connected by four repeaters. Of these five segments only three may have active nodes (that's why this guideline is better known as the *three-four-five rule*). If you can keep these simple principles in mind when laying out a network, you can solve problems during the design phase, which is by far the cheapest time to work them out!

ETHERNET RESOURCES:
BIBLIOGRAPHY AND STRATEGIES

For general networking references, please consult Appendix C, "A List of Networking Resources." The magazines and other publications listed there can help you find out lots of information about NICs. The following references are particularly helpful for the information they contain about network interface cards:

Chappell, Laura A., and Dan E. Hakes. *Novell's Guide to NetWare LAN Analysis*, 2nd ed., Sybex Books, 1994, Alameda, CA: The most comprehensive, clear and concise coverage of NetWare-related protocols, across the whole ISO reference model (which means great coverage of Ethernet, token ring, ARCnet, and more). $44.99.

Derfler, Frank, Jr. and Les Freed. *How Networks Work.*
 Ziff-Davis Press, 1993, Emeryville, CA: An illustration and example-intensive description of how networks actually operate. Includes good discussions of most basic networking components, including NICs. $24.95.

Derrick, Dan. Network Know-How: *Concepts, Card and Cables.*

Osborne McGraw-Hill, 1992, Berkeley, CA: In addition to being a good source of general networking information, this book includes an entire chapter devoted to NICs. At $19.95, it's a useful addition to any networking professional's library, even if only to lend to newbie users.

Lowe, Doug. *Networking for Dummies.*
IDG Books Worldwide, 1994, Indianapolis: This is a good gentle introduction to networking, including useful overview on network interface cards. At $19.95, it's a useful addition to any networking professional's library, even if only to lend to newbie users.

Network Interface Technical Guide
MicroHouse, Inc., 1992, 1993, Boulder, CO: This $99 technical reference includes over 1,000 pages of information on just about every NIC known. If you find an old NIC with no manual, chances are good that this book can supply an adequate replacement; at the very least, it's sure to document all of the switch and jumper settings you'll need to know about to properly configure the card.

Newton, Harry. *Newton's Telecom Dictionary*, 7th ed.
Flatiron Publishing Company, 1994, New York: Harry Newton is a towering fiigure in the telecommunications industry, and his dictionary isn't bad either. Even though it purports to be telecom specific, it's one of the best sources for looking up PC-related acronyms, standards, and other terms that we've ever found anywhere. At $24.95 for 1,200 pages of text, it's a bargain to boot!

Novell Ethernet Supplement NetWare
Novell, 1991, 1992, 1993, 1994, Provo, UT: This gem of a manual explains how to install an Ethernet network with NetWare, and it also includes detailed descriptions of NICs and configuration information for the NE1000, NE2000, and NE3200 network interface cards originally designed by Novell, but now marketed by Eagle Technology (a divi-

sion of Artisoft, Inc.).

Sant'Angelo, Rick. *NetWare Unleashed.*
Sam's Publishing, 1994, Indianapolis: This book is a must for Novell NetWare users. It
basically covers everything in networking from A to Z. $45.00.

Sheldon, Tom. *The LAN Times Encyclopedia of Networking.*
Osborne McGraw-Hill, 1994, Berkeley, CA: A general sourcebook for networking terms
and technologies. Includes discussions, some lengthy and detailed, about nearly every
conceivable networking topic. $39.95.

Theakston, Ian. *NetWare LANs: Performance and Troubleshooting.*
Addison-Wesley Publishing Company, 1994, Wokingham, UK: A good troubleshooting guide for several different networking schemes, especially for Ethernet LANs. Pricing information not available.

THE TOP FIVE ETHERNET VENDORS

3Com Corp.
PO Box 58145, 5400 Bayfront Plaza
Santa Clara, CA 95052-8145
800-638-3266; 408-764-5000
FAX: 408-764-5001
Tech support: 800-876-3266
Tech support BBS: 408-980-8204

Standard Microsystems Corp. (System Products Division)
350 Kennedy Dr.
Hauppauge, NY 11788
800-SMC-4-YOU; 800-833-4-SMC (CD); 516-273-3100
Direct sales: 516-435-6255
FAX: 516-273-7935
Tech support: 800-992-4762
Tech support BBS: 516-434-3162

Intel Corp. (Personal Computer Enhancement Division)
5200 N.E. Elam Young Pkwy.
Hillsboro, OR 97124-6497
800-538-3373; 503-629-7354
FAX: 503-629-7580

Tech support: 503-629-7000
Tech support BBS: 503-645-6275

Microdyne Corporation
3601 Eisenhower Ave., Ste. 300
Alexandria, VA 22304-9703
800-255-3967; 703-329-3700
FAX: 703-329-3722
Tech support: Use toll-free no.
Tech support BBS: 703-960-8509

Eagle Technology (division of Artisoft, Inc.)
2865 Zanker Rd.
San Jose, CA 95134
800-524-3245; 408-577-3900
Direct sales: 800-733-2453
FAX: 408-577-3901
Tech support: 800-726-5267
Tech support BBS: 602-670-7444

10

TOKEN RING

TOKEN RING?

OK, this name takes some getting used to. *Token ring* makes us think of elves sitting in a circle out in a forest somewhere, all concentrating madly on some sort of magical device. While this image may suffice as a high-level explanation of token ring networking, it has the distracting tendency to lead to musings on three-footed beings with pointed ears instead of network operating systems.

Getting past this fantastic image takes some doing, but once you look closely at token ring technology, you'll discover a speedy, elegant alternative to Ethernet access methods that is gaining wider acceptance in the networking community.

Nodes on an Ethernet network broadcast messages out to the network. Because frames are broadcast all over the LAN, they are received and interpreted by all connected nodes. In a token ring network, transmission access to the network is limited to the node that holds the token, and all network messages move in a specified direction around the ring.

On a per-segment basis, Ethernet nodes are connected to a common bus, or cable, and nodes contend for the bus using CSMA/CD to avoid collisions and confusion on the network. Nodes on a token ring network are connected by two wire pairs. Both ends of the cable pair attach physically to a common hub (known in IBM-speak as a MAU, or medium access unit), which acts as a central point for communications and wire management.

Logically, a machine attached to a token ring network ships its information to the next node on the ring (known as its *downstream neighbor*), and receives its data from the preceding node on the ring (known as its *nearest available upstream neighbor*, or NAUN). The last node on the ring is logically connected to the first, closing the circle of transmission so that a logical ring is formed. Because all messages move in a predefined direction around the ring and each node mode must take possession of a circulating token before it can transmit, collisions are avoided, along with the resulting degradation in network performance.

A ring is usually arranged in a star topology, with both wires from an individual node connected to a wire concentrator that establishes a logical, rather than a physical, ring. A token is a specific pattern of data encapsulated in a packet that circulates around and around the ring. All nodes on a ring network have the opportunity to take possession of the token and send messages to other nodes out onto the ring. We'll find out more about the specifics of token ring operation, but first let's take a look at how token ring came into existence.

ORIGINS OF THE RING

Newcomers to the networking world might think Ethernet is the be-all and end-all for business networking, but as early as 1969, a token ring access method was proposed by Olaf Soderblum. As with Ethernet, many different organizations took up the study and development of ring access techniques. Different vendors of ring technologies came up with their own flavors of token ring networking. Apollo Computers developed Domain, a 12 Mbps token ring access network operating system. Proteon developed a 10 Mbps token ring system, ProNET-10. There were others, and they all performed acceptably, but none of them ever achieved the broad acceptance of Ethernet.

Specs:

In the early mid 1980s, token ring began to come into much wider acceptance. There were two major factors to this acceptance. The first major factor was IBM's endorsement of the token passing access method. IBM created and dominated the personal computer market in the 1980s, and its acceptance of token ring access made most companies looking for network technology take a closer look at token ring. By the mid 1980s, the Institute of Electrical and Electronic Engineers (IEEE), finally defined token ring standards in the IEEE 802.5 series specifications, which were based closely on the token ring method standards that had already been adopted by IBM.

TOKEN RING EXAMINED

Let's start by breaking token ring networks down into the key elements, and then we'll start to get a little more complex.

Check the Ring

Both Ethernet and token ring networks operate over a shared transmission medium. Token ring carefully defines which network node can use the medium and when this can be done.

As mentioned earlier, all the nodes on a token ring network are attached to a shared medium, called the *ring*, by two wire pairs. One pair delivers incoming data and the other carries outgoing data. The final node connects logically to the first, completing the ring. Originally, token ring was designed to use shielded twisted pair (STP) wiring to provide separate transmissions and reception pairs.

Physical Rings

In the early days of token ring implementation, the ring was actually physically set up just as described in the preceding paragraph with one pair coming in and one wire pair going out. This setup works acceptably, but there are some major drawbacks to consider:

- All the nodes on a physical ring must be turned on and operating for the network to be enabled.
- If a network node on the ring goes down for some reason, then the ring is broken and the network ceases to function.
- Adding and deleting nodes from the ring is difficult, time consuming, and disables the entire network while it takes place.

Although a physical ring topology might be perfectly acceptable under laboratory conditions, it would be of limited usefulness in a business environment for obvious reasons. Very early in the development of token ring networks, the wire pairs from every node were linked to a central unit. These central units go by many names:

- wire centers
- Multistation Access Units (MAUs)
- hubs
- concentrators

but they provide more or less the same major function on a token ring network.

The central units act as the nerve center and control for the token ring network, and they use internal relay switches to connect and disconnect nodes from the ring. In this configuration, a physical star, the cable from the node to wire center becomes a multipara cable, with the transmission and reception pairs both contained in one cable.

MAUs

Wire centers, MAUs, hubs, and concentrators designed for token ring networks are all based on the MSAUs designed by IBM for use as concentrators on the original 4 Mbps token ring networks. The typical MAU has eight ports for input/output cable connection to connect nodes on the network, and a ring in port and ring out port for connection to additional MAUs. Using MAUs, an extensive token ring network can be established and maintained.

Relays inside the MAU switch the transmission and reception wire pairs from a node into the ring when a node wants to join the network and out of the ring when the node wants to leave. Thus the MAU ensures that one node can't break the ring and bring down the network.

MAUs make it much easier to manage a token ring network. They make it possible to add and remove nodes without disrupting network service. They make wiring considerations much simpler, as only one cable containing the wire pairs is run from the node to the concentrator. And finally they give network administrators considerable flexibility in the layout and design of token ring networks.

Logical Rings

Now we recognize that if each node is physically plugged into the MAU and not connected directly to two other nodes on the ring, then the physical ring has become a physical star, with cables radiating out from a central hub to the individual nodes. The MAU preserves the ring, but *logically* inside the unit as opposed to physically.

In fact, the physical location of the nodes on a token ring network is not important as long as the integrity of the logical ring is maintained. Nodes may be attached to MAUs from any location depending on restrictions on cable length. Multiple MAUs can be attached to one another as well, up to the maximum ring node capacity. Capacity is 260 nodes per ring using shielded twisted pair cabling and 72 nodes per ring using unshielded twisted pain.

The Token

In a token ring network, a 3 byte packet is constantly passing from node to node in the proper direction around the logical ring. This packet is known as the *token*. Access to the network is determined by which node is in control of the token. Any node wishing to transmit must wait until it receives the token. The transmitter takes possession of the token then transmits its message out onto the network. When the transmitter receives word of successful delivery of the message by the receiver, it releases the token, which goes back into circulation around the ring.

In this way token ring networks avoid the collisions and resulting retransmissions that invariably occur during peak load times on Ethernet networks. There is only one token, and only the holder of the token can transmit onto the ring. Lets take a look at the frame for a token ring token, shown in Figure 10.1.

Start Delimiter (1 byte)	Access Control (1 byte)	End Delimiter (1 byte)

Figure 10.1   *A token ring token is a very short packet.*

TOKEN RING IN OPERATION

Token ring network operations were defined by the IEEE 802.5 committee with no operation speed specified. IBM, which set the standard for token ring implementation, designed the first token ring controllers to operate at 4 Mbps. Later implementations released were designed to operate at 16 Mbps.

However, a token ring will not support controllers operating at 4 Mbps and 16 Mbps on the same ring. But most 16 Mbps controllers can be set to operate at either 4 Mbps or 16 Mbps. First we'll take a look at how token ring transmission and reception occurs on a 4 Mbps ring, and once that's understood, we'll examine how token ring implementation was optimized to operate at 16 Mbps.

4 Mbps Token Ring Operation

In a token ring network all the packets transmitted by the nodes move in one predefined direction around the ring. Likewise, the token itself is constantly circulating. A particular node that wants to send a message must take possession of the token as it passes on the ring. Because is only one token is on the ring and only one node can have possession of the token at any given time, only one node can transmit at a time.

Technobabble: Capturing the Token

The node wishing to send captures the token and changes one bit, which converts the token to a start-of-frame sequence. A field in the token frame shows the type of priority required by the sending node for the transmission. The priority setting is the sending node's request to the other stations for use of the token. The other stations compare the sending node's request with their own priority levels. The sending node that has a higher priority it gets possession of the token. Taking possession of the token, also called *capturing the token*, takes the token off the ring. The node that captures the token then transmits its data onto the ring in packets. Each station on the ring will receive the newly transmitted information.

When it receives the SD field, the next node on the ring, the downstream node, looks into the packet to find out if it is the sender or receiver of the packet. If it is the receiver then the node copies the packet, resets the copy bit to show the packet has been copied, and sends the packet on around the ring. If the node is not the receiver, then it simply repeats the frame back onto the ring in its original state without copying the frame.

Note that all nodes on the ring act as repeaters. Under normal circumstances, only the node that originally sent the packet out can take the packet off the ring in a process known as *stripping*. The original sender of the packet strips the data from the ring and releases the token back on to the ring at the same time.

Simply put, each node on a token ring network may be in one of three states:

*   repeat mode
*   transmit mode
*   copy mode

When a node has no data that it wants to transmit to the network, it stays in normal repeat mode. If a node wants to transmit, it captures the token and goes into transmit mode. If a node downstream from the transmitter finds on examination of the packet that it is the destination node, then it goes into copy mode, copying the data and resetting the copy bits to let the original sender know that transmission was successful. When the sender receives the packet and determines that transmission was successful, it strips the data from the ring and releases the token. If, for any reason, the transmission was not successful the sending node will recapture the token and send again.

Figure 10.2 shows the format of a token ring frame carrying data.

Start Delimiter (1 byte)	Access Control (1 byte)	Frame Control (1 byte)	Destination Address (6 bytes)	Source Address (6 bytes)	Data	Frame Check Sequence (4 bytes)	End Delimiter (1 byte)	Frame Status (1 byte)

Figure 10.2   *The format of a data-carrying token ring frame.*

Reading from left to right, here's what each of the fields is about:

- *The start delimiter* signals the beginning of a data frame.
- *Access control* contains information about reservation of the token. Other nodes on the ring will grant the token if they have a lower priority.
- *Frame control* defines the type of frame, whether it is media access control information or information intended for a node on the ring. All nodes read media access control information.
- *The destination address* is a particular node, a combination of nodes, or all nodes on the ring to which a frame can be sent.
- *The source address* is the frame sender's address.
- *The data* contain the frame's payload. If the frame is a MAC frame this is where control information resides. If it's a data frame, it's size is determined by the access speed (bigger packets for 16 MB than 4 MB token ring; details follow).
- *The frame check sequence* contains error checking information. This ensures the integrity of the frame as delivered.
- *The end delimiter* announces the end of the frame.
- *The frame status* indicates whether the frame was received by the intended station or stations on the ring and the copy status of the frame.

Active Monitor

Error conditions are monitored and corrected by a node on the ring known as the *active monitor*. Any node on the ring can be designated the active monitor. Usually the first workstation on the ring when the LAN is initialized becomes the active monitor.

The active monitor ensures that the network functions efficiently and deals with error conditions such as lost tokens, tokens and frames that circle the ring more than once (if the sender receives a packet it has transmitted without the copy bits set, then some type of error condition exists), checks for other active monitors on the ring (only one per ring is allowed), and controls the synchronization of transmissions. If for any reason the active monitor should fail, the remaining nodes on the ring bid for the position of active monitor.

The active monitor periodically sends out a MAC frame to notify the other nodes on the ring that the ring clock is being managed. One of the most important functions of the active monitor is to manage phase shift on the ring, known as *jitter*. Although a transmission is repeated by each node as it goes around the ring, certain factors such as cable tolerance cause the signal to get out of phase with the reference phase on the active monitor.

The active monitor is responsible for resetting the phase to the reference phase. The amount of phase shift depends on the number of nodes, cabling, and the frequency of transmission. If the phase shift gets too great, a node will lose the timing of the transmission, causing error conditions. Buffer memory, known as *elastic buffer*, on the active monitor's controller resets the phase of a transmission as it passes by on its way around the ring. At 4 Mbps, the elastic buffer is 30 bits.

16 Mbps Token Ring Operation

The first release of token ring by IBM was designed for 4 Mbps operation at 8 MHz. In 1989, switchable controllers, capable of operating at 16 Mbps at 32 MHz or 4 Mbps were released to the market.

The 16 Mbps token ring is made possible by *early token release*, which is supported only at 16 Mbps. Early token release makes it possible for multiple packets to circulate the ring at the same time and therefore multiple nodes to transmit packets simultaneously without a collision.

Early token release is exactly what it sounds like. On the 4 Mbps ring, only one packet circulates the ring at any given time. The transmitting node strips the data from the ring after one round and releases the token to allow other nodes access. On the 16 Mbps ring, the transmitting station releases the token immediately after it finishes transmitting the data frame.

Because of the synchronized timing of the frames as they move around the ring, another node wishing to transmit will either copy or repeat the data frame before it receives the token. The second transmitting node may capture the token and send out a data frame, also releasing the token immediately after transmission. Frames travel in only one direction around the ring and pass around the ring only once and there must be some delay while the second node captures the token and transmits its message, so there is no chance that packets can collide or be mixed in transmission.

Data frames and the token may circulate simultaneously on the ring. Theoretically, all of the nodes on the ring may transmit data as the token passes around the ring. On a 16 Mbps ring, the active monitor must have

126 bits of elastic buffer to compensate for the jitter built up by the higher frequency of transmissions.

Getting on (and off) the Ring

When a node initializes and wants to join the ring, it must carry out certain operations to ensure that it causes no error conditions that would bring down the ring. The controller in the node will carry out a four step initialization routine to seek entry onto the ring:

1. The cable from the node to the MAU, known as the *lobe* is tested. The node sends packets over the lobe that are looped back from the MAU to the node. If there are no problems, then step 2 is begun.

2. The controller sends a signal to the MAU to allow it to be inserted onto the ring. A relay in the MAU is tripped, causing an interruption on the ring. The active monitor resolves the error condition caused by the interruption and sends frames reporting the new active status of the ring.

3. The new node's controller sends frames with the source and destination addresses set to its own address. This routine checks for duplicate addresses on the ring. If duplicates are found, the node removes itself from the ring. If none are found, the node moves to the next step.

4. The node identifies itself to its downstream neighbor (the one that passes frames to the node) and to its upstream neighbor (the one that the node passes frames on to).

If there are no errors during any of these steps, the new node enters the ring and is able to transmit and receive data. If for any reason the node senses an error condition, it may remove itself from the ring at any time.

Error Conditions

Two types of errors, hard and soft, can occur on a token ring network:

1. Soft errors can cause bad data transmission but do not cause the ring to go down. Soft errors are reported to the network management software and are usually corrected dynamically.

2. Hard errors recur in data transmission or cause ring failure. Typical hard errors include bad cable segments, faulty controllers, or some type of physical break in the ring.

Hard errors are relatively easy to isolate due to the characteristic design of the ring. If a hard error should occur, the node immediately downstream from the break will start sending out beacon frames. In this condition the ring is said to be *beaconing*. The source address of the beaconing node is contained in the beacon frame. The presence of the source address should give the network management software all the information it needs to isolate the position of the hard error.

SUMMARY

In its early years, the 4 Mbps token ring might have seemed an unlikely choice for networking when compared to the blazing 10 Mbps speed offered by Ethernet. But with the release of the 16 Mbps controllers for token ring, the obvious benefits of a token passing system started to get much more attractive.

Compared to the relative anarchy of an Ethernet network, token ring is much more refined and contains more built-in factors that provide stability to data transmission and the ring itself. The synchronized passage of data in one direction around the ring is easy to comprehend, and error conditions are much easier to isolate and correct than on an Ethernet network. These factors have led to increased interest in token ring networking, and more rings continue to come on-line every day.

BIBLIOGRAPHY AND REFERENCES

Bird, David. *Token Ring Network Design*: Addison-Wesley, Reading, MA: 1994. Everything you need to know about token ring, simply presented and easily understood.

Miller, Mark A. *LAN Protocol Handbook*: M&T Publishing, Redwood City, CA: 1990. A little bit about everything, a lot about some things. Great for comparisons.

Sheldon, Tom. *LAN Time Encyclopedia of Networking*: McGraw-Hill, Berkeley, CA: 1994 Covers every network subject you can imagine and in good detail. An excellent reference, especially for beginners.

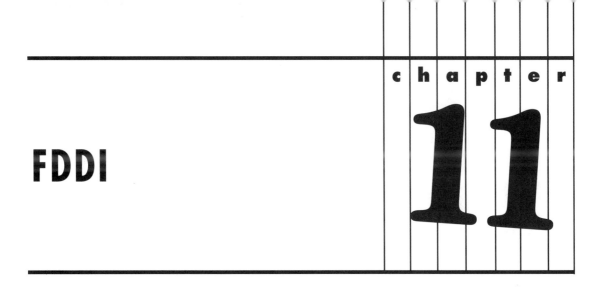

FDDI

FDDI Defined

FDDI stands for Fiber Distributed Data Interface. It is a networking standard defined by the American National Standards Institute X3T9.5 committee. The original standard calls for operation over a dual token passing ring at 100 Mbps over fiber optic cable. An FDDI ring may be as much as 120 miles long and can support up to 500 network stations.

An FDDI ring is made up of nodes connected in series by ANSI defined cable segments that form a closed ring. Data frames are transmitted from one node to another in a serial stream of bytes. Nodes receive the stream from their upstream neighbors, then regenerate that stream or repeat the symbol stream and pass it to their downstream neighbors.

When stations join the ring they agree through a bidding process on a guaranteed service time. Just like token ring networking, the node holding the token is the only one with the right to transmit. The transmitting ring transmits as needed, or as long as the agreed service time permits, and then puts the token back into circulation. When the data frame returns to the sender from its upstream neighbor the sender strips the data frame from the ring.

An FDDI ring is made up of dual, counterrotating rings. These two rings act independently unless a fault occurs, such as a break in the cable. If this happens, the rings are joined, or wrapped, so that the ring is not broken and may continue to operate. Dual rings provide redundancy and therefore add a high degree of fault tolerance to the ring.

FDDI offers a significant boost to LAN and WAN technology. Needless to say, this attractive technology standard has been the subject of lots of attention in the worldwide networking community.

WHY FDDI?

To really understand the need for FDDI networks, we have to go back to the early days of PC networking. Back in the bad old days, of course, there were no networks. PC technology was brand new, and PC users were pleased as punch to have their powerful new 8088 processors and their 5 megabyte hard drives and 128K RAM. I can remember wondering why anybody would ever need 5 megs of storage.

But, as PC popularity grew, users thought up more uses for them and developers built applications to use all their capacity. Managers charged users with more and more duties to perform on their processors, and businesses started to depend more and more on this new technology. Pretty soon, this new and seemingly limitless technology started to run into natural limits.

Once these limits were reached, new technologies were developed. Immediately, users, developers, managers, and theorists started to push the technological envelope out a little farther.

Managers dreamed of linking up all their PCs into one organizational unit. Users wanted access to more and more information. Developers scrambled to fulfill their wishes. The first Ethernet and token ring networks, flying along at 10 Mbps and 4 Mbps respectively, set new standards for business computing and ushered in a revolution in the way information was disseminated and processed in an organization.

Networking provided simple solutions to a lot of complex business problems. Once the technology was proven, everybody wanted to get in on the act. All the departments had PCs, then those PCs were networked, next departmental networks were connected, and throughout the process computers were being used for more and more tasks. Network cowboys flocked onto the wide open prairies of corporate networks and internetworks; life was good. But network administrators started to see some fences on the horizon.

More and more users for the network eventually consumed all available network resources. Engineering work groups using CAD programs, advertising and marketing sharing sophisticated graphics and design applications; developers working together on multifunctional applications—everybody competing for limited bandwidth on the network range. And like the 5 MB hard drive that seemed so big in 1985, the 4, 10, and 16 Mbps network systems started to clog up as more users took advantage of their capability.

Specs:
The ANSI X3T9.5 standards for FDDI were set to take advantage of some emerging technologies in communications and give network users and administrators more bandwidth, extending those "wide open (networking) spaces."

FDDI STANDARDS

Standards for Fiber Distributed Data Interface are defined and updated by the ANSI X3T9.5 committee. They have also have been approved by the International Standards Organization (ISO). The following sections provide an overview of the standards for FDDI adopted by the ANSI.

FDDI LAN Defined

FDDI, by definition, is a 100 Mbps timed token passing LAN. The FDDI LAN is made up of two independent, counter-rotating rings. FDDI can connect up to 500 nodes on a distributed system over a total fiber cable length of 200 kilometers (124 miles). Because fiber is used for both of the dual rings in constant operation, the effective span of an FDDI system is 62 miles.

In fact, those dual counterrotating rings that make up an FDDI ring represent the basic concept behind FDDI operation. One ring is defined as the primary ring, and the other is the secondary ring. Ordinarily the primary ring is used for data transmission and the secondary ring is used as a backup. Although the FDDI standards allow both rings to be used for data transmission, normal usage is as described. In fact, for high bandwidth transmissions, it is the recommended configuration.

In the event of a break in the ring or a node failure, the signal is wrapped back to the backup ring to preserve the continuity of the ring.

Cable

The first cable defined for the ANSI standards was multimode fiber-optic cable. But because of the need for longer network spans, additional standards were also adopted for single-mode fiber-optic cable. Recently, standards have been implemented for more traditional twisted-pair copper wire cables to supply attachments to FDDI rings over short distances (usually 300 feet or less).

Components

Component standards for FDDI are segmented into layers that can be mapped to the OSI model for network architecture. FDDI standards deal with operations that occur at the physical and datalink layers of the OSI model, as we will define in more detail later on.

Technobabble:

ANSI standards define two sublayers at the physical layer of the OSI stack:

1. The Physical Layer Medium Dependent (PMD) layer defines the requirements for cabling and connector types on the fiber ring.
2. The Physical Layer Protocol (PHY) defines the rules for operation of the lines, synchronization, and data encoding on the FDDI ring.

At the data link layer of the OSI model the ANSI committee defines an FDDI media access control (MAC) layer. The timed token protocol, frame formats, and addressing are defined at this MAC layer of FDDI.

Overlapping the physical layer and the MAC layer is the FDDI station Management (SMT) standard. As its name implies, SMT includes mechanisms for management of the PMD, PHY, and MAC layers of FDDI. SMT standards also provide the rules for establishing communications and fault protection on the FDDI ring.

Hardware

ANSI standards for FDDI also define the devices to be used in fiber networking. The following devices are the most important for this chapter:

- *Concentrators.* Concentrators act as repeaters on the FDDI ring. The concentrator allows for the attachment of multiple single or dual attachment stations to the ring. There can be single attachment concentrators (SACs) or dual attachment concentrators (DACs) which both act as connection points and allow connection through M ports. SACs attach to the ring through their own S ports, DACs attach through A and B ports and can be directly attached to the primary or secondary ring.

- *Single attachment stations (SAS).* SAS stations have one S port and connect to the ring through the M port of a concentrator.

- *Dual attachment stations (DAS).* DAS stations have two ports, A and B. The A port connects to the B port on another station and the B port connects to another station's A port. The DAS can connect to both primary and secondary rings.

Physical Layer Medium Dependent (PMD) Protocol

The PMD layer of FDDI is where the power levels, node interface requirements, acceptable error levels, and cable and connector specifications are defined. Standards exist for multimode fiber-optic cable, single mode fiber, and for twisted-pair cable. Fiber-optic cable is not designed to carry electromagnetic impulses, like traditional copper cable. Fiber-optic cables carry an optical signal, a ray or mode of light is used to transmit instead. Fiber optics offer some significant advantages over copper cable:

- Immunity to electrical or magnetic interference.
- Security—no bleeding of the signal outside the cable means there can be no monitoring of cable traffic from outside the ring.
- No impedance, as is associated with copper cable. This means fewer transmission errors and a resulting decrease in traffic on the network
- Distance—fiber-optic cable can convey signals over long distance with limited degradation

Optical fiber is made up of a central core of flexible glass surrounded by a glass tube called the *cladding tube*. The two central tubes are in turn surrounded by an outer coating that protects the optical fibers from damage.

Multimode Fiber

Multimode fiber carries multiple modes (rays) of light emitted by light emitting diodes (LEDs). It is used to connect nodes spaced no more than 2 kilometers (1.2 miles) apart.

Single-Mode Fiber

Single-mode fiber is used where distances between nodes are much longer. The signal is transmitted by a laser light source. Single mode fiber can support much larger distances between nodes. The link distance for single mode fiber is slightly more than 20 kilometers (12.4 miles).

Twisted-Pair

Standards exist for using STP and UTP cable for links of no more than 300 feet.

Connectors

Media interface connectors (MICs) are used to physically connect a fiber cable to a node on an FDDI network. MICs are polarized to ensure the quality of the signal over the link.

ST-type connectors are also used to provide a lower cost alternative to MICs. ST connectors are not polarized

Ports

FDDI standards allow only certain types of connections to make sure that no nonstandard links can be constructed on an FDDI ring. There are four port types: A, B, M, and S. Dual attach stations have two ports, A and B. A single attach station has only one port, the S port. Concentrators have several M ports for connecting to the A, B, or S ports on connected nodes.

Physical Layer Protocol (PHY)

At this level of FDDI, the nonmedia dependent physical layer is defined.

Clock and Data Recovery

Every node on the FDDI ring has a locally generated clock responsible for synchronizing transmission on the ring. A receiving node synchronizes its local clock to the incoming symbol stream from the upstream node and decodes the data using the new setting. When the node repeats the stream for transmission, it uses its local clock as the timing source.

Encoding

On an FDDI ring, symbols are used to transmit information between the nodes. The symbol is the basic unit of FDDI encoding. When the PHY layer receives information from the MAC layer, it converts the information into an *encoded bit stream,* using either of two encoding schemes:

4B/5B

NRZ/NRZI

The encoding process creates uniform 5-bit code groups for transmission and reduces the bandwidth necessary for the transmission.

Symbols

32 symbols are used for FDDI transmission. The symbols are grouped into three main types:

Data. Of the defined symbols, 16 are used to represent data in hexadecimal form on the FDDI ring.

Line state. When a connection begins, groups of line state symbols are transmitted between the PHY layers on the nodes. Idle symbols are sent between frames for synchronization.

Control indicator. These symbols indicate the status of a frame.

Elasticity Buffer

The PHY layer of FDDI controls the elasticity buffers that make up for phase shift as frames are repeated around the ring. As in 4/16 Mbps token ring, the elasticity buffers can store enough bits from the transmission to ensure that clock frequency differences create no error situation.

Smoothing

The start of an FDDI frame is a preamble containing idle control indicator symbols. The smoother function of the PHY layer is to replace any bits lost from the preamble as it is repeated around the ring. Loss of the preamble can cause a receiving node to not recognize an incoming frame and lose it.

Repeat Filter

The repeat filter basically ensures the proper functioning of the ring. The repeat filter will not allow code violations and invalid line states on the ring. The repeat filter is also invaluable in locating error conditions on the ring.

Media Access Control (MAC)

Like 4/16 Mbps token ring, FDDI uses a token passing access method. The token passes around the ring and is captured by any node that wants to transmit. The transmitting station sends frames downstream on the ring until it is finished or until it reaches end of its predetermined transmission interval.

When finished, for whatever reason, with the transmission, the node releases the token back onto the ring. Releasing the token gives other nodes a chance to take control of the token and transmit. Frames from multiple nodes can coexist on the ring. When the destination node repeats a frame, it recognizes its own address, copies the data into local memory and sends the copy symbols along to its downstream neighbor. When a transmitting node receives its transmission from its upstream node, it strips the data from the ring.

The MAC layer also oversees operation of the timed token protocol (TTP). The TTP allows for the nodes on the ring to negotiate and determine the target token rotation time (TTRT). TTRT is used by TTP to guarantee that each node will have access to the token at predetermined intervals.

Three types of frames carry information around the ring. MAC frames carry MAC control data, SMT frames carry ring management information, and LLC frames carry link level service information. Even though the Logical Link Control (LLC) layer is not defined by FDDI standards, FDDI assumes and requires that IEEE 802.2 standards defining LLC at the data link layer of the OSI stack are implemented.

Station Management (SMT)

Management of the ring processes is defined by the SMT standard. SMT provides the monitoring and control functions in an FDDI node. Three major functions are handled by SMT. *Connection management* handles traffic between instances of PHY and MAC layers within a node, listens for errors on the ring, and takes care of insertion and removal of nodes at the physical layer. *Ring management* detects error conditions on the ring and reports to SMT and higher level processes operating on the node. SMT *frame services* sends out frames of different types to aid in mapping the ring and reporting on the status of the ring nodes.

FDDI Transmission Modes

FDDI supports three different modes of transmission on the ring. The first two modes, synchronous and asynchronous, are part of the original FDDI standard. The new FDDI-II standard also supports circuit-based, or guaranteed-bandwidth connections as well as the original two standards.

Synchronous
Synchronous transmission allows for bandwidth to be reserved for transmission and guarantees that time-sensitive transmissions arrive at a preset time. The network manager is responsible for setting aside the dedicated bandwidth.

Asynchronous

This is the standard timed token transmission mode. The station holding the token broadcasts over the network as needed and is bounded by only the preset time it is allowed to hold the token.

Circuit Based

Live video, and multimedia transmission can suffer on an FDDI ring by having to contend with other frames on the ring. FDDI-II was created as an upgrade to FDDI to provide for time-sensitive transmission. The circuit-based mode creates a dedicated link between nodes and reserves assigned bandwidth for the transmission.

SUMMARY

The FDDI standards define a fast, efficient method of transport for networking on a timed token ring. Fiber-optic technology and fiber cabling combine with the protocol standards to provide for fault tolerant transmissions over extremely long distances. FDDI is an excellent choice for the backbone of an extended internetworking system.

BIBLIOGRAPHY AND REFERENCES

Michael, Wendy H., William J. Cronin and Karl F. Pieper. *Fiber Distributed Data Interface: An Introduction*. Digital Press, Burlington, MA: 1993 The definitive guide to FDDI.

Sheldon, Tom. *LAN Time Encyclopedia of Networking*. McGraw-Hill, Berkeley, CA: 1994 Covers every network subject you can imagine and in good detail. All the FDDI basics.

ISDN

The first network technology to revolutionize the way we live and do business has been in place for almost 100 years. That's right. The world's first telephone network, created with state-of-the-art technology, was already being assembled over 100 years ago. This chapter will explore how developments in telephone and computer technology have combined to provide a new digital communications network, the *integrated systems digital network*, or ISDN.

ISDN Defined

ISDN is the name for a worldwide communications network that will provide end-to-end digital connectivity among user devices of different types and functions. The ISDN has evolved from existing technologies in the computer and telephone communications industries. Standards for ISDN call for the integration of voice, video, audio, and data transmission over a single communications link.

ISDN Standards

Standards may be defined as follows: a prescribed set of rules, conditions, or requirements concerning definition of terms; classification of components; specification of materials, performance, or operation; delineation of procedures; or measurement of quantity and quality in describing materials, product, systems, services, or practices.

Several standards organizations have involved themselves in defining the standards for the proposed ISDN. The preeminent body in this group is the International Telegraph and Telephone Consultative Committee (CCITT).

The CCITT definition of ISDN follows: "An ISDN is a network, in general evolving from a telephony IDN, that provides end-to-end digital connectivity to support a wide range of services, including voice and nonvoice services, to which users have access by a limited set of standard multi-purpose user-network interfaces."

Specs:

In 1984 the CCITT defined the following *principles* for ISDN.

1. ISDN should support a range of voice and non-voice applications. Service integration for an ISDN should take place using a limited set of connection types and user–network interface arrangements.

2. ISDNs support a variety of applications, including switched and nonswitched connections. Switched connections should include both circuit-switched and packet-switched connections.

3. New services introduced into ISDN should be arranged to be compatible with 64 kbps switched digital connections.

4. ISDNs will contain intelligence to provide service features, maintenance, and network management functions. This intelligence may not be sufficient for some new services and may have to be supplemented by either additional intelligence within the network or, possibly, compatible intelligence in the user terminals.

5. A layered protocol structure should be used for the specification of the access to an ISDN. Access from a user to ISDN resources may vary depending upon the service required and the status of implementation of national ISDNs.

6. It is recognized that ISDNs may be implemented in a variety of configurations according to specific national situations.

Further, the CCITT recommends the following evolutionary pattern for the move to ISDN.

1. ISDNs will be based on concepts developed for telephone ISDNs and may evolve by incorporating additional functions and network features, including those of any other dedicated networks such as circuit switching and packet switching for data to provide for existing and new services.

2. Arrangements must be developed for the interworking of services on ISDNs and services on other networks as the transition from pre-ISDN to ISDN networks proceeds.

3. An evolving ISDN may also include, at later stages, switched connections at bit rates higher and lower than 64 kbps.

As this chapter unfolds, we'll see how these standards have been implemented in various ways and explore the parts of the ISDN. Right now, let's check out how we got this far.

EVOLUTION OF ISDN

ISDN, which may seem like a revolutionary new technology, is really a merging of computer technologies that have been developing over the past 50 years and telephone technologies that were in their experimental stages almost 150 years ago. No one could have predicted the exponential growth in computing over the past 10 years, but this concatenation of technologies has been anticipated for some time.

Analog Communication

Telephone communication is based on human speech. The original goal of the telephone's developers was to provide a means to transport the human voice faithfully (or at least audibly) over long distances. In its beginning phases, digital telephony wasn't even a pipe dream. Early practitioners of the telephonic arts used the human voice, which they were determined to transmit and re-create, as the basis for development of their systems.

Human voices generate sounds that travel through the air in continuous waves. These waves are known as *analog* signals. Analog voice signals cause vibrations on a membrane in the human ear, which converts the waves into recognizable sound. Not surprisingly, a conventional telephone receiver acts much like the human ear: speaking into the phone transmits vibrations onto a membrane, generating electric impulses that are transmitted as a continuous wave over the phone lines. On the other end of a connection, telephone receivers interpret these electrical impulses and re-create corresponding sound waves as close to the original as the limits of the equipment will allow.

Because these electric pulses are analogous to the sound waves that generate them, telephony is said to be based on analog transmission, in the same way that human speech is based on analog transmission.

The original phone system was made up of a single transmitter connected to a single receiver over a single wire. Early commercial telephone implementations offered phone service only to sites directly connected by discrete wires. As the popularity of phone service grew exponentially, the basic components that now make up the international telephone network began to be developed and brought on line.

The first addition to the phone system was the addition of *central offices* (COs), which provided a common switching point for all the phone lines in a given geographical area. All telephone system end users were connected to the CO by their *subscriber loops*. A call would come through the central office over a subscriber loop and a connection to the receiving subscriber would be made. At first these connections were made manually by operators by physically connecting wires on patch panels to establish the connections between subscribers.

In the next phase of elaboration, COs were linked by trunk lines. Multiple COs could also be linked by *tandem offices*. A tandem office contains a *tandem switch* that can switch transmissions over trunk lines and handle the routing of calls between COs. Tandem switches lower the cost of phone transmission by providing links between COs that do not require a dedicated direct trunk line.

Since 1984 the United States has been divided into 161 *local access and transport areas* (LATAs), made up of local loops, COs, and tandem switches. Long distance calls are handled by inter-LATA carriers. COs or tandem offices switch calls to the inter-LATA carriers, where calls are transmitted and switched between LATAs in the same way they are transmitted and switched between COs. This may sound complex (and in many ways it is), but it also means that almost any call in the United States can get between caller and callee by going through less than six involved parties: two local loops, two LATAs, and one or two inter-LATA carriers. Logically, this bespeaks a complex and pervasive communications grid.

Computer Design

While the telephone network was extending worldwide, the development of modern computing began. All communications inside computing machines, between computers and their peripheral devices, and between interconnected computers is handled digitally.

Although telephone system was originally based on analog transmission and evolved from that point, there has never been a precedent for analog transmission in a computing environment. Computers have always been based on digital information and instructions. Thus, communications inside the computer and among devices attached to computers has always been digital.

Coming Together Digitally

Telephony has always had two major concerns in implementing telephone networks: transmission and switching. Transmission is concerned with the lines that carry telephone connections. Switching has to do with the way the transmission links are requested, maintained, and broken once a call is completed.

Digital First Carriers

The first major use of computer, or digital, technology in the phone network was in transmission. Although most local subscriber loops in the United States are still analog, the more sophisticated transmission functions of telephony have been converted to digital. The first digital lines used in the United States were *digital first carrier systems* (T1), made up of two wire pairs, one for transmission and one for reception. T1 lines were introduced into the phone network to provide a high volume link between COs and between COs and tandem offices. Analog signals are converted to a digital bit stream and transmitted over the T1 line.

Switches

The first switching devices on the telephone network were electromechanical switches called *step-by-step* switches. Like their name implies, step-by-step switches reacted to each digit dialed by the user and made physical connections in the switch to route the call. The next step in switch development was to provide *common control* of the switching function within the switch. Common control switching is based on a series of electromechanical relays in the switch. Instructions for electromechanical switching were defined by the wiring of the switch.

Stored program switches, made possible by the development of the transistor, were implemented next to allow for easier reprogramming of switches in the phone network. Stored program switches began to be installed in the network in the early 1970s. Essentially they were digital switches, and their inclusion into the telephone network, taken together with the implementation of T1 transmission lines, marks the beginning of the digitalization of the telephone network and the beginning of the evolution of ISDN.

Inclusion of digital switches and high volume digital transmission lines made for a high volume of analog to digital and digital to analog conversions within the network. Although these conversions were practical and necessary, considering the evolution of the phone network, they also added considerable overhead and cost to transmission of phone calls without adding any value to the connection. Engineers in the phone network immediately began to convert more of the transmission and switching functions from analog to digital to deal with this overhead and cost by reducing the number of conversions.

Digital Communications

Computers have always used digital communication for controlling devices and for communication over the local bus. The development of the local area network (LAN) led to a slightly more complex form of digital communication—communication between computers. LANs allowed for powerful new applications of computer technology. The development of LAN technology was the first step toward the linking of LANs into wide are networks (WANs).

Widespread adoption of WANs led to large-scale use of the telephone network to complete the links in a WAN. Computer network nodes on a WAN may be connected not only by local cable but by telephone links. Digital computer signals are converted to analog signals and reconverted on the receiving end to digital by modulating and demodulating equipment (modems). Even though this conversion causes considerable delay and increases network overhead, the benefits of wide area networking made it practical and necessary. Widespread use of telephone lines for data transfer created a new use for phone switching and transmission equipment and was an important factor in the push for a fully digital telephone system.

Getting Together

Computers have come to be used almost as much for communications as for processing and they depend on telephone lines for much of the transport of their information. The telephone network has become increasingly dependent on digital technology developed for computers to provide more bandwidth on trunk lines and enable faster switching and signal conversion. As these two related technologies come to rely more and more on one another, we have seen the realization of many of the standards that have been created for ISDN.

Telephony standards have been in place for quite some time that call for the implementation of an *integrated digital network* (IDN). The *I* in IDN stands for the integration of digital switching and transmission into an end-to-end digital link for transmission.

As innovations in telephone and computer technology make the IDN more of a reality than a specification, computer users have pushed for the next step, the ISDN, the creation of a worldwide digital network that will offer not only seamless digital connectivity but also allow the network to provide a variety of services to users on request.

END-TO-END ISDN

An ISDN local loop, the line from the CO to the user location, is designed to carry digital signals from the user out onto the digital communications network and deliver these signals to their destination. This connectivity is achieved using various ISDN channels, access interfaces, functional devices, and reference points. Further, the ISDN is expected to provide a set of services defined in the standards and a larger subset of supplementary services.

Reference Points and Devices

To describe the way an ISDN is arranged architecturally, we'll start with a discussion of the standards for ISDN devices and then describe the way these devices are connected by defining the reference points between them.

Functional Devices

ISDN standards define several types of devices. Separate devices may have different purposes and functions, which may exist physically or not. Here is a list of the various recognized types of ISDN functional devices:

- ISDN terminal equipment (TE1)
- customer premises switching equipment (NT2)
- local loop terminator (NT1)
- ISDN local exchange (LE)
- non-ISDN terminal equipment (TE2)
- terminal adapter (TA)

Reference Points

Many device-to-device connections are defined in the ISDN standards. Each connection type, or interface, requires a defined protocol. Each of these interfaces is described as a *reference point*.

Specs:
Four reference points are defined by ISDN standards:

1. The R reference point describes the interface between non-ISDN terminals (TE2) and terminal adapters (TA).

2. The S reference describes the interface between an ISDN terminal (TE1) or terminal adapter (TA) and a network terminating device (NT1 or NT2).

3. The T reference point is the interface between a local switching device (NT2) and the local loop termination (NT1).

4. The U reference point exists between the NT1 and the ISDN local exchange (LE) and defines the standard for communications between the two. CCITT international standards define the NT1 device as a part of the local network and therefore do not deal with standards on the local subscriber loop. ANSI standards in the United States define transmission standards over the local loop.

ISDN Channels

An ISDN local or subscriber loop is designed to carry only digital signals. The loop will be composed of distinct logical channels used for signaling between users and the network and for transmission of user data. ISDN standards define the following channels:

- The D channel is designed to carry signals from users to the network and vice versa. Though it is intended for signal transmissions it may be configured for data transmission
- The B channel provides bearer services. It carries voice, data, audio, and video data at a rate of 64 kbps.
- The H channel provides bearer services at a much higher capacity than the B channel.
- B-ISDN channels will enable applications requiring transmission speeds and bandwidth at much higher rates than those defined for H channels. The standards allow for transmission rates as high as 622.08 Mbps.

Access Interfaces

ISDN standards define two common access interfaces to the digital network, the basic rate interface (BRI) and the primary rate interface (PRI).

Basic Rate Interface

The basic rate interface is made up of two B channels and one D channel. The designation for this configuration is 2B + D. The D channel operates at 64 kbps. Each B channel is configured for transfer at a rate of 64 kbps. The combined maximum user data rate for the BRI is 144 kbps.

Primary Rate Interface

In the United States, the PRI is defined as 23 B channels plus one D channel operating at 64 kbps. The PRI can also be configured as 24 B channels, all operating at 64 kbps. Other possible configurations of the PRI are aggregations of B channels combined to provide necessary bandwidth.

BEARER SERVICES

A *bearer service* is the method for transporting end user data from one location on the ISDN to another. ISDN standards define a set of distinct bearer services that they feel are sufficient to fill all the requirements for end user data transfer.

Bearer services are defined by attributes of three general types:

- access
- transfer
- general

Different users use ISDN for different purposes at different times. Some users will use the ISDN primarily for voice communication, others will use it often for the transfer of large files. The committees that set the standards for ISDN had a choice. They could attempt to define a separate and distinct bearer service for each use and potential use or they could define general categories of bearer service that would be flexible enough to encompass any new developments.

Standards developers decided that a large number of defined bearer services would add unwarranted complexity to the ISDN. As the purpose of the ISDN is to simplify communications, the developers settled on description of three types of general categories of bearer services.

Circuit-Switched Voice

Traditional phone conversations take place over *circuit-switched voice* channels. A circuit switched voice connection is established at the start of a call. The transmission bandwidth and network switches necessary to complete the call are assigned to the connection at the beginning and belong to the caller for its duration.

With ISDN, the voice connection is made over one of the B channels. The signaling needed to establish the connection is made over the D channel. The call initiator exchanges messages with the network, and the network exchanges messages with the destination user, using *SS7* messages that are forwarded over the D channel.

Because ISDN standards provide for two B channels, there is the potential to make two voice calls over the ISDN at the same time. Messages can be exchanged between the call end points over the D channel at the same time. This represents significant improvement over traditional telephone calling.

Circuit-switched voice transmission over ISDN also allows users to invoke *supplementary services* that add an ever-increasing list of capabilities. Many of these supplementary services are already in common use on the phone network. Many more are being added to ISDN services each year. A brief listing of some of the more important supplementary services follows:

- Direct Dialing In (DDI) allows an ISDN user to forward a call through a PBX or private network directly to the destination without operator interference.

- Calling Line Identification Presentation (CLIP) delivers the ISDN number of a caller to the destination

- Malicious Call Identification (MCI) traces prank, obscene, or just plain nuisance (JPN) calls

- Call Transfer (CT) allows the transfer of an established call to a third party.

- Call Waiting (CW), the network notifies the ISDN user of an incoming call when no B channel is available.

- Conference Calling (CONF) allows multiple users simultaneous use of the call circuit.

- Priority Service allows users to set priority of incoming and outgoing calls.

There are many more supplementary services. The point is that all of these services will be available to the ISDN user, and they can be accessed at any time. A user will simply request the service by signaling to the network.

Basically, circuit mode voice transmission over ISDN feels the same as traditional telephone voice transmission. The benefits of the ISDN connection will be faster call setup and the availability of a variety of supplementary services.

Circuit Switched Data

Most data communication over the phone network today is handled by modems that convert digital computer signals into modulated signals for transmission over the analog phone line and then demodulate the signal to reconvert it to digital for the receiving computer. Analog modems handle this function.

On the ISDN, there is no need for this conversion. The ISDN circuit connection for data transfer has been compared to a "digital extension cord," in which the ISDN transfers unconverted digital information between computers.

A circuit-switched data transmission over ISDN takes less than 1 sec to be established and can allow for data transmission speeds over a 64 kbps B channel at a throughput rate of up to 128 kbps using compression algorithms. This marks a significant improvement over modem setup and transfer times.

Packet Switched Data

When a circuit-switched voice or data call is made, the entire 64kbps bandwidth is reserved for the channel. This bandwidth is held by the circuit for the duration of the call. Packet-switched transmission the channel is divided into several logical channels. One B channel could be used to provide several simultaneous connections for packet switched data transfer. Even the D channel can be used for packet switched transfer requiring bandwidth of less than 16 kbps.

Packet-switched connections make for more efficient use of available bandwidth and lowers the cost of the transmissions.

ISDN PROTOCOLS

As it is described, ISDN maps to the lower three levels of the OSI model for network architecture. A full analysis of ISDN protocols is too complicated to present here, but for simplicity's sake, we show the ISDN protocols as they map to the OSI model.

The CCITT describes ISDN as consisting of the control plane (C plane), the user plane (U plane), the management plane (M plane), and the transport plane (T plane). The *transport plane* corresponds to the physical layer of the OSI model and deals primarily with the transport media involved in communication. The *user plane* carries information between user applications. The *management plane* handles communications between the different protocol levels in the stack.

Most ISDN protocols deal with the interface between the user and the ISDN network, done over the D channel, which operates at the C plane. ISDN protocols for the D channel can be mapped to the lower three layers of the OSI model:

- Layer 1 protocol defines the physical connection, the coding scheme, and frame construction of the connection between the local network terminator and an ISDN terminal.

- Layer 2 uses the link access procedures to handle fault tolerance over the link and set up logical connections between users and the network.

- Layer 3 protocols provide for signaling between the customer network and the network provider switching equipment.

BROADBAND ISDN

The description of ISDN up until this point has been directed at an explanation of what is called *narrowband* ISDN (*n*-ISDN). N-ISDN is so called to distinguish it from a type of ISDN transmission that will provide exponentially increased bandwidth to applications that suffer from the delay imposed by the 1.5 Mbps speeds provided by PRIs. This new type of ISDN is known as *broadband* ISDN (B-ISDN).

Some ISDN services will need transmission speeds greater than those that can be delivered by a single PRI. These services are to be delivered by *broadband* ISDN. B-ISDN services are loosely divided into two main groups, communications services and distribution services

Communications Services

Communications services include all of the services delivered over the traditional analog telephone network, as well as conversational, messaging, and retrieval services. Here's a bit more detail on each of these subjects:

- *Conversational* services are two-way real-time communications between remote user stations. Video teleconferencing is one major service made possible by B-ISDN.
- *Messaging* services enable the transfer of user-to-user mail applications including voice, video, and document services in any combination.
- *Retrieval* services offer users access to databases of information stored as video, text, images, documents, or data.

Distribution Services

Distribution services will provide users of the B-ISDN access to network services such as high density television (HDTV), pay-per-view television, video libraries, interactive multimedia applications, news services. They are defined as being *user controlled* or not. Access to on line video databases might be described as user controlled, because users can choose when they want access and to what they want access at any given time.

Services outside user control would be HDTV programming, which can be understood as analogous to present-day TV programming. The network provides broadcasts of programs and information at scheduled times, and users may choose access to them are not.

Asynchronous Transfer Mode

A new type of data delivery mechanism, similar to packet delivery, is being provided as the transport mechanism for B-ISDN. Called asynchronous transfer mode (ATM), it is carried out by cells similar to frames and allows for delivery of data within preset transmission parameters with a high degree of accuracy.

The next chapter will deal exclusively with ATM and B-ISDN.

Summary

The first worldwide technological network was the telephone network. The telephone was developed to provide communication facilities analogous to human speech.

As more and more users got into the phone network, various additions and improvements were made to allow for the increase in demand and keep the cost of services as low as possible. Original telephone operations were improved and linked up with the new technologies to create network of telephone links that covered the entire world.

Computers have always been based on communication using a stream of binary bits. In other words, computers have always used digital communication. At the end of the 1980s, computers started to become more powerful, more flexible in their uses, and more affordable. Traditional mainframe batch processing has been mostly phased out and replace with distributed, or enterprise, systems, made up of multiple desktop computers linked together in local area networks (LANs) are in turn linked, often over telephone lines, to form wide area networks (WANs).

Developments in the computer field made possible the creation of digital switches and transmission lines to make telephone communication simpler and cheaper. Introduction of the first digital trunk lines in the 1960s and the first digital switches in the 1970s marked the beginning of the transformation from analog to digital telephony.

The overhead and time required to transform digital stream computer signals to analog signals for transmission over the telephone network causes sluggish or downright unacceptable performance on computer networks. The demand for faster and more accurate transmission of computer information over telephone systems has pushed the move to a completely digital phone network, the Integrated Services Digital Network (ISDN).

ASYNCHRONOUS TRANSFER MODE

ABOUT ATM

ATM or *asynchronous transfer mode* is a technology based on cell formation and a type of multiplexing that provides users with broadband Integrated Services Digital Network (ISDN) services requiring extremely high transmission rates (see Chapter 12 for a discussion of ISDN). ATM can supply users access to this high bandwidth, over a broadband ISDN channel (B-ISDN) where voice, data, audio, video, and network signal traffic may be fully integrated.

Standards for ISDN, defining the basic rate interface (BRI) and the primary rate interface (PRI) allow for integrated transmission over ISDN. The predefined channels of the BRI and PRI provide access to *narrowband* ISDN (N-ISDN) services. These may be handled by conventional telephone lines for local access services. ATM, on the other hand, provides significantly greater bandwidth and usually requires fiber-optic media for long-haul transmission.

The CCITT, which set the standards for ISDN, have designated ATM as the transmission technology to provide transport for *broadband* (B-ISDN) services on the ISDN. B-ISDN standards deal with services requiring high transmission rates, like video information services, high-speed data transfer, and real-time video teleconferencing. ATM standards deal with the organization of data into *cells* for transmission, and describe the way bandwidth is multiplexed for carrying B-ISDN services.

ATM technology has been adapted for use over a seamless digital network made up of ATM devices ranging from network interface cards to high-volume digital network switches acting as backbones linking multiple LANs. In this chapter we take a look at broadband ISDN, present the standards for ATM, and look in to how the network and communications worlds are coming together over ATM.

BROADBAND ISDN

Broadband ISDN services, defined in CCITT standards, are characterized by their need for high bit rates in transmission. B-ISDN is differentiated from the original *narrowband ISDN* by its need to meet the high bandwidth requirements as they occur.

The BRI offers a considerable degree of functionality to ISDN users, and the PRI multiplies available bandwidth by a significant amount. Standards for BRIs and PRIs define what is now known as narrowband ISDN. ISDN standards calling for high bandwidth services define a new category of ISDN, broadband ISDN.

Most B-ISDN services call for much higher transfer rates than the PRI can provide. B-ISDN services such as high-speed data transfer, and real-time video teleconferencing need lots of bandwidth, as much as 25 Mbps for compressed high resolution video. A customer requiring these services would need a bundle of PRIs to provide the necessary bandwidth, and transfer of all that information would monopolize a standard N-ISDN channel. Conversely, when high bandwidth services aren't being accessed, lots of interface bandwidth will be unused.

Customers using N-ISDN are paying for available bandwidth. B-ISDN customers have similar requirements for N-ISDN services, but sometimes require higher bandwidth for access to services unique to B-ISDN. B-ISDN channels must still be able to handle tasks like packet transfer and telephone calls, but the B-ISDN standards also call for the integration of bandwidth-intensive services over the same access loop. So the B-ISDN channel must be *scalable*. This means that the channel must allow high bit rate transfers for B-ISDN services when needed, so that the customer using a B-ISDN channel pays for bandwidth that is used, not a static preassigned bandwidth like that supplied by N-ISDN channels.

Asynchronous transfer mode is the technology defined in the standards as the bearer of broadband ISDN services. A B-ISDN channel is multiplexed using ATM to provide a single channel over which traditional N-ISDN services and B-ISDN services may be integrated. In this chapter we'll take a look at the basic unit of ATM technology, called a *cell*, and describe how ATM cells and switches allow integration of bandwidth-intensive applications.

ATM TRANSPORT

N-ISDN access interfaces, the BRI and the PRI, depend on a time division multiplexing scheme called *synchronous transfer mode. Synchronous*, in this context, refers to the division of the physical frames used in transmission into time-dependent slots that occur at preset intervals. Synchronous transmission depends on regularly occurring slots in physical layer frames that define different channels for the access interface. In synchronous transfer mode (N-ISDN), a framing bit that is always followed by an 8-bit slot for the first B-channel, occurs at regularly timed intervals (with strict time synchronization enforced between senders and receivers). The next 8 bits define the second B-channel, and so on. Physical layer frames always contain channel-defining bits, whether a channel is idle or in active use.

B-ISDN services could be carried over N-ISDN channels, but the potential for wasted bandwidth is unacceptably high. Because ISDN customers pay for bandwidth, reserving B-channels for short, high-speed transmissions doesn't make economic sense.

To provide a pay-as-you-go allocation for bandwidth, and to allow high bandwidth transmission when needed, B-ISDN services are transmitted *asynchronously*. Synchronous transmissions provide channel access at preset intervals determined by available bandwidth, but asynchronous transmissions employ channels that are created as they are needed to carry data. Certain types of transmissions are assigned priority and are placed in contiguous slots in the cell. This gives high-bandwidth traffic immediate access to the physical link and explains how ATM is able to supply bandwidth on demand.

ATM Cells

The basic unit of ATM technology is the *cell*. ATM standards call for a fixed-size cell composed of 53 bytes. Header information is contained in 5 bytes, and 48 bytes are used to carry user data, called the *payload*. Packets, used in other types of data transmission, like LAN access methods or frame relay systems, can vary in length. Differences in length can cause delays, as longer packets take more time to prepare and switch than shorter packets.

The uniform size of ATM cells is one of the keys to the speed and accuracy of ATM transmission. The uniform size of the ATM cell allows for faster transmission and switching with predictable delivery times. A common analogy used to describe this situation is to compare packet traffic to automobile and truck traffic on a city street. Although cars can flow right along through the traffic switches—which can be viewed as intersections controlled by traffic lights—a couple of trucks or buses can really slow things down. Taking this analogy a few steps further, we could picture ATM cell traffic as a long line of identical Volkswagens, all traveling at the same speed, with all the drivers scrupulously obeying traffic laws. All the drivers get where they're going as quickly as possible, in this scenario.

Cell Structure

An ATM cell is the fundamental unit of ATM technology. The cell is always 53 bytes in length, with 48 bytes used for carrying data and 5 bytes containing header information. Figure 13.1 shows the fields in an ATM header.

Generic flow control (4 bits)	Virtual path identifier (8 bits)	Virtual channel identifier (16 bits)	Payload type (3 bits)	Cell loss priority (1 bit)	Header error check (8 bits)

Figure 13.1 *An ATM header.*

The header of an ATM cell identifies the destination, type of cell, and the priority of the transmission. The generic flow control (GFC) field can be used to define the type of B-ISDN service being carried and allows multiple ATM devices access to the B-ISDN network at different bit rates. The virtual path identifier (VPI) is used to assign virtual paths between users or between users and the B-ISDN network.

The virtual channel identifier designates a particular virtual channel linking users or users and the network. The *payload type indicator* (PT) tells whether the information transported is user, network, or management data. The cell loss priority field contains priority values. Higher values mean lower priority for transmission, with a zero signifying that no cells can be dropped. Header error control (HEC) provides a capability for error detection and correction at the bit level.

ATM Switching

ATM switches are the heart of the ATM beast. ATM provides a connection-oriented transport service for networking. Connection identifiers are assigned to each cell and are used for switching instead of full addresses. A virtual circuit connects ATM end stations. ATM cell headers provide only enough routing information to give the ATM switch enough information to route cells to the correct output links. The routing label and incoming link are used to determine outgoing links at the ATM switch.

ATM connections can be point-to-point or multipoint, and they are of two distinct types—*virtual channels* and *virtual paths*. ATM devices may act as endpoints, generating and receiving cells, or as connecting points, handling switching over the ATM.

Virtual Paths

Logical connections between endpoints in the ATM network are known as virtual paths. A virtual path is a collection of virtual channels that have the same endpoints. A virtual path connection is the combination of a series of virtual path links between endpoints and their associated connecting points. Multiplexing of the virtual path allows for switching of several virtual channels at the same time over one logical connection.

Virtual path identifiers. Virtual path identifiers identify a particular link formed by a virtual path between endpoints or between an endpoint and a connection point. VPIs can be thought of as port addresses within the ATM network.

Virtual Channels

Virtual channels represent the connection between ATM equipment at both ends of the transmission. A virtual channel connection is made up of all the virtual channel links between ATM switches.

Virtual channel identifiers. A virtual channel identifier is used to identify individual channels associated with a particular virtual path.

ATM Protocol Architecture

ATM's model is a subset of the protocol model for B-ISDN. Standards for B-ISDN result in a segmented model that maps to the physical and data link layers of the OSI stack.

B-ISDN Model

Note that the B-ISDN model is made up of planes just like the ISDN model. The control and user planes cut across the model from the higher layers right down to the physical layer. The management plane is divided into two parts, with a layer management plane that manages interfaces between each layer in the control and user planes, and a plane management plane which provides a framework for the structured interaction of the protocols in the stack.

ATM Protocol Stack

In this chapter we're primarily interested in the ATM layers related to the B-ISDN planes. These layers really describe ATM function—the physical layer, the ATM layer, and the ATM adaptation layers (AALs).

Physical Layer

The physical layer is made up of two sublayers: the *transmission convergence* (TC) sublayer and the *physical medium* (PM) sublayer. The PM sublayer interfaces with the physical medium used to provide the link and passes the transmitted bit stream up to the TC sublayer.

The TC sublayer puts ATM cells into the bit stream in frames and recovers the frame's extract cells from the stream. These cells are either received from the ATM layer or are handed up to the ATM layer.

ATM Layer

The ATM layer handles mutiplexing, switching, and control actions. At this layer the information from the ATM cell header is decoded to provide necessary information for ATM layer actions. Conversely, at this layer the ATM header is created and encoded with transmission information.

At the ATM layer, information is generated and interpreted that provides for the fast switching capabilities of ATM. The ATM layer protocols create the route for transmission using the VPI and VCI fields in the cell header and direct the stream of cells over virtual channels and virtual paths. The ATM layer passes information up to the AAL layer after stripping the header and adds the header to cells passed down from the AAL.

The ATM layer generates and attaches the header for each cell passed down to the physical layer and removes the header on the receiving end.

AAL Layer

This layer is subdivided into two sublayers, which is appropriate, because this layer has two functions. One of these functions is to provide an interface with higher level applications and protocols in the B-ISDN stack. The *segmentation and reassembly sublayer* (SAR) takes packets from higher level applications and segments the information into the right length for insertion into ATM cells. Naturally, the SAR performs the converse action of reassembling high-level messages from fragmented information coming in from ATM cells. The convergence sublayer (CS) presents network services to the higher level apps and protocols.

MIGRATION TO ATM

Should you move your organization to ATM? Should you drop everything and head up to the CEO's office shouting "bandwidth on demand!" repeatedly? Or should you just sit back and keep using proven technology to optimize your LANs and WANs? Let the other guys take the chances?

The answer to all those questions above is, of course, "It depends." There's been a lot of talk about ATM, a lot of expectations, and a lot of frustration. Only an experienced corporate bungee jumper would shout anything in the CEO's office, but chances are that she or he has heard about ATM, is interested, and secretly can't wait for the day a tired CEO can watch *The Sound of Music* on the desktop PC while waiting for accounting to crank out the year-end trial balance. The word out in the communications and networking worlds is that ATM is going to happen. The question now isn't "when will ATM happen?" but "when will it happen to you?"

As a matter of fact, ATM is happening already in many places. Lots of vendors are offering ATM hardware and ATM management software. Applications are being written to take advantage of ATM. Lots of companies are installing ATM equipment. Many companies, large and small, are planning migrations to ATM technology, and lots of them are already implementing the early stages of their plans.

A suggested migration path is based on capital outlay for ATM technology. The most expensive part of an internetwork, and the most critical, is the backbone, which carries traffic between connected LANs or LAN segments. Corporate managers, faced with integrating a new technology are always out to get the most "bang for their buck." Network managers moving to ATM systems often see the high cost justified when applying the new technology to this part of a complex internetwork. ATM switches used as backbones can provide significant increase in total throughput over a large internetwork. On the other hand, trusting a mission critical production network to a new technology is not a move to be taken lightly. To provide fault tolerance in this critical area, many organizations are implementing ATM backbones into corporate- or campuswide systems that run parallel to the backbones already in place.

After implementing an ATM backbone, the next step would be to replace the lower level of routers and gateways in the organization with ATM switches connecting high performance devices and servers throughout the enterprise. The final step, taken after ATM technology has become more pervasive and more economical, would be to install ATM interfaces in desktop PCs.

In other organizations, one workgroup will be selected as a test group, to implement ATM technology directly from the desktop. ATM interface cards are already on the market, and ATM devices are available to route and switch ATM cells from a user's PC out over existing digital communications facilities. With the test group taking the point, identifying useful technology, and addressing problems along the way, the rest of the organization can move forward toward ATM connectivity in relative safety.

At any rate, you can expect a surge in interest in ATM systems over the next five years. Lots of organizations are in the midst of their migration to ATM, and many more are considering the advantages over the risks.

ATM ON THE MARKET

The cost of ATM devices currently coming online more or less defines how quickly ATM can move into common usage. When you get into any leading-edge technology, you've got to be prepared to pay, and every investment in a new technology has an associated risk. This section takes a look at a few instances of ATM technology and their costs, and might help you calculate the value of an ATM investment in your organization.

ATM on the Desk

- IBM markets 25.6 Mbps adapters priced in the $400 range (this is a proprietary IBM implementation, so be aware that you're climbing into bed with IBM if you go this route).
- Interphase 155 Mbps adapters are available at $650 for a copper version and $850 for a fiber version.
- Adaptec adapters start at $349 for 25 Mbps and $895 for 155 Mbps NICs.

Switches

Cabletron Systems Inc. offers a scalable line of ATM switches. Its competitor and ofttime partner, Fore Systems, is also moving ahead with a line of ATM switching components designed for heavy use on backbones and as intermediate switches over LANs and WANs. A 24-port ATM switching module to add to its popular MMAC Plus is available for less than $20,000. ATM access modules are also available for the entire intermediate MM hub line, including the MMAC and MicroMMAC hubs. Available from Fore Systems is the ASX-200 ATM switch, with support for up to 24 ATM ports, with prices also in the $20,000 range.

Software

Newbridge Networks has created application management tools for ATM. Its VIVID System Manager provides general network management capability for the ATM network, including a physical view of the net and logical grouping of workgroups. Newbridge's 46020 MainStreet Network Manager displays network topology on a graphical user interface. Both these products are in the $10,000 range.

Prices for these very sophisticated network management tools are expected to drop significantly as other companies release management software now in development.

CONCLUSION

ATM technology gives users access to B-ISDN services, providing the bandwidth necessary to carry services such as high resolution video, video teleconferencing, and high-speed data transfer. ATM uses asynchronous transmission of uniform cells, and switching technology based on virtual paths and virtual channels multiplexed and addressed over the physical medium.

ATM can assign as many virtual channels as needed at a given time through asynchronous transmission, effectively providing the same type of bandwidth on demand that is expected on LANs. ATM effectively channelizes an entire link, eliminating the need for D- and B-channels apportioned by access providers in the original N-ISDN standards. ATM users will pay only for bandwidth used, not a predefined rate interface.

The B-ISDN protocol model maps to the physical and data link layers of the OSI stack, while some of the addressing associated with the ATM layer can mapped to the network layer of OSI.

The high cost of moving to ATM networks at this time, weighed against the obvious benefits of ATM, calls for careful planning when migrating to ISDN. A number of ATM products have been released to the market, and network managers contemplating and planning their migration to ATM technology should do their homework carefully before making an expensive move.

BIBLIOGRAPHIES AND RESOURCES

Hopkins, Gerald L. *The ISDN Literacy Book*. Reading, MA: Addison-Wesley Publishing Co., 1995. This is a compendium of ISDN and ATM knowledge written for real human beings.

Kessler, Gary C. *ISDN*, 2nd Ed. New York: McGraw-Hill, 1993. This is a scholarly work on a complex subject. Lots of technical information is presented sensibly and clearly.

McDysan, David E., and Spohn, Darren L. *ATM Theory and Application*. New York: McGraw-Hill, 1995. Lots of information is presented on a technical level.

Musich, Paula. "Desktop ATM Advances: NICs to Proliferate as More Firms Enter the Fray." *PC Week* 12, no. 7 (Feb. 20, 1995):55.

Stallings, William. *ISDN: An Introduction.* New York: Macmillan Publishing Co., 1995. Lots of fundamental technical information is in here. You might want to wait for the Classics Illustrated version.

Wallace, Bob. "Cabletron Readies ATM for Entire Hub Line." *InfoWorld* 17, no. 8 (Feb. 20, 1995):6.

MORE ACCESS, MORE TRANSMISSION

14

ACCESS

As we've already said repeatedly in this book, in the early days of networking, numerous access methods were developed as proprietary or ad hoc systems. Some of these systems or their general approaches to networking evolved into some of the more robust or widely used access methods that are still in use today. Others served as the basis for protocol suites and network operating systems, some defunct, some also still in use. In the preceding five or six chapters, we've covered the most common and popular access methods; in this chapter, we'll depart the topic with a quick trip off the beaten track to some of the other access methods that you might encounter in your trips into the back country of networking.

ARCNET

ARCnet is another token-passing networking system. Based on technology developed at the Datapoint Corporation in San Antonio, Texas, in the early 1970s, ARCnet was the first widely used local-area networking technology used for office automation. Although Datapoint was the first company to bundle networking in with its workstations, ARCnet didn't become a standard form of networking until 1992, when ARCnet finally became an ANSI standard. The company's decision to keep the technology proprietary probably cost it a leading role in networking technology.

ARCnet is not too difficult to implement, and one of its primary virtues is its low cost when compared to other access methods. ARCnet's 2.5 Mbps bandwidth can't compare to Ethernet and token ring. At one point, ARCnet accounted for a little over a third of all LAN-attached nodes, but today ARCnet's only major market remains its installed base (not too many new ARCnet networks are being installed these days).

BROADBAND LANS

In the 1970s, a number of vendors developed proprietary broadband LAN technologies. Companies like Allen-Bradley Corporation and Ungerman-Bass developed systems that offered from 1 to 2 Mbps bandwidth, primarily using coaxial media. These products were widely deployed in manufacturing and factory floor environments because of their high reliability and relative immunity to environmental interference.

Although you may still see these technologies from time to time, especially on the shop floor, they have been supplanted by more conventional network access methods (e.g. Ethernet and token ring). These newer implementations usually employ fiber-optic media, because of its complete immunity to environmental interference, and provide better access to other organizational networks and data resources (it's hard to find a router or bridge to interlink these older technologies with any of the more standard ones).

TRANSMISSION

Wide area network transmissions of all types sooner or later involve the services of a communications carrier. The phone companies have implemented a number of *public* data transmission services to offer their subscribers sophisticated data transmission at attractive prices.

X.25

We've already talked about X.25, the popular and ubiquitous public packet switching network. The X.25 network is spread around the world and offers extremely reliable transport service for its clients. You can still obtain X.25 connections at almost any location, but with fully digital services with greater bandwidth available from the same common carriers, X.25 networks are less prevalent than they used to be.

Nevertheless, in environments like Europe, where national telecommunications companies can complicate international communications, X.25 is a commonly-understood and therefore widely deployed method for international internetworking.

SYNCHRONOUS OPTICAL NETWORK

Synchronous Optical Network (SONET) is the communications world's equivalent of Ethernet. SONET defines physical layer standards for all kind of communications over a *worldwide* fiber-optic network. SONET standards deal with all the physical characteristics and capabilities necessary for high speed transmission technologies like SMDS, frame relay, and ATM.

SWITCHED MULTIMEGABIT DATA SERVICES

Switched Multimegabit Data Services (SMDS) is a high speed transfer service that offers subscribers high bandwidth transmission capability, but it's not a worldwide service. SMDS is a local exchange service that can provide clients the public equivalent of a metropolitan area network (MAN). SMDS transport is based on the use of fixed size cells, just like ATM.

FRAME RELAY

We've already touched on frame relay. It's included here to emphasize that frame relay is a public access network, where access can be supplied to any organization that can afford the tolls. Frame relay is a data-link level transmission method based on ISDN standards.

HIGH (BIT RATE) DIGITAL SUBSCRIBER LINE

High bit rate Digital Subscriber Line (HDSL) is yet another data transmission service offered by local exchange carriers. HDSL permits high speed data access over normal telephone lines that competes with ISDN, but at a higher cost for higher bandwidth (HDSL offers a maximum bandwidth of 784 Kbps, and features full-duplex communications). Today, HDSL is not widely used, except for applications that require access from a local copper loop to the SONET network.

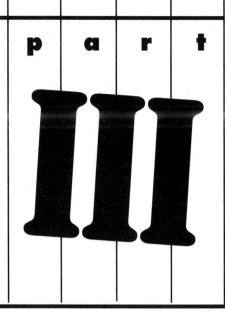

part

III

NETWORKING PROTOCOLS

Once you set up a network and link its components together, your computers will only be able to use the network's capabilities if they have a way to talk to each other. Networking protocols supply the means of communication among computers (as long as they have a protocol in common) and define the basic communication methods and formats computers use to exchange information, requests and responses.

Here in Part III, you'll learn about the various kinds of networking protocols you're likely to encounter on your network as you explore the software that makes communication possible. We'll discuss specific services and applications individual protocols support to help you understand the capabilities and appeal of some of the individual protocol collections.

Because protocols seldom occur as singletons, most so-called networking protocols are best termed "protocol suites" since they are collections of interrelated and cooperating individual protocols that together define the capabilities of one particular suite or another. In Chapter 15, as we begin our discussion of all things protocol-related, we will expound on what makes a protocol so "suite," and how these collections of protocols cooperate and interoperate to get things done.

Following the protocol overview, we move on to a discussion of the Internet protocol suite called *TCP/IP*. Funded by some of the most enlightened dollars ever spent by the U.S. Department of Defense, *TCP/IP* has become the world's most popular and talked about protocol suite. Chapter 16 explains what TCP/IP is all about. In Chapter 17, we discuss Novell's Internetwork Packet Exchange/Sequenced Packet Exchange (IPX/SPX)—the networking protocol used on more desktops around the world than any other—and explore its capabilities.

In Chapters 18 and 19, our mood turns Blue as we investigate IBM's Networked Basic Input/Output Systems (NetBIOS) and the ubiquitous and undying Systems Network Architecture (SNA). Since SNA is not only widely used but also served as the inspiration for the ISO reference model for networking, so you'll probably be surprised by some of its contents and capabilities.

The final two chapters in Part III, Chapters 20 and 21, tackle the simple and elegant AppleTalk protocol suite and a grab bag of other protocols and related buzzwords you may encounter in your perambulations in the networking world. We think you'll find some interesting ideas in AppleTalk, and some unusual variety in our grab bag!

Our basic intention in Part III is to explore the communications capabilities inherent in the protocols you're most likely to encounter on your network, and to point you to some hopefully useful resources for more details should you ever need them. After you're read this Part, you'll probably agree that when it comes to networking, protocols and diplomacy have very little in common!

PROTOCOLS

15

PROTOCOLS DEFINED

Commonplace use defines the term *protocol* as "a code prescribing strict adherence to correct etiquette and precedence." In other words, a protocol is a rule used to dictate behavior in certain situations—so that certain situations have associated protocols to govern them.

As you grew up, you learned a variety of protocols and sets of protocols that you had to master to move into new situations and activities. You had to learn a protocol for eating, for dressing, for speaking, and for a lot of other things. And each of these things didn't have just one protocol to manage how it was done, everything had a whole host of protocols.

At first these protocols probably seemed difficult to understand or put into practice. But as you became more and more familiar with the protocols necessary to complete a task, you tended to forget them. They were still there of course, but they receded into the background. After a certain amount of learning, the rules that govern behavior become less important than the behavior itself, and this is the level at which most adults focus their attention. Because diplomacy is a delicate art and the stakes are much higher than for everyday interaction, protocol remains an overwhelming concern and helps to keep diplomats and politicians out of hot water as much as possible.

Protocols = "Rules of the Road"

Here's an example of a very important set of protocols that you probably take very seriously without giving a lot of conscious thought. I'm talking about the rules that manage how you drive and how traffic flows.

At a certain level traffic is governed by laws, and you have to follow them or you'll get a ticket or, maybe, get killed. Following this model, protocols are laws. The traffic laws keep us all from going crazy out on the road by making sure we have an agreed on set of rules that we are all going to go by. One of the first sets of traffic protocols we learned are the traffic light protocols. Stop on the red, go on the green, yellow means look out (and don't get caught by Mr. In-Between). We stop at red lights because we know the drivers crossing the intersection are looking at green lights that give them permission to occupy the intersection. We drive confidently through the green lights because we know the drivers crossing our road will stop for their red lights.

The Dating Game

UNIX geeks can just skip this section. There are so many protocols managing relations between the sexes that just mentioning them well might be a violation of one of them. But these protocols make good examples because we all had to learn them. There are protocols for meeting, going out together, and everything that happens after. What happens if you violate one of these protocols?

Think back, you'll remember.

Miss Manners Suggests . . .

Table manners. One of our mothers kept a big book on table manners at the dinner table and used it as a reference and guide. One of our dining protocols was that no one ever mentioned how disturbing this habit of hers was to digestion. But Mom had a mission: she was trying to teach us as many of the thousand protocols associated with eating as she could before we got away from her and flew out into the wide world. We started with the simple stuff—don't juggle your biscuits—and worked our way into which fork you use to eat snails. Now, we're grateful because we can eat in a fancy restaurant without making fools of ourselves.

What's It All Mean?

These are just some examples of some common protocols that have been adopted in some form or fashion in every culture on the planet. Sometimes protocols are laws, and sometimes they are just suggested ways to behave. Either way, you can see that protocols are the basic precepts that guide us in our relations with other people.

NETWORKING PROTOCOLS

Just as human beings need to have to have myriads of protocols to help them handle their interactions with one another, machines need them, too.

Technobabble: Regarding Protocols

The IBM *Dictionary of Computing* has this to say about protocols: "A set of semantic and syntactic rules that determines the behavior of functional units in achieving communication." In network communications language, this means three things:

- Form (syntax) and meaning (semantics) in a network communication are defined by a set of rules, called a *protocol* (or more commonly, a *suite of protocols*)
- *Functional units* can mean hardware or software; either way, functional units do all the work. Protocols just define how they are assigned and how they operate.
- Protocols establish a method of communication that resembles the rules for a language (but doesn't describe every possible utterance, like any syntax).

Computers can do only exactly what they're told to do, neither more nor less. For computers to communicate, for any information to be delivered, every little bit of information to be exchanged between sender and receiver must be supplied, not implied. For computers to communicate they must begin with a complete agreement about every stage of that communication. A set of rules regarding communications must be completely mapped out and then implemented in software before computers can communicate with each other.

Likewise, every situation that can arise during computer-to-computer communications needs at least one of these rules to manage or control it. In other words, every conceivable set of circumstances that might arise between (or among) computers communicating with one another must be fully understood to enable computers to communicate. The collection of all these circumstances and their understandings forms the basis of a set of rules about how network communications occur, and how to react when things don't work, for whatever reason.

Sets and Suites

One of these collections of communications rules might be called a *network protocol* and would govern the way the computer accesses the networking medium. Another set of rules might describe how an application, like an electronic mail package, could send and receive messages. Still other collections of rules are necessary to diagnose the health and availability of the network (to see if it's working, and if it's OK to use it). Lots of collections of rules are needed to make computer networking a going concern.

In short, all of the networking protocols necessary for computer communications to take place, taken as a group, are called a *protocol set*, or a *protocol suite*. For computers to communicate successfully, they must share a common protocol suite. In fact, when computers are communicating through the use of common protocols they are communicating as *peers*; even if one peer is playing the role of *client* and the other the role of *server*, at some level, they are just two computers exchanging information across a network with each other.

Stacks

We've already had a look at the OSI reference model for network communications. This OSI reference model is an official networking standard (it's important to know what a standard is also, so we'll take a look at that later). The OSI model breaks down networked communications into layers. These layers are stacked one on top of the other. For this reason protocol suites, or sets, are also commonly known as *stacks*. At each layer of the stack certain networking tasks are grouped, as are the protocols that govern those tasks, and the services that permit those tasks to be completed.

Networking Standards and Stacks

Standards

Building a complete set of communications rules is a difficult and time-consuming job. Nearly every possible type of network interaction must be taken into account and corresponding protocols must be developed. In the early days of the computer industry, individual companies or groups would assign development teams to create networks. These companies and groups may have created successful networks for themselves, but one group's implementation would inevitably have little or nothing in common with another group's. Over time, this process led to too many ways of handling network communications and not enough agreement to make widespread networking easy or convenient.

It soon became obvious that standards needed to be applied to networking. Groups and companies sent representatives to sit on standards committees and boards that grappled with the tough issues that had to be solved to make network standards workable. These boards worked hard to reach a consensus on the best set of protocols for networking. They had to listen to everybody in the networking world grinding his or her individual ax, and then they had to reach agreement on sets of standards that would do the greatest good for the greatest number of network users.

At the same time, numerous private companies were selling their own proprietary brands of networking hardware and software. These companies also sought to define sets of protocols that would be widely accepted and used in the computer world so that they could sell their products and make lot of money. To stay competitive, they all wanted to get their own work done before their competitors could bring their products into the same markets.

This led to the inevitable development of two types of networking "standards." One was a set of "official" standards, created by committees who agreed on every aspect of network architecture and communications. The other was a set of incompatible (and often contradictory) "proprietary" standards, designed to protect the markets of individual companies or consortia.

Standards Committees

Standards committees represent a sincere effort by leaders in a particular field to develop, or recognize, the best possible way to do something. Like all committees, networking standards committees take a long time to make decisions. That's the bad news; the good news is that standards committees make their decisions publicly, and they share the details with the public after the decisions get made. Consequently, almost all standards committees put forth what are known as *open standards*.

An open standard is available as a model for anyone concerned with the technology or functionality covered by that standard. Anybody who wants to can use an open standard, copy it, or develop products based on it (although they may have to pay a licensing fee to use copyright trade names or to obtain copyrighted materials incidental to the standard; it's essential to understand that *open* seldom means "free of charge"). Open standards go a long way toward seeing that everyone in a particular arena is playing the same game. Vendors can adopt open standards, and then assure their customers that their product complies to the latest and greatest version of that standard. Customers and organizations can be confident that they aren't committing themselves to a "flash in the pan," but rather to a technology that has some muscle and momentum behind it.

Proprietary Standards

Given the value and availability of official open standards, why then do proprietary technologies (which vendors like to call *standards* whenever possible) continue to flourish and grow? The secret's based on capitalism. Private companies live and die in a free marketplace. A company that makes a product or service nobody wants is doomed. If, on the other hand, Company B builds a better mousetrap ... you know what happens then. "Better mousetraps" all too often tend to be proprietary as well.

Sometimes companies have a product or service that everybody in that market wants. If that condition persists for any length of time, like it or not, that product or service becomes a "standard" in its market, even if it is proprietary. Such standards weren't created by committees who carefully studied the needs of the market. They were created by factors in the open market and became standards through a process of capitalistic natural selection. Like them or not, we have to accept them and live with them, simply because they work!

The Best of Both Worlds

The network architectures and associated protocols that we deal with in this book are the most widely used members of their classes. Because the networking marketplace is neither totally organized nor totally rational, they are an amalgamation of *open standards* and *proprietary standards*. Either way, all of the protocol suites covered in the chapters that follow are in widespread use all over the world.

The "Short and Suite" List

Here's a list of the networking protocol suites we'll cover in the next several chapters:

1. TCP/IP
2. IPX/SPX
3. NetBIOS and derivatives
4. SNA
5. AppleTalk

Every one of these protocol suites was developed in response to a clearly defined need:

TCP/IP was developed as a joint effort at the behest of the U.S. Department of Defense, an organization that not only has a way of getting what it wants but also has a bad habit of buying one or more of everything there is, including computers. TCP/IP was invented because the government had lots of different kinds of computers and wanted to be able to make them talk to each other..

IPX/SPX is the name of the family of protocols created by Novell Corporation, building on work done by the geniuses at Xerox PARC (for the Xerox Networking System, or XNS), to enable PCs to provide business-level local networking services.

NetBIOS was developed by IBM and Sytek, Inc., as a standard for applications that wanted to interface with IBM PC networks. It turned out to be so easy to program that lots of programmers used it and continue to use it to this day.

The systems networking architecture (SNA) is IBM's big-gun networking entry. It was developed in particular to allow an assortment of *IBM* network devices to exchange information efficiently. It also turned out to be the foundation for a way of doing networking that has been emulated and enshrined in many forms, including the much-mentioned OSI reference model for networked communication.

As for AppleTalk, it was developed as Apple's way of simplifying networking for chowderheads—er, normal users—who just wanted to plug their computers together and have them automatically be able to communicate. This was the first "plug and play" form of networking ever introduced and, 11 years later, it's *still* pretty impressive stuff!

The OSI Stack

At every layer of the OSI reference model different protocols, or groups of protocols, operate to carry out the functions required for that layer. For messages to travel from computer to computer on a network, the processes represented in the OSI model must be implemented, but they need not be the same implementation in every instance (only between pairs of computers trying to communicate).

Different protocol suites invariably implement different mappings for protocols and related functionality in their particular stacks. Nevertheless, the same tasks must be completed on the sending and receiving stations (in reverse order) for effective networking to occur. For this reason nearly all protocol stacks, even the ones that weren't based on the OSI model, have some resemblance to each other and can be mapped to the OSI model for purposes of explanation.

Encapsulation

Information that is processed within any given computer must be transferred over the internal bus between the CPU and the memory, or between the memory and secondary storage, and so on. Throughout this process, system designers can safely assume that data formats and transfers are predictable and timely. Information that travels across a network, on the other hand, needs special formatting to protect and maintain its contents, so that it can survive the trip intact, where it's never safe to assume that data formats or transfers will be either predictable or timely.

Information transferred across a network travels down the protocol stack through a process of packaging and repackaging that is completely described by the formats and representation schemes defined for the protocols in operation at every level of the stack. At the topmost level—the application layer—data is transmitted from (or received by) some application running on your computer.

Starting at the presentation layer (layer 6 of the OSI reference model), the data is *encapsulated,* or enclosed in a header that adds some information to identify and help route the data before it is passed down to the next level. At each subsequent layer in the stack, the prevailing protocol adds another header to the previous layer's data and its header and may even break up a single long message into numerous short ones. Finally, at the data link layer (layer 2) the local protocols assemble packages of data with their layer 2 headers into a *frame*, which is handed over to the physical layer for transmission over the network medium, where the whole laborious process will be repeated in reverse by its recipient on the other side of the network connection.

There are many techniques for data encapsulation that will be discussed in the following chapters, but generally speaking, when data is passed up and down protocol stacks it is passed in *packets*. When these packets of data actually travel across a wire, they are encapsulated in *frames*. Packets are passed back and forth over virtual connections that are said to exist between *peer layers* (identical protocols and services) in the sender's and receiver's protocol stacks, but frames are transmitted over the physical medium that defines a particular networking access method or technology. Because different protocol stacks have slightly different methods for organizing these packets and frames, their methods will also be discussed in the succeeding chapters.

When the data arrives at its destination it is completely encapsulated, but these layers of encapsulation are stripped away, one by one, as the data travels back up the stack on the receiving computer. When it arrives at the application layer, it's supposed to be an identical copy of the data transmitted by the sending computer (but it may have been adjusted for cross-platform differences between different types of computers, so that a Macintosh format may get converted to a PC analog, or vice versa).

Inside the Seven Layers of the OSI reference model

If we take a look at the types of protocols in operation at each of the seven layers of the OSI reference model, it can illustrate the activities and functions that will be implemented in most protocol stacks. That's why the OSI reference model is the commonly accepted standard for network architecture and why it is so often used as a benchmark for comparison with other network architectures.

Starting at the top, at the *application layer*, users interact with the network and take advantage of network applications or services. Data, or requests for data, are passed from these applications down to the lower layers. This is the layer where protocols define the applications, or services, that let users interact with the network. Some examples of services at this level include Telnet, the network control protocol (NCP), and the AppleShare filing protocol (AFP).

At the *presentation layer*, the data is formatted for the application that requested it. Presentation layer protocols deal with formatting the data in the network transmission and not with the actual transfer of the data. At this level data is usually encrypted or compressed and then passed down to the session layer.

In the *session layer*, host computers are synchronized for communication, and communications between processes on separate hosts are requested, established, used, and then terminated when a session is complete. The session layer is usually implemented with the network basic input/output system (NetBIOS) or a similar protocol, which provides applications a link to network transfer services in the lower layers of the stack.

The *transport layer* breaks long messages up into smaller units (*packets*) and makes sure of various delivery services to transport messages to the receiving station. TCP and SPX are just two of the protocols that operate at this level. Both of these are concerned with the quality of a network transmission. That is, they want to make sure the right message got through to the right station. Other transport protocols, like UDP, are concerned only with proper transmission and don't include built-in checks on actual delivery and data integrity. These differences provide varying levels and speeds of network delivery that application developers can use as they see fit.

The data, now segmented into packets, move down to the *network layer*, which establishes the path (or route) from the sending computer to the receiving one. The switching, routing, and control of these packets is handled at this layer. IPX, IP, and DDP are a few of the different protocols that operate at this level. These protocols are in different stacks, but they are all concerned with *addressing* the packets that make up a network transmission, checking to find the most appropriate *route* for sending the packets to their destination, and passing the packets down to the lower levels in the stack for transmission.

Packets are sent down from the network layer to the *data link layer*, where the mechanism is provided to send the packets, also called *frames* at this layer, down to the physical layer for transport down the wires that connect the network nodes.

You already know about the *physical layer*. That's because the connectors and wiring and other physical links that the data move over as it passes between computers over a network provide one of the few parts of networking that you can actually see! Protocols at this level define the minimum standards for voltage or current levels, pinouts, connector sizes and shapes, and anything associated with moving bits across a physical transmission medium. At this layer, protocols define the way hardware is designed and manufactured, to ensure that products from different vendors can interconnect and interoperate.

Connections

In a network, the network medium—usually, a cable—provides a *physical* link between computers that are sharing information. This type of connection is easy to check. If there is a signal crossing the cable between machines on the network, then a physical connection can be presumed to exist. Naturally, for proper data transmissions to occur, there must be a valid physical connection.

The different layers of the protocol stack must also establish and maintain connections with one another to transfer data on a network. These are called *virtual* connections. Virtual connections are the links between the protocols operating on the various levels of the stack. The protocols responsible for encapsulating application data at the top of the stack must establish connections with the layers directly under them to pass the data along. At every layer protocols are in operation that communicate with the layers above them and below them. Virtual connections are just as real as physical connections while networking is taking place.

All the virtual connections depend on the physical connection to transfer the frames encapsulating all the data being transmitted. At the other end of a connection, whether virtual or real, the lower layers begin to unwrap headers from the data as they pass it up the stack on the receiver.

For network communications to occur, each protocol in operation on the sender has a corresponding protocol in action on the receiver. These corresponding protocols are called *peers*. In properly defined network communication, layers of the protocol stack are also communicating with the layers above and below, and with their peers on the receiver.

Connection Handling

One way to classify protocols is whether they are *connection oriented* or *connectionless*. The most common way used to describe a connectionless protocol is to compare a datagram, or packet of information as it's commonly called at this level, to a piece of regular snail mail. A datagram has data encapsulated with an address and a route to a receiver, and off it goes. Connectionless protocols don't check to see if the datagram made it to its destination intact, they just send them out. They're counting on higher level protocols to take care of error detection and reliability checks. Snail mail is similar. You give the mail the correct address and drop it into a mail box. You're counting on the mail service to handle delivery, but you've got no built-in way to check. You've just taken part in a connectionless communication. Connectionless packets aren't sent out in any special sequence and they don't necessarily arrive in the same order that they're sent. Connectionless protocols don't care about sequencing.

Connection-oriented communications are a little more formal. They don't just send datagrams out onto the network. They send out and receive a carefully constructed and monitored stream of data to their peers, and they're very careful about checking the status of the connection between sender and receiver. They use a *handshake* to start communications, so that the peers communicating at that level can check on the status of the communications, including the sequence of the packets. Connection-oriented protocols are aware of delivery success or failure and can send error messages if the delivery is unsuccessful.

Connectionless datagram protocols are low in overhead and keep the memory costs of networking to a minimum. Connection-oriented protocols may carry significant overhead because of the extra services they provide to monitor and maintain the quality of the connection between peers.

Building the Frame

Lets take a look at how a frame is assembled for transmission to a receiver in the OSI stack:

- At the application layer, a service sends a message (data) to a corresponding service on a receiver. The application layer protocols add a header to the data and send it down to the presentation layer.

- At the presentation layer, the original data, with the application header applied is treated as a complete data unit. A presentation layer header is added and the data unit, with the two appended headers, is passed down to the session layer.
- The session layer, transport layer, and network layer receive the data unit in turn and add their particular header information to the data unit.
- When the data unit reaches the data link layer, it is further encapsulated in a frame for transmission over the physical link. Framing information, address information, and control information is added as the data link header. Trailer information—the frame check sequence and additional framing characters— is added, forming a completely assembled frame.
- On the receiving end, the frame is picked up by the data link layer as it comes in over the wire, and the process of assembly is reversed as the data unit passes up the layers of the receiver protocol stack. Finally, at the application layer, the application layer header, the last one left on the data unit, is stripped away and the data are delivered to the application corresponding to the one on the transmitter where the process was begun.

The Shape of Things to Come

The next several chapters cover different protocol suites that define several different types of network interaction. We will examine each of these protocol stacks in detail, covering the following topics:

- Where did this protocol suite come from?
- How does the subject stack compare to the OSI model?
- What protocols are active at each layer of the stack?
- What functions are provided by the protocols?
- How is a packet formatted for transmission by the protocols in the stack?

Finally, we'll follow a message from the top layers of the subject protocol stack down through the layers to the receiver.

Pay Close Attention to the Man behind the Curtain!

Remember that protocols are sets of rules. Networking protocols are the rules for networking. If you want to install and maintain a working network, you've got to understand the rules and how they govern networking behavior!

16

TCP/IP

TCP/IP REVEALED

Commissioned by the same benevolent U.S. government that brought us the Vietnam war and the P-38 can opener, TCP/IP is designed to be independent of hardware considerations, operating systems, network operating systems, physical transmission links, and other criteria that were once stumbling blocks on the path to internetwork communications.

TCP/IP is a set of protocols that were created specifically to allow development of network and internetwork communications on a global scale. Although the origins and definition of TCP/IP date back more than 25 years, TCP/IP remains the most durable and common set of protocols in use in network communications today. TCP/IP supplies extended network capability to machines and networks of different types, using many different operating systems and communicating using a wide variety of technologies, which can include local and asynchronous links, packet radio transmissions, and satellite links.

The development of TCP/IP has paralleled the growth of the Internet, the most tangible manifestation of the widely publicized and much ballyhooed "information superhighway." The Department of Defense (DoD) helped to create and evaluate TCP/IP, beginning in the late 1960s and throughout the 1970s. By 1984 the DoD adopted TCP/IP as its official Internet protocol. Many people believe that TCP/IP's adoption as an internetworking standard was the most significant step on the way to creating the worldwide internetwork we call the *Internet*. In this chapter, you'll learn about the beginnings of the TCP/IP protocol, why it's been around so long, how the TCP/IP protocols interoperate, and the kinds of services and capabilities they provide.

WHAT MAKES TCP/IP TICK?

One reason for the TCP/IP suite's legendary flexibility is the fact that it was not developed as a top-down set of protocols created to structure communications but as a ground-up set of protocols that has always responded, and continues to respond, to available technologies. What this means is that the original developers of the TCP/IP protocol, most of whom are still cruising around the Internet, came up with their designs based on currently available technology.

From its very beginnings the developers of TCP/IP encouraged—and continue to do so to this day—user involvement in the development of the protocols. As new technologies (like new hardware, software, or communications links) become available, approved protocols for including them can be—and often are—added to the TCP/IP protocols.

For TCP/IP, all definitions and descriptions of its protocols and services are contained in requests for comment (RFCs). RFCs constitute the collection of documents that specify and describe what TCP/IP is and what it does. RFCs are assigned in numeric order and are referred to by number. They may be submitted by anyone who feels that additions or modifications to the protocols already in use are called for. In this way, additional TCP/IP protocols are developed for new technologies.

Specs: RFC1720

The current document that describes the Internet official protocol standards is RFC1720. Even though the phrase *request for comment* sounds more like a question to solicit feedback on an idea (which is how the bulk of RFCs actually function), standard RFCs have the weight of law in the Internet and TCP/IP communities.

RFCs actually dictate how protocols behave and what functions they must perform. Failure to conform to these definitions, especially for required or recommended protocols, can cost a vendor the opportunity of doing business with the United States government and all the other bodies and agencies that adhere to its guidelines. Access to the RFCs may be obtained from the Internet host ds.internic.net via FTP or electronic mail, or via the Word Wide Web at http://www.cis.ohio-state.edu/hypertext/information/rfc.html.

Next, you'll examine the history of TCP/IP, and how it parallels the history of computer networking, but first it might be helpful to define some common terms from the TCP/IP world.

COMMON TCP/IP TERMINOLOGY

While TCP/IP isn't really all that complicated, it's going to be hard to explain all of its ins and outs without agreeing on some terminology. All of these terms are common in the networking community, but restating them here should make sure you know what we're talking about when we use them!

Addressing

In the network world, every device needs an identifying number that is unique to that device. Usually these identifiers are made up of some combination of numbers. For network, and internetwork communications to occur, each device needs to have this unique numeric ID, or address. For purposes of this discussion there are two important types of addressing: IP addresses and MAC layer addresses.

IP Addresses

IP addresses are unique numerical addresses based on a standard scheme and assigned by a central governing body. They are used to communicate between nodes on an internetwork.

MAC Layer Addresses

Media access control addresses are the hardware addresses used by nodes on a network to identify and locate one another. They are used to communicate between nodes on the same wire and are most often built right in to the NICs used for network communications. MAC addresses are the lowest level of network identifiers and provide the final links by which information is passed from device to device on a network.

Datagram

A packet that contains data and delivery information is a datagram.

End Nodes

These are the machines (devices) on a network at which users perform their work. Desktop PCs, printers, and file servers connected to a network are all examples of end nodes.

Gateway

A gateway is a machine that connects a network of hosts to another network. On the Internet, gateways function as routers, passing messages along until they reach their destination.

Host

A host is any machine (device) connected to a network or internetwork.

Internet

Most network schemes are controlled by routers that handle network communications and monitor network activity for the rest of the connected nodes. An internet is a set of two or more network routers that are connected and able to share processing and data.

The Internet

The formal name for a worldwide matrix of gateways and hosts transferring and sharing information. This is the specific internetwork constantly being referred to in the newspapers and broadcast media. This is by far the largest internetwork in the world, connecting universities, military installations, research facilities, corporations, and much more.

Network

A network is any collection of machines or devices connected physically by some type of physical transport medium (i.e., wire). Network devices may all be on the same wire or they may be connected over a series of wires using bridges or repeaters.

Node

A node is any machine (device) connected to a network or internetwork.

Packets

Information is carried across networks in blocks of information called *packets*. Transmission of uniform packets of information allows for many hosts on a network to communicate simultaneously over the same transport medium. Packets also contain information about themselves that allow for error detection and correction across the network. Packets have two parts: the header and the body.

Header

The header carries information such as the source and destination of a packet.

Body

The body is the raw data carried by a packet or, in many cases, another type of (encapsulate) packet that contains its own header and body.

Protocol

A protocol, in networking, is a set of rules that specifies the formation of network packets and sets forth the ways these packets are handled on the network. Each protocol is designed to deal with a specific function or collection of functions (see Chapter 15 for a more detailed explanation of this all-important networking concept).

Routers

Routers are machines that connect nodes on a network. Routers perform all the functions offered by the network operating system and are responsible for knowing how the network topology is configured and transferring information from one part of the network to another.

Because of its origins and because TCP/IP and internetworking (and the Internet itself) are so intertwined, we're going to examine the beginnings of computer networking, the origins of TCP/IP, the development of the TCP/IP protocols, and how all these have combined to give us the global internetwork known to users, TV commentators, politicians, and software vendors worldwide as the *Internet*.

THE ORIGINS OF INTERNETWORKING

Today, when millions of computers of all kinds communicate freely across a worldwide internetwork of machines and LANs, it's hard to relate to a time when computers, both large and small, did all their work in isolation. But that's the way it was in the early days of computing.

The original computers were developed for the U.S. Department of Defense during World War II to aid in the war effort. These machines were lavishly expensive monstrosities that labored around the clock to solve complicated mathematical problems related to artillery targeting, logistics, and accounting. They required pretty large teams of engineers, scientists, and technicians, for maintenance and operations support. These teams of computer "babysitters" all worked more or less in splendid isolation. Any sharing of information between these teams happened over the telephone, or at the odd meeting or conference, on a more or less as-needed basis. Communication between these machines just didn't happen, or it was based on a primitive version of "sneakernet," where highly paid technicians lugged crates of punch cards or paper tape from one computer or computing center to another.

It didn't take long for the brain trust at the Department of Defense, which was responsible for all these machines, to recognize a real need to tie the machines together and eliminate the expense and duplication of effort involved in computing as practiced in its most prehistoric form. One particular agency, the Advanced Research Projects Agency (ARPA), was formed inside the Department of Defense with a charter to find an effective method to enable computer-to-computer and, ultimately, network-to-network communications. It would serve as the source of funding and inspiration for the efforts that have culminated in the Internet so widely used around the world today.

Machine Talk

The first links between isolated computing machines involved simply stringing wire between two or more machines and creating some kind of program that would allow them to communicate with each other. The same approach worked pretty well for tying peripheral devices like printers, storage devices, and any terminals that were required. Of course, the limitations of this approach are obvious. The length of the wire itself physically defined the strength of the signal it carried. This method worked fine, up to a point, for linking computers in the same room or the same building, but wasn't much help when it came to linking machines separated by many miles (as was the case with the small number of widely scattered computers originally acquired by the U.S. government).

Devices were developed to modulate computer signals into the audible tones required for phone transmissions and to demodulate them back into computer signals at the other end of the phone transmission. These 'modems' allowed computers to communicate over phone lines and enabled a great leap forward in communication between remote computing machines and networks. But these early telephone links, or circuits, allowed only one machine to talk to one other machine at a time.

Some method had to be developed to allow telephone circuits to be fragmented to allow multiple computers to be networked. Various approaches were tried. Multiplexing, or the decomposition down of a single circuit into multiple but limited channels, was the most common method. Even the success of multiplexing was clouded by the fact that it depended on breaking down the already limited bandwidth of a telephone line into even smaller "pipes," thus limiting the amount of traffic on the line.

Packet Switching

Around the end of the 1960s a method of transmission was developed that allowed more efficient communications, called *packet switching* This method, which is still used today, involves breaking down arbitrarily long messages into equal-sized packages of information and choosing the best route available for shipping them from a sender to one or more receivers, rather than using a predefined channel or band.

The development of packet switching environments provided the step necessary to enable the networking and internetworking world that we now know. All that is necessary in this environment is that packets be properly labeled when a message is disassembled in preparation for shipping and that these labels can be clearly read on delivery to permit proper reassembly of the pieces into their original format and layout.

In a packet-switched environment, the links between computers are called *lines*, and the computers where lines come together are called *nodes*. Computers add a special set of tags to each packet during assembly, including a sender and receiver address, a sequence or ID number, and some flavor of quality-control information to ensure the accuracy of the transmission. Individual packets can be sent using any available route, or line, in any sequence, as long as the receiving node has the ability to translate the addressing and reassembly information of each packet. This type of communication is called a *packet switched network*, because packets of information are constantly being switched from one line to another by the connected nodes as they forward information between sender and receiver.

Packet switched networks allow many machines to communicate simultaneously over a single, common transmission medium because the packet labels keep the individual transmissions distinct as they are routed between the interlinked nodes. This lets multiple users share the same network and makes all receivers at least theoretically available to all senders.

The ARPAnet

In the late 1960s, ARPA provided the funding for a number of universities where Department of Defense research was ongoing to set up the first internetwork based on packet switching network. The idea was to link computers of different types—that is, to interconnect machines made by more than one manufacturer—and to provide a broad range of capabilities across this network. These capabilities included remote access to other computers on the network, and the exchange of files and sharing of peripheral resources including things like printers and storage devices. This network came to be known as *the ARPAnet* or more simply *ARPAnet*.

ARPAnet used a special set of communications rules, called the network control protocol (NCP), to handle its network traffic. Specially programmed computers called interface message processors (IMPs) were developed and installed to handle the packet-switching duties that this network required. By late 1969, the ARPAnet was successfully up and running, linking computers in California and Utah. The early success of

ARPAnet caused an explosion of interest in networking and internetworking and quickened the pace of the development of networking technologies. Within three years of ARPAnet's introduction, several new internetworks were set up around the United States, and links to the international computing community were also established.

The Origins of TCP/IP

The rapid proliferation of ARPAnet-derived technologies soon pointed out fundamental weaknesses in its internetworking capabilities. NCP, the protocol developed to handle messaging across the ARPAnet, was too dependent on the characteristics of the original ARPAnet itself to accommodate some of the new and radically different networking and transmission technologies that were coming on-line around the world. The initial investment in IMPs, which were required by ARPAnet for packet switching duties, also restricted internetworking access from the growing world networking community.

In 1972, ARPA, now renamed the *Defense Advanced Research Projects Administration* (DARPA), formed the InterNetworking Working Group (INWG). Vincent Cerf, the chairman of the group (and one of the original developers of ARPAnet), and his team began work to create what would become an internationally agreed-upon set of standard networking protocols for a networking environment to be designed to replace the original ARPAnet implementation.

Even then, it was widely believed that a new suite of protocols would be necessary to support the proliferation of new and radically different networking technologies. Based on experience with the ARPAnet, this new design also had well-defined parameters: it needed to provide mail services, to enable mail delivery and reception between remote hosts; it needed to provide terminal services to allow remote terminals to connect to and execute commands on a remote host; and it needed to provide file transfer services to enable files to be moved easily and efficiently from host to host. In answer to all of these needs, Cerf's INWG team created the necessary specifications and developed a new suite of protocols and related services, which were named the *transmission control protocol/internet protocol* (TCP/IP).

THE TCP/IP ARCHITECTURE MODEL

The OSI reference model for network architecture is covered in detail in Chapter 15, so in this chapter, you'll have a chance to examine a layered model of the TCP/IP protocol suite, as you learn how this model corresponds to the corresponding OSI layers. The OSI reference model demonstrates the activities necessary at each level of networking activity to implement working networks and categorizes the operations required for successful networking, based on the layers it introduces to break up networking into a sequence of logically related tasks. Since the OSI reference model was created after the development of TCP/IP it does not share the same exact view of how networking should be subdivided into logically disjoint tasks. Nevertheless, mapping the TCP/IP suite to the OSI reference model should help you obtain a better understanding of TCP/IP implementation.

The Open Systems Interconnect Reference Model

If you recall, the OSI reference model has seven layers or levels. Starting from the bottom, they are

- Physical layer
- Data Link layer
- Network layer
- Transport layer
- Presentation layer
- Session layer
- Application layer

The OSI model is designed to separate network activities into different levels and allows for separate and distinct connectivity issues to be dealt with independent of one another. So is the TCP/IP implementation; in the section that follows you'll have an opportunity to explore the differences between the two outlooks.

The TCP/IP Model

The TCP/IP Model has fewer layers than the OSI model, because TCP/IP doesn't define distinct layers for either sessions or presentations. Distinct TCP/IP applications provide services corresponding to those two layers of the OSI model as they are required, without sharing common abstractions of those layers. This leaves the following "layered look" for the TCP/IP view of networking:

- Physical networks
- Network interface protocols
- Internet protocol
- Transmission control protocol
- Applications

In the sections that follow, you'll learn how this TCP/IP view corresponds to the view developed in the OSI reference model.

Mapping OSI and TCP/IP

Mapping the TCP/IP model to the OSI model can shed light on what TCP/IP is doing at each level. Each particular layer is covered in one subsection that follows.

Data Link and Physical layers

The physical layer of the OSI reference model corresponds to the physical network layer of TCP/IP. The data link layer of the OSI model maps to the network interface protocol layer of the TCP/IP model.

For these layers of the OSI model, TCP/IP supplies no protocols that are not already in existence but does interface with protocols provided by others for local and wide area networking. TCP/IP can interface with any data link layer that provides a communications pathway from the sender to the receiver. TCP/IP was originally developed for use with packet-switched networks using interface message processors (IMPs) or packet switching nodes (PSNs) and now supports almost all types of local area networking technologies, including Ethernet, token ring, and ARCnet, and most wide area technologies, including X.25 and X.25, SMDS, serial link interface protocol , point-to-point protocol, and many others.

As this is being written, support is being created for frame relay transmission and for asynchronous transfer mode transmission. Delivery of these protocols is expected sometime in 1995. As newer, more capable technologies are developed, it's reasonable to assume that TCP/IP implementations will be among the first networking capabilities built for such technologies.

Network Layer

The network layer of the OSI model maps directly to the Internet protocol level of TCP/IP. This layer of the model is where the TCP/IP protocol set begins to do its work. Additional protocols at this layer, all of which are associated with IP more or less directly, include the address resolution protocol, reverse address resolution protocol, internet control message protocol, and a variety of routing protocols: the exterior gateway protocol, routing information protocol, border gateway protocol, and the open shortest path first protocol.

The Internet protocol is the core TCP/IP protocol operating at this level, and as its name might suggest, one of the central protocols in the TCP/IP suite. Additional TCP/IP protocols at the network layer provide enrichment and support to IP. IP's major function is to move data between transmitting and receiving hosts by assembling packets of information called *datagrams* from the upper protocol layers into the proper size on the transmitting host, attaching address and delivery information, and establishing a path to a receiving host. In this chapter you'll be exposed to more detail on all of these protocols, particularly IP and its helpers, but for now let's continue our tour through the relationship of the TCP/IP model for networking to the OSI reference model.

Transport Layer

The transmission control protocol layer of TCP/IP maps to the transport layer of the OSI reference model. This layer contains two major protocols, the transmission control protocol (TCP) and the user datagram protocol (UP), whose function is to formulate messages and establish virtual connections between communicating hosts. Both of these protocols are encapsulated in IP packets to provide access to particular programs, or services, running on internet hosts.

IP is concerned at the network layer with the reception and delivery of data. After the data arrives at its destination, TCP and UP decode a final level of addressing in a packet, which allows the packet to find the particular application within the receiving device that requires the data. This next level of addressing is called a *port number* or *socket address*. Port numbers are unique addresses of services represented as simple integers. Port numbers are specific to the type of protocol used in transmission and are unique to an application. The numbers are in the TCP or UDP headers contained in IP packets.

Application Layer

The layered model of the TCP/IP protocol combines the functions of the presentation layer, the session layer, and the application layer of the OSI reference model and therefore maps to the top three layers of the OSI model. The application layer of TCP/IP will appropriately format the data that are to be communicated to the receiving application and performs all the presentation and session management services necessary. These data are then passed to the transport layer for further processing.

A wide range of TCP/IP services are available to users at the application level, and many of them will be covered later in the chapter. Services provided by this layer include name services, so that pathways between hosts can be determined; file transfer services, so that files can be transferred between dissimilar processors; mail services, so that letters and files can be exchanged between users; and TELNET services that allow terminal devices on one host to interface with and perform actions on remote hosts. In addition, some TCP/IP implementations include remote command execution services so that commands can be executed on a host to which one is not directly connected.

Avoiding Confusion

At this point it might be helpful to make some distinctions.

A *protocol* is a rule for conduct. The book of manners your Mom used to read at the dinner table was a book of agreed-on protocols for dining and interacting. A suite is a collection or set of interrelated protocols. The TCP/IP protocol suite was created to give an agreed-on form and structure to internetwork communications.

An *application*, sometimes known as a *service* in the TCP/IP world, is a routine or series of routines that performs tasks for the users on a node. A TCP/IP application is compliant with the protocols that pertain to its level of the stack, but it is not a protocol.

One reason some find TCP/IP hard to understand is that protocols in the TCP/IP suite and applications that comply to these protocols and aid in internetwork communication often share the same name. A case in point is FTP, or file transfer protocol: it's not just a set of rules for transferring files between remote hosts, it is also an application, compliant with the TCP/IP protocols, that provides a range of file system navigation and transfer functions to its users.

THE TCP/IP BREAKDOWN

If you could follow a message sent from your host computer to another host somewhere out on the Internet, you'd see what happens to the message at each level of the TCP/IP stack and where it goes from there. At every level of the stack (*stack* is just another name for the TCP/IP model, the layers are stacked one on top of the other), separate and distinct protocols or services are in operation. By following an example message through a metaphorical TCP/IP stack, you can examine some of these protocols as you pass through the layers.

Application Layer

At the top of the TCP/IP stack, a TCP/IP application sends a request or message to the corresponding application on the remote host. This message is sent down to the next layer as a stream of asynchronous data. At the application level, you'll find a variety of TCP/IP-based applications that perform user tasks. In the sections that follow, you'll be exposed to a few of the most important and commonly used TCP/IP applications.

Telnet (Terminal Emulation over a Network)
Telnet was developed early in the evolution of internetworking. Before the development of Telnet services, users working at a terminal station who wanted to communicate with a remote host had to establish a link using a

modem or dedicated ports on the target machine. The cost for several remote logins to a CPU could be high, because the CPU was required to manage the translations between the various terminal codes in use. Telnet provides a virtual link (network virtual terminal) with a logical printer and a logical keyboard at each end of the connection, and it takes over responsibility for translation of terminal codes, thus relieving the CPU of the burden of translation. This makes network access easier, cheaper, and allows more different kinds of computers to communicate with one another (since only one translation has to be implemented for each "end" of a terminal emulation session).

Users desiring to connect to a remote system and interact with the various servers on a remote system can use the Telnet command. Executing Telnet with the name of the remote host causes a login session to begin on the remote host. The user who is connected to the remote host enters commands from his or her terminal as if sitting at a terminal on that host. Telnet commands are available to control the connection with the remote host and perform various remote functions.

FTP (File Transfer Protocol)

Transferring files or groups of files between hosts is accomplished using the FTP command. FTP also establishes a virtual terminal link between two hosts. Users must log in to a remote host using a preset password, or they can log in anonymously. A user who is connected to a remote host using FTP can browse directories remotely and select files for transfer. Although *transfer* is the word used, files are not actually moved across the connection, they are copied. FTP also allows the user to switch back and forth between the file structures of the local and remote hosts. Multiple selection criteria can be used to select which files to transfer. FTP also offers a command language so users can create scripts of file commands for unattended operation.

DNS (Domain Name Service)

Machines like to communicate with numbers, and they can remember lots of them. But the folks that use the machines have way too many numbers to remember already. We all know lots of people by their names, but it would be pretty unusual to remember them all by their driver's license or social security numbers. That's the reason the domain name service exists.

Every machine on a TCP/IP network has an identifying number, its IP address, that is unique for that network (for the Internet, this means addresses need to be unique for the whole world). That's how IP knows where to deliver all those packets flying around the Internet to the right host on the right network. Since it's a lot easier for those of us who use TCP/IP to remember names, rather than numbers, for the host we want to contact, DNS provides the all-important service used to resolve the symbolic name of a host with its IP address.

SMTP (Simple Mail Transfer Protocol)

SMTP is provided as a part of the TCP/IP protocol suite to allow users with different mail applications to exchange mail across the Internet. The function of SMTP is to deliver mail reliably, by establishing a link to a remote host and handling the translation of the different mail file formats between hosts. To arrange for electronic mail delivery, mail utilities running on a particular host must make a call to SMTP, which then handles the delivery from there on out. SMTP uses standard internet domain and user names to find a connection, relying on DNS to supply the translations to IP numbers.

SNMP (Simple Network Management Protocol)

SNMP was developed specifically for use in the TCP/IP environment. SNMP is technically the name of the protocol used to carry network management information, but the name also refers to the whole set of management databases, operations, and agents needed to control a network. SNMP is used primarily to gather statistics about network operation.

This concludes our discussion of the TCP/IP application-level protocols and services, which also include presentation and session level capabilities. Under the next heading, you'll find the equivalent information for the TCP/IP transport layer.

Transport Layer

At the next layer down the stack, a message is received by TCP and segmented into packets. The length of each packet is defined by TCP, and a header is attached to each packet containing a checksum and sequence number (if the original message requires more than one packet to be accommodated).

TCP can establish *two-way* communications with a remote host at the transport layer by creating a connection known as a virtual circuit. If this is requested, then a unique number called a *socket* is assigned by TCP and transmitted to the remote host. The receiver responds by sending its own socket number. These numbers are used to identify the connection for its duration. After the connection is established, the segmented data is sent down to the IP layer.

Two important protocols are in operation at this level, both responsible for message formulation and transmission.

UDP (User Datagram Protocol)

UDP is a connectionless datagram-based protocol. This means that UDP transmissions are restricted to a maximum size in the amount of data that can be sent in one packet, and they can be forwarded to an internetwork regardless of their delivery status. UDP is known as an unreliable, or best-effort protocol. This doesn't mean that UDP is shiftless and lazy, it just means that UDP doesn't contain the measures to ensure reliable data transfer, it expects the machine taking delivery to be responsible for data integrity. UDP is most often called when a very low transmission error level is expected. Two other well-known best-effort protocols are Ethernet and IP.

TCP (Transmission Control Protocol)

TCP is a stream-oriented protocol, which means it doesn't have to worry about the size of a transmission. TCP is connection oriented, which means that it works like a circuit that connects two remote hosts. TCP breaks information up into small pieces and maintains a close eye on the reliability of the transfer of data. In fact TCP is known as a reliable protocol. This doesn't mean that TCP is any better at delivering and receiving messages than UDP, it just means that TCP is constantly monitoring the data stream for error messages and delivery status. TCP delivers data if it is possible to do so and reports back to the sender if it is unable to do so. Because of the wider range of service provided, TCP has considerably more overhead than UDP.

This concludes our discussion of the transport layers protocols; in the sections that follow, you'll move on to explore the networking layer, know in the TCP/IP model as the *internet protocol layer.*

Internet Protocol Layer

This layer contains the protocols most important for delivery of messages across an internetwork. The most important of these is IP, which provides a connectionless datagram service. *Connectionless* means that IP transfers packages of information that might be designated for one, many, or for every node on an internetwork and that IP offers no guarantee of delivery. Handling error control for IP is ICMP (Internet control message protocol). Routing of IP messages (datagrams) is handled in different ways by the routing protocols at this layer.

At the IP layer three distinctive processes occur. First, IP is responsible for fragmenting message segments to be transmitted into datagrams that will be forwarded to the physical network layer; second, for addressing the transmissions that will be forwarded; and third, for routing the datagrams across the internetwork. IP applies the proper header to the datagram before it is passed down the stack. This header contains all the information pertinent to the datagram's ultimate delivery, including the length of the datagram, the sequence number, the sending and receiving addresses, and a checksum for the header field. Once the proper information is applied, the datagram is passed down to the physical network layer.

One more piece of header information added by IP is called its *time to live* (TTL). This sets a maximum time for transmission of the datagram. If the datagram isn't transmitted in this time it is dropped. This information keeps lost or corrupted datagrams from wandering the Internet until the end of time.

IP Addressing

IP requires that each host and gateway in an internetwork have a unique address, called the *internet address*, or *IP address*. Any device that wishes to send and receive messages over a TCP/IP network must use such an address to specify both sender and receiver.

Addresses used with TCP/IP are 4-byte (32-bit) numbers, which are formally called *TCP/IP addresses*. Because each piece of the IP address is 1 byte, its value must be between 0 and 255 inclusive. These addresses are written in standard dot notation. IP addresses have two components, a network component and a host or node component. For every network gateway on an internet there is a unique IP network number. Every host or node connected to each gateway has a unique number within the network. This ensures that no two nodes on an internet will have the same network ID and node ID. The combination of network and host numbers is referred to as an IP number.

IP Network Address Classes

To provide for efficient address use and allow for expansion on an internet, IP addresses are divided into classes by the value of the first byte. Three classes of networks are A, B, and C. Classes D and E do exist, although they are not commonly assigned at this time.

Class A addresses are determined by the value of the first bit in the address. A limited number of networks can be in class A—in fact no class A addresses are now available—but class A networks allow for the largest number of connected hosts.

Class B addresses are determined by the value of the first 2 bits in the address. They allow for many more networks to be connected to the internet, but a substantially lower number of hosts. Although some unused Class B addresses still remain, they are nearly impossible to obtain for public use today.

Class C addresses, by and large the only addresses left to be assigned on the Internet, allow for many more network connections. Because the first value of the first 3 bits of the address is used as identifiers, only a limited number of hosts can be connected to any single network when using a Class C address.

Network numbers can belong to any one of the three classes, which are broken down as follows:

Class	Network IDs	Host IDs	Usable
A	126	16,777,214	1–126
B	16,328	65,534	128.1–191.259
C	2,097,150	254	192.0.1–223.255.254

Table 16.1   *TCP/IP classes of addresses.*

An IP network is defined by the IP address whose host portion consists of all zeroes. Hence, 137.103.210.2 is a class B address that has a network portion of 137.103 and a host portion of 210.2. This network, the 137.103.0.0 network, can support up to 2 byte's worth of hosts (for a maximum of

65,535 possible addresses). Each of these hosts will have a unique IP address, yet they all will share the same first 2 bytes of information, 137.103.

IANA (Internet Assigned Numbers Authority)

Node-to-node information transfer on local area networks that are isolated from all other networks is routed by MAC layer ID. MAC layer IDs are most commonly hard-coded into the communications cards that allow local area networking. The local network router knows the location and ID of each node and manages the flow of data across the link.

But internetworking, as we have learned, depends on each device on the entire internetwork having a unique identifier independent of hardware or network operating system requirements. So the question is, who comes up with all these IP numbers? And the answer is IANA. To get an IP address for Internet operations you've got to contact the IANA IP address registry. The IANA is part of the Internet network information center, which operates on behalf of the Internet Activities Board (IAB) that manages the Internet.

Most IP devices require manual configuration. The person installing the device must obtain a unique and correct IP address from the local network administrator or from the IANA and type it in to some configuration program or console, usually along with other information such as IP broadcast address, subnet mask, and default gateway address. IP is helped along in its job by an additional set of protocols at the IP level. These are involved primarily with address translation and resolution and routing of messages on the internet.

ARP (Address Resolution Protocol)

ARP is a protocol that maps internet addresses to hardware addresses. Even though the ARP function is provided as a required part of the IP layer, the data link layer uses the ARP function directly. The data link layer needs the hardware address of a node to send messages to the correct node. ARP can be requested by the data link layer to inform it as to the hardware address of the internet host.

ICMP (Internet Control Message Protocol)

ICMP provides many of the error-reporting mechanisms that can be used to regulate performance of the network. This protocol is used by IP to report errors and transfer control information between gateways and hosts, ICMP delivers messages about failed deliveries and network time-outs, as well as delivering network addresses for dial-up connections. ICMP is most commonly used to echo traffic across an internetwork for a TCP/IP application operating at the IP level called Ping. Ping is used to check the availability of a node at a given IP address.

ICMP also ensures that your host has an up-to-date routing table by dynamically updating the table and providing route redirection as needed. ICMP needs no configuration and is supplied by requirement in every TCP/IP implementation.

RARP (Reverse Address Resolution Protocol)

Just as its name should suggest, RARP maps hardware addresses to internet addresses. The data link layer will need to translate hardware addresses into internet addresses so that it can determine which host sent a particular message. This translation is provided by using the reverse address resolution protocol.

Routing Protocols

The basis for all IP routing decisions is a table of routing information maintained by the stack and the routing protocols. The routing table is one of the most frequently accessed structures in the TCP/IP stack. Each entry in the table contains a destination and IP gateway address. For a given destination address, the router address indicates the host to which an IP datagram should be forwarded to reach that destination. Routers use various flags to find the way from host to host so that gateways on the internet can exchange path information automatically and update any route changes dynamically. Various protocols are involved in the routing of the messages across an internet.

EGP (Exterior Gateway Protocol)

This protocol advertises what it wants the internetwork to see to the core gateways that link an internet. The first routing protocol developed for internetworking, EGP lets organizations offer servers and services to the networking community without allowing "visitors" into the entire network. EGP does not supply dynamic route information, merely advertises one route.

BGP (Border Gateway Protocol)

A second generation replacement for EGP; BGP uses TCP as a transport mechanism for establishing connections. Full path information is exchanged between routers using BGP, thus establishing the best route between hosts.

RIP (Routing Information Protocol)

RIP uses the hop count (number of gateways crossed) as its metric to provide the best route across and internet. RIP learns the number of hops to its destination. If the router learns of another patch to the host using fewer hops, it switches to that route dynamically. RIP is limited to 15 hops, thereby limiting its utility on the Internet.

OSPF (Open Shortest Path First Protocol)

OSPF can exchange routing information with other routing protocols, such as RIP and EGP. There is no limit to the number of hops that OSPF can traverse, so it is a significant, and lower cost, improvement over RIP.

This concludes the discussion of the network layer protocols for TCP/IP, which it calls the *internet protocol* layer. Once the TCP layer and the IP layer have prepared and encapsulated, the message with the proper header information, it is handed down to the physical network layer as a datagram, or a series of datagrams, depending on its original length.

Physical Network Layer

At this level the datagram is encapsulated in a frame (network operating system header information is added) and transmitted to the next gateway.

At the receiving node, the datagrams pass back up the same stack. As they move up the stack, the headers are read, the proper header information is interpreted, and the pertinent header piece is stripped away. Messages arrive at the applications layer as asynchronous stream transmissions.

Whew! That's an awful lot to digest. But you probably recognize most of these acronyms, and more than likely you have been using some of these TCP/IP services while browsing on the Internet.

Now that you know where TCP/IP came from, who developed it, what the TCP/IP protocol suite is and what it does, when the various protocols and services are invoked, and how the protocols and services operate, you're ready to move on to the next step—installation.

INSTALLING TCP/IP

TCP/IP was developed to be nonspecific to operating systems (OSs) and network operating systems (NOSs). TCP/IP was originally included with 4.0 BSD Unix, an OS that was widely used and distributed by mainframe and minicomputer companies. Most Unix vendors still include the TCP/IP protocol suite with their OS to this very day.

Since the development of TCP/IP was funded by the government, the source code for the suite was freely distributed, resulting in TCP/IP implementations for most available computing platforms. Installation and configuration instructions for the variety of operating systems that presently support TCP/IP would fill up a book larger than this one, but they all have similar requirements. In this section we'll discuss installation for DOS/Windows There are more OSs and NOSs, of course, and there is usually a flavor of TCP/IP available for each one.

Before You Install . . . Here's a short list of things you'll need to know before you start to install:

1. The hardware configuration of your machine (i.e., what interrupts, I/O base addresses, and RAM base addresses are being used)
2. The name of your network interface card (MAC layer address)
3. Your IP address, your subnet mask, and your broadcast address
4. The IP address of your domain name server
5. The IP address of your default gateway

6. Don't forget to make backups of all the files that configure the environment on your machine (i.e., win.ini; system.ini; program.ini; net.cfg., etc.)

Installing TCP/IP for DOS and WINDOWS

There are several ways to install the TCP/IP kernel into a DOS/Windows environment. The three most common are

- as TSRs
- as dynamic link libraries
- as VxDs

Each of these methods provides some benefits and drawbacks when it comes to cost (both in memory use and hard cash) and performance. For now it's just important that you choose the method of implementation most productive for your PC or network..

TCP/IP implementations for DOS or DOS/Windows install just like any other DOS or Windows application. During the installation you will be prompted for certain information. Correctly entering the requested information will ensure proper configuration of TCP/IP on your machine.

The following files on your PC will probably be altered during the installation (this will vary depending on your exact environment and the particular TCP/IP implementation in use):

1. autoexec.bat
2. config.sys
3. protocol.ini (NDIS only)
4. win.ini
5. system.ini
6. net.cfg

As always, remember to reboot your PC after installation so the changes can take effect.

ADMINISTERING TCP/IP NETWORKS

An important part of managing a TCP/IP network after it is installed is to set up and maintain several tables of information that TCP/IP requires to properly handle access and interoperability.

Hosts

Nodes in a network are registered in a file called /etc/hosts on a Unix system. Any node entered into this file can be sent a message. Nodes not in this file can be reached if the IP address is known, or if a name server is accessed to obtain the proper address. Thus, the *hosts* file usually plays a role only in dealing with access to local (or nearby) network nodes.

Equivalent Hosts

The hosts.equiv file in the /etc directory lists all the hosts that can be connected and make use of remote commancs on the local host. Passwords are not required for equivalent hosts.

Rhosts

The *rhosts.* file is a list of users who are allowed access to the local host without supplying a password. This file is kept on the home directory in the etc/passwd file.

Password files

This file, named either password or passwd, in the etc/ directory holds the names and passwords of all users who will be allowed access to the host.

Services File

In the /etc/services file the port number and protocol specified by an application are listed. Port numbers for the assorted TCP/IP services are assigned by the Internet Architecture Board so any service that wants to communicate with another application on a remote host knows what port number to use. The assigned port number is called the *well-known port address* of a service. New services can be added, and port numbers can be assigned, but none of the well-known addresses currently in use can be duplicated.

Your Mileage May Vary

This is a perfunctory overview of some common elements for TCP/IP environments, mostly from a Unix perspective. For the real details on your own environment, consult your system manuals (or *man* pages). Also, be sure to check out the many references on TCP/IP listed in the References section at the end of this chapter.

TCP/IP SOFTWARE VENDORS

The following is a list of TCP/IP software provided by commercial vendors. The important things to look for when purchasing TCP/IP software are what operating systems, network operating systems, and TCP/IP protocols are supported. Make sure the product you select will provide all the services that you require and that it is compatible with the operating system or systems on your machine.

TCP/IP REFERENCES

The Internet is the subject of two books by the same authors, John R. Levine and Carol Baroudi. *The Internet for Dummies*, 2nd ed. (Indianapolis: IDG Books, 1994) and *More Internet for Dummies* (Indianapolis: IDG Books, 1994). Both of these books are a good place for beginners to start investigating the basics of TCP/IP.

John Quarterman and Smoot Carl-Mitchell are the authors of *Practical Internetworking with TCP/IP and UNIX* (Reading, MA: Addison-Wesley, 1993). This book is aimed at the system or network administrator who works on a TCP/IP network, and wants to understand how things work and why.

TCP/IP for Dummies by Marshall Wilensky and Candace Leiden (Indianapolis: IDG Books, 1995) is a great place to continue your TCP/IP investigations. In addition to covering the topic in wonderfully amusing detail, it provides a gentle introduction to TCP/IP that is hard to beat.

Matthew Flint Arnett is the first in a series of 14 coauthors for *Inside TCP/IP* (New Riders Press, 1994), another book aimed at helping those who must run a TCP/IP network or internetwork or those who must oversee an Internet connection.

O'Reilly and Associates covers TCP/IP with a Nutshell Handbook for Unix system administrators, *TCP/IP Network Administration*, by Craig Hunt.

A truly definitive look at TCP/IP comes from Douglas E. Comer, author of *Internetworking with TCP/IP*, a 3-volume set (Englewood Cliffs, NJ: Prentice-Hall, 1991, 1991, 1993; Volumes 2 and 3 were written with David L. Stevens). Comer's books are widely regarded as the best general references on the subject.

Another comprehensive two-volume treatise on TCP/IP is available from W. Richard Stevens (assisted by Gary R. Wright on the second volume; Reading, MA: Addison Wesley, 1994). Called, *TCP/IP Illustrated, Volume 1 and Volume 2*, these books are more up-to-date than Comer's and offer detailed "war stories" taken straight from life on the Internet. For a reference that brings many salient TCP/IP details together in one place, this is a good choice.

The ultimate authority on TCP/IP comes from a standards body called the Internet Architecture Board (IAB). Within the IAB, the Internet Engineering Task Force is responsible for drafting and maintaining Internet standards of all kinds, including those for protocols, in the form of numbered documents called requests for comment.

For a listing of all the current protocol-related RFCs, consult RFC 1720 *Internet Official Protocol Standards*, which is available in at least three ways (if 1720 isn't current any more, it'll tell you it's been replaced by a new document, and you can follow a link to the new reigning standard).

Tip: The Real TCP/IP Info

If you take the time to poke around in the RFC collection (Table 16.2 on page 202), you'll be going straight to the horse's mouth, where TCP/IP and related matters are concerned!

Service	Method
e-mail	Send e-mail to mailserv@ds.internic.net with "file /ftp/rfc/rfc1720.txt" in the message body
FTP	Anonymous FTP to DS.INTERNET.NET (password = your e-mail address) or look in directory rfc/ for the file named rfc1720.txt
Web	<URL: http://www.cis.ohio-state.edu/htbin/rfc/rfc1720.html> for the contents of RFC 1720
	<URL: http://www.cis.ohio-state.edu/hypertext/information/rfc.html> has general RFC info

Table 16.2   *Three methods for examining RFCs.*

IPX/SPX: THE NETWARE PROTOCOLS

NETWORKING FOR BUSINESS

In the last chapter we talked about TCP/IP and how the U.S. government came up with the TCP/IP protocols to get the maximum benefit from its widely separated and expensive computers. Now, it's time to take a look at a more business-oriented approach to some similar issues.

Dawn of an Era

Some corporations took to computers from the earliest days of the *mainframe*. These companies could share files, their groups could work together, and their overall productivity increased markedly. Then, as now, managers generally agreed that more productivity was a good thing.

All these users were linked together using the only suitable technology available at the time: everybody had a dumb terminal on his or her desk, and all these terminals were tied into a monolithic central processing unit called a *mainframe*. This approach wasn't fancy, but it proved to be effective enough to represent a giant leap forward for business computing.

But this was a leap that only giants could make at first. The overwhelming majority of businesses couldn't afford the initial start-up costs of *mainframe* computing. They read about it. They knew about it. And they were buying computing from services who sold processing time and services, using somebody else's equipment. Thus, the real benefits of data processing were beyond the immediate grasp of most businesses.

As electronic data processing became more sophisticated and more available, more and more businesses jumped on board. Mainframes got a little smaller and a little easier to use, and the prices started to come down. By the mid 1970s computers were common in businesses of all sizes, except for the smallest "mom and pop" operations.

Enter the PC ...

When the IBM/PC and its immediate successor, the PC/XT, hit the market in the early 1980s, nearly every business bought one, or two, or a hundred. More and more people companies had access to computers or had their own computers. Businesses started to see a dramatic upswing in the quality and the timeliness of their output. At the same time, workers at all levels of business were beginning to feel the power of personal—as opposed to institutional—computing.

Sales divisions created their marketing projections on computers, making them more accurate and therefore more useful to the organization. Sales representatives began to keep their contacts electronically. Customer data were organized more efficiently.

Over in accounting, these computers made possible a much wider range of reporting, and dramatically increased the timelines of that reporting. Personnel departments started keeping employee data electronically, making access to information much more practical and bringing more science to management. Pretty soon almost everybody had a computer on his or her desk, and the outlook for business seemed brighter than ever.

Trouble in Paradigm

But the some of the same problems that the Department of Defense had been trying to solve with the TCP/IP protocols started to crop up in business. All the different departments had been computerized, but all those computers around the company were working in splendid isolation. The information they were creating wasn't being shared throughout the organization because the machines weren't talking to each other.

In a few company divisions, networks were set up. Accounting might have one, but it was a closed system. Only people in accounting had access to that information. The guys in sales got their own network. When the accountants wanted to share some information with sales, and vice versa, they all just got together over lunch.

"Sneakernet" was practiced on a grand scale. Computers had made more information more readily available, but sharing of information between machines and therefore between different parts of the business was cumbersome. It didn't take long for the businesses that had jumped onto the computer bandwagon to realize the need for some type of connectivity between all of their machines and between all of their networks.

We'll Send You a Copy

By an unremarkable coincidence, others had anticipated that need. Over at Xerox, a company already famous for business automation, work was going on with the stated purpose of setting up business computers to be linked up in networks and to share information. Xerox researchers at the Palo Alto Research Center (PARC) created an architecture for linking business computers, called the *Xerox Network System* (XNS), that paved the way for local office networks to be created for businesses. And those networks were to be linked to other networks.

The research and development of the XNS protocols is a story in itself. What's important here is that the XNS architecture, and its associated protocols, were released as an *open standard*. That meant anybody could use and extend this suite of protocols, and several companies released network operating systems inspired by the XNS design.

Novell NetWare X.x

Lots of companies created proprietary network protocols based on the XNS architecture. One of the most successful of these companies was Novell, Inc. Novell built its own set of protocols and message formats around XNS starting at a time when Zilog ruled the integrated circuit world and the ruling operating system was called CP/M, not DOS.

Novell's implementation of XNS is embodied in the family of network operating systems called *NetWare*. The set of protocols that govern its operation are called *IPX/SPX*. IPX and SPX are two of the central protocols of this suite, but taken together IPX/SPX is the name for the aggregation of protocols that make up the Novell stack.

Today, IPX/SPX is the most commonly used network architecture on the planet. The IPX/SPX protocols operating in NetWare provide the same services of any network protocols. Different tasks are isolated on different levels in the stack, and protocols handle the transfer of information between the layers of the stack and across the physical medium.

The following is a graphic representation of the IPX/SPX protocol stack:

NetWare core protocols (NCP)		
NetBIOS (optional)		
SPX (sequenced packet exchange)		
SAP (service advertising protocol)	IPX (internet packet exchange)	RIP (routing information protocol)
ODI (open datalink interface) Access protocols (Ethernet, token ring, ARCnet, FDDI, etc.) Physical media		

Figure 17.1   *The IPX/SPX protocol stack.*

Although the IPX/SPX architecture stack differs slightly from the OSI reference model, the layers correspond roughly and the actual functions of the protocols operating in the layers provide similar definitions and services. It might be helpful at this point to map the Novell architecture to the OSI reference model.

Physical Layer

The physical layer is defined by the type of network interface card and the physical medium (type of wire or cable) used to physically connect the machines operating on a network. Network interface cards are usually designed to operate with one particular access method.

Data Link Layer

In its proprietary architecture, Novell combines the physical and data link layers. Open data—link interface (ODI) is implemented as a software driver at this layer and handles the communication between the physical medium and the higher level protocols in the stack. Following a common

OSI	Novell Architecture
Application Presentation	NCP
Session	NetBIOS (optional)
Transport	SPX
Network	IPX, SAP, RIP
Data Link	ODI driver—link support layer ODI driver —media access layer Access protocols (Ethernet, etc.)
Physical	Wiring

Table 17.1   *Comparison of the OSI reference model and the Novell Architecture.*

approach, Novell chooses to divide the data link layer into two layers so the interaction between the physical layer and the upper level protocols may be more clearly defined. The media access control sublayer provides an interface to the physical layer. The link support layer (LSL) is a sublayer that provides the interface between the higher level protocols in the stack and the access methods used to get packets onto the physical layer.

Network Layer

At this layer Novell provides the Internet packet exchange protocol. IPX provides addressing data for network transmissions and provides the delivery system for this data. IPX is a connectionless datagram protocol like IP in the TCP/IP suite. Like IP, IPX is concerned with the addressing and routing of packets. Although it makes its "best effort" to deliver a packet, IP is not concerned about the connection between hosts, only about the addressing and the delivery of the packets.

The services advertising protocol, running in a NetWare router or a related routing module, broadcasts information about the services offered by servers on the network. A table of services is maintained within the router, and the information on the table is periodically broadcast (every 60 sec) onto the internet. Information broadcast by other connected routers is received by SAP and used to update the local table.

Routing information protocol, holds address information about other routers on the internet and constantly broadcasts and updates this information onto the internet. Routing tables are maintained on a router, and the information on the tables is broadcast periodically (every 60 sec) over the internet. RIP receives broadcast information from other connected routers and uses this information to update its own table.

IPX originally depended on RIP and SAP to find whatever services were available on the network or internetwork and to find the best possible route to the requested network service. Over small and uncomplicated internetworks, RIP and SAP perform acceptably, but complicated LANs and larger WANs need more optimal performance. For this reason Novell developed the NetWare link state protocol (NLSP). NLSP is supported by NetWare version 3.x and later versions. Its purpose is to provide more efficient use of network resources. Because it is a dynamic update protocol, NLSP helps to reduce the constant traffic fomented by SAP and RIP by broadcasting information only when the network's configuration changes, instead of once every minute.

With the introduction of NetWare 4.x, and the NetWare directory services (NDS) that help to organize and control NetWare 4.x-based (and hybrid) networks, SAP's behavior has also been changed. Because NDS can provide information about all of the services available in a particular NDS directory tree, the only services that have to advertise in such environments are directory services, which can then provide a method to inquire about all other services that might be available. This helps cut down on the "chatty" nature of SAP.

Transport Layer

For the transport layer Novell provides sequenced packet exchange. SPX provides the virtual connections between hosts that are necessary for applications to share processing information. Since NetWare is designed for high-quality transmission at the data link layer and since NCP takes care of some error control and sequencing on the server and the client, SPX is rarely used. It is used primarily for peer-to-peer communications between the NetWare client and server, for utility programs such as RCONSOLE, and PCONSOLE, and for SNA and other gateways.

Session Layer

NetWare supports the NetBIOS interface, which provides a link between external network applications and the operating system. Novell's own approach to NetWare communications does not use NetBIOS, however; it is supported primarily for the benefit of applications seeking to take advantage of this service, which is easy for programmers to use to build networked applications. NCP handles session issues for applications, in addition to its application layer role.

Presentation and Application Layers

Novell's network architecture, like that of XNS, does not distinguish between the presentation and application layers. The application programs that allow users to interact with the network operating system operate at this level of the NetWare stack, which employ protocols that are used by IPX and SPX to enable network and internetwork communication.

At this layer IPX/SPX provides NCP, the NetWare core protocol. NCP contains the protocols that define and govern all of the services provided by the NetWare operating system. Through NCP clients can have client/server access to a NetWare server, including file, print, directory, chat, and all the other services that NetWare offers.

We'll take a closer look at each of these protocols in the sections that follow. Each of the major Novell protocols will be examined, and we'll see how they work together to provide for reliable network and internetwork communications.

ODI

Novell's ODI driver specifications provide a way for a network workstation to utilize different access methods (token ring, ARCnet, Ethernet) and their associated protocols and defined frame types while simultaneously providing access to different protocol stacks operating on an internetwork (including protocols like TCP/IP, IPX/SPX, OSI, or AppleTalk).

Specs: Multiple Link Interface Drive (MLID)

ODI provides this functionality by coordinating the operations of drivers operating in two sublayers. The multiple link interface driver (MLID) layer is the ODI specification for a network interface card driver that can support all the various access methods in use. The MLID handles communications between all access methods in use on the physical layer and the link support layer. Using an MLID allows higher level protocols access to any of the various access control methods and the types of physical links that they support. This provides some welcome flexibility on widely used networks like Ethernet, where a single ODI driver can provide simultaneous support for 802.2, 802.3, and SNAP Ethernet headers without introducing confusion or complications among the separate data streams that are typically involved for each frame type.

Specs: Link Support Layer

The link support layer switches communications between the access control methods supported by the MLID and the higher level protocols that operate above the data link layer. In the case of IPX/SPX, the LSL hands data link information up to IPX, which is operating at the network layer of the protocol stack. If multiple stacks are in use, the LSL can handle switching among the different protocols in use. Here again, Novell's ODI driver technology offers unparalleled support for multiple protocols in simultaneous use (we've regularly run NetWare servers capable of handling all of the following en masse: IPX/SPX, TCP/IP, SNA, OSI, and AppleTalk).

IPX

The key protocol in the Novell network architecture is IPX. IPX works together with all the other protocols in the stack, providing a backbone for network and internetwork communication. IPX provides a connectionless, unreliable, datagram service to workstations and servers on an internetwork or a network. Remember that unreliable doesn't mean undependable and lazy in this case, it just means that IPX makes a best effort attempt to deliver a packet to a destination but requests no acknowledgment to make sure the packet has reached the right spot or to find out if packets have arrived in the proper sequence.

IPX depends on protocols operating at higher levels in the stack to provide guaranteed delivery and other services that it does not include. SPX and NCP, both of which we'll cover later in this chapter, are examples of higher level protocols in the NetWare suite that are concerned with the quality and reliability of network transmissions.

IPX has two major duties. Its first duty is to format packets. The second is to provide for their delivery. An IPX packet consists of a header (30 bytes) followed by a data section, which can be up to 546 bytes long (in most cases). Because IPX provides no facilities for packet fragmentation,

IPX implementations must ensure that the packets they send are small enough to be transmitted on any physical networks they want to cross.

IPX requires that all physical links be able to handle IPX packets that are 576 bytes long. (Therefore, the safest approach is to send no packet larger than 576 bytes.) Many implementations refine this process slightly by detecting when they are sending packets directly to a destination that shares a common segment of networking medium. If it can handle packets larger than 576 bytes (as with Ethernet, which supports packets up to 1,500 bytes, or token ring, which can handle packets of either 4,472 or 17,888 bytes, depending on the particular implementation in use), larger packets can be used.

Formatting IPX Packets

Any data that are to be transmitted on a LAN need to be formatted for transmission over the network. All data handed down to IPX from an upper-layer protocol are encapsulated into an entity known as a *packet*. IPX is responsible for taking data from the higher levels in the stack and segmenting the data into the packet size determined by the physical transmission media.

Once the packets are cut down to size, IPX adds some information to each packet to ensure its proper delivery to the final destination. This process is most often compared to the way letters are sorted, addressed, and forwarded to their destinations. When you decide to send some type of data through the mail, you find the right size envelope (packet) to put the letter in. On the front of the letter you put its address (destination) and your return address, so the receiver knows who sent the letter.

Once all that is done, you're ready to drop the letter in the mailbox so it can be forwarded to its destination. This is similar to the process IPX uses to format the data to deliver it to the network.

The Anatomy of an IPX Packet

An IPX packet contains the following fields:

Checksum—The checksum can be thought of as a fancy parity check. Its objective is to ensure that the bits transmitted are the same bits that are received. In other words, it seeks to ensure that no bits in the packet have been transposed or altered during the transmission. The sending station performs the checksum algorithm on the packet and puts the result in this field. The receiving station will also perform a checksum on the IPX portion of the packet and generate its own checksum. That checksum is checked with the checksum in the packet. If there is a match, the packet is said to be good. If the two do not match, that packet is said to contain an error, and the packet will be discarded. Since this algorithm is performed at the data link layer in many networking technologies, Novell has opted to disable this feature by default for IPX, considering it to be redundant and time consuming—with unnecessary cost. It can be enabled, however, as a configuration option.

Length—This field is used to indicate the total length of the IPX packet, including the IPX header checksum field. This means the length of the IPX header and the entire data field. The minimum length allowed is 30 bytes (the size of the IPX header) and its maximum number is typically said to be 576. For communications on a LAN, this number may be as high as the transmission medium allows.

Transport control—This field is initially set to 0 by the sending station. This field counts the number of hops (the number of routers) the packet encountered along the way. Since the maximum number of routers a packet is allowed to traverse is 15 (a network 16 hops away is considered unreachable), the first 4 bits are not used. This is also used by routers and other file servers that support service access protocol, reporting to indicate how far away a server (providing certain services) is from the recipient of the packet. When a packet is transmitted onto the network, the sending station will set this field to 0. As the packet traverses routers on its way to the destination, each router will increment this counter by 1. The router that sets it to 16 also discards the packet.

Packet type—This field is used to indicate the type of data in the data field. This is the Xerox registration number for Novell NetWare. It identifies the XNS packet as a NetWare packet. Since IPX is a derivative of XNS's IDP protocol, it follows the assigned types given by Xerox.

Destination network—This 32-bit field contains the physical address of the destination network on which the destination host resides. An analogy is that a network number is like the area code of the phone system. It is used by IPX in routers and workstations to determine if the destination host resides on the local network or a different network.

Destination host—This 48-bit field contains the physical address of the final, (not any intermediate hosts) destination network station. An analogy of this is the address displayed on the letter. Another analogy is the seven—digit number (not including the area code) on the phone system.

Destination socket—This 16-bit field is an indicator of the process to be accessed on the destination station. A socket number is an integer number assigned to a specific process running on a network station. Each service that runs on a file server will be assigned a socket number. Any workstation requesting a service must set this field to the proper socket number for the service requested to be properly serviced. Some socket numbers are constant, called *well-known sockets*. Well-known socket numbers are assigned to specific applications and services and they never change. Other socket numbers are assigned dynamically.

Source network—This 32-bit field contains the network number of the source network. This indicates the network number from which the packet originated. A network number of 0 indicates the physical network of the source is currently unknown. If a router receives a packet with no network number, it will assign one. When IPX is initialized, it may obtain the number from the workstation. It may also find its network number from the router. Network numbers are not assigned to the workstation.

Source host—This 48-bit field contains the physical address of the source host (the network station that submitted the packet). This represents the host number from which the packet originated. Like the destination host field, if the physical address is less than 6 bytes long, the least significant portion of this field is set to the address and the most significant portion of the field is set to 0s. Otherwise, it is set to the 48-bit address of the LAN interface card.

Source socket—This 16-bit field contains the socket number of the process that submitted the packet. This number is usually defined dynamically at the source requester.

Figure 17.2 on page 214 is a representation of the makeup of an IPX packet header.

Sockets Explained

Multiple processes may be running on a workstation and will definitely be running on a file server. Sockets are the addresses that indicate the end points for communication between like processes. A unique socket number indicates which process running on the network station should receive and transmit data.

Checksum (2 byΩtes)	Packet length (2 bytes)	Transport control (1 byte)	Packet type (1 byte)	Destination network (4 bytes)	Destination node (6 bytes)	Destination socket (2 bytes)	Source network (4 bytes)	Source node (6 bytes)	Source socket (2 bytes)

Data
(546 bytes minimum)
Ethernet (1500 bytes)
IEEE 802.3 (1496 bytes)
token ring (4472 or 17888 bytes)

Figure 17.2   *An IPX packet header.*

Sockets represent an application process running on a network workstation. There are two types of sockets: static and dynamic. Static sockets are reserved sockets assigned by the network protocol or by an application or service. Static sockets are the "property" of a particular service and cannot be used by any other process on the network. Their socket number never changes. For this reason they are called well-known socket numbers. Dynamic sockets are assigned randomly and can be used by any process on the network.

For example, to access the file services of a server, IPX would fill in the destination and source network, the destination host number of the file server, and source host number of its workstation. The destination socket number would be set to 0451 (hex). This is a well-known socket number defined by Novell. The source socket (assigned by IPX at the source workstation) will be a dynamic number and IPX will choose an unused address in the range of 4000 to 6000 Hex.

The source socket is used by the destination as a socket number to reply to. It indicates the socket number that made the request. In this way, when the packet arrives at the server, the server will know that the packet is destined for it (the host number) and will also know the transmitting station is requesting something from the server (socket 0451). Deeper into the packet will be an NCP control code that defines exactly what the transmitter of the packet wants to do (create a file, delete a file, directory listing, print a file, etc.).

Once the command is received and decoded, the server will return data to the transmitter of the packet. But it needs to know which end point of the workstation will receive this data (which process submitted the request). This is the purpose of the source socket number. The file server will format a packet, reverse the IPX header fields (source and destination headers), set the destination socket number to the number indicated in the received packet of source socket number, and transmit the packet.

Finally, the socket number (source or destination network number, source or destination host number, and source or destination port number) is the absolute address of any process on the network. With the combination of these fields, any process on any network on any network station can be found. IPX controls all socket numbering and processing.

That was one of the functions provided by IPX—the formatting of data into a packet so that it may be transferred across the network. The next function provided by the IPX protocol is routing packets directly to workstations on the same LAN or to a network station on a remote LAN.

IPX Routing

The routing function allows packets to be forwarded to different networks through the use of a device known as a router. Two types of routers are available on a Novell network, internal and external.

The internal router is usually performing some other tasks as well as the routing function. These tasks may be file and print services or a gateway service to SNA. Internal routers usually are concerned with maintaining the flow of data through a LAN. The external router is a PC with more than one network interface card installed. Its sole function is to route packets. External routers are usually used to link one LAN to another to create internetworks. Where Novell used to ship software for external routers with the NetWare OS, it now sells a separate product called the Novell Multiprotocol Router (MPR) that competes with routers with similar capabilities from other companies like Cisco Systems, or Bay Networks.

In fact, a number of companies manufacture and install routers that are compliant with Novell's IPX/SPX scheme. Usually these are *multiprotocol routers* that will route other types of packets (TCP, AppleTalk, DECnet, etc.) as well as NetWare packets. The protocols are routed simultaneously in the same router.

To route a packet, routers will accept only packets directly addressed to them and will determine the best path on which to forward the packet. Then, they will either forward that packet on to a local workstation or server (if it's destined for delivery on a segment of medium directly accessible to the router) or onto another router (if it's not directly accessible to the present router).

IPX Routing Tables

Routers need to know of all other available routers and therefore all other active networks on its internet. The IPX router keeps a complete listing of the networks listed by their network numbers. This is known as a *routing table*. Each router in a NetWare internetwork will contain a routing table. The entries in the routing table will let the router determine which is the best path for forwarding packets. Routers on an internetwork exchange information about one another through the routing information protocol.

A routing table contains a listing of network numbers and an associated path to deliver the packet to its final destination network. The entries in the routing table do not contain any physical addresses of the network stations that reside on the internet. The only physical addresses in the table are those of *other routers* to which packets, destined for a remote network, may be addressed. Routers do not know which other end stations are on the networks they connect to. The final destination (physical address of the final destination) is embedded in the IPX header (the destination host). Once the router determines that the final destination network number is directly attached to the router, it will extract the destination host number from the IPX header, address the packet, and deliver it over the directly attached network segment.

Routing Information Protocol

To exchange their tables with other routers on the internet, IPX uses the routing information protocol or RIP. RIP is a service residing on the network layer of the stack. Its purpose is to provide IPX with up-to-date address and route information so that packets can be expeditiously forwarded to their destination.

The functions of RIP are to allow:

1. Workstations to attain the fastest route to a network by broadcasting a *route request packet* that will be answered by the routing software on the Novell file server or by a router supporting IPX RIP.

2. Routers to exchange information or update their internal routing tables.

3. Routers to respond to RIP requests from workstations

4. Routers to become aware when a route path has changes.

When an IPX router starts up, it puts the network numbers of the directly connected routers into its routing table. These network numbers are entered by the network administrator when the router is installed. Once integrated, the router will then send a broadcast packet to the network (on each of its directly connected cable segments) containing these routes (the network numbers of the directly attached cable segments) that the router will now make available. Other routers on those cable segments will read this information and update their tables.

The router will then transmit another RIP packet requesting information from other routers on its directly attached network segments (an RIP request). This request will be responded to by any other active routers on the directly connected segments. The term *directly connected segments* is used here because request and response packets are sent in broadcast mode. This means that all stations on the local network will receive and process this packet. These broadcast packets are not forwarded to other networks by the routers. Routers update their tables and, in turn, will broadcast their updated tables to routers that they are directly connected to. The router will then compare the received table to its own table and make any changes necessary.

Once these events have taken place, the IPX router will place itself in the operation of receiving information processing RIP requests, routing packets, and maintaining its own routing table. In addition to these updating tasks, all routers will broadcast their routing tables every 60 sec.

Determining a Local or Remote Path

When a router is fully operational, other network stations may then use it to forward a packet to those remote networks. Any time a network station wishes to send information to a destination station, it must have the network address as well as the physical (data link or MAC) address of the destination station. If the two stations are communicating on the same network (sharing the same network number), the transmitting station can send the packet directly to the destination without using a router.

But if the destination station is on a different network, the transmitting station must find a router to submit the packet to. The transmitting station depends on that router to find the best route to the destination.

To find a router, the network workstation must transmit a RIP request packet. Inside this packet is the destination address (network number) of the final destination. This request will be answered by routers only on the immediate (same network as the requesting station) network. Routers that are not directly connected to the same network will not see this request because it is broadcast only over the network. Local routers can respond to this type of packet but will not forward this or any direct broadcast packet. Any router that has a path to that destination in its own routing table will respond, and the network workstation will choose the router to forward the packet to. Usually, this will be based on the lowest tick (time) or hop count (number of routers involved in forwarding the transmission).

On receipt of a request, a router sends out a response packet containing its own router's physical address. The requesting network station will use this address to physically address its packet to the router. The router is responsible for finding the location of the destination and for forwarding the packets.

RIP request and response information is encapsulated by IPX for transmission onto the network. These IPX packets, since they don't contain user data or requests, are known as *control information packets* or *overhead*. They aren't participating in user data transfer, but they are necessary for the proper functioning of the network.

Service Advertising Protocol

Another type of control information is provided by the service advertising protocol, which, like RIP, operates at the network layer of the stack. For a workstation to find a server on the network, to log in or out of the network, to use print, e-mail, or file services, it must be able to locate a server and the services running on that server. Routers keep tables of server names, their full internet addresses, the services they provide, and their distance from the workstation. The process of maintaining and sharing this information across the network is carried out by SAP.

Routers and file servers maintain tables of service information. SAP is a routing service, but routers update their SAP tables in the same way that they update RIP tables.

When a server is initialized on the network, it broadcasts its table of services to the network to let the network know that these services are now available. Service identity packets, encapsulated in IPX headers, are used to carry this information. They are periodically broadcast over the network and attached routers and servers update their own SAP tables accordingly.

When a server is brought down for any reason, it broadcasts that its services are no longer available, and the other routers and servers attached delete the services provided by that server from the SAP tables.

Workstations seeking services send out service query packets, encapsulated in IPX headers, to find any active server offering the required service. Routers that receive these packets check their SAP tables and respond by broadcasting service identity packets that contain the full internet addresses of the requested servers. The workstation takes the address information and uses it to address it's request directly to the server in an IPX packet.

NetWare Link Services Protocol

RIP and SAP were both designed to provide a capability for transparent access to servers and routers on an internet. But when a large number of servers and routers are in operation, the overhead from the RIP and SAP broadcasts becomes considerable and slows down network performance; as increased bandwidth is devoted to updating and maintaining information in the RIP and SAP tables.

NLSP differs from RIP and SAP in that it is a "link state protocol." Rather than broadcasting service or route information every 60 sec whether there has been a change in the internetwork or not, NLSP updates the routing or service tables only when a change has been made to the state of the network. NLSP periodically checks the connection to links on the network. If a primary link should go down, NLSP switches automatically to another link so that service is not completely interrupted.

NLSP also removes the limitation of no more than 15 routers between end points on an internetwork. In the early days of networking, this seemed like a logical and prudent limitation. But as networks grew and began to be linked up through routers, the limit of 15 routers became a problem and a limitation on internetwork sizes and reach.

NLSP can be a replacement for RIP and SAP, or it can operate in conjunction with the older protocols, allowing it to act as a gateway protocol for separate RIP and SAP domains. Each router using NLSP maintains an adjacency database (table), where information about the router's direct links and immediately connected nodes is located; and a link state database (table), which is a connection map of the entire internetwork.

Specs: NLSP packets

Three new types of packets are used by NLSP to carry out its functions:

- Hello packets
- Sequence number packets
- Link state packets

Through the use of hello packets, an election process occurs among the routers on an internetwork. One router is elected the designated router and thereafter maintains a pseudonode, or logical representation of the internetwork, in its link state database. Hello packets are also used to send out alerts to neighboring routers whenever a router link has failed for some reason (which might indicate a router failure or perhaps just a machine being shut down for some reason).

Link state packets (LSPs) are sent out by a router that detects a change in the network topology. The router that finds such a change builds an LSP and sends it out to its neighboring routers. The LSP does not contain a completely redrawn network map. Only the area affected, which therefore needs to be changed, is transmitted in the LSP.

Sequence number packets come in two types. Partial sequence number packets are used by routers to acknowledge receipt of LSPs. Sequence number packets contain a list of all areas reported as changed in LSPs, and the sequence of their arrival (sequence number). A router receiving the LSP can compare it to its own table and request the necessary update.

NLSP may be implemented over NetWare 3.x as an add-on NetWare loadable module, but it is included as part of the standard NetWare 4.x release. Network routers may use either NLSP or RIP/SAP, or they can be used simultaneously. This latter approach is common where older NetWare networks need to be interconnected for intermittent or occasional use; it obviates the need to update every router, yet permits the old 15-hop limitation to be overcome and reduces the overhead that a pure RIP/SAP routing scheme might otherwise impose.

NetWare Core Protocols

The NetWare core protocols provide the definitions for the NetWare operating system and the services that operating system gives to its users. All of the services contained in NetWare are contained in one kind of NCP packet or another. In this way, NCP defines a language for communication between the servers and clients on an internetwork.

NCP messages are prepared and sent using the formats and conventions specified by Novell's defined NCP standards. NCP is the language Net-Ware servers and clients speak when they are requesting or delivering services from or to one another.

Clients make requests of servers using the NCP workstation shell or its virtual loadable module (VLM) equivalent. The client transmits messages defined by NCP to request file reads and writes, to create print jobs or monitor print queue status, to determine drive mappings, to search through directories on a file server, and so on.

Servers answer NCP requests by providing access to services that have been defined by NCP. Some examples of such services include:

- Accounting services—keep track of server transactions
- Bindery services/directory services—provide access to a database of information about network resources
- Message services—allow messages to be broadcast to servers or clients on a LAN or WAN
- Print services—allow clients on the network to access network printers
- NetWare loadable modules (NLMs)—external programs running in a Novell server that are not governed by NCP yet still act like a direct servers. NLMs may be developed by Novell as additions to predefined services or by third party application developers wishing to extend NetWare's services

NCP requests and replies are encapsulated in IPX headers for transmission across the network or internetwork. But the various types of NCPs define most of what makes NetWare the most popular network operating system in use anywhere in the world today.

SPX

The sequenced packet exchange is the Novell transport layer protocol It was derived from the Xerox sequenced packet protocol (SPP).

SPX provides a reliable, connection-oriented, virtual circuit service between network stations. SPX uses the IPX datagram service to provide a sequenced data stream. This is accomplished by implementing a system that requires each packet sent to be acknowledged. It also provides flow control between the network stations and ensures that no duplicates are delivered to the remote process.

SPX reduces the number of times that an unneeded retransmission occurs to decrease the congestion on the network. Retransmissions normally occur after the sending station has timed out waiting for an acknowledgment of a packet that has been lost, damaged, or dropped. SPX uses an algorithm to estimate accurate retransmission times. It also uses historic information to determine the initial time, and it then increases the time by 50% if a time-out occurs. The process continues until a maximum time-out value is reached or until acknowledgments return in time and retransmissions are no longer required. In the second case, the time-out stabilizes at a value that is workable for prevailing network conditions.

SPX adds 12 bytes to the IPX packet header, mostly to carry connection control information. Added to the 30 bytes of the IPX header, this results in a combined header of 42 bytes. The maximum size of an SPX packet is the same as the maximum for an IPX packet (which means that the data portion is 12 bytes less, because of the overhead that SPX itself adds).

The developers of NetWare were concerned with reliable and efficient transfer over LANs and WANs. Software was implemented in NCP to provide some of the services of the transport layer, where SPX resides. The NetWare client shell and VLMs also have some simple transport functions included. For this reason SPX is rarely used in Novell networking, except for server-to-server communications and applications that require a special degree of reliability.

In Conclusion ...

This pretty much covers the basics of Novell's IPX/SPX protocol stack. By now you should have a good foundation in the basics of NetWare operations. To summarize, here's a brief rundown of how this stack operates:

- Data is formulated for transmission at the application layer of the stack and passed down to SPX.

- SPX is used to provide a virtually error-free connection between remote applications.

- Data from the higher layers of the stack are sent down to IPX, where the data are segmented into packets of the correct length and addresses are added to allow network and internetwork transmission.

- IPX attaches the proper header information and hands the packet down to the LSL at the data link layer.

- The LSL hands the packet down to the MLID, a driver designed to communicate with the various access methods in use for the various physical transmission media.

- The access method defines the way that packets are transported over the intervening physical media used for the network transmission.

One reason IPX/SPX is the most popular protocol suite in use today is that IPX supports nearly every conceivable interface method and physical transmission medium in use in the networking world.

In subsequent chapters, we will describe some other protocol suites currently used in networking. In the next chapter we'll take a look at NetBIOS, and explain a lot more in detail about how this interface allows external application developers a way to tap in to networking protocol suites. For more of the details on IPX/SPX, please consult the resources that follow in the "Bibliography" section.

BIBLIOGRAPHY AND RESOURCES

Bearnson, Stephen. "Communication Basics and Open Data-Link Interface Technology." (Basics of protocol stack operation, lots of ODI.) *NetWare Application Notes*, vol. 3, no. 11 (November 1992): 51.

Chappell, Laura A.; and Hakes, Dan E. *Novell's Guide to NetWare LAN Analysis*, 2nd ed., Alameda, CA: Sybex, Inc., 1994. When you want the real thing, go right to the source!

Miller, Mark A. *LAN Protocol Handbook*. Redwood City, CA: M&T Publishing, Inc., 1990. Good technical reference for those already in the know.

Mosbarger, Myron. "A Review of Bridging and Routing Technologies." *Novell Application Notes vol. 5, no. 3*, (March 1994): 101. (What is bridging? Routing? Good background on how networks and internetworks are assembled)

Naugle, Matthew. *Network Protocol Handbook*. McGraw-Hill, Inc., 1994. All the important protocol suites are discussed in detail. For a broad range of protocols, this is a good, informative work.

Tittel, Ed; Connor, Deni; and Follis, Earl. *NetWare for Dummies,* 2nd ed. Indianapolis: IDG Books, 1993,1995. An informative light hearted look at a serious subject, and a good general introduction to networking.

18

NETBIOS

NETWORK BASIC INPUT/OUTPUT SYSTEM

Even though the network basic input/output system (NetBIOS) was developed by Sytek, Inc. for the IBM PC broadband network in 1984, precious little information is available on the subject. Many pundits thought that NetBIOS would eventually fade away, but internetworking equipment capable of carrying SNA and NetBIOS traffic efficiently have preserved NetBIOS and extended its life well past what some might consider its usefulness.

Products like Microsoft LAN Manager, OS/2 LAN Server, Microsoft Windows for Workgroups, Windows NT Advanced Server, and some LAN Manager for UNIX products all use NetBIOS or the NetBIOS Extended User Interface (NetBEUI). Even though the demise of this protocol has been predicted for years, we don't think that NetBIOS will fade away with these vendors behind it!

Most of our references at the end of this chapter point to older articles or books. Nevertheless, we encourage you to look them up as a good starting point for more in-depth information on NetBIOS than is available from this brief chapter.

NetBIOS: Myths and History

NetBIOS was originally designed to run on an IBM PC network adapter board and was added as a networked extension to the PC's own basic input/output system (BIOS). A PC's internal BIOS lives on its motherboard and scans for the existence of NetBIOS; if the onboard BIOS finds NetBIOS, the regular BIOS initializes NetBIOS during the system's boot routine.

Older PCs required a BIOS upgrade so they could perform this scan during the boot. Later versions of NetBIOS were implemented using memory resident software (TSR) called *NetBEUI* that runs on the client PC. This occurred about the time that Token-Ring was introduced. Still later, companies like Novell designed software that emulated NetBIOS, to let NetBIOS client services run in the NetWare environment (as they do to this day). Many other companies followed suit, but unfortunately, not all emulators were compatible.

IBM developed the IBM PC LAN support program which included a DOS device driver labeled DXMT0MOD.SYS that acted as a NetBIOS emulator for use in its PC network broadband and baseband versions and in token-ring network adapter cards as well. This software provides all kinds of functionality for host access over a local area network, including terminal emulation of several kinds and file transfer capabilities. The IBM PC LAN support program currently sells for about $55 and includes software drivers that permit source routed token-ring nodes to connect to 3745 communications devices in the SNA world. Because PC Network is a 1 Mbps technology, it's not too widely used anymore, but it, too, still supports the PC LAN Support software.

Specifically Speaking

NetBIOS Explained

NetBIOS has been around for 10 years and has been used heavily in the IBM world. Many users and network managers assume that it's either a networking protocol or a network standard. The truth is, it's neither!

In reality, NetBIOS is a high-level application programming interface (API) that defines all kinds of useful high-level network access services. Programmers can write code that requests a 5CH interrupt that invokes NetBIOS services. NetBIOS redirects an application to file and print services over the network. NetBIOS is easy for programmers to use, which explains most of its persistence in a marketplace that has long since advanced past this API's rather limited capabilities.

Let's take a look at a typical PC in an IBM PC LAN environment that relies on NetBIOS to talk to other network devices. This PC will use software interrupts in the form of DOS device drivers to link the application to the NetBIOS interface.

Use of IBM PC LAN over token ring required a way to link applications programs, NetBIOS, and the token ring (IEEE 802.5) network. The IBM PC LAN Support Program DOS device drivers were developed to provide this service to the IBM PC LAN.

The IBM PC LAN Support Program supports base services in 1.2, and extended service in version 1.3. Base services resides at the client workstation in the form of a requester. The requester can be configured in the following four ways:

1. *Redirector* (RDR). In communications between a local client and a network server, the RDR intercepts the client's I/O requests, reroutes the requests to a network server, and accepts the server's response. (This is similar in concept to the shell in NetWare—NETX.COM or the later VLM.EXEs.)

2. *Receiver* (RCV). This provides redirector services plus logging capabilities. The RDR is not able to log messages, so the RCV is used to perform RDR services and to log messages.

3. *Messenger* (MSG). This provides all of the services of RDR and RCV plus additional services related to message handling.

4. *Server* (SVR). This resides on a file or print server in the network and provides a server's basic I/O functions.

As the name suggests, the extended service version provides additional capabilities for administrative controls over multiple servers.

RDR is the most commonly used configuration of a requester in client installations. When an application on a client requests to print, the request is sent to the RDR on the workstation. The RDR determines whether the printer is local or a network printer. If the request is to a network device, the RDR converts the request into a server message block (SMB) message and sends the newly formatted request to the print server using INT5CH, the NetBIOS interface. So, in this case, the client redirector is used to determine whether to use local or network devices. NetBIOS provides a way for the client to access and communicate with the other devices, but it is not in charge of formatting messages, sending files, and so forth.

Interestingly enough, it is possible to access a Novell network using IPX.COM and NETX.COM (or their VLM equivalents) and simultaneously access an IBM LAN using NetBIOS and the PC LAN Support Program redirector. We did that several years ago when we migrated away from IBM PC LAN to a Novell network. Connection to both kinds of servers from a single workstation permitted us to transfer data from the IBM PC LAN file server directly to the Novell NetWare file server using the DOS XCOPY command!

Interrupts

MS-DOS operating systems provide services in the form of interrupts. DOS has several interrupts, with INT21H the most commonly used by programmers. Within each interrupt is a hexadecimal number that performs a specific function. For example, INT21H, function 5CH provides file locking and unlocking services, as where INT21H, function 39H provides a service to create a subdirectory.

Prior to DOS 3.X, no networking interrupt functions were available. So, if an application issued an interrupt to print, DOS assumed it was directed at the local parallel port. Once LANs were introduced, users needed a way to redirect the print output from a local printer port to a print server on a network. This is just one of the functions needed and includes other functions like file services and file server disk access.

NetBIOS was designed as an API in the form of an interrupt that provides a network extension to the PC's onboard BIOS. It is called *INT5CH* but is not to be confused with DOS INT21H function 5CH. NetBIOS is an API that provides a programmer access to network devices.

The boot-up routine of a PC includes loading all of the interrupts into a look-up table location in memory. Hardware interrupts from the PC's BIOS and software interrupts from device drivers and TSRs are all examples of interrupts that get loaded into memory. As you might guess, if any interrupts have the same hexadecimal number, unpredictable results can occur. Because DOS uses INT21H, no other TSR programs or other APIs can use that interrupt number.

Once the interrupt table is loaded into the PC's memory, an application can invoke an interrupt and the processor is asked to stop and service the interrupt. An interrupt initiates the following sequence when invoked:

1. The invocation tells the processor to stop what it's doing and service the interrupt request.
2. The processor jumps to a lookup table in memory where all of the interrupts are stored and finds the appropriate interrupt.
3. The processor looks at the value in the interrupt memory location and finds an address of where the actual interrupt program routine is stored.
4. The processor then jumps to that address and executes the program. This program is called an *interrupt handler*. It will services the actual print request, file access, or whatever other service the application has requested.

Figure 18.1 on page 229 shows a an application requesting local DOS services which are serviced through the PC's own BIOS. Figure 18.2 on page 230 depicts the path a request travels when an application call is to a network device using the NetBIOS interface. This should help you to understand the logical flow of operations in both sets of circumstances.

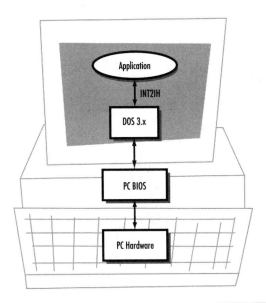

Figure 18.1   *Message path for local device.*

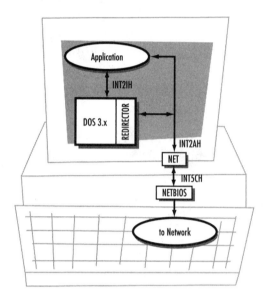

Figure 18.2   *Message path for network device.*

Two additional interrupts are available to a programmer using NetBIOS. INT2F permits the programmer to call a file server directly, while INT2A serves the same purpose, but sends a call directly to a print server. So, when programmers write code for an application, they have a few choices for how to access these services on the network. Here's a list of the ways in which programmers can invoke network services:

1. DOS application sends an interrupt to DOS and then is redirected through the workstation redirector.
2. Network application can either request interrupt 5CH directly or use extended DOS INT21H extended network calls in DOS 3.X releases.
3. Application can use special interrupts 2AH and 2FH to access servers directly on the network.

The DOS networking extension functions that were added to versions 3.X and above provide basic services only. NetBIOS, was specifically designed to provide networking services bypassing DOS interrupts. As we mentioned earlier, this approach is simple to use and easy to program. That's why NetBIOS is still broadly used in many networked applications to this day!

THE OSI CONNECTION

No networking services discussion is complete without comparing its functionality and organization to the OSI model. Because NetBIOS acts as an interface between the session layer and the higher layers of the OSI model, NetBIOS does not support the network layer. This makes it difficult to use in large internetworks. NetBIOS can be used at this layer through a process known as *tunneling*, in which NetBIOS calls are encapsulated by frames of a routable protocol like TCP/IP. The TCP/IP protocol has defined standards in RFC 1001 and RFC 1002 that provide the ability to encapsulate NetBIOS traffic. Windows NT is an example of an application that tunnels NetBIOS packets in TCP/IP to make them routable. NetBIOS also interfaces with the data link layer where the frames are formatted for transmission.

The following functions are provided by NetBIOS on a network:

- create a session and exchange information with another user on the network,
- support names and aliases,
- send and receive broadcast information on the network, and
- diagnostics to provide information on network adapter status and control.

On a NetBIOS network, a user gains access to the network by declaring a particular name. A broadcast is sent out on the network to see if that name is already in use. Naturally, if the name is in use the user won't be permitted access. These names are generally in the form of an alphanumeric alias rather than a hexadecimal address, which would be difficult to remember. This type of broadcast is fine on a small LAN with only a couple of nodes, but isn't really practical on a large internetwork, where broadcast traffic can steal precious bandwidth, especially over WAN connections.

Let's take a look at a typical path from a client request to a NetBIOS's service:

1. Client PC sets up a network control block (NCB) to communicate with NetBIOS.
2. The NCB interrupts NetBIOS's INT5CH.
3. NetBIOS tells the processor which service is requested by the client PC.
4. NetBIOS, operating at the session layer, bypasses the network and transport layers and sends the message to the data link layer to be formatted as an 802.2 or 802.5 frame.

NetBEUI was developed to work as a transport for NetBIOS and operates at the transport and network layers of the OSI model. Many people commonly refer to NetBIOS and the NetBEUI as just the NetBIOS protocol. But remember, NetBIOS is not a protocol! Regardless of whether you use NetBEUI, TCP/IP or any other network transport method, NetBIOS needs one of them to work in a large enterprise network.

NETBIOS AND NETBEUI: BIBLIOGRAPHY AND STRATEGIES

For general networking references, please consult Appendix C, "A List of Networking Resources." The magazines and other publications listed there can help you find out some information about NetBIOS. A trip to your college or city library may also prove helpful, because they usually carry back issues of periodicals where most of the details on NetBIOS are likely to found. Also, we encourage you to contact companies like IBM and Microsoft for their white papers on NetBIOS and NetBEUI.

The following references can be particularly helpful for the information they contain about NetBIOS.

Glass, Brett. "Understanding NetBIOS." *Byte* 14, no. 1 (Jan. 1989):301. As the name suggests, this article explains NetBIOS in depth. *Byte* magazine usually has very good technical articles. Because this one dates back to 1989, you may have to go to the library to find it.

Grehan, Rick. "Two Tin Cans and Some String (AppleTalk and NetBIOS—Part 1)." *Byte* 14, no. 10 (Oct. 1989):303. Part 1 of a two-part series discussing in depth AppleTalk and NetBIOS protocols.

Grehan, Rick. "Two Tin Cans and Some String (Integrating NetBIOS—Part 2). *Byte* 14, no. 12 (Nov. 1989):427. This article discusses the capabilities of NetBIOS and compares it with the AppleTalk protocol.

Haugdahl, J. Scott. *Inside NetBIOS*, 3rd ed. Minneapolis: Architecture Technology Corp., 1990. This is a small but powerful book. If you need to use NetBIOS, you might want to start with this book as a primer so you understand it better. $57.95

Brain, Marshall. "Network Communications Using the NetBEUI Protocol: Named Pipes and Mailslots for NT and Chicago." *Dr. Dobb's Journal* 19, no. 11 (Oct. 1994)82. A short, very technical discussion meant only for the guru.

Brough, Tom. "Tuning Novell's NetBIOS Emulators: Through Manipulation, the Power of NetBIOS Emulators Can Be Yours." *NetWare Technical Journal* 2, no. 4 (Oct. 1990):53. This article is intended for programmers but is also useful in a general understanding of NetBIOS.

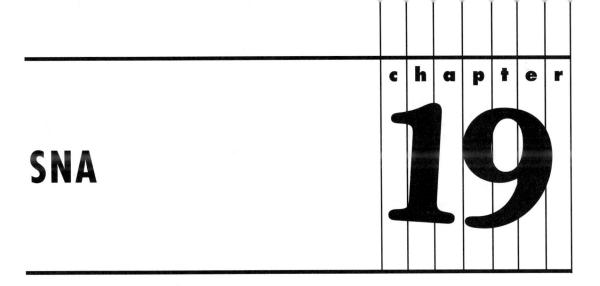

SNA

TO READ OR NOT TO READ

A lot of LAN managers know nothing about SNA. There's a good reason for this. SNA started out in the mainframe world, and mainframe gurus haven't been very forthcoming about sharing their information. SNA networks are essentially networks of mainframe and mini-mainframe computers and devices.

Like most other mainframe technologies, SNA networks have traditionally been managed and run from a centralized location. Lots of companies that use LANs made up of PCs still have SNA networks up and running. Nevertheless, there's no communication, except a very complicated sneakernet process, between the two systems. More and more companies are looking for links between their SNA and LAN systems. The network administrator has to find a way to carry SNA traffic on the LAN, and LAN traffic on the SNA network.

Migration to LANs and WANs often means moving from legacy mainframe systems to distributed network-based architectures, but that invariably involves a long period of transition. One of the main challenges that faces a LAN or WAN administrator is connecting an SNA network with disparate LAN systems. In this chapter, we'll try to point out important terminology, equipment, and techniques for bringing together the LAN and the mainframe networking worlds.

By the time you finish this chapter, you should have a basic understanding of SNA. We hope you'll also have more insights for solving typical

LAN-to-host connection problems. The scope of this chapter can't include every detail about interconnecting SNA networks and LAN systems, but we invite you to consider it a good starting point. While you're considering, be advised that if your organization does not have any IBM mainframes or minicomputers, you can consider yourself lucky!

SNA Architecture

The SNA architecture is a host-centric network system arranged in a hierarchical topology. Dumb terminals and other devices communicate with the host using private networks and packet-switched services. The host maintains the brains and the processing power, while the dumb terminals serve as screen displays for its users. Typically, mainframe host management and control is centralized because the host is itself in one place, but the centralized management model also offers a cost-effective way to deal with expensive resources.

Today, that structure is disintegrating. The evolution of LANS and the deployment of client–server-based networks has caused an erosion of central control. In client–server networks, the client plays an important role in the processing of programs, instead of serving as a dumb terminal. The processing is therefore distributed instead of host centric. Obviously, distributed processing demands new technologies and architectures. The mainframe is nowhere near dead and buried, so the two worlds must also be able to get along.

OSI ... AGAIN?

Most protocol books or chapters include the obligatory discussion on the OSI model. We discussed the OSI reference model for networking in Chapter 15 and repeatedly throughout this book. We will need to refer to it from time to time as we compare the OSI model to the SNA model. If you haven't read the introduction or any of the other chapters on protocols and access methods, then you might take a few minutes now to cover that material so that you can better understand this chapter.

SNA History

The International Standards Organization (ISO) began its development of open systems interconnection (OSI) standards 20 years ago and published its seven-layer model in 1979. The OSI model is based on a layered approach to networking just like its predecessor, SNA. While organizations were still waiting for the OSI standards to emerge, IBM's SNA architecture was able to slip into large organizations and gain a strong foothold in e industry. Because of the high costs of SNA, which involves mainly mainframes and stratospheric prices, most small organizations were not able to afford SNA networks, but many of them rented access to time-sharing networks that permitted them to partake of SNA services and applications without absorbing all of the associated costs. Even so, although "big iron" isn't always a "big company" phenomenon, big iron expertise is much more common in larger organizations than in smaller ones.

SNA Releases

SNA was designed to connect various devices like terminal controllers, microcomputers, minicomputers, and mainframe computers. SNA began as an architecture in 1974. There have been several subsequent versions of SNA, most recently the advanced peer-to-peer networking (APPN) specification, which is also called the *new* SNA. The following list represents IBM SNA and APPN releases over the years along with a brief description, where the kind of hierarchical network organization that SNA supports is called a *tree structure:*

- *1974.* Original release of a tree structure that provided support of only one host and its terminals.
- *1976.* A tree structure that allowed for multiple hosts each with its own trees, with communications between trees permissible by communicating through the root of each tree.
- *1979.* This provided for more general communications and eliminated the need for communications having to go through the root of each tree.
- *1985.* Certain topologies of LANs and hosts were supported.
- *1986.* APPN routing was introduced on System/36.

- *1988–1991.* Some IBM systems could single-hop to adjacent nodes, AS400 could multihop beyond adjacent nodes.
- *1991–1993.* APPN routing capability delivered to AIX and SAA environments.
- *1993.* APPN delivered to mainframe via free upgrade of VTAM and NCP.

Piecing Together the Jigsaw Puzzle

IBM had a near lock on the computer world before the explosion in LAN computing occurred in the 1980s. One consequence of its dominance is the large number of corporate networks that started out as SNA networks. Many companies started out with an IBM SNA system, but added LAN technologies to their enterprise networks over time.

Today, a major puzzle for these organizations is how to integrate their existing and evolving SNA network, and the newer but rapidly expanding LANs. Many companies still maintain two separate WANs, one of them for connecting mainframes and devices using SNA, and the other for connecting LANs using PC technology.

IBM introduced Advanced Peer-to-Peer Networking (APPN) to aid in linking its customers in an SNA network to an enterprise networking environment that incorporated dissimilar networks. APPN has never been the solution it was intended to be. APPN didn't perform well in internetworking, but provided for much more efficient internetworking between SNA networks. One of APPN's greatest contributions is that it changes SNA from its hierarchical structure to a peer-to-peer structure.

IBM Wakes Up!

In 1994, IBM began announcing products and strategies that would prove it was serious about connecting its own SNA products to the rest of the world. We'll discuss some of these products along with other vendors' solutions later in this chapter. The industry is still debating whether IBM waited too long to jump on the LAN bandwagon. APPN took a long time to step up to the plate, and some organizations simply couldn't wait. Some say that SNA and APPN are dying, yet others claim that SNA is regaining strength. We're not sure whether it's poised for higher heights or ready to croak, but either way, it's not dead yet, and must be dealt with.

SNA BRIEFING

SNA was designed to operate at the data link layer (layer 2) of the OSI model. It is a connection-oriented protocol that predetermines the path that data will travel through the network before data are sent. The protocol is designed so that the communications devices on the network request a connection or session with the receiving node and then make sure the data are sent. The timing of transmissions involved in SNA messaging makes SNA unsuitable for transmission in a LAN-based environment. We'll talk more about that later in the chapter. In the meanwhile, here's an introduction to important SNA terminology and concepts.

Nodes

SNA has different components in its architecture. These components are defined as *nodes*, which are physical points in an SNA network that contain one or more network components. Any device that conforms to SNA's specifications and houses SNA components can be considered an SNA node. There are four types of SNA nodes:

Type 1. Terminals—devices that interface with a user.

Type 2. Controllers—cluster devices that manage multiple terminals.

Type 3. Ooops, there isn't a type 3 node!

Type 4. Front-end processors—devices that manage communications with a host and controllers; FEPs poll the controllers periodically.

Type 5. Hosts—the brains of the network (*host* means an autonomous computer, which in the IBM world is often synonymous with mainframe).

Figure 19.1 on page 240 depicts a basic node configuration. At first glance, you'll probably notice the tree structure or hierarchical topology for these

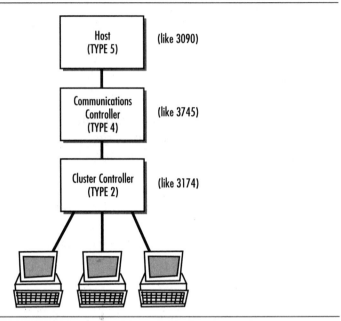

Figure 19.1   *Basic node configuration in an SNA network.*

nodes. This comes from the original design of SNA, which required data to travel up and down this tree structure to go from sender to receiver.

IBM's 3174/3274 controllers were typically connected via dedicated SDLC WAN links (9.6–56Kbps serial connections, often leased telephone lines) to an IBM front-end processor at the mainframe site. Dedicated lines guarantee bandwidth in an SNA network but don't allow commingling of SNA with LAN-based traffic. These dedicated links were important to SNA because of its time-sensitive nature. The FEP's most important job, therefore, was to poll controllers and wait for a response, usually at 10-second intervals. If it did not receive a response from a controller within this time frame, the FEP assumed the controller was down and terminated the session.

Physical Units

As the name suggests, physical units (PUs) are the physical devices or hardware that can be found in an SNA network. Each SNA node contains at least one PU along with its associated services to manage the physical device. PUs are given the same designations as their corresponding node types.

PU Type 1—terminals.
PU Type 2—controllers.
PU Type 3—not defined.
PU Type 4—front-end processors
PU Type 5—Hosts.

Logical Units

Logical units (LUs) are software-based access points through which users can communicate with the rest of an SNA network. Each LU in the following list represents functions that software programs provide in an SNA network.

LU0—generic function.
LU1—printer support.
LU2—3270 screen management.
LU3—3270 printer management.
LU6.2—program-to-program communication (used for APPC/APPN).

System Service Control Points

Simply put, system service control points (SSCP) is the software that provides the overall management services for a particular domain of the SNA network. Obviously, without this service, chaos would abound on an SNA network. System service control points are found on Type 5 nodes or host processors.

Network Addressable Units

Each node contains one or more network addressable units (NAUs) and path control network components. PUs, LUs, and SSCPs are all network addressable units. In addition to the address, these units are given a network name (or alias name) that can be easier to remember than a set of hexadecimal numbers. For example, an IBM 3820 printer has a unique network address and name. The *name* might be representative of the city and floor where the printer is located (i.e., HOU22). The *address* will be its hexadecimal address.

Domain

This is a collection of SNA nodes in a network that are managed by an SSCP. This SSCP management is a soup-to-nuts management service including devices, physical wiring, software, and microcode. Domains typically contain several subareas in a medium- to large-size SNA network.

Subareas

A subarea can be considered a branch of the domain in a hierarchical topology. Each subarea within a single domain communicates with the same host.

Multiple Domain Networks

When more than one host (Type 5 device) is present, multiple domains exist. Devices in domain A, for example, can communicate with devices in domain B. A host in domain A and a host in domain B set up communications that allow for devices in the two domains to communicate as well.

The Pictorial View

Sometimes you can describe a concept until it's dead and your readers may still not understand what you're trying to convey. We believe the old adage about a picture being worth a thousand words. Figure 19.2 on page 243 depicts all the items mentioned in the preceding sections in a simplistic setup that should help you understand their functions and relationships.

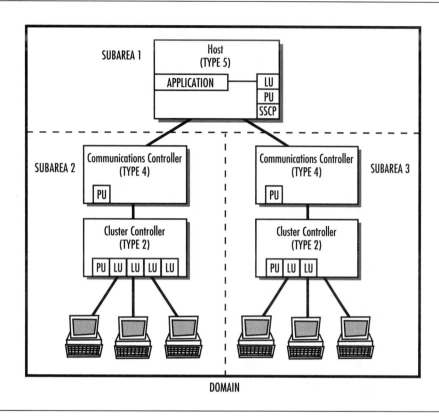

Figure 19.2   *A basic SNA network.*

SNA vs. THE OSI MODEL

Table 19-1 shows a comparison of the SNA architecture to the OSI model. The SNA model only has five layers compared to the seven layers of OSI. Even though layers 1 and 7 of the OSI model are important even in the SNA world, they are defined outside the SNA model. Nevertheless, we've placed them here as a reference.

Layer	OSI Model	SNA Model
7	Application	Application
6	Presentation	Function Management
5	Session	Data Flow Control
4	Transport	Transmission Control
3	Network	Path Control
2	Data Link	Data Link Control
1	Physical	Physical Control

Table 19.1   *OSI model vs. SNA model.*

A Layered Approach

Each layer in the SNA model is assigned functions to perform and services to provide. We'll go through each layer individually, but first we want you to look at the layers as a whole, and see how each layer communicates with the others.

Figure 19.3 on page 245 shows two basic nodes. Node 1 would like to communicate with node 2. The user at node 1 passes the information on to the function management layer. That layer may add information to the message, as determined by its function, and then will pass the data down to the next layer—data flow control. Each layer continues to add information and passes its data to the next layer below until the physical control layer is reached. When the data reach this layer, they are placed onto the wiring and sent across to node 2.

Node 2 reverses the process by sending the data up through the layers until the data reach the user at node 2. As the data are passed up through node 2's layers, each layer strips off any information that its function may have added in node 1. By the time the data are received by the user at Node 2, all extra information is stripped off, leaving only the data. This description may make the layer information seem extraneous, but it's vital to the accurate packaging and delivery of data across the network from one node to another.

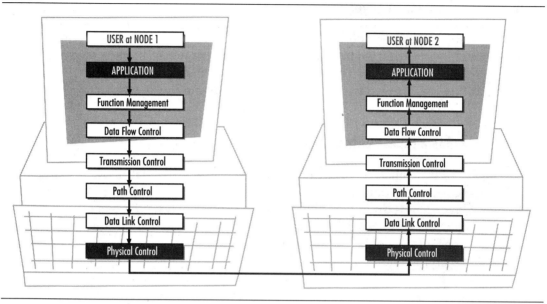

Figure 19.3 *Node-to-node communication.*

Physical Control Layer

The physical control layer is defined outside of the SNA architecture; like the physical layer in the OSI reference model, it is concerned with sending bits over the wire. This layer doesn't concern itself with interpreting bits or trying to decipher how many bits are grouped together. It simply knows that it has some bits that need to get onto the wire but doesn't check to see where the information needs to go.

Data Link Control Layer

The data link control layer operates one level above the physical control layer. This layer concerns itself with transmitting the data from one node to the next with the routing information provided by the path control layer. The data link control layer is also responsible for detecting and recovering from transmission errors that may occur on the physical link.

Path Control Layer

This layer is responsible for providing routing information for the data. This layer defines the end-to-end path that a message must take to the data link control layer. The path might include the various nodes that a message must visit to get from its sending to its destination address.

Transmission Control Layer

The transmission control layer maintains session status and tracks packet sequencing, data integrity, and data pacing. Once a session is initiated, this layer keeps an eye on the session's progress. It also looks at whether the data are received in the same sequence they were sent. If the sending node encrypts the data, the transmission control layer decrypts the data on the receiving end.

Data Flow Layer

The data flow layer is charged with managing the overall flow of data during a session.

Function Management Layer

The function management layer is too complex for one layer, so it is functionally divided into two sublayers:

*   function management data services and
*   the NAU services manager.

The function management data services sublayer is the manager of the interface provided to the user as well as the presentation of that interface. A completely separate function of this sublayer is to manage the overall network and its associated sessions.

The NAU services manager layer is the nebulous layer. It is usually described only as a layer that provides services to layers beneath it. We're not exactly sure what IBM does here, and neither are any of the references we've checked.

Application Layer

The application layer is not part of the SNA model, but is defined outside of the SNA architecture. This layer represents the users of the network and the network software.

INTERNETWORKING SNA

Today it is common to find SNA users connected over a LAN through a gateway server to the mainframe world. Novell has been the leader in this technology with its NetWare for SAA product. Microsoft NT now offers a remote office gateway product that matches Novell's product (and, some would say, exceeds it in ease of use and functionality). Regardless, a gateway generally has options to connect to the SNA network using SDLC or the channel attach method. Because this forces network administrators to support two backbones, this is a desirable interim step.

The real challenge involved in internetworking the enterprise into one homogeneous network is to provide network services with only one backbone technology, not several. Network management and security are critical issues in this challenge. Some router vendors include SNMP-to-NetView mapping modules to overcome this problem by interlinking TCP/IP-based SNMP with IBM's NetView network management environment. A tightly monitored SNA network can look scary when viewed through a TCP/IP environment and vice versa. Vendors are now attempting to address security issues to overcome this problem.

LAN Traffic vs. SNA Traffic

So, what's all the hubbub about connecting SNA networks over an enterprise backbone? If the enterprise backbone carries LAN traffic, SNA nodes could run into some congestion problems. Because LAN traffic can be classified as "bursty" traffic, meaning that there are times when the pipe is quiet and times when the entire bandwidth of the pipe might be utilized, this can pose a serious problem for time-sensitive SNA communications.

For example, if an FEP shares the same backbone with a file server on a LAN, the FEP may not be able to communicate, or poll its controllers, if a user is transferring a huge graphic file across the backbone. Until recently, this problem could be solved only by separating the two types of networks, using separate and distinct backbones. This solution is not only complex and but requires organizations to maintain trained support personnel for each type of technology. Clearly, a better common solution was needed.

Vendors and Groups Lead the Way

Because IBM has been slow to release standards and strategies to help SNA networks integrate with LANs, vendors have been slow to provide products. Cabletron, Hewlett-Packard, 3Com Corp., and CrossCom, Inc. are router vendors that have announced support for something called the DLSw specification (data link switching, a backbone technology that mixes support for guaranteed bandwidth required for SNA or other time-sensitive traffic with bandwidth on demand suitable for LAN traffic). These vendors were involved in an interoperability test where IBM rigorously tested the DLSw specification with various products from the vendors.

In October 1994, an APPN Implementors Workshop (AIW) was held. The AIW is involved in finalizing its high-performance routing (HPR) standard. HPR is a high-speed standard for multiprotocol backbones is enterprise networks. AIW is also involved in the completion of the DLSw standard mentioned earlier. It's still too early to tell what contributions this group will be able to make, if any, but its very existence augurs well for IBM LAN-to-host connectivity issues.

Vendor Products or Futures

- 3Com will provide DLSw in Release 8.0 of its NetBuilder II software, as well as advanced peer-to-peer network node over frame relay support.
- CrossCom plans to offer DLSw on its routers by mid-1995.
- Cabletron will support DLSw in its hubs.
- HP currently supports DLS capabilities in some of its AdvanceStack routers.

- Cisco Systems Inc. will support Data LInk Switching (DLSw) in its routers.

SNA Internetworking Protocols

Data LInk Switching Specification

IBM originated this informal specification and implemented it in the 6611 router. The DLSw specification defines a way to send SNA traffic over TCP/IP-based backbones. IBM then submitted DLSw to the Internet Engineering Task Force as a proposed standard, RFC1434, in 1994. At present, this standard is nearing completion and will probably be an official standard by the time you read this.

DLSw allows routers to protect the time-sensitive nature and data integrity of SNA networks and hence should be adopted by most major router vendors (as the set of products in the preceding section should illustrate).

Frame Relay

Frame relay is well suited to respond to the challenge of integrating SNA and LAN-based traffic. Frame relay requires less error checking, which can slow down other transmission methods, and it works well in a "bursty" environment. Because SNA provides its own error checking, it can combine elegantly with frame relay. Because frame relay also handles "bursty" traffic well, it appears able to serve both sets of networking concerns more or less equally.

In addition, frame relay has gained popularity as a means for SNA internetworking because it is less expensive than leased lines and can achieve higher speeds. It is a fast-growing industry that is expected to replace a lot of the leased lines and X.25 network backbones.

ATM

IBM has chosen ATM as its future internetworking direction. ATM technology is well suited for data, voice, and video because it uses small, fixed-length packets called *cells* (for more details on ATM, please consult Chapter 13). ATM's most attractive feature for the SNA community is that it will include "bandwidth on demand" services. It allows organizations to pay for the transmission bandwidth they actually consume, instead of paying a fixed monthly cost for a prespecified level of bandwidth on a leased line. All of these should help prolong the usefulness of SNA.

TCP/IP

TCP/IP appears to be the predominant protocol for internetworking enterprises. A recent push in this direction is IBM's draft proposal of DLSw, which is designed to route NetBIOS and SNA traffic over TCP/IP-based networks. Many of the router companies are already implementing the DLSw specification in their router technologies.

SUMMARY

SNA continues to provide networking connections and technologies for many organizations, especially those who have been involved with networks the longest. Because so many of these organizations have substantial investments in SNA, the protocol appears destined to stick around for the foreseeable future. As these organizations grapple with the problems in internetworking SNA- and LAN-based networks, they have pushed IBM and the networking industry toward a variety of interesting and workable solutions. We've only scratched the surface of SNA in this chapter, though, so we invite you to consult the information in the following section, if you're in need of further details.

BIBLIOGRAPHY AND RESOURCES

Martin, James. *SNA: IBM's Networking Solution.* Englewood Cliffs, NJ: Prentice-Hall, 1987. This book thoroughly describes the SNA architecture and is geared toward the technical guru; novices beware.

Cerutti, Daniel, and Donna Pierson. *Distributed Computing Environments.* New York: McGraw-Hill. A good summary of the SNA architecture can be found within a few pages of this book.

Pedersen, Elinor. "The APPN Connectathon." *Midrange Systems,* 7, no. 15 (August 12, 1994):39. This is a great overall article on APPN.

Krivda, Cheryl D. "Where the Action Is." *Internetwork,* 5, no. 11 (November 1994):28. This is an excellent article to read if you are attempting SNA internetworking. This article includes address and phone numbers of vendors that provide SNA internetworking products.

TOP FIVE SNA INTERNETWORKING VENDORS

3Com Corp.
PO Box 58145, 5400 Bayfront Plaza
Santa Clara, CA 95052-8145
800-638-3266; 408-764-5000
FAX: 408-764-5001
Tech support: 800-876-3266
Tech support BBS: 408-980-8204

Cabletron Systems, Inc.
35 Industrial Way, PO Box 5005
Rochester, NH 03867-0505
800-332-9401; 603-332-9400
FAX: 603-337-2211
Tech support: Use toll-free no.
Tech support BBS: 603-335-3358

CrossCom Corp.
450 Donald Lynch Blvd.
Marlborough, MA 01752
800-388-1200;508-481-4060
FAX: 508-229-5535
Tech support: 800-933-0143
Tech support BBS: 508-229-5600

Hewlett-Packard Co.
3000 Hanover St.
Palo Alto, CA 94304-1181
800-752-0900; 800-387-3867 (CD); 415-857-1501
Direct sales: 800-637-7740 (HP Direct)
FAX: 800-333-1917
Tech support: 800-858-8867
Tech support BBS: 415-852-0256

International Business Machines, Inc.
Old Orchard Road
Armonk, NY 10504
800-IBM-CALL or 800-IBM-CARY
FAX: 800-2-IBMFAX or 800-IBM-4FAX

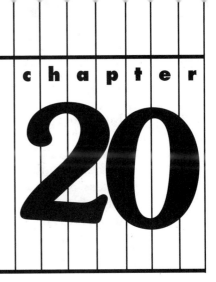

AppleTalk Protocols

Apple Philosophy

Users First

There's a scramble on in the computer world right now. Systems designers, developers, and even managers spend a lot of time talking about "end users." Graphical interfaces for applications, object-oriented operating systems, and graphical development environments give systems users more power than ever before to do what they want to do the way they want to do it.

It wasn't always this way. Computers are complex, technically oriented machines designed by complex, technically oriented people. For lots of reasons it always made more sense to computer system designers for users to adapt to the system than for the system to adapt to the users. In the beginning, system designers and implementers thought a lot about hardware and code and not so much about the people who had to use it.

Apple Computer, Inc., changed all that. Apple brought a new philosophy to the computer world—their computers were designed and built with users in mind. The company's stated philosophy is to provide greater power to individuals through computer technology. Before Apple, computers had been dedicated to a mission or to a business goal. Apple computers, represented by the Apple II and Macintosh family, have always been dedicated to their users, allowing direct manipulation of resources and capabilities.

Let Them Talk

The designers at Apple realized early on that no person is an island. Even in the beginning, when they were making some of the first personal computers, Apple designers wanted to make "interpersonal" computers. In other words, they wanted users to maximize their own potential, and they wanted to allow interaction between users through their computers.

If the Macintosh is devoted to a user, then AppleTalk, the Apple networking protocol family, is dedicated to giving users access to resources and information outside the confines of their own desks, offices, or homes. As the Macintosh operating system was created to allow seamless control of a machine, the AppleTalk networking system was created to allow seamless access to other machines, devices, and the world.

Why Bother?

Apple's philosophy of giving users the power to make their own world carried over into their philosophy of how networking should take place. Back in the early 1980s, when AppleTalk was being created, the network world was a disorderly and confusing place.

In the Beginning ...

It had been hard enough to solve the big technical problems and create computers that worked reliably. It was easy for designers and builders of the first generations of computers to focus on the machines, and save the worry about the users of the machines for later.

Once the machines worked—more or less reliably—designers and builders turned their attention to networking. They brought with them their technically oriented, machine-centric philosophy. Networking technology was developed as a kind of adjunct, or add-on, to computer technology.

The Apple Touch

Apple engineers took a different approach—the Apple approach. They didn't want to give their users more complicated things to learn and worry about. So they decided to make networking technology an integral part of, and sometimes a seamless extension of, the basic Macintosh operating system. They didn't want users to have to learn a machine operating system and then a network operating system. They wanted to create networking and internetworking with no extra baggage. They came to the conclusion that the network technology then in existence would not favorably extend their system, so they designed their own.

AppleTalk Goals

AppleTalk's designers had a list of goals in mind when they created their protocol suite and its related services:

- *Versatility*—Design a network system that allows any machine or device to participate in the share of information.
- *Plug-and play capability*—Always an Apple specialty network devices should be plugged in to a network and begin to operate immediately with no special configuration necessary.
- *Peer-to-peer architecture*—Save money and increase flexibility by making all network machines equals. Save the money for dedicated file servers or devices, and spread the processing load over as wide a net as possible.
- *Simplicity*—The simpler the network operating system is, the less overhead necessary to implement it. With less overhead comes the ability to build network capability right into the machine operating system itself.
- *Link independence*—Since technology will advance and take unforeseen directions, network architectures cannot be too closely linked to current hardware and software.
- *Seamless extension of the user's computer*—Maintain the look and feel of the individual machine's operating system throughout the network operating system.
- *Open architecture*—Allow users and third party vendors to add to and extend the operating system in ways not originally contemplated.

The Apple Stack

AppleTalk's architecture corresponds closely to the OSI model for network operating systems. Let's take a look at the AppleTalk model (Figure 20.1), then we'll see how it "stacks" up against the OSI model.

AppleTalk filing protocol		PostScript	
AppleTalk data stream protocol (ADSP)	Zone information protocol (ZIP)	AppleTalk session protocol (ASP)	Printer access protocol (PAP)
Routing table maintenance protocol (RTMP)	AppleTalk echo protocol (AEP)	AppleTalk transaction protocol (ATP)	Name binding protocol (NBP)
Datagram delivery protocol (DDP)			
TokenTalk link access protocol (TLAP)	EtherTalk link access protocol (ELAP)	LocalTalk link access protocol (LLAP)	AppleTalk address resolution protocol (AARP)
Token ring hardware	Ethernet hardware		LocalTalk hardware

Figure 20.1   *The AppleTalk stack.*

This is a graphic representation of the AppleTalk protocol stack. Like all protocol stacks, each layer operates independent of the other layers, providing for ease of maintenance and flexibility in implementation.

Figure 20.2 maps the AppleTalk protocol stack to the OSI reference model. You might note that AppleTalk's architecture very closely resembles the well-known OSI reference model.

Since they were starting from scratch to create a user friendly, plug-and-play network architecture, the developers of AppleTalk were able to build discrete, well-defined protocols to operate at each layer of their stack. Let's take a brief look at each layer of the OSI stack and the protocols that operate at the corresponding layer of the AppleTalk stack.

Physical Layer

As we've said before, the physical layer is defined by the type of network interface card and the medium (type of wire or cable) used to physically connect the machines operating on a network. Network interface cards are usually designed to operate with one particular access method. Because different networking systems are in operation and therefore different hardware in use, AppleTalk's designers created protocols that could support a variety of methods, including Ethernet, token ring, ARCnet, FDDI, and Apple's own LocalTalk (a 230 Kbps twisted-pair networking technology).

OSI	AppleTalk			
Application Presentation	AppleTalk filing protocol		PostScript	
Session	Routing table maintenance protocol	AppleTalk echo protocol	AppleTalk transaction protocol	Name binding protocol
Transport	Routing table maintenance protocol	AppleTalk echo protocol	AppleTalk transaction protocol	Name binding protocol
Network	Datagram delivery protocol			
Data link	TokenTalk link access protocol	EtherTalk link access protocol		LocalTalk link access protocol
Physical	Token ring hardware	Ethernet hardware		LocalTalk hardware

Figure 20.2   *Mapping AppleTalk onto the OSI reference model.*

Let's move on to the data link layer, since it operates so much in conjunction with the physical layer, and we'll take a look at some of this variety.

Data Link Layer

Every Apple computer made comes with the physical connection hardware and the protocols to transfer information from a machine or from the higher layers of the stack onto the physical transport medium.

The hardware, LocalTalk hardware, and the LocalTalk link access protocol (LLAP) operating at the data link layer are built into every Apple computer. Taken together, these are enough to enable real peer-to-peer networking. All you need is some cable to connect the machines.

AppleTalk's creators knew that some popular networking access methods and hardware were already in use. That's why their protocol stack provides support for many of the most popular ones: token ring, ARCnet, FDDI, and Ethernet, as well as LocalTalk.

At the data link layer the TokenTalk link access protocol (TLAP) and EtherTalk link access protocol (ELAP) provide the translation between the higher layers of the AppleTalk stack and their corresponding supported physical link. Similar data link protocols operate for the other networking technologies.

Also operating at this layer is the AppleTalk address resolution protocol (AARP). AARP is responsible for translating protocol addresses from higher up in the stack into hardware addresses.

Network Layer

This layer of the OSI stack corresponds to the AppleTalk layer that features the datagram delivery protocol (DDP), the workhorse protocol of the AppleTalk suite. Data link layer protocols provide for the delivery of information between different stations, or nodes, on a LocalTalk network. DDP extends this capability by providing for delivery of information between internet sockets—higher layer process addresses. We'll discuss how AppleTalk defines a socket later on in this chapter.

Like its counterparts in other networking stacks, DDP is a connectionless, best-effort protocol. It handles the necessary segmentation and addressing of packets to be transported, and lets other protocols worry about error control and transmission reliability.

Transport Layer

This layer of the OSI stack holds the protocols that are the key to the operation of an AppleTalk internetwork, in that they provide the key services needed by DDP for locating, addressing, and routing transmissions on the internet.

The routing table maintenance protocol (RTMP) maintains, updates, and broadcasts internet addresses and routes. RTMP operates on an AppleTalk internet router, maintaining and providing information about destination addresses on the internet.

The AppleTalk echo protocol (AEP) operates out of a designated socket on each node in an AppleTalk internetwork. AEP finds out if a particular node is accessible on the internet and finds out the time for roundtrip data transfer to a particular node.

AppleTalk transaction protocol (ATP) provides reliable transport services between sockets on a node. AppleTalk defines a transaction as a request from one socket to another to perform a high layer function and report on the status of the requested service.

The name binding protocol (NBP) is the protocol that provides for resolution of the names of devices and machines on the AppleTalk internetwork. NBP translates internet numerical addresses into the actual names and aliases of machines and devices. An AppleTalk internetwork has no designated name server. NBP takes care of maintaining information about all reachable names and addresses.

Session Layer

At the session layer of the OSI stack, the AppleTalk developers were determined to provide the flexibility that is uncommon in network architectures by providing session protocols tailored to very specific needs as well as general ones.

The zone information protocol (ZIP) allies itself with the routing protocols in operation at lower levels to allow networks and internetworks to be broken down into less unwieldy partitions. We'll define what *zones* mean in an AppleTalk internetwork later on.

AppleTalk data stream protocol (ADSP) is designed to provide general session layer services between any two sockets on an internetwork. ADSP establishes and maintains data stream transmissions between sockets with full duplex capability.

AppleTalk session protocol (ASP) was included specifically to be used by ATP to establish two-way communication between workstations and servers on an AppleTalk internet.

The printer access protocol (PAP), also allied closely with ATP, was originally included in the stack to handle communications between Apple computers and LaserWriter printers. Today, PAP is used to provide a connection-oriented communication between clients and servers, as well as between nodes and printers. Like ASP, PAP uses ATP and NBP to establish and maintain connections between clients and servers on the internetwork.

Presentation and Application Layers

In the AppleTalk stack, the line between the presentation and application layers of the OSI stack is somewhat hazy. Two protocols are operating at this layer, the AppleTalk filing protocol (AFP) and PostScript.

AFP allows workstation users to share files by providing information on the location of a file on the network and a means of accessing the file. PostScript is a particular page description language developed by Adobe Systems, used for transferring information between Apple computers and PostScript-capable printers (like LaserWriters) on the network.

LocalTalk (Data Link and Physical Layers)

As we've already mentioned, all Apple computers are delivered to users network ready. What this means is that the networking protocols necessary for peer-to-peer networking are included in the basic Macintosh operating system. The necessary physical links are provided for by including a network interface built into each machine.

In fact, all you need to set up a LAN with Apple products is some cables to hook all the computers and devices together. Even LaserWriter printers are shipped network ready. This readiness to network is important evidence of the goals that motivated the AppleTalk developers. In most ways that count, LocalTalk networks really are an extension of the Macintosh operating system.

The capability to just hook machines and devices together and provide automatic network capability is very important to Apple. Very little special configuration is necessary to install or configure a LocalTalk network. This is the embodiment of Apple's "plug and play" philosophy.

An Apple network that is not connected to another network works just fine with the basic protocols and physical connection media included with each machine and device. Apple, Inc. has indeed provided all the physical layer and data link layer protocols necessary for simple networking. Today, its more recent Quadra and Power PC models come equipped with Ethernet, perhaps in recognition that LocalTalk's 230 Kbps bandwidth is inadequate for higher end network access.

LocalTalk Link Access Protocol

LLAP headers include the addresses of the source and destination nodes and a type field that specifies the packet type contained in the packet's data field. A node's address is dynamically assigned by LLAP when it starts up.

Different specifications operate for data packets and control packets. After the packet type comes a data length field followed by the data itself. A frame trailer follows with a frame check sequence (FCS) number, a flag value, and an abort sequence indicating the end of the frame.

Figure 20.3 gives us a look at the internals of an LLAP frame.

Control packets are used to provide information to the LAN and do not contain data. Data packets can contain up to 600 bytes (called *octets*, in network-speak for some reason lost in the dim history of data communications) of information.

Frame preamble	Destination node ID	Source ID	LLAP Type	Data length	Data	FCS	FLAG	Abort

Figure 20.3   *The layout of an LLAP frame.*

Ethernet and Token Ring Link Access Protocols

AppleTalk developers designed support for other popular networking methods into their protocol architecture. This includes ELAP and TLAP, as well as other link access protocols.

The EtherTalk link access protocol encapsulates the information contained in an LLAP frame in an Ethernet frame by adding an Ethernet destination source field, Ethernet source field, and Ethernet type field. Some padding may be added to reach the minimum length requirements for Ethernet frames. TokenTalk link access protocol operates exactly the same. A token ring destination field and a source field are added to the LocalTalk header.

AppleTalk Address Resolution Protocol

The AppleTalk address resolution protocol is implemented at the data link layer to provide a way to handle transmissions between the higher level protocols and hardware addresses. AARP uses three types of packets to do its job: probe, request, and response packets. Here's how they work.

When a network node initializes AARP assigns an address for the higher level protocol stack on the node and then broadcasts *probe* packets to find out if any other nodes are using that address.

Each node keeps an address mapping table for any protocol stacks on the device. *Request* packets are sent out to locate specific nodes on the link so that a transmission can occur. If a node gets a request for a protocol address that matches its own it sends out a *response* packet containing its hardware address. If a match is not found then a request packet is sent out.

Datagram Delivery Protocol

Every protocol suite involved in an internetwork needs a connectionless protocol in operation at the network to provide for delivery of packets. While LAN transmissions are enabled by data link and physical layer protocols, the protocols at the network layer make internetworking possible.

In fact, all the AppleTalk protocols in operation above the DDP layer depend on DDP to let them do their work. The data link layer frames we've already discussed deliver information between nodes on a LAN. DDP is responsible for delivering packets between sockets on the internet. A *socket* is defined as the addresses of higher layer processes on any given network node.

Sockets Explained

All high level processes operating at protocol stack layers above DDP are dynamically assigned socket numbers by DDP, or they have statically assigned sockets reserved for use by protocols such as the name binding protocol and routing table maintenance protocol. Internet socket addresses are made up of a 16-byte network number, an 8-byte node ID, and an 8 byte socket number.

DDP gets a node's AppleTalk address when it initializes. DDP takes information from the underlying data link in use by the node, and from internet routers on the data link, to get this address.

Socket clients are implemented with socket listeners that receive datagrams addressed to that particular socket. Socket listeners are able to receive asynchronously either through an interrupt of some type of input/output routing. A sockets table is implemented in DDP to maintain the location and type of each open sockets listener. Calls to the socket listener are used to open a dynamically assigned socket, close a socket, send datagrams, and receive datagrams.

DDP in Operation

Datagrams are transmitted by internet routers from source to destination sockets. DDP on the source node checks the destination network number of the datagram and finds out if the destination is on the local network or somewhere beyond the local link. If the destination node is on the LAN, then DDP hands the packets to be sent down to the data link layer for transmission. If the destination is not local, then DDP encapsulates the transmission in its header and uses the data link protocols to send the packet to a router. The router uses its routing tables and the associated routing protocol to determine the best path to the destination and forwards it onto the internetwork. A router on the destination network is eventually reached and hands the datagram down to the data link layer for forwarding to the destination node.

DDP Packets

DDP packets are made up of a 8-bit hop count field, 8-bit datagram length field, 16-bit DDP checksum, 16-bit destination network number, 16-bit source network number, 8-bit destination node ID, 8-bit source node id, 8-bit destination socket number, 8 bit-source socket number, and an 8-bit DDP packet type field encapsulated in a LLAP frame along with the accompanying data. Figure 20.4 shows an example of the formation of a DDP packet. It is a representation of the makeup of an DDP packet header.

Hop count (2 bytes)	Datagram length (2 bytes)	Destination network (2 bytes)	Source network (2 bytes)	Destination node (1 byte)	Source node (1 byte)	Destination socket (1 byte)	Source socket (1 byte)	DDP Type (1 byte)	Data (0-to-586 bytes)

Figure 20.4   *The anatomy fo a DDP packet header.*

Routing Tables

Routers need to know the addresses of all other available routers and therefore about all the other active networks reachable on its internet. AppleTalk routers keep a complete listing of these networks, listed by their network numbers. This is known as a routing table. Each router in an AppleTalk internetwork will contain a routing table. The entries in the routing table let the router determine which is the best path for forwarding packets.

A routing table contains a listing of network numbers and an associated path used by DDP to deliver packets to their final destination network. The entries in the routing table contain no physical addresses of the network stations that reside on the internet. The only physical addresses in the table are those of *other routers* to which packets, destined for a remote network, may be addressed. Routers do not know which other end stations are on the networks they connect to. The final destination (physical address of the final destination) is embedded in the DDP header. Their job is to get the packets to the right network, not to the precise workstation (this is handled at the local level by the final router in the chain between sender and receiver).

Routing Table Maintenance Protocol

RTMP operates on AppleTalk internet routers. RTMP establishes and maintains the routing tables used to transmit datagrams over the internet between source and destination sockets. Every AppleTalk router has RTMP in operation on a statically assigned socket known as the RTMP socket. Routers get RTMP packets from other routers on the internet and use the information they contain to maintain and update their own routing tables.

Each entry in the routing table includes the port number through which packets must be forwarded by the router, the network number and the node address of the next router, and the distance to the destination network measured in hops.

RTMP provides for the construction of routing tables and keeps track of other routers initializing or going down on the internet. When a router initializes it starts its own table by examining each of its enabled ports. Any port with a network number other than zero connected to one of the router's ports tells the router that it is directly connected to that network. RTMP creates table entries for these network numbers.

Each router in the internetwork broadcasts its own table periodically (every 10 sec) by sending data packets through its enabled ports to the RTMP socket. If a router receives RTMP table information not included in its own table, then that information is added to its own table. In this way, information about a network's configuration gets updated regularly and reliably.

AppleTalk Echo Protocol

The AppleTalk echo protocol is used to find out if a node is accessible over the internet. AEP operates on a statically assigned socket and listens for packets addressed to this socket. If a packet is received the echoer determines if the packet is an echo packet. If it is, then a copy of the packet is made and transmitted to the same socket on the sending node.

AEP is used to determine if nodes can be reached and the roundtrip time for a packet to reach a remote node and be returned (much like Ping in the TCP/IP stack). This information is valuable for certain proactive network management functions and is used by higher level protocols in estimating the time-outs specified by protocols at higher levels in the stack.

Name Binding Protocol

AppleTalk protocols rely on numbers—node ID numbers, socket numbers, network numbers, etc.—to provide addressing capability. But, as we all know, numbers, which are easy for computers to remember, are not so easy for users to remember. Names are a more usable type of identification for the average user. When a user refers to a network device or computer by name, that name must be converted into a network address that can be understood by the computers on the internetwork. NBP handles the translation of numbers into names, and vice versa.

Since node address assignments are done dynamically by AppleTalk, the number assigned to a node may change often. The name of that particular node does not change so readily. NBP is valuable in keeping up with dynamically assigned names and addresses.

Network Visible Entities

Each node on the network maintains a names table that keeps the names to entity internet address mappings of all the NVE in that node. A network visible entities is any entity accessible to DDP on an AppleTalk network. Nodes on the internet are not NVEs but the services in those particular nodes are. A network server is not an NVE but the services offered on defined sockets in that server are NVEs.

The NBP process is statically assigned to a socket and responsible for keeping the node's names table and handling lookup requests from the network and from the node itself.

NBP Services

NBP provides four basic services:

- Name registration
- Name deletion
- Name lookup
- Name confirmation

NVEs enter their names and socket numbers into the names table by notifying NBP on the node. NBP is responsible for entering these names into the table. If an entity stops operation for some reason, it sends a name deletion call to NBP and the corresponding mapping is removed from the names table.

When a user or higher level protocol wants access to an entities service, it issues a name lookup call to NBP. NBP performs a search through the names table and returns the address to the requester. In some circumstances, NBP issues a name confirmation call to confirm that a mapping is still valid.

AppleTalk Transaction Protocol

AppleTalk transaction protocol, operating in the transport layer of the stack, is concerned with end-to-end data flow between sockets on the internetwork Earlier, we described DDP, working at the network layer, as a best-effort or connectionless protocol. That means DDP is interested only in forming up a packet, addressing it, and sending it on its way.

ATP, being concerned with end-to-end data flow, is connection oriented. That means ATP wants to make sure that all its packets are delivered error free. Also, ATP is concerned with the state of the connection and the results of a transmission.

Transactions

ATP is designed to create and maintain an error free, transaction-based, connection between sockets. When a socket client on an AppleTalk internet requests a service from another socket client, it sends a request to that socket using ATP. The socket client receiving the request performs the service as requested and then sends an ATP response out to the requester reporting the outcome. This interaction between the requester and service performer is called a *transaction*. ATP was designed specifically to take care of this type of network activity.

Two types of transactions are the responsibility of ATP:

- At least once (ALO)
- Exactly once (XO)

When a socket client on a network node sends out a request for services it makes the determination whether the requested transaction is a ALO or an XO transaction.

ALO transactions make sure that the requested service is performed at least once, and ATP ALO is concerned if the service is performed more than once. If the requesting socket doesn't receive an ATP response from the service provider, it just sends out another request. If for some reason the response packets aren't getting through, then the transaction requested is performed each time a request comes through. Asking a remote node for its ID is an example of an ATP ALO transaction.

XO transactions can't be executed more than once without causing some type of unwanted change. Some protocols higher up in the AppleTalk stack, like the printer access protocol and AppleTalk session protocol require this type of service to maintain the integrity of their transmissions. ATP XO maintains a list of requests and corresponding responses. When a request for a transaction is sent out with ATP XO, the receiving socket checks the list to see if the transaction has been received and responded to already. If this is the case, ATP XO ignores the request.

Session Layer

On the next level of the stack, the sessions layer, AppleTalk provides four protocols concerned with establishing and maintaining connection-oriented reliable data transfer: PAP, ASP, ADSP, and ZIP. For more details on these protocols, please read on.

Printer Access Protocol

The printer access protocol is a session layer protocol that sets up connection-oriented communications sessions between workstation and server socket clients on the AppleTalk network. The protocol was originally designed strictly for workstation communication with LaserWriter and ImageWriter printers but it can be used for any asymmetrical communications between servers and workstations.

PAP defines a node as having multiple processes that are available to workstations on the internetwork. These processes are made available by the server to the client workstation through PAP, which is itself a client of

ATP and NBP. Servers advertise their availability to the network through session listening sockets.

When a workstation wants to establish a connection with a server node, it will call NBP for the address of the server's session listening socket, then call the address to request a connection session. PAP uses ATP, in exactly one mode, for the data transmission.

PAP servers can handle many transactions simultaneously, depending on their configuration. If all available connections are in use on the server, it will ignore other PAP requests for session connections.

AppleTalk Session Protocol

ASP opens up sessions between sockets on the internet and is responsible for maintaining the connection and closing down the session once the transmission is complete. ASP uses ATP as a delivery mechanism to perform four basic functions related to communication between the workstations requesting services and servers provided the requested services:

- Opening sessions
- Session request handling
- Session management
- Closing sessions

ASP requests between clients are sent out to open a session. Session request handling describes the transfer of messages and data between the sockets involved in the session. Session management is concerned with the integrity of the data flow and the status of the sockets involved in the session. At the end of a session, ASP closes down the connection.

When ASP initiates a session or connection between two network entities, it assigns a session number to the connection, so that more than one workstation may access the server at the same time. ASP commands are sent to the server and ASP replies are returned to the workstation. ASP does not provide for the server to make demands on the workstation, but it does allow the server clients to let the workstation know when it needs attention.

ASP's reason to exist is to establish and maintain direct connections between the higher level protocols in the stack with a minimum of alteration by the lower level protocols. A server entity on the network makes its service known by opening an ATP socket and then registering a unique name on this socket with the Name Binding Protocol. Once the name is registered, ASP is notified of the address on the ATP socket. ASP listens at this socket for session requests from workstations that want to use the advertised service. Workstations call NBP to learn the socket's address and then call ASP to open the session.

AppleTalk Data Stream Protocol

ADSP takes the functionality of ASP a little bit further. ADSP is a connection-oriented protocol that allows client sockets to establish and maintain a two-way byte stream of data. ADSP concerns itself not only with the reliability of the transmission but also the flow control and sequencing of bytes by assigning sequence numbers to the bytes in the stream. With ADSP, the flow of data between two socket clients is directed to and from the connected nodes simultaneously.

Making the Connection

A connection end of ADSP communication is identified by its internet socket address, made up of the socket number, the node ID, and the network number. ADSP assigns a connection ID to each session so that each sequenced byte transmitted can be forwarded to the right process on the right node at the right time.

Byte Numbers

ADSP also assigns a sequence number to each byte in the data stream between the two connection ends in a network transmission Each packet transmitted carries a sequence number that ADSP uses to maintain error-free delivery of the packet flow.

Flow Control

ADSP also uses the sequence numbers to maintain flow control, so that slow receivers aren't flooded with more packets than they can deal with. Periodically, ADSP checks the receive buffers on the node to make sure that they aren't filling up with data. Information about the buffer status is exchanged between the ADSP socket clients.

Zone Information Protocol

AppleTalk's designers built AppleTalk with the ability to service up to 16 million nodes on a single internet. An internet is made up, of course, of a number of local area networks connected by routers to form an internet. With AppleTalk, the nodes on an internet can be segmented into zones, allowing the administrators to exercise additional control. There is no strict relationship between zones and network numbers on an internet. Nodes on the same network could be in different zones, at the discretion of an administrator with sufficient privileges to assign and modify AppleTalk zones.

Like RTMP, ZIP operates on AppleTalk internet routers. NBP makes calls to ZIP on the router to find out what networks or network nodes belong in what zone. ZIP maintains the zone information in zone information tables maintained on the router. Zone information is transmitted to other routers on the internet through a statically assigned socket known as the *zone information socket.*

AppleTalk: Application Layer Services

At the top of the stack, AppleTalk provides some specific services to users of the AppleTalk network. Two distinct protocols operate more or less along the border between the presentation and application layers of the stack. PostScript, the language used for Apple printer communications, and the AppleTalk file protocol.

AppleTalk File Protocol

AFP is a presentation layer protocol, a client of ASP. AFP is used to manipulate files on remote workstations and servers. AFP contains translators that can translate file formats between end-user nodes on the internet.

Workstation clients request and manipulate files using the workstation's native file system commands. The native file system manipulates files on physically connected resources. A file data structure in local memory on the workstation indicates whether the requested file is local or if it resides in an external file system. If the file is local it is handled by the native file system. If the file is on an external file system, the native file system routes the command to an AFP translator.

The AFP translator translates native commands into AFP and sends them to the file server where the requested file resides. The translated commands are forwarded through the AFP AppleTalk filing interface.

PostScript

PostScript is the presentation language used by AppleTalk stack when printer data is transferred from workstation clients to servers on the internet. PostScript is designed to be carried by ASP.

Finishing the Core . . .

This chapter has presented the basic operating concepts of an AppleTalk internetwork. AppleTalk's designers decided early on in network history to design and build their own protocol stack. They succeeded in creating an elegant set of networking protocols that met the designer's goals of creating a plug-and-play internetwork requiring an minimum of user configuration and operating as a natural extension of the native operating system. Even today, it remains among the simplest and easiest of networking technologies to use.

BIBLIOGRAPHY AND RESOURCES

Andrews, Richard F.; Oppenheimer, Alan B.; Sidhu, Gursharan S. *Inside AppleTalk,* 2nd ed. Reading, MA: Addison-Wesley, 1990. This is the definitive work on AppleTalk, written by the Apple guys who helped design and create the AppleTalk protocols.

Apple Computer, Inc. *AppleTalk Network System Overview.* Reading, MA: Addison-Wesley, 1989. Apple's own introductory overview of Macintosh networking and AppleTalk technologies (dated, but still useful).

Apple Computer, Inc. *Planning and Managing AppleTalk Networks.* Reading, MA: Addison-Wesley, 1991. A book aimed at helping network administrators plan, install, and manage AppleTalk networks (dated, but also still useful).

Howard, Stephen. "AppleTalk: Old Protocol Poised for Speed, Mobility." *MacWEEK*, *vol. 8, no. 1* (January 3, 1994): 82.

Kosiur, Dave and Joel Snyder. *The Macworld Networking Bible*, 2nd ed. Indianapolis: IDG Books Worldwide, 1994. An outstanding comprehensive treatment of AppleTalk networking, from protocols, to hardware, to software, to troubleshooting and installation.

Miller, Mark A. *LAN Protocol Handbook*. Redwood City, CA: M&T Publishing, Inc., 1990. An introductory look at AppleTalk, not a bad place to start.

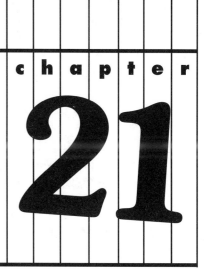

A FEW MORE PROTOCOLS

The preceding chapters provide a pretty comprehensive look at those protocol suites most commonly used on LANs and WANs. But numerous other protocols are used in networking, which you're likely to encounter from time to time. Here's a short list of some protocols suites and architectures that are important to know about. They just didn't make the cut to get their own chapters in this book!

DIGITAL NETWORK ARCHITECTURE

The Digital Equipment Corporation, affectionately called DEC (pronounced "deck"), has been a player in the great game of networking since the early 1970s. In 1977, DEC released a line of hardware and software products to implement what they called DECnet. DECnet-compliant devices and applications conform to the Digital Network Architecture (DNA) protocols, which describe the DNA architecture, the basis for DECnet.

In 1980 DEC was of the big three companies, along with Xerox and Intel, that designed Ethernet. Naturally, DNA protocols are supported by Ethernet and vice versa. DNA protocols are implemented in accordance with OSI protocol specifications and support TCP/IP and other widely used WAN protocols. Outside the DEC computing world, you're unlikely to encounter this protocol suite, however.

Best Buy:
For an excellent discussion of DECnet, please consult Carl Mala-mud's book; *DEC Networks and Architectures* (New York: McGraw-Hill Book Company, 1989).

XEROX NETWORKING SYSTEM

The foundation for almost all PC network protocol suites came from the Xerox Networking System (XNS) protocols. The developers of Novell Net-Ware and Ethernet were inspired rather directly by XNS.

If you know IPX/SPX networking and understand its architecture, then you already know more about XNS than you think you do. The layers and protocols in operation in XNS are almost identical to IPX/SPX. Only the names have been changed to protect plausible deniability.

OSI

If you don't know what OSI stands for by now then you haven't been pay-ing attention at all. The Open Systems Interconnection (OSI) model is the basis we've used for describing every protocol discussed so far in this book and in every other book on networking. Back when this architecture was proposed by the Organization for Standardization (ISO) in the early 1980s lots of networking protocols were already in use and in the late stages of development. The reason for the impact of the OSI protocols was their re-lease as an *open standard*.

The OSI model was quickly adopted as a standard for most network ap-plication developers because it makes it easy for systems analysts and de-signers to compare apples. OSI protocols didn't take long to become standard for industry comparisons, but their acceptance as standard *imple-mentations* has yet to occur.

Pundits speculate that this is because OSI is what's sometimes called a *kitchen sink* protocol suite (that is, it contains everything imaginable, in-cluding the kitchen sink). Developers believe that OSI's acceptance has been savagely hindered by a lack of standard application programming in-terfaces (APIs) and interlayer communications models that permit Compa-ny A's OSI implementation to operate freely with Company B's (which, alas, is not the case today).

LAN MANAGER

When you're the richest man in the world you can develop and implement your own set of network protocols. That's what Bill Gates did at Microsoft. Back when IBM and Microsoft were working together to develop the OS/2 operating system they came up with a network architecture to run over that OS.

Ask yourself this question: "Do I run a network over OS/2?" If the answer is no, then LAN Server does not apply. If the answer is yes, then you know LAN Server (formerly known as LAN Manager) is really more of an operating system than an architecture. The real importance of LAN Server to this discussion is its implementation of Server Message Block (SMB) protocols at the application and session layers of the OSI stack. SMB provides the file structure for LAN Server as well as the interface to the user of the network.

SERVER MESSAGE BLOCKS

Microsoft bailed out of OS/2 and LAN Manager development processes and subsequently developed its own networking systems, Windows for Workgroups and Windows NT. One thing all their architectures have in common is the implementation of SMB at the application and presentation layers of the stack, running over NetBIOS and NetBEUI.

Server Message Block provides file structure on many types of networks, the aforementioned included. *File structure*, in this case, means that remote files and directories appear local to the network user. SMB creates a distributed file structure across the network and lets NetBIOs handle the transport.

UNIX

The ubiquitous UNIX operating system, extended by the TCP/IP protocols for distributed operation, should be known, if not familiar, to you. UNIX networking has its own distributed file architecture, which is worth mentioning here, the Network File System (NFS). NFS is the application and presentation layer protocol for the TCP/IP stack, but it jumped more or less fully formed out of the Sun Microsystems implementation of the UNIX OS (known at the time as SunOS).

Network File System

NFS got its start in the UNIX world and is the core of the TCP/IP network management. But NFS sits over more stacks than just TCP/IP. It's been adopted by vendors and developers for a variety of distributed architectures, providing robust structure and file management capability for very large wide area networks.

IBM

LAN Manager isn't IBM's only foray into networking. Back when PC networking was just a dream, IBM had implemented its SNA architecture for mainframe and minicomputer networking. We already hit the high points of SNA but want to mention Advanced Peer-to-Peer Networking (APPN).

ADVANCED PEER-TO-PEER NETWORKING

APPN is the protocol at the top of the SNA stack, and it's mentioned here because it's another type of distributed file architecture protocol. APPN implements dynamic network structures of files and directories.

Best Buy:
For a good discussion of this architecture, please consult Alex Berson's book, *APPC: Introduction to LU6.2* (New York: McGraw-Hill, 1990). Suffice it to say here that this technology represents IBM's try at a distributed processing environment, which has not been widely accepted or deployed outside the IBM environment.

PROTOCOL ANALYZERS

chapter 22

BASIC OVERVIEW

Network management is a broad topic, spanning many disciplines and include a variety of tools and technologies. In Part V of this book, we discuss network management at length.

In this chapter, we will discuss a specific tool, the protocol analyzer, as one of the many tools available to network administrators. Protocol analyzers can play a significant role as one of the tools in troubleshooting networks. They can help an administrator in diagnosing network problems, gathering statistics, and simulating certain conditions. Protocol analyzers can play a significant role as one of the tools in troubleshooting networks. They can help an administrator in diagnosing network problems, gathering statistics and simulating certain conditions. The following is brief list of some of the invaluable things that can be done with an analyzer.

- Locate nodes generating excessive errors,
- Filter packets for viewing by protocol or type of packet,
- Determine which nodes generate the most traffic,
- Analyze network performance,
- Set network thresholds that produce alerts when they are exceeded.

Without access to theses types of information, without knowing what's going on inside the wiring and what data are flowing, where the data are flowing, how much data, and how fast data are flowing, network problems could go undetected and uncorrected until a failure occurs. Of course, this assumes that a trained or skilled technician can understand the information that is gathered by an analyzer. Some analyzers come with built-in artificial intelligence that analyzes captured data, determine what events are causing error conditions, and then provide information as to the possible causes of the events. Others rely more on the intelligence and experience of their operators.

Until several years ago, protocol analyzers costs were in the range of $30,000—far too expensive for most organizations. However, competition and rapidly dropping prices have made protocol analyzers affordable for most businesses. Consequently, more and more analyzers are popping up on networks. For about $15,000, a network administrator can now purchase a portable analyzer with built-in artificial intelligence, including the necessary software, hardware, NIC card, and color display. That's not a lot of money for a device that can diagnose at least 85% of all network problems!

THE ANALYZER

Protocol analyzers are designed to permit network administrators to capture packets on a network segment and analyze those packets for information and diagnosis. A good working knowledge of protocols down to the frame level is necessary to interpret captured information. Knowledge of access methods like Ethernet and token ring is critical in understanding captured information from a protocol analyzer.

To put analyzers into perspective, let's use an example that everyone might understand. Assume that you have an injury in your leg that's tremendously painful. If pain won't go away, you go to the doctor. Your doctor can touch your leg and move it around to narrow the problem down, but you'll probably be sent to a diagnostic clinic for a magnetic resonance image (MRI) so your doctor can see exactly what's going on inside your leg. An MRI is an expensive diagnostic tool, but it can show the exact nature of the problem in your leg.

Specs:
You can think of a protocol analyzer as something much like the MRI. It's expensive, requires skilled technicians to operate and interpret,

and provides a layered breakdown of data on a LAN. This layered breakdown usually includes packet decodes from various layers within the OSI model. In addition to diagnosis, a protocol analyzer can help determine your needs for network expansion and can be used to simulate network traffic loads and operating conditions. Using an analyzer to capture network trends provides information over time to the network administrator and is an invaluable aid in forecasting growth needs. An analyzer can generate traffic on a network, assisting the administrator by simulating "what if" scenarios before they are installed.

Analyzer Types

Older Analyzers

Older analyzers typically shipped as hardware/software combinations in barely luggable cases. Schlepping around this kind of analyzer was not terribly handy for the administrator (nor too kind on his or her back). These analyzers provided raw data that only technowizards could understand. These analyzers were also priced in the $30,000-plus dollar range. They were status symbols of a particularly nerdy kind, and only people on IEEE committees could interpret the data they returned.

Software Only

Along came the concept that an analyzer could be put on a PC by purchasing software, along with a special NIC that operates in a "promiscuous" mode (i.e., grab all packets passing by on the network medium, no matter what their address). That reduced the cost of analyzers greatly, but this approach was still not very portable. Because analyzers typically must be plugged into individual segments, this was not always a practical solution, even though it was cheaper.

The Whole Enchilada

Around 1990, Network General came up with a solution to analyzer implementation problems that many buyers felt was the best of both worlds. The solution took the luggable analyzer and incorporated it into a notebook PC. Needless to say, these are much easier to move around! Network General also provided choices to load on the notebook. The software could be plain vanilla software with no artificial intelligence capabilities or expert software that did include AI. All of this comes bundled together today for $15,000. And numerous other companies, including NCC, Spider, Novell, and others, offer reasonable solutions that can cost significantly less.

How Does It Work?

An analyzer's basic function is to capture and display data. An analyzer basically sits on the network as an "eavesdropping" device, monitoring traffic but not generating any additional traffic of its own. Everything that goes through the wire is essentially dumped into the analyzer's buffer. Specific filters can be set to eliminate certain types of traffic from capture. Let's look at the basic functions.

Capturing

An analyzer captures data packets as they travel through a network segment and puts a time stamp on every packet. Most analyzers are used to capture traces (collection of frames) during a specific time period or during a specific event. The analyzer receives data through its buffer and usually offers options to save the buffer contents to a file on a floppy or hard disk.

An analyzer captures data in its buffers, so when it runs out of buffer space, it cycles back and writes over data captured in the beginning of the buffer. Because of this behavior, it is advisable to buy as much memory and hard disk space as you can afford. The more space to store your captures, the more data you'll have available for use in later analysis. Due to the way analyzers write to the buffer, leaving an analyzer connected to the network all day can cause data collected early in the day to be lost, because it may be overwritten by data collected later in the day.

Tip: Filtering

Capturing every single packet on a network could provide more information than you need to troubleshoot a problem. If some information is known prior to the capture, filters can be set that eliminate all but a certain type of traffic. The filtering can be done by node, server, protocol, destination class, or network event. For example, if you know that the problem is IPX-based, then you can set a protocol filter to capture only IPX packets, eliminating all others. If you know that the problem is with a particular node, you can set the filter to examine all packets going to and from that particular node.

Filtering can be done at the capture level or the display level. For example, you may want to capture all of the frames during a particular time frame, but for troubleshooting purposes you may want to view only certain frames at a time.

Decoding

Once packets have been captured, they can be decoded using a protocol interpreter. Some protocol analyzers decode only one type of protocol; others have multiple protocol interpreters that can be purchased separately or may come as an add-on package when the product is purchased. The decoding process involves breaking down each captured packet in sequence, then decoding the various protocol layers in the captured frames. This information is usually displayed in a summary presented in plain English.

Depending on the analyzer in use, certain correlations to the OSI model can be made in the decoded information. For example, Table 22.1 shows the correlation of Network General's decoded information to the layers of the OSI model.

OSI layers	Expert sniffer analyzer layers
Application Presentation Session	Application
Transport	Connection
Network	Network station
Data link	DLC station
Physical	

Table 22.1 *Network General's Analyzer Layers Compared to OSI Model*

As you can see in Table 22.1, Network General does not provide a layer-to-layer decode to compare with the OSI model. Let's look at what each of the Sniffer's layers does provide:

1. The Sniffer merges the upper three layers of the OSI model into one layer called the *application layer*. It does this because only a small number of protocols (like NetBIOS) operate at the session or presentation layers. Of concern to the analyzer at these three layers is how two end nodes in a connection are set up by an application and how those two end nodes communicate with each other through an application. Items like slow file transfers can be detected.

2. At the transport (or connection) level, the Sniffer analyzes the efficiency of end-to-end communication and error recovery.

3. The network layer (or network station) is concerned with network addresses and routing issues. Duplicate network addresses are detected at this decoding layer.

4. At the data link and physical layers (or DLC station), the analyzer is concerned with the actual transmission of the data and the physical errors that occur along the way. Throughput, broadcasts frames, and CRC errors are decoded at this level.

A typical decoded NetWare frame might contain information like frame number, length of frame, number of errors, station ID, checksum, hop count, and network number.

Displaying

A protocol analyzer would be useless unless it displayed the decoded information for an administrator. This display can be done in a separate stage from the capture or while the capture is active. The latter method is the more helpful. It permits the administrator to toggle back and forth between screens to analyze what is happening in real time.

Most of the analyzers provide graphical displays for items like network utilization, protocol utilization, and more. We love graphs that display in real-time mode!

Once a frame makes it past the display filter, it can be displayed in summary mode, detail mode, and hex with ASCII mode. Some analyzers permit all three types of display to appear on the screen at once. We don't like to torture ourselves that way and prefer to stick to the summary and detail mode mostly. We can remember a time when you had to take a hex dump, locate the beginning of the frame, and break out the frame into fields until you reached the end. The analyzer takes the information in that form and summarizes it for you in plain English!

Analyzer Features

Depending on the type of analyzer you purchase, the following features could be considered as standard, extra purchase features, or downright unavailable.

Thresholds

Thresholds provide a network manager a proactive approach to monitoring the network. Some analyzers allow an administrator to set thresholds on the analyzer that produce alerts when exceeded. For example, setting a 25% utilization threshold on an Ethernet network could provide a valuable alert before the network becomes congested. Most analyzers come with default thresholds that are set to commonly acceptable levels. These settings shouldn't be adjusted unless the adjuster is extremely skilled.

The thresholds can be broken down by protocol layer and interpreted layer by layer. For example, if you want to be notified of application errors once a database server is set up, then limits can be set and monitored proactively at this layer only.

Triggers

An administrator can set the analyzer up to recognize an "event." When the analyzer detects the event (such as a duplicate network address), it begins recording or capturing to a disk and can optionally stop capturing after the event occurs. This is useful in situations where you know what events you want to capture but not when they might occur. Rather than turning capture on and then checking the analyzer every hour or so, it can be programmed to turn itself into capture mode. Like the thresholds, triggers can be set to look for events occurring in one particular protocol layer.

Baselines

Some analyzers provide capability to plug an analyzer in during normal operations of a network so that it can learn "normal" levels of network activity. This information is used it as a baseline for comparison if problems occur out on the network. Alternately, a capture can be stored that can later be used to reproduce a particular error or inject an error into a healthy network for research purposes (after hours of course!).

Simulation

Some analyzers permit the analyzer to be used as a traffic generator. This can be useful to an administrator that needs to experiment with "what if" scenarios after hours. Simulations give the network administrator a look at how the network will behave if subjected to certain conditions.

Symbolic Names

It's not very interesting to read a bunch of hexadecimal numbers and not much fun collecting them in the first place. Trying to maintain a table of MAC layer hex addresses that corresponding to users is like having minor surgery just to entertain yourself! Some analyzers can translate MAC layer hex addresses into symbolic names, like login names, that are easier to recognize on a decode.

NETWORK PERFORMANCE ANALYSIS

The analyzer, used properly and skillfully, can provide the administrator with a lot of statistical information about a network. The information can be used proactively to head off some potential problems before they become real.

Utilization

Utilization is a percentage calculated by a ratio of the number of bits that travel across the network divided by the total number of bits a network can convey. The numerator is generally referred to as throughput and the denominator is generally referred to as the bandwidth of a network. For example, if your network supports a bandwidth of 10 million bits/sec, and a throughput of 5 million bits/sec, the network's utilization is 50%. You can then say that 50% of the bandwidth is being utilized. In a token ring network, this is in the okay range, but in an Ethernet network, this is nearing the trouble zone.

Utilization information is critical for a network administrator. You can think of utilization like plumbing. Your pipes have certain diameters that can only hold a certain amount of fluid. If you exceed that amount, you'll get an overflow somewhere, with unexpected and unwelcome results. The same can happen with a network. If more data is put onto the wire than the wire can handle, saturation occurs and data can be corrupted. Also, one workstation that consumes the entire bandwidth with broadcasts, prevents other users from transmitting or receiving data. Protocols designed for LANs and WANs have incorporated mechanisms right into the protocols to keep this from happening, but older protocols still in use may allow complete saturation to occur.

Utilization is usually presented in the form of current, peak, and average percentages. It's helpful to know that you have peaks when your network activity is high but that, generally or on average, the utilization doesn't exceed 15%. You can further subdivide utilization down by protocols, so that you can see if one protocol is hogging your network's bandwidth.

Network administrators should also look at the average utilization over a period of time to determine whether the network needs to be further segmented. Critical utilization percentages are different for Ethernet networks and token ring networks. For example, a utilization of reading of 30% is considered time to segment in an Ethernet network, but 65–75% on a token ring network is the point where a network administrator should consider segmenting the token ring.

Traffic

Analyzing the traffic patterns on a network can provide more key information to the administrator. For example, an air traffic controller has to know the start and stop points for flights. If too many flights are in a certain flight pattern, a decision can be made to reroute certain flights or change the timing of certain flights to avoid possible collisions. The same holds true in networking: If two nodes are jamming the airways, it might behoove an administrator to separate those two nodes by placing them on separate segments.

Another way to analyze network traffic is to look at the number of frames and their average lengths to determine what kind of traffic is traversing the network. Shorter frames could indicate lots of database queries, while larger frames might indicate file transfers. Knowing what kinds of traffic is moving and when peak periods occur can prove helpful in scheduling times for performing certain activities. For example, if a user transfers files to another node on a daily basis in the morning, perhaps these transfer should be rescheduled at night, when the network is less busy.

Errors

The ability to measure and analyze errors on a network is also crucial. A node sending a frame that produces an error it must retransmit that packet. A faulty node retransmitting packets could generate a lot of unnecessary traffic on a network. Increasing frequencies of errors on individual segments should always be investigated, because they are often the first indicator of impending equipment failure (hubs, concentrators, NICs, etc.).

Delays

Ever have your customers tell you that the network is running awfully slow? With an analyzer, you can break down this problem into two measurements: channel acquisition time; and network response time. channel acquisition time measures the delay time for a frame, beginning when it is ready to be transmitted and ending when it actually gets onto the LAN. Network response time measures the time it takes for a packet to make a loopback—that is, the time it takes for a packet to get from the sender to the receiver and then back to the sender. Both measurements can be useful in isolating the actual causes.

THE SECURITY DISCUSSION

Use of a protocol analyzer in organizations requires that you take proper security measures. Information like corporate e-mail, salaries, and accounting that flow through your network is nevertheless considered confidential. Because an analyzer collects all information traveling over the network, confidential information can sometimes show up "mysteriously" in the IS department.

It is also common to capture information in a diagnosis and then send that information to an outside organization like Cisco for further examination. Network administrators should check with their legal departments to make sure that they are complying with all of their organization's binding nondisclosure or confidentiality requirements before sending any such information to outsiders.

WHAT TO BUY

Until recently, protocol analyzers cost $30,000 or more and consisted of specialized hardware and software. These older units were luggables that were clumsy to carry. Today, vendors provide software-only solutions that can cost as low as $500. Price is directly proportional to features and functionality, so be careful not to buy something that provides too little functionality! In the Bibliography and Strategies section at the end of this chapter, we provide information for locating a good buyer's guide to all the available products. You might want to obtain a copy of that article and look at the products.

The following list may help you narrow your focus on these features that you require in a protocol analyzer:

1. *Budget.* What is the amount of money you can spend on an analyzer? If your budget is $1,000, then your choices are narrowed down so far you might not need to go onto the next few questions. Don't forget to factor in training costs.

2. *Size of network.* How many segments do you need to analyze at one time? If you need to analyze only one segment at a time, you could purchase a portable analyzer. If your budget is large enough that you can purchase an analyzer for each segment, you might want to look at an overall network management strategy discussed in Part V of this book.

3. *Type of analyzer.* Software only or a hardware/software combination? We recommend that you buy the hardware/software solution in a notebook PC. You can usually buy one that is ready to plug into the network without any messy installation. This type of setup gives

you the most flexibility and the best migration path to a larger management platform later.

4. *Amount of RAM.* As the analyzer captures, it stores the data it captures to RAM known as buffers. The higher is the analyzer's RAM, the more data that can be captured before overwriting occurs.

5. *Hard disk space.* Analyzing and saving traces over time can fill up a small hard disk in no time. It is important to buy the largest hard disk you can afford. You won't be sorry!

6. *Monochrome or color monitor.* We strongly urge you to pay the few extra dollars and make sure you can display your results in color. You'll thank us when you're looking at a decode that breaks down into colors for different protocols. When you're analyzing graphical displays in several colors instead of just orange, you'll be glad you spent the extra dollars.

7. *Protocol interpreters.* You should look for an analyzer that modularizes the protocol interpreters and thus allows you the flexibility of adding a protocol to your analyzer if necessary. However, if the analyzer permits you to install protocols only on an all or nothing basis, it could prove to be overkill for a network that only runs one protocol!

Our best advice to prospective LAN administrators is that you learn as much as you can about the major protocols like TCP/IP and IPX/SPX, right down to the frame level. Then, you can purchase an analyzer and learn how to use it as a tool on your network. You will not regret it!

Top Five Vendors

Network General Corp.
4200 Bohannon Dr.
Menlo Park, CA 94025
800-764-3329; 415-473-2000
Direct sales: 800-764-3337
FAX: 415-321-0855
Tech support: 800-395-3151

Hewlett-Packard Co.
3000 Hanover St.
Palo Alto, CA 94304-1181
800-752-0900; 800 387-3867 (CD); 415-857-1501
Direct sales: 800-637-7740 (HP Direct)
FAX: 800-333-1917
Tech support: 800-858-8867
Tech support BBS: 415-852-0256

Novell, Inc.
122 East 1700 South
Provo, UT 84606-6194
800-453-1267 or 801-429-7000
Tech Support: use either number above
http://www.novell.com/

Wandel & Goltermann, Inc.
2200 Gateway Centre Blvd., Ste. 207
Morrisville, NC 27560-9228
800-277-7404; 919-460-3300
FAX: 919-481-4372
Tech support: Use main no.
Tech support BBS: 919-460-3336

Azure Technologies, Inc.
63 South St.
Hopkinton, MA 01748-2212
800-233-3800; 508-435-3800
FAX: 508-435-0448
Tech support: Use toll-free no.

Digilog, Inc. (subsidiary of NumereX Corp.)
2360 Maryland Rd.
Willow Grove, PA 19090
800-DIGILOG; 215-830-9400
FAX: 215-830-9444
Tech support: Use main no.

GN Navtel, Ltd.
6611 Bay Circle, Ste. 190
Norcross, GA 30071
800-262-8835; 404-446-2665
FAX: 404-446-2730
Tech support: Use main no.

PROTOCOL ANALYZER RESOURCES:
BIBLIOGRAPHY AND STRATEGIES

For general networking references, please consult Appendix C, "A List of Networking Resources." The magazines and other publications listed there can help you find out lots of information about protocol analyzers. The following references are particularly helpful for the information they contain about protocol analyzers:

Best Buy:

Chappell, Laura A., and Dan E. Hakes. *Novell's Guide to NetWare LAN Analysis;* 2nd Ed. Alameda, CA: Novell Press and SYBEX, Inc., 1994. This is a wonderful book for understanding LAN analysis! Details of Ethernet and token ring LANs are thoroughly discussed, with a separate section devoted to protocol analyzers. This book is extremely useful also for non-NetWare LANs. We consider it a must-have book for a LAN administrator's library. $44.99.

Miller, Mark A. *LAN Protocol Handbook.*
    Redwood City, CA: M&T Books, 1990. A good book that first discusses the various protocols, along with analysis of protocols. The book ends with chapters that analyze NetWare, 3Com, Vines, token ring, and AppleTalk. $34.95.
Steinke, Steve. *Guide to Managing PC Networks.*
    Englewood Cliffs, NJ: Prentice-Hall, Inc., 1995. Steve Steinke presents the material in this book clearly. Part One of the book discusses the business aspects of network management; Part Two discusses fault management, configuration management, performance management, and planning secure networks. Part Three goes on to discuss network management platforms along with the future direction of network management.

Steinke, Steve. "Sorting Out Network Tools!" *LAN Magazine* 9, no. 13 (December 1994): 125. Great article that separates network management tools into groups and provides a discussion on each group. The article takes a 30,000 foot view of network management with a discussion on how protocol analyzers fit into the big picture.

"Network Management." *LAN Magazine* 9, no. 11 (October 1994): 185. This is the Annual Buyer's Guide that contains name, address, and telephone numbers of vendors that supply protocol analyzers along with a paragraph about their products.

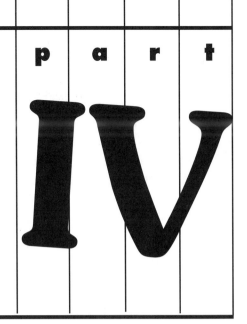

NETWORKING EQUIPMENT

Like engines to car nuts, so networking gear is to the networking enthusiast. While we can't be sure how enthusiastic you are about your network, you are definite about your needs for one or more items of equipment to make it work.

Here in Part IV, you'll learn about the various kinds of networking equipment you're likely to encounter on your network, both from the standpoint of operation and capabilities and some of the options available. We'll also discuss specific items of equipment or software—software is as important for servers as the hardware that it runs on—and identify the top vendors in a few of these areas.

We'll march up the ISO reference model as we look at equipment, starting with the gear you'll use to interconnect network wire, elements, and even applications. This is where we examine the whys and wherefores of wonderful widgets like network interface cards, hubs and concentrators, and the ever-popular bridges, routers, and gateways.

From the equipment that makes connections possible and workable, we'll move on to the equipment and software that lets your network actually do something useful—the server. Here, we'll examine the many kinds of general purpose and specialized servers you're likely to find.

We conclude Part IV with a look at network peripherals thatcan bring sophisticated input/out and communications services right to your network. We'll discuss printing, faxing, communications and scanning options that can extend your network's capabilities in new and interesting ways.

Our purpose in Part IV is to explain what your network is made of and how to go about adding new capabilities to its smorgasbord of services and applications. By the time you get through, you should be able to build a collection of networked goodies to rival the best networks available today!

THE NETWORKING BESTIARY

In medieval times, a bestiary was a collection of fanciful stories about animals, often with morals aimed at the human audience who listened to them. Raconteurs could draw on real or imagined resemblances between members of the audience and members of the animal kingdom and deliver pointed commentaries or satires without having to name any names.

The medieval times are long since past, and bestiaries have lost their moral components to become more catalogs of members of a group of animals or inhabitants of an area. Although the sense and entertainment value of the bestiary has declined somewhat since Chaucer's day, we'll treat the next set of chapters in the book as a bestiary of networking components. In this part of the book, we'll examine the equipment that you're likely to find on a network, and the kinds of roles it can play in the network's operation.

The interdependency of the animal kingdom has never been in doubt, but it has always been the custom of animal (and human) predators to eat their prey. At least, in the networking bestiary, you'll be free of such concerns. Although you may have to upgrade or replace the occasional item of equipment, there's no need to fear that "Nature, red in fang and claw" will cause you to lose items of your networking inventory!

CONNECTION EQUIPMENT

At the most basic level of networking, a variety of equipment is required to attach computers to the networking medium, and to interconnect individual media segments or different types of media into a single logical network. This kind of equipment is the focus of our first group of chapters, including the following elements:

- The network interface cards (NICs) used to attach computers to the medium,
- The hubs and concentrators used to aggregate wiring and handle networking media,
- The bridges, routers, and gateways used to interlink multiple networks, access methods, or media segments.

All in all, this part of the bestiary connects up the network and makes it possible for the many computers that seek to use its services to communicate with one another.

SERVERS OF MANY FLAVORS

Once the networking connections are in place, the network becomes a natural breeding group for client/server applications. These, in turn, depend on a variety of servers to meet client's requests for network services of many shapes and forms. Although incredible hybrids that combine multiple services are common on smaller networks, as networks grow larger and more complex, servers tend to become more specialized, offering rather less diversity in any one package but rather more power and functionality in those narrower areas.

When it comes to network servers, here are the members of the network menagerie that we cover in Chapters 27 through 33:

- A general overview of servers that concentrates on the features they all have in common,
- A look at the most common and widely used member of the genus, the vanilla file and print server, which provides the all-important access to shared files and printers that justified networking in the first place,

- A look at more exotic (and expensive) multiprocessing and special-purpose servers, which can deliver high levels of performance and service for most client/server applications,
- A discussion of the ever-popular database server, which handles DBMS services for its client base,
- A review of communications servers, which bring the outside world together with the network (coming and going),
- An examination of the fax server, which can bring the fax machine to each user's e-mailbox, if not to the very desktop
- A rumination on special printing servers, that can handle printing without benefit of other servers if need, or that can provide exotic and advanced print capabilities.

Our objective in introducing the servers is to tell you what marvelous network draft animals they are, able to carry the heaviest loads and deliver the most useful and interesting of services to your users' desktops. As you come to know these powerful and loyal beasts, you'll come to depend on them for the bulk of what your network delivers.

NETWORKED PERIPHERALS

Although servers are among the most powerful and interesting members of the bestiary, a new family is springing to life on the network. These are peripheral devices—printers, scanners, fax machines, copiers, and more—that can attach directly to your network, ready to provide their special abilities to your users.

In Chapters 34 through 39, we trot out the most common members of this increasingly numerous family, for your entertainment and edification. The critters you'll encounter here include the following:

- An overview of network peripherals and their many talents,
- A quick look at the Small Computer Systems Interface, so commonly used to connect such devices to the network (or to other computers),
- An inquiry into networked printers, which supply advanced print services and output right to the network (some of which even feature built-in print servers),

- An investigation of networked CD-ROM devices, which can deliver astonishing amounts and variety of data to your network's users,

- An introduction to networked fax/modem devices, which can forever eliminate your users' needs for their own phone lines and private fax machines or modems,

- An inspection of networked scanners, which can bring fascinating images to life on your network or provide the means to bring paperbased documents into the electronic embrace on your network.

By bringing special-purpose devices to the network, everyone can share their capabilities. Even better, because they can attach directly to the networking medium, you can put them anywhere the network goes. And because it goes everywhere you want to be, what could be better than that?

SUMMARY

The next few chapters are going to explain the habits, character, and benefits of the members of the networking bestiary in a lot more detail. We'll get a look at the most common pieces of equipment for interlinking networks and providing their most important services and capabilities. While we're touring this metaphorical zoo, please don't feed the animals!

NETWORK INTERFACE CARDS

chapter

24

WHAT'S IN A NIC? BASIC OVERVIEW

The network interface card is the piece of hardware that sits between a computer and the network. It moves information off the network and into the computer when receiving data and moves information from the computer to the network when sending data. NIC is the common abbreviation for network interface card and is pronounced "nick." NICs are also called *network adapters* or *LAN adapters*, but all this terminology adds up to the same thing.

Because a NIC sits between the computer and the network, it handles several important tasks to let the two communicate. First, its job is to convert incoming signals from the network medium—which may, or may not, be a cable (don't forget wireless networks)—to a form that computers can understand. At the same time, it has to be able to go the other way—that is, to convert outgoing communications from a form that the computer understands to something that can be transmitted over a network.

The second major task of the NIC is to provide a proper physical connection to the network. This means it must include the right kind of plug, socket, or other attachment to hook up with the type of network and connection technology in use. If you can't make the connection, you can't use the network!

Third, NICs handle information that arrives in bursts or in large chunks (typically, this happens only from the computer side of this connection) and they also handle information that arrives in a stream, one bit at a time (typically, this happens from the network side, where communications occur as a sequence of signals, one right after another). NICs have to be able to accommodate the bursts or chunks as they arrive and break them up to ship them out one bit at a time to talk to the network. They also have to be able to collect the bits (or signals) as they arrive and put them together into chunks to deliver them to the computer. Either way, this means they need some space to store things while they're being assembled or broken down.

Beyond that, many NICs offer additional capabilities, but these things provide the basic common functionality that all NICs share (at least the working ones). In the next section, you'll learn more about the different forms that NICs can sometimes take (please see the section entitled "Pieces and Parts of a NIC" for more details on their makeup and layout).

The Many Forms of NIC

As you've learned NIC stands for network interface card and is sometimes called a network adapter or a network interface. All of these things stress the notion that a NIC is something you plug into a computer to make an attachment between it and a network. In many cases, a NIC will actually be a computer card that plugs into a socket or other special connector inside your machine. Because they go inside the machine, NICs don't have to be packaged in enclosures or include their own sources of power. Even though we focus on PCs in this book, other computers—like Macintoshes, many UNIX workstations, and many minicomputers—include built-in network capabilities. This means that they already have a network interface of some kind built in or inserted during the manufacturing process. Although many PC vendors will gladly sell you preconfigured machines that include NICs, this is still not the norm in the PC world. It's also unusual to find PCs that feature built-in network adapters. Figure 24.1 on page 301 shows a common kind of PC network adapter, an NE2000 from Eagle Technologies (recently acquired by Microdyne, Inc.).

Sometimes, network adapters can't fit inside a particular kind of computer. For PCs, laptops and notebook computers are a great example. They're so compact and crammed with other essential pieces of gear that most of them can't accommodate a standard internal NIC. For these machines, you'd have to use an external adapter to attach them to the network, or put them in a docking station that might include an internal adapter.

Figure 24.1   *An NE2000 NIC.*

It's also possible to use a plug-in type of interface called a personal computer memory card international association (PCMCIA) shaped and sized much like a credit card to attach to network. We may be fudging to call this an external interface, but because it slides in and out, and usually includes its own separate power supply, we've decided it belongs in the external category. Figure 24.2 on page 302 shows a PCMCIA network adapter.

Today most network adapters belong to one of these three types. But as new technology comes along, don't be surprised to find others popping up here and there in the marketplace.

Things Are Wonderful—When They Work!

It's a sad truism that nobody notices networks when they work like they're supposed to, but that everybody notices when they don't work properly or

Figure 24.2   *A PCMCIA network adapter.*

even at all. Because proper physical connections are so vital to a network's normal operation, NIC difficulties often figure in the ultimate diagnosis when things go wrong on a network.

We'll cover some of the common causes for NIC trouble in the section entitled "Common NIC-Related Problems" later in this chapter, but you should already know that, because the NICs are where the cables hook the network to the computers, they're often near the scene of the crime when things on the network go awry! This means that checking NICs and their connections is a great place to start looking when network troubleshooting is called for.

TOURING BY BUS

When it comes to PCs, the bus isn't a vehicle you ride, it's a highway for moving data around the system from the motherboard where the central processing unit (CPU) lives, to and from the other adapters and devices that make up a complete, functioning system. The bus provides a set of data- and signal-carrying lines that let the "brains" of your computer—the CPU and its associated memory, etc.—communicate with the other components needed for things like your display (a graphics adapter makes this connection), your disk drives (a disk controller makes this connection), or various communications ports (like the serial port your mouse uses and the parallel port common for attaching printers). If you have a network, the NIC adds the components necessary to make the connection needed to use it. For PCs, and for many computers, it all happens over the bus.

PC Buses vs. Other Buses

As we look at five of the most popular PC buses in the sections that follow, we'll also be taking a tour of PC history and development trends. As PCs have gotten bigger, faster, and cheaper, so have the buses that serve them: what began as a relatively slow, 8-bit technology in the earliest PCs is complemented by fast, 32- or 64-bit technologies in current machines.

The number of bits a bus can handle is determined by the number of parallel lines it can support; each line can handle 1 bit's worth of information. Thus, it takes 8 parallel lines to support the data for an 8-bit bus (usually there will also be one or more additional lines needed to carry signals that coordinate the activities of adapters and the CPU to keep them from interfering with each other) and 64 lines to support the data for a 64-bit bus. The number of data lines is often called *the data path width* and is sometimes called the *bus width*.

Today, in 1995, PCs support two different types of buses. One hearkens back to the original bus architecture of the very first IBM PC. It could also be called a *system bus* or *PC bus*. The number of adapters this kind of bus can handle varies from 8 to 16, and they're widely used for all kinds of devices and system attachments.

The other is a more recent development, introduced to accommodate the higher speeds and bus widths common for newer PC CPUs, like the Intel 80486 or Pentium processors. They can handle data so quickly and efficiently that this second type of bus was developed to connect subsystems where speed and capability are particularly important—today, subsystems to access a computer's disk drives, graphical displays, and its network connection are viewed as particularly performance sensitive. This type of bus is called a *local bus*, because it handles only a small number (typically 3 or less) of fast adapters with wide (32 or 64 bit) data paths.

As we explore the buses in the PC fleet, you'll learn something about the characteristics, speed, and path width for each one, in addition to their best applications and uses.

Industry Standard Architecture

In retrospect, one of the best things that IBM ever did for PC users was to widely and freely disseminate the specifications for the original IBM PC, including the PC's bus, which has now become known as the *industry standard architecture* (ISA) *bus* (before there were other alternatives, it was simply known as the *PC bus*). Of course, this didn't do IBM much financial good, but it did open up an enormous market that continues to this day for so-called PC clones and for many different kinds of ISA-based adapters, including NICs.

ISA comes in two flavors. The original flavor has an 8-bit data path and typically runs at a speed of either 4.77 or 8 MHz. With the introduction of the PC/AT, IBM doubled the width of the ISA bus from 8 to 16 bits, but maintained a compatible socket layout, so that a 16-bit socket can accept either 8- or 16-bit ISA adapters. Figure 24.3 shows a standard 16-bit ISA socket with matching edge connector for a 16-bit card (an 8-bit version would include only the pins on the first of the two connector sections, starting from the "front" of the card.

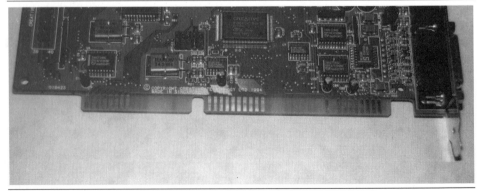

Figure 24.3   *A 16-bit ISA adapter.*

MicroChannel Architecture

MicroChannel Architecture (MCA) represents IBM's attempt to close the door to the technology barn after the livestock had already departed. From its inception, IBM launched MCA as the logical successor to ISA for its PS/2 PC line and touted its 32-bit bandwidth, easy configuration, and superior design to try to attract more customers. Unfortunately, MCA never really caught on, primarily because

- MCA uses a completely different form-factor from ISA. Users apparently decided that MCA wasn't good enough to justify tossing out all their old ISA adapters.

- MCA adapters hit the marketplace at a price premium of at least 100% (that is a typically MCA card would cost at least twice as much as its ISA equivalent). Users also decided that this wasn't necessarily worth it.

- The real killer in this deal for IBM was their attempt to control MCA technology tightly and maintain its proprietary nature. They instituted a fairly expensive licensing scheme for vendors to use MCA, backed this up with some aggressive talk about lawsuits, and generally put too many hurdles in front of MCA adoption to make it financially attractive to the same hardware vendors who had been getting rich off ISA.

Nevertheless, MCA did prove attractive to some customers, especially larger corporations who had long-standing relationships with IBM prior to the introduction of the PC. Its 32-bit architecture could initially run at speeds up to 33 MHz (even faster versions are available today). Figure 24.4 shows an MCA bus socket and displays some of IBM's attempts to improve bus adapter ergonomics (rocker cams to seat/unseat the boards, guide rails, smaller footprint, etc.).

MCA also supported advanced bus control capabilities that would let certain MCA cards handle data transfers with minimal CPU involvement (for more efficient processing). Finally, MCA adapters were designed to be configured mostly through software, instead of requiring the tedious learning curve required to manually configure ISA cards with DIP switches, jumpers, etc. (we'll cover these beauties in the "Pieces and Parts" section later, so don't worry about these terms for now). Today, industry analysts figure MCA adapters constitute less than 5% of the total population; for

Figure 24.4   *An MCA adapter.*

NICs this proportion is higher, at about 11%, primarily because of IBM's position in the token-ring marketplace.

Extended ISA

At about the same time that MCA started garnering press coverage and market attention, Compaq spearheaded a group of "clone" vendors in developing an alternative 32-bit bus, called *extended ISA* (EISA) because any of its sockets permit either 8-or 16-bit ISA cards to be inserted, or 32-bit EISA cards. The "secret" to EISA lies in the depth of insertion: an older ISA card fits into only the first quarter inch or so of the socket, down as far as the key slots indicated on Figure 24.5, which depicts a typical EISA NIC. The edge connector on the EISA card is deeper and fits around the key slots, so that the additional 16 bits' worth of edge connectors make contact in this lower area that is inaccessible to the normal ISA cards.

Figure 24.5   *An EISA edge connector.*

EISA technology is applicable in computing environments, like network servers, where multiple high-performance adapters (and related peripherals like disk drives, CD-ROM players, and scanners) operate in parallel. EISA uses an intelligent bus master (where a CPU is part of the design of the NIC or other adapter) that can reduce the processing burden on a PC's main CPU by handling data transfers between the adapter and the computer's main random-access memory (RAM).

To maintain compatibility with ISA, EISA buses can support the standard 8 MHz bus speed. True EISA adapters are capable of transferring data in so-called burst mode (clumps of data, rather than a steady stream) at speeds up to 24 MHz.

Like MCA, EISA never really caught on in the same kind of volume as ISA. Part of this phenomenon had to do with expense: like MCA adapters, EISA adapters typically cost at least twice as much as their ISA counterparts. Another reason for this phenomenon, though, has to do with what we can only call rapid obsolescence. This is the result of CPU technologies in the past few years, when clock speeds and data paths have doubled in 12- to 18-month cycles or less. With CPUs like the Pentium available today with 100 MHz clock speeds and 64-bit bus widths (a 128-bit bus is already under design at Intel), a 32-bit wide, 24 MHz bus doesn't have a lot of sex appeal! That's why it's difficult—but not impossible—to find PCs that offer EISA bus support in the 1995 marketplace.

VESA Local Bus (VL or sometimes, VLB)

You've finally reached the zenith of computer-speak in this chapter: VLB includes an acronym, VESA, within itself, making it an acronym within an acronym. VESA stands for video electronics standards association. It's name is a dead giveaway to its origins: VLB originated as a bus specifically designed to support graphics adapters for higher-resolution Super VGA monitors for PCs. It didn't take other adapter manufacturers to realize that a 32-bit bus that could support burst-mode rates of up to 160 MHz might have applications beyond driving displays for newer, faster computers. Because NICs can show immediate benefits from faster clock speeds and higher bandwidths, VLB NIC cards became popular quickly.

VLB is laid out so that the local bus portion of the edge connector ties in at the back of the card. This lets PC manufacturers lay out motherboards so that a slot can support either an ISA (or EISA) and VLB adapter (even some dual-capability adapter cards are available that plug into both sections of the socket area). This layout is depicted in Figure 24.6, which calls out the VLB and ISA sockets and a matching VLB edge connector.

Figure 24.6   *A VLB connector.*

Like EISA, VLB supports bus mastering and high-volume burst-mode data transfers, making VLB a good bus choice for demanding applications—like network or other servers, or high-end workstations. Put another way, machines that have to move large amounts of data across the bus—whether to get on and off the network or to and from a large-format, high-resolution display device—are good candidates for VLB adapters for things like disk controllers, NICs, and graphics adapters. One of VLB's biggest limitations is that the number of VLB adapters a single bus can support is only three. Consequently, it hasn't really taken off as a bus of choice for servers, though it is still pretty popular for workstations.

Peripheral Component Interconnect

Peripheral component interconnect (PCI) is the current darling in today's fleet of PC buses. It's newer, shinier, and more capable than any of its compatriots. PCI is a local motherboard bus to enable high-performance, high-bandwidth peripheral components to connect to the PC bus.

PCI was developed by Intel to provide a high-speed data path between the CPU and up to 10 peripherals (video, disk, network, etc.), as opposed to only 3 for VLB. Like other expansion buses, the PCI bus coexists in the

PC with ISA or EISA. With PCI, ISA and EISA boards still plug into an ISA or EISA slot, while high-speed PCI controllers plug into a PCI slot. Figure 24.7 shows a PCI slot and matching edge connector.

Figure 24.7 *A PCI edge connector.*

The PCI bus runs at 33 MHz and supports 32-bit and 64-bit data paths and bus mastering. Because of Intel's considerable clout, more vendors are supporting PCI adapters than any other kind of expansion bus (including VLB and EISA). For this reason, we recommend that you consider adding PCI NICs to your servers and power users' machines, if PCI is an available option for them.

Future Buses

Given that the past 12 years has seen the introduction of five different PC buses, with major and minor modifications to nearly all of them, it's not unreasonable to assume that it's just a matter of time before something new comes along (again). We don't have any inside information, but we expect to hear talk about a 128-bit bus, with 100-plus MHz clock speeds no later than 1997. After that, it's anybody's guess!

Speeds and Feeds

In computer-speak, *speeds and feeds* refers to the performance characteristics and bandwidth for a given technology—in this case, we're talking about the various buses you've looked at here. Table 24.1 summarizes much of what we've covered in the past sections for each of the various buses. It's a way to compare the various contenders and see what's got the performance edge (currently, it's PCI; despite the apparent advantages shown for VLB, there simply aren't enough VLB NICs available to make it a technology worthy of serious consideration).

Name	Width	Sustained max transfer rate (MBps)	Burst-mode max transfer rate (MBps)	Devices per bus	Max clock (MHz)
ISA	8 & 16	8 & 16	8 & 16	16	8
MCA	32	32	32	16	16
EISA	32	16	32	16	8
VLB	32	132	264	3	40
PCI	32 & 64*	66	132 & 264*	4 (10)**	33

* No 64 bit PCI boards are currently available.

** Theoretical maximum is 10 PCI slots, but bus loads and timing issues have limited implementations to 4 slots.

Table 24.1   *Speeds and Feeds for PC Buses.*

Which Bus Should You Catch?

There are two answers to this question. First, for purchase of new machines, it's wise to compare prices and capabilities for machines that support the top buses available (in this case VLB and PCI). For heavy-duty server use, the 3-adapter limit on VLB means that you should buy a PCI machine that can support up to 10 adapters.

Second, for existing machines, compatibility dictates that you buy whatever kind of adapter the machine will support. Most computers that support all of the higher speed buses (except MCA) typically ship with ISA bus slots as well. For these hybrid machines buy an adapter that matches the type of the fastest technology open slot available.

PIECES AND PARTS OF A NIC

In this part of the chapter, we'll focus a microscope on a typical NIC, to take you on a guided tour of its pieces and parts. Figure 24.8 on page 311 is your point of departure; to figure out where you're going, simply follow the arrows and read the labels along the way! Just for your touring pleasure, we're going to follow a path across the card as the data moves from the network to the PC, pointing out items of interest along the way.

Figure 24.8 *Another look at an NE2000 NIC.*

Media Interface

It's easy to see where the network connects to most NICs, because that's where the wires hook up. As you can see, the front edge of the card is where the two plugs reside. The barrel-shaped connector on the lower end of the front edge is called a *BNC connector*. This BNC connector is for a type of Ethernet called 10Base2, which is also known as *thinwire Ethernet* because it uses a thin, pliable coaxial cable (please see Chapter 9 for more of the details).

Technobabble:

The 15-pin D-shaped female plug above the BNC connector on the front edge is known as an *AUI* (attachment unit interface) or a *DIX* (Digital Intel Xerox, the co-inventing companies behind Ethernet) connector. This connector is used with a type of Ethernet called 10Base5, also known as *thickwire Ethernet*, because it uses a thick, fairly rigid coaxial cable. To use 10Base5 Ethernet, you'll also have to use an additional cable, called a *transceiver cable,* to connect the NIC to a transceiver of some kind (you'll learn more about transceivers later).

This makes the NE2000 what's known as a *two-way card;* that is, by selecting one connector or the other, this NIC can actually attach to two different kinds of cables. The three rows of pins immediately to the left of the AUI connector is called a *jumper block.* When the black plastic and metal connector bridges the lower two rows of pins, you've selected the BNC connector as the "live" network attachment. If the connector bridges the upper two rows of pins, you've selected the AUI connector. Hint: an easy way to tell if the jumpers are properly selected is to look at the relative position of the jumper block to the media connectors. If the AUI connector is uppermost on the front edge, to use it, you'll have to bridge the upper two rows of pins; if the BNC connector is lowermost on the front edge, to use it, you'll have to bridge the lower two rows of pins.

Media Interface: Transceiver

The network signals enter the NIC through either the transmitter or the receiver (together, the transceiver). What happens next depends on whether the card is being used with 10Base2 (BNC connector) or 10Base5 (AUI connector) Ethernet. Because 10Base5 requires the use of an external transceiver, if you are using this connection to hook up to your network, the external transceiver delivers or accepts signals that have been "cleaned" up for further processing by the NIC (if incoming) or by the transceiver (if outgoing). If you're using 10Base2, the transceiver circuitry is built right onto the NIC itself. It is composed of many of the elements on the right-hand side of the NE2000, with the exception of the large socketed chip labeled *Ethernet controller*. Figure 24.9 shows an external Ethernet transceiver and a transceiver cable.

Figure 24.9 *An external Ethernet transceiver, with cable.*

As the title for this section is supposed to indicate, the transceiver on a NIC handles the conversion of a stream of bits into electrical signals that can be transmitted across a wire or vice versa (a stream of signals into a corresponding stream of bits). This is where digital representations of data get turned into signals for outgoing communications and where signals getting turned into digital data for incoming information.

Because we're using an Ethernet card as an example here, we're bound by the requirements of Ethernet technology to talk about transceivers. But, actually, a transceiver is a special case of what we can more generally call a *media interface*. A media interface is that part of the NIC that handles conversion of digital data streams to whatever type of signals are needed to drive the networking medium or converts such signals to digital data to accept incoming data from the medium. That's why it's called a *media interface*. For whatever type of NIC you're using, the components near the connector or connectors that support the media attachment are probably involved in making this kind of conversion.

Controller Chips

Both types of connections—BNC and AUI—converge at the next stop on our tour: the Ethernet controller chip. This is the "brains" of the NE2000. It's where most of the really interesting stuff happens, and it's actually what coordinates the activity of the rest of the NIC. It decides when to send data and reacts to incoming data, to ensure its proper reception.

Again, nearly every kind of NIC will have a controller of some kind, to coordinate communications between the PC and the network. Although the details will differ among different networking technologies (e.g. token ring, ARCnet, Ethernet), the coordination and handling of incoming and outgoing messages remains a constant requirement.

Controller chips usually deal with three kinds of tasks:

1. Media access control. Every networking technology has rules about when it's OK to communicate and what to do if errors occur. The controller monitors of incoming signals and network activity and decides when it's OK to transmit (and what to do if transmission fails, for whatever reason).

2. Serial to parallel and vice versa. Most networking media work like a garden hose; information has to move across the medium one signal at a time. Computers work with bits in chunks (called *bytes* or *words*). The controller also converts these chunks into streams for outgoing information and from streams to chunks for incoming data.

3. Special message handling. Some networking technologies, like token ring, use special messages to control how the network

behaves. It's the controller's job to recognize and react to such messages, reconfiguring itself or changing its behavior in response to them. Basically, it controls how the NIC behaves and interacts with the network.

Buffers

One interesting aspect of network communications is that the messages users send and receive are quite different from the ones that travel across the network. By the time a message reaches the NIC, it's been prepackaged to closely resemble the kind of message that needs to travel across the network. But a bit of repackaging and disassembly work still is required to turn chunks of bits into streams of signals and vice versa. Also, work is required in sending and receiving chunks of bits between the computer (across the bus) and the NIC.

Incoming network data arrives in a serial fashion, where bits show up one at a time. Outgoing network data arrives in chunks but has to be broken into a stream of bits. To allow communication to take place, both sides of this conversation need a place to put things—that is, a place to store incoming bits as they arrive, until they represent a complete message, and a place to put a message from the computer, so that it can be broken into bits and pushed across the network.

This happens in a set of memory chips on the NICs that are called *buffers*. On the NE2000, the buffers live in the memory chips on the left-hand side of the card Most NICs use fairly sophisticated buffers, so that the computer can move chunks of data into one side of the buffer while the NIC is turning bits into signals and pushing those signals out onto the networking medium for outgoing data. For incoming data, the process is reversed, so the NIC can move complete chunks of data to the computer, even as it's assembling incoming chunks on the NIC for delivery later on.

In the grand scheme of things on a NIC, buffers act like holding tanks to store information that is being sent or received until it's ready to be moved to the computer or out onto the networking medium.

Boot ROM

Many NICs are capable of accepting a second "brain" in addition to the controller. This second brain is called a *boot ROM* (ROM stands for read-only memory). Boot ROMs provide the intelligence to let a computer talk to the network as it's starting up (called *booting up* or *boot up* in computer-speak) to read the information the computer needs to make itself work from across the network, instead of from a local hard or floppy disk.

Technobabble:

Boot ROMs are used primarily in tightly secured environments where the PCs in use have no hard or floppy drives (to prevent users from copying sensitive information onto a diskette, for example). They are also used where computers provide a narrow range of functions—such as an information kiosk or electronic directory—and general-purpose capabilities aren't needed. Such machines are often called *diskless workstations* because they don't need local hard disks. This just shows you how important the network can be in some operations: for a diskless workstation, network failure means that the machine can't be used! Figure 24.8 on page 311 shows the socket where a boot ROM could be plugged into the NE2000 if we needed to use one.

Bus Interface

The final major component in our journey is the NIC's bus interface, which consists of the circuitry and connectors that manage the transmission and reception of information across the PC's bus (primarily from the CPU or the computer's RAM memory). The most evident representation of this interface is the edge connector at the bottom edge of the NIC: we've seen these charmingly referred to as *golden fingers* in some Taiwanese adapter manuals. While we can't necessarily see the resemblance, except for their gold-bronze color, it's an unforgettable phrase to remind you of how the edge connector plugs into your PC's bus!

Software Components

Some of the most important components that let your PC talk to the network don't appear on the NIC at all: they're the software pieces that instruct your PC how to communicate with the NIC and the various additional pieces of code that extend the functionality of your local operating system (usually DOS or Windows, but possibly OS/2 or some flavor of UNIX) to include access to the network. This collection of software provides the detailed instructions for your PC to understand how to address the NIC, and how to exchange information with it.

One of the most important software components for your NIC is something called its *driver*. Also called a *device driver*, a driver is a small program that understands the exact details of how your computer needs to communicate with the NIC. In the DOS world (with or without Windows), the driver is a piece of code that is always ready to run; because the network may deposit data on it, or a program may want to access the network at any time, the driver has to lurk in the background, ready to send or receive data as soon as it's needed.

In addition to the driver, which manages access to the NIC, it's also necessary to provide software that understands how to communicate over the network (or how to handle incoming messages from the network). This function is handled by software that implements whatever protocols, which are basically a formal set of rules for communication (see Part III of this book for a detailed discussion of the most common networking protocols), you need to use the network. Like the driver, this software has to lurk in the background, because it handles the translation between the messages that users or applications send to the exact formats and layouts required by the networking technology in use.

The final software ingredient in the recipe for successful networking supplies some form of application links to the other programs that run on your network. For DOS, this typically occurs through a piece of software called a *shell* or a *redirector*.

A shell program surrounds DOS with additional networking and intercepts input from the keyboard or applications to see if network services are needed or not. If they are, the shell takes care of requesting them; if not, the input is passed on to DOS to be handled locally. Incoming information from the network is handled by the shell and passed along to the appropriate application.

A redirector augments DOS with network capability so that requests for services, resources, or information that can't be satisfied locally get passed on (or redirected) to the network. Both kinds of software require precious DOS memory to run, but add in the ability to interact with the network.

Windows is more like other operating systems—like Windows NT, UNIX, and OS/2—in that it supports networking drivers directly and makes them a part of its working environment if they're loaded before network services or resources are needed. No matter what type of operating system is in use though, this last layer of software adds the final crucial link that lets applications send and receive information to and from the network.

Picking Compatible NICs

When it comes to selecting the right NIC for your needs, you'll quickly learn that the choices are constrained by a number of factors. While this won't totally narrow down the number of options you'll have to choose from, it'll definitely lower the number of choices you'll have to make.

First, you can use only NICs that support the networking technology in use. This means that you can use only Ethernet NICs on an Ethernet network, no matter how many kinds of token ring or ARCnet cards you might have in your storeroom. You have to match the NIC to the network or your PC won't be able to connect.

Second, you can use only NICs that accommodate the right kind of connector to attach to the networking medium you want to use. Our sample NE2000, for instance, would be worthless on a 10BaseT Ethernet network, because it requires an RJ-45 connector, rather than the BNC and AUI connectors present on the card. You have to be able to plug in or otherwise connect to the networking medium to establish a working connection.

Third, you'll have to match the NICs bus connector to an open bus socket on your PC. This means that an EISA card will do you no good, if all you've got are ISA and PCI slots. You have to match the card's bus connector to the slot you want to plug it into, to make it work.

Fourth, you'll want to ponder some other considerations before making your final choice. If the NIC you're looking for is for a server or a very busy workstation, you'll want to consider a number of factors that could improve network performance. A bus mastering NIC can offload processing from the main CPU and speed up network access. Given the choice between ISA and PCI, for example, you'd want to choose the faster, more powerful (but alas, more expensive) PCI NIC. Finally, you need to make sure that your chosen NIC will work in your local networking environment. If there's no NetWare driver for the new Quack5 PCI 64-bit Ethernet NIC, it's speed will do you no good—if your server can't talk to that particular network adapter.

In the end, compatibility is as important for networking as it is for most other things in life!

INSTALLATION SECRETS

OK, so you've found a NIC that passes all the compatibility tests. Now, you're just itching to get that sucker installed and jump on the network with both feet. Does this mean you should rush right over and rip the case off your PC to stick your NIC where you think it belongs? Despite your commendable enthusiasm, the answer for now has to be "Not yet!"

Before you can install a NIC in a PC, you have to do some homework. If you want your new NIC to withstand the ultimate networking test— namely, does it work?—you have to prepare yourself, and your machine, to maximize your chances of passing.

Know the Process

To begin with, it's important to understand the overall installation process and what it means to add another adapter to a PC that may have half a dozen cards of various kinds working away inside, unseen, already. Every such combination of existing interfaces—for disk drives, CD-ROM players, multimedia, telecommunications, or whatever—results in a particular configuration that must be accommodated any time something new gets added.

Tip:
Given that you now understand that anything new has to fit in among the existing components (or, perhaps, replace one of them), here's a high-level view of the typical sequence of events involved in installing a NIC:

1. **The background check.** Before you do anything else, check the dates on the driver files and other software for the NIC. If they're more than 6 months old, call the manufacturer or check with other sources to see if newer versions are available. Also, review the manual for the NIC to determine its default configuration (the way it's set up at the factory) and its configuration options.

2. **Configuration review.** If your computing environment is well-run, you should be able to locate a file (either on paper or on the machine) that fully documents what's already installed in the PC that's supposed to receive the NIC and all the configuration details for each adapter it already includes. If you don't have access to this

information, you'll have to figure it out for yourself. We'll tell you how a little later on.

3. **Finding a slot.** It's also important to know what kind of slot your NIC requires and to be sure that the right kind of bus socket is unoccupied so that the NIC can take residence in the right location. Here again, if your PC is well-documented, you'll already know what slots are taken and which ones are available. If not, you'll have to take a peek inside to see what kinds of slots are open. While you're in there, make sure that the area above and around the open slot offers sufficient clearance to accommodate your NIC. Skip to step 6, "turning off and opening up," for instructions on how to do this and then continue with the next step.

4. **Understanding NIC limitations.** Many NICs require the selection of certain settings or combinations of settings, to work. Review the NIC's manual to find out which settings it will accept and which ones it won't or can't.

5. **Planning the new configuration.** If all of the settings the NIC can handle are already taken, you have two choices: (1) you can rearrange something else in the machine to free up the settings your NIC needs or (2) you can try to find a different NIC that will work with the open settings that are still available. Whatever you end up doing, make sure you find a combination of settings that will work with the NIC that ultimately winds up in your PC.

6. **Turning off and opening up.** OK, now you've done your homework; the rest should be easy. If it's running, turn the machine off and remove the power cord. Then, remove the screws or fasteners that hold on the PC's case. Make sure you have a small paper cup or other receptacle for screws nearby and put any such items you remove from the PC into the receptacle. This makes them easier to find when you need them.

7. **Adding the NIC.** Firmly seat the NIC in its designated bus socket. The best way to do this is to gently lower the card into the available space, until the edge connector is resting at the bus socket opening. Then, grasp the card with both hands, using thumb and forefinger positioned at the upper right- and left-hand corners, and gently rock the card while pushing down. The NIC should slide right in and attain a firm seat. When it's seated, give it an extra push to make sure that the edge connector is fully engaged. If you can, shine a flashlight along the top edge of the connector to make sure the card

is fully inserted.

8. **Closing up and testing out.** Now, you're ready to test your work. This means replacing the power cord and powering up the machine (don't put the cover back on just yet). If the PC boots, you're off to a good start. Next, install the drivers and other software, and try to connect to the network. Eventually, you'll get things working or realize you need to get or do something else before you can make the NIC work. At that point, remove the NIC if necessary, replace the case, and continue on.

9. **Off and running.** If you're lucky and living right, you'll be off and running with a new connection to the network on your PC!

This concludes the overview of what it's like to install a NIC. In the next sections, we'll cover a few of the finer points, along with some tips and tricks to help you complete each step with éclat and panache.

Preparation

In case we haven't already made this clear, preparation is the most important activity in installing a NIC. If you do your homework and get everything you need together before you start the installation process, you'll be that much surer of a successful consummation. Over the years, we've learned (the hard way) that the real time wasters come from "small inconsequential details that probably aren't important anyway." So here are some foolproof tips to help you prepare.

Tip: RTFM, Babe!
When they ship from the factory, almost every NIC includes a manual in its box. Find one and at least skim the whole thing looking for configuration requirements and details, potential gotchas, and the vendor's technical support number. If you have a NIC, but no manual, try to locate information on your NIC in one of the references in the "NIC Resources" section.

FYI, *RTFM* stands for "read the fabulous manual," except the F-word sometimes varies!

Avoiding Stale Software

A diskette with driver software on it should also accompany your NIC. Check its vintage (look at the file creation dates using a directory listing command). If the files are more than 6 months old, you should call the vendor's technical support number and find out if newer versions are available. For more details on how to dig up vendor and product information, please consult Appendices D and E in this book.

Asking for Trouble

Your next step in the installation process should be to ask around to find out if there are any known problems or gotchas! related to the NIC you plan on installing. Check with your local networking guru, the company that sold you the NIC, the vendor's technical support line, or the on-line sources of information covered in Appendix D. If you're armed for trouble, it can't take you by surprise. This step may also keep you from having to go on a wild goose chase for which there may be no happy ending.

Your List of Ingredients

Before you crack open the PC and install a NIC, here's a checklist of the items you'll want to have on hand:

- All the manuals you can lay your hands on for the system, including the system manual itself, and the manuals for every adapter already installed on the PC, plus the manual for your NIC (if you have to start moving other adapter's settings around to accommodate the NIC, you'll need their manuals, too).

- A comprehensive list of all of the settings already in use on the system, including as many of the elements inTable 24.2 on page 323 as they apply to each and every adapterThe combination of settings you want to use for your NIC. Select these and write them down on the same list you built for the previous step. If you can't accommodate the NIC using the open settings available on the system, you'll have to see if other adapters can be reconfigured to open up settings that the NIC can use. This is where the other manuals will come in handy. Don't actually do anything until you're convinced that you can make all the pieces fit together.

- The latest drivers and other software for the NIC. Obtain them and make sure you have those files close at hand.
- The technical support numbers for the company that sold you the PC and for the PC's and NIC's manufacturers (if you have to move other cards around, get their technical support numbers, too).

Setting type	Explanation
IRQ	A PC depends on special signal lines on the bus, called *interrupts*, that are used by adapters and other devices to signal the CPU for attention. Interrupts are numbered 0–15 and commonly, each adapter must have its own unique IRQ assigned to it. Common NIC IRQs include 3, 5, 7 (some also support interrupts in the range from 10–15). Setting IRQs usually involved setting DIP switches or jumpers.
DMA	*DMA* stands for direct memory access, which provides a way to tie a region of RAM on the PC to buffer memory on the NIC. Although this method for transferring data across the bus is less common than it was in the 1980s, working with DMA requires a DMA channel ID and a DMA channel address to be supplied to manage the memory transfers between the CPU and any adapters that use DMA.
Memory base addresses	Also called *MEMBASE*, this address is used to handle status information flow between the PC and adapters. Each adapter must have a unique MEMBASE address, which is usually expressed as a hexadecimal number (e.g., C000h). This address defines a region of main CPU memory to which the contents of the NIC's buffers will be stored for incoming data or copied from for outgoing network traffic. For DOS and Windows, this memory will usually be assigned in the High Memory Area, which occupies addresses A000h through FFFFh (most NICs use the addresses C000h, C800h, D000h, or D800h). You must watch out for potential address conflicts and steer around them. It's normal to use jumpers to set MEMBASE addresses.
I/O port addresses	An input/output (I/O) port is used to send and receive data between the PC and adapters on the bus. Each adapter must have its own unique I/O port address, where certain addresses are reserved for particular types of interfaces, especially video cards. NICs usually offer a range of possible port addresses that range from 2E0h to 380h, and the most common default address is 300h.

Table 24.2   *Research all adapter settings prior to installation.*

Once you've got all this information together, you'll finally be ready to do something about that NIC you've been itching to install for so long.

Going Through the Motions

In smaller offices and networks, you may not have the luxury of having a test machine to work with. If you don't, make sure you've figured out a fallback strategy before starting a first-time installation. That way, if you can't complete the installation for some reason and the PC remains out of service, you won't be leaving its user in the lurch. For this reason, we recommend making a complete backup of any system in which you're installing something (hardware or software), and that you figure out a way to boot from a floppy and restore the backup without having to rely on the potentially mangled contents of that system's hard drive.

If you do have a test machine, you can practice the installation in a less pressured environment before you go out and do it for real. We recommend this approach whenever possible, because hidden gotchas can emerge during the installation process, no matter how well you've planned and prepared.

Back to the Future!

Every install should start with the same thing (or at least with the assurance that a current one is available): a complete backup of the system on which something is to be installed. It's also a good idea to make sure you have a set of boot floppies (with access to the backup software included), too, so you can be sure of being able to restore the backup, if necessary.

Practice Makes Perfect

For larger networks, where wholesale installations and upgrades are normal, this test procedure goes double or triple. Practice indeed makes perfect, and it can greatly speed up the time it takes to repeat the same installation or upgrades tasks many times over. For this kind of situation, practice means working in a test lab that duplicates the common machines and configurations on the network. If you make sure you can install the NIC and its software successfully in this environment, you should encounter far fewer difficulties when it's time to go into full-scale production mode.

Write It Down!

When you start shuffling configurations or deciding on adapter settings for your NIC, it's all too easy to just go with the flow and neglect to record your activities and selections. Take notes on anything unusual or significant about the installation, so you can refer to them later, should you ever have to do it again.

If you get in the habit of keeping good records about your systems and their settings, you'll have to do far less work in the long run. Any time you change a setting or install a new piece of hardware or software, record the changes that result. It'll keep you from having to crack the case next week just to look up the new IRQ settings, etc., when that user needs to install a SCSI adapter for their new quadspeed CD-ROM drive!

Hooking up for Real

Once you're past the experimental phase, you can get serious about your installation. By reviewing your notes and working with your setting information, you should be able to install one NIC, or a thousand, by marching through your planned-out process.

Tip:
Be sure to test as you go, to catch potential mistakes along the way. For instance, once you've seated the NIC in the system's bus, reattach the power cord, keyboard, and display. Keep your hands—and other conductors—away from the computer's innards and power up the machine. If it boots, you can be assured that you didn't introduce any serious settings conflicts during the installation. Repeat this incremental testing after you install the drivers, and then when you attach the network cable. This lets you focus on solving a small number of potential problems, instead of having to backtrack all the way through the installation process to figure out where things went awry.

Tip:
Here's another tip from the school of hard knocks: even though the temptation may be nearly irresistible to go out and find the fastest, most innovative NIC every time you need to put another machine on the network (or add another interface to a server), diversity can be

counterproductive. If you research a dependable, functional NIC (or product family of NICs), you can concentrate on learning how to deal with two or three models, instead of as many models as there are machines on your network. This may not be as exciting or as much fun, but it is a much more manageable approach to running a successful network if you standardize on a limited number of NIC makes and models. You'll also have to learn much less esoterica, keep tabs on a smaller number of drivers, and be better able to develop a relationship with the same team of folks for technical (and moral) support.

Remember this, too, while you're installing a NIC in a computer: the real fun starts *after* the machine's attached to the network!

COMMON NIC-RELATED PROBLEMS

It's not within the purview of this book to provide a complete troubleshooting list for all the ills that can ail a NIC, but we thought it would be a good idea to prepare for some of the most common, everyday problems you're likely to encounter. Each section that follows is titled with a symptom, follows with a brief diagnosis, and then goes on to suggest some possible cures.

PC Won't Boot

If this happens right after you've tried to install a piece of hardware, it means that something is interfering with the operation of the computer. Generally, this is one of two things:

1. The power isn't getting to the PC or to some other vital component. Turn off the power first. Then, check the power cable and make sure everything's properly plugged in. While you're at it, make sure all the other cables are correctly attached (we've been fooled by a loose video cable more than once) and that all of the adapter cards in the bus are firmly seated. Turn the power back on. If the machine still won't boot, proceed to Step 2.

2. Congratulations! It looks like you managed to introduce some kind of settings conflict into the PC. To check this, power down the PC and remove the NIC. Try to boot again. If it boots, you know the

problem's been introduced by the NIC. If it still won't boot, something else is wrong. Make sure all of the cards are seated and all the cables are OK. If it still won't boot, try to boot from a floppy disk with a minimal configuration. If that works, you'll probably be able to get back in operation by removing the drivers and other software you added to support your new NIC. If that doesn't work, you'll have to restore the system to its previous state from your backup—you did make a backup, didn't you?

If none of these approaches do you any good, the PC will have to go into a repair shop, where a real professional can try to figure out what happened. Don't feel too bad, though, you'll probably learn that a system component—very often, the power supply is a culprit—decided to give up the ghost at an inopportune moment. When this happens, it's a good idea to have a fallback scheme—like an extra PC, or a loaner from the repair shop—lined up and ready to put into action.

No More Network

Sometimes, the network will apparently just "go away." It'll be completely inaccessible, no matter what your users try. When this happens, the most common cause is loose cabling. If this happens on a bus topology (like 10Base2 or 10Base5 Ethernet), the whole network will go down, so you'll have plenty of notice that something's wrong.

Gotcha:
There's no alternative to checking all cable connections to make sure everything's properly hooked up. Chances are better than average you'll run into some user who says, "I didn't know I couldn't disconnect that cable any time I felt like it," or some other lame excuse. If that's the case, the fix is easy, and you can only hope he or she gets the message that this is extremely inconvenient for the rest of the user community. Repeat offenders are usually shot!

A more pernicious cause of such problems is when cables become damaged or broken. If you expect service people, like air conditioning technicians, electricians, or telephone repair staff, to be in the vicinity of your network cables, it's almost always a good idea to warn them what to watch out for. For campus environments, be aware that there's an almost mystical connection between backhoe operators and cable runs: when there's going to be digging in your neighborhood, please do what you can to keep these two ingredients at a safe distance from one another!

Network Not Accessible

In cases where a single cable or connection can fail or be disconnected without affecting the entire network—as with 10BaseT and most other star-wiring schemes (like token ring and some flavors of ARCnet)—loss of network access for a single workstation often means that the NIC simply isn't able to talk to the network.

Here again, the cable and the connection closest to the NIC are the most likely causes, but such failures could also be due to

- A NIC failure or configuration error that renders the NIC inoperative.
- A disconnect at the other end of the cable (i.e., at the hub, concentrator, or other device where the network medium plugs in).
- Software changes on the affected PC have interfered with the NIC driver's ability to function.

The only way to figure this one out is to go through a process of elimination. You'll have to question the user whose machine is having a problem about recent changes to his or her environment, but don't always believe what you hear. Another dead giveaway is to check local files that reflect configuration changes: for DOS, look at the modification date for CONFIG.SYS and AUTOEXEC.BAT; for Windows, check WIN.INI and SYSTEM.INI as well.

Gotcha:
Sometimes entire sections of the network may become inaccessible. When this happens, you're dealing with a failure that's very likely not NIC related (except for server NICs, which often function as routers for individual cable segments). The best thing to do in this case is to figure out where all of the affected elements converge (at a server, hub, or router) and start from there.

Driver Difficulties

Sometimes a PC will boot quite happily but then fail to load the network drivers. Because no drivers means no network access, this too will keep users off the network. The most common causes of this symptom are as follows:

- **Loose connections.** Make sure the connector is properly seated on the NIC, but be sure it's plugged into something on the other end, too!

- **Installation problems.** Check to be sure that the drivers are still where they're supposed to be, and that their directory is referenced explicitly or included in the DOS PATH definition. If the computer can't find the drivers, it can't run them, either. Sometimes things get moved around—or accidentally deleted—when new software gets installed. Be sure to check the driver versions, too—we've run into some installation programs that actually overwrote newer versions of a driver with older (and useless) replacements. Same file names, just wrong versions!

- **Conflicting settings.** The NIC may have been working properly, but now another adapter's been installed or an old one has been replaced by a newer incarnation. Just as the introduction of the NIC can conflict with other system elements during installation, adding another interface can have the same effect on the NIC. Try all the other adapters and see if another isn't working, either—this can very often help to pinpoint the cause of a conflict. The latest addition to the system is also a good place to start looking for problems.

Gotcha:
Remember that most network problems are caused by loose connections or configuration errors. If it's not one of these two "usual suspects," you'll need to get serious and do some real sleuthing work.

Lights on, Nobody Home

Sometimes you'll make a successful connection to the network, or at least a reasonable facsimile of one, and then be unable to communicate using that connection. When this happens, it's a more subtle variety of the preceding problems. The big difference here is that this symptom can be caused by application conflicts as well as driver difficulties or NIC/cable/connection problems. Only by working through a careful process of elimination can you get to the bottom of this mystery: all we can say is "Good luck!" Think hard, step through recent changes and additions to the system, and remember to take lots of breaks. Given enough time, you can figure *anything* out! Just remember that it's OK to ask for help.

Change the Rules, Change the Game!

Any time a PC's configuration or its software changes, trouble is liable to pay a visit. This is another reason why you might want to consider writing things down: if there's a record of system changes available, you won't have to figure things out the hard way. Keeping track of things one at a time is quite a bit easier than working your way back to a PC's original installation profile.

BUYING TIPS: NEW OR USED, LOCAL OR MAIL ORDER?

When it comes to buying NICs, there are lots of options to consider. There are also certain things that you should insist on and others where it's OK to be flexible. Here's a shopping list of features, functions, and information to look for:

- **Warranty/guarantee.** Don't ever compromise on a warranty. Even if you're buying used equipment, insist on a money back guarantee. If the NIC doesn't work for you, the money you've spent on it is wasted. For new equipment, a 90-day warranty is fairly common, but you can find plenty of vendors who warranty their NICs for one, two, and even three years. Why settle for less?

- **Technical support.** Many vendors can no longer afford to give their customers free telephone support, but they should still be willing to answer questions from their customers. Finding a vendor with free, unlimited phone support is the exception these days, but we'd advise against buying NICs from vendors who don't offer free on-line support over the Internet or CompuServe or who don't offer faxback support for faxed-in questions. When you need help, you want the party on the other end of the conversation to be ready, willing, and able to help you.

- **Easy access to driver updates.** Here again, on-line access is the key: you want to be able to locate and download the latest and greatest drivers for your NIC without having to move mountains. Vendors with BBSs or on-line file libraries are preferable to those who don't offer such convenience.

- **Clear, readable manuals.** Don't be bashful about asking a salesperson to find you the manual for a NIC you're thinking about buying. Even if he or she has to break the shrinkwrap on a new package, you should persevere and take a look at what kind of information the vendor provides about its products. This will often tell you a lot about a vendor's concern for quality and workability.

- **Vendor certification.** If you're going to be using the NIC with a particular brand of networking software, be aware that most of the major players have certification or testing programs. The purpose of the programs is to provide buyers with a reasonable expectation that the hardware and drivers will work with the networking software in question. Novell has been the leader in this area with its NetWare Tested and Approved program, but Microsoft, Banyan, and Artisoft, among others, also have similar programs. This certification is not an absolute guarantee of compatibility, but it does indicate that the NIC and its drivers have been tested and found workable in the vendor's test labs.

- **Multi-way capability.** Most Ethernet NICs available today offer support for at least two of the three most popular connectors: BNC (10Base2), AUI (10Base5), or RJ-45 (10BaseT). Even though you may be using 10Base2 today, it could be a smart purchase to get a two- or three-way NIC that includes RJ-45 as well (it's the fastest growing segment of the Ethernet marketplace today; many new office buildings come prewired for 10BaseT networks).

- **Buy the best you can afford.** Given a choice between an ISA and a PCI card, you might be tempted to opt for the ISA card, even if the target machine for the NIC has an empty PCI slot. If you can afford the difference in cost, go for the faster card: it'll continue to serve you well in the future, even if you change from vanilla to switched Ethernet (which offers significantly higher bandwidth). Newer models are also likely to be supported longer by their vendors (they can't write drivers for all the cards they've built since the beginning of time, you know) in the future.

Don't forget the basic requirements when shopping for NICs: guarantees, tech support, media interfaces, etc., don't matter at all if you don't get the right kind of NIC for the right bus socket for your machine.

Price vs. Value

When you're shopping around for NICs, look for multiple sources of information. Don't just take the word of whatever salesperson you happen to run across while you're out shopping. The most expensive NIC isn't always the best one (but it usually produces the largest commissions, so be wary).

Best Buy:
Read the networking journals, ask fellow users, and visit the vendors' on-line forums whose names you see receiving favorable mention. This will also give you the opportunity to see what kinds of horror stories existing customers are telling and how the vendor responds to them. The bottom line is this: don't buy strictly on price, but don't assume that the highest price is the best value, either.

You Bought It, You Own It!

When buying used equipment, guarantees are going to be hard to come by. But you should never buy a used NIC without at least a verbal money-back agreement. Ask the question, "If I can't get this to work, will you give me my money back?" If the answer is no, keep looking; there are plenty of sources for used networking gear that won't have a problem with such a request. Be prepared to accept a time limit on this offer, though: it's not unusual for used-equipment dealers to offer refunds for only the first 10 to 30 days after purchase.

Used Doesn't Mean Used-Up

If you do decide to buy used equipment, inspect it carefully to make sure it hasn't been damaged or broken. Even if you can return it, it's better not to hassle with returns in the first place. Look for obvious signs of wear and tear. Jiggle the connectors on the NICs to make sure they haven't come loose. Make sure all of the important components are still in place. Just because many NICs have a single empty socket for the Boot ROM doesn't mean that empty sockets are a good thing! If you buy from a dealer, rather than an individual, most of them will be glad to test the NICs you want to buy for you, just to make sure they're working. If you buy from an individual, consider asking to borrow the NIC first so you can "try it before you buy it."

Separating the Players from the Fly by Nighters

With price differentials as high as 30–35% off retail, it's almost impossible to avoid doing business with mail order outfits. Here again, careful buying is the key to avoid shoddy service or outright rip-offs.

First, make sure the dealer's listed in its local phone directory. *Never* do business with an unlisted mail order dealer; such outfits spring into existence only long enough to milk the response business from magazine or newspaper ads and then disappear forever, often leaving customers with only bills to show for their purchases (no merchandise).

Second, call the Better Business Bureau in the mail order vendor's home town and ask how many complaints about it is on file. If that number is higher than three or four, look for another candidate: there are hundreds to choose from.

Third, ask the vendor about payment terms and charges. We don't recommend doing business with a company that charges your credit card before the merchandise ships. When possible, make arrangements to establish credit and pay with a purchase order.

Fourth, ask the vendor for a list of reference accounts. If it has customers in your area, these are especially useful. Likewise for customers in the same line of business you're in. Both can be valuable sources of all kinds of information, not just about this particular mail order vendor. They can become a part of your "other" network (the one you maintain with peers and colleagues as part of your workaday world).

Fifth, don't be afraid to push on prices. Most mail order outfits will bargain with you, especially if you can quote them chapter and verse on a better price you saw in somebody else's advertisement. Some may not meet the other price, but you may be able to get them to meet you halfway. This can be worth a lot, if you find a mail order vendor you're comfortable doing business with and that gives you good service to boot.

Finally, if you do encounter bad treatment or get ripped off, make sure you tell somebody. Call the vendor's local BBB and register a complaint. Call the magazine that printed the ad and complain (sometimes they can even get your money back). Send a letter to the vendor's home state's Attorney General, Consumer Affairs Division. One good turn deserves another but a bad outfit should be reported.

NIC Resources:
Bibliography and Strategies

For general networking references, please consult Appendix C, "A List of Networking Resources." The magazines and other publications listed there can help you find out lots of information about NICs. The following references are particularly helpful for the information they contain about network interface cards:

Derfler, Frank, Jr., and Les Freed. *How Networks Work.*
Emeryville, CA: Ziff-Davis Press, 1993. An illustration and example-intensive description of how networks actually operate. Includes good discussions of most basic networking components, including NICs. $24.95.

Derrick, Dan. *Network Know-How: Concepts, Card and Cables.*
Berkeley, CA: Osborne McGraw-Hill, 1992. In addition to being a good source of general networking information, this book includes an entire chapter devoted to NICs. At $19.95, it's a useful addition to any networking professional's library, even if only to lend to newbie users.

Lowe, Doug. *Networking for Dummies.*
Indianapolis: IDG Books Worldwide, 1994. This is a good gentle introduction to networking, including useful overview on network interface cards. At $19.95, it's a useful addition to any networking professional's library, even if only to lend to newbie users.

Network Interface Technical Guide.
Boulder, CO: MicroHouse, Inc., 1992, 1993. This $99 technical reference includes over 1,000 pages of information on just about every NIC known. If you find an old NIC with no manual, chances are good that this book can supply an adequate replacement; at the

very least, it's sure to document all of the switch and jumper settings you'll need to know about to properly configure the card.

Newton, Harry. *Newton's Telecom Dictionary*, 7th Ed.
New York, NY: Flatiron Publishing Company, 1994. Harry Newton is a towering field in the telecommunications industry, and his dictionary isn't bad either. Even though it purports to be telecom specific, it's one of the best sources for looking up PC-related acronyms, standards, and other terms that we've ever found anywhere. At $24.95 for 1,200 pages of text, it's a bargain to boot!

Novell Ethernet Supplement NetWare.
Provo, UT: Novell, Inc., 1991, 1992, 1993, 1994. This gem of a manual explains how to install an Ethernet network with NetWare, but it also includes detailed descriptions of NICs and configuration information for the NE1000, NE2000, and NE3200 network interface cards originally designed by Novell, but now marketed by Eagle Technology (a division of Artisoft, Inc.). It's free with the purchase of Novell's NetWare 3.x operating system.

Sheldon, Tom. *The LAN Times Encyclopedia of Networking*.
Berkeley, CA: Osborne McGraw Hill, 1994. A general sourcebook for networking terms and technologies. Includes discussions, some lengthy and detailed, about nearly every conceivable networking topic. $39.95.

Tittel, Ed, Deni Connor, and Earl Follis. *NetWare for Dummies*, 2nd. Ed.
Indianapolis: IDG Books Worldwide, 1995. An introduction to NetWare that includes a good discussion of networking basics, with special emphasis on NIC terms, setup, and configuration. $19.95.

THE TOP FIVE NIC VENDORS

1. 3COM Corporation
2. Standard Microsystems Corporation (SMC)
3. Intel Corporation
4. Microdyne Corporation
5. International Business Machines (IBM)

HUBS AND CONCENTRATORS

chapter

CONNECTIVITY 101: BASIC OVERVIEW

Concentrators originated in the mainframe world as telecommunications devices that could connect several slow-speed communications links into a central point, and provide higher speed links emanating from the concentration point. You can think of a concentrator as a boxlike device with several incoming lines and one or more outgoing lines. The concentrator is then linked to another device, usually as a component of a hierarchical network topology.

Before LANs, mainframes stalked the earth like dinosaurs, and concentrators played an important role in their function. A concentrator was able to link several slow-speed terminal type devices through a higher speed link to a mainframe front-end processor or another concentrator. Because many terminal devices were attached to a mainframe, concentrators were a popular technology in that realm.

As LANs came along, concentrators played a similar role, linking several incoming workstation lines. Outgoing lines from early LAN concentrators operated at   the same speed as the incoming lines. Basically, in the LAN world, early concentrators served merely as a centralized wiring hub.

Concentrators Grow Up!

As usual, the computer industry is never satisfied with having just one term for one technology. Today, simple wiring concentrators have grown up to become intelligent wiring hubs with management capabilities. As early concentrators evolved, it has become common for the terms *concentrator* and *hub* to be used interchangeably.

LAN CONCENTRATOR DETAILS: WHAT IS A CONCENTRATOR?

The basic concentrator is a dumb, or passive, device. A concentrator collects wiring into a central location so that management of the wiring is simplified. A token ring multistation access unit (MAU) is a good example of a concentrator. An IBM 8228 MAU houses 10 ports, 8 ports used for workstation connection and 2 ports used for daisy-chaining the MAU to another MAU if needed.

Up to eight workstations can be centrally connected into one MAU concentrator. These MAUs have no intelligence and simply pass the token from one workstation to another. The MAUs have relays but no electrical components like power supplies.

Any network administrator operating in a token ring environment is familiar with racks of MAUs and clumsy shielded twisted pair cable. When a problem arises, the LAN administrator has to isolate the errant MAUs by a process of trial and error, unplugging each workstation from the MAU, and then plugging the workstations in one by one to isolate the problem workstation. This is tedious and time consuming—and time is of the essence for a LAN administrator. Soon after concentrators came into common use, the demand for more intelligence started to grow.

On Ethernet LANs, hubs were used to connect more devices to the LAN bus. Token ring and Ethernet are distinct access technologies, but the uses for concentrators and the common drawbacks to their use are pretty much the same for both access methods. With a supply push from both major business networking technologies, improvements in concentrator design and function weren't long in coming. Enter intelligent hubs.

HUB DETAILS

Earlier implementations of Ethernet involved snaking cabling through the walls of buildings, connecting one workstation or network device to another in a daisy chain that eventually brought together all of the separate segments. After all this trouble to make the physical connections, powering up the server and workstations often produced no kind of LAN at all. Network functionality was prevented by cabling faults, misconnections, and other problems related to physical links.

Hubs were designed to eliminate this daisy chain of nodes and devices and make troubleshooting easier. Hubs, by design, provide a single connection between each workstation and the hub. The connection is typically made over twisted pair cabling. A problem in the wiring affects only a single workstation instead of bringing down an entire network segment of multiple workstations. Figure 25.1 depicts early Ethernet implementations

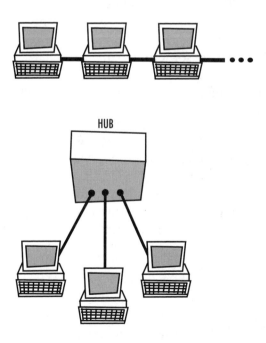

Figure 25.1   *Daisy chain vs. hub connection of workstations.*

using daisy chains of workstations, compared to a hub connecting multiple workstations.

The first hub implementations consisted of eight ports, allowing eight workstation connections. If more workstations needed to be connected, another hub was connected into the first one. Daisy chaining hubs involved shelling out more money for additional chassis, electrical components, and so forth. As LANs grew in popularity and average size, modular hub chassis were introduced. These permitted additional hub modules to plug in to a single chassis and eliminated the need for separate electrical equipment, cutting out some of the cost of extending LANs by combining hubs.

Hub Types

In its most basic form, a hub is a box that connects together wiring from workstations. Early hubs, still used in LAN architectures today, were of two basic types: active and passive. A passive hub houses a few ports for workstations but has no electrical connections. Therefore, a passive hub cannot regenerate the signals that it receives; it merely passes them along. An active hub has electrical connections as well as ports and can regenerate the signals it receives. This ability to rebroadcast signals from the hub is why hubs are sometimes called *repeaters*.

As hub design progressed, additional features and uses were defined for them. Intelligent and enterprise hubs include such additional features.

- Intelligent hubs provide features like fault tolerance, remote management capabilities, Simple Network Management Protocol (SNMP) support, and backplanes with multiple buses and multiple media type support.
- Enterprise hubs incorporate all of the features of intelligent hubs, with the addition of switching and high-speed backbone capabilities.

Let's take a look at the pieces of a hub, then we'll discuss in detail the situations in which we might use each type of hub.

Hub Components

A hub is composed of a chassis, backplane, modules, management software, wiring, and power supplies. Figure 25.2 shows the components of a hub.

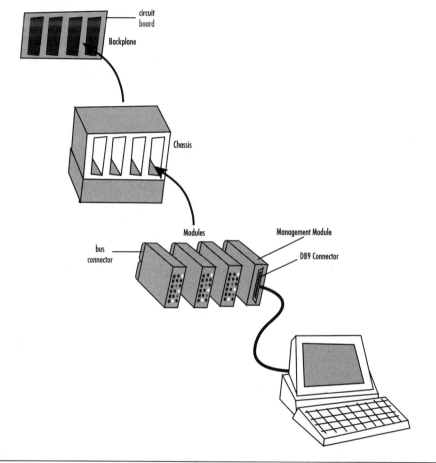

Figure 25.2 *Components of a hub.*

Chassis

The chassis is the box that houses all the hub parts. It includes connections for the power supply and for additional hub modules. If a chassis only has a four-slot capacity, then it is limited to four module cards that can be inserted to provide for multihub connections. If a chassis has eight slots, obviously the capacity is doubled.

Backplane

The backplane is the brains of the hub. Just as the name suggests, the backplane is located at the back of the hub. It is similar in concept to a motherboard of a PC but much smarter and faster than a motherboard. All the module slots plug directly into the backplane, which serves as the bus for the entire hub. A hub's bus can be configured as follows:

1. *Standard bus*. This bus can be an MCA or EISA bus into which each module is plugged. The modules then must generate an interrupt to get onto the bus. These buses are generally found on hubs where only one network type, like token ring or Ethernet is needed.

2. *Multiple bus*. This bus has more than one bus on the backplane into which modules can be plugged. Only one type of traffic can be carried on each bus. A multiple bus backplane has two or more buses that are physically separate. For example, a multiple hub could have three buses on the backplane, one bus for Ethernet, one bus for token ring, and one bus for FDDI. When an Ethernet module is plugged into the backplane, it plugs only into the Ethernet bus. The same is true for the token ring and FDDI modules.

3. *Segmented bus*. This type of bus is segmented and then tied together with common connectors. Ports on one module card can be connected logically with ports on other module cards via the backplane, as long as the ports being connected are of the same network type. For example, port 5 on Ethernet module card 1 can become part of a LAN segment with port 7 on Ethernet module card 3. Because the module cards must be of the same network type, port 5 on token ring module card 2 cannot become part of a LAN segment with port 7 on Ethernet module card 4. Segmenting the ports is this manner connects the ports so that they share the same network address.

4. *Multiplexed bus*. This bus provides much the same capabilities as the segmented bus but is different in that it is a single bus logically divided into several buses, with each bus being a separate channel. So, each module plugs into the one bus on the backplane, and the bus is logically segmented into channels by multiplexing.

Modules

Modules are also known as *cards*. They slide into the hub and plug into the backplane. Each module generally has anywhere from 8 to 24 RJ-45 connectors that provide the workstation connections. Modules come in different types:

- Ethernet,
- token ring,
- bridge,
- router,
- FDDI and
- management cards.

Housed on each card are status lights for the module as well as individual port lights. The module lights represent things like ring speed for token ring cards, and port lights represent a port's status. The usual standard for the lights is green for active okay status, yellow for inactive okay status, and red for trouble status.

These indicator lights are useful if you are looking at them in a wiring closet. However, most LAN administrators are all over the building or campus and spend very little time in closets until stress really starts to become a problem. To isolate and correct faults, and to provide more proactive management, network administrators look to management software.

Management Module and Software

Most hubs provide a management slot and a management card that can be configured either through a terminal connection or through a workstation with management software. A management card provides information on the segmentation of a hub, if any, and also operates on its own bus to interact with a backplane to gather statistical information about hub performance.

Managing a hub from a Windows-based workstation PC is the optimal choice. Information about multiple hubs can be gathered and analyzed from one location. In addition, hubs can be configured from a workstation PC instead of going to each hub individually, which can be undesirable in large campus environments. In fact, it is undesirable even in hubs separated by floors contained in one building because it requires a trip to each wiring closet every time there is a change in configuration.

Hub management software is generally SNMP-compliant and writes information to MIB databases. Each device in the network is given a TCP/

IP. Each device writes information to an MIB, which is then collected by the central management software. The LAN administrator can set certain threshold levels in the software that will generate an alert if the threshold is reached or exceeded. This is extremely helpful to the administrator when trying to analyze network segments for traffic and congestion or deciding whether or not to further divide a network segment.

Wiring

Wiring plays an important role in hubs because the wiring is what connects the workstations to the hubs. Wiring and cabling is covered in detail in Chapters 1 through 4. You should refer to those chapters for specifics on cable length and troubleshooting. In this chapter, our focus is on connecting the workstation wiring to the hub. This is typically done using a patch panel that has wiring receptacles on one side and RJ-45 connectors on the other side. This is so that the wiring—twisted-pair cabling, for example—can be punched down permanently into the back of the patch panel from the workstations. On the front side, jumper cables are used to connect the patch panel to the hub. Using jumper cables to move workstation connections requires only unplugging the cable and then replugging it into another plug.

Without patch panels, each time a workstation is moved, wires have to be physically moved and repunched with a punchdown tool. Using a patch panel adds an additional connection in the wire, which will cause a small dB loss in signal, but the advantages outweigh this negligible loss.

If you plan to connect workstations to a patch panel using twisted-pair cabling, it is recommended that twists in the cable be maintained all the way to the back of the patch panel. Because the back of a patch panel may connect wires for 96 ports, there can be a lot of crosstalk, along with all its related problems, if the twists are not maintained per the specification.

Power Supplies

All hubs, except the most basic passive hubs, have at least one power supply. Intelligent hubs often have more than one power supply for fault tolerance. If one power supply fails, the hub switches over to the second power supply with no interruption or downtime for the hub. Generally, the power supplies are hot-swapable, which means you can replace the bad power supply without turning off the hub. This can be a significant and necessary feature if your shop works 24 hours, 7 days a week!

Tip:
As a general rule, hubs should be located on an isolated circuit, with an uninterrupted power supply (UPS) connected. Many times, in buildings, the power can go out, causing failures in the cards or the hub itself. A UPS will provide the hub with an uninterrupted power supply until the power is restored. Some computer rooms are equipped with a systemwide UPS system like a Liebert system. If you're lucky enough to have one of these in the building, you can tie in the hubs on each floor to the computer room UPS system. You can still buy UPSs—just use the cheapest and most reliable method.

Get the Right Hub!

As we discussed earlier, there are several hub types: basic, intelligent and switching hubs. Let's take a look at typical scenarios where you might use each hub.

Basic Hub

A basic hub is generally used in very small companies where the workstations and file server total less than 20 or so devices and where only one media type like Ethernet or token ring is used.

In medium to larger companies, this hub can be used if the organization is divided into departments that typically don't share data. For example, the marketing department might have its own file server and several workstations that need to talk only with each other but not with the finance department.

Intelligent Hub

This type of hub is used in medium to large organizations where twisted-pair cabling connects workstations to a wiring closet hub. Each hub in a wiring closet is then connected to some sort of backbone hub which is usually located in a central computer room. The topology described in this example is quite common, but wiring structures may vary considerably between organizations.

One of the main reasons network administrators add intelligent hubs in networks is the central management capability they provide. Being able to gather statistics down to the port level from a hub located several floors away is obviously much easier than traveling to each wiring closet. Statistics coming back from the hubs provide more information to the network administrator so that he or she can determine the best way to segment the traffic on congested LANs without have to make subjective decisions or use complicated protocol analyzers.

Another reason to add intelligent hubs to a network design is to add support for additional media types. The addition of a backplane with multiple buses to the intelligent hub provides the ability to mix media types in one chassis.

Enterprise Hub

An enterprise hub is designed to incorporate all the networking needs of an organization. This includes all the features of intelligent hubs plus a few additional capabilities. These hubs typically have built-in redundancy, advanced management capabilities, switching ability, and very high-speed backbones and buses. Hub vendors have begun implementing ATM switching capabilities in their enterprise hubs for high-speed transmission.

Switching in a hub incorporates all of the features of an intelligent hub and an enterprise hub. Switching provides port-to-port segmentation and bridging circuitry so that each port can act as a separate LAN segment and use the entire bandwidth available to that segment. Because each port can talk directly to another port using this special bridging circuitry, without having to go through a backbone, individual ports need not worry about access or contention on the bus. Implementations other than switching require a bridging module that must talk to a backbone device. This process is much slower and does not isolate the LAN down to the port level.

What Should I Look for in a Hub?

We recommend that if you plan to purchase a hub, your first step is to sit down and put on paper what your networking needs are right now. For example, there is no need to add multiple media capability if your organization uses only Ethernet. Step 2 is to carefully examine the future expected use of hubs in your organization. For example, if you plan to migrate to

ATM capability, then it is best to purchase hubs that include that functionality now, rather than upgrade or purchase new hubs later.

Tip:
We recommend the following minimum features you should look for in a hub. To these, add your organization's specific needs, and you will have a good plan for hub integration.

1. *RJ-45, AUI, and BNC Connectors.* These are absolutely essential. They allow you to physically change the ports on a network easily, as well as provide backbone-type connections. The more interface connections supported, the more flexibility you will have.

2. *Four to Eight Slots.* Eight slots is preferable because it allows room for future growth and addition of workstations, but four slots is acceptable where not much growth is expected.

3. *Multiple Media Type.* It should support Ethernet, token ring, and FDDI connections.

4. *UTP and Fiber Support.* Because many organizations employ twisted pair cabling horizontally, connected to fiber runs vertically, it is preferable to have dual capability at the time of purchase. If fiber proves to be too expensive now, its costs may lower significantly as it becomes more common, and you want to be ready to plug in.

5. *Management Capabilities.* Take a good look at the management software and make a checklist of the various reporting capabilities that can be gathered. If the management software is limited in what it can report, there is no point in buying hardware that you can't keep an eye on. It's a good idea to balance the network topology and the capabilities of your net management software.

6. *Hot Swapable Parts.* Even if you're sure your hub is not mission critical, parts are certain to fail during business hours! If a card fails then, you not only have 16 users down, you have to take down the whole hub along with all the other connected users, just to swap out the card. Keeping things up and running is an excellent reason to buy hot-swapping capability.

Special Hub Features

The following special features can be found on either intelligent or enterprise hubs. Basic hubs provide none of these features.

Bridging Modules

These modules can replace PC-based bridges that operate very slowly—in the area of 3,000 packets per second (pps). Bridge modules can cost around $6,000 and can increase the pps threefold, up to around 10,000 pps.

Print Server Modules

Remote offices managed from a central location can use print server cards in their hubs. This is an excellent idea for a remote office where no network administrator is present. Remote office personnel need not fiddle with the components of the print server or even configure it. Everything can be done remotely by an experienced network administrator.

The physical wiring of the hub has to be done locally, as well as connection of the printer(s) to the print server module. Because distance is a factor, if a remote office spans more than one floor, some care must be given in designing this type of configuration.

File Server Modules

Like print server modules, file server modules are ideal for remote offices and small businesses. Because backplanes can be segmented, the file server can be configured as a separate backbone.

Router Modules

Sometimes bridging cards and router cards are combined so that a single card can provide bridging or routing functions. For organizations where space is at a premium, this option can provide a nice compact way to organize the network. Additionally, router vendors like Cisco and Bay Networks are working in conjunction with the hub vendors to provide hooks into one another. Bay Networks Corp. is the product of a merger between a router company (Wellfleet) and a hub company (Synoptics).

Fault Tolerance

Depending on the mission critical role of a hub in an organizational LAN, fault tolerance can play an extremely important role. One feature of fault tolerance offered by vendors is multiple power supplies. As discussed earlier, this permits one power supply to keep a hub running in the event that another power supply fails.

In addition to keeping a hub from powering down, hot-swapable parts are available so that changing failed components does not require turning off the hub.

Hub Costs

The cost of a hub generally consists of the chassis, the module cards, the management station, and the cabling. Those costs show up on purchase orders and paper.

When you buy a hub, the obvious costs like chassis, module cards, management station, and cabling are going to show up as line items on the purchase order and the invoice. These costs are bad enough, but the ones that don't show up on paper—the hidden costs—can really jump up and bite you. Examples of hidden costs are required training, installation, maintenance, and any additional wiring components needed.

Training. The training issue is an often overlooked item. Intelligent hubs are very sophisticated tools and not simple to set up and learn. Early hub and concentrator administration didn't involve things like SNMP, MIBs, TCP/IP, or autodiscovery on networks. But these all come out to play in intelligent hubs. Administrators should plan on attending a two-day structured training course offered by the vendor, which probably will add significant costs to the basic purchase order.

Installation. Installation is another tricky item. Many computer room wiring technicians are dying to get their feet wet with this new technology. Nevertheless we recommend that you pay a little extra for the vendor's trained technicians to complete the first hub installation. Your wiring guru can watch, learn, and go for coffee while learning the proper connection methods. This first installation can serve as a model for those that come after.

Wiring workstations. Wiring can seem like an unnecessary item in the hub installation but can prove to be a major consideration later. For example, let's say your plan is to, among other things, use the hub as a repeater so that you can run workstations to the hub at 100 Mb/sec over twisted-pair cabling. To run at 100 Mb/sec over twisted pair requires each connection in the run to be rated at Category 5 wiring.

Gotcha:

If your overall hub installation plan does not include replacing the wall receptacles in each office with Category 5 rated receptacles, you may have to ask for additional money later. In addition, the patch panels that will be used must also be rated for Category 5 wiring. The point is this—consider your wiring.

Maintenance. You might not consider maintenance of network parts a hidden cost. But, if you don't address specific issues of maintenance up front and get an itemized cost, issues can pop up later that have to be addressed. So, let's address them now so there will be no surprises later on.

Consider this: Will you purchase all your equipment and have it shipped up front, or will you purchase the equipment just in time for the installations. Let's say that you plan to purchase and ship all of the equipment at once and then perform successive installations. If the equipment has a 90-day warranty and your installations take more than 90 days, you could end up with untested equipment no longer covered by warranty. Be sure that you know your warranty before purchasing, and make sure every piece of equipment is in place and has been tested before time runs out.

Gotcha:

Will you keep some hot spares in your organization? If so, some vendors offer a different maintenance rate for hot spares. They know that the spares are not powered up all the time. If your organization is large enough, it behooves you to keep at least one set of hot spares around, or find another company in your area and work out some sort of mutual support agreement.

Some local wiring organizations keep a warehouse of hub components and will offer you a cheaper maintenance agreement. Sometimes this is very appealing if these companies are often in a 60-mile radius to your organization. This is a cheaper alternative to housing hot spares, but be sure to ask the company if its warehouse of parts is available after hours and on weekends. After all, some parts do break on the weekend! In addition, ask the vendor what is the turnaround time on its shelf items. There's no point in saving five percent of a maintenance contract from the hub vendor by going with someone local only to find out that the local parts are six months old and might not work with your state of the art equipment!

Of course the ideal setup would be to have a standardized setup so that you could maintain just one set of hot spares for each component. However, we've yet to see an organization that is standardized like that!

So before we go onto the hardware costs, let's summarize a plan to make sure you've addressed the hidden costs and minimized the need for additional funds at a later date.

Plan to Address Hidden Cost Items up Front

1. Hold a meeting with the following persons: telecommunications chief, wiring specialist, LAN administrator. In this meeting, blueprints or floorplans should be included in the discussion and should detail the current wiring and electrical connectivity. The wiring technician should be able to provide these details.

2. All persons in the meeting should be advised of future plans for the hubs, the purpose the hubs will serve, and possible installation and training dates. For example, if the hub will house a router, the telecommunications person needs to be advised and available for training.

3. Ask the wiring technician to look at the blueprints and see if you have overlooked any connection issues that relate to category levels and so on. The wiring technician should trace a typical path on the diagrams from the workstation through the walls and ceilings to the wiring closet or computer room to see if any additions or changes will be needed. See Figure 25.3 for an example.

4. Obtain an accurate count of the number of workstations that will be connected to the hub or hubs if you're in a medium to large company. Factor in future expansion plans or possible growth of the number of employees needing workstations to your count. Sometimes this employee count is the hardest number to estimate. Human Resources is usually reluctant to give out this number. A good rule of thumb is to add 10% to your current number of workstations. Also, don't forget to count your server devices and bridge devices if they are already existing as PCs.

5. Discuss installation with everyone involved.

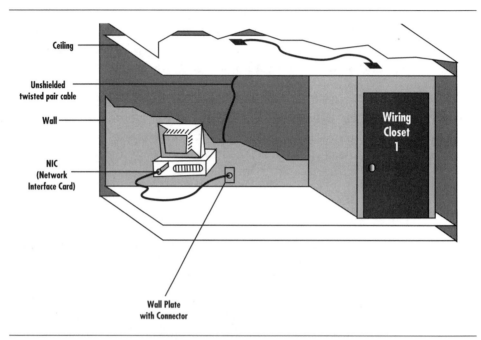

Figure 25.3 header labels:
- Ceiling
- Unshielded twisted pair cable
- Wall
- NIC (Network Interface Card)
- Wiring Closet 1
- Wall Plate with Connector

Figure 25.3   *Wiring schematic from workstation to computer room.*

Gotcha:

Don't forget that installing hubs means that you'll have to reconnect workstations to new patch panels, and that's going to entail disconnecting the workstations. This means workstation downtime, so we recommend that you plan the installation for weekends and advise the users. If you have 50 nodes per floor or so, we recommend that you do one floor per weekend, then test each node afterwards. Weekend work can sometimes involve overtime pay, so don't forget to factor this into your overall cost. Trying to save money by installing all nodes over few weekends may end up costing more in the long run. Our advice is to leave a fair amount of time per installation that leaves some breathing space for testing and troubleshooting.

6. Do your homework before meeting with the vendors.

Gotcha:

Not to make vendors sound bad, but they can eat you alive with unnecessary items if they feel they've found someone green around the ears. Okay, we admit, there are still a few good vendors out there looking out for your best interests, but it's still easier to plan for the worst than hope for the best.

7. Now that you have covered these topics, it's time to hold a meeting with your vendors to explore their technologies and costs. Don't forget to include the telecommunications and wiring specialists in the meeting. They will provide invaluable insights that you might not think of. Do not try to play expert in this installation by omitting key people from important decision making meetings!

Nonhidden Costs (Hardware)

Let's take a look at the hub costs that weren't discussed yet. We can break them into low-end, medium-end and high-end costs. We searched through information from several competing vendors and provide these tables merely to point out costs associated with features. Table 25.1, Table 25.2 and Table 25.3 do not include vendor-specific items that may factor into the cost (such as management software, if available). Also, these are selected samples and each vendor can provide you with complete information that will meet your needs.

Product	Lattis System 3000	MMAC-M3FNB	LinkBuilder MSH (3C18000)
List Price	$1,095–$6,195	$825–$1,995	$3,195
Number of Devices Supported	10	65	240
Networks Supported	FDDI, E, TR	FDDI, E, TR	E, TR
IEEE Standards Supported	802.3 and 5, 10BaseT	802.3 and 5, 10Base2, 5, T & FL	802.3 and 5, 10Base2, 5 & T
LAN Speeds Supported	4, 10, 16, 100 Mbps	4, 10, 16, 100 Mbps	4, 10, 16 Mbps
Interfaces Supported	DB-9, MIC, RJ-45	AUI, BNC, RJ-45, DB-9, SMA, ST, MIC	AUI, BNC, RJ-45, DB-9, ST

Table 25.1   *Low-end hub costs (under $10,000).*

Company	Bay Networks	Optical Data Systems	3Com
Product	Lattis Switch System 28115	ODS 1085-8	LANplex 5004 Switching Hub
List Price	$16,950	$13,800	$16,800
Number of Devices Supported	18	8	8000
Networks Supported	E	FDDI	E, FDDI
IEEE Standards Supported	802.3, 10BaseT		10Base T & FL
LAN Speeds Supported	10, 100 Mbps	100 Mbps	10 and 100 Mbps
Interfaces Supported	RJ-45	MIC	AUI, 50-pin Telco, RJ-45, ST, MIC

Table 25.2   *Medium-range hub costs ($10,000–$20,000).*

Product	Lattis System 3000	MMAC-M3FNB	LinkBuilder MSH(3C18000)
List Price	$1,095–$6,195	$825–$1,995	$3,195
Number of Devices Supported	10	65	240
Networks Supported	FDDI, E, TR	FDDI, E, TR	E, TR
IEEE Standards Supported	802.3 and 5, 10BaseT	802.3 and 5, 10Base2, 5, T & FL	802.3 and 5, 10Base2, 5 & T
LAN Speeds Supported	4, 10, 16, 100 Mbps	4, 10, 16, 100 Mbps	4, 10, 16 Mbps
Interfaces Supported	DB-9, MIC, RJ-45	AUI, BNC, RJ-45, DB-9, SMA, ST, MIC	AUI, BNC, RJ-45, DB-9, ST

Table 25.3   *Low-end Hub costs (Under $10,000).*

Company	Optical Data Systems	Cabletron	3Com
Product	ODS 1090	FDCDMIM-34	LANplex 6021 Switching Hub
List Price	$21,425	$25,950	$31,900
Number of Devices Supported	42	4	8000
Networks Supported	FDDI	FDDI	E, FDDI
IEEE Standards Supported			10Base 5 and T
LAN Speeds Supported	100 Mbps	100 Mbps	100 Mbps
Interfaces Supported	MIC	MIC	AUI, 50-pin Telco, RJ-45, ST, MIC

Table 25.4   *High-end Hub costs ($20,000 and higher).*

HUB AND CONCENTRATOR RESOURCES: BIBLIOGRAPHY AND STRATEGIES

For general networking references, please consult Appendix C, "A List of Networking Resources." The magazines and other publications listed there can help you find out lots of information about hubs and concentrators. The following references are particularly helpful for the information they contain about hubs and concentrators.

Derfler, Frank, Jr. and Les Freed. *How Networks Work.*
Ziff-Davis Press, Emeryville, CA: 1993. An illustration and example-intensive description of how networks actually operate. It includes good discussions of most basic networking components, including NICs. $24.95.

Derrick, Dan. *Network Know-How: Concepts, Card and Cables.*
Osborne McGraw-Hill, Berkeley, CA: 1994. A good source of general networking information. At $19.95, it's a useful addition to any networking professional's library, even if only to lend to newbie users.

Lowe, Doug. *Networking for Dummies.*
IDG Books Worldwide, Indianapolis: 1994. This is a good gentle introduction to networking. At $19.95, it's a useful addition to any networking professional's library, even if only to lend to newbie users.

Newton, Harry. *Newton's Telecom Dictionary*, 7th. ed.
Flatiron Publishing Company, New York: 1994. Harry Newton is a towering field in the telecommunications industry, and his dictionary isn't bad either. Even though it purports to be telecom specific, it's one of the best sources for looking up PC-related acronyms, standards, and other terms that we've ever found anywhere. At $24.95 for 1,200 pages of text, it's a bargain to boot!

Sheldon, Tom. *The LAN Times Encyclopedia of Networking*.
Osborne McGraw Hill, Berkeley, CA.: 1994. A general sourcebook for networking terms and technologies. It includes discussions, some lengthy and detailed, about nearly every conceivable networking topic. $39.95.

TOP FIVE VENDORS

Bay Networks, Inc.
4401 Great America Pkwy., PO Box 58185
Santa Clara, CA 95054
800-776-6895; 408-988-2400
FAX: 408-988-5525
Tech support: 800-473-4911

Cabletron Systems, Inc.
35 Industrial Way, PO Box 5005
Rochester, NH 03867-0505
800-332-9401; 603-332-9400
FAX: 603-337-2211
Tech support: Use toll-free no.
Tech support BBS: 603-335-3358

Chipcom Corp.
118 Turnpike Rd., Southborough Office Park
Southborough, MA 01772-1886
800-228-9930; 508-460-8900
FAX: 508-460-8950
Tech support: Use main no.

3Com Corp. (Switching Division)
85 Rangeway Rd.
North Billerica, MA 01862-9943
800-992-2446; 508-670-9009

FAX: 508-670-9015
Tech support: Use toll-free no.

Optical Data Systems, Inc.
1101 E. Arapaho Rd.
Richardson, TX 75081-2336
214-234-6400
FAX: 214-234-1467
Tech support: Use main no.

ROUTERS, BRIDGES, AND GATEWAYS

BASIC OVERVIEW

What Is Internetworking?

By definition, an internetwork is a "network of networks." Internetworking devices are needed to connect disparate LANs and remote offices into a single, seamless network system that behaves like one large logical network. The need to share data across multiple platforms as well as span multiple locations has spurred the growth of internetworking products to keep pace with ever-increasing demand.

Bridges, routers, and gateways are internetworking products that can connect LANs, WANs, and MANs, to enable users to share data across multiple platforms.

What is the Open Systems Interconnection Model?

The Open Systems Interconnection (OSI) model is a data communications standard that promotes interoperability among different vendors' communication equipment. The OSI model has seven layers, with layer 1 the lowest. Layer 7, the highest layer, serves as an interface with the user and layer 1 and with the hardware. In this chapter, we will focus on layers 2 through 7, also known as the data, network, and application layers. Layer 1, the physical layer, is covered in other chapters.

You may find it helpful to refer back to Chapter 15 where the OSI model is discussed in depth before continuing with this chapter. Because internetworking devices work at certain layers of the OSI model, we recommend you develop a good understanding of these layers and the roles they play in networking.

In this chapter, we cover internetworking concepts from the standpoint of three basic devices:

- *Bridges* are devices that connect and pass packets between networks. They operate at the second layer of the OSI model, also known as the *data link layer*. Bridges are media dependent but protocol independent.

- *Routers* are devices that connect two or more LANs, each with its own network addresses. Routers operate at the third layer of the OSI model, also known as the *network layer*. They are protocol dependent but media independent. Until recently, purchasing a router was a fairly simple choice since two competitors garnered most of the market share—Cisco and Wellfleet. In 1994, Wellfleet and Synoptics both merged to form Bay Systems Network, Inc. Other companies like 3Com and IBM have marketed and sold routers, but were not as pervasive in the marketplace as Cisco and Wellfleet. Today, the choice is more complex as internetworking technologies converge and more vendors merge their organizations.

- *Gateways* are devices that connect networks and translate between protocols or applications. They operate at the top four layers of the OSI model. If your organization has a mainframe, you may already use a gateway. A gateway can convert data formatted for the mainframe into data that the LAN can read and vice versa. A gateway is needed to convert the mainframe protocol and data into the LAN protocol. A user would receive garbage if there was no gateway between the two.

BRIDGES

In this section, it may be helpful to think of a bridge that connects an island to the mainland. Without the bridge, the island people could not travel by car to the mainland. In the data communications world, two LANs cannot communicate with one another without some type of link between them.

This link can be a bridge that sits between the two networks and passes packets back and forth. The type of bridge you use depends on the size and location of the networks in your organization.

Why Use a Bridge?

If you have a small office, you may be wondering why even use a bridge. There are several reasons for using bridges, even if your LAN has only 50 nodes or less.

- *Expand distance of a LAN.* Adding one bridge that connects two networks of similar length effectively doubles the total span of a network.

- *Expand the number of nodes on a LAN.* Token ring networks have a 72 node limitation on each ring. Bridging rings together separates the LAN traffic as well as increases the number of nodes. For example, if you have two rings you can bridge them together and increase the total node count to 144 nodes.

- *Segment LAN traffic.* Tying together network segments A and B with a bridge keeps traffic on each segment separate. If a packet on segment A has a destination address of segment B, only then does the packet travel across the bridge to segment B. Segment A's traffic will always stay on Segment A unless there is a request to deliver a packet to Segment B. Sometimes it takes some analysis to know what the traffic patterns are on a network and how best to segment the LAN.

- *Link unlike LANs together* (i.e., Ethernet and token ring). Ethernet and token ring networks can be bridged together but require special translating bridges like IBM's 8209 bridge. The reason for the translation type bridge is that the packet structures of Ethernet and token ring differ in size as well as in other topology. In an Ethernet to token ring bridge, the bridge takes the Ethernet packet data and repackages the data in a token ring format before passing it on and vice versa.

How Does a Bridge Work?

A bridge looks at each packet's media access control (MAC) destination address and decides whether it should forward the packet onto the next segment. The data link layer of the OSI model is divided into two sublayers: the MAC sub-layer and the logical link control (LLC) sublayer. Devices that support the MAC specifications of the IEEE 802 standard can be bridged with other devices that conform to the 802 standard.

Bridges link together network segments that have the same network address. A bridge on a network examines each packet and stores the packet's source address in its cache. The bridge then looks at the packet's destination address and compares it with the addresses in its cache. If a match is found, the bridge forwards the packet onto the interface specified by the address, unless the packet originated from the same address. In that case, the bridge discards the packet, assuming that it was a bad packet going in circles. If the bridge does not find the address in its cache, the bridge forwards the packet onto all of the interfaces except for the interface where the packet originated.

What Does a Bridge Do?

1. *Frame forwarding.* As we discussed earlier, a bridge looks at each packet and determines whether the packet should be forwarded to the next segment. If a packet on Segment A is addressed to a station on Segment A, the bridge does not let the packet pass, which keeps the locally addressed traffic from flooding the network.

2. *Loop resolution.* Some bridges are able to detect and stop a packet that is looping endlessly in a large LAN implementation.

3. *Learning addresses and table updates.* Older LAN administrators may remember the old days when bridges required manual entry of station addresses! Now, bridges build their own address tables by examining packets that pass through them as well as learning the addresses from explorer packets that travel through and learn the network routes.

Types of Bridging

Local

A local bridge links two network segments at a local site or within the same building. We have been discussing local bridging thus far in this chapter. Local bridging for small networks is as simple as putting two network cards in a PC, loading the bridge software, and naming the segments. In larger networks, local bridging can become more complex and lead to problems like looping bridges.

Remote

A remote bridge links two network segments at different sites, using either analog links with modems or leased digital links like T1 lines. Remote bridging can be a less expensive alternative to routing, if traffic is not heavy over the wire or if you're linking only two locations. However, a router might be more practical for linking multiple locations, providing backup links and satisfying heavy traffic needs.

Methods of Bridging

Transparent Bridging

Transparent bridging was developed by DEC and later adopted by IEEE's 802.1 committee. With transparent bridging, seen only in Ethernet topologies, the bridge starts learning and building its address tables as soon as it is powered up. It does this by examining every packet that it receives. It then takes the source address of a received packet and adds that address to its cache table. The bridge repackages the packets destined for a different segment before sending them on.

Transparent bridging uses a discovery process if it cannot find a packet's destination address in its cache table. In this discovery process, a bridge sends out a discovery packet to all LANs except the originating packet's LAN. The destination node sends back address information to the bridge and the bridge updates its cache table. Eventually, a bridge will learn the address of every node on a network using a combination of learning and discovering.

Source Route Bridging

Source route bridging is found in the IBM world. Unlike transparent bridges, source route bridges do not hold address information of the nodes on a network. Instead, source route bridges hold address information of other bridges in a network. Nodes hold path information and tell a bridge the path a packet should take to get to a destination node.

A node sends out an explorer packet to determine the path a packet should take to get to a destination node. If there are multiple routes, multiple explorer packets are sent out by the source node to the destination node. The destination node receives the explorer packets and responds to each packet by sending packets back to the source node. The source node then looks at the packets it receives back from the destination node and determines which of those packets contains information on the best path. Once the path is determined, the bridge stores the path information in its cache table for future use.

Source routing requires a workstation terminate-and-stay resident (TSR) and a server capable of source routing, In NetWare environments, this requires a ROUTE.COM command to be loaded at the workstation and a ROUTE.NLM to be loaded on the file server. If the TSR is not loaded on the workstation, it will not connect properly to the file server because it can't find the server. If the workstation has the TSR loaded, but it's not needed because a different type of bridging is used, the workstation will work for a while and then crash. This is important to know in environments that use mixed bridging where there are a lot of moves, additions, and changes in the network topology. Moving workstations requires the network administrator to check each PC's configuration after it is moved to make certain that the correct bridging method is run on the workstation.

Bridges and Tolls

Tip:
On the low end of the bridge spectrum, bridge software can be purchased for $500 or less. Add to that the cost of the PC to run the software and handle the traffic. We recommend only 486-based processors and 32-bit NIC cards if your organization can afford that. The faster your bridge can process packets, the less congestion and lost packets your network will have.

On the high end of the spectrum, bridges can be installed as cards in hubs like Cabletron's bridge modules. These types of bridges require no software because everything is contained on the hub card. The bridges can be configured through a terminal-type connection directly to the hub, or if desired, software can be purchased to manage the hubs as well as the bridge cards in the hubs. These bridge cards in hubs generally cost about $6,000. The hub cost is additional and will depend on the vendor and the topologies in use.

ROUTERS

Routers work at the network layer of the OSI model and have more capabilities and processing power than bridges. Routers can be found mostly in WAN environments, linking sites to one another. Because they have more intelligence and flexibility than bridges, routers can make decisions about the routes that a packet will take to get to its destination.

Why Use a Router?

There are several reasons why your organization may want to use a router to connect networks together. Let's take a look at some major router functions.

Collapsed Backbone

A router can be used to form what's called a collapsed backbone. This was not practical until several years ago when companies like Cisco began adding multiport cards in routers. Prior to that, routers and cards had a one-to-one relationship that permitted only one LAN segment to use a router card. Early routers had limited slots, so this method of linking network segments became cost prohibitive since larger LANs would require multiple routers.

Now, with quad-port cards, 16 or more networks can be linked together. Routing packets is much more efficient than using a bridge, because routers have more intelligence for uses like multiprotocol translation and frame filtering.

To Link LAN Sites

In our previous case study, remote offices in New York, Florida, and Chicago are linked together with routers and leased lines. The remote sites log onto the HOU-1 file server in Houston and transfer data easily. As new upgrades to software on the routers at the remote sites becomes necessary, the network administrator in the Houston office can simply download the upgrade to the routers using the flash memory download capability.

To Service Multiprotocol Needs

Although bridges can pass multiple protocols between them, they cannot filter out and route protocols in any type of manner. Routers can filter out packets by protocol and routers can allow a backbone in a WAN to consist of only one protocol. For example, if a WAN links networks that use IPX, TCP/IP, and SNA protocols, the router can encapsulate everything across the WAN link so that all the packets look like TCP/IP.

Speed Considerations

Routers can be setup to determine what the fastest path is for a packet to travel. The path can be determined by the number of hops, the amount of congestion, or other factors. For example, if a packet needs to get to LAN A, and the shortest number of hops is four to get to LAN A, but that path is currently congested, a router is smart enough to route the packet through a path that may take five hops but is less congested. This feature of routers improves the throughput of the network.

Frame Filters

Filtering can be set on a router so that certain frame types or packets do not cross certain routers. For example, the Houston office may not want to accept any TCP/IP packets from the remote sites but may want to receive NetWare's IPX traffic. A router in the Houston office can be set to discard TCP/IP traffic and accept only IPX traffic. In addition, a router can be configured to discard service advertising protocols (SAPs) from other IPX devices like print servers or file servers. This is extremely helpful in a large internetwork where many server type devices are connected and broadcasting themselves.

How Does a Router Work?

Network Layer of the OSI Model

A router operates at the network layer of the OSI model. As discussed earlier, this is layer 3, which interacts with layers 2 and 4. A router does not merely pass packets between LAN A and LAN B but uses its intelligence to determine what packets will move and what route they will take. Unlike bridges, a router connects two LAN segments that have *different* network addresses.

Strips off Physical and Data Link Portions of Packets

A router first strips off the physical and data link portions of the packets it receives and then is able to examine the network layer portion.

Maintain Tables, Look at Packets, Determine Best Route

To determine the best path for a packet to travel, the router has to maintain it's own internal tables. These tables consist of other routers addresses as well as other resources across a network. For example, when a NetWare file server sends out a service advertisement protocol (SAP), that advertisement is sent to all routers on the internetwork that are accepting SAPs. The SAPs from a router are then passed onto a NetWare file server that stores them in memory. A NetWare user can issue an SLIST (server list) command and receive a listing of other NetWare servers available. If a router is not accepting SAPs, then the NetWare server is not updated either, and an SLIST command would return a null string. A router can be configured to deny certain types of SAPs, such as printing SAPs.

A router is most efficient in its ability to determine the best path for a packet to travel. Once the tables are set up, when a packet arrives, the router looks at the destination of the packet and determines what route would be most efficient. This is very useful in congested WANs because the router might find a least congested path even if it is more hop counts.

Filter, Discard, or Pass On

Because a router has processors on board, along with configurable software, it is able to perform some logic and calculations. A router can look at packets, compare the destination and type of packet with the router's configuration, and determine if the packet should be forwarded on to the next router.

A router can look at the hop count in a packet and determine if a packet has reached the 16-hop limit. Routers can discard packets that have reached the limit. This prevents packets from endlessly floating around a network. A router decides that a packet is lost if it reaches its hop count limit and discards the packet.

Single Protocol, Multiprotocol, or Encapsulated Protocol

Routers come in different varieties to serve different needs. Some organizations only use one protocol like IPX or TCP/IP and therefore have no need for a router that can service multiple protocols. A multiprotocol router has software that understands certain protocols. Depending on the vendor, you can purchase a basic router with software, and then add protocols at an extra cost. Most basic routers support the IPX, TCP/IP, Vines IP, and AppleTalk protocols.

Some protocols like NetBIOS are not routable protocols and therefore must be made to look like another protocol. This, called *encapsulation*, is performed by the router. The router takes a NetBIOS packet and adds a header and trailer so that the original packet looks like a TCP/IP packet, which can forwarded through the router. This obviously causes some overhead and is not advisable unless absolutely necessary. Earlier implementations of Lotus Notes supported only NetBIOS not IPX or TCP/IP. Therefore, those organizations using Notes had to encapsulate their NetBIOS data to pass Lotus Notes data back and forth across routers between remote sites.

What Flavor Is That Router?

Routers come in several different forms and can be tailored to meet any organization's needs. Deciding what type of router to purchase is going to depend on your organization's size, distance between sites, number of protocols in use, and amount of traffic. The following describes the most commonly used routers today:

Best Buy:
PC-based with software. This type of router involves a PC with software that can be configured. This is a good route for very small

offices that need a link with other small offices but little change and upgrade to the routers is required.

Best Buy:
External multiprotocol routers. This device looks like a box with ports on it. Companies like Cisco, 3Com and Bay Systems Network sell these types of routers. The basics of these routers come with at least one WAN port, one Ethernet/token ring port, on-board processors, and software. Some of these routers have flash memory that allows administrators to download upgrades to the software on the router across the wire.

- *Internal cards in a hub.* This type of router is similar to the bridge modules except for the way in which they operate. Router cards plug directly into the backplane of the hub and can be configured using a terminal type device or through software loaded on a PC that is connected to the hub.

Minimum Router Requirements

Whether you have a small network or a large one, we recommend the following configuration for a router as the bare minimum:

- two WAN ports (either FDDI, T1, or ISDN)
- two local LAN ports
- multiple processors
- multiprotocol support for at least IPX and TCP/IP

Contents of the Advanced Router

- *Flash memory chips.* These chips provide the capability to download future upgrades to the software in the router directly across the WAN link from a remote site. This is desirable in large organizations that are maintaining remote offices from a centralized site. The router specialist no longer has to travel to the remote site to replace chips.

- *Fault tolerance.* Some routers have extra fault tolerance like dual power supplies. This is recommended in places where a link is considered vital and has to be up and running. If one power supply fails, the other power supply kicks in with no downtime for the router.

- *Hot-swapable parts.* The ability to replace a bad power supply (if using dual power supplies) while the router is up and running is essential in shops that do not close down. The more hot-swapable parts a router has, the greater the flexibility is to change out parts without bringing the network links down.

What Do I Need to Hook up a Router?

The most basic form of hooking up a router consists of the following: communications link (ISDN, leased line), DSU/CSU device, and router software and hardware.

How Do I Manage My Router?

Managing routers used to be somewhat complex. Most WANs have sprouted up in organizations rather than being planned. In some cases, organizations used all one type of router. However, some were not as efficient and have many different types of routers.

The ideal setup is to be consistent with one type of router and have a centralized administration of the routers. Many internetworking devices today are adding simple network management protocol (SNMP) as one way to manage routers. An SNMP agent is loaded onto the router, and information is gathered from the agent as to the status of the router. The information is collected and analyzed from a central location.

A popular product, Network General's Distributed Sniffer is actually an extension of their LAN Sniffer. This device is a protocol analyzer that allows one to examine data at the frame level. Just as this is extremely useful (and sometimes necessary) in the LAN area, so it is helpful in the WAN world. Prior to the distributed Sniffer, the regular Sniffer had to be carried around to each LAN segment to analyze problems.

Companies like HP have written platforms in network management like OpenView. This is a base management system that allows other vendors to write applications to work over OpenView. For example, Cabletron has Lanview, which works over OpenView's platform and has hooks into OpenView.

Cisco Systems has announced an effort to establish its Common Internet-working Topology Initiative (CITI) as a networking standard. CITI proposes to provide a common networking topology standard that allows internetworking devices, network design and optimization tools, and network management platforms from different vendors to share configuration data. This would be helpful to those companies that have a mixture of products instead of a homogeneous environment. A few companies like SunSoft and Cabletron Systems support CITI, but others like HP and Bay Networks are still uncertain.

If You Have to Ask What It Costs ...

At the low end, you can expect to spend $10,000 or less. For smaller organizations, this range's features and functionality might suffice. Here's a sample of what you can purchase in this range: Cisco AccessPro PC card. Each card has either one Ethernet or token ring port, one ISDN BRI port, two synchronous serial ports, and one asynchronous serial port. Price ranges are $2,500 to $4,500 for the card, depending on the features selected. The PC and ISDN monthly lease lines are additional costs.

If you step up to the middle range, prices fall in the area of $10,000-20,000. This range will probably suit most organizations with complex internetworking needs. Mid-range routers provide features like those found in the low end, but with the addition of RISC processors, high-speed buses and backplanes, dial on demand, bandwidth on demand, data compression, and more.

High end routers will run $20,000 or more and probably will be more than most organizations need—unless you're a company like Coca-Cola, Intel, or GM. If you're the network administrator for one of these companies you need to quit reading this and hire some help right now!

GATEWAYS

Gateways operate at the top four layers of the OSI model, converting data from one protocol to another. You can think of a gateway in terms of the language translator sometimes used in television when a speaker on television does not speak the native language. The translator will listen to what the speaker is saying, and then convert the speech into the native language so the listeners can understand what the speaker is saying. A gateway works in a similar manner, taking the information it receives from one source and converting the language or protocol into another source.

Why Use a Gateway?

- *Convert protocols.* Let's say your organization has an IBM mainframe and a NetWare LAN. IBM mainframes use the SNA protocol but NetWare LANs use the IPX protocol. The NetWare LAN expects to see IPX packets and cannot understand SNA packets unless a gateway is used that converts the SNA packets to IPX format.

- *Terminal emulation to a mainframelike host* (3270, 5250, DEC, etc.). There are many ways to perform terminal emulation to a mainframe. One way is to put a gateway between a LAN and a mainframe, with the gateway providing terminal emulation functionality to the LAN-based users.

- *Printing* (IBM world to LAN printer don't have to use IBM 3820 printers). Until several years ago, printing mainframe data required mainframe printers that could understand the print jobs sent from the mainframe. With the advent of gateways like Novell's SAA gateway product, printing to local LAN-based printers became possible. Sometimes modifications or additions need to be added to the mainframe software programs so that they recognize a local printer, but the change is minute and not always needed. Printing to a LAN-based printer eliminates high costs associated with maintaining mainframe laser printers.

How Does a Gateway Work?

As mentioned earlier, a gateway operates at the top four layers of the OSI model. A gateway takes each packet and then repackages it into the protocol desired on the receiving end.

What Types of Gateways Are There?

1. *IBM host.* This type of gateway converts IBM's mainframe SNA protocol to a LAN-based protocol like IPX or AppleTalk. The gateway can optionally provide terminal emulation and printing capabilities.

2. *DEC.* DEC gateways are similar to IBM host gateways except that DEC uses a different protocol (LAT) and therefore the gateway converts LAT protocol to a LAN-based protocol.

3. *TCP/IP, AppleTalk.* These gateways can be LAN-based to LAN-based where an AppleTalk LAN is connected to a Banyan Vines LAN. Because the two speak different protocols, the gateway performs the conversion.

4. *eMail* (X.400). An eMail gateway performs two basic functions: translating messages from the format of one system to the format of another and synchronizing the user directories or mailing lists between two or more messaging systems. For example, if your organization has Microsoft Mail and Lotus cc:Mail, a gateway is needed between the two systems for users to send mail to one another. If your organization has only one vendor's product like cc:Mail, then no gateway is needed.

5. *Communications gateway* (ACS). A communications gateway is popular today on LAN systems for dialing into and out of the LAN. The gateway converts the LAN protocol to a serial protocol that can be transmitted out of the LAN to a service like CompuServe. On the incoming end, the communications gateway receives data in a serial protocol and converts the data to a LAN-based protocol that can be sent across the LAN and interpreted.

6. Basically, these are extensions of the TCP/IP gateway concept (since TCP/IP is the protocol used on the Internet) that provide access to common Internet services—usually, terminal emulation (telnet), file transfer (ftp), e-mail (SMTP or a derivative), or World Wide Web access, by providing links between local applications and their Internet equivalents. Normally, users of such gateways need not support TCP/IP directly, nor do they have to run specific Internet applications.

What Form Does a Gateway Come In?

Gateways generally come in one of two forms: as a PC-based hardware and software combination or a box with a processor.

In the PC form, a board is needed to provide the connectivity, and software is needed to configure the protocols and emulation sessions as they are required. The other gateway form, a device that resembles a box with a processor, is generally used for simple conversion only, with little or no configuration needed (i.e., simple packet conversion but no terminal emulation).

What Does It Cost?

This price is hard to define because much of the cost will depend on the type of gateway, number of gateways, and types of features like terminal emulation and printing needed. The number of nodes will add to the cost in addition to the cost of the hardware.

WHAT TO BUY

The *LAN Times* 1994-1995 Buyers Directory Issue has a terrific listing of routers and bridges with addresses and telephone numbers of the various vendors, as well as a paragraph or more on each product. See the Resources section at the end of this chapter for more details.

TOP VENDORS

Bridges

Cabletron Systems, Inc.
35 Industrial Way, PO Box 5005
Rochester, NH 03867-0505
800-332-9401; 603-332-9400
FAX: 603-337-2211
Tech support: Use toll-free no.
Tech support BBS: 603-335-3358

Bay Networks, Inc.
4401 Great America Pkwy., PO Box 58185
Santa Clara, CA 95054
800-776-6895; 408-988-2400
FAX: 408-988-5525
Tech support: 800-473-4911

IBM (International Business Machines)
Old Orchard Rd.
Armonk, NY 10504
800-426-3333; 914-765-1900
Direct sales: 800-426-7695 (IBM PC Direct)
Tech support: 800-237-5511
Tech support BBS: 919-517-0001; 800-847-7211 (OS2)

Toshiba International Corp.
13131 W. Little York Rd.
Houston, TX 77041

800-231-1412; 713-466-0277

FAX: 713-466-8773
Tech support: Use toll-free no.

Routers

Cisco Systems, Inc.
170 W. Tasman Dr.
San Jose, CA 95134-1706
800-553-6387; 408-526-4000
FAX: 408-526-4100
Tech support: Use toll-free no.

Bay Networks, Inc.
4401 Great America Pkwy., PO Box 58185
Santa Clara, CA 95054
800-776-6895; 408-988-2400

FAX: 408-988-5525
Tech support: 800-473-4911

3Com Corp.
PO Box 58145, 5400 Bayfront Plaza
Santa Clara, CA 95052-8145
800-638-3266; 408-764-5000
FAX: 408-764-5001
Tech support: 800-876-3266
Tech support BBS: 408-980-8204

IBM (International Business Machines)
Old Orchard Rd.
Armonk, NY 10504
800-426-3333; 914-765-1900
Direct sales: 800-426-7695 (IBM PC Direct)
Tech support: 800-237-5511
Tech support BBS: 919-517-0001; 800-847-7211 (OS2)

Hewlett-Packard Co.
3000 Hanover St.
Palo Alto, CA 94304-1181
800-752-0900; 800 387-3867 (CD); 415-857-1501
Direct sales: 800-637-7740 (HP Direct)
FAX: 800-333-1917
Tech support: 800-858-8867
Tech support BBS: 415-852-0256

Gateways

Novell, Inc.
122 East 1700 South
Provo, UT 84606-6194
800-453-1267; 801-429-7000
FAX: 801-429-5155
Tech support: 800-638-9273

Lotus Development Corp.
55 Cambridge Pkwy.
Cambridge, MA 02142-1295
800-343-5414; 617-577-8500
Direct sales: 800-426-7682
FAX: 617-693-3512
Tech support: 800-223-1662
Tech support BBS: 617-693-7000

RESOURCES: BIBLIOGRAPHY AND STRATEGIES

For general networking references, please consult Appendix C, "A List of Networking Resources." The magazines and other publications listed there can help you find out lots of information about bridges, routers, and gateways. The following references are particularly helpful for the information they contain about internetworking.

Perlman, Radia. *Interconnections Bridges and Router.* Addison-Wesley Publishing Company, Reading, MA: 1993. Great detailed book on bridges and routers—down to the packet level.

Williams, Dennis. "A Route to a Bridge Through a Gate: Determining the Best Setup for your Data Communications Interconnectivity." *LAN Times Magazine* 11, no. 17 (September 1994) 58. Excellent article on the definitions of bridges, routers, and gateways.

Merenbloom, Paul. "Your Bridge/Router Selection is Key to a Successful WAN." *Info-World*, 16, no. 18 (May 2, 1994) 90. A good article on building a successful WAN, including how to analyze and project for future needs.

Bridges, Routers, Repeaters (1994–1995 Buyers Directory Issue) *LAN Times Magazine*, 11, no. 18 (September 12, 1994) 43. Includes information on over 300 products in the bridges, router, and repeater area. Information such as company name, product name, phone number, and product description is included.

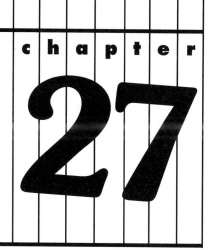

SERVERS: AN INTRODUCTION

NETWORK SERVICES

Personal computers provide an increase in efficiency and give a boost to production, but only for one user at a time. Networks channel that efficiency throughout an enterprise and allow multiple users in all parts of an organization to share their information, therefore can give productivity an even bigger boost. PCs give a user personal power; networks give power to entire organizations.

Networks empower organizations by channeling individual efforts across the enterprise, delivering both information and *services*. Network services are provided by network operating systems that are presented to network users by specialized devices called, appropriately enough, *servers*.

Services provided by networks fall into three very broad classes. They may have to do with *sharing information* through an enterprise. They may be related to *sharing resources* on a network. Or they may deal with communications—handling various methods of communication between or among users or servers—on a network (or attaching to the network from a remote location).

AT YOUR SERVICE

The following chapters describe different kinds of network servers. The workload on a network is shared among the clients, or desktop PCs that typically consume lots of information, and the servers, which provide functions and information to the network. A network is like a skeleton, in fact, so that a diagram of a network can display at least some information about an organization's composition and makeup.

Servers are the organs that make the business function. In other words, they're the heart of the enterprise network, whose job is to keep the information flowing.

The Original Servers

The original computer servers were the first mainframes. Every application, every database, and every file was stored somewhere on a mainframe which could therefore be a very intelligent server, indeed.

If mainframes were smart servers, they were pretty lame in the area of client relations. All processing power and intelligence was used up providing services. Not much was left over to empower the terminals attached to the mainframe. which were often described as *dumb*.

The power and intelligence of a mainframe terminal is minimal. The terminal depends on the mainframe processor for its intelligence, and anyone who's ever used a dumb terminal knows the mainframe doesn't have too much intelligence to spare for those poor brutes.

Peer-to-Peer to Client/Server

The creators of the first mainframes couldn't wait to get them linked up. Early computer developers didn't waste much time coming up with ad hoc access methods that would let their mainframes communicate. There were lots of good reasons for this, but the underlying reasons for mainframe connectivity still hold true in the world of modern distributed computing.

Networking allows information to be shared quickly and easily. Sharing information accelerates the process of obtaining or creating knowledge. Increased knowledge and awareness leads to heightened ability to perform tasks. Increased task performance leads to increased productivity. Increased productivity leads to more profits for the organization.

The bottom line is this: Profits are good!

Peer-to-Peer Networking

These early networks of two or three mainframes were peer-to-peer networks. That is, they all shared access to one another's peripheral devices and files as equals or peers. This was a tremendous leap forward in computing but only the first step toward modern networking.

Not that we've evolved beyond peer-to-peer networking. Peer-to-peer networking remains ideal for small workgroups that focus on a single task or need only basic services, and it is widely used to this day. Novell's Personal NetWare and Microsoft's Windows for Workgroups are just two examples of widely used, modern peer-to-peer network systems. But peer-to-peer networking is limited in the types of service it can provide. And it relies totally on the processing power of the attached stations.

Client/Server Networking

Modern networks, even some mainframe networks, are based on the concept of *clients* and *servers,* both attached to the network. Clients are the desktop computers that users rely on for their output. Clients do most of processing related to the presentation of information. Servers are repositories of information and provide processing-intensive services to their clients. This puts some of the more demanding networking functions on servers, which can be specially configured to take care of these functions elegantly, and frees up clients to spend their processing power in other ways.

That's one of the keys to establishing and running a client/server network. If a majority of the clients on the network are using their processing power for the same function, then that function can be moved to a server. The clients still have access to the function and its benefits, but they don't have to do the required processing. The processing is done by a specially configured server.

Network Servers

Here's a short list of some basic server functions:

- Repository for application programs,
- Repository for data,
- Repository of the network operating system,

- Manager and storage for directories and files,
- Manager for the network.

File Servers

If you have only one server on your network, it perforce fills all these roles. These tasks are usually handled by a *file server*, which acts as the core for such a network. A user can store files on the file server so that others in the organization may access them. The file server appears to its connected users as if it is part of their own personal PC.

You might encounter two categories of file servers. *Dedicated* file servers are standalone computers; they usually have considerable hard disk space for file storage and run specialized file server software. Dedicated servers can also provide file management and be configured to provide file security at different levels of access. *Nondedicated* file servers are the servers you'd find on a peer-to-peer network. Users can allow other network users access to some of the individual files and directories on their hard disk. They have access to certain designated files on their peers' disks.

Dedicated servers run file management software so that clients don't have to. Nondedicated file servers require every attached peer to run the file management software. One of the advantages of dedicated servers is that they take away processing overhead from the clients and handle it themselves. If one or more of a dedicated server's tasks start to take up an inordinate amount of resources, then other file servers can be added to a network to share the load.

Backup Servers

Also called *archive servers*, these machines are optimized for storage of data that must be accessed occasionally but is not critical to dynamic function of the organization. Backup servers use different storage techniques including high density magnetic storage (tape), or optical storage. Software to manage access to and structure of the stored data runs on backup servers. Backup servers may use sophisticated storage techniques and compression utilities to maximize storage space.

Communications Servers

A communications server manages connections between network stations and remote sites that need access to the network. Usually a communications server includes a bank of modems used to provide dial-in and dial-out services for attached users. A communications server may also provide gateway services to a network, translating between different access methods, protocols, and presentation formats. E-mail to remote sites is usually handled by a communications server as well.

Applications Servers

On some networks, applications are not installed on the individual client machines. They are installed, reside, and operate on special servers called *application servers*. Management and control of such applications is certainly simpler when they are centrally located, and it's much easier to establish and control access rights for server-based applications. Updates on an application server need be made once, as opposed to updating every client machine.

Some organizations like this central control, but it has its drawbacks. Performance of networked applications can sometimes be sluggish. An application server has to offer extremely good performance to provide dynamic access to applications. Usually the processing load will be split up between the server and the attached clients to optimize network performance.

Database Servers

Database servers provide some core functionality for client/server systems. Sophisticated database software runs on the server and provides services crucial to information processing. Database software also provides an orderly process for the storage and manipulation of shared data. Additionally, database servers ensure data integrity by maintaining an orderly approach to updates and rollback of incomplete or spoiled transactions.

Mail Servers

The mail server is the central post office of the network. Whole books have been written about electronic mail; e-mail can be the glue that holds an organization together. The mail server manages mail traffic through an organization, making sure that the right messages go to the right users. It provides a central repository for client mail and is usually the location for the central mail directory, the corporate e-mail address book.

Fax Servers

If you send and receive faxes, then you're in business. Businesses generate and receive tremendous amounts of fax traffic. Critical information moves through a business fax system almost 24 hours a day.

Management of all this fax traffic can be a major problem, but fax servers can provide an elegant solution. Because fax servers supply centralized management and storage for all fax traffic, inbound faxes can be routed to their proper destinations, and outbound fax traffic can be queued on the server for transmission at any time. These key functions provide access to fax services for a large number of users without incurring the expense of investing in fax hardware individuals. Instead, users share a common pool of fax hardware, fax software, and fax printing facilities.

Print Servers

One piece of PC hardware that everyone needs is a printer. Today, printers are manufactured to fill a variety of needs, from simple text output to sophisticated desktop publishing and multicolor graphics. Pick any particular type of print output and chances are good that there is a printer designed for that need.

But buying all users printers for their special needs can be expensive. One of the earliest factors driving the adoption of corporate networks was the need to share printers. Having a printer attached to your desktop is handy but having a selection of printers attached to your network is even handier (and certainly more affordable).Print servers concentrate the management and operation of multiple printers attached to the network. Print servers also define, contain, and control the queues of jobs waiting to be printed.

Directory Services Servers

When you need information about your network or your internetwork, you need access to directory services. Examples of things that are listed in directory services include the number of network stations and devices, the network addresses for these stations and devices, and information about various network resources available.

A directory server brings all this information together in one place. On a small network this might be a luxury, but on a large corporate network or internetwork it is absolutely essential. Network managers must have dynamic access to these types of information to keep their networks functioning smoothly.

WHO NEEDS SERVERS?

You do! If you're reading this book then you're interested in establishing, maintaining, and extending networks and network services. No matter what type of networking is involved, it involves using servers.

Small businesses or small workgroups in a larger organization can make use of a network of nondedicated servers, acting as clients while simultaneously acting as file and print servers. Larger businesses will depend on a number of dedicated servers carrying out well-defined functions for network operation and client support.

How those servers are configured and where they are located on the network depend on the nature and needs of the organization. Multiple services may be provided by one server. It is common in smaller businesses for the functions of the file server, directory services server, mail server, and print server to be combined on one machine. As an organization grows larger and its needs more diverse, more servers can be added to the network, and their individual functions can be separated and become more focused.

SUMMARY

Productivity is the key to networking. Standalone PCs became popular in business because their use brought about a significant increase in productivity. Networks are used in business today because they bring additional gains to business productivity.

Desktop PCs attached to a network can perform many functions. When a significant number of PCs attached to the network all perform identical functions, that particular function should become a candidate for server installation. A single server can be used to provide multiple network services, but when a single high performance server gets overloaded with requests for assorted services, then those services should be split onto additional servers. Remember, though, that the cost of additional servers must always be weighed against the productivity gains they can provide!

VANILLA FILE/PRINT SERVERS

IN THE BEGINNING: BASIC OVERVIEW

A file server centrally stores files on a PC-type machine's hard disk for shared use. It is composed of hardware and software to accomplish this task. The software is known as the network operating system (NOS) and can be purchased from IBM, Novell, Microsoft, or Banyan as well as other vendors. Hardware on a file server is generally referred to as memory, disk drives, controllers, and a PC. A file server also permits users to share peripherals on a LAN-like scanners, CD-ROMs, and printers.

People sometimes refer to a file server generically to mean either the NOS, the hardware, or both. The correct terminology is file server hardware and NOS.

A print server allows users on a LAN to share printers. A print server can consist of hardware and software also and is used in conjunction with a file server. Print server hardware consists of a PC or similar processor-type device that manages print jobs sent to a printer. Software on a print server is generally part of the NOS, but can also be purchased separately from another vendor.

A Look Back

The earliest file server NOSs like MS-NET from Microsoft were designed to run on top of DOS. DOS is not a multitasking operating system, so this caused problems because LANs were architected for more than one person to share resources. A NOS running on top of a non-multitasking operating system presented plenty of bottlenecks and performance issues.

Later NOS architectures like Microsoft's LANMAN and Banyan's virtual network system (VINES) rode on top of multitasking operating systems like OS/2, or modified UNIX System V, respectively. Novell's NetWare was designed around its own multitasking operating system. This allowed NetWare administrators to purchase the product and obtain a NOS integrated with an operating system.

File server NOSs and hardware have come a long way since their inception over a decade ago. The file server was originally used to simply store files in a central place so that regular backups could be performed and users could share files and printers. Not much money was put into the LANs at that time and not much was expected in return. However, today, institutions like banks are shifting their entire operations from mainframe-based to LAN-based. This puts more demand on the entire network in every conceivable way.

Let's take a look at the basics of file and print servers today.

File Server Components

Hardware components of a basic file server generally consist of RAM, CPU, hard disk and controller and one or more NICs. The NOS is software that controls the operation of a file server. These components must be present to build a vanilla file server.

Software

NOS

The NOS is the brain of the LAN. It maintains node connections and user information, processes file read and write requests, queues print jobs, and provides data security tools for administrators. Until recently, those were the basic services a NOS provided. However, newer NOSs like Microsoft's

NT Advanced Server can issue TCP/IP addresses and replicate drivers to workstations, allow dial-up, and more. Novell's NetWare, Banyan's Vines, Apple's AppleTalk, Microsoft's NT Advanced Server, IBM's OS/2 LAN Server are all currently popular.

Technobabble:

Novell, Inc., first introduced its concept of a NOS in 1983 with its debut of S-Net, which ran on a Motorola 68000 processor. This NOS provided basic file and print sharing across a LAN, along with administrative and security aspects, but ran on proprietary hardware. Novell later ditched that NOS and introduced NetWare 86, which was designed to run on an IBM XT, an 8086 processor! NetWare incorporated mainframelike security, and that was a hot item back then. Remember, most organizations were still mainframe-based at that time. As the microprocessor industry grew, Novell grew up along with it, garnering 67% of the LAN market share.

Microsoft's first NOS was MS-NET, designed to run on top of DOS, but it suffered from many performance problems. Microsoft then decided to market its NOS through 3Com along with other OEMs. In 1991, 3Com decided to leave the networking market, and Microsoft took over and developed LANMAN that ran over OS/2.

Microsoft's NOS has probably seen the most change over the years. NTAS supports AppleTalk's file system without having to load any special software. In addition, NTAS can be loaded onto RISC processors as well as Intel processors.

Hardware

Because a NOS can't operate on thin air, hardware must be selected on which to run it. Buying a great NOS and then loading it onto a file server that's old and slow is not a good idea. You can figure on spending between $10,000 and $20,000 for a good file server that leaves room for growth in the future, depending on the number of users you want that server to support. (Note: these costs may sound high, but they include the costs for the necessary hardware and software to deploy a production-grade network server for commercial use.)

Tip:
Just as there are different NOSs to choose from, so are there different
hardware vendors to choose from. We always recommend that you
do your homework before purchasing a system that will be expected
to last for several years. Also, we'd recommend that you stick to standard systems rather than proprietary ones. Proprietary means that
you will always have to stick with that vendor for future upgrades to
your file server.

In this chapter, we look at hardware components of an Intel-based system. Although NOSs like NetWare 4.X, and NTAS are designed to become
more processor independent, we still feel that the majority of file servers
are based on the Intel 80X86 chip family.

CPU

A CPU is the processor that executes instructions from the NOS. Generally,
the faster the CPU, the better is the performance. But this is more likely to
be true, if other performance areas of the file server are properly tuned.
That is, if you have a file server with a Pentium processor and run it on a
LAN that services 150 nodes but has only one NIC card, the performance
provided by the Pentium will be offset by the bottleneck that a single NIC
can create. In fact, a 486/66 CPU will work fine for a 100-node network that
supplies mostly file and print services, provided that the network has been
segmented to keep bottlenecks from slowing down the server.

The minimum CPU requirements for a file server will depend on the size
of your organization's network and budget. Also, if your organization
already has PCs sitting on a shelf, purchasing a new PC may be out of the
question.

If you are evaluating whether or not to upgrade an existing server or
purchase a new server, look at the user's expectations and average
observed performance. This will help you decide whether your current
server will meet the current and future demands that will be placed on it.
If your server is a 386-based processor and you have more than 40 users
operating in a Windows environment, we recommend that you upgrade to
a Pentium-based multiprocessor. Some NOSs already support multiprocessing and others are releasing versions soon that will support multiprocessing. Purchasing a multiprocessor now will secure your ability to

quickly upgrade your NOS and take full advantage of the multiple processors.

RAM

RAM on a file server is important. Many NOSs use RAM to cache recently accessed data, instructions, or other information in memory. This provides an essential performance boost for a network server, because retrieving information from memory is faster than retrieving it from storage. Some NOSs, like NetWare, employ specific formulas for determining the amount of RAM to install in a file server. Some companies like Compaq recommend that you use their RAM with their computers because their RAM employs its own timing algorithms to reduce the risk of memory crashes.

Tip:
We recommend that your file server include a minimum of 32 MB of RAM. Because RAM is inexpensive, adding RAM is an affordable way to improve the performance of your file server. The more you can afford, the better.

Older file servers may have a ceiling on the total amount of RAM they can support. For example, the first Compaq SystemPros could house only 96 MB of RAM (today that ceiling is an astonishing 1.5 GB!).

Bus Interface

The file server's bus provides the data path between the NIC and the CPU (and other peripherals and system components, like disk controllers, as well). The wider the data path, the better the resulting performance. The width of the path is determined by the number of bits that the bus can transfer in a single clock cycle. When it comes to a file server, forget about ISA because it's too slow. An EISA or 32-bit bus (like PCI or VLB) is a good choice (PCI and VLB are preferable because they provide higher transfer rates than EISA).

Disk Drives

One of the primary purposes of a file server is to share files, so a disk drive plays another important role in the architecture of the file server. A disk drive can be internal or external to a file server. If it is internal, total disk space is limited to the capacity of the machine and its available slots. If the disk drive is external, the limit of total space then becomes a function of the NOS.

Earlier implementations of NOSs did not include mirroring and duplexing of disk drives. As file servers became increasingly important in organizations, so did the data that were stored on them. Although tape backup systems were available, they were often slow in restoration of data. Organizations needed fault tolerance built in so that little or no downtime occurred. With the introduction of mirroring and duplexing in file server NOSs, organizations got their wish, but with an extra added cost burden.

Mirroring requires double the amount of disk space needed on a LAN because the file server writes data to two disks instead of one. In this fashion, if one disk crashes, the NOS is prepared to retrieve and store data on the other drive with no interruption of services to the users. Unfortunately, mirroring is set up so that the two disk drives share only one disk channel. If the channel fails, the whole system fails.

A more reliable, but more expensive route is to duplex the mirrored drives. This involves providing a separate disk controller for each drive. Of course the higher the fault tolerance, the higher the cost.

Technobabble:

When redundant array of inexpensive disks (RAID) was first introduced, it provided for striping the data across several disks that acted independent of one another. By striping data across the drives, retrieval of data can be done in a parallel fashion because the disks act independently of one another. This presents an obvious performance gain in reading information off several disks instead of one but adds to the disk space required because RAID was designed to reserve one drive as a parity drive. A parity drive holds information about the other drives' data so that if one drive fails, the parity drive is used to reconstruct the failed drive. RAID comes in six different levels called RAID 0–5.

The original Compaq SystemPro contained something like RAID, called *data guarding*. If you had four disk drives, one was reserved as the parity drive. This meant that 25% of your disk space was taken up for the parity drive. In addition, the system had to calculate the parity drive, which resulted in a 25% performance degradation. So unfortunately, fault tolerance has both benefits and tradeoffs.

Many vendors now sell 4 GB disk drives. We recommend file servers to at least have 2 GB drives that are externally housed with Fast Small Computer System Interface (SCSI). If the drives are internal to a file server, maintenance on a disk drive means taking down the file server. Many vendors now sell "hot-swapable" drives. This means that you can replace a bad disk drive while the file server is up and running, with no interruption to the users, depending on how your system is configured.

NIC

A NIC connects the file server to the rest of the LAN community. More than one NIC can be placed in a file server to act as a bridge in linking several different LANs. A 32-bit NIC is generally preferred in file servers, because all traffic to and from the file server must pass through it. This requires as wide as a data path as an organization can afford. Refer to Chapter 24 for an in-depth discussion of NICs.

DIFFERENT TYPES OF FILE SERVERS

Dedicated vs. Nondedicated

When the concept of a file server was first introduced, many organizations were not yet convinced of its cost vs. its benefits. Therefore, many earlier file servers were implemented in a nondedicated mode. Nondedicated means that a file server can be used as a workstation while also providing file and print services to the rest of the LAN users. Although this was not a recommended or preferred method, smaller organizations almost always implemented file servers in a nondedicated fashion to use existing hardware investments.

A dedicated file server can't be used as a workstation. This method is the preferred method, especially on large LAN implementations. As LANs grow, more organizations are splitting off other services from the file server like printing, communication, and sharing of other peripherals. This frees up the file server to process files and sends the processing of other services like printing onto another processor.

High-Powered Processors

The first Intel-based NOSs were designed for the 8086 processor. Imagine that! We remember installing our first file server with NetWare 2.X, which was designed for the 80286. At that time, the file servers ran some applications and menu systems as well as handling the printing. However, the first migration to file servers was not a leap but a slow trek. Most PCs already had software loaded on them and users were able to perform their work without connecting to the LAN. And, LAN-based applications were not readily available at that time, so many file servers simply became central repositories for shared files and also handled print tasks but ran few applications. In this context, 286-based file servers were appropriate.

As more vendors provided LAN-based software, more applications were loaded onto and run from the file server. Loading applications centrally on the file server greatly reduced the amount of time it took an IS department to perform software upgrades. However, this meant that the file server was handling more of the processing function of applications instead of the workstation. Some organizations found that the 286-based processor was not able to keep up with the new workload demand on the server. As the applications were loaded centrally on the server and the workstations were acting as dumb terminals to the server, the need to invest more power in the file server's processor became obvious.

As the demand toward a high powered file server grew, 386-based PCs became the new standard for those organizations that could afford to upgrade their file server hardware. Vendors also supplied 32-bit NOSs that were capable of utilizing the power of these new processors. Novell, for example, released its NetWare 3.X line that was designed specifically for the 386-based processor.

Because some organizations were slow to implement LANs, and continued to maintain a mainframe-based viewpoint, many LANs were slow and clumsy at best. As the industry grew, LANs became more widespread and the cost of file server hardware dropped dramatically. Lower up-front costs justified corporate expenditures for 486-based file servers.

Until recently, having a 486/66 MHz PC as a file server was considered a luxury for some organizations. But with the advent of the Pentium processor, the 486-based processor has to take a back seat. The 486 file servers still provide the network core in smaller organizations, but larger organizations are moving rapidly to Pentium-based servers.

Superservers

Superservers are touted as monolith file servers. In reality, they are servers that have streamlined the I/O process on the server. Most bottlenecks are I/O related, and superservers address these I/O problems very well. Companies like Tricord and NetFrame sell superservers that have quasi-proprietary hardware.

In addition to better I/O performance, these superservers offer multiprocessing However, with Compaq and HP now offering symmetric multiprocessing for $20,000 and less, Tricord and NetFrame have had to scramble. They've had to watch some of their market share slip away to this competition. Also, as the PCI and VL buses gain more popularity, superservers will probably drop out of the general LAN marketplace entirely and be shifted over into special niche markets.

Multiprocessors

The latest shift in network computing involves combining more than one processor to handle the workload. Terms like *symmetric* and *asymmetric multiprocessing* are common today. Asymmetric processing involves dedicating certain CPUs to certain tasks; symmetric processing allows all CPUs to be used for any task. Symmetric processing is more desirable because there is less chance that a CPU will sit idle while waiting for a task.

Novell, in a later release for NetWare 4.X, is making plans to provide a three-phase approach to symmetric multiprocessing. Microsoft ships NTAS with support for symmetric multiprocessing built in and companies like HP and Compaq are already shipping file servers with multiprocessing capabilities. For a thorough discussion of multiprocessing, refer to Chapter 29.

Rack-Mounted Servers

If your organization is like most, your computer room has been overcrowded by e-mail servers, communication servers, hubs, leftover hardware, cabling, and more. Space is at a premium. Let's forget about the fact that mainframes used to take up entire floors, needed special water cooling systems, raised floors and other expensive niceties.

Today, the focus is on squeezing as much into a room as possible so that everything can be centrally located and managed. Because many LANs were not planned but grew up like mainframe stepchildren, lots of organizations left little space for the LAN computer room. If this is the case in your organization, you may want to take a look at rack-mounted servers. Compaq and other vendors are supplying rack-mounted file servers that fit nicely into the standard 19″ rack.

PRINT SERVERS

Some of you may recall early print sharing prior to networks. Electrical switch box devices were popular, but required getting up from one's desk and flipping a switch to share a printer. Needless to say, the distance between users sharing a printer this way was limited. The alternative was to buy a printer for each desktop. Budget-minded managers still gnash their teeth over this solution.

With the advent of networking, printing on a network was redirected across the network, enabling the sharing of printers through the LAN. Early networking software included provisions built into the NOSs for network printing. Printing on a network has not changed dramatically over the years. Some slight variations and new additions have changed printing a little, but for the most part, printing hasn't changed much.

Methods of Network Printing

Printing on a network can be done in three ways: attaching printers directly to a file server, printing through a workstation attached to a printer, or printing through a dedicated print server.

Printer Attached to a File Server

One early method in network printing was to attach printers directly to a file server so users could send their jobs to print at the file server. This method worked okay, but distance was limited and it forced network architects to keep file servers in open public areas instead of secure locations. Some smaller organizations, with a negligible need for file server security, still attach printers to their file servers. We don't recommend this method, because print jobs have caused lockups at the file server, and a locked file server often means network failure.

Remote Printer Attached to a Workstation

The remote printer method attaches a printer to a nondedicated PC that could be used both as a workstation and as a print server. The workstation attached to the printer has to be turned on to permit the rest of the users to print. For very small offices, this may work well, but not for the organization with heavy printing needs. This method is very slow because the printing speed is rated by the speed of the parallel or serial port that the printer is attached to.

Printer Attached to a Dedicated Print Server

Using a dedicated print server is the most expensive option. This method requires a separate PC or similar processor-type device dedicated to managing the printers attached to it. Most organizations that have heavy printing needs use dedicated print servers. With more applications like desktop publishing providing graphics capabilities, demands on network printing have grown substantially.

Let's take a look at how print servers work in general, then we'll move onto the different varieties of print servers available today.

1. An application sends a file to a software driver on the workstation.
2. The software driver prepares the file for a specific type of printer.
3. The workstation sends the file to a directory on the file server via the network cabling.
4. The file server notifies the print server that it has something to print.
5. The print server signals file server that the requested printer is available.
6. The file server sends the file to the print server through the network cabling.
7. The print server sends the file to the printer.

Most of the common NOSs like NetWare, VINES, and NTAS print using these steps. Until a few years ago, it was possible only to use a PC as a dedicated print server. Nowadays companies like Intel and Milan provide small boxes with processors inside them that act as dedicated print servers. There are essentially three types of dedicated print servers:

1. *PC print server.* This type involves setting up a PC as a node somewhere on the network and then connecting printers to the PC, using either parallel or serial cables. The speed of printing here is limited to the parallel or serial port speed. This can be slow and unsuitable for heavy graphics printing. Also, this method does not permit multiprotocol printing.

2. *External print server box.* This is a processor housed in a small box that attaches directly to the network. On the box are serial and parallel ports to which printers can be attached. Again, the printing speed is limited to the parallel and serial port speeds on the box. Some companies have enhanced the speeds of these ports, but generally they are still slow.

3. *Internal print server box.* HP provides JetDirect cards that slip into a slot in an HP printer. The card provides both a connection to the network and print server functionality. This method allows printing speeds to be rated at the network speed because there are no parallel ports to print through.

Print server boxes also have the ability to print more than one protocol. This is extremely important in medium to large organizations where several protocols may be in use.

Print Queues

A print queue is an area on the disk where a file is spooled while it waits its turn to be printed. In a network environment, several users may be spooling files at the same time. To prevent a jam at the printer, files are redirected by the workstation network drivers to an area on a file server. The files stay in a queue until the requested printer is available. The print server is responsible for notifying the file server when the requested printer is available.

In the simplest of setups, there is a one-to-one relationship between a queue and a printer. That is, each printer has its own queue. In more complex setups, each printer can service more than one queue and the administrator can set priorities on the queues so the president's print request is always serviced first, on the printer closest to his or her office.

The order of the queue can be rearranged, canceled, or placed on hold by an administrator or a by a user with special print manager privileges.

So, although a print queue manages the order of files to be printed, the print server manages the queues. Therefore, there can be several queues assigned to a print server.

Printer Management

As networks grew in size, so did the amount of printers attached on a LAN. Because printers can be dispersed anywhere on the LAN today, printer management on the LAN has become an issue. Printers and print servers had little management capability, forcing the user or network administrator to physically visit the printer to view its status (out of paper, on/off, etc.).

Vendors now sell printers that have bidirectional communication capability. This means that an administrator can collect information like serial number, available memory, tray sizes, and printer model from a central location. In addition, more vendors are supplying print devices with simple network management protocol (SNMP) agents built in.

FACTORS TO CONSIDER WHEN BUYING A FILE SERVER

Tip:
1. Determine the number of people that will be using the file server.
2. Determine applications that will be running. Will the applications be primarily database, file, print, Windows-based, or what?
3. Determine how much disk space is needed currently and for future expansion.
4. Will this file server house e-mail like cc:Mail or Microsoft Mail? If so, add these needs to number 3.
5. Determine the budget ($0, $5,000, $10,000, or $100,000).
6. Determine fault tolerance needs (i.e., will your server need 100% uptime even on weekends?).
7. How many NICs will you need? See Chapter 24 for assistance in NICs.

8. Determine which NOS and version will best fit your organization's needs (i.e., NetWare 4.X, NT Advanced Server, etc.)

9. Do you already have a tape backup system? If you do, get a system with more capacity; if you don't, get one right away! We feel this is a requirement for file servers housing data for multiple users.

10. Determine where the server will be located and how much space is available (i.e., you may need a rack-mounted server).

FACTORS TO CONSIDER WHEN BUYING A PRINT SERVER

1. How many protocols will this print server service? Is it important for the printer to be based in IPX but interpret other protocols like TCP/IP? Or is it important for the printer to be based in TCP/IP with ability to interpret other protocols like IPX? Multiprotocol servers understand and can print various protocols. But, you should ask what is the native protocol for the print server.

2. Is printing speed important? If so, look at HP or Intel's solutions. They offer products that print at network speeds.

3. What type of topology do you have (token ring, Ethernet?). Some print servers do not support ARCnet or token ring.

4. If using token ring, what speed is your ring? Some solutions do not support 4 Mb/sec, others don't support 16 Mb/sec.

5. If using NetWare, do you want to stick with PCONSOLE? Some solutions provide their own software installation and management.

6. Do you want to manage the printer remotely or from a centralized location? Find out if the printer supports SNMP.

7. What type of printers do you have and how many printers are you trying to hook up?

TOP FOUR FILE SERVER VENDORS

Compaq Computer Corp.
20555 State Hwy. 249
Houston, TX 77070-2698
800-345-1518; 713-370-0670
Direct sales: 800-888-5858 (Compaq DirectPlus)
FAX: 713-378-1442
Tech support: 800-OKCOMPAQ

Tech support BBS: 713-378-1418
IBM (International Business Machines)

Old Orchard Rd.
Armonk, NY 10504
800-426-3333; 914-765-1900

Direct sales: 800-426-7695 (IBM PC Direct)
Tech support: 800-237-5511
Tech support BBS: 919-517-0001; 800-847-7211 (OS/2)
Tricord Systems, Inc.

3750 Annapolis Lane, Ste. 105
Plymouth, MN 55447-5438
800-TRICORD; 612-557-9005
FAX: 612-557-8403
Tech support: Use toll-free no.

NetFRAME Systems, Inc.
1545 Barber Lane
Milpitas, CA 95035
800-852-3726; 408-944-0600
FAX: 408-434-4190

TOP THREE PRINT SERVER VENDORS

Hewlett Packard, Inc.
3000 Hanover St.

Palo Alto, CA 94304-1181
800-752-0900; 800 387-3867 (CD); 415-857-1501
Direct sales: 800-637-7740 (HP Direct)
FAX: 800-333-1917
Tech support: 800-858-8867
Tech support BBS: 415-852-0256
CIS: GO HP

Castelle Inc.
3255-3 Scott Blvd.
Santa Clara, CA 95054
800-289-7555; 408-496-0474
FAX: 408-492-1964
Tech support: Use main no.
Tech support BBS: 408-496-1807

Intel Corp. (Personal Computer Enhancement Division)
5200 N.E. Elam Young Pkwy.
Hillsboro, OR 97124-6497
800-538-3373; 503-629-7354
FAX: 503-629-7580
Tech support: 503-629-7000
Tech support BBS: 503-645-6275

MicroTest, Inc.
4747 North 22nd St.
Phoenix, AZ 85016-4708
800-526-9675; 602-952-6400
FAX: 602-952-6401
Tech support: 602-952-6650
Tech support BBS: 602-957-7716

RESOURCES: BIBLIOGRAPHY AND STRATEGIES

For general networking references, please consult Appendix C, "A List of Networking Resources." The magazines and other publications listed there can help you find out lots of information about file and print servers. The following references are particularly helpful for the information they contain about file servers NOSs.

Siyan, Karanjit. *NetWare The Professional Reference,* 3rd ed.,
New Riders Publishing, Indianapolis: 1995. This is an excellent book on NetWare 2.X, 3.X and 4.X. It includes thorough discussions on topics where the Novell manual ends. If you don't have this book, your library is not complete. $38.25.

Cowart, Robert. *Windows NT Unleashed,* 2nd ed.,
SAMS Publishing, Indianapolis:1995. This is one of the most comprehensive books available on Windows NT, including installation, administration and internetworking. $39.99.

Krochmal, Jim, Mark E. Conner, Gary Hughes, Andre M. Malarcher, and Karanjit Siyan: *Banyan VINES The Professional Reference.*
New Riders Publishing, Indianapolis: 1994. The Professional Series by New Riders Publishing is one of the best that we have seen. The series includes all NOSs and is very comprehensive. $50.00.

Ackermann, Ernest, *et al. Using UNIX,* Special Edition.
QUE Publishing, Indianapolis: 1994. This is another comprehensive tool for the network administrator's library. This book covers everything from e-mail to the Internet to internetworking. $39.99.

MULTIPROCESSING AND SPECIAL-PURPOSE SERVERS

c h a p t e r

29

OVERVIEW

Multiprocessing (MP) computer architectures have been in used since the early 1980s on larger scale computers such as minis and mainframes, primarily in the academic and scientific worlds. As more organizations begin to rightsize and shift from older mainframe or minicomputer to client/server environments, additional horsepower is being demanded from the network servers being widely deployed as a function of rightsizing. Today, the trend toward multiprocessing architectures has reached the network operating system, so it's time for savvy network administrators to take a look at MP technology and to understand its strengths and weaknesses.

As its name implies, MP involves more than one CPU in handling routine processing. For many network administrators, this approach diverges from more convention computing methods. In fact, most organizations today use only a single processor per computer, whether for network servers or other processing, which does all of the work by itself. In the past, this made good sense because operating systems and applications have traditionally been designed to handle only one process at a time. Shifting to an MP environment, therefore, involves substantial changes in a computer's hardware, in its NOS or OS, and in its application software as well. Despite these across-the-board changes, the results of adopting MP can still be quite rewarding, as we'll attempt to explain in this chapter.

The Many Flavors of MP

MP architectures are available in several different scales, which we'll refer to as small, medium and large scale. It will be helpful to understand these scales before we go into the specifics of how any of them works. Although no industry standard as yet defines these scales, you can use the following definitions as a guideline for this discussion.

- *Small-scale MP*—The low end of the MP spectrum typically includes systems that house two to four CPUs, along with 32–64 MB of RAM, several gigabytes of fast and wide SCSI-2 storage, and six or more EISA or PCI bus slots. Vendors like Compaq, AST, ALR, and Dell are jumping into the emerging marketplace. As the lowest prices for small scale MP systems has plummeted to $5,000 and as NOS vendors like Novell, IBM, and Microsoft now provide network operating systems that support and take advantage of MP, such systems are becoming commonplace in the medium-sized organizations.

- *Medium-scale MP*—Systems in the medium scale typically house 4 to 32 CPUs and generally are Unix-based. This class of systems boasts the largest installed base, supported by vendors like Sun, DEC, and Sequent. Compared to small-scale MP, this range houses more CPUs, so more memory (typically 16–64 MB per CPU) and disk space (2–4 GB per CPU is customary) come along with these systems. Medium-scale MP systems often play host to larger databases and mid-range on-line transaction processing systems. Prices for medium-scale MP systems typically begin at $150,000 and can go up into the low millions.

- *Large-scale MP*—This range occupies a small niche that requires copious computing resources processing on a grandiose scale. Large-scale MP systems usually house more than 32 CPUs, along with large amounts of memory and disk space. Generally, heavy-duty scientific modeling and financial applications requiring intense floating point processing or massive amounts of data manipulation are found in this range. Specialized applications, including full-blown on-line transaction processing systems (like airline or car rental reservation systems) or decision support software, must be written specifically to handle large numbers of CPUs. Given the cost of the software and the hardware involved, prices for large-scale MP systems typically start in the millions and go up from there.In this chapter, we'll concentrate on small-scale MP, since that is the market sector that is growing most rapidly and is also where the largest number of organizations are likely to get involved with this technology.

THE POWER OF SYMMETRY FOR MP

Two different implementations of MP are available as products today: symmetric (SMP) and asymmetric multiprocessing (AMP). The current trend for both software and hardware vendors favors SMP, even though some special-purpose applications lend themselves to an AMP environment. Let's take a look at each of these implementations so that you will understand which, if any, might be suitable for your organization.

Asymmetric MP

AMP assigns specific tasks or services to each CPU in a system. These CPUs may or may not be housed in the same box. Because the CPUs in an AMP system can be housed in different computers, they typically manage their own dedicated memory and peripherals and do not require that common resources be shared among multiple CPUs.

AMP is not as efficient as SMP because any given CPU will sit idle if its particular services are not needed, while another CPU might be overtaxed when its services are in heavy use. One important advantage of AMP is that it allows a variety of different computers to work harmoniously together to act as a single "virtual computer" (i.e., a collection of machines that acts as if it were a single machine). Another of AMP's advantages is that it supports both loosely and tightly coupled systems (which we discuss in a later section in this chapter).

Symmetric MP

In SMP systems, all CPUs are housed in a single computer, and all of them share the system's memory, its I/O devices, and all other system resources. The basic premise behind SMP is that any service or task must be capable of running on any CPU—meaning that the CPUs will typically be identical. If a computer houses different kinds of CPUs and a service that can run on one type of CPU cannot run on another kind, SMP will not work.

Because of the sharing of resources that SMP normally entails, the operating system for such a computer must be able to provide tight synchronization and accurate timing to all CPUs; in other words, it must operate as a tightly coupled processing environment. Here's why: if one CPU gets too far ahead of another and ties to retrieve data that another CPU has not finished processing, any results obtained would be questionable, if not downright wrong. Because all CPUs in an SMP system must be housed in one enclosure, any SMP system's scalability is limited by the maximum number of CPUs the enclosure can support. For small-scale MP systems, this provides sufficient scalability at a relatively low cost. As the number of CPUs in a single enclosure increases, however, designers must be aware that the "law of diminishing returns" is never absent and that increased complexity may sometimes outweigh increases in processing power or performance.

Loose vs. Tight Coupling

Tightly coupled processors share common resources, including a computer's backplane or its bus, which connects a computer's CPUs to its other attached devices (and sometimes its memory). This means that each CPU in a tightly coupled system has to be aware of other CPUs' activities whenever it attempts to run a task or utilize a service. Failure to coordinate results in inaccurate data or system failures, so considerable effort in hardware, operating system, and software design is needed to keep tightly coupled systems from going awry. Tight coupling can result in great performance, but it also imposes greater hardware costs and is subject to diminishing performance returns as the number of CPUs increases. For example, Windows NT supports tightly coupled processors and runs on commodity server platforms from IBM, Dell, AST, ALR, and other companies that offer two to four CPUs.

In loosely coupled systems processors are linked together that do not share memory and system resources. Consequently, less synchronization and coordination is required to assign, manage, and complete tasks. In a loosely coupled system each processor provides its own services and complete its own tasks, and it needs to worry about synchronization and coordination only at the task level. Because loosely coupled systems can run on more than one computer, the scalability of these systems is far less limited than for tightly coupled systems. Loosely coupled systems lend themselves to large-scale MP environments, especially those that may adapt well to AMP-style implementations.Underlying MP System requirements

Specs:
When it comes to MP, you might be tempted to ask, what about standards? In other words, it might be interesting if there were a collection of MP standards to govern the ways that hardware, operating systems, and software should operate in such environments. From a systems standpoint, here are the requirements necessary to make MP technology work. Alas, the standards in this area are few and far between!

Hardware Issues

Tip:
Intel introduced a multiprocessing hardware specification called MPS 1.1. This advanced programmable interrupt controller (APIC) architecture was introduced with the new 82489DX interrupt controller chip, which serves as a replacement for the older 8259A interrupt controller used in conventional uniprocessor PCs. The APIC controller acts as a traffic cop for interrupts from I/O devices by setting priorities on the interrupts and sending them along to the processor in an MP systems that is least busy. Not all vendors are supporting Intel's spec, but it offers some interesting capabilities for building workable small- and medium-scale MP systems.

Another approach, jointly developed by a group of vendors including companies like Advanced Micro Devices, Cyrix Corp., Compaq, Motorola, IBM, and Apple is called the *open programmable interrupt controller* (OPIC) architecture. OPIC was unveiled in March 1995 to the usual round of self-promotional industry hoopla, but it appears to offer some interesting capabilities as well. For instance, Microsoft got involved to ensure compatibility with MS-Windows. It will be instructive to see which of these competing MP approaches—

APIC and OPIC—is supported in the marketplace and even more so to see which one will eventually win out.

Another company, Evergreen Technologies, has introduced its REV To SMP system—their systems offers a way to convert a single-processor, 486-based PC, into a dual processor PC, by adding a processor of the same type and clock speed to your existing one. The Evergreen hardware plugs into any 168-pin 486-compatible CPU socket, and provides sockets for two processor chips.

That's one way to upgrade your current system to bare-bones MP—to do this, you need only purchase Evergreen's system and one additional CPU chip (you can use your current CPU chip on this new system and avoid having to purchase two chips). As usual, you'll want to call Evergreen and ask them the customary litany of questions to make sure their system enhancement will be compatible with the operating system and applications you want to use.

OS Strategies

As we mentioned earlier, changes in hardware and software, including both operating systems (OS) and network operating systems (NOS), and applications as well, are needed to take advantage of an MP environment. Adding more processors to your server alone will not boost your system's performance because your server might not be able to use those additional processors as is.

By adding a NOS or OS that is MP aware and therefore able to assign tasks (known as multithreading) to run efficiently on multiple processors, you could obtain a significant performance gain. Of course, the actual gain will depend on what type of applications the system is running and the application's ability to benefit from multiple processors as well.

Some operating systems like Windows NT are already able to support MP, without requiring additional software or a special implementations. In fact, Windows NT supports up to four processors in its standard implementation. When it comes to using any operating system on an MP computer, you'll be well-advised to make sure the version you purchase supports MP, whether or not that means buying a standard or special version of the operating system. This is especially true for Unix implementations, since Unix Systems Laboratories delivered an MP-capable version of its software to its many licensees in 1994.With the introduction of NetWare 4.1, Novell began with the first of three phases in its move to provide full-fledged MP support in its operating systems. Here's an overview of Novell's three phases for MP support:

- *Phase I: SMP enabled*—A pending release of NetWare scheduled for the summer of 1995 is slated to provide SMP support for NetWare, so that certain pieces of the OS can run on multiple CPUs.

- *Phase II: Domains*—Currently Novell allows NLMs to run in one of two operating system domains. Ring 0 is where the OS resides. This ring must always function for the server to continue running; adding functionality to Ring 0 can therefore be a truly risky business. When testing an NLM for the first time, many system administrators run the new NLM in a domain separate from the OS to prevent possible crashing of the system. In Phase II, every NLM will be allowed to run in its own protected OS domain. Instead of having only two domains in which to load NLMs, many domains will be available, with improved communication between them. This makes MP much easier to implement, because it allows processes to run wherever NetWare wants to put them, without having to worry about compromising the integrity of the entire network operating system.

- *Phase III: Clusters*—Clustering allows work to be spread among multiple CPUs that span multiple networked servers (or other computers). This lets work appear to be unified in one system or virtual system using high speed links to distribute, manage, and coordinate tasks across the network. Ultimately, this will let an entire network function as a single virtual computer.Software Issues

Software Issues

Some newer applications are written explicitly to take advantage of MP and multithreading. Typically, these applications include database and imaging software like Adobe's Photoshop. Ask your vendors if their software was written to take advantage of MP before you make any purchases. You may need to talk with a technical support representative rather than a sales representative to obtain this level of information, but it will help you to understand if the software supports MP.

Is More Better?

The burning question that keeps popping up when discussing MP is, does a system's performance increase for every additional processor? The debate over this issue continues to surface, with some believing that there are limitations to the scalability of MP on Intel-based platforms.

Jim Greene, product manager for NetWare server products at Novell said, "For SMP, all of our tests have shown that with the fifth processor, you are actually decreasing your performance. The fourth processor is a wash, but with two processors, you can expect to get more than 200 percent" in an interview with Bradley F. Shimmin, *LAN Times*, January 23, 1995 p.1, Intel multiprocessing has hidden limitations (Novell's UnixWare 2.0; SMP support for NetWare 4.1). Diminishing returns is a reality that can occur because all processors share the same memory pool. This means that at some point, the burden of the overhead necessary to coordinate processors will outweigh the benefits of adding another processor. This also means that you will seldom see fully linear performance improvements when you add more CPUs to your MP system. It's inevitable that, at some point, more will cease to be better. This is as true for MP as it is for the other good things in life!

THE TOP 5 MP VENDORS

OS Vendors

SCO Unix MPX
Sun Microsystems Computer Corp. (unit of Sun Microsystems, Inc.)
2550 Garcia Ave.
Mountain View, CA 94043-1100
800-821-4643; 800-821-4642 (CA); 415-960-1300
FAX: 415-969-9131
Tech support: 800-USA-4SUN

Windows NT Advanced Server 3.5
Microsoft Corp.
One Microsoft Way
Redmond, WA 98052-6399
800-426-9400; 206-882-8080
Direct sales: 800-MSPRESS
FAX: 206-635-6100
Tech support: 206-454-2030; 206-637-7098 (Windows)
Tech support BBS: 206-936-6735

OS/2 3.11
IBM (International Business Machines)
Old Orchard Rd.
Armonk, NY 10504
800-426-3333; 914-765-1900
Direct sales: 800-426-7695 (IBM PC Direct)
Tech support: 800-237-5511
Tech support BBS: 919-517-0001; 800-847-7211 (OS2)

NetWare 4.1
Novell, Inc.
122 East 1700 South
Provo, UT 84606-6194
800-453-1267; 801-429-7000
FAX: 801-429-5155
Tech support: 800-638-9273

Vines
Banyan Systems Inc.
120 Flanders Rd.
Westborough, MA 01581-1033
800-222-6926; 508-898-1000
FAX: 508-898-1755
Tech support: Use main no.
Tech support BBS: 508-836-1834

Hardware Vendors

Compaq Computer Corp.
20555 State Hwy. 249
Houston, TX 77070-2698
800-345-1518; 713-374-0484
Direct sales: 800-888-3298 (Compaq DirectPlus)
FAX: 713-374-4583
Tech support: 800-OKCOMPAQ
Tech support BBS: 713-378-1418

AST Research Inc.
16215 Alton Pkwy., PO Box 57005
Irvine, CA 92718
800-876-4AST; 714-727-4141
FAX: 714-727-9355
Tech support: Use toll-free no.
Tech support BBS: 714-727-4132

Advanced Logic Research, Inc. (ALR)
9401 Jeronimo Rd.
Irvine, CA 92718
800-444-4257; 714-581-6770
FAX: 714-581-9240
Tech support: 714-458-0863
Tech support BBS: 714-458-6834

Dell Computer Corp.
2214 W. Braker Lane, Bldg. 3
Austin, TX 78758-4033
800-289-1260; 512-338-4400
FAX: 512-338-8700
Tech support: 800-624-9896
Tech support BBS: 512-728-8528

IBM (International Business Machines)
Old Orchard Rd.
Armonk, NY 10504
800-426-3333; 914-765-1900
Direct sales: 800-426-7695 (IBM PC Direct)

Tech support: 800-237-5511
Tech support BBS: 919-517-0001; 800-847-7211 (OS2)

Bibliographies and Resources

Many of the articles that follow are from *Windows Sources*, (February 1995). We found that issue to be particularly relevant to our MP discussion and hope you will obtain a copy of *Windows Sources* and read through the articles listed here.

Lamb, Jason. "The New NetWare: SMP Workhorse." *LAN Magazine*, vol. 9, no. 12 (November 1994): 42. With NetWare 4.1, Novell implements distributed parallel processing, a multiprocessing technology that may change the way you network. (Novell's NetWare 4.x network operating system)

Jones, Mitt; Penrod, Paul S. "SMP: Multiprocessing Hits the Desktop." Symmetric multiprocessing, includes related article on SMP terminology. *Windows Sources*, vol. 3, no. 2 (February 1995): 162.

Jones, Mitt. "For the Few: Learn What SMP Can't Do, and You'll Begin to Understand What It Can. " *Windows Sources,* vol. 3, no. 2, (February 1995): 165.

Jones, Mitt; Penrod, Paul S. "NT Builds in SMP." *Windows Sources*, vol. 3, no. 2, (February 1995): 172. Windows NT 3.5 operating system; symmetric multiprocessing, includes related article on testing methodology

Jones, Mitt; Penrod, Paul S. "O/S 2 Adds SMP." *Windows Sources,* vol. 3, no. 2, (February 1995): 177. (IBM's OS/2 for SMP 2.11; symmetric multiprocessing.

Shimmin, Bradley F. "Intel Multiprocessing Has Hidden Limitations." *LAN Times*, vol. 12, no. 2, (January 23, 1995): 1. (Novell's UnixWare 2.0; SMP support for NetWare 4.1)

DATABASE SERVERS

DATABASE HISTORY

The Mainframe Way

The way data are collected, organized, and managed in an organization is one of the most critical factors in the success or failure of an enterprise. One of the first uses of mainframe computers was for databases, those large electronic collections of rigidly structured records that act as data repositories for everything from personnel records, to financial transactions, to product inventories and sales information.

Even the first unwieldy database management systems (DBMSs) offered to mainframe users were a tremendous boost to business. Early mainframe database computing was completely transparent to end users, who were encouraged to enter data, but rarely given a chance to manipulate the information their databases contained. Even today, large mainframe-housed databases are typically managed and maintained from a centralized location.

Centralization gave the IS department total control of database use. Dedicated programmers and mainframe personnel were employed to manage these databases and provide reports to users. Predefined reports, in preset formats, were available to users, but if a department wanted a report from the database that wasn't on the different than the list of available reports, it had to make a special request to the IS department. If a change in a data-entry or reporting program was necessary to reflect new business practices, another call was placed to the IS department and yet another request would have to wait for an IS response and the request was placed in a queue. Needless to say, this method was slow, cumbersome, and created an opportunity for endless friction between users and IS personnel.

PCs Replace Dumb Terminals

Users and business managers alike could see that funneling all special requests through the IS department was too slow to be practical in rapidly changing business environments. Therefore, IS and department managers alike were constantly seeking ways to streamline access to their companies' database management systems.

The rise of desktop computing on PCs brought about some important changes in database use. As PCs began to replace dumb terminals, database and spreadsheet software provided a much more user-friendly way to acquire and manipulate large quantities of data. Users could download data from mainframe databases to their PCs and were able to massage the data into the formats they needed. Users began creating their own databases and reports from packages like dBase and Report Writer. Some of them even dared to think that their dependence on central IS was forever broken.

Databases on LANs

As LANs began to emerge in businesses, so did LAN-based database software. LAN administrators could place LAN DBMS on their file servers, allowing multiple users to share the databases. File and record locking was a basic feature in early LAN-based database software and prevented users from opening the same database simultaneously and overwriting each other's data.

But human nature created some important drawbacks to early LAN database implementations. Users, who always want their data in widely varying formats would often work independently and at cross-purposes, resulting, in unique home-grown versions of databases. It didn't take long for the LAN to become home to a variety of differently structured databases that often contained redundant data.

This, of course, is the downside of pulling centralized IS out of the database picture: when users rule the database world, they don't spend much time worrying about niceties like "fifth normal form" or "the redundant data problem." Unfortunately these concerns, although esoteric, can be ignored only at some risk to the integrity and accuracy of the data in the databases involved. That's why leaving behind the professionals, even though it may speed things up considerably, may not always be the best idea!

Database Servers on LANs

Over time, the solution that IS had already reached became equally obvious to LAN administrators: collect all the data in one place, exactly as had been done in the mainframe environment. The theory was that the database could be kept on the LAN itself. Vendors released database applications designed to run on servers attached to the LAN.

Then, as businesses began to migrate to LAN computing, database management on the LAN became more important in the enterprise. Gradually, database servers took over all database management functions, separating the databases from the file and print functions. Often, the DBMS software and its related data stores would be housed in its own machine. Most early database servers were designed to run over Novell's NetWare, because NetWare was the most popular network operating system for business use.

WHAT'S A DATABASE?

In the simplest terms, a database is a collection of information. A desktop Rolodex is a good example of a simple database: it contains specific, well-understood data elements for each entry. A typical rolodex has information like name, address, city, state, zip code, and phone number. In database-speak, these elements of information are known as *fields*.

A Rolodex is generally further subdivided so each individual name or company is represented by a single Rolodex card. On that card, all the fields we mentioned above might be represented or perhaps only a subset of those fields. In a database, each collection of information about an individual item, corresponding to a Rolodex card, card is called a *record*. Following this definition, a record is a collection of fields.

A Rolodex on your desktop may have one or more cards that contain information; this Rolodex, with all its associated cards and data, corresponds to a *database*. The problem with a Rolodex is that it is manual; every time you want to make a change, you have to either retype or rewrite a paper card. In addition, you have to manually sort the cards in whatever order you want to view them.

As it happens, most people sort their Rolodex cards in alphabetical order. But what happens if you want to send a customer mailer out to people in zip code order? For a paper-based Rolodex, this would require resorting the cards by hand, this time in zip code order.

To computerize a Rolodex, you would first need to design the structure of the database. In other words, you would need to tell the database software specifics about the database fields like length and type. For example, if your database has a field called State, and that field will hold two-letter designations of states (i.e., TX), then the field length can be defined with two characters. The field's *type* will be character, and the *length* of the field will be 2.

But let's say you have another field called Zip and you would like to put the person's zip code in that field. Because zip codes can be of two lengths: five-digit or nine-digit, depending on whether you use the old system or new zip code numbering system, this field must contain numbers so the field *type* should be defined as numeric instead of character, and the *length* of the Zip field should be long enough to accommodate the nine digits present in the new form. You'd also want to flag an error if a ZIP code of 0–4 digits or 5–8 digits was entered because this would be an invalid entry.

Once you've designed the structure of the database, you then have an empty shell. This is just like having a house with no furniture. The next task is to input data into that database. Once this step is completed, reports can be generated, the database can be indexed or sorted by fields, and a variety of functions can be performed.

Now you're the envy of the office because you've just created a database of information on all your customers. Everyone in the organization will want to use your information. Unfortunately, it's on your PC—and that means your co-workers will have to use your PC to use your database. If you want to share that information effectively, the logical place for your database is on the LAN!

Relational Databases

Relational databases can be compared to a spreadsheet. A relational database is made up of tables of data containing rows and columns. The rows represent individual records, and columns hold representations of the values of individual fields (i.e., the labels for columns correspond to field names). Users can compile reports by querying database tables and relating them based on common fields between all the tables.

For example, an organization might have a relational database where the tables relate to one another by the customer name field. In that relational database, there might be an address table and a purchase order table connected by a common customer name value in particular fields. Typically, you would have only one record for a customer in an address file, but you might have several records in the purchase order file that relate to the customer file. The relational database gives you the ability to combine all the data from related tables into a single report. Relational databases effectively give users a chance to display and manipulate all their organization's data in easy, intelligible forms (at least, all the data they're allowed to see, anyway—data security is as much a concern for most organizations as is network security).

Object-Oriented Database

Using the preceding Rolodex example, an object would represent a customer. The customer object contains information about an individual customer, as well as functions that operate on customer data.

Novell's NetWare 4.0 implements an object-oriented database for all the users, resources, services, and other entries contained in NetWare Directory Services (NDS). Those of you who have installed NetWare 4.x might be familiar with the objects used by this NOS, like user objects, volume objects, and server objects. Clicking on an object pulls up information about those objects.

WHAT'S A DATABASE SERVER?

LAN database servers are designed to increase performance of databases and eliminate unnecessary data flowing across the LAN. If clients run their own standalone database programs, even though the databases they manipulate are housed on a file server, the server does not process user requests. Instead, all the data required to process the request must be shipped over the LAN to the user's PC. Thus, if a user submits a request to sort an entire database, that entire database must be sent across the LAN from the file server to the user's PC. The database is then sorted and sent back to the file system on the file server. Not only is this process slow, it takes up crucial bandwidth on a LAN if the database is large.

Database servers were developed to solve this problem. A database server is sometimes called a *database engine,* but either way, this technology involves splitting the database functions off into a special set of server software. For heavily used databases, this software may be the only major service offered by a particular server, which may then rightfully be called a *dedicated database server.*

Following this approach, users submit requests to sort a database, and the sorting is done by the database server. Only the request from the user travels across the wire, not the entire database. For the database server to operate over the LAN, it has to run on a network operating system platforms, like UNIX or Novell's NetWare. Most early database servers were based on the UNIX and then ported to other network operating systems.

Early implementations of these database servers were clumsy to install and difficult to configure. Today, companies like Oracle and Compaq have teamed up to ship systems that practically install themselves.

Database Engine

Database engines or servers are composed of hardware and software. Each of these components is important to overall system performance. Selection of these items requires careful examination of your organization's current and future data processing demands. Such systems can cost up to $200,000 for a large organization, so the selection process should be careful and thorough.

Tip:
We strongly suggest that you get your database engine tuned by a trained professional once the system is in place. Failure to do so could result in lower performance than expected, to the detriment of your users and your organization.

Hardware
Determining the hardware for a database server is a critical step in the process. Failure to match up hardware to the needs of the enterprise can result

in unacceptable performance. The following lists covers some of the database server platforms you can choose from:

1. Intel-based single processor (i.e., IBM Mod 90), recommended for small organizations.
2. RISC-based single processor UNIX servers (i.e., IBM RISC 6000 590), designed for medium-size organizations.
3. Multiprocessor server (i.e., HP 9000, Compaq ProLiant 2000), for medium- to large-size organizations.
4. Mainframe server (only if you have one hanging around).

We recommend that you do your homework thoroughly before choosing your hardware platform. Server hardware prices can range from $50,000 to $200,000. The Compaq ProLiant 2000 is in the $55,000 range and houses multiple RISC-based processors. The advantage of going with a multiprocessor server is that specific database engines can be tied to specific processors, permitting the database to have full access to the resources of the processors without worrying about scheduling clocked algorithms.

Newer technology, called *parallel processing,* allows a single query to be split up into several and distributed among multiple processors—a technique called *query distribution* that is similar to the way disk access requests are decomposed and distributed by RAID controllers. A single query arrives at the server and gets divided up and distributed among the available processors. When the query is completed, it is reassembled.

System Memory and I/O

Once the hardware platform is chosen, the next step is to look at the memory and I/O of the system. Although 256 MB is considered a lot of memory for file servers, the amount required for database use is an important matter. Factors such as the number of users and the nature of reporting must be considered. Because memory is faster than disk, it is important to scale memory accordingly if speed is a factor—and our experience has been that wherever databases are concerned, speed is *always* a factor.

The disk I/O of the system is critical. It is important that the database server employ disk drives of the same type from the same vendor. Mixing disk drives from different vendors with varying latencies can cause degradation to the whole system. Striping the disk drives using RAID technology will also increase the overall system performance. We recommend large amounts of storage (at least 4–8 GB for a typical server) and the fastest 32- or 64-bit disk controller(s) or RAID subsystem you can afford.

Software

Database Management System (DBMS). This software is similar in concept to a network operating system. The DBMS is the brains of the whole system. When choosing this software, you will need to evaluate the vendor as well as the software. You also need to match your software with the hardware you intend to buy. For example, if you've selected a multiprocessor hardware engine, you need to ask the vendor if its software can support multiprocessing. The following list gives an example of vendor software and an associated hardware platform:

- Intel-based single processor: Microsoft SQL Server
- RISC-based single processor: Sybase SQL Server
- Multi-processor server: Informix On-Line
- Mainframe server: Oracle7

A DBMS provides tools to manage the database system. These software tools manage data storage and retrieval, security and integrity and administration of the database system. The following features are found in most DBMS systems.

Database Design. The design for a database must be in place before any data are input. Most databases use a data definition language (DDL), which is a database programming language, to drive the design process. DDL is used to build the structure or definition of the primary database. Another maintenance tool, called a *data dictionary*, stores the definitions for the elements of the primary database in another database, along with information about table structures, functions, and other relationship data.

Data Administration. No system is complete without a way to manage access. If all the users on a LAN were permitted to read and write to all areas of the file server, chaos might result. Administration tools can limit or grant users varying levels of access to the data. A separate class of user, called an *administrator*, is the only user permitted to change the structure of the database. This class of access is generally restricted to one or two specially trained individuals (called *database administrators,* or DAs) in the IS department.

Data Entry. Data entry control features help control the process of entering data into a database; they can include simple prompts or may use elaborate screens with decision-making capabilities, error checking, and more.

Report Generation Tools. Programmers use such tools to produce canned reports for the users. These documents generally consist of common reports frequently requested by users. By using predefined reports, users need not waste valuable time continually rebuilding the same report.

"Ad Hoc" Query Tools. Sometimes users want to extract information that is not on the list of canned reports. After all, the IS department can't think of every type of report users may need. These tools help users to query the database for information without having to know all the database internals and other specifics.

Integrity Tools. Unfortunately, servers go down at the worst time. For database servers processing transactions, this can lead to disaster. Integrity tools help prevent disaster from happening on a database system.

Let's say you're inputting data for several customers. You complete your input and proceed to update the database. In the middle of updating, the database server crashes. When the server comes back up, you're not sure which transactions were processed and which weren't. Integrity tools provide a way to track the transactions of a database so that, in the event of a failure, the database can be rolled back to a state before the transactions were processed, or at least so that no incomplete transactions leave the database in a questionable state.

Structured Query Language (SQL). SQL is pronounced "ess-kyoo-ELL" or "SEE-kwill" and is provided by the DBMS. As the name suggests, it's a language used for creating, maintaining and viewing database data. Originally invented by IBM for its mainframe databases, ANSI now has a standard SQL definition across all computers.

Some organizations have several types of database systems in-house, and having a standard for SQL across platforms and operating systems allows these different systems to communicate and exchange data. We think you'll find this to be a technology well worth investigating.

Deploying the Workhorse

Some organizations may have or plan to have only one database engine. However, heterogeneous organizations that are attempting to connect several engines along with many sets of databases must decide how to distribute the data and how to control database access over the network.

Distributing data can be defined as spreading data across multiple servers in a network. A DBMS on one server can manage the distributed data, or it can relinquish that responsibility to the network. For the network to handle the distributed data, it must be using a distributed file system (like NFS).

Distributing control means that multiple servers manage the database structures and access. DBMSs on every server in the network must work together so that changes are synchronized. This can be quite complicated if an organization is not using the same DBMS system!

Oracle's SQL*Net V2 is an excellent example of distributed computing. It permits data to be located on several servers throughout an organization. These servers can run different operating systems or use different hardware or networking technologies, but to the users, it all appears as one unified system.

What Is Client/Server?

Client/server is an architecture that permits the client to perform some or all of the application processing. A long time ago, in the mainframe world, dumb terminals were used to extract data from mainframe databases. The mainframe handled all of the processing and requests and then sent screen dumps back to the terminal. When PCs came along and then became powerful desktop processors, companies started to migrate from centralized computing to what is now called client/server technology. Client/server architectures separate the data storage and the data manipulation functions in the network. Storage and some network functions are performed by servers, while memory-intensive processing is performed by clients associated with those servers.

Client/server architectures are important to business for many reasons. Most importantly, they allow data and reporting to be done in the departments where they are most needed and best understood rather than by technicians in a central location. This makes a business more flexible and better prepared to respond to factors in the marketplace.

BACK TO THE FUTURE

Up to now, we have only discussed storing, retrieving and managing text. However, as multimedia proliferates, video, text, graphics, and digital sound will all be classified as data, and, inevitably, stored in database servers.

The movie industry is a good example of an industry whose data storage needs go considerably beyond traditional text. An emerging technology that can handle these storage-intensive types of data is called *binary large object* (BLOB). Accommodation of multimedia promises to greatly enrich DBMS capabilities while increasing its already prodigious appetites for CPU power, RAM, and disk space!

SUMMARY

Of all of the services a network can deliver, database access is probably the most important. Today's data-hungry organizations demand high performance and immediate access to LAN-based database servers. In this chapter, we've tried to cover the basic concepts and terminology for database design, creation and management. We've also introduced the key elements involved in selecting and deploying usable database services in your organization. Here again, we could write a book—if not many books—on this fascinating topic. Please consult the bibliography section at the end of this chapter for more information on the subject.

THE TOP FIVE DATABASE VENDORS

Oracle Corp.
500 Oracle Pkwy.
Redwood Shores, CA 94065
800-633-0596; 415-506-7000
Direct sales: 800-ORACLE-7
FAX: 415-506-7200
Tech support: 415-341-4333 (PC); 415-341-3003

Borland International, Inc. (InterBase Division)
100 Borland Way
PO Box 660001
Scotts Valley, CA 95067-0001
800-245-7367; 408-431-1000
FAX: 408-439-9208
Tech support: 800-841-8180

Microsoft Corp.
One Microsoft Way
Redmond, WA 98052-6399
800-426-9400; 206-882-8080
Direct sales: 800-MSPRESS
FAX: 206-635-6100
Tech support: 206-454-2030; 206-637-7098 (Windows)
Tech support BBS: 206-936-6735

Sybase, Inc.
6475 Christie Ave.
Emeryville, CA 94608
800-8-SYBASE; 510-596-3500
FAX: 510-658-9441
Tech support: Use toll-free no.

Informix Software, Inc.
4100 Bohannon Dr.
Menlo Park, CA 94025
800-331-1763; 415-926-6300
Direct sales: 800-688-INFX
FAX: 415-926-6593
Tech support: 415-926-6626

DATABASE SERVERS:
BIBLIOGRAPHY AND STRATEGIES

For general networking references, please consult Appendix C, "A List of Networking Resources." The magazines and other publications listed there can help you find lots of information about database servers. The following references are particularly helpful for the information they contain about database servers and vendors.

Gillette, Rob, Dean Muench and Jean Tabaka. *Physical Database Design for Sybase SQL Server*. Englewood Cliffs, NJ: Prentice Hall, 1995. A 225-page book written for the experienced SQL Server database designers. $49.00.

Myers, Marc. "Choosing a Database Server." *Data Based Advisor* 12, no. 10 (Oct. 1994):86. A good article on selecting a database server and showcases products of the six largest vendors.

Linthicum, David. "Database Servers Rise to New Demands." *PC Week* 11, no. 36 (Sept. 12, 1994):S27. (NetWorld + Interop Technology Review supplement). Good article discussing Oracle's Parallel Query Option on symmetric multiprocessors (SMP), massively parallel processors (MPP) and clustered multiprocessing machines. Also discusses binary large object (BLOB) technology and replication servers.

Watt, Peggy, Edward Dowgiallo, and Amy H. Johnson. "Databases Conquer New LANs." *InfoWorld* 16, no. 46 (Nov. 14, 1994):128. Excellent overall comparative article on Microsoft Corp's SQL Server for Windows NT 4.21A and Oracle Corp's Oracle 7.0.16 software packages. This in-depth article includes three spreadsheets that cover various SQL-related database engine capabilities and features.

"Database Servers and Host DBMSs" (1994 Database Buyer's Guide and Client/Server Sourcebook). *DBMS* 7, no. 6 (June 15, 1994):34. At the time of this writing, we did not see the 1995 issue out, but this is an excellent starting ground if you are just beginning to research database servers and DBMSs. The Buyer's Guide lists names, addresses and phone numbers of the vendors, along with a paragraph on the product.

Sheldon, Tom. *The LAN Times Encyclopedia of Networking*. Berkeley, CA: Osborne McGraw Hill, 1994. A general sourcebook for networking terms and technologies, it includes discussions, some lengthy and detailed, about database technology. $39.95.

THE TOP FIVE DATABASE VENDORS

Oracle Corp.
500 Oracle Pkwy.
Redwood Shores, CA 94065
800-633-0596; 415-506-7000
Direct sales: 800-ORACLE-7
FAX: 415-506-7200
Tech support: 415-341-4333 (PC); 415-341-3003

Borland International, Inc. (InterBase Division)
100 Borland Way

PO Box 660001
Scotts Valley, CA 95067-0001
800-245-7367; 408-431-1000
FAX: 408-439-9208
Tech support: 800-841-8180

Microsoft Corp.
One Microsoft Way
Redmond, WA 98052-6399
800-426-9400; 206-882-8080
Direct sales: 800-MSPRESS
FAX: 206-635-6100
Tech support: 206-454-2030; 206-637-7098 (Windows)
Tech support BBS: 206-936-6735

Sybase, Inc.
6475 Christie Ave.
Emeryville, CA 94608
800-8-SYBASE; 510-596-3500
FAX: 510-658-9441
Tech support: Use toll-free no.

Informix Software, Inc.
4100 Bohannon Dr.
Menlo Park, CA 94025
800-331-1763; 415-926-6300
Direct sales: 800-688-INFX
FAX: 415-926-6593
Tech support: 415-926-6626

COMMUNICATIONS SERVERS

For the past 10 years, LANs have been sprouting up and growing all over the world. Today, it's probably easier to name the businesses that don't use LANs than the ones that do. The use of client/server applications and architectures has exploded, along with white-hot demand for group productivity products like corporate e-mail packages and Lotus Notes. With more and more mission-critical applications being rightsized onto LANs from mainframe environments, even the most dyed-in-the-wool mainframe users have grown to depend on the services of their LANs.

Because of the Clean Air Act mandated by the U.S. government in 1990, companies are looking at ways to reduce the number of cars on the roads carrying their employees. Some organizations have implemented pilot studies on telecommuting, where selected employees work in home offices, connecting their home PCs to their office PCs. And every company's sales representatives need a way to communicate with the home office and exchange information while traveling. Many salespersons already have laptops that they can take with them on the road but still lack the ability to connect to their home office LANs.

All of these trends have spurred a growing interest in remote communication. In this chapter we discuss different ways for users to dial into and out of their LANs.

GENERAL COMMUNICATION

Let's take a brief look at some basics of modem and LAN communications and then move on to a discussion of communications servers. Discussing the basics here will lay the groundwork for the rest of this chapter.

PCs and Modems

A modem connects to a PC's serial interface using an RS-232 modem cable. Modems send data in a serial fashion, one bit at a time in an "unclocked" or asynchronous manner. A start bit and stop bit signal the beginning and end of the data transmission.

As a modem sends data to a PC's serial interface, a UART (universal asynchronous receiver/transmitter) chip, located on the serial interface, intercepts the data. The UART chip converts the data from an RS-232 format to a PC bus format by stripping off the start and stop bits. Next, the UART chip generates an interrupt to the microprocessor to indicate that it has data ready to go to the communications software loaded on the PC. The processor hands this data over to the communications software that is in charge of processing the incoming data.

Technobabble:

On earlier PCs, older model 16450 and 8250 UART chips were commonly used. These chips processed data 1 byte at a time. If the processor did not process the data in the buffer by the time the next byte arrived, the first byte would be lost. Newer PCs generally ship with a 16550 UART. This newer model processes data 16 bytes at a time. But in a system whose sole function is to process communications among many users, even a 16-byte buffer would quickly become overloaded. In this case, it is best to look at intelligent serial I/O cards like the AccelePort cards from DigiBoard, or ARTIC (pronounced "arctic" as in the North Pole) cards from IBM. These cards typically have an onboard processor with extra memory to process and buffer incoming data.

LANs and Modems

A LAN does not send data one bit at a time like a modem, but rather in packets in a "clocked" or synchronous manner. The clock specifies the beginning and end of each data transmission. When a user dials in from a remote location, his or her modem sends the data to the LAN in serial format, which the LAN is unable to interpret.

LANs don't expect data to come with start and stop bits; your network operating system is looking for data that have appropriate header, trailer, and address information. Because modem data and LAN data use different formats, data will be interpreted incorrectly if there is no translation between the two. A communications server functions as a gateway between these two worlds and provides the necessary translation of the two formats.

Communications Servers

Communications servers are typically high-powered PCs with 486 processors (or better), multiport serial boards, high-speed modems, and communications software.

Communications servers manage modem pools attached to a server. A modem pool consists of two or more modems connected to a multiport serial card. The card is shared by users who dial in for LAN access or dial out of the LAN using one of the modems in the pool. The software loaded on the communications server manages tasks like connecting and disconnecting modems, managing network connections, and keeping track of what's going on with all the various devices it must control.

X.25 pads and LAN-to-mainframe gateways are also considered communications servers, but in this particular chapter we'll keep it simple, and focus on dialing into and out from a LAN.

The Popular Dial-up Methods

We've grouped dial-up communications into the four most popular and widespread areas of use today:

1. single-user remote control
2. multiuser remote control
3. remote node
4. dial out

The three items on the list represent dialing into an office or LAN, the fourth item, dial out, deals with communicating from an office or LAN to a computer resource outside the office environment. Examples of an outside computer resource would be an on-line service like CompuServe or a technical bulletin board service that a vendor's technical support might offer its customers. Single-user remote control does not typically involve the use of a communications server, but we describe it here because it is important in the evolution of multiuser remote control.

Remote Control

Remote control gained popularity around 1985 when file-sharing software like Carbon Copy from Microcom appeared on the market. With a remote control program, a user is able to load communications software on an office or host PC and use it to support a connection from a remote PC at home or on the road.

This connection requires a modem at each end and an analog phone line to carry the data. These remote control applications allow remote users to take control of a PC over the modem connection. The remote site acts like a dumb terminal to the host PC, so only the keyboard and screen are active on the remote PC. Applications are executed on the host PC, with the remote user receiving screen updates back to the remote PC.

The remote control method requires a dedicated host PC to be up and running in host mode to support a remote PC connection. This proves to be a major disadvantage for organizations, both large and small. Not many businesses can afford to dedicate a PC exclusively to the task of waiting for a call to come in from a remote user.

In addition to a dedicated PC, the remote control method requires an analog line and a modem for each host PC. If an organization occupies several floors or has a campus environment, this method can cause administrative nightmares as well as high setup costs for extra lines and modems. If a user dials in only occasionally, remote control hardware costs could be prohibitive.

Multiuser Remote Control

Large organizations looking to save money on modems, PCs, and telephone lines can use multiuser remote control technology to connect remote users to resources at a host site, while saving on hardware costs. Basically, multiuser remote control takes the remote control we described in the previous section and adds the ability to share modems, analog lines, and PCs. Instead of having a separate line, modem, and PC for each user, an organization can set up a pool of these resources to be shared among remote users. Because this pool of resources is centrally located at the host site, administration of an organization's dial-up access is simpler.

Gotcha:

Multiuser remote control works only if users connect occasionally and do not remain connected for long periods of time. To share resources, resources must be free occasionally. If you have four modems with four users who remain logged on constantly, they leave nothing free for other would-be remote users.

Implementations of multiuser remote control at the host site typically include a communications server, several high-speed modems, and communications software. A communications server typically contains one or more high-speed processors like 486 CPUs.

Gotcha:

On servers where there is only one processor, service can be divided among as many as 15 sessions. However, when one processor is divided into 15 virtual machines, the virtual machines behave like XT-type processors, both in terms of capability and performance. For example, if you take a 486 PC and divide it so that it has 15 XT speed processors, you haven't really gained anything useful unless your dial-up needs are only for file transfer. A better approach is to add several 486 processors, and to allow each processor to handle a single session. That way, each remote user gets his or her own real computer, instead of a pale virtual imitation of one!

On the remote side, little horsepower is required because the remote site does not handle the processing; it merely acts as a dumb terminal. If your organization has a lot of high-powered PCs at the office, but your users have low-end PCs at home, multiuser remote control is an excellent choice.

Speed was once a problem for remote users running graphics-intensive software like Windows. Early versions of communications software were originally designed for DOS programs, so older programs used to repaint the whole Windows screen at the remote site every time the user moved the mouse. Now, newer software like ReachOut from Ocean Isle, sends only differential changes, thereby eliminating the need to send large graphics screen dumps back to the remote user. This significantly speeds up remote control for Windows, so sluggish performance is no longer an issue.

Companies like Cubix and J&L Communications are the leaders in the remote control industry. They provide proprietary hardware that comes in a special cabinet housing a backplane for attaching individual processors. These vendors build fault tolerance into their boxes, and some of these machines include built-in multiplexers so individual processors can share a common monitor and keyboard. Most remote control hardware comes bundled with the vendor's proprietary software, DOS, Windows, and a set of communications applications.

Both Cubix and J&L have been in the remote control industry for a long time. Their products have matured into reliable, secure servers. Network administrators from middle size companies need to seriously consider getting one of these special servers, if you don't have one or two already. Cubix, for example, works hand in hand with *system integrators*, technicians who do nothing but install and configure Cubix boxes.

Take our word for it, setting up a communications system can be a frustrating, tedious chore. You'll have lots of chances to start over. We've done it, so we speak from firsthand experience! We recommend that you pay a little extra and have an integrator come out and perform the installation. You can watch over his or her shoulder and ask lots of questions, so don't worry about getting bored!

Lots of satisfied remote dial-up users are looking at a new twist on remote access, called *remote node access*. In this approach, the remote machine establishes a virtual connection to its home network, where it can access all kinds of resources, not just the capabilities of a single machine.

We spoke about remote node technology with Tom Kayser, a communication specialist at a major oil company. Tom has been a longtime proponent of multiuser remote control for dial-up access. Although he feels there will always be a market for remote control, he also sees a big future for remote node communications. Tom has been involved in remote access computing since its inception, and has written a book on remote access, *Telecommuting—The Future Present*.

Remote Node

The remote node method became popular for users who needed to share files with a host site LAN, but didn't need to run applications from the host's LAN. By loading special software on a remote site PC, users are able to connect to a host site's remote node server (RNS) and tap in to all the resources available on a LAN.

The RNS handles the communication between remote nodes and the LAN. RNSs are typically based on Motorola's 68000 processor. Unlike the remote control server, an RNS server commonly can handle up to 32 virtual sessions for each inbound call, because the RNS server is only translating the data's serial format into a LAN format and keeping an eye on each session.

One way to picture remote node access is to visualize an exceptionally long LAN cable stretching from a remote PC to a host LAN. All of the LAN services provided to LAN users can be accessed over telephone lines linking the LAN and the remote node.

As more users purchase home PCs with 486 and Pentium processors, the need for remote control access diminishes. Users can run applications on their home PCs, along with their familiar GUI interfaces at the same speeds they expect at work. But remote node access still provides users with the ability to transfer files to and from a host or a LAN or to send e-mail over the link.

Remote nodes work best if remote users have all their executable files running locally, although this is not strictly required. Be advised, however, that running applications at a host site from a remote node yields significantly lower levels of performance, as applications get downloaded to the remote node using slow phone links, instead of running at local PC speeds. For example, if you're trying to log onto a Novell LAN at a host location, it is faster to have the LOGIN.EXE file executing locally on the remote node than to run it from the host.

If you're running Windows, the remote node method is faster than the remote control method only if you have the Windows executable files residing on the remote node PC's hard disk. Any time you're trying to run applications from the LAN, especially graphical ones, the remote control method will be faster. If you must transfer large graphical files to and from a LAN, the remote control method will be faster as well.

Certain applications run better in a remote node session. These typically include client/server applications where the executable file was designed to reside on the client. Examples of such applications include Lotus Notes, Windows for Workgroup, and e-mail software.

Dial-Out

With more and more business computer users accessing bulletin board services for information and support and with increased dependence on on-line service providers, companies are facing a dramatic increase modem and phone line usage. Businesses are always on the look out for cost effective ways to provide their users access to all these services.

Before technology for sharing resources like modems became widely available, analog phone line access, modems, and communications software were awarded only to users who were deemed worthy of the privilege. But, as more employees required this access for increasingly critical functions, it became too expensive to outfit each individual user in this fashion.

A more modern method to dial out of a LAN is to share modems and analog lines so that users can pool resources. This sharing can occur only if the users don't dial out and stay connected all the time. Sharing available resources only works if there are resources available to share!

A good example of how on-line access can streamline operations is to examine how Environmental Health and Safety departments function in most typical organizations. This department is usually responsible for keeping up with the latest rulings affecting safety regulations and distributing that information throughout the organization. Before governmental bulletin boards were available to EHS departments, government agencies mailed out volumes of paper that were usually old by the time anyone got around to sifting through it. Now that all those documents are available through a bbs, safety bulletins can be passed on to employees the day they are issued. On-line services sometimes allow users to do electronic searches for information they need, which is much faster than trying to sift through paper, and usually results in fresher information.

Some companies like Telebit, provide dial-up services to the LAN as well as dial out from the LAN, all in one server. Other companies require that you have separate modems and servers for each function. Some communication software, like Norton's PC Anywhere, can be used for both dial-out and dial-in, but other software, like CrossTalk MK 4, is geared for only dial-out.

When dialing out of the LAN, the workstation dialing out needs a redirector that takes the data from the PC and redirects it to the communications server. Two important network protocols that support this process are Interrupt 14 and Novell's Asynchronous Services Interface (NASI). When using a modem pool to dial out of the network, some software packages require that a serial port be designated as a target for redirection. This can require some contortions to work around in a network environment (such as mapping COM: ports to devices elsewhere on the network, in much the same way that LPTx ports get mapped to network printers).

Other packages are "modem pool aware." This means that the software supports redirection of the data from the serial port of the user's PC through the network card to a serial port on the communications server.

Technobabble: Interrupt 14

Interrupt 14 is a redirection protocol that uses IBM PC's standard BIOS calls to intercept data going to the serial port on a PC and sends it to a NIC card for forwarding to a communications server. This protocol is character oriented and much slower than the NASI protocol that we discuss later.

Although the Interrupt 14 protocol is much slower, it is most prevalent among communications software packages today.

Technobabble: Novell Asynchronous Service Interface

The Novell asynchronous service interface (NASI) protocol is much simpler to use than the interrupt 14 protocol. NASI is a byte-oriented protocol, as opposed to of interrupt 14's character-oriented protocol. This makes NASI much faster for the transfer of data—and speed can be crucial in communications. Be aware, though, that some software does not support the NASI protocol. Some manufacturers have a driver that you can load on your PC to supply NASI support.

None of the Above

If you need to use a modem pool but your software does not support it, you can purchase a Multi-Tech redirector card for each workstation for about $40. This solution works only with Multi-Tech's proprietary modem-sharing hardware. We are not in favor of purchasing additional hardware for each user to get software to work. But this is available, and sometimes it will be necessary for special needs.

SECURITY

Most communications servers provide a feature called *callback*. This feature allows a remote user to call into the server and identify himself or herself to the communications server. The communications server disconnects the call and calls back the remote site, thereby ensuring LAN security. This method works great for users who frequently dial in from the same number at the same remote site However, for salespersons trying to access the LAN from a different number every 4 or 5 hours, updating this security becomes an administrative problem.

On most systems, passwords are optional but, in our view, they are absolutely necessary. By requiring every user to enter a password to connect to a communications server and requiring an additional password to connect to a LAN, administrators can implement a two-tiered security system that will be sufficient for most organizations.

Some organizations implement security for remote users by assigning individual PIN numbers to each user. This method works as long as PIN numbers remain secure and only if your communications server requires a password to permit access.

HOW NOS VENDORS HANDLE COMMUNICATIONS

Novell has been a leader in developing communications technology for LANs. It and a host of third parties, sell products compatible with NetWare 3.x and 4.x that permit remote access to a Novell LAN. Remote node solutions for NetWare are also available.

Microsoft uses the remote node method in their Remote Access Server (RAS). RAS permits Windows clients, Windows for Workgroups PCs, DOS workstations, and Windows NT clients to access NT servers across phone lines. The NT server must be connected to the RAS server and both must use the same protocol to provide NetBIOS services. As many as 256 remote nodes can connect up to a single RAS server

COMMUNICATIONS SERVERS
THAT INCLUDE FAX CAPABILITIES

Just as more and more modems ship with fax capability built in, communications servers coming online now may offer fax capability in addition to dial-up services. Nowadays, lots of organizations have fax and dial-up services available from one server. High levels of use might even dictate separating these functions onto two different servers.

RESOURCES: BIBLIOGRAPHY AND STRATEGIES

For general networking references, please consult Appendix C, "A List of Networking Resources." The following references are particularly helpful for the information they contain about communication servers.

Newton, Harry. *Newton's Telecom Dictionary*, 7th. ed.
Flatiron Publishing Company, New York: 1994. Harry Newton is a towering field in the telecommunications industry, and his dictionary isn't bad either. Even though it purports to be telecom specific, it's one of the best sources for looking up PC-related acronyms, standards, and other terms that we've ever found anywhere. At $24.95 for 1,200 pages of text, it's a bargain to boot!

Sheldon, Tom. *The LAN Times Encyclopedia of Networking*.
Osborne McGraw Hill, Berkeley, CA: 1994. A general sourcebook for networking terms and technologies. It includes discussions, some lengthy and some detailed, about nearly every conceivable networking topic. $39.95.

Humphry, Saraand and Peter W. Goften. *Mastering Serial Communications*. Sybex, Alameda, CA: 1994. This is a great book detailing serial communications at very advanced levels. $26.95.

Opening Gateways in the LAN Maze: Using Data/Fax and Remote Node Servers for Dial-up Communications, 3rd ed. MultiTech Systems. This white paper is superbly written for all levels of experience to understand. MultiTech is listed in the vendor section at the end of this chapter.

Remote Network Communications for DOS and Windows Environment, Shiva Corporation. This white paper is more of an overview and discussion of the pros and cons of different dial-up methods. It's free! Shiva Corp. is listed in the vendor section at the end of this chapter.

THE TOP SEVEN
COMMUNICATIONS SERVERS VENDORS

Readers take note: Lots of reliable vendors provide excellent products in this area, so we wanted to present you with more than the usual five nominations.

Cubix Corp.
2800 Lockheed Way
Carson City, NV 89706
702-883-7611

J&L Information Systems, Inc. (division of Astro Sciences Corp.)
9600 Topanga Canyon Blvd.
Chatsworth, CA 91311
818-709-1778
FAX: 818-882-9134
Tech support BBS: 818-709-5899

Microdyne Corp.
3601 Eisenhower Ave., Ste. 300
Alexandria, VA 22304-9703
800-255-3967; 703-329-3700
FAX: 703-329-3722
Tech support: Use toll-free no.
Tech support BBS: 703-960-8509

Shiva Corp.
63 Third Ave., Northwest Park
Burlington, MA 01803
800-458-3550; 617-270-8300
FAX: 617-270-8599
Tech support: 617-270-8400
Tech support BBS: 617-273-0023

Telebit Corp.
One Executive Dr.
Chelmsford, MA 01824
800-989-8888; 508-441-2181

FAX: 508-441-9060
Tech support: 408-734-5200

Novell, Inc.
122 East 1700 South
Provo, UT 84606-6194
800-453-1267; 801-429-7000
FAX: 801-429-5155
Tech support: 800-638-9273

Microdyne Corp.
3601 Eisenhower Ave., Ste. 300
Alexandria, VA 22304-9703
800-255-3967; 703-329-3700
FAX: 703-329-3722
Tech support: Use toll-free no.
Tech support BBS: 703-960-8509

FAX SERVERS

TECHNOLOGY OVERVIEW

According to BIS Strategic Decisions, there is an installed base of 20 million fax machines worldwide. That's a lot of machinery out there! All those fax machines are manual, some are located in unsecured locations, others may be sitting idle due to underuse. Because the majority of these fax machines are manual, and technology is moving toward automatic, unmanaged equipment, manual fax machines are giving way to the more convenient form of fax modem boards in computers and fax servers.

Fax servers have been around since 1987 and have been popular for outbound faxing. However, inbound faxing has been difficult through fax servers until recently, hampering their widespread use. Consequently, network administrators have installed many individual PC-based fax modem boards while waiting for inbound fax routing methods to improve. In many such circumstances, installing one fax modem per user is overkill.

This has led to many fax modem boards sitting idle throughout the average working day. The good news for network administrators is that these idle boards are not as noticeable to upper management as a big fax machine sitting out in the hallway might be. The bad news is that there is no cost justification to upper management for installing a fax modem board for every user. The only possible justification for this practice is convenience.

Nonetheless, as inbound routing methods begin to improve, more vendors are jumping into the fax server market with additional features such as e-mail routing, OCR routing, and many others.

What Is a Fax Server?

Simply put, a fax server is a resource on a network for handling incoming and outgoing faxes for users on a network. The basic requirements for a fax server include some kind of machine to host a fax modem board (which may be a proprietary fax-only server, an existing server to which fax services may be added, or a new general purpose server to be dedicated to serving up faxes to its network users), server (proprietary, existing, or new), some kind of client software to let users send and receive faxes, and finally, a network to interconnect users and the fax server (among other things).

The benefits of fax server technology include the following:

- *Cost savings*—Instead of putting a fax modem on each PC, a servers lets resources be pooled to enable maximum use of a single modem. For an excellent worksheet on computing the financial pro's and cons of purchasing a network fax system, consult Harriett Hardman's book (it's listed in the Bibliography section at the end this chapter).

- *Better accountability*—A fax server can track incoming and outgoing faxes and can charge departments or individuals appropriately. Manual fax machines cannottrack incoming faxes for charge-back purposes, and many of them lack accounting functions altogether.

- *Better output*—The output quality of a fax received through a server or fax modem board is better than a fax transmitted through a manual fax machine, simply because it will in all likelihood be printed on a higher resolution printer.

- *Time savings*—By sending and receiving faxes via your network, you can reduce the time it takes to handle faxes. Using a fax server typically means fewer trips down the hall, less waiting in line, less looking up phone numbers, and less time spent waiting for faxes in general.

- *Overhead savings*—Since a fax server can be centralized, this simplifies maintenance, support, and security for the administrator. In addition, analog lines can also be centralized and administered more simply.

    Vendors are taking three different approaches in providing fax servers. These solutions follow next. The three industry players in this arena include Intel, Castelle and Cheyenne Communications. Although each vendor has taken a unique approach, which requires different hardware and software, each has a fairly secure niche in today's marketplace.

- Cheyenne's Faxserve is an NLM-based server. This approach will work best in a small company that wishes to maximize use of an existing file server. Faxserve's list price is $1,195 for 100 users or $4,995 for 1,000 users. This is the least costly solution of the three we discuss, but it does requires access to file server resources that may cause the server to bog down, especially when it's heavily used. Although Cheyenne offers its NLM for as many as 1,000 users, we recommend that you look at another approach if you have that many users or that you dedicate a server strictly for faxing if you're trying to service a large user community.

- Castelle's FaxPress is a proprietary, standalone box that attaches directly into the network. Their approach uses proprietary hardware and hence will not add to the load on your existing file servers. FaxPress lists for $4,295, including all necessary hardware, software, and gateways (and a print server for unlimited users).

- Intel's Net SatisFAXtion creates a PC-based server for one or more of Intel's fax modem adapters.This approach requires you to purchase or tie up a standalone PC that is attached to the network. Since the cost is only $1,995 for up to 1,000 users, if you already have a PC available for such use, Intel's is really the cheapest solution. If you have to purchase a machine, though, you'll want to factor its cost in with the $1,995 for the Intel components. Recently, Intel has added support for a limited set of third-party modems to its software, including the GammaLink GammaFax family of products.

Underlying System Requirements

Although many current solutions are built around Novell's NetWare platform, other solutions can support multiple platforms, including mini- and mainframe computers. Biscom, Inc., is one company that offers these kinds of multiplatform products. Other solutions might not offer support for minicomputers or mainframes, but they may support a variety of NOS solutions. If you have an IBM network, you will have to rule out Cheyenne's NLM solution. If you have a mixed environment of minis, mainframes, and LAN NOSes, you might want to look at specific products that support all three environments. Your ultimate purchase decision will depend on your current environment and local configurations.

Type of Services Offered

Tip:
You should expect to find these basic services in most fax servers on the market today:

- *Send and receive faxes from the desktop*—This feature requires careful selection of the client interface. Even though some fax servers bundle client software along with their other components, much care still needs to go into your evaluation of the client-side software. There's simply no point in offering a great system, if its users find it too difficult to understand. As Windows-based faxing software is improving daily, there is no need to consider any package that your users can't point and click on (sorry DOS users!).

- *Delayed faxing*—Queuing up faxes and storing them to send during off-hours (when rates are cheaper) can provide significant cost savings to any company that can afford to wait to send its faxes. Any company that sends a lot of international faxes can recoup its investments in such technologies quickly.

- *Priority fax handling*—When the financial group needs to send a myriad of faxes, but the president needs to send an urgent fax to the chairman of the board, you'll need a method of to keep any single group from monopolizing your fax server. Priority settings or overrides and priority queues are two types of "special handling" services you'll want to look for.

- *Fax routing*—many products offer a choice between automatic or manual routing for incoming faxes. Automatic routing eliminates the need for human intervention, but requires set-up effort to locate individual recipients by e-mail address, mail stop ID, or telephone number. Manual routing is more prone to human error but requires less administrative effort. Most fax-handling systems also offer an option to print incoming faxes as they arrive, just as they would on a regular fax machine.

- *Centralized electronic phonebook*—By replacing a random collection of arbitrarily stale lists of phone numbers with a single shared database, a centralized electronic phonebook eliminates duplicate fax numbers. For a properly maintained database, this can also do away with the need to go searching high and low for Joe Schmo's fax number.

- *Improved security*—Since faxes can be routed to individuals' electronic mailboxes instead of being printed on a public, shared machine, security controls over incoming faxes can be improved 10-fold.

- *Individual cover pages*—Users can customize and individualize their cover pages. In some companies this is an absolute must, in others it is another handy feature.

- *OCR*—Computer-based fax receipt automatically confers the ability to convert faxes to editable documents, provided the fax package includes optical character recognition (OCR) software or its formats are intelligible to a third-party OCR package (like Caere's OmniPage).

- *Centralized fax management*—Network administrators can usually manage the fax servers right from their desks or from some centralized location on the network. Less knowledgeable network users even handle more routine fax server management tasks, provided that they don't require extensive network knowledge, leaving the more network intensive management duties to the LAN administrator.

Some fax servers even offer gateway connectivity to e-mail systems, so that incoming faxes can be routed to their recipients via electronic mail. If this is a requirement for your company, be sure to call any prospective fax server vendors and ask them which e-mail systems they support.

Hardware Requirements (Extra Interfaces, Memory, Disk Space, Etc.)

Some fax server vendors, like Castelle, require you to purchase proprietary hardware, while other vendors, like Intel, require you to provide your own computer to house a fax server. Until recently, Intel's fax server worked only with Intel's fax modem boards. Today, their Net SatisFAXtion software also works with GammaLink fax modem boards. In Cheyenne's solution, there is no additional hardware required—other than the server in

which the NLM runs and the fax modem boards that the software uses—
which is possibly why their software is priced on a per-user basis.

To PC or Not to PC

Gotcha:
Where a dedicated PC is required, it is best use nothing slower than a
386DX PC. Actually, we'd prefer to see you use a server with nothing
less than a 486 DX/33 or a Pentium processor. Remember, this
machine will act as a server on your network. Fax files are large, primarily because they are actually bitmapped images—that's why
you'll want to plan to have a machine with enough power to handle
images flying across the network.

Additional Disk Space on the Server?

Plan on adding extra disk space to your new fax server, too. Administrators
may be asked to log, track, and archive incoming or outgoing faxes for legal
or other reasons. Use an estimate of 40–50 KB per page of text as a guideline. For large numbers of users (or faxes), you will find the availability of
multigigabyte hard disks to be a real lifesaver (sometimes, adding a single
drive can add all the capacity you'll need—providing, of course, that it's
big enough!)

Wiring and Communications

Every fax server installation requires some attention to the following communication issues:

- Additional phone lines may need to be installed (typically, one to
  four per fax modem board in your server).

- Inbound call routing methods need to be determined (this is especially important for private branch exchange or Centrex-based telephone systems).

- Consider DID (direct inward dial). On a DID system, each user on
  the network is assigned an individual fax number. This method is
  highly desirable because it requires no manual intervention for incoming faxes (even though a single fax server may actually field all

incoming faxes, using DIDs allows them to be routed directly to their designated recipients).

- DTMF (dual-tone, multifrequency) may save time. Each user on the network has a unique telephone extension. This is less convenient for senders, senders are required to dial a fax number and then insert the recipient's (or recipients') extension(s) when transmitting faxes into such systems. Because it requires system knowledge from users likely to be unfamiliar with the telephone system, it imposes an extra educational burden on all users.

- OCR may save time, too. The person or program transmitting a fax must include some type of predetermined code in a specific area on the cover page. For example, some fax systems require the sender to put the recipient's name in Courier 12 typeface in the left-hand corner of the cover page, so that it can be scanned and then recognized to drive the routing process. While workable, this approach is not terribly convenient and, like DTMF, requires educating all users, both inside and outside the organization using this approach.

The basic goal driving the fax server-related communications is to avoid using analog lines punched down all over a building. The more data, be it for faxes or normal network traffic, that you can run over the same set of wires (what you know as your network), the less frayed you will find yourself at the end of the day. Installing individual fax modems in every PC requires you to maintain a set of analog wires in addition to your LAN cabling. (Note: if you're not already responsible for your organization's cable plant, you should go and get friendly with that person now, since you're going to need his or her help when you set up your fax server.)

Interface and Fax Modem Boards

Fax servers require network interface boards along with fax modems. Companies like GammaLink and Brooktrout provide multichannel boards that permit more than one phone line to be attached to a single PC interface card. This is useful in companies where large numbers of users are involved.

Also, fax modem boards for use in servers should be CAS 2 compliant, and they should supply as much on-board processing as possible, to prevent incoming or outgoing faxes from tying up your server's CPU. Once a fax job arrives at your server, that server wants to be able to forward the job to the fax modem card for processing as quickly as it can. This frees up the processor to service other requests.

All of your fax modems should operate at a minimum of 9600 Kbps, but we'd recommend at least 14.4 Kbps fax modems (V.32 or V.32bis, with V.42bis compression), because prices have dropped so dramatically for this kind of equipment. In fact, we'd recommend taking a long hard look at the newer V.34 and V.34bis modems available today, to see if your organization could benefit from their use.

In addition to buying the fastest equipment you can afford, your fax modem boards should include support for CCITT Group III operation. Some fax modem boards offer error checking (i.e., MNP5 or V.42), even it is not strictly required for use in fax server. Nevertheless, we feel strongly that spending the small extra sums of money needed to obtain such features will quickly be repaid if they are ever needed.

Software Requirements

Here again, depending on the type of fax server you select, you may not need certain software. The following list is essentially the bare minimum software requirements you'll need for a successful fax server installation:

- Fax server software
- Client fax software (drivers and client interface)
- TWAIN support (optional, but really good idea—for the details on TWAIN, please consult Chapter 39)

FAX SERVER PRODUCTS

Mini-Reviews of the Top Three or Four Products

Best Buy:
Throughout this chapter, we have mentioned the top three fax server vendors: Intel, Castelle and Cheyenne. We will use this section to discuss a review by Elizabeth Eva, Victor R. Garza, Robert Gryphon and Andre Kvitka, entitled "Evolution of the fax" that appeared in *Info-World*, April 3, 1995, vol. 17, Issue 14, pp 62–76. Reviews of those three vendor's products are summarized in Table 32.1, taken from page 64 of *Infoworld's* article.

Performance	Weighting	Castelle FaxPress 2K/3.5	Cheyenne Faxserve 2.0c	Intel Net Satisfaxtion 3.0
Install and config	100	Good	Satisfactory	Good
Send/receive fax	150	Good	Satisfactory	Excellent
Interoperability	100	Very Good	Good	Poor
Routing	100	Good	Good	Good
Administration	150	Satisfactory	Satisfactory	Good
Other features	50	Good	Satisfactory	Satisfactory
Speed	50	Good	Satisfactory	Good
Support/Pricing				
Documentation	50	Satisfactory	Satisfactory	Good
Support policies	75	Very Good	Very Good	Good
Technical support	75	Poor	Good	Very Good
Pricing	100	Satisfactory	Satisfactory	Satisfactory

*Point values as follows: Excellent = 1.0, Very Good = .75, Good = .625, Satisfactory = .5, Poor = .25

Table 32.1   *Fax Server Evaluation Report Card.* Infoworld, April 3, 1995.

This table is handy because it uses a weighting system that allows you to plug in your own weighting factor value and then calculate the product winner for your particular company needs. The formula to calculate this is to multiply your weighting value by *InfoWorld*'s, April 3, 1995 product rating, sum the values and divide by 100. Got it?

FAX SERVER RESOURCES: BIBLIOGRAPHY AND STRATEGIES

For general networking references, please consult Appendix C, "A List of Networking Resources." The magazines and other publications listed there can help you find out lots of information about fax servers. The following references are particularly helpful for the information they contain about fax servers, modems, and communications.

Hardman, Harriett. *Network Faxing: Choosing and Using Your Computer-Based Fax.* New York: McGraw Hill, 1995. A very straightforward book on weighing the pros and cons of purchasing a network fax system as well as a comprehensive look at various different products. $25.45.

Held, Gilbert. *The Complete Modem Reference: The Technician's Guide to Installation, Testing Trouble-Free Communications.* 2nd ed., New York: John Wiley & Sons, 1994. A great book on modems and communications with a special chapter dedicated solely to fax modems. $29.70.

TOP FIVE FAX SERVER VENDORS

Intel Corp. (Personal Computer Enhancement Division)
5200 N.E. Elam Young Pkwy.
Hillsboro, OR 97124-6497
800-538-3373; 503-629-7354
FAX: 503-629-7580
Tech support: 503-629-7000
Tech support BBS: 503-645-6275

Castelle Inc.
3255-3 Scott Blvd.
Santa Clara, CA 95054
800-289-7555; 408-496-0474
FAX: 408-496-0502
Tech support: Use main no.

Cheyenne Software, Inc.
3 Expressway Plaza
Roslyn Heights., NY 11577
516-484-5110
Direct sales: 800-243-9462
FAX: 516-484-3446
Tech support: 800-243-9832
Tech support BBS: 516-484-3445

Biscom, Inc.
321 Billerica Rd.
Chelmsford, MA 01824-9837
800-477-2472; 508-250-1800
FAX: 508-250-4449
Tech support: 508-250-8355

U.S. Robotics, Inc.
8100 N. McCormick Blvd.
Skokie, IL 60076-2999
800-USR-CORP; 708-982-5010
Direct sales: 708-982-5001
FAX: 708-982-5235
Tech support: 800-982-5151
Tech support BBS: 708-982-5092

SPECIAL SERVICES

TECHNOLOGY OVERVIEW

Enter the Hydra

A new breed of networking products, nicknamed *hydras*, after the multi-headed mythological creature, work together to combine printing, copying, faxing, and scanning. Another nickname for this technology combo is PFC (printer/fax/copier). Hydras are an "all in one" answer to a manager's prayers, providing central management for several common business functions.

Although this technology was first introduced in the late 1980s, it never really took off because of high equipment costs. More recently, lower cost equipment has been released to the market by vendors like Panasonic and Hewlett Packard.

Early forms of hydras, like QMS's 2001 Knowledge System, which uses a high-end laser-based technology, were introduced at $3,000 or thereabouts. A processor was typically included along with that price. However, it was too expensive for the market niche that hydras are best suited for—SOHOs, or small office/home office installations. QMS's 2001 Knowledge System is now priced at a more affordable $1,600 without a processor. Most customers these days want to select and purchase that item separately.

Where Are They Now?

The more recent low-end versions of hydras or PFCs list for under $1,000. Now, that becomes affordable for small offices where desktop space is at a premium, and for home offices where $1,000 or less gets you one device that provides multiple services. Because this technology combines four technologies into one, it is offered by only a few vendors at the time of this writing. Because the vendor offering is very limited, the few products that are offered may not be mature enough to fit into a medium or large sized organization.

Sometimes when a technology is emerging, the cost is high and the functionality is low. In this case, the cost is relatively low, but the functionality is low as well. For example, the hydra's four technologies, combined in one unit (remember, some vendors offer scanning capabilities) do not match the power of the four technologies operating in separate dedicated units. The downside of purchasing dedicated units is that you might not find all four technologies from one vendor at a comparable price. However, if you shop around, especially in the *Computer Shopper Magazine*, you might find better bargains for equivalent items, if purchased separately.

LAN Hydra-ting

As with any technology, hydras will eventually end up on a LAN somewhere. We can expect to see this technology improved, and enhanced, and available for medium to large organizations in the near future. A number of vendors, many more than are currently in the market, are racing to supply hydras for the intermediate to large business market. But right now only a limited number of vendors are supplying hydra technology suited for a LAN or workgroup environment. Even though products like Ricoh's MV715 and Okidata's DOC*IT look promising, we feel that the PFCs time has not yet come.

A CLOSER PEEK AT THE TECHNOLOGY

Let's start with the SOHO market products and vendors (Panasonic and HP) and then move up into the LAN arena (Okidata and Ricoh). Examining the individual features of each product will help you decide if a PFC is suitable for a remote office, or a network, or maybe just not suitable at all. This is just a sampling of the features provided, so it is best if you contact the vendor directly and get more information or, better yet, a demonstration!

If you plan to purchase this type of technology for your LAN, remember that any central technology center can also serve as a single point of failure for several functions that can be deemed critical. Make sure that you get a good service or maintenance contract for this single point of failure technology!

The SOHO Market

The most popular vendors providing products for the SOHO market are Panasonic and Hewlett Packard. We rate the Panasonic as the better choice of the two vendors because it has better printing speeds, supports Macintoshes and IBMs, and has better paper handling capacities. Interesting features to note are laser emulation, which is generally that of an HPII or HPIII instead of an HP4, and fax modem speeds that often achieve blinding speeds of up to 9,600 bps!

Best Buy: Panasonic KX-SP100

- Price: $999
- *Printer:* b/w, 4 ppm, 300 dpi
- Printer emulation: HP LaserJet IIP (PCL 4)
- Interface: Parallel
- Compatible with Apple Macintosh; IBM PC
- Base/max RAM: 2MB/4MB
- In/out paper capacity: 70/50 sheets
- Paper size: Letter, legal, A4, envelopes
- Duty cycle: 2,000 pages/mo.
- *Fax:* Group 3, 9,600 bps, 10 page sheet feeder
- *Copier:* 300 dpi

Best Buy: Hewlett-Packard OfficeJet

- Price: $959
- *Printer:* b/w, 2.5 ppm, 600 dpi
- Printer Emulation: Equivalent to HP DeskJet printers
- Interface: Parallel
- Compatible with IBM PC
- Input paper capacity: 20 sheets
- *Fax:* Group 3, 9,600 bps, users cannot transmit files directly from word processors
  5. *Copier:* limited capabilities

Higher End Markets

Some of these systems may be fine for lower output needs on small LANs or if money and space are an issue. Ricoh's product promises the best bang for your buck even though it's asking for a lot of your bucks. The most promising feature we saw in that product was its optional ISDN feature. This told us that Ricoh is already looking towards the future to enhance its product!

QMS 2001 Knowledge System

- Price: $1,649
- *Printer:* b/w, 6 ppm, 600 dpi
- Interface: Parallel
- Compatible with IBM PC; Apple Macintosh
- Base/max RAM: 2MB/10MB
- In/out paper capacity: 100/50 sheets
- Paper size: letter, legal, executive, half letter, A4, A5, B5, envelopes, transparencies, A6, B6, postcards
- Duty cycle: 2,000 pages/mo.
- *Fax:* Group 3

- *Copier:* 400 dpi
- *Scanner:* 400 dpi grayscale scanner

Okidata DOC*IT 4000

- Price: $2,999
- *Printer:* b/w printer, 8 ppm, 400 dpi
- Printer emulation: HP LaserJet III (PCL 5); Postscript Level 2
- Interface: Parallel
- Compatible with IBM PC
- Base RAM: 7MB
- In/out paper capacity: 200/100 sheets
- Paper size: letter, legal, A4, envelopes
- Duty cycle: 16,000 pages/mo.
- *Fax:* Group 3
- *Copier:* 8 ppm
- *Scanner:* 10 ppm, 200-400 dpi

Ricoh Corp. MV715

- Base price: $5,995; all options, $9,425.
- *Printer:* 300 dpi, 10 ppm
- Printer emulation: HP LaserJet III compatible, 300-dpi, 10-ppm
- *Fax:* high-end Group 3 (optional Group 4 fax for ISDN)
- *Copier:* 15 ppm
- Options: Four 250-page paper drawers, a 30-page automatic document feeder, and a sorter with three output trays give you plenty of paper-handling options.

When you get right down to it, there still aren't a lot of products to choose from! We expect to see some joint agreements in the future that will have various vendors that specialize in one or more of the combined technologies teaming up to produce superior PFC products. Vendors like HP might couple with Intel to provide a great combination of printing and faxing as well as scanning and copying. Right now some individual vendors are struggling because they lack the requisite experience in all four of the technology areas.

So if you're planning a foray into the PFC market, you might do well to just sit back, watch, educate yourself, and wait till this promising technology stops taking baby steps and starts stomping around the network technology market.

RESOURCES: BIBLIOGRAPHY AND STRATEGIES

For general networking references, please consult Appendix C, "A List of Networking Resources." The magazines and other publications listed there can help you find out lots of information about networking. However, because this technology is very recent, we found very little material available so we've listed all of the magazine articles here as a starting point. We recommend, however, that you contact the vendors for more up-to-date information.

Brown, Bruce. "Cool Color, Crisp Copy: Buying an Inkjet or Laser Printer."
   Computer Shopper 15, no. 3 (March 1995) 282.

Lake, Matthew. "Panasonic PFC KX-SP100: It Prints, Copies, Faxes and Zooms."
   PC-Computing 8, no. 3 (March 1995) 61.

"Panasonic PFC (multifunction I/O device)."
   PC World, 12, no. 12 (December 1994) 124.

Gardner, Fred. "Panasonic Targets SOHO Arena with PFC."
   Computer Reseller News no. 592 (August 22, 1994) 26.

Damore, Kelley. "Vendors Pack Peripherals."
   Computer Reseller News no. 591 (August 15, 1994) 191.

TOP FIVE VENDORS

Hewlett-Packard Co.
3000 Hanover St.
Palo Alto, CA 94304-1181
800-752-0900; 800 387-3867 (CD); 415-857-1501
Direct sales: 800-637-7740 (HP Direct)

FAX: 800-333-1917
Tech support: 800-858-8867
Tech support BBS: 415-852-0256

Panasonic Communications & Systems Co. (Office Automation Group)
2 Panasonic Way
Secaucus, NJ 07094-9844
800-726-2797; 201-348-7000
FAX: 201-392-4441
Tech support: 800-222-0584
Tech support BBS: 201-863-7845

Okidata Corp. (division of Oki America, Inc.)
532 Fellowship Rd.
Mt. Laurel, NJ 08054
800-654-3282; 609-235-2600
Direct sales: 800-654-0018
FAX: 609-778-4184
Tech support: 609-273-0300
Tech support BBS: 800-234-5344

Ricoh Corp. (subsidiary of Ricoh Co., Ltd.)
5 Dedrick Place
West Caldwell, NJ 07006
201-882-2075
FAX: 201-882-2506
Tech support: 800-955-3453 (Printers and Scanners)

QMS, Inc.
1 Magnum Pass
Mobile, AL 36618
800-622-5546; 334-633-4300
Direct sales: 800-523-2696
FAX: 334-633-0013
Tech support: 334-633-4500
Tech support BBS: 334-633-3632

Introducing Network Peripherals

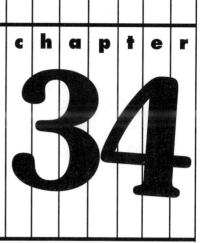
As networking has become more and more important to business information technology, the ability to provide services using a network has also increased in importance. In the last five years, the following articles of office equipment have been delivered to the public in a "network-ready" form:

- printers
- CD-ROM players
- fax machines
- modems (usually available as fax modems nowadays)
- scanners

In this chapter, we'll take a quick look at what's motivating the appetite for such devices, and at some dramatic architectural work underway at several major networking vendors to make this kind of thing even easier in the future. Then, in the four chapters that follow, we'll examine each of these kinds of devices, with a special emphasis on networked versions.

THE KEYS TO THE NETWORK

The simple explanation for the proliferation of network attachable peripherals is convenience. Although it's always been straightforward to attach peripherals to computers (that's what the name actually implies), this has introduced some interesting contortions in the past.

In the past, two approaches to attaching peripherals for network access have been the most broadly used. One approach has been to plug them into a server, typically using the appropriate interface cable (SCSI for CD-ROM, scanners, or external storage; parallel cables for printers; and serial cables for modems or fax machines). The other approach has been to plug them into a networked client machine, using the same cables.

Server-Connected Peripherals

When a peripheral is attached to a server, it goes where the server goes. Because most people like to keep their servers out of harm's way, typically in restricted-access server rooms (or more simply, a locked but well-ventilated closet), this poses some immediate limitations on where peripherals can be situated.

Because printers are the most commonly used peripherals, this invariably requires the use of longer-than-average printer cables to enable the printer to be in a publicly accessible place yet still attached to the server. This is no problem for modems, because physical access isn't often required, but it can be a problem for fax machines (but only if they include a printing/scanning unit). Any SCSI-attached device, which here includes both a CD-ROM and a scanner, can be a problem, because physical access to the device is required (to change CDs on the CD-ROM player and to manipulate materials being scanned on a scanner). And because the length limitations on SCSI cables are pretty stringent (and such cables are expensive), this can be a real problem under some circumstances.

Then, too, servers will require device drivers for the peripherals that are attached to them. For printers, fax modems, and CD-ROM players, this is no longer the problem it once was (most of the major NOSs ship with drives for all three kinds of elements included), but it's still a problem for many scanners today.

Client-Attached Peripherals

When a peripheral is attached to a client, it goes where the client goes or at least fairly nearby. But because clients are all over the place in most organizations and are often affordable enough to be worth dedicating one to a peripheral attachment, they don't suffer from most of the access or proximity problems that you might find with some servers.

Also, because most peripherals are initially used as end-user devices, finding drivers for just about anything won't be too hard, as long as you stick to something fairly common, like DOS, Windows, OS/2, or the Macintosh OS. The problem with using clients for peripheral attachments are different and sometimes most subtle.

First, if a desktop machine actually sits at somebody's desk, the user tends to regard that machine as his or her own private computing province, no matter what the legalities of the situation might indicate. This means users feel perfectly empowered to turn the machine on and off whenever they need to and reboot whenever things start getting weird.

Gotcha:
This has unfortunate side effects if the same machine has a networked peripheral attached—namely, that the availability of the peripheral depends on the availability of the network interface that's plugged into the desktop machine, which in turn depends on that machine being up and running, and logged into the network. Each time the machine is rebooted or turned off, the network connection goes away!

Gotcha:
Also, using a client-attached peripheral as a network device usually means that the desktop machine to which the peripheral is attached must run extra software, in addition to the normal network redirector or shell programs. This extra software acts as a kind of "request catcher" that handles incoming jobs to be printed, scanned, faxed, or whatever (mostly printed, as in common practice). This, too has some unfortunate side effects on the client's user:

- Adding another driver or TSR to a desktop machine adds to local complexity, memory requirements, and sometimes adds unwanted instability.
- Each time the client machine is used to print, scan, or whatever, this activity steals precious CPU cycles from that machine's user, often to the detriment of that person's ability to get work done.
- The peripheral attached to the client's machine will cause other people to stop by to pick up output, change a CD, scan materials, or

whatever. This, too, can lead to distractions that detract from productivity.

All in all, what client-attachment adds to convenience for other users, it can take away from the poor user to whose machine the peripheral is attached. But if your organization should have an older or unused PC sitting around, remember that using such a machine as a dedicated "client peripheral server" is not only a good use of resources, it's the only way to beat the downsides of this technology that we've just covered!

Do It the Direct Way

By now, we hope you understand why direct-attached peripherals are the wave of the future. Because they communicate with servers (or clients) directly over the network, they can be situated wherever it's appropriate. Because they include built-in network interfaces, you can use whatever cables your workstations use to attach to the network to attach the peripherals, also. This supports a much better fit to the networked environment and should help to explain why so many devices ship network-ready today, or why it's easy to buy add-in or add-on network interfaces for such devices.

As you should know from our review of networking technology, however, a simple network connection is not enough. This is where some really interesting work is going on with network-attached peripherals. Some printers, fax modem servers, and scanners are actually shipping today able to not just replace their normal computer cable attachment to a client or a server with a network attachment but also to act as standalone servers in their own rights.

That means that peripheral vendors are building enough smarts (CPU power) into their peripherals to let them act like servers, but it also means that they're aggressively licensing technologies from companies like IBM, Novell, and Microsoft, that will let their equipment look and act just like a "real LAN Server" box to a LAN server client, a "real NetWare server" to a NetWare client, and so on. It also means that they're building disk storage and RAM into these devices in sufficient amounts to let them handle file queuing, status information, job completion notification, and the rest of the things that a dedicated peripheral server must do.

Sometimes, vendors will opt for a lesser implementation—namely, using the network connection as an often speedier replacement for the cable that would have attached the peripheral to the client or server machine in the past. Either way, the watchword remains convenience. And because either implementation offers a significant value added for customers, this lets vendors charge more for such equipment, always a welcome ability in an era when hardware costs, sales prices, and margins seem to be shrinking with frightening speed (to vendors that is; buyers tend to love these kinds of markets).

Convenience Is Valuable!

So, if there was any doubt in your mind before you started reading this chapter about the value of attaching peripherals directly to the network, we hope we've dispelled it. If not, you'll have to take our word for it that this is definitely a "good thing" and that it promises to usher in a whole new era of convenient computer peripherals. Don't be surprised to see networked copiers, electronic routing of faxes via e-mail, much stronger integration of computers and telephone systems, and the like popping up all over the place in the next year or two.

Some of the networking vendors think it's such a good thing in fact, that they're trying very hard to broaden the scope of what's regarded as a network peripheral and are making their connection technologies available to a broad spectrum of industries and uses. In the next section, we'll take a quick look at some of these options.

WHERE THERE'S A CPU, THERE GOES THE NETWORK!

The concept behind extending the reach of the network speaks to an accelerating technological phenomenon—it seeks to capitalize on the increasingly ubiquitous presence of CPUs in lots of different kinds of equipment. Today, most of the office equipment, nearly all consumer electronics and appliances, and even most motor vehicles include one or more microprocessor. Because it's a fairly small extension of functionality and cost to bring the network to many of these things, network vendors are starting to ask themselves the question "Why not take networking anywhere it can go?" In different terms this could be restated as "Why not attach the network anywhere there's a CPU?"

Because of the budgets for office equipment and the ongoing plans to make the network ever more available in the workplace (not to mention that it's the focus for this book), we're going to narrow the rest of our discussion of this technology to home and workplace applications that have obvious networking potential. It's important to realize, however, that, in the vision of the vendors involved in this area (and thinking about jumping in), the market is incredibly huge and it encompasses much more than just office equipment. In addition to discussions of the more obvious elements—telephones, television sets, centralized climate and lighting controls—we've also heard discussions of some pretty far-out or industrial things like pagers, cellular telephones, factory floor systems, automobiles, and major appliances.

Embedded Systems

The most common buzzword for this kind of technology is *embedded systems*, which is meant to refer to the microprocessors included in devices with other primary purposes (i.e., a computer may be part of a device but computing will not be its primary function or capability). This might sound like a wild idea on first blush, but it's actually one that's likely to produce some major benefits for users in the future.

For the purposes of this discussion, the notion of the network attachment encompasses people utilizing traditional equipment in the workplace to manage information flow. Equipment like printers, fax machines, telephones, copiers, scanners, multifunction devices, video/imaging equipment, storage systems, and personal digital assistants (PDAs) will ultimately become information appliances. Widespread access to information should derive from their interconnection and from the interoperation of different types of devices, independent of specific manufacturer or application requirements. The ultimate goal is to provide access to information that people need.

The key benefits for vendors that participate in this outlook on networking include

- Enhanced participation in a large and growing market,
- Access to advanced services, capabilities, and information through networked communications, including advertisement of services, resources, and capabilities to all network users,

- The ability to send status and monitoring information, as well as record repair and maintenance history and to install new firmware, to control device configurations and operations, all to and from intelligent devices attached to the network.

Several vendors appear to believe today that extending the reach of the network offers significant opportunities to those companies that participate, both to expand their existing markets and to develop major new opportunities. In the sections that follow, we'll examine Novell's and Microsoft's views on this subject.

NOVELL'S EMBEDDED SYSTEMS TECHNOLOGY

In the summer of 1993, Novell Embedded Systems Technology (NEST) was first introduced to the marketplace. Its efforts have continued unabated ever since, and they represent Novell's attempt to participate directly in the convergence of intelligent devices of all kinds with networked communications technology.

Novell is convinced that networking is well on its way to becoming pervasive, so that most environments and activities are already in the process of "getting connected" to a network of some kind. Their view of the history of computing technology is that it demonstrates incredible levels of expansion in use, from its initial deployment in purely financial and scientific applications in the 1960s and 1970s. In Novell's view, the 1980s witnessed the introduction of the PC and the concomitant explosion of desktop computing and office automation, while the 1990s appear to ushering a new era of mobile connectivity, where roving workers in the field link up with their counterparts in the office.

Novell also believes that the next decade will witness an incredible proliferation of computing technology, as the home begins to catch up with the workplace. As ever-cheaper and more intelligent CPUs find their way into all kinds of products, they expect the advent of truly "pervasive computing"—that is, where computers are everywhere and all are interconnected with one another—within the next 10 years.

Following these views, NEST includes efforts focused at multiple market segments, including the factory floor and other production environments; office environments of all kinds; the home, with all of its communications capabilities and other contrivances; and the communications infrastructure that reaches into all of these areas that ultimately tie them together. As all of these environments become increasingly computerized, Novell expects that they will also become increasingly better equipped to communicate with one another.

That's why NEST spreads its focus across control networks used to manage and physically manipulate equipment, devices, and human environments and data networks, which deal with the exchange of information and other kinds of intangible transactions. This vision is neatly depicted in Figure 34.1.

As the capabilities of the elements that compose human environments change, the societal organizations that use and serve them must change apace. Novell notes that the phenomenon known as the "virtual corporation," which uses technology to bring collaborators together from many

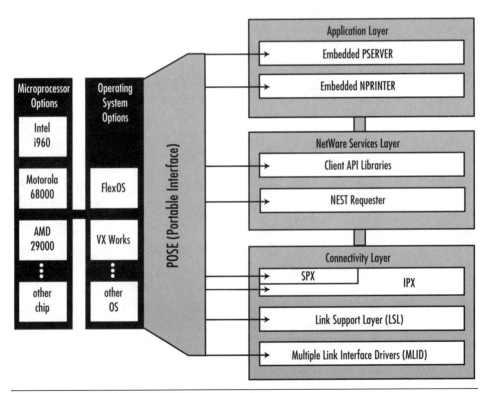

Figure 34.1   *Novell's Embedded Systems Architecture*

organizations that nevertheless acts "like a single company" for the duration of the project that unites them, is probably the first step toward an ever-more virtual workplace.

Novell appears convinced that increased networking and communications capabilities will make such groups the norm. They would argue that the concept could more accurately be called a *virtual workgroup*, because it is the key unit that gets things done and it no longer matters whether its members belong to the same corporation or different corporations. In an era where mobility and ready communications are combined, workgroups can work in a distributed fashion, no matter how dynamic they may be.

The office of the future will therefore have to unite workers from different locations, with different specialties and points of view, to support these virtual workgroups. This means that the broad range of information devices, applications, and services will have to be as available and interconnectable to everyone as the telephone is today. Novell's contention that networking is critical to this vision stems from its realization that the network provides the common link that connects users, resources, and services. In the future, it must do so seamlessly and dynamically.

The Network Is the Key

It's no exaggeration to say that the network, in fact, is where all of these trends toward increasing intelligence, communications, dynamism, and virtuality converge. That's why Novell believes that networking provides the intersection where all of these trends and their underlying technologies can meet. With both host machines and desktops moving toward the network, information access is clearly already being consolidated. With the network providing the transport for information and work flows between colleagues and coworkers, it also provides a confluence for all the data currently handled in today's enterprise. As other data sources—such as telephone systems, document management system, and paperwork processes—make their way onto the network and as the distinction between "the office," "the home," and "remote access" disappears, the convergence of networking and applications will be total.

 Tip:
Novell's chief objectives with NEST are to speed up and smooth out this process. Because the information flows that drive organizations

in general and business in particular will drive everyone toward convergence, this explains the impetus behind Novell's concept of what they call the intelligent office.

An Overview of the Intelligent Office Initiative

The intelligent office represents Novell's concept of what it means to make it easy for office devices of all kinds, including those traditionally not attached to networks, to attach directly to the network. This will allow them to partake of full access to networking resources and services and should enable the creation of new ways to manage and move information within and around the work environment.

Already, Novell has established significant relationships involving its embedded systems technologies with certain key office equipment vendors, especially those who offer devices traditionally shared over a network. This includes several major printer and print server vendors, and vendors of specialized network servers of all kinds (including fax servers, copiers and document servers, and communications servers).

But the idea of intelligent office seeks to go beyond those elements that will obviously benefit from improved network access to include other technologies and capabilities that will make it useful for connections in the office for most kinds of equipment. The concept of "intelligence" in the intelligent office stems from Novell's recognition that, because so much office equipment includes embedded microprocessors and some kind of computational ability, such equipment becomes much more able to connect to a network and partake of the benefits of its resources and services.

More than Just Embedded Systems Technology ...

There's more to the intelligent office than connecting embedded systems to a network, however. At the same time that NEST makes it possible for equipment vendors to add networking to their devices' capabilities, Novell is engaged in other significant technology and development efforts to provide a collection of resources and services to extend worker productivity. A key concept behind the intelligent office is to improve the reach of the network, to be sure; but even more important, this effort is intended to enhance workers' abilities to take advantage of both conventional and extended networking environments. These other efforts include such things as

- **Telephony services.** The telephone is the only piece of office equipment more ubiquitous than the PC; the convergence of these two technologies can provide significant advantages and permit automation of telephone-related tasks and activities, which represent a significant chunk of most office workers' time. Novell's Telephony Services Application Programming Interface (TSAPI) has already garnered support from leading telephone switch and PBX manufacturers and promises to help unite telephone systems and computer networks in new and powerful ways.

- **Groupware functionality.** This lets office workers communicate about their work directly over the network, fostering an electronic method of cooperation for sharing information, managing group schedules and activities, routing assignments, and monitoring work flow and progress as never heretofore possible. Novell's GroupWise product family includes all of these capabilities, and more, all of which are available programmatically as well as through specific end-user applications.

- **Document management.** This lets office workers replace paper flow with network deliveries; that is, it permits the exchange all kinds of documents electronically, including works in progress and images of legally binding documents needed to authorize activities, expenditures, and more. Document management also permits work flow to be documented and controlled, supports both images and editable documents, and can help to speed up information flow throughout an organization. Novell has licensed important document technology from Collabra Corporation and intends to make it a key part of the workings of an intelligent office.

- **NetWare enhanced services.** These make up a key component in the overall functioning of the intelligent office. NetWare Directory Services (NDS) is, in fact, the cornerstone for this concept, because it provides a transparent way for programs, devices, and end users alike to locate one another and the services and resources they need to perform their designated tasks. In the same vein, NetWare 4.1's support for work flow, networked multimedia, video teleconferencing, and other state-of-the-art capabilities make it a platform suitable for tomorrow's networking needs, as well as today's.

Also, by pursuing relationships with third parties to extend what is possible in the networked office environment, Novell is seeking to further leverage the productivity of office workers and increase the automation of traditional office work. Today, these efforts span the full range of the OSI Reference Model, from high speed wide and local area networking media and access methods at the Physical Layer (like ATM and ISDN) to advanced interactive whiteboard and work-sharing services at the Applications Layer (like CU-SeeMe and Intel's VideoConferencing architecture).

In short, Novell's vision of the Intelligent office is to create an office environment where information and work flow smoothly between colleagues and coworkers and where basic tasks and activities are automated as much as possible. This draws in all kinds of office equipment and facilities, but it also makes the human workers much better able to communicate and control their interactions with each other and their working environment. Now, let's take at look at Microsoft's views on the subject.

MICROSOFT'S AT WORK ARCHITECTURE

Unfortunately, Microsoft's Windows At Work Architecture (AWA) although no less ambitious but somewhat less far-ranging than Novell's NEST, has unfortunately been shelved (if not canceled outright, at least according to stories in the trade press we read). We can't, therefore, provide the level of detail for this architecture that we did for NEST, but a quick look at AWA is worthwhile in any case.

AWA was intended to link most office devices, including telephones, to computer networks, so that users could access and operate all the devices from their Windows mail and office applications. By July 1993, over 60 office equipment and computer companies had announced support for this new architecture, including carriers like AT&T, MCI, and Sprint, and equipment manufacturers like Ricoh and Minolta.

At Work applications require Microsoft Windows on the computers in the picture, so that users could transfer calls, send voice mail, route faxes, and run copiers from their PCs. Such devices could be remotely programmed, and transmissions could be scheduled to occur at the least expensive times of day.

The multipart At Work architecture was to have been based on a real-time, preemptive multitasking operating system which sounds suspiciously like Windows NT designed to work with office devices and a number of application programming interfaces (one of which later came to be known as WinPad, an implementation of Windows for touchpad devices, PDAs, etc.). In the At Work environment, each such connected device would have a Windows-like graphical interface with pop-up features keyed to events or user input.

At one point, Microsoft developers planned to include a rendering system for transmission of graphics and fonts, to let networked devices provide better looking displays and outputs. They also wanted to provide the option of secure communications to allow multiple data formats to be safely transported over a variety of supported connections. The connections technologies that Microsoft mentioned during At Work's heyday included standard networking technologies, plus all kinds of wireless links (like infrared, cellular phone, and packet radio, etc.).

Another key component of At Work was the Windows printing system. This component was one of the two most widely adopted components of At Work and was the subject of support announcements at Comdex in November 1994, which included companies like Texas Instruments, NEC Technologies, Epson America, Canon Computer Systems, Lexmark International, and Olivetti. At Work was designed to separate print tasks between the computer and the printer, as opposed to other solutions that are exclusively host based (the host drives the printer) or require intelligent printers (the printer drives itself).

The remaining key component of At Work was Microsoft's Telephony API (TAPI). This component is still quite alive and well and has been implemented by many vendors, especially those aiming at the small office/ home office market. TAPI's distinguishing features are its linkage between individual telephones (up to four lines, in most of the implementations we researched) and individual computers. Whereas Novell's Telephony Services API (TSAPI) is aimed at integrating PBX systems or telephone switches with a (NetWare) network server, Microsoft's TAPI makes it easy to turn the telephone into an extension of the desktop computer.

TAPI includes some terrific capabilities that help to explain its survival, even following the demise of its parent architecture:

- Pop-up Windows to indicate call arrival, call status, and Caller ID information, called *screen pops,*
- built-in call records, including logging, indexing, and call history,
- Support for multimedia voice mail, voice annotation, and networked voice message-handling services,

- Computer-driven dial and redial, from an online phone directory,
- Advanced call blocking, call forwarding, and call handling where the underlying telephone service supports them.

Today, more than 50 TAPI-compliant products are readily available, with many more scheduled for market delivery in the next six months (by year-end 1995). With this kind of momentum, TAPI appears poised to stake a claim on computer telephony at the desktop level.

It's hard to say what led to Microsoft's decision to back away from the At Work architecture. Perhaps it was related to a lack of widespread vendor support (though they have always been able to muster support from "big names" for announcements). Perhaps it was the delays that plagued the architecture: what was originally announced for delivery by mid-1995 had slid until 1997 by the time the plug was pulled.

But if there's one thing we've learned from watching Microsoft closely over the years, good ideas never die—they just come back in a different form (with a different name) a few years later. Even though Microsoft isn't actively challenging Novell's push into the embedded systems marketplace right now, there's no guarantee that it will stay that way forever.

The most interesting thing about At Work and NEST, taken together, is the idea that the convergence of the network and the workplace is at hand. We couldn't agree more, and that's the main reason why we think networked peripherals is the wave of the future and not just another technological flash in the pan!

SUMMARY

When it comes to making device services available, there's no better way than to hook the device itself right up to the network, where it can happily deliver the services required from just about any location. Even though vendors may not deliver full-fledged peripherals with built-in network server capability, there are still clear advantages of convenience and placement to be garnered by purchasing such devices. And, as we look into the future of networking, it seems pretty clear that the number and kinds of such devices that can attach directly to the network will be exploding in the next decade, as we grope toward the era of "pervasive computing."

BIBLIOGRAPHY

Franklin, Curtis, Jr. "The ABCs of APIs." *VARbusiness* 11 no. 6 (April 15, 1995): 123.

Gillooly, Caryn, and Stephanie Stahl. "Grand Expansion Plan: Novell's NEST Connects Uncommon Devices Over a Common Network." *Information Week*, no. 515 (February 20, 1995): 16.

Miner, Nicola. "Printer Makers At Work on Microsoft's Office OS: Faster Printing, Mixed Media," *Infoworld* 16, no. 46 (November 14, 1994): 14.

Morgan, Cynthia. "At Work Architecture Gives Windows Users the Key to the Whole Office." *Government Computer News*, 12, no. 15 (July 19, 1993): 35.

"Novell Ships NEST Developers Kit, Redefines Network Printing." *The Hard Copy Observer* (February 1995): 1–5.

Novell, Inc. "NEST: Novell Embedded Systems Technology." 1994, publication number 461-000262-001.

Novell, Inc. "Novell Embedded Systems Technology (NEST): Technical Overview," July 1994, publication number 471-000035-001.

Novell, Inc. "Novell Strategic Direction: White Paper," October 1994, publication number 462-000462-001.

35

INTERFACES

HARDWARE INTERFACES: BASIC OVERVIEW

This chapter briefly covers hardware interfaces like SCSI (small computer system interface) and IDE (integrated disk electronics). This provides some background that will be necessary before we go onto Chapters 36–39, which focus on network peripherals that require an interface for connection.

A hardware interface is a device that connects two separate devices so they can communicate with one another. Normally, one of the devices is the PC (or other computer) itself and the other is a peripheral device of some kind. To make such a connection work, the hardware is usually accompanied by software, to provide drivers for the specific device involved.

For example, a SCSI host adapter is an interface card that can be installed between a CD-ROM drive and a PC's motherboard (which includes the PC's all-important CPU) to enable the devices to communicate with one another. This chapter is intended to briefly discuss SCSI and IDE interface technology available for peripherals as well as the future interfaces on the horizon. It is our hope that in knowing more about how peripheral components connect, you will be able to pose questions to your vendor on their current and future directions before you purchase any network peripherals.

Some of the information that we will discuss may not be at the level of detail you desire. Some future interface technologies are still very new, and therefore, not a lot of information is currently available about them. However, we present it here so that you may be aware of new trends and so that you can keep an eye out for more information as you read about these technologies in the future.

The interfaces that we will discuss in this chapter include SCSI-1, 2, and 3, IDE, Enhanced IDE (EIDE), FireWire, SSA, and Fiber Channel.

SCSI Fundamentals

Specs:

SCSI (pronounced "scuzzy") is an industry standard Input/Output (I/O) intelligent, parallel bus specification originally approved by the American National Standards Institute (ANSI) in 1986. It is a PC expansion bus that takes the form of a host adapter to permit peripherals to connect through it to pass data to and from a PC. Each SCSI device is connected in a daisy-chain format as shown in Figure 35.1. SCSI devices are designed and manufactured with intelligence that permits the device to understand commands from the SCSI host adapter card in the PC independent of one another.

As Easy as SCSI 1-2-3

Work on SCSI (also called *SCSI-1*) began in the early 1980s, when it became apparent that Seagate's ST506 disk interface transfer rate of 300 Kbytes/sec was insufficient to handle new applications that needed higher levels of hard disk performance. SCSI-1 boasted a transfer rate of 1 Mbyte/sec—three times faster than Seagate's ST506 interface.

SCSI 1 for the Money

SCSI-1 originally only incorporated two devices: the host adapter and the disk drive (SCSI initiator and SCSI target, respectively). At that time, there were no CD-ROMs or other I/O-intensive peripherals other than disk drives, so that's what SCSI-1 was designed around. Because of this, the SCSI-1 standard is simple and straightforward and lacks many characteristics necessary in today's complex computer environments. Since SCSI-1 was intended for only one device and a host adapter, little or no attention was paid to the possibility of bus contention. Therefore, you will find no provisions for bus arbitration, drive parity, or asynchronous operations. All of these "frills" turned into serious problems as soon as users wanted to

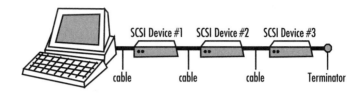

Figure 35.1   *SCSI devices in a daisy-chain.*

hook up more than one device to their PC's SCSI bus. In addition, many vendors loosely interpreted the finalized 1986 standard in their designs and implementations, creating interconnectivity nightmares for those network administrators who tried to use products from a variety of SCSI vendors.

SCSI 2 for the Show

These compatibility problems made it obvious that a stricter interpretation of the SCSI-1 standard was needed to support multi-vendor SCSI configurations. In 1986, the common command set (CCS) was proposed as a solution; it was intended to define a common subset of the SCSI-I command set but actually became the beginning of the SCSI-2 standard in 1986.

The SCSI-2 standard took four years to complete before it was submitted to ANSI for approval in 1990. It took an additional three years until 1993 before it was finalized by ANSI. By the way, ANSI is not a government standards body, but a voluntary standards organization that publishes standards in the United States. X3T10 is the name of the ANSI subcommittee that develops standards in the area of SCSI. Table 35.1 on page 484 compares a few of the features between SCSI-1 and SCSI-2.

SCSI 3 to Get Ready

As the information age continued to pound us with more and more graphics and data-intensive applications, we needed a way of moving data more efficiently between a PC and its peripherals. SCSI-2 bus speeds of 10 or 20 MB/sec were no longer sufficient to keep up with demand, especially on

	SCSI-I	SCSI-2
Transfer Rate	1 MB/sec	10 MB/sec
Overhead	90%	30%
Mode	Asynchronous	Asynchronous, syncronous
Interface	Single-ended	Single-ended, differential
Bus Width	1 byte	Up to 4 bytes
Compatibility between vendors	Poor	Great

Table 35.1   *SCSI-I and SCSI-2 comparison.*

high-performance PCs—like a Pentium sporting a PCI (peripheral component interconnect) bus.

Since the first version of SCSI came along, PCs and their I/O interface counterparts have been playing leapfrog with each other. For example, as the CPU technology went to Pentium, 120 Mhz, utilizing a PCI bus that can handle speeds of up to 100 MB/sec, the I/O channel, even at SCSI-2's 20 MB/sec became a *big* bottleneck. A PC might be able to process the data real fast, but it just can't spit it out quickly enough.

ANSI is currently finalizing specifications for SCSI-3 or Ultra SCSI, the latest SCSI standard, which boasts speeds of up to 40 MB/sec, and is expected to be approved by mid-1995. This may or may not be fast enough for some systems, but it's a move in the right direction. Those users requiring even more speed will have to look to the future at some newer serial interfaces (they're described in a section of this chapter later on).

For the remainder of this chapter, we will put SCSI-1 in the same category as the XT computer—dead. We will discuss SCSI only in terms of SCSI-2, because it is the most widely used SCSI interface in use today. SCSI-3 promises higher speeds, but is not yet finalized.

Speeding SCSI

When we first set out to find a simple chart of SCSI-1, 2, and 3, along with their respective speeds, we found none in existence clear enough to understand. One of the confusing things we found is that every vendor has come up with its own alias for a particular SCSI standard. For simplicity's sake in this chapter, Table 35.2 on page 485 addresses only SCSI-1, 2, and 3.

Under each of those categories, we will talk in terms of fast and wide technology, where appropriate.

Before you read the table, we have one more item to clear up for you. When you see SCSI-2 on the chart, you'll see four different burst transfer rates. The way to calculate the burst transfer rate of a SCSI bus is to take the width of the bus in bytes and multiply that number by the number of megabyte transfers per second. For example, in the basic SCSI-2 interpretation, the following calculation applies:

$$1 \text{ byte} \times 5 \text{ megabyte transfers/sec} = 5 \text{ MB/sec.}$$

However, in the fast SCSI-2 interpretation, the following different calculation is used to determine the burst transfer rate:

$$1 \text{ byte} \times 10 \text{ megabyte transfers/sec} = 10 \text{ MB/sec}$$

The trick to understanding Table 35.2 is to note that the term *fast* in SCSI has to do with the number of 10-megabyte transfers per second regardless of whether you are discussing SCSI-2 or 3. A 5-megabyte transfer per second is not considered fast SCSI, but is termed *normal speed*. The *wide* term has to do with the bus width. *Wide* adds a second data path—therefore, you

Type of bus	Width (bytes)	Transfer rate	Highest burst transfer rate (MB/sec)
SCSI-1	1	5	5
SCSI-2	1	5	5
Fast SCSI-2	1	10	10
Wide SCSI-2	2	5	10
Fast and wide SCSI-2	2	10	20
SCSI-3	4	5	20
Fast SCSI-3	4	10	40
Wide SCSI-3	8	5	40
Fast and wide SCSI-3 (serial?)	8	10	80

Table 35.2 *SCSI transfer rates.*

must multiply the normal bus width by 2. A bus of 1 byte or 8 bits is not considered wide, but normal bus width. In SCSI-2, wide is considered to be 2 times 1 byte or 2 bytes. In SCSI-3, wide calculates out to be 2 times 4 bytes or 8 bytes. The *double wide* term means the bus width is 32 bits or 4 bytes wide. (You don't see this in SCSI-2 because, in that standard, it is essentially dead by ANSI.)

As you can see in Table 35.2, SCSI-3 is the new kid on the block. Actually, it's still in the womb waiting to be born. SCSI-3's expected arrival date is sometime in the third quarter of 1995. It essentially extends the life of the parallel SCSI standard for disk drives, controllers, and adapters. This new extension to the SCSI standard has garnered the support of not only ANSI, but industry giants such as Conner, HP, Quantum, and Seagate. The appealing part of SCSI-3 is that with little change to the firmware of a PC and no change to the physical connection, you can effectively double a disk drive's burst transfer rate to 40 MB/sec.

Here's one last thought on speed that we'd like to share with you—faster speed and timing must be accommodated by both adapter and any attached SCSI peripherals, to take full advantage of the potential maximum speed. If, for example, you hooked a SCSI-2 fast peripheral to a SCSI-1 host adapter, it would work but only at the top SCSI-1 speed (5 MB/sec). These devices negotiate their operation speeds at boot-up time. This always ends up being the lowest common denominator between the adapter and the slowest peripheral.

Tip: Nuts and Bolts of SCSI

We need four basic items to install up to seven SCSI devices in a PC:

1. PC loaded with SCSI software drivers
2. SCSI host adapter card
3. SCSI cable
4. SCSI devices, each with its own unique SCSI ID

All Apple MacIntoshes ship with a SCSI port built in—so if you own a Mac, you can eliminate item #2 from your purchase order. However, the SCSI port on the Mac is not the standard port, but uses DB 25 connector. A special cable is needed if you are purchasing a SCSI peripheral that was not designed specifically for the Mac (this SCSI cable is a DB 25 to Centronix type connector cable).

Each SCSI interface or controller card permits the PC to talk with up to seven SCSI devices linked together in a daisy chain. Also, you can have more than one SCSI controller in a PC at a time. Theoretically, you can install up to seven SCSI controller cards in one PC for a total of 49 SCSI devices controlled by that one PC. We've yet to see a computer that had more than four SCSI controllers installed in it! But, they say it can be done.

So, why use SCSI? What are the advantages of this technology? Here are a few reasons why SCSI is popular today:

- *Speed*—SCSI has several different transfer rates.

- *Multiple connections*—One SCSI card can support connections for up to seven SCSI devices. This is far better than a standard parallel or serial connection, which supports only one device per port. Also, SCSI can hook up to 49 devices to one PC without draining the PC's main processor.

- *Industry support*—In addition to hard disk drives, many peripherals in the industry today support the SCSI standard, including CD-ROMs, scanners, and tape drives.

Asynchronous SCSI Operations

One feature of SCSI that makes it stand out above other interface technologies is its ability to logically connect and disconnect from its host adapter, freeing the adapter and the PC's CPU to process other work while the device is busy handling pending requests (this feature was not available in SCSI devices until the SCSI-2 standard was approved). SCSI-2 (or newer) devices incorporate a connect and disconnect feature. Since each SCSI device has its own processor, once it receives a command from the host adapter, it can disconnect and process that command while the host adapter is working with another SCSI device in the chain (or doing something else). All this can occur simultaneously, thus creating more efficient use of SCSI devices.

TOP SCSI VENDORS

Some of the top vendors in SCSI technology are Adaptec, BusLogic, NCR Microelectronics Products Division, and QLogic.

And, if we haven't given you enough information on SCSI in this chapter, you can dial into a SCSI BBS provided by Symbios Logic, Inc., at 719-574-0424. We found this BBS to have quite a bit of information on SCSI and standards available for download. Ancot Corporation is a company that specializes in SCSI technology. If Ancot doesn't know it, it probably doesn't exist. It can be reached at 415-322-5322. Another company that really knows this stuff inside out is M5 Electronics. It offers disk drive technology classes either at your company or at their own locations in Boulder or San Jose. I spoke with the owner, Mike Machado, and he really did know his SCSI stuff. Mike and his crew can be reached at 303-499-0976.

Don't forget to call your vendor for information, either. Many of them have written white papers on various technologies and standards. Storage Dimensions sent us their white paper on *The Advanced SCSI-2 Technology Guide for NetWare Servers*; it contained lots of useful information that we put to good use in this chapter!

INTEGRATED DEVICE ELECTRONICS

Integrated device electronics (IDE) is also sometimes known as *AT interface* or *attachment*. IDE drives contain the electronic circuitry needed to control them right on the drives themselves, as opposed to requiring a separate controller for the hard disks. IDE first surfaced around 1986 when Compaq was working with Western Digital to design a hard disk drive for the Compaq Portable II, where it was essential that no available slots in the portable were used by a disk controller. Since necessity is the mother of invention, this proved to be an idea with appeal way beyond the confines of the Compaq Portable, and it has become the most popular PC drive controller technology in use today.

IDE became more and more popular with disk drive manufacturers and PC manufacturers alike and was approved as an ANSI standard in 1991. This standard is more commonly known as the AT attachment interface, but we call it IDE, because it's shorter that way!

One good example of an IDE disk drive comes in the form of those so-called hard cards (i.e., a disk drive mounted on an adapter card) that could be plugged into the bus of a PC. Some of the disk drives that called themselves IDE also had an adapter card (not a controller card) that plugged into one of the PC's expansion slots or had a cable somewhere on the motherboard. With this type of arrangement, two disk drives could be hooked up to a single adapter. Usually, most users hooked up only one hard disk drive to the adapter and had a free connection dangling unused.

When CD-ROMs gained popularity in the computer arena, users needed a way to hook up a CD-ROM drive to a PC. Knowing that the IDE drive had an extra dangling connection likely to be unused, it became an issue for hardware vendors to figure out how to connect a CD-ROM player to a PC using that extra connection.

This was not simple because CD ROM players typically use a SCSI interface, and they also have audio needs as well. Enter the enhancement to the AT interface called the ATA packet interface (ATAPI). By means of this new interface, a CD-ROM device could now be connected as the second device on an AT interface adapter card—with the hard disk drive being the first device. No more dangling, unused connection.

Technobabble:

Not wishing to stop with ATAPI but to continue to improve and expand on the ATA specification, some manufacturers came up with two different new enhancements they coined *ATA-2* and *Enhanced ATA*. The purpose of these two extensions or enhancements were to essentially beef up the AT interface to enable it to handle the higher speeds of newer, faster products. In addition to speed, higher storage requirements were needed on local LANs as rightsizing to client/ server environments began to emerge in the industry. Current IDE standards only allowed for 528 MB capacity.

Seagate and Western Digital, two popular disk manufacturers, have been molding their own picture of what they envision the future of ATA to be. Seagate uses the term *fast ATA,* Western Digital prefers to use the term *enhanced IDE.*

Now that you know a little history on IDE, let's take a peek at the possible future of IDE coined *EIDE* by Western Digital.

Enhanced IDE

In future chapters, especially Chapter 37, you're going to hear about Enhanced IDE or EIDE. Western Digital came up with four improvements to IDE that they claim define EIDE:

- *Allow more than two drives per system*—This involves installing another AT adapter in the PC that can hook up two drives to the card. Add those two to the two already installed and you have four. However, to address these 4 drives, your PC's BIOS has to be changed.

- *Permit more than 528 MB storage capacity*—This requires a change in the BIOS as well, since EIDE addresses the disk drive using logical block addressing (LBA) method instead of the traditional cylinders, heads, and sectors method you are currently familiar with.

- *Increase speed*—An increase to 11 MB/sec in speed can be obtained by switching control from the host microprocessor to the hard disk drive and allowing the hard disk drive to decide how much data will flow in the channel. Unfortunately, this requires a PC designed to permit the device to take control. Another EIDE method of increasing speed is to utilize direct memory access (DMA). This is where the device takes the data and sends it directly to memory, bypassing the host microprocessor. This effectively would increase the speed to 13 MB/sec. Using DMA, you would also need a new BIOS and new device drivers.

- *Permit devices other than disk drives to be connected*—EIDE continues to use the ATAPI enhancement.

As you can see, moving to EIDE seems to involve a lot of work with very little return on your investment. SCSI still boasts higher speeds at this time and we recommend that you stay on the SCSI path which, will lead you into the serial interface world we will discuss next. Let's take a look at what appears to be unraveling.

FOOD FOR THOUGHT: FUTURE CEREALS?

Technobabble:
Okay, so we really meant future serial connections! In this section, we'll take a peek at three future serial interface standards coming down the pike, resulting from IEEE's P1394 serial bus draft standard: FireWire, *SSA* (storage system architecture), and FC/AL (fiber channel/arbitrated loop). Of these three future serial port standards, industry giants all have differing viewpoints as to which one will be the replacement interface for IDE and SCSI.

IBM is betting on its direction, known as SSA; while Apple is betting on FireWire as a future serial interface. IEEE's intent behind proposing P1394 is to replace all of the ports on the back of your PC with one type that is low cost, serial and high speed (100 MB/sec). This means that your parallel, SCSI, etc. ports would be eliminated and only one type of interface would need to be used. A P1394 serial bus could carry synchronous data as well as isochronous, multimedia communications. Sounds too good to be true!

All three future serial interfacing schemes have several things in common. First all boast speeds somewhere in the neighborhood of 80–100 MB/ sec! Also, future upgrades to P1394 include speeds of 200 and 400 MB/sec! Second, all support greater cable distances using twisted-pair cabling, with fiber channel supporting twisted-pair and fiber. And, third, all support a higher number of peripheral devices that can be interconnected. Because the interface is serial and smaller, more devices such as camcorders can be connected in the future. Although none of these directions has been finalized, you need to keep a close eye on the direction of these interfacing standards. If you own Apple PCs, you need to understand FireWire. If your direction is with IBM products, you need to familiarize yourself with their SSA directions. Information will be your best tool when deciding which technology to buy.

	Current			New			
	IDE	**SCSI-2**	**EIDE**	**SCSI-3**	**FireWire**	**SSA**	**FC**
Data rate (Mbytes/sec	3–4	20	13.3	40	40	80*	200*
Number of peripherals	1	7	4	15	16	127	126
Cable length	> 1 ft	6	18″	6	72′	20	100
Medium	None	Ribbon	Ribbon	Ribbon	TP**	TP	TP, fiber
Cost/node (dollars)	> 1	5–8	2–4	10	20–25	> 20	20–100

* Dual-ported
**Twisted-pair

Table 35.3   *Interfaces.*

Many analysts are currently wondering if serial interfaces will replace the current IDE and SCSI interfaces. We think IDE and SCSI will be around (like DOS) for a while on the desktop, but will fade away quickly on servers when serial interfaces support more than just disk drives. Dell computers have already begun shipping PCs designed to be servers using IBM's SSA serial interface.

The following are a few of the companies that are supporting the direction of the P1394 serial interface: Maxtor, Adaptec, Western Digital, IBM, TI, Apple, and NCR, HP, Quantum, Seagate, Conner, Micropolis,

Table 35.3 was taken from *OEM Magazine* (February 1995) p. 54. We found it extremely useful in putting interfaces into perspective.

BIBLIOGRAPHY

Basics of SCSI, 2nd ed. A SCSI tutorial written by Ancot Corporation. Contact Ancot for availability information at phone: (415) 322-5322; fax: (415) 322-0455.

Fujitsu, Inc. *Fast Track to SCSI, A Product Guide*. Englewood Cliffs, NJ: Prentice-Hall, ISBN 0-13-307000-X

Rathbone, Andy. *CD-ROM Drives for Dummies*. Indianapolis: IDG Books Worldwide, 1994. A lighthearted but informative discussion of CD-ROM drives and related technology, including PC-multimedia, that covers installation, troubleshooting, and everyday use of CD-ROMs.

Rosch, Winn L. *The Hardware Bible* 3rd ed. Indianapolis: Sam's Publishing, 1994. A detailed source book of hardware technology on every conceivable topic from A to Z. A book that should be on everyone's bookshelf. $29.70

SCSI Interconnection Guide Book, an AMP publication (dated 4/93, Catalog 65237) that lists the various SCSI connectors and suggests cabling schemes. Available from AMP at (800) 522-6752 or (717) 564-0100

SCSI: Understanding the Small Computer System Interface, NCR Corporation. Englewood Cliffs, NJ: Prentice-Hall.

Sheldon, Tom. *The LAN Times Encyclopedia of Networking*: Copyright 1994, Osborne McGraw Hill, Berkeley, CA. A general source book for networking terms and technologies. Includes discussions, some lengthy and detailed, about nearly every conceivable networking topic. $39.95.

The SCSI Bench Reference, *The SCSI Encyclopedia*, and *SCSI Tutor*. Saratoga, CA: ENDL Publications.

What Is Fibre Channel? A Fibre Channel tutorial written by Ancot Corporation. Contact Ancot for availability information at: Pphone (415) 322-5322; fax: (415) 322-0455.

Zadian SCSI Navigator (quick ref.erence book) and *Discover the Power of SCSI* (first book along with a one-hour video and tutorial book), Zadian Software, Suite 214, 1210 S. Bascom Ave., San Jose, CA 92128, (408) 293-0800

Rosch, Winn L. *The Hardware Bible:* Copyright 1994, Sams Publishing, Indianapolis, IN. 3rd Edition. A detailed sourcebook on hardware technology on every conceivable topic from A to Z. A book that should be on everyone's bookshelf. $29.70

SCSI: Understanding the Small Computer System Interface, written by NCR Corporation. Available from: Prentice Hall, Englewood Cliffs, NJ, 07632 Phone: (201) 767-5937 ISBN 0-13-796855-8

Basics of SCSI, 2nd Edition, a SCSI tutorial written by Ancot Corporation Contact Ancot for availability information at Phone: (415) 322-5322 Fax: (415) 322-0455

What is Fibre Channel? A Fibre Channel tutorial written by Ancot Corporation. Contact Ancot for availability information at: Phone (415) 322-5322 Fax: (415) 322-0455

SCSI Interconnection Guide Book, an AMP publication (dated 4/93, Catalog 65237) that lists the various SCSI connectors and suggests cabling schemes. Available from AMP at (800) 522-6752 or (717) 564-0100

Fast Track to SCSI, A Product Guide written by Fujitsu.Available from: Prentice Hall, Englewood Cliffs, NJ, 07632 Phone: (201) 767-5937. ISBN 0-13-307000-X

The SCSI Bench Reference, *The SCSI Encyclopedia*, and the *SCSI Tutor*, ENDL Publications, 14426 Black Walnut Court, Saratoga CA, 95070 Phone: (408) 867-6642

Zadian SCSI Navigator (quick ref. book) and *Discover the Power of SCSI* (First book along with a one-hour video and tutorial book), Zadian Software, Suite 214, 1210 S. Bascom Ave., San Jose, CA 92128, (408) 293-0800

36

PRINTERS

ANATOMY OF A PRINTER: BASIC OVERVIEW

A printer is a hardware device that converts the binary output of your PC into printed text on paper. A printer can be hooked up directly to your PC or it can be installed on your network and made accessible through a print server.

To start printing out the work you're doing on a standalone PC, or on a networked PC, you must first have a printer. This can be one of the many types of printers: impact, inkjet, or laser. But just setting a printer on top of your desk isn't going to produce text on paper. You also need some basic equipment to go with it. The second piece of equipment you'll need is a cable to connect your PC to your printer. This cable can either be a parallel or serial cable, depending on what type of port you're planning to plug your printer into, and it's usually sold along with the printer.

Third, you need a printer driver that's compatible with the application from which you are trying to print. A printer driver is a piece of software that translates the application's print request into a format that your printer can understand. This software driver needs to be one that either shipped with your printer, came with your application software, or was installed along with your operating system. Printer drivers can be downloaded from CompuServe or the Internet, and printer manufacturers also supply them through their BBSs.

Let's run through an example of printing, and trace the actual events that occur when we print a word processing document:

1. We tell the application we want to print by choosing the *print* command.
2. The application loads its printer driver and converts the internal document format to a series of explicit printer commands.
3. When the conversion is complete, the application sends an interrupt request to the CPU that says it wants to send something to the parallel (or serial) port where the printer is attached.
4. The CPU responds by taking the data and sending it out the port.
5. The data travels through the cable to the printer, already formatted in the printer's language by the printer driver
6. Finally, the printer interprets the data and prints the document

That's assuming that your printer is turned on! If it isn't, you'd get a message back from the print driver around Step 2 telling you the printer couldn't be found.

Ways to Print

This example illustrates printing to a desktop printer—of all the possible methods, this is by far the easiest one. Standalone printing used to be the only way to connect a printer until networks came along. Today, there are three common ways to hook up a printer:

1. Standalone, where a printer is connected directly to a single PC.
2. Multiple PCs sharing a printer, typically using some sort of print-sharing device.
3. Printing over a local area network (LAN), using a print server with a directly attached printer, a remotely attached printer, or a printer attached to the networking medium.

As you can see, methods 2 and 3 introduce some complications that standalone printer users never have to encounter. Let's take a look at each of these methods.

Standalone Printing

There are two types of ports on the back of your PC that can support a printer connection: parallel and serial. Because the port sends the data to be printed over the cable, you're going to want the fastest connection available.

The fastest of the two types of hookups is the a parallel port. As its name is meant to suggest, this type of connection transmits data 8 bits (1 byte) at a time across parallel lines. In contrast, a serial port sends the data out 1 bit at a time, with a resulting reduction of throughput. In some cases, this choice will be dictated by a printer's design—that is, it may support only a serial or parallel connection but not both. Some printers offer both types of ports (and even include add-ins for network media interfaces as well).

Using a Serial Printer Connection. Hooking up a printer using a serial connection is slower and more tedious to install, making it the less desirable method. But, if you absolutely have to do this, there are some things you should know.

First, since serial communications transmit the data asynchronously from your PC's COM port 1 bit at a time, the printer at the other end has to know when the PC is finished sending the data and it has to have a way to make sure that the data got there all in one piece. So the data has to be padded with extra bits that communicate this information to the printer. This extra padding, which includes baud rate, character length, parity, stop bit, XON, XOFF, and more, creates some overhead that further slows things down when it's been properly defined. If it's not defined properly, the printer probably won't work at all!

Second, there has to be a traffic cop on the PC end to handle the traffic going to and from the PC. This cop is a little chip called a UART (universal asynchronous receiver/transmitter) that resides on the serial port. This UART chip is important because it determines a serial connection's speed.

Older PCs shipped with 8250 UART chips installed, which include only a 1 byte buffer. For that reason, they operate extremely slowly and can't handle fast data transfers. Likewise, the newer 16450 UART also includes only a one-byte buffer. It, too, is hampered by speed limitations, but they're not as extreme as for the 8250.

Many newer PCs include a 16550 UART, which features a 16-byte buffer that can handle much higher speeds. Just because you bought your PC recently, doesn't necessarily mean you have the 16550 UART chip. To check your serial port, run MSD.EXE (Microsoft Diagnostics) from either Windows or DOS. If you have one of the older chips, you can upgrade by replacing an older version with a 16550 (for serial/parallel cards with socketed chips, it will cost about $15 to replace your current chip; for soldered chips, you'll have to spend about $30 to replace the entire serial/parallel card).

Using a Parallel Printer Connection. In most cases, all you'll need to do can be completed in three short steps:

1. Configure your printer to use the parallel port.
2. Attach the parallel cable from the printer to the PC's parallel port.
3. Configure the print driver for the proper parallel port ID (LPT1:, LPT2:, etc.).

After that, you'll probably be ready to print to your heart's content!

Printer-Sharing Devices

If you absolutely have no money and no network, but you have to share a printer, then this is one way to go. We won't spend a lot on time on this option since it's not commonly used, but you do need to know it's available.

Technobabble:

This method requires that you purchase a device that looks like a power strip. The device comes with software that you install on each PC that's going to be sharing the printer. Typically, one PC becomes the master and all additional PCs are connected to the device as slaves. The master PC keeps the printer-sharing software loaded and resident in memory and has to be up and running for the other PCs to be able to print. Something to look at carefully is whether or not the device handles buffering and, if so, how well it works. Also weigh the costs of the cables, hardware, and connections for print sharing against the costs of dedicating a PC for printing that people can walk diskettes over to and share (networking bigots call this *sneakernet* because data moves when people carry it around on foot).

Networking a Printer

If you want to hook your printer up to a network, here are some additional points to consider:

1. You must have a LAN of some sort, complete with a file server.
2. You need to have a connection to the LAN for each PC that wants to access the networked printer.
3. You're going to need some sort of networked print server to handle network print jobs for those networked PCs.

As you can see, printing on the LAN differs from printing to a printer directly attached to your PC.

Common ways that administrators hook up their printers include

- PC print server,
- external print server box,
- internal print server box.

See Chapter 28 on "Vanilla File/Print Servers" for a more detailed explanation of print servers and printing on the network. That chapter will cover all of these connection options, including the hardware and software necessary to make them work.

Handy Terms in the Printer World

Speed—This is how fast a printer works. Speed can be measured in pages per minute (ppm), characters per second (cps), or lines per minute (lpm). Generally, the higher is the number, the higher the price, no matter what metric is used.

Throughput—This is the overall rate of printing speed. Factors included in this calculation are the PC's ability to send the data, the rate at which the printer's port can receive the data, and the time it takes for the printer to process and spit out the data.

Resolution—This is usually measured in dots per inch (dpi). It means just that. If you have 300 dpi, your image will be good. If you have 10 dpi, your image will be really bad. Generally, the higher is the resolution, the higher the price tag and the more memory your printer will need.

Memory—All printers come with initial memory (1–2 MB for lasers), which usually has some ceiling that you can up your printers memory to. The more graphics type data that you're trying to print, the more memory you'll need.

Font—Essentially, this is the look, size, and format of the printed text. You might already be familiar with fonts such as Letter Gothic, Courier, Times Roman. Fonts can be built into the printer (internal), plugged into the printer via a cartridge, or generated from software.

Language support—You will hear the terms PCL and PostScript. Both are languages that printers understand. Your software sends a set of text commands in one of these languages that the printer interprets and then prints on a page. If you're buying a laser printer you'll want your printer to be capable of understanding both languages. PCL stands for printer control language and was designed originally for use in HP LaserJet printers. However, many printers now use this language. PostScript is another printer language, developed by Adobe Systems Inc. It's best to purchase a printer with a built in interpreter to translate these languages into text, otherwise you'll have to go the old software route, which is slower.

Emulation switching—Now that you know the difference between PCL and PostScript, you'll want a printer that can automatically switch between the two languages.

Paper handling capacity—This is how much paper the printer can support.
Input bin—This is the paper tray that takes paper into the printer.
Output bin—This is the reservoir or holding area where the output goes.
Envelope feeder—An option on some printers that feed envelopes into the printer.

Duty cycle—Measurement of operating time to total elapsed time (i.e., #pages/month)

Duplexing—This means that the text is printed on both sides of the page. Some printers support it, but not all.

Multitasking printer—Some printers can manage their buffer and memory well enough to handle queuing of one print job while printing another. They can print more than just one document at a time.

Printer driver—A piece of software installed in applications that translates the application's print request into something understandable by the printer. Print drivers have versions, so always make sure you have the *latest* version of the driver for a particular printer.

SNMP support—SNMP stands for simple network management protocol. If your printer is going to be in a networked environment and you want to collect information about the printer across the wire from a remote area or a different floor, you'll want a printer that supports this protocol. For a nitty gritty discussion of this, see Chapter 20.

Centronics cable——A parallel cable that fits in only centronics plugs on printers. If you look on the back of most laser printers, you'll see that big, ugly looking plug. It is a 36 pin cable on one end, 25 pin connector on the other end.

Bi-Tronics cable (bidirectional centronics)—This is basically a centronics cable that has bidirectional capabilities. It fits into the centronics plug in your printer. It lets your printer communicate with your PC in a two-way method, transmits data faster, and allows printer drivers to be automatically configured (if you have software that supports that).

DIFFERENT KINDS OF PRINTERS

Now that we know what a printer is, and the different methods in which it can be hooked up, let's take a look at some of the more common types of printers out there: impact printers, inkjet printers, and laser printers.

Impact Printers

Old timers will remember that impact printers were the first printers available for desktop use. I can remember getting my first impact printer a long time ago—an Okidata. Impact printers have a print head (see Figure 36.1) that holds the ribbon up against the paper and strikes through it in a way that's similar to the way typewriters do. It also uses a ribbon cartridge instead of a toner cartridge. Remember the old ribbons? They came on two spools and getting them into the printer was tricky and messy. Now, you can snap that cartridge into the printer in a jiffy—no more ribbon spools.

The printers themselves have pins on the print head that formulate the typed text. The greater is the number of pins, the better the output. These printers can operate in draft mode or in what's called NLQ mode (near letter quality). NLQ mode takes longer because the printer makes at least two passes to print each character, but the output is somewhat more presentable. Because of the design, the printer can print only one character at a time. Thus, this printer's speed is usually measured in characters per second or cps.

Regardless of speed, you will be limited to the fonts that the printer can print. For impact printers the pickings are slim. You'll have to check to see which fonts your impact printer will support.

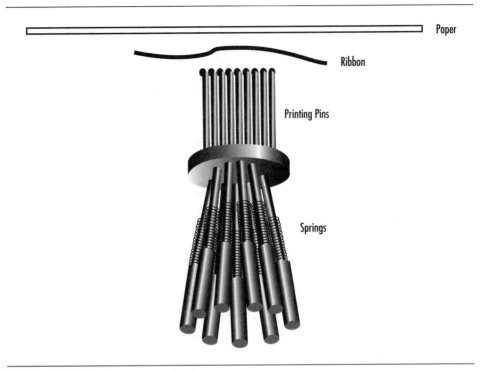

Figure 36.1   *Dot matrix print head.*

There are basically two ways that paper is fed into printers, sheet feed and tractor feed. Sheet feed means that one sheet of paper at a time is fed through the printer. Tractor feed printers have gears where the paper is installed, and as the gears turn, the paper is fed through the printer. Most impact printers are tractor feed, although many will support sheet feed also. Almost all laser and inkjet printers are sheet feed.

Impact printers can print on standard cut sheet paper or on what's called *continuous form feed paper*. This kind of paper comes in a box and when stretched out, looks like one continuous piece of paper with perforations so it can be separated. The continuous form paper is tractor fed and comes handy if you have to print out forms that come preprinted, such as some AS/400 data, or checks, or if you are printing out massive accounting reports that hardly anybody is going to read anyway.

The printer comes in a narrow carriage or wide carriage versions. Always better to buy the wide version since you never know what you're going to end up having to print later on. Why limit yourself from the start?

Best Buy:
Generally, these printers are known for their low prices. You can get one for as low as $125, and most of them are in the $150 to $200 range. But you can spend as much as $9,000 for a real heavyweight heavy duty version. The amount of money you spend is directly proportional to the speed of the printers and the features they include. Table 36.1 lists impact printers as chosen by *PC Magazine*.

Company	Printer Model
Epson America	Action Printer 5000+ [*†]
Okidata	Microline 590 [*]
Okidata	Microline 591 [*]
Mannesmann	Tally MT360 [*]
Fujitsu	DL6400 [†]

[*]November 1993 issue.
[†]November 1994 issue.

Table 36.1   *Printers chosen by PC Magazine for Editor's Choice Awards.*

InkJet Printers

An inkjet printer is a next step up from an impact printer, and generally costs a little more. You will, however, get more features and capabilities for the extra money.

An inkjet printer does not use a print head that strikes a ribbon; instead, it uses a print head stored inside a disposable ink cartridge (see Figure 36.2 on page 504) that heats the ink and sprays it onto the paper. These ink cartridges sit in the printer and draw ink from an ink holding reservoir through long, thin nozzles shaped like miniature garden hoses. The more nozzles in the print head, the better the output will be (similar to number of pins on the impact printer). Color inkjet printers generally use four colors—black, yellow, cyan and magenta—to produce a full range of colors. The output generally is 360x360 dpi.

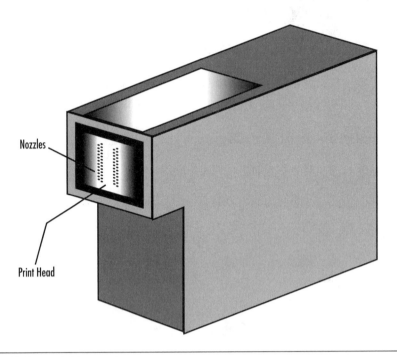

Figure 36.2   *InkJet cartridge.*

Installation is pretty easy for the inkjet. Usually, you snap in four ink cartridges, prime the cartridges, plug in the printer, load the printer driver, and away you go.

Inkjet printers are faster than impact printers; speed is therefore measured in pages/minutes instead of characters/second. On the high end of the spectrum, a good inkjet can print 5 ppm for black/white, but graphics and color can slow printing to 1 ppm or less. Some inkjet printers have bitmapped (nonscalable) fonts built-in and some have TrueType (scalable) fonts built-in for use with Windows applications. If you're planning on using your printer primarily with Windows, we'd strongly recommend the latter over the former.

The big plus in buying an inkjet is increased quality at a low price. This makes inkjet printers attractive to home computer users and the companies with low-volume output requirements.

On the down side, inkjet printers have higher maintenance costs after purchase. Replacement monochrome (black) ink cartridges cost around $7,

Company	Printer Model
Canon	BJ-100
Canon	BJ-200e
Hewlett-Packard	DeskJet 540

Table 36.2   PC World *Best Buys on InkJet Printers (January 1995)*.

while color cartridges ring in at a more hefty price tag of $20 and up. Depending on your output needs, you may have to buy special paper to get the best results. This special paper must be used when regular paper causes ink to bleed or smudge. But where ordinary paper costs 1 or 2 cents per page, the special stuff goes for around 13 cents. Ouch!

Best Buy:
Generally, the inkjet printers that go for under $500 usually only print in black, but some of them—notably the HP DeskJet 540—offer add on color products for a modest $35 to 40. Table 36.2 on page 505 lists some inkjet printers chosen by *PC World*.

Laser Printers

The next printer up the ladder uses laser technology to output pages. It works almost exactly like a copier machine: the laser printer relies on a photosensitive drum to apply toner to a page. The toner is housed in a toner cartridge, by far the biggest printer cartridge of them all. Typically, toner is a black powder that sits in the toner cartridge (although some vendors, like Canon, offer other colors as well). Toner can be a real pain in the neck to remove if you ever have an accident, so a certain amount of care in handling is strongly recommended. The good news about these cartridges is that they're easy to install and can even be recycled (normally, they're good for at least $5 in trade-in value on a refill).

Laser printers are built with some serious brains—typically, they've got a processor inside equivalent to a 68000- or 80386-class CPU or better. Some of the higher end lasers have RISC based processors that range in speed from 20–33 MHz!

Output speed is generally in the range of 8–15 ppm for a typical laser printer, and their duty cycles range from 20–35,000 pages per month. They've got input/output bins that hold from 100 to 500 sheets of paper.

Laser printers usually come with 1 or 2 MB of built-in RAM, where the RAM can do I/O buffering. Most lasers today have automatic font switching between PostScript and PCL, which saves the printer from having to download the fonts every time they're switched. Some of the newer ones are being shipped with a bicentronics interface for increased speed and to support planned network management capabilities.

Last, many higher end laser printers come equipped with a network interface slot so that you can plug these guys right onto a LAN that has the appropriate hardware and software. Some are even capable of acting as standalone print servers. But for each additional bell or whistle, expect to pay extra. A high-speed, heavy-duty network laser printer can easily cost more than $10,000.

Best Buy:
For home use, we've seen good lasers on the market for under $500. Their output is slower to be sure, but it is usually sufficient for more modest printing needs. The only drawback to laser-based printing is that most of them can print in only one color—black. Color versions are available at higher costs, as we'll cover in the next section. Table 36.3 lists some laser printers recommended by *PC World*.

Company	Printer Model
Brother	HL-630 (personal printer)
Lexmark	Optra R (midrange printer)
Texas Instruments	microLaser PowerPro (low-end workhourse laser)
Hewlett-Packard	HP 4MV (network laser)

Table 36.3   PC World *Best Buys on Laser Printers (February 1995).*

Company	Printer Model
Hewlett-Packard	Color LaserJet
QMS	Magicolor
Xerox	4900

Table 36.4   *Color laser printers worth investigating.*

Color Laser Printers

Best Buy:

QMS released the first color laser printers about in early 1993. You don't see a lot of them around offices yet, because prices are still pretty high. Even basic models run anywhere from $7,000–10,000, and the sky's the limit on higher output, higher capability color laser printers. In exchange for color, you'll end up compromising on output speed. Generally, color laser printers can deliver only 2 full color pages per minute, while most monochrome machines can deliver 10 ppm. The cost for a printed color page is about 6 cents per page, compared to a penny or so for monochrome pages. Table 36.4 lists some color laser printers.

NETWORKED PRINTERS

Networked printers will be handled in more detail in Chapter 28, "Vanilla File/Print Servers." Here, let's trace the path data takes to go from a PC application to a networked printer.

- File goes to software driver.
- Software driver prepares file.
- File is sent to a directory on the file server via network cabling.
- File server notifies printer that it has something to print.
- Print server signals file server that it is ready to print.
- File server sends file to print server through network cabling.
- Print server sends file to printer.

Some of these steps may vary, depending on what kinds of print servers you're using and the version of LAN OS involved. Also, speed considerations will vary depending on how you have your printer attached to the network.

INSTALLATION

This section will focus on installing a standalone printer of any type. For installation tips on hooking a printer up to a LAN, see Chapter 28, "Vanilla File/Print Servers."

For installation purposes, it does not really matter which type of printer we are dealing with. The main differences in the types of printers will become important when it comes to installing the ribbon, toner, or ink cartridges. So, for this section, we will focus simply installing a printer. In the checklists that follow below, we'll take you through the steps of preparation and installation, for both hardware and software.

Preparing to Install a Port-Attached Printer

✓ Gather all the printer and PC manuals.

✓ Get the printer and the correct cables (make sure the printer cable and power cords are long enough to meet your needs).

✓ For serial connections, make sure you have the right cable (do not use a modem cable). Also, make sure you have the right cable for the number of pins in use.

✓ Position the printer where you want it.

✓ Get printer paper ready.

✓ Check the printer driver—is it more than six months old? If so, call and ask if a more recent version is available. Make sure to use the Windows driver for Windows, etc.

✓ Have a piece of paper handy to document the installation, including the printer's serial number, port ID, etc.

✓ Look through manuals for configuration information; resolve any questions that emerge before starting the installation

✓ Have the tech support number of the companies that sold you the PC and the printer, should you need them.

Installing a Port-Attached Printer

Hardware

✓ Make sure your PC and printer are turned off.

✓ Hook up the printer cable. This should be easy—the printer cable fits only one way, either to a parallel or serial connection. Make sure you don't have a modem cable.

✓ Turn your PC on.

✓ Now, it's time to add the toner, a ribbon, or inkjet cartridges to the printer. This requires getting out the manual and looking at the how-to diagrams.

✓ Toner cartridges require you to pull out a long plastic strip—again, refer to the manual to make sure you pull out the right strip. Don't get toner on your hands!

✓ Some inkjet printers have you go through a process called *priming* to get the ink flowing.

✓ If your printer is a serial printer, you'll have to check for dip switches to set the speed, parity bits, etc. This definitely requires the manual.

✓ The last step is to add paper, close the paper drawer, and turn on the printer.

Software

✓   If you're using a serial cable, you'll have to add the following to your AUTOEXEC.BAT file—MODE COMZ:YYYY,X,W where Z is equal to the COM port you're trying to connect to and YYYY is equal to the speed (i.e., 9600), X is equal to the parity, and W is equal to the number of stop bits.

✓   Driver installation for Windows: Windows allows you to install the driver once in the Windows install program and be finished. Each application will then use what you have set. To install the driver in Windows, simply click on Control Panel from the MAIN group and then choose printers. If you don't see your printer there, click on the ADD button (don't forget to insert your diskette that came with the printer into Drive A or B). You'll need to tell Windows which parallel (LPT1, LPT2, or LPT3) port or which serial port (COM1 or COM2) you're using. There are some other options you can choose to customize your printer.

✓   Driver installation for DOS: DOS is not so friendly since each DOS application works on its own. That means you will need to go into every application that you use and install the appropriate printer driver. Each application installs the driver a different way so it will be hard for us to lead you through this. Our best advice is to get rid of that primitive DOS system and move to a Windows environment (but only if it's practical to do so).

✓   **The test**: Go into your application and print! If you encounter problems, consult the basic troubleshooting section that follows.

COMMON TROUBLESHOOTING FOR PRINTERS

•   Is the printer turned on? Don't worry, this happens to everyone at least once.

•   Does the printer have a power save feature that may have turned the printer off?

- Loose cable? Check the cable at both ends to make sure it's plugged in snugly.
- Out of paper? This too happens to everyone at least once.
- Toner, ribbon, or ink run out? You shouldn't have this problem with a new printer, but things have been known to foul up on the assembly line. Try a different cartridge and see if there's any change.
- Do you have the latest printer driver? This is pretty important and warrants a call to the tech support person to make sure you've got the latest and greatest.
- Paper jam? Clear it out and get on with it.

WHAT TO BUY

Here are some important factors to help you select the right printer for your needs.

Volume and capacity supported by the printer. If you need very high volume, then an impact printer won't do. Try to figure out the volume in terms of monthly output and then match it up with the printer's ability.

Cost. If you only have $500 dollars to spend, then that severely limits your choices. Determine your budget and eliminate printers outside your range.

Speed required. If you've got high volume needs, then you also will need a printer with good speed.

Is color required? This is an important question. If you need color, you can eliminate certain printers right off the bat. Will there be primarily color printing or only occasional?

Heavy graphics printing required. If so, you'll probably want to get more memory right now.

Future plans for use of the printer. While you might be purchasing the printer now, will your printing needs change in a short time? Do you have plans for the printer to serve as a fax paper printer? If so, spend a little more on your purchase to allow room for growth.

Will it be a networked printer? If so, then you should look at printers that have networking capabilities built-in. It will make your life simpler in the long run.

How reliable is the vendor? Does the vendor have a BBS? Can you call tech support without being put on hold for one hour? Is the tech support toll free? Is the vendor involved in standards bodies?

Ease of management. Choose the printer with the best controls and remote management features, especially when deciding among apparently equivalent makes and models (when in doubt, ask around on CompuServe or at user's groups).

TOP FIVE PRINTER VENDORS

Hewlett Packard, Inc
3000 Hanover St.
Palo Alto, CA 94304-1181
800-752-0900; 800 387-3867 (CD); 415-857-1501
Direct sales: 800-637-7740 (HP Direct)
FAX: 800-333-1917
Tech support: 800-858-8867
Tech support BBS: 415-852-0256
CIS: GO HP

Canon Computer Systems, Inc.
2995 Redhill Ave.
Costa Mesa, CA 92626
1-800-848-4123; (714) 438-3000
Fax: (714) 438-3099
Support: 1-800-423-2366, 8 a.m. to 11 p.m. weekdays, 11 a.m. to 6 p.m. Sat. (EST); Fax: (714) 438-3317; BBS: (714) 438-3325

QMS, Inc.
One Magnum Pass
Mobile, AL 36618
800-622-5546; 205-633-4300
Direct sales: 800-523-2696

FAX: 205-633-7253
Tech support: 205-633-4500
Tech support BBS: 205-633-3632

Lexmark International, Inc.
740 New Circle Rd., NW
Lexington, KY 40511-1876
800-358-5835; 606-232-2000
Direct sales: 800-438-2468
FAX: 606-232-2403
Tech support: 606-232-3000
Tech support BBS: 606-232-5238

Epson America, Inc.
20770 Madrona Ave.
Torrance, CA 90509-2842
1-800-289-3776 Support: 1-800-922-8911, 9 a.m. to 9 p.m. weekdays
(EST); Faxback service: (310) 782-4214; BBS: (310) 782-4531; CIS:
GO EPSON

PRINTER RESOURCES:
BIBLIOGRAPHY AND STRATEGIES

For general networking references, please consult Appendix C, "A List of Networking Resources." The magazines and other publications listed there can help you find out lots of information about printers. The following references are particularly helpful for the information they contain about printers.

Knorr, Eric. "Laser Printers"
  PC World, (February 1995), p. 129. Excellent article comparing different models of laser printers. Includes Best Buy choices.

Weibel, Bob. "The Frugal Printer: How to Save Money on Toner, Cartridges, and Paper."
  PC World, vol. 12, no. 4 (April 1994), p. 175. Great article on tips for saving money on the printers' consumables.

Stone, M. David. "Fit to Print: Choosing a Personal or Color Printer
  Computer Shopper, vol. 14, no. 1 (January 1994) p. 326. Very good article on selecting the right printer for you.

CD-ROM

DISSECTION OF A CD-ROM: BASIC OVERVIEW

CD-ROM stands for Compact Disc—Read Only Memory. A CD-ROM is a small disc-shaped item that can store a vast amount of text, graphics, audio, and video for retrieval. In most cases, data cannot be written to these discs (but it is possible to purchase CD-ROM mastering equipment to create such disks, in the $3,000–4,000 price range).

The disc itself measures 4.5 inches in diameter and resembles an old 45 RPM record in shape and size. While you may already have CDs for your stereo system., but we will discuss CD-ROMs for the computer in this chapter. We'll continue to make references to audio CDs since they've been on the market for years now and you should be familiar with them.

Basically, audio and computer CDs are the same except that audio CD players can only play audio, but cannot read the text, graphics, and video you'll normally find on a CD-ROM. We'll also discuss the drives that play CD-ROMs—called *CD-ROM players* or *CD-ROM drivers*—in this chapter.

You can think of the CD-ROM drive as being equivalent to your audio CD player in terms of what it does for CD-ROMs. Just as audio CD players come in many forms (portable, five-disc player, single-disc player, player for the car,) so do your computer CD players. You can hook up some types of CD-ROM players inside your PC, these are called *internal* drives; otherwise, you can purchase some models that are housed in their own enclosures with their own power supplies, these are called *external* CD-ROM players. There are also models that will fit inside notebook PCs, and you can even buy "jukebox" versions of CD-ROM players. Like the jukeboxes you'd find in a bar or a diner, a CD-ROM jukebox will allow you to place many CDs in a single enclosure for easy access.

The Benefits of CD-ROM Technology

Even though the need for such a device might not already be apparent, there are several reasons why you or your company might want to consider purchasing CD-ROM devices: 650 MB of storage capacity per disk, a wide range of commercial data resources, durability, and affordability. Unlike tape, a CD-ROM does not degrade with repeated use: these devices read data using a laser, so there's no physical contact with the medium involved that will ultimately cause a recording to wear out.

More Room, More Convenience

CDs store beaucoup information and are very portable. That's a lot of data for something so small and portable. Remember installing your first Net-Ware file server? It came with over 30 diskettes. Remember sitting in front of the file server and doing nothing but swapping diskettes in and out of the file server? Today, NetWare 4.1 and 3.12 each ship on a single CD-ROM. Installation takes about 15 minutes and requires only that you pop in the CD and just answer the questions posed by the installation program

The numerous "suites" of software available today—like Microsoft Office, WordPerfect Office, or Lotus Computing's SmartSuite—provide another good example of the benefits of CD-ROM publication. It's cheaper for vendors and considerably easier for users to deal with a single CD-ROM than to manage the 20 or more diskettes that these suites typically require.

Likewise, microfiche is starting to give way to CD-ROM or other optical forms of on-line storage. These can let you view your company's records on your computer, instead of having to go down the hall to that special microfiche reader.

Built-in Retrieval Software and Access Methods

Second, most CDs come with their own retrieval software to manage access to the databases of information they typically contain. Rather than dealing with hardcopy versions of magazines or other trade publications, you can subscribe to CD-ROM digests or obtain full-text versions of the same materials. Thus, when you want to research a particular topic, you could perform a keyword or topic search using the retrieval software for the CD-ROM, rather than having to leaf through a pile of paper. In general, the computerization of text and other forms of data makes it much easier to sift through, analyze, or examine than a paper-based equivalent.

A Wide Range of Topics and Mountains of Data

Today, many subjects and topics are covered by CD-ROMs, ranging from medical references to a full catalog of ZIP codes for the entire United States. Assuming the information these CD-ROMs contain is of interest, the collections of information they represent, coupled with the search engines they include for perusing their contents, make such CD-ROMs incredibly useful.

You can find items like dictionaries, encyclopedias, and technical databases. You can find entries for categories such as Education, History, How-to's, and Games. If there's an audience of even modest size for large collections of information, chances are you'll find either a mass-market or a specialty publisher offering a related CD-ROM!

Durability, Reliability, and Longevity

Best of all, CDs are made to last a long time. This is because of the special manufacturing of the disc, which employs materials designed to meet or exceed governmental data storage requirements—this means that they're guaranteed to remain accurate for at least 10 years of shelf life—and also because no parts actually touch the disc when reading.

A laser is used to read CD-ROMs, so nothing but a focused beam of light ever touches the CD-ROM inside the reader (this is also a good reason for keeping your fingers off the back side of a CD-ROM, where the data is actually stored). Other types of recording technologies depend on physical contact between the playback systems and the medium. On a phonograph, the needle touches the record; and on a VCR or other tape recording technology, the heads touch the tape. All this means wear and tear on the playback device and on the medium. Both will wear out over time. This is not a problem for CD-ROMs or other forms of optical storage.

Affordability

Finally, CD-ROM drives are affordable, and the discs are cheap to manufacture. Today, you can purchase a reasonable internal CD-ROM drive for your PC for $250 or less for drives with average performance, and $500-600 will buy you a state-of-the-art single-disk device. Even jukeboxes are becoming more affordable—recent announcements from companies like NEC and Panasonic have mentioned plans for delivery of three- to five-disk CD-ROM jukeboxes for under $1,000.

Likewise, CD-ROMs themselves are quite inexpensive. When produced in volume (typically, 5,000 copies or more), they cost less than a dollar apiece to manufacture. Even recordable CD-ROM blanks are much cheaper than other forms of media: They cost $10-15 apiece, far cheaper than the prices for equivalent amounts of other kinds of media, whether tape, diskette, or removable magnetic media of other kinds.

All in all, CD-ROM technology offers too many good qualities to be overlooked for more computer installations these days. For vendors, it's a way to provide lots of data inexpensively and reliably; for users, it's a perfect combination of price and access that makes collecting large amounts of data easy to afford, manage, and use.

DETAILS, DETAILS, DETAILS

Now that you know a little about CD-ROMs and why you might find it useful at home or at the office, we'll take a closer peek at the technology involved. First we'll examine the medium, the CD-ROM discs themselves, and then we'll take a look at the drives that house them.

CD-ROM Discs

If you've ever been moved by simple curiosity, or perhaps frustration with a malfunctioning diskette, you've probably taken one or more of them apart. Even a cursory examination of either a 5.25" or 3.5" floppy shows a surprising number of moving parts that basically consists of a round piece of recording film enclosed by a shell of some kind, with a variety of tabs and openings used to control read/write capability. Well, you can't do that with a CD disc—what you see is what you get: they're composed of a single piece of plastic recorded on the back side (the side that usually has no printed information on it). Figure 37.1 on page 519 illustrates a CD-ROM.

Figure 37.1   *A typical CD-ROM.*

CDs are a new type of storage medium developed by a multinational company, Philips. These discs store information in binary format that the PC already knows how to read. That part is not different from your floppies and hard disk drives. But, as we learned earlier, it does not use magnetics to store and retrieve data. It uses another method, optics. This involves light, lenses, and mirrors.

The surface of a CD or CD-ROM looks completely smooth. But, in reality, it incorporates some tiny indentations on it that are not visible to the human eye. The disc also has areas on it that are unindented. The unindented portion between the indentations is treated as a sequence of identically sized areas called *lands*, each of which represents a binary zero. The tiny indentations are referred to as *pits*, where each pit represents a binary one. Lands are the same size as pits, with a small amount of separation on either side to promote accuracy. The spacing of these pits and lands on the disc is extremely dense, giving the CD-ROM its large storage capacity. Figure 37.2 on page 520 shows a cross-section of a CD-ROM with pits and lands.

As you might guess, the process of creating a CD-ROM, requires that it be populated with the pits and lands that represent the binary data to be

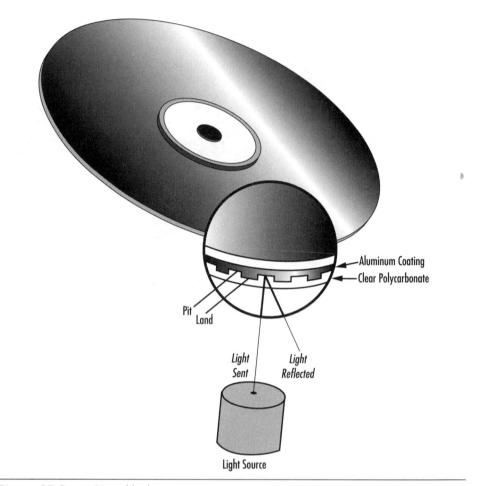

Figure 37.2   *Pits and lands.*

stored. The process of recording this information is quite different from that of saving a file to your hard disk. The process is complex and requires a background in physics and chemistry to be fully understood.

We'll supply a simplified explanation instead. At a high level, creating a CD works something like this:

1. To begin with, someone has to arrange the CD's ID, data, error detection and synchronization behavior. This is similar to the typesetter who has to design and arrange a page before it can be printed.

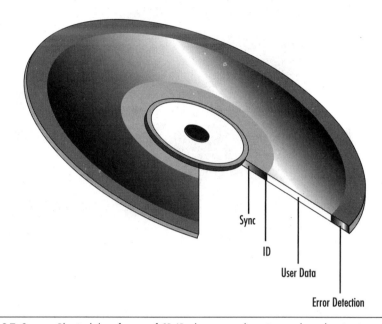

Sync

ID

User Data

Error Detection

Figure 37.3   *Physical data format of CD ID, data, error detection, and synchronization.*

This work is performed on some kind of magnetic medium at the re-cording plant, typically on large, fast disk drives. Figure 37.3 on page 521 and Figure 37.4 on page 522 show the physical data format of a CD-ROM.

2. Once the exact sequence of binary information has been recorded on disk, this sequence must be transferred from the magnetic medium to a glass disc by a laser etching method to inscribe the pits onto the disc for each binary one that the data contains. This results in the creation of a disc that is used as a master for creating additional CD-ROM discs.

3. The glass master is used to create additional molds (like the two sides of a stamp used for minting coins), from which CD-ROMs or audio CDs can be pressed in a pressing mill. One of these molds, called a *stamper*, is used to produce playable versions of the disc.

4. The CDs or CD-ROMs will then be packaged individually in a con-tainer of some kind (usually a plastic shell called a *jewel box*), shrink wrapped, and then delivered to a distributor or reseller, from whom you might purchase it.

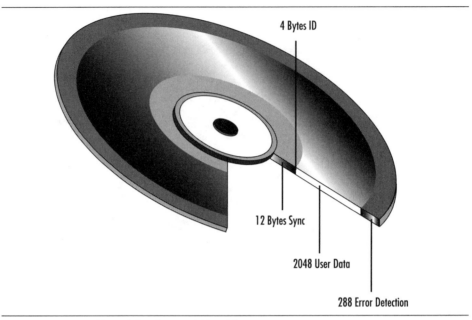

4 Bytes ID

12 Bytes Sync

2048 User Data

288 Error Detection

Figure 37.4   *Physical data format of CD and byte representation.*

Even though the process of producing CD-ROMs is very like the process of printing books or stamping records, the underlying difference is that the data is purely binary and uniquely suited for computer use.

The Physical Makeup of a CD-ROM Disc

CD-ROM discs are made of polycarbonate plastic. Each one has a coat of aluminum deposited as a thin film atop the plastic to optimize the surface's reflectivity, covered by an outer coat of clear lacquer for protection against oxidation and fingerprints. While affording some level of protection against ordinary use, this coating won't protect your disc if you accidentally step on it or run it over with the vacuum cleaner. Thus, it's always a good idea to exercise some care while handling CDs or CD-ROMs.

Retrieving Data from a CD-ROM

Once a disc is printed, it's worthless unless you can read its contents The data—in the form of pits and lands—is read optically by a small infrared laser. The CD-ROM drive throws a beam of light onto the surface, looking for lands and pits. The aluminum coating helps to reflect this light as brightly and accurately as possible. If the light hits a pit, it scatters and reflects less light back to an optical sensor than if it had hit a land. A lower reading converts to a binary 1, a higher one to a binary 0. The reader supplies the circuitry and timing information necessary to synchronize the rotation with the placement of lands and bits, to avoid incorrect data recognition.

The Software Side of CD-ROMs

Now let's look at the software side of the CD-ROM world. First and foremost, the data on the discs require some sort of format to make them readable. When it comes to optical storage, about nine different formats are available. Fortunately, we need to be concerned with only the two most common formats: ISO 9660 and HFS.

Specs:
ISO (International Standards Organization) 9660 is derived from an older data format called *High Sierra*. It is an international format that defines the overall structure, the file structure, and the database structure of the CD. The HFS (hierarchical file system) format is used on Apple Macintosh PCs. As the name suggests, it's a hierarchical structure or tree structure file system. If you are purchasing a drive for a standard PC, then make sure it can read the ISO 9660 format. Most of them now read ISO 9660 and HFS structures interchangeably.

Once the format is determined, the data has to be laid out on the disc. This is done in a spiral method from the inside of the disc to the outside. All of the indexes, synchronization data, and error detection information are found on the inside portion of the disc. Please keep in mind that the inside portion of the disk is smaller in circumference and therefore holds less data than the outside of the disk. This will come into play when we are discussing how drives manage rotation speed in the next section.

CD-ROM Drives

CD-ROM drives come in a variety of flavors. When it comes to selecting the package that's right for your needs, you'll have to choose among external drives, internal drives, drives for laptop or notebook PC, or a multidisc box for your network or standalone PC. CD-ROM drives also come in four different speed ratings: single, double, triple, and quad speed.

In addition to these speed ratings, there are also variations on what's called *seek time* for such drives, which refers to the average amount of time it takes for the drive to locate a particular region anywhere on the disc. Seek time becomes important when you are doing graphics, video, and animation, where faster access and smaller seek times are invariably better.

CD-ROM drives support a variety of interfacing schemes, including SCSI (small computer systems interface), IDE (Integrated Drive Electronics), parallel port interfaces, and a variety of proprietary interfaces. Some of them come with devices called *caddies* or *magazines* (see Figure 37.5 on page 525), which are basically special holders in which you must insert a CD (or CDs) before inserting the caddy or magazine into the drive. It will be helpful for you to understand as many of these capabilities of a CD-ROM drive prior to purchasing one, so we'll take a look at most of these features and options in greater detail in the sections that follow.

CD-ROM Drive Basics

As an analogy, most audio CD players come disguised as a box with LEDs and control buttons on the front. These controls include functions like play, skip, eject, sample, etc. Some players have LED readouts to tell you what track you're currently playing, and most have a button to open and close the door where you put in the CD. They also normally feature multiple sets of RCA jacks to plug your player into a stereo receiver or preamplifier.

A CD-ROM drive is not all that different from its audio counterpart Most basic PC model feature only a single button on the front to insert or eject a CD-ROM, with a single LED to indicate drive activity. Other drives include a volume control and a headphone jack (typically a mini-jack, like you'd find on a portable audiotape or CD player).

Some CD-ROM drives require caddies, while others use a tray drawer. A caddy is a plastic enclosure that houses the disc and then slips into the drive. A tray is basically a built-in caddy: when you push the eject button on the drive, the CD drawer slides open and you put the disc directly into that drawer.

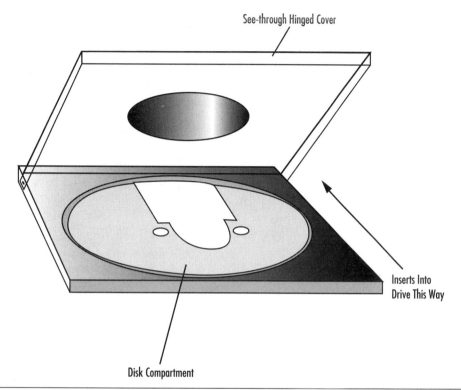

See-through Hinged Cover

Inserts Into
Drive This Way

Disk Compartment

Figure 37.5   *CD-ROM caddy.*

When it comes to audio, CD-ROM players can usually play audio CDs, as well as binary data discs. Most CD-ROM players include both RCA and mini-jack connectors for sound, but most PCs require a sound board (like a SoundBlaster or AdLib board) to be installed to take full advantage of a drive's audio capabilities. When purchasing a multimedia system, you'll have to decide what kinds of audio capabilities you want and make sure the system can support the kinds of connections you plan to use.

Internal vs. External Drives

When selecting a CD-ROM drive, you'll have to choose between a unit that mounts inside the PC itself and one that is externally housed. Internal drives use the PC's power supply and are part of the PC in which they're installed. External drives come with their own power supplies and are considered somewhat portable because they can be moved from one PC to another, as long as both support the kind of external interface that the drive uses. Truly "portable" drives differ from external drives because they're designed to be taken on the road with a laptop or notebook PC. Figure 37.6 and Figure 37.7 on page 527 show the front and back of an external CD-ROM drive.

The kind of CD-ROM drive you choose depends on your needs, the type of PC you need to use it with, and the degree of portability you're looking for. When deciding between an external or internal drive, speed won't play much of a role, because both offer the same ranges of speed and performance. In this case, your decision will probably be based on the interface type and computer's processor speed.

To install an internal drive, you must have an open 5.25" half-height bay available in your PC that opens from the front. In addition, you will need an open slot in your PC for the CD-ROM drive's adapter or interface card. Also, since the drive is going to use the PC's power supply, you'll need to make sure that there is an open pigtail connector on your power supply

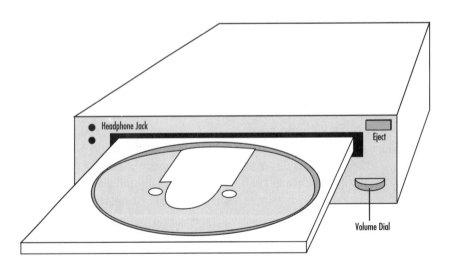

Figure 37.6   *External CD-ROM drive.*

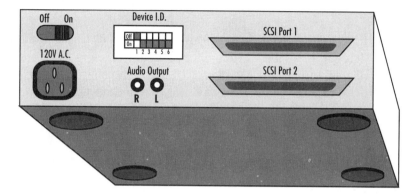

Figure 37.7   *The back of an external CD-ROM drive.*

cable. Internal drives use thin ribbon cables instead of the sturdy parallel cables used to attach external devices. Internal drives are usually cheaper right because there they include fewer parts and are therefore cheaper to build.

External drives cost slightly more than internal drives because they incorporate more parts and labor, including an external power supply and a case for the drive. Since the drive is outside the PC, it also requires a special cable to interconnect the two. It also requires an open slot inside the PC for the drive's adapter card, unless you plan on attaching it to an already-installed interface (like adding to an existing chain of SCSI devices).

Adding CD-ROM to a Portable PC

If you have a laptop or notebook PC, you might want to consider a portable external CD-ROM drives. Typically, portable CD-ROM drives connect through a parallel port adapter that offers printer passthrough capability (so you don't lose your printer attachment by using a parallel-port CD-ROM drive).

It's also possible to find notebook PCs that include an internal CD-ROM drive. For these kinds of machines, there are several issues you should consider. You'll want to observe how the CD-ROM is mounted (some machines require that you unhook and lift up the keyboard, with the drive underneath). Because they're fairly sizable devices, you'll want to consider what else you might have to give up, or how much extra weight you'll have to carry for the privilege of incorporating an internal CD-ROM drive.

Some vendors do without a floppy disk drive and insert a CD-ROM drive in its place. Others, like IBM, allow users to interchange their floppy drives with CD-ROM drives of the same shape and size—but then, you'd need to have both drives available whenever they were needed.

The biggest issue regarding CD-ROM drives in laptops or notebooks centers around battery life. Regular or frequent use of a CD-ROM drive will appreciably shorten your machine's battery life and may force you to add to your load on the road with additional batteries to compensate for the extra power drain they can impose.

Jukebox CD-ROM Drive

A jukebox CD-ROM drive houses multiple CD-ROMs. Typically, a jukebox CD-ROM drive will accommodate anywhere from 5 to 100 or more discs in a single magazine. Some are designed to run mainly on networks like the Optical Access's CD-Maxtet 4X drive, while others like Pioneer's DRM-604X drive, are designed to work on standalone PCs.

The important things to look at when buying a jukebox are the following:

- Speed. Most CD-ROM drives are rated in terms of their data transfer speed. CD-ROM drives are rated as 1x, 2x, 3x, or 4x (single, duplex, triplex, or quad). A higher number means a higher transfer rate, which translates into better performance when reading data off the drive. Like any other CD-ROM drive, a faster transfer rate on a jukebox's playback units will serve your users better than a slower one.

- Seek time. Seek time is the delay between requesting that a drive read data from a particular location and the time when the data can actually begin to be read. Drives with lower seek times are preferable to those with higher ones, but there is a corresponding increase in cost for the increase in performance. Most jukeboxes use the highest quality components available at the time they were designed, so you should expect their performance to be on a par with the fastest single-play units on the market.

- Number of playback units. When pricing a jukebox, be sure to determine the number of separate playback units that it contains. You may get a better value for your money if you bought 3 or 4 single-unit drives and paid an operator to mount discs for users who needed them than if you bought a 100-platter drive with only a single playback unit.

- Ease of operation. Be sure to examine and consider the operation of a jukebox when selecting one. How hard is it to swap discs in and out of the machine? How long must users wait when switching from one disc to another? How does the operator interact with the unit, and how easy is it to configure and manage? The best equipment can be rendered useless by a difficult installation or by poor controls or management facilities.

- Cache handling. Because of the volume of data they handle, many jukeboxes include special cache handling. This usually consists of extra RAM in the jukebox, available to each playback unit, and lets users access information from RAM rather than the disc, for better overall performance and behavior.

- Format. Most jukeboxes will support both the ISO and Macintosh CD-ROM formats; nevertheless you should make sure the device supports the CD-ROM data formats that your users need to access.

- Supports your network. Since the majority of jukeboxes are employed in networked environments, you'll also want to be sure that the device supports the types of file servers and networking software in use on your network.

By working your way through your hardware and software requirements, you'll very often be able to narrow the field of choice to an acceptably small number. Then, you can try a little hands-on testing or ask for a demonstration to help you decide which one you want. For expensive devices like a jukebox, it's also a good idea to ask the vendor to supply you with the names of some reference accounts that you can contact for more information about the equipment. Sometimes, you'll want to check other sources—like CompuServe, the Internet, or local users' groups—for information, to avoid the kinds of glowing references that vendors always try to supply.

Other CD-ROM Drives

Kodak and other vendors produce CD formats that differ from the ISO and Macintosh formats mentioned earlier. The Kodak Photo CD allows you get your photographs developed and then have them digitally recorded on a CD-ROM for playback. To view the images, you'll need a Photo-CD capable drive. Many of the newer CD-ROM drives support this data format in addition to the others. But if you want to do anything complicated with these images on your PC, you'll need to purchase additional software from Kodak. If you simply want to view them on your TV set, they have a drive that will do this.

One other type of CD-ROM drive is called a CD-recordable (CD-R) drive. We won't go into heavy detail on these devices here, but you should be aware such devices are becoming increasingly available. CD-R drives allow you to actually create your own CDs, taken from information on your own PC. Such devices used to be prohibitively expensive and weren't in widespread use. But in 1995, prices have fallen drastically to $4,000 and lower, so many users are taking a closer look. We expect that recordable CDs will become a popular computer medium some time in the next five years.

What About Interfaces?

In addition to the many varieties of CD-ROM drives available, several types of interfaces are available for connecting them to your PCs These range from SCSI, to IDE and parallel interfaces, to various kinds of proprietary interfaces. Whenever you're negotiating to buy a CD-ROM drive, be sure to ask your vendor if the price they are quoting includes the interface. Sometimes, you can get one as a part of the deal just by asking.

Small Computer System Interface. SCSI is an ANSI standard for high-speed parallel interfaces. Because it's a standard, anyone can make SCSI devices such as adapter cards and cables. The trick here is that lots of folks have had problems with the original SCSI-1 interfacing because it involves hardware, software, and devices. Sometimes, you might have a new device, but not the latest software driver. So even though it's a standard, there are components with revision levels that have to agree to work together properly.

Your best bet is to go with 16-bit SCSI-2 (a second generation of SCSI design). As an interface standard SCSI-2 is faster and suffers from far less interface incompatibilities than its predecessor. Other options include

SCSI-3, fast SCSI, and wide SCSI. These offer higher performance still, but as new technologies may suffer from some vendor incompatibilities. If you feel you must get the highest possible performance—and are willing to pay the price—be sure to ask for a compatibility guarantee from your vendor or reseller, so that if your equipment choices prove incompatible, you'll at least be able to swap them for units that should work together.

SCSI interfaces allow you to interconnect multiple devices (up to seven per SCSI adapter) to the first device. A single computer will support up to seven distinct SCSI adapters. Theoretically, you could have 49 CD-ROM drives attached to a single PC! Just remember, if you want to support Macintosh users as well as PC users, you'll have to supply a CD-ROM drive that handles HFS as well as ISO CD-ROM formats.

Proprietary Means "One Vendor Only". As the term is meant to imply, a proprietary interface is the sole and exclusive province of a single vendor. This therefore limits you to one vendor, both for the adapter and the CD-ROM drive. Some vendors, such as Sony and Mitsumi, sell interfaces and drives as matched sets. They claim that this works better or that they've added enhancements that you can't. For the most part, this is probably true. But, you should ask yourself why you should choose a nonstandard route for a little more speed or a few more features. You're essentially tying yourself to that vendor exclusively. Should it ever change its designs or go out of business, you might have to replace that equipment just because you couldn't get the right spare part. In general, we counsel most users to avoid proprietary solutions whenever possible. There's simply less risk involved and more options to choose from.

IDE for CD-ROMs: A Little Ahead of its Time. One last option you could choose for your CD-ROM drive is the enhanced IDE interface. You may already be familiar with this technology from your hard disk studies. It has now broken into the CD-ROM arena, but only with a few vendors utilizing and updated version of the integrated drive electronics technology devised in the late 1980s to help make larger hard disks more affordable for PC users.

If your PC already has an enhanced IDE hard disk drive, you can now get a CD drive for this interface. Some options are also available for the older unenhanced version, but they may not be compatible with your IDE controller. If you're willing to upgrade your disk controller to an enhanced IDE model, vendors are catching and riding this wave. It looks like you will have plenty of quad drives to select from if you take this route, but be warned: most network servers currently support only SCSI interfaces for CD-ROM drives. Thus, where you plan on attaching the drive is almost as important as what you want to use it for!

For CD-ROMs, Speed Does Not Kill!

Once you've decided how you're going to connect your CD-ROM drive to your PC, you'll need to decide what brand of drive to buy. Choosing an interface, and selecting the format requirements will help to narrow your search. But an important question remains: What difference does speed make?

Two important measurements to look at when evaluating different drives include seek time and data transfer or throughput rates. A drive's seek time measures how long it takes the drive to find the data on the disc. If the seek time is above 350 milliseconds, you might find it too slow for your needs.

When it comes to the data transfer rate, CD-ROM players come in different flavors. That is, they come in single, double, triple, and quad speed. And, as you might have already guessed, the higher is the transfer rate, the higher the drive's price tag, but also, the higher its speed.

The very first CD-ROM drives supported a data transfer rate that has now come to be known as single speed. As Table 37.1 indicates, this implies a transfer rate of 150 kilobytes per second. The next generation of CD-ROM drives to be produced offer a transfer rate exactly double that of the single speed drive—hence the name *double speed*. The same ratio holds true for triple and quad speed drives; each represents a higher multiple of the initial rate for single speed drives.

Drive speed	Throughput (KB/sec)
Single Speed	150
Double Speed	300
Triple Speed	450
Quad Speed	600

Table 37.1   *CD-ROM Drive Speeds.*

As an example, Table 37.2 lists some quad speed drives with seek, access and throughput rates as well as prices. This data is taken from *Multimedia World Magazine* (February 1995), pages 96–99.

Vendor	Model	Price	Access Time (ms)	Transfer Rate (KB/sec)	Interface Type
Optical Access	CD/Allegro 4X-ext	399	110	600	SCSI-2
Toshiba	XM-3501B-int	470	120	600	SCSI-2
	XM-3501E-ext	600	120	600	SCSI-2
Procom	MCD-4X-int	755	120	600	SCSI-2
	SICD-4X-ext	665	120	600	SCSI-2
CD Technology	CD-Porta Drive-ext	500	120	600	SCSI

Table 37.2   *Quad Speed Drive Sample Statistics.*

Another speed related consideration involved built-in drive caching. A CD-ROM drive that offers a built–in cache will typically deliver better performance. Some drives offer no built-in cache, some include as little as 32K, and others offer as much as 256K. Plextor has a quad speed CD-ROM drive that includes with 1 MB of cache; not surprisingly, it is a leading performer in many speed comparisons. When trying to decide how much cache you need, the price you're willing to pay for a drive will help to set a reasonable limit.

NETWORKING CD-ROMS

Before you purchase any kind of CD-ROM drive for your network, you must determine your needs and requirements. Here are some basic questions you'll want to consider:

- Will only a handful of users share one drive and one CD?
- Will it be more than a handful—more like a work group?
- Will it be the whole company sharing multiple CDs?

- What type of applications will be run from the CDs (Multimedia, text, databases, etc.)?

There are a couple of ways to hook up the shared CD-ROM drive(s) to the network. For Novell, most of the vendors supply NetWare Loadable Modules (NLMs) that work with the drive plugged into a SCSI port on the file server. Another method resembles HP JetDirect concept where an external device out on the network lets the drive function as a distinct network node that communicates with special software on the file server. Another design lets the CD-ROM drive act as a server to the network. Some of the vendors in this arena include Corel, Meridian, Opti-Net, MicroDesign, and Optical Access.

In a NetWare environment, the users can access the CD-ROM discs as if they were mounted volumes. To them, using a CD-ROM works like just another drive assignment. For example, Optical Access's Maxtet 4X works as a SCSI device plugged into the NetWare server. An NLM loads on the server side which permits the server to mount the CDs as separate volumes. The Maxtet features seven CD bays, each with its own separate reader.

Technobabble:
Some of the Network Operating Systems (NOSes) require a redirector. This is a piece of software that lets the CD-ROM drive appear local to workstations on the network. One device driver that performs this redirection is called MSCDEX.EXE (Microsoft CD-ROM Extensions). If you have DOS 6.2, MSCDEX is included. Windows NTAS 3.5 offers embedded support for ISO 9660 (remember that's a CD data format) and MSCDEX.

If you purchase a system that holds enough CD-ROMs to satisfy everyday needs, then you won't need an operator to run the computer and swap out discs on demand. That's the last thing a busy network administrator needs. If a jukebox is beyond your means, consider attaching multiple single-play units to a server, one for each of the most commonly used CD-ROMs on your network.

If you do install a CD-ROM on your network, be especially careful about software licensing. If a quick perusal of the license for the software makes no mention of network use, call the vendor before you make any CD-ROM available over your network and ask about licensing and compliance. Some vendors require that you buy a license pack for network use, while others require different versions (and charge you more money) for networked versions of their software, as compared to standalone versions.

Finally, if you're planning to use multimedia on your network, ask yourself if your network has enough bandwidth to handle the huge files that this technology typically involves. Be sure to consider your users' needs for audio and video services carefully, because these services require additional equipment, which typically means increased hardware costs for everyone who wants to participate.

WHAT'S THE MULTIMEDIA WAVE?

Multimedia means combining text, voice and sound, music, and video or animation. To experience multimedia on a PC, you must have a sound card, loudspeakers, software and usually, a CD-ROM drive with multimedia capability (known as MPC, short for multimedia PC).

A multimedia CD-ROM drive is nothing more than a regular CD-ROM drive that conforms to the MPC2 hardware specification. To meet this specification, it must be a double-speed drive or faster, with a seek time less than or equal to 400 ms with only a 60% CPU utilization.

In addition, the Multimedia Marketing Council has set forth specifications for PCs to run multimedia. They recommend that the following as an absolute minimum: a 486SX/25 processor, 4MB RAM, 16-bit color video, and a 16-bit sound card able to play 8-note synthesized sound and MIDI. Anything that has an MPC logo means that the product has been approved by the council or meets its specifications. This also holds true for multimedia software.

Here's an example of something you can do with multimedia. You can pop in your World Atlas CD and narrow in on a country. You can run an animated video about your selected country and then play that country's national anthem. Or, you could plug in your Myst CD and get lost in an adventure game with animated video and sound. According to a recent study in *Information Week* (February 1995), over $2 billion was lost to such activities in the U.S. workplace in 1994!

What Type of PC Do You Need?

In a computing utopia, all creatures possess Pentium machines with 20″ monitors and ergonomic keyboards. In the real world, people possess all kinds of different processors with different monitors and few ergonomic keyboards. This chapter lives in the real world, so we'll discuss your PC needs in those terms.

For those XT gurus reading this section to see if you can still hang on to your bookend and try to squeeze the last bit of life out of it—yes, you can install a CD-ROM drive on an XT, 512K RAM, hard drive, and DOS 2.11 or older if you only intend to use text. But why bother? Why not junk it and upgrade? You're not going to like the performance if you go that route.

Earlier, we discussed what the Multimedia Marketing Council recommended. If you plan to only use CDs for text and never anything more, than you can choose a slower model like a 386/20 Mhz. The basic rule to remember: the faster your processor and drive are, the better the output will be. It doesn't get any more complicated than that.

Installation

This section focuses on preparing and installing a standalone, external SCSI CD-ROM drive. Put your pilot's cap on!

Preparing to Install the CD-ROM Drive

- Gather up all your installation disks, your CD-ROM drive manuals, and your PC manuals

- Unpack the CD-ROM drive, make sure you have the correct cable (for internal CD-ROM drives, this means a ribbon cable with enough connectors attached for the number of devices to be hooked up to the controller; for external drives, this means an additional external cable for the device you're intending to add). Check the cable to make sure the connector or connectors match up to the desired devices.

- Be sure to have a few small screwdrivers handy—get both flathead and Phillips, just to be on the safe side. Only a few drives or computers use Torx screws, but you may want to check to see if you'll need some of those as well.

- For external drives, set the drive on your desktop where you want it; for internal drives, position it in the bay where you intend for it to be located. Make sure you get a snug fit and that the drive isn't touching other components nearby.

- Keep a CD-ROM (and an audio CD, if you're planning on using the drive to play music) handy for testing.

- Round up the necessary device drivers—you'll also need to modify PC configuration files (either AUTOEXEC.BAT or CONFIG.SYS) depending on the drivers, so it's a good idea to back the original versions up now.

- Keep a piece of paper handy to document installation settings, serial numbers, and other activities during the installation process.

- Read through your manuals for configuration settings and information; write down any unanswered questions that occur to you as you're reading. Try to get all of these questions answered before you actually begin the installation process.

- Make sure you have the tech support number for the CD-ROM drive vendor, and for the company that sold you the drive.

Installing the CD-ROM Drive

Hardware

- ✓ Make sure your PC and drive are completely powered down.

- ✓ Disconnect the power cable to the PC to make sure. Disconnect any other cables that are in the way in the back of your PC.

- ✓ Pop the hood on the PC.

- ✓ Put on a static wrist guard if you have one to prevent zapping the card.

✓   Find an open slot in your PC and plug the card in, but don't tighten the card with a screw yet. Always wait until the thing works before battening down the hatch.

✓   Plug the SCSI cable into the back of your PC and also into the top plug on the back of your CD-ROM drive (if applicable). Or do something similar for your IDE or proprietary interface.

✓   Plug the terminator plug that came with the drive into the bottom plug on the drive. Some drives will work without this, but we prefer to plug it in to avoid future problems.

✓   SCSI devices require that you set a device ID number (in case you have more than one device). Since presumably this is your first SCSI device on your PC, you shouldn't have to change the factory setting but you may want to check the manual and make sure it's set correctly. You can look on the back of your drive and you'll see some dip switches, a thumbwheel, or some other kind of switch with settings from 0 to 7.

✓   In some cases, you may have to set the IRQ if it is needed and the factory default settings conflict with other devices you may be using in the PC already.

✓   Plug all your cables back into your PC and into the power in the wall. Don't forget to connect the drive's external power source.

✓   Turn everything on. Ideally, you're going to see lights everywhere. On the PC and on the drive. If not, check all of your cables and make sure you plugged in the power plugs and sources.

✓   Push the little button on the drive door to see if it opens. Now close the door by pushing the button again. That was fun.

✓   If everything works, batten down the hatch. If not, it's time to start troubleshooting!

Software

✓ This part is pretty involved and is really going to depend on the drive you buy. It's important that you know that there will probably be changes made to your AUTOEXEC.BAT and CONFIG.SYS files. To be on the safe side, always make a backup of them before installing anything. Another thing we always do is make a backup of our Windows INI files. All this only takes a few minutes, but it has saved our bacon more than a few times.

✓ Most CD-ROM drives include self-installing programs that will do the work for you and reconfigure things, set parameters, etc. The first thing we do with disks we receive is to look for a README.TXT file and then look for an INSTALL.BAT or INSTALL.EXE or SET-UP.EXE. Any of those will get you started.

✓ We hate to leave you alone from this point on, but you're going to have to pull out the manual and let them step you through their processes. Good luck!

TROUBLESHOOTING COMMON CD-ROM PROBLEMS

- Did you remember to load the appropriate software before trying to access the drive? Did you load the device driver in your AUTOEXEC.BAT or CONFIG.SYS or both?
- If you're working with an internal drive, did you remember to connect the pigtail connector from the power supply on the PC to the drive? Is the cable loose?
- If you're working with an external drive, is the cable loose? Is the power source plugged in? Is the interface card snugly plugged in? Try reseating it.
- SCSI connector—did you flip the switches to identify the device ID?
- Do you have the CD disc inserted upside down? Some want them inserted label up, some label down. Try flipping it over. Remember,

since the drive works only with light, and no parts touch the CD, you will not harm it by doing this.

- Do you have the right CD? Meaning, did you buy the Macintosh CD instead of the PC version (HFS vs. ISO 9660)?

WHAT TO BUY

Here are some important factors in selecting the right CD-ROM drive for you.

- Will this be a networked drive? If so, how many folks need access to the drive? One work group or everyone? Will the users need to access more than one CD? That would require a jukebox type arrangement. Will you pull large graphics or video across the wires? You'll need to check your bandwidth.

- Will this be a standalone drive sans network? If so, check the PC you're going to connect this to. Make sure it has the minimum processor and memory requirements.

- Cost—if you only have $400 dollars to spend, then that limits your choices. Determine your budget and then rule out drives out of your range.

- Speed required? If you've got needs such as animation or heavy graphics, then speed is very important and quad should be your only choice.

- How good is the vendor? Does the vendor have a BBS? Can you call tech support without being put on hold for one hour? Is the tech support toll free? Is the vendor involved in standards bodies?

- Read all the comparison charts you can find. We find them all the time in PC magazines. You can too.

- Don't forget that friendship is powerful—check to see if any of your friends has purchased, researched, or installed anything in this area? Pick their brains apart. Don't be bashful.

TOP FIVE VENDORS

Toshiba International Corp.
13131 W. Little York Rd.
Houston, TX 77041
800-231-1412; 713-466-0277
FAX: 713-466-8773
Tech support: Use toll-free no.

NEC Technologies, Inc. (subsidiary of NEC Corp.)
1414 Massachusetts Ave.
Boxborough, MA 01719-2298
800-632-4636; 508-264-8000
Direct sales: 800-374-8000 (NEC Select)
FAX: 508-264-8673
Tech support: 800-388-8888
Tech support BBS: 508-635-4706

Pioneer New Media Technologies, Inc.
(Optical Memory Systems Division)
2265 East 220th St.
Long Beach, CA 90810
800-444-6784; 310-952-2111
FAX: 310-952-2990
Tech support: 408-496-9140

SONY Electronics, Inc. (Computer Peripheral Products Co.)
3300 Zanker Rd.
San Jose, CA 95134
800-352-7669; 408-432-1600
FAX: 408-943-0740
Tech support: 408-894-0555
Tech support BBS: 408-955-5107

Mitsumi Electronics Corp., Inc.
(division of Mitsumi Electric Co., Ltd.)
6210 N. Beltline Rd., Ste. 170
Irving, TX 75063
800-MITSUMI; 214-550-7300
FAX: 214-550-7424
Tech support: 408-970-0700

Top Ten CD-ROMs

This list is taken from *Multimedia World* magazine, which mentions the source as PC Data (703-435-1025), October 1994. An interesting thing to note is that the top two are games. We've got Myst and it's great entertainment, but an incredible time-waster!

- Doom II
- Myst
- 5 Foot 10 Pak Volume II
- Quicken CD-ROM Deluxe
- 5 Foot 10 Pak Volume I
- Print Shop Deluxe CD Ensemble
- Encarta
- Corel Gallery
- 7th Guest
- Compton's Interactive Encyclopedia

CD-ROM Resources: Bibliography and Strategies

For general networking references, please consult Appendix C, "A List of Networking Resources." The magazines and other publications listed there can help you find out lots of information about CD-ROMs. The following references are particularly helpful for the information they contain about CD-ROMs:

Benford, Tom. *Welcome to . . . CD-ROM*. New York: MIS: Press, 1993. Great book on everything about CDs, including their manufacturing process. $16.95.

Wodaski, Ron. "Quad Speed CD-ROM Drives: The Race Is On!" *Multimedia World Magazine*, (February 1995) , p. 85. Great evaluation of 37 quad-speed CD-ROM drives. Includes comparison charts of the different drives, and buying tips for the novice user. If you're planning to purchase a quad-speed CD-ROM drive, then this an article worth reading!

Poor, Alfred. "Multimedia Takes Center Stage, CD-ROM Drives, Sound Cards, and Speakers:" *Computer Shopper*, vol. 14, no. 11(November 1994), p. 306. An absolute must-read article before purchasing any CD-ROM drive. Includes buying tips and guidelines for installation.

NETWORK FAX/MODEM

FAXING AWAY: BASIC OVERVIEW

Fax is a common abbreviation for facsimile transmission, which in turn refers to the process of transmitting printed material across a communications medium—typically, the telephone system—to a receiver. Both sender and receiver must have fax equipment that can interoperate to pass information back and forth. Beyond that, senders and receivers have all kinds of options about where the data comes from (hardcopy, electronic formats, electronic mail, etc.) and a similar set of options of how the data gets delivered.

On the receiving end, a transmission is usually printed out or stored in some kind of electronic format. All that is required on the sending end is a source for outgoing data, a telephone line, and one or more valid fax machine numbers to which to ship the data.

Some Forgettable Fax History

Today faxing is pretty simple; but it wasn't always that way. We can remember the days of acoustic couplers, which required inserting the handset of a phone into a couple of rubber boots (one for the mouthpiece, the other for the earpiece). Then came the fancy footwork with the paper. Transmissions took forever and were notoriously difficult to read. Back then, very few offices used these devices because they were expensive, difficult, and balky.

As the price of the technology dropped and the technology became faster and more improved, more and more companies purchased fax machines. Eventually, the state of the art as we know it today arrived. Even so, there are still some inconveniences in using conventional, paper-based fax technology.

Many fax users still have to start with a hard copy of the data they want to transmit. This means either printing a document to the printer, or making a copy of the document if it was preprinted material. Then, you have to get to the fax machine, which is all too often down the hall, far away from your office. When you get there, you might have to queue up behind other users already waiting with their hard copies ahead of you. If you're thinking something like "What a waste of time and money!" we can only agree.

Receiving a fax isn't much easier, when paper is the medium of exchange. Whenever you receive an unexpected fax, you can almost count on its contents being made public—or at least perused by anyone who stops by the communal fax machine—and it might occasionally get tossed into a public bin, rather than your in box. Unless you remember to check that bin, you'd be out of luck.

Then, there's the hassle of sharing that fax with other recipients. If you wanted to send that fax to somebody else, you'd have to copy it and route still more hard copies. It's not convenient nor is it a step toward the much-ballyhooed, but still remote, pipedream called the *paperless office*. Worst of all is to come into the office early in the morning only to find that your fax machine is out of toner and paper because some company or companies sent a ton of junk faxes overnight. We hope it burns you up as much as it does us to pay part of somebody else's advertising bills.

A Brave New Fax World

What if you could send a fax directly from within a word processor or spreadsheet right from your own PC? What if you were to receive a fax, by e-mail or be notified by a little notice on your computer screen (electronic notice, not a little yellow sticky notice) that you had a fax waiting for you?. Then, you'd be able to view the fax on your PC's screen and decide if you wanted to print it or just delete it. If you wanted to route that fax, you could do it electronically instead of routing more paper. And best of all, junk fax is gone with the push of a single button!

By using the latest in fax modem technology, you can do all that today. In this chapter, we discuss fax modem technology in detail. You'll also look at different ways to implement this technology that could save money, and make faxing more efficient.

Details, Details, Details

Let's start with a more detailed look at how a fax machine works and how it transmits and receives data with other machines. Next you'll learn about some advanced fax modem technology and about the standards that prevail in this field.

How a Basic Fax Machine Works

Most companies have a fax machine of one kind or another today. The most common type is the one that sits by itself in a corner and is usually busy—especially when you want to send a fax.

A basic fax machine consists of a boxlike device with a built-in telephone keypad and handset, fax paper, and, an analog connection. It can operate as a telephone or a fax machine or the world's most primitive copier. Inside the enclosure, there is a roller similar to the drum inside a laser printer or a copier. Paper with printed material is fed into the fax machine typically face-side down, and is placed on the roller. The fax machine scans each line individually by reading the reflection from an intense beam of light shined at the copy passing through. Figure 38.1 on page 546 shows a basic fax machine.

Basic fax machines can read only monochrome images, so the reflected light bounces back from one of two sources: either the black or white area on the paper. When a beam of light is emitted, the type on a page absorbs some of its energy and therefore reflects back less light than the white space. Using these two different intensities, the fax machine can create a binary representation of the black and white areas on a page. Thus, each scanned line results in binary information, a series of ones and zeros to represent light and dark areas.

As far as a fax machine is concerned, each line on a page is composed of dots or picture elements (PELs), which can be either white or black. There are 1728 PELs per line on an 8.5 x11 page, and 98 lines per vertical inch. For

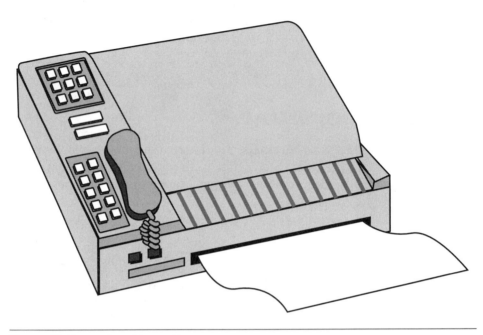

Figure 38.1   *Manual fax machine.*

example, a capital letter of the alphabet might take about 5–7 lines depending on its font size. This also implies that a single page of text contains approximately 1.4 million PELs.

This helps to explain a number of other additional features built into fax machines. These devices customarily compress the page data before sending it. But if the sender compresses the data, the fax on the other end of the connection has to know how to decompress it. Likewise, speeding up data transmission rates means it takes less time to transmit a page. Here again, the receiving machine has to be able to match any speed increases on its end. These two features, and some adjustable rates for page resolution, constitute the standard features built into most fax machines available today.

Some considerable advantages are to be gained by moving fax machine capability into PCs, however. Despite the lack of paper, many of the same principles apply, but the information can be kept in electronic format for easier access, storage, and retrieval. And nothing compares with the convenience of working with faxes on-screen on your own PC, instead of sharing a communal fax machine with your coworkers. All that's required is a computer device called a fax modem, and you're ready to walk away from the communal machine for good! Even better, it's also possible to set up a networked fax server that can handle the multitudes, each on the privacy of his or her own machine.

What Is a Fax Modem?

A fax modem is a device for transmitting and receiving faxes from within an application at the user's desktop. It's almost as if took the fax machine from down the hall and squeezed it inside your PC. Fax modems conform to the same international standards as standard fax machines (fax standards were developed and approved by the CCITT, the Consultative Committee for International Telegraphy and Telephony, which we'll discuss later). Better yet, fax modems don't operate by scanning paper to transmit data, but instead use software that converts application files—like spreadsheets and word processors—into graphic images called *bitmaps*. A bitmap is literally a bunch of bits mapped out on a page or a screen to form an image. Figure 38.2 shows a bitmapped font.

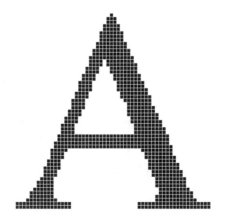

Figure 38.2   *Bitmapped font.*

A fax modem has several components that combine to make it work. As its name implies, the device includes a modem to manage the telephone connection. Modems can be used on individual machines or they can be shared over a network in what is known as a *modem pool*, which is nothing more than a collection of first-come, first-served devices available for the asking. As always with computer devices, driver- and application-level software is required to talk to modems and interface with their users. For the modem to work, it also requires access to a telephone connection, typically an analog line of some sort. Finally, there needs to be link of some kind between the modem and the PC (depending on the interface chosen, a PC may even need to be upgraded to support it). See Figure 38.3 which illustrates the components of an external fax modem.

The components of a fax modem system can be manufactured and sold by different companies or they can be bundled together in a single package. Some companies manufacture only fax modem boards, along with their drivers and the APIs (application programming interfaces) that they need, but don't provide any user interface software (Brooktrout is a good example). Brooktrout's main focus is on producing the best fax modem board, so the company licenses its APIs to other companies so they can produce end-user applications to utilize the hardware.

Sending and Receiving Fax Modem Transmissions

A closer look at an actual fax transmission from point A to point B, should help to illustrate the different steps and stages involved. For this example, we'll refer to two hypothetical companies, known as Company A and B,

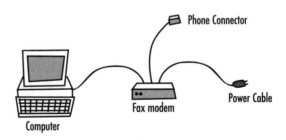

Figure 38.3   *Components of an external fax modem.*

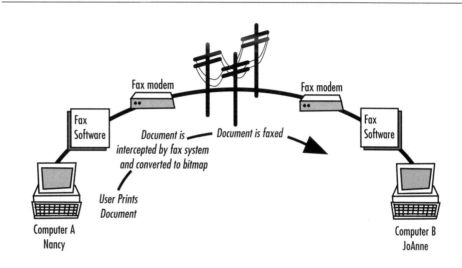

Figure 38.4   *Nancy faxes to JoAnne.*

and two equally hypothetical users, whom we'll call Nancy and JoAnne. In this scenario, Nancy is the transmitter, and JoAnne the receiver. Use Figure 38.4 as a guide while you read.

- The user tells the PC application to print to COM port. Nancy has just finished an Microsoft Excel brochure that she'd like to fax to JoAnne. From her desk, Nancy tells the Excel application to print by choosing FILE/PRINT, and choosing her fax modem as the output device.

- The fax server software driver goes to work. Nancy's fax software intercepts this print request, takes the file, and converts it to a bitmap file. It then sends the file to the fax modem for transmission.

- The modems hold a conversation. Nancy's fax modem dials JoAnne's fax modem and sends it a hello signal. JoAnne's modem replies by sending a signal back that describes JoAnne's modem's features, including it's maximum data rate and resolution. The signal that JoAnne's modem just sent told Nancy's modem that it could transmit data at 14400, at medium resolution.

- Operation: send fax, decompress, and begin error check. Nancy's modem transmits the data line by line. After each line, JoAnne's modem sends an acknowledgment that it received the line. It does this by counting the total number of PELs—expecting that number to be 1728. If Nancy's modem uses data compression, then JoAnne's modem has to decompress the data before it acknowledges receipt of the complete line.

- The end of work for sender Nancy.
- The beginning of work for JoAnne's fax modem. JoAnne's modem processes the incoming fax and sends JoAnne an electronic notification of the fax to her computer screen.
- The user decides what to do worth the fax. JoAnne retrieves the fax, examines it on-screen, and forwards it to her boss via electronic mail.
- Transmission is complete.

The Types of Fax Modems

There are multiple types of fax modems available in today's marketplace. They differ primarily in terms of speed, resolution, and the kind of interface (internal vs. external, and PC bus or connection type) that they support. Before we get into the details, though, we'll take an important detour to consider some important related communications standards.

Specs: Let's Talk Standards in this Technology
The CCITT is the international standards body that governs most aspects of telephony and telephone-based communications. They have designated four groups of fax systems, numbered Group 1 through Group 4. Our primary focus is on Group 3, simply because 95% or more of the fax machines in use today belong to Group 3.
The CCITT's Group 3 standard specifications are as follows:

- Width = 8.5".
- Resolution = 100x200 dpi.
- PELs/line = 1728.
- Data compression = modified Huffman encoding.
- Error correction = none.
- Modem modulation = V.27ter at 4800 bps.

Both in terms of speed and resolution, these standards are on the low end of the scale of capabilities for most modems today. If you purchase a fax modem that claims to be a Group 3 modem, you can expect it to meet or exceed those specifications. High-end fax modems will usually exceed these minimum requirements on some of their features. For example, modem modulation can go as high as the V.17 standard or 14,400 bps, and the resolution can be fine, which means 200x200 dpi (horizontal and vertical resolution).

When buying a fax modem, be aware that there are sometimes two designations for their performance: one for data, the other for fax. When the modem boasts a 28.8 speed, ask if it is for the data or fax. Chances are 100% that it is a data specification, because fax speeds top out at half that rate—14,400 bps—today.

Specs:
In addition to the CCITT, the EIA (Electronics Industry Association) has also defined some modem classifications, known as Class 1 and 2. Class 1 fax modems do all the processing on the PC's CPU, which typically means that all other PC work must halt while a fax is processing. Class 2 fax modems allow some of the fax processing to be handled directly by the fax modem, offloading some of the CPU's work. Another standard, known as CAS (communications application standard), originated at Intel—the company that originated PC CPUs—allows the PC's CPU to offload most of fax processing onto the fax modem.

Internal vs. External vs. PCMCIA Fax Modems

Fax modems come in several different forms. Internal modems, which plug into the internal bus of a PC, are the most common type and can be found inside standalone PCs, file servers, or PC servers. Internal fax modems are similar in concept to the internal CD-ROM drives in that they use the PC's power supply. Figure 38.5 on page 552 shows an internal fax modem setup.

Another type of internal fax modem is a PCMCIA II fax modem. This type consists of a "modem on a card" that fits into a PCMCIA II slot. We call it internal because it slides into a slot in a notebook or other PC, but in reality, PCMCIA represents an interesting combination of internal and portable equipment technologies (internal, because it fits inside a PC; portable, because it can be easily removed and carried from one machine or location to another).

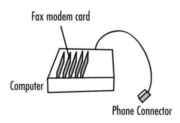

Figure 38.5   *Components of an internal fax modem.*

External modems are similar to external CD-ROM drives in that they need enclosures to house them, as well as requiring their own separate power supplies. There's no real advantage in going the external fax modem route unless you enjoy reading the blinking status LEDs that most such external units offer (and when it comes to troubleshooting hardware problems or bad connections, these displays can be very useful indeed).

Multiple Fax Modems

In a server environment, you might require multiple fax modems when multiple users fax documents. In this case, you could dedicate a PC to handling a collection of modems, thereby supplying many open slots available for fax modems to plug into and a way of keeping communications processing separate from other kinds of network services.

As we mentioned earlier, there are different classes of modems. In a multiple fax modem arrangement, you'll want use CAS class devices, to allow faxing functions to pass directly from the user through the server to a fax board. That frees up the server's CPU to work on the next fax request. Remember, too, that Class 1 or 2 fax modem boards tie up the CPU because these kinds of fax modems offer little or no on-board processing capabilities. At the end of this chapter, we'll take you through the installation of a dedicated PC fax server with several fax modems to better help you understand this process.

What Features Vary in the Fax Modems?

As you examine the offerings available in the marketplace, you'll observe that fax modems with different speeds and capabilities are widely available. In the following sections, we'll examine some of the features you should investigate, to help pick the equipment and software that best fits your needs.

Speed

If you're sending long-distance or international faxes, speed is important. Of course, this assumes that the fax on the receiving end can operate at the speeds your fax modem can handle. Although, at least 90% of today's modems operate at 9600 bps, but we recommend at modem with 14.4K fax capabilities since such boards are becoming increasingly more popular (a faster board can always fall back to a lower speed but the reverse is not true for most kinds of computer hardware).

Fax Queuing

Fax queuing allows users to queue up their faxes and schedule them for after-hours transmission, when rates are typically cheaper. Unless your current setup also supports queuing, this feature alone can help to repay the costs of an upgrade to equipment that can provide this support.

Inbound Routing

There are five methods of routing incoming faxes to their recipients:

- DID (direct inward dial) hooks into a local telephone system like a private branch exchange and requires technology to recognize or supply a telephone number from a user's name or telephone number.
- DTMF (dual-tone, multifrequency) requires inclusion of a local telephone extension code, but provides the same capabilities as DID.
- OCR (optical character recognition) uses OCR technology to decode the recipient's name and address and handle forwarding.
- E-mail interfacing provides a direct link to electronic mail systems, but usually requires a sender to include the recipient's e-mail address as part of the fax's header.

- Manual routing requires an operator to examine faxes and forward them to their intended recipients. Manual routing can be electronic or paper-based.

DID requires that you have a phone switch (i.e., ROLM, Northern Telecom) installed which can be expensive if your company doesn't currently have one. DID provides a separate fax phone number for each user on the system. This requires the sender of the fax to remember only a phone number when transmitting the fax to the recipient. DID is the most desirable method.

DTMF requires that each person have a four-digit extension to identify him or her on the system. Putting in this type of system will probably cause the number of your incoming faxes to dwindle drastically. DTMF requires the sender to input the four digit extension after dialing the recipient's number and obtaining a fax connection. Unfortunately, the DTMF method won't work at all if you're trying to queue up your faxes to send overnight.

The OCR method scans the first page for familiar text that it recognizes to properly route incoming faxes One vendor we spoke with said that the sender has to put information about the recipient in Courier 12 point font in the upper left-hand corner of the cover page to use the OCR feature of its software. Here again, special handling requirements can make fax routing troublesome for the uninitiated.

The e-mail method routes the incoming fax to the receiver via the e-mail package. All vendors do not support every e-mail system. Some do not support a particular e-mail package, but fake support by using Novell's message handling system (MHS). So, if you decide to go this route, call the vendor and ask which e-mail interface or package it supports. Since you can't pick a solution that will accommodate everybody, pick the one that accommodates the greatest part of your recipient population.

Manual routing is the easiest method of all, but it requires that an administrator view the cover page and route the fax to its designated recipient. Thus, although it is the most simple method, it's also the most expensive and, owing to human fallibility, the most error prone.

Number of Channels Supported

Fax modems may be either single channel and multichannel boards. The number of channels indicates the number of phone lines a fax modem can support. Thus, if a fax modem is able to support only one phone line per board, you'll run out of slots in a communications server quickly, unless your needs are fairly modest (typically, eight lines or less). Multichannel boards like those offered by Gammalink and Brooktrout can support multiple phone lines per board, making them more suitable in medium to large networking environments.

Phone Book Support

Most fax modem software permits its users to create and maintain an electronic phone book. In reality, this phone book is nothing more than a centralized database that can store a shared collection of fax and company contact information. If you find this feature appealing, be aware that some of the vendors' software permits the existing database file formats (i.e., dBase, FoxPro, etc.) to be imported. If you need to manage this kind of data transfer, make sure to pick a package that supports a data format that you can use.

Recognized File Formats and Emulations

Some fax systems recognize multiple graphics file formats (i.e., PCX, DCX, BMP, etc.). Other systems are more limited in the number of formats they support directly. Likewise, printer emulations may vary. If you're concerned about Hewlett-Packard compatibility, be sure to ask the vendor which PCL revision that its fax system emulates.

Here's another important aspect to note here about fax modems: modems accept incoming data in one graphics format or another. If you have anything on paper to send through such a system, it must be scanned into the proper format to be used. We'll talk more about scanners in Chapter 39.

NETWORKING FAX MODEMS

Networking fax capabilities usually involves installing multiple fax modems into a file server or designating a dedicated PC to act as a fax server. For NetWare, such an approach requires the installation of special NLMs on one or more file servers, where fax modem hardware must then be attached directly to a designated server that will handle incoming and outgoing faxes. Figure 38.6 shows the path a fax travels through a network.

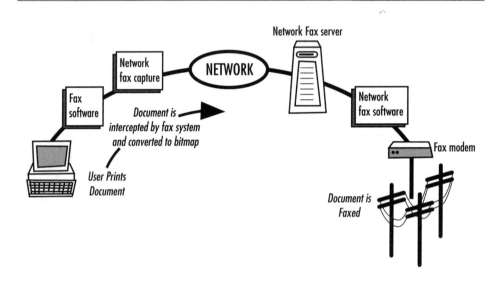

Figure 38.6   *Path of a network fax.*

For those of you not using NetWare, a number of products support network fax services for a wide variety of other network operating systems. These include Alcom Corporation, Biscom, Delrina Corporation, Futurus Corporation, NUKO Information Systems, Inc., and Tracs Computer Distribution. Biscom is an especially good choice because it markets fax products for a wide variety of platforms, including the AS/400, IBM System 36 machines, Banyan Vines, and DEC Pathworks.

For network use, a fax modem must be at least CAS class or better. Forget about Class 1 or 2 modems, because these modems tie up the server's CPU and can cause it to bog down. CAS modems include on-board processors that can handle fax transmission or reception and free up the CPU to perform other tasks.

Issues such as security, inbound routing methods, and the number of phone lines needed for fax use should be addressed before purchasing any network fax system. You will need to work closely with the telephone person at your company and plan your network fax system within the capabilities of your phone system. For a good book on purchasing a fax modem or networked fax server please consult Harriett Hardman's *Network Faxing* (a full citation is available in the Bibliography at the end of this chapter).

WHAT TYPE OF PC WILL I NEED?

When selecting a PC for use as a dedicated fax server, choose a machine that has as many open slots as possible. You'll also want to provide plenty of hard disk space; even though they're compressed, fax files do contain graphical information, and can often be quite large. As with any server, there's no pressing need for color, but you will need a monochrome VGA monitor at minimum. If you're planning to replace a number of standalone fax machines with one or more fax servers, it's a good idea to use nothing slower than a 486/33 processor (but buy as powerful a processor as you can afford).

On the other hand, standalone PCs seldom require changes or upgrades to accommodate a fax modem. Here again, we recommend at least a 486/25 SX for today's demanding desktops, with a minimum of 4 MB RAM for DOS, or 8 MB for Windows use.

Installation

This section will focus on preparing and installing a networked fax modem on a dedicated PC (i.e., a machine other than your friendly neighborhood file server). For this example, we'll install an internal modem that conforms to the CAS standard.

Note: this means we won't need to upgrade our existing 486/33 DX PC with its 410 Mb hard disk. For the server, we'll use Windows-based fax modem software and assume that the users all have Windows and that the local phone system supports a DID interface.

Preparing to Install the Fax Modem in a Dedicated PC Server

✓ Gather the installation disks, modem manuals, and PC manuals

✓ Get the fax modem and correct cable and place nearby.

✓ Have a few small screwdrivers handy (flathead and Philips).

✓   Have another fax phone number and person ready on the other end
    to test sending and receiving a fax.

✓   Gather up all necessary device drivers—you'll also need to modify
    the CONFIG.SYS or AUTOEXEC.BAT (depending on driver re-
    quirements), so now's a good time to make a backup of these files on
    floppy.

✓   Have a piece of paper handy to document the installation, including
    the fax modem's serial number and make and model number.

✓   Dog-ear the manual pages that contain the configuration section.
    Look through any sample configurations to see if there are any po-
    tential gotchas that you might need to anticipate (and avoid).

✓   Write down technical support numbers for the company that sold
    you the modem system, and the numbers for the support operations
    at the equipment and software vendors whose products you're go-
    ing to be installing, should you need them.

✓   Set up a LAN user ID for the server PC (the server you're installing
    must be connected to the LAN and logged in as a user to provide
    networked fax services).

✓   Set up the server PC as if it were a workstation on the LAN: this re-
    quires a NIC to be installed in the PC, along with the appropriate
    LAN drivers needed to establish a network connection. Operating
    system software (DOS) and Windows should also be installed and
    running prior to installing the fax software and hardware. Make
    sure there's a free connection on the network for this PC near the
    telephone lines intended for fax use (since this PC will be a dedicat-
    ed server, it's wise to place it in your telecommunications room if at
    all possible).

✓   Inform your telecom person that you need two analog lines and may
    need additional lines in the near future. Also let the telecom person
    know that you'll be using the DID feature of the fax modem—he or
    she will need to get you a bank of DID numbers that you can assign
    to individual fax users. Also, ask the telecom person for a satin cord
    (satin cord goes from modem line jack to telephone jack in wall.)

Installing the Networked Fax Modem

Hardware

- ✓ Make sure your PC and modems are completely powered down.

- ✓ Disconnect the power cable to the PC to make sure. Disconnect any other cables that are in the way in the back of your PC.

- ✓ Pop the hood (cover) on the PC.

- ✓ Put a static wrist guard on to prevent zapping any interface cards with the static electricity from your body.

- ✓ Find two open slots in your PC and plug the modem cards into those slots. Do not screw them down just yet. Wait until you have successfully sent and received a fax before making this installation permanent.

- ✓ Depending on the software you choose, you may need to configure your modems to use COM1 or COM2. This is usually done by a switch block on the modem cards or via an installation program.

- ✓ In some cases, you may have to reset the IRQ and Base I/O on the fax modems if the factory default settings conflict with other devices. In most cases, these settings can also be configured with the same installation software.

- ✓ Your modems need to be connected to the power source of the PC. This can be done by using the pigtail connector.

- ✓ Take your satin cables and plug them in from the line jacks in the modems to the analog jacks in the wall.

- ✓ Plug the NIC into the network connection.

- ✓ Plug all your cables back into your PC and into the power in the wall.

✓ Turn everything on. Ideally, you're going to see lights on the PC. Most likely, you will not see lights for the modem since it's an internal card. Some cards have lights on the outside in the back of the PC. If not, check all of your cables and make sure you plugged in the power plugs and sources.

✓ Log onto the LAN with the server PC.

✓ Don't close the hood and tighten the screws yet! Wait until the software part is configured and working then close the hood.

Software

✓ The software part is a two-step process. The first step involves configuring the software on the dedicated PC server. The second step involves configuring an end user's workstation.

✓ It's important that you know that changes probably will be made to the AUTOEXEC.BAT and CONFIG.SYS files. To be on the safe side, always make a backup of them before installing anything. Another thing we do is make a backup of our Windows INI files. All this only takes a few minutes, but is well worth the extra time.

✓ Most of them have self installing programs that will do the work for you and reconfigure things, set parameters, etc. The first thing we do on disks we receive is look for the README.TXT file and then look for an INSTALL.BAT or INSTALL.EXE or SETUP.EXE. Any of those will get you started for the dedicated server end of things.

✓ You will have to go to each PC that you want to fax across the network and make it fax modem aware. This is essentially another installation except it is done at the end-users' PCs and is typically not as involved a process as the server-side installation.

✓ Hate to leave you alone from this point on, but you're going to have to pull out the manual and let them step you through their process. Good luck!

TROUBLESHOOTING FAX MODEMS

- Did you remember to load the appropriate software before trying to access the modem? Did you load the device driver in your AUTOEXEC.BAT or CONFIG.SYS or both?

- If it is an internal modem, did you remember to connect the pigtail connector from the power supply on the PC to the modem? Is the cable loose?

- If it is an external modem, is the cable loose? Is the power source plugged in?

- Are you trying to dial the correct number? Does your system require that you dial a 9 to get out of the building?

- Is your modem plugged into the analog line? Is the analog line punched down properly? Try hooking up an analog phone to the line and see if you get a dial tone. You might have to get your telephone person involved especially if you're setup with DID inbound routing.

- Is your interrupt number in conflict with other devices in the PC? Try a different IRQ by using a DOS diagnostic tool (like MSD.EXE, DIAGSOFT, or Quarterdeck's Manifest) to locate an unused IRQ number.

WHAT TO BUY?

When determining the kind of network fax modems to purchase, you must first ask yourself a number of questions. Depending on their answers, you can narrow your choices down quite a bit. For example, if you absolutely must have a system that supports inbound routing using DID technology, then you could immediately eliminate those vendors who do not even support such routing.

- Does your company have moderate or heavy faxing needs? Most fax machines print out a ledger. You should be able to collect all the registers from all of the fax machines and count the outgoing/incoming faxes for one month. If the number per machine exceeds 200 faxes per month, you should consider switching to a networked fax server.

- Does your company need the inbound routing capability? If so, which inbound routing method can you utilize? DTMF? DID? OCR? E-mail? Manual? Is security an issue in the inbound routing? Will you have to hire an additional fax administrator to handle this function?

- What type of network does you company have? Will you need to fax from the AS/400 and UNIX boxes as well as PC's? The answers to these questions could drastically reduce your choices. For example, several of the options support only NetWare. So if you have Vines, you can rule those items out immediately. A handful of products support multiprotocol environments and multiple hosts, but these tend to be more expensive than narrowly targeted products.

- Will your company have need to connect the fax system to the e-mail system? If so, what e-mail packages and interfaces does the fax vendor support?

- What are the workstation requirements? If you have a DOS shop and the system supports only Windows and OS/2, you can trim down your decision even more.

- What type of file formats and printer emulations does the fax modem support? If all of your work is stored in BMP files, and the fax vendor doesn't support that file format, then you're going to have some converting to do.

- How good is the vendor? Does the vendor have a BBS? Can you call technical support without being put on hold for one hour? Is the technical support number toll free? Is the vendor involved in standards bodies?

- Read all the comparison charts you can find. We find them all the time in PC magazines. You can, too.

- Use the power of friends, associates, and professional associations— have any of your friends purchased, researched or installed anything in this area? Pick their brains apart. Don't be bashful. Do you regularly converse with your associates at other companies? If not, you should begin to do so immediately. It proves to be invaluable. Do you belong to any professional organizations such as CNEPA? If not, join up right away so you can take advantage of the information and contacts these organizations can provide.

Top Five Vendors

Intel Corporation
5200 NE Elam Young Parkway
Hillsboro, OR 97124-6497
800-538-3373

Castelle Inc.
3255-3 Scott Boulevard
Santa Clara, CA 95054
408-496-0474
408-496-0502 (fax)

Cheyenne Software, Inc.
3 Expressway Plaza
Roslyn Heights, NY 11577
516-629-4453
516-627-2999 (fax)

Delrina Corporation
895 Don Mills Road,
500-2 Park Centre
Toronto, Ontario
Canada M3C 1W3
416-441-3676

Biscom, Inc.
321 Billerica Road
Chelmsford, MA 01824
508-250-1800
508-250-4449 (fax)

Networked Fax Modem Resources: Bibliography and Strategies

For general networking references, please consult Appendix C, "A List of Networking Resources." The magazines and other publications listed there can help you find out lots of information about fax modems. The following references are particularly helpful for the information they contain about fax modems:

Hardman, Harriett. *"Network Faxing."*
McGraw-Hill, Inc., New York: 1995 A good source for comparisons of different fax modem software in additional to analysis of hardware needs. $25.45

Held, Gilbert. *The Complete Modem Reference 2nd ed.*
John Wiley & Sons, Inc., New York: 1994. A great technical look at every aspect, feature and standard of modems. One chapter is specifically written on fax modems. A must for every bookshelf. $29.70

SCANNERS

39

SCANNING 101: BASIC OVERVIEW

What Is a Scanner?

A scanner is a hardware device that converts printed text or graphics into a binary file format. Scanners use a sensor to detect reflected light from images and convert those images into binary file formats. A scanner is similar to a camera except that it records images in binary format, not on photographic film. Scanners function as a "pair of eyes" for your computer, in much the same way as a camera acts as a replacement for the human eye. A scanner can be hooked up directly to your PC, or it can be installed on a server on your network.

Scanning Basics

To begin with, to scan an image into a standalone PC or onto a networked PC, you must first have the right equipment—a scanner, along with the cables and software needed to get the scanner to communicate with your computer. Scanners come in many types: handheld, flatbed, sheetfed, or drum. Whatever kind you use, it's the foremost piece of equipment you'll need to bring scanning capabilities into your computing environment.

The second piece of equipment you'll need to establish a working connection is a cable to connect your PC (or server) to your scanner. This cable may be parallel, serial, or SCSI, depending on what type of interface your scanner supports. If you're lucky this cable will be included with your scanner; if not; be prepared to spend somewhere between $10 and $40 for an appropriate cable.

The third ingredient for a working computer-to-scanner hookup is some kind of application software that allows you to edit and manage the image files you record using the scanner. Typically, this software includes some or all of the following items:

- image scanning and enhancement software
- OCR software
- document management software
- desktop publishing software

The application software that usually comes with a scanner may originate from a variety of companies, even though it's been sold to you as a bundle.

What Can I Do with a Scanner?

Let's take a look at some of the things you can do with a scanner.

Scan Text into OCR Programs

Without a scanner, the only way to incorporate a document available only in paper or printed form is to retype the whole durn thing. If you have a scanner and the appropriate optical character recognition (OCR) software, you might be able to eliminate the need for retyping (or at least 90% of the retyping; no OCR software is 100% accurate). Despite the need for touchup, using a scanner with OCR typically involves a great deal less work than rekeying a document.

OCR lets a scanner convert a text image into a stream of text characters that can be interpreted using software specially designed to recognize characters in the binary data created by a scanner's input functions. OCR packages may be sold individually or bundled with a scanner. Whether you get such software with your scanner or not, obtaining an OCR program is probably a good idea, since it's one of the main applications for scanners in the first place.

Capture Images into a Faxable Format

Scanning a paper document into a bitmap file allows you to use fax software to send out that image. You can use your fax software to broadcast this information to numerous people—something that isn't as easy to do from an old-fashioned fax machine. By combining the power of a fax modem with a scanner, you've recreated the input side of an old-fashioned standalone fax machine; if you've also got a printer, you can throw that dinosaur away!

Scan Images to Use as Templates

Some software programs work exclusively to trace the outlines of scanned images. Once an image has been scanned, this software takes over to provide a complete trace of the image. This creates an electronic template that can be reused as needed to drive shop floor or manufacturing equipment. Such templates can also be edited electronically or combined with other designs to facilitate better consumption of materials or more convenient production techniques. Here again, a scanner can serve to better integrate existing equipment, because of its ability to provide fully digitized images and input information.

Scan Line Art for Publications and Desktop Use

Using a scanner to import line art into a document is often faster, cheaper, and more efficient than the traditional methods. Rather than sending line art to a typesetter or photo shop for layout and plate generation, a scanner can let you do your own image capture and manipulation. Electronic editing and layout changes are easier to manage and permit alterations right up until the moment the film or plate is imaged for final printing.

Scan Photographs

It used to be both complicated and expensive to scan photographs into documents. The most common manual technique for composition of final documents is called *paste-up*, because it depends on precise cutting and positioning of printed photographs and type to prepare pages for final imaging. Today, photographs can be scanned easily into existing electronic documents, making it easy to do final compositions electronically, rather than physically. As with the previous example, electronic methods permit far more flexibility and let changes be introduced more readily into the production process, right up to the final stages.

How Does a Scanner Work?

Scanners vary by make, model, type, and scan engine manufacturer. Because of these differences, the mechanics of a scanner's operation will differ from one kind of scanner to another. Regardless of any differences in the hardware, all scanners share the following characteristics:

- some type of light source
- some means of reflecting light back from the image to a sensor
- some type of circuit to convert analog information to a digital format

Let's run through an example of scanning a document using a monochrome flatbed scanner and trace what happens as we scan a page of text. Let's assume that the page we're scanning was printed on a laser printer from a Windows word processing document:

1. Place the page face down on the glass surface of the flatbed scanner (just like a copier).
2. The scanner moves a light source under the glass surface, directed at the paper, moving from one end to the other until the whole surface has been scanned. The amount of light reflected back to the scanner triggers on or off (black or white) states in an array of sensors.
3. The sensor array reads the light reflected back from the paper. Black areas on the paper absorb more light and reflect less light back to the scanner. The white areas on the paper absorb very little light and reflect back more light than the black areas.
4. This light is reflected through a set of mirrors on the scan head to a light sensitive diode. The diode converts the amount of light returned to the scanner into electrical current. A white area on the

scanned image reflects more light back and generates more voltage than a black area.

5. An analog-to-digital converter in the scanner translates analog voltage values to digital pixel values. These pixel values will be one of two states: black or white.

6. The scanner stores the image on the PC's hard disk in a graphics file format determined by the user. The image is now ready to be used in conjunction with the various software packages that permit editing, and so on.

It's easy to think of a scanner as a kind of copying machine. It is in fact, except that it produces an electronic copy of the input page, rather than a positive image on paper.

Ways to Connect a Scanner

There are five common ways to connect a scanner to a PC:

1. *Parallel port (usually on the back of the desktop PC or laptop)*—This method is for use mainly with portable scanners on notebook and laptop PCs. However, a scanner can be hooked up to the parallel port on a desktop PC.

2. *Serial port (on the back of the desktop PC)*—This connection method is becoming less and less common as SCSI connections take the lead. This method is the least desirable because it is the slowest of all the methods mentioned here (see Chapter 36 for a detailed description of serial communications).

3. *PCMCIA slot*—This method is used with scanners that will be connected to notebook and laptop PCs with PCMCIA slots.

4. *SCSI interface*—The preferred and fastest method for attaching scanners to PCs. This interface requires a SCSI card in the PC and a scanner that supports a SCSI connection. Not all scanners include a SCSI port, but some vendors bundle SCSI boards with their scanners. If you're planning on using a scanner heavily, this is a feature worth shopping for!

5. N*etwork interface*—Some vendors like Fujitsu offer a select few scanners that include a built-in network interface, which allows such scan-

ners to be plugged in as nodes on the network. This type of scanner will be available to anyone on the network with the right driver software installed (and the right permissions to use the device).

Handy Terms in the Scanner World

Pixel—Picture element (or PEL). This is the smallest element representing part of an image—usually a dot.

dpi—Dots per inch, a measurement of the density of an image. The more dots per unit of measure, the denser it is and the higher its resolution (e.g., resolution is directly proportional to density).

Drawing—An image type that is represented by only black and white dots.

Halftone—Process of grouping black dots of the same size into groups such that they can appear to be one larger dot. The process is used to create the appearance that an image uses continuous tones even though it can print only black dots of the same size.

Dithering—Same as halftone, it represents the gray areas on an image by grouping black dots into certain patterns so that they appear both gray and continuous.

Grayscale—The range of gray values pixels can take on in any part of an image.

Line Art—Drawings that have only black and white areas on the image, but contain no shaded, grayscale, or halftone areas.

Raster graphics—An image represented by dots or a bitmap.

Vector graphics—An image represented by lines instead of dots.

OCR, or optical character recognition—The process of scanning an image, recognizing any text and converting it into an editable binary file.

Gamma correction—A process for controlling features such as brightness, resolution and contrast by enhancing the black tones in an image. Some scanners handle gamma correction in the hardware, other scanners rely on software.

Interpolation—increasing the resolution of an image by adding four dots where there was only one dot. Using this 4:1 ratio and replacing every dot with four dots for the whole image increases the resolution. Figure 39.1 on page 571 shows an image scanned at 300 dpi. Figure 39.2 shows the same image interpolated to 600 dpi.

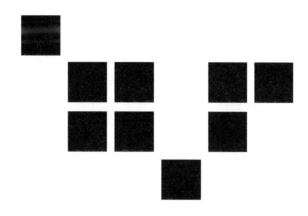

Figure 39.1   *Image scanned at 300 dpi.*

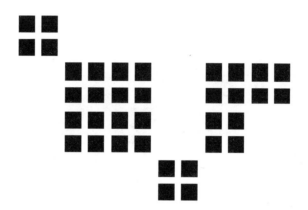

Figure 39.2   *The same image interpolated to 600 dpi.*

TWAIN, or toolkit without an interesting name—This is an industry standard application interface for image capture. For example, if a program is TWAIN compatible, then you'll be able to use it to edit a scanned image. Such editing may only consist of brightness and contrast controls, but it may save steps by eliminating the need for an image editor.

DIFFERENT KINDS OF SCANNERS

Now that we know what a scanner is and the different connection methods you can use to attach one to a PC or the network, let's take a look at some of the more common types of scanners available. These include handheld scanners, sheetfed scanners, flatbed scanners, and drum scanners.

Handheld

Handheld scanners come in a variety of shapes and sizes. Of the two most frequently used types of hand scanners, one model resembles a highlighter pen and another model resembles a mouse with a wide head (see Figure 39.3). As their names suggest, users must hold these types of scanners in their hands and move the scanner over the page manually. The scanner must be moved steadily and evenly. Because of the need for steady, even motion, handheld scanners work best on a flat surface.

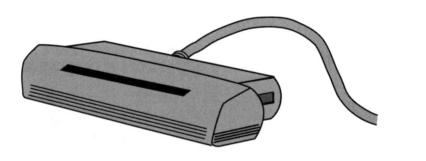

Figure 39.3   *Handheld scanner.*

Some advantages of handheld scanners include

- low price, $150–400 range
- small, size of pen or mouse
- good resolution, ranges from 100–400 dpi
- ability to scan large areas, scan small areas and patch together

Although its handheld nature contributes to low cost and ease of use, the very nature of handholding introduces the possibility of human error, like incomplete scanning, or improper sequences; and the scanning process with handheld models is often quite slow. A handheld scanner is not a good option for anyone with high volume scanning needs or anyone with shaky hands.

Best Buy:
Some of the companies in the handheld scanner market include Log-itech, Kyocera, Chicony, UMAX, and Niscan. If you plan to buy a handheld scanner, look at the end of this chapter for the book by David D. Busch; it's a reference that focuses completely on handheld scanners.

Sheetfed

A sheetfed scanner works much like a fax machine. Paper is handfed into a sheetfed scanner until a pinch roller grabs the paper, which then feeds it through the scanner one line at a time. The sensor and the light source in the sheetfed scanner do not move, only the roller moves, taking the paper along with it. Figure 39.4 illustrates a sheetfed scanner.

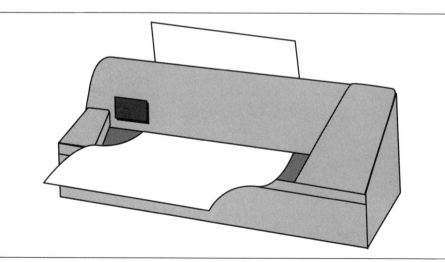

Figure 39.4   *Sheetfed scanner.*

The advantages of using a sheetfed scanner include

- low cost
- small footprint
- automated paper feed.

Sheetfed scanners range from $500-1,000 in cost. This is affordable, both for home and office users. Also, their small size—compared to the flatbed scanners covered in the next section—and automated paper feed is a big step up from the handheld scanner's manual processing. Sheetfed scanners typically allow pages up to 8.5″ x 17″ to be scanned.

A sheetfed scanner's main disadvantage follows from its resemblance to a fax machine—if the paper does not feed properly or jams, you must manually clear the mechanism and reinsert the paper. And if it's mangled beyond the machine's paper-handling abilities, well, you're out of luck (better have an extra copy handy, just in case)!

Some of the companies in the sheetfed scanner market include Logitech, Plustek, Fujitsu, Canon, and HP. Canon has an IX-3010 scanner and HP has a ScanJet 3P. Both the Canon and HP models are worth investigating further if you're shopping for a sheetfed scanner.

HP ScanJet 3P Sheetfed Scanner

List cost: *$599*

Resolution: *300 dpi with interpolation 1200*

TWAIN compliant? *Yes*

Software bundle by HP that includes the following:

- WordScan OCR v3.01 (by Calera)
- PicturePlace Editor (image editing)
- PictureScan (HP scanning software)

Does it support color? *No*

What type of interface? *SCSI*

Does the interface come bundled? *Yes*

What type of software is required to run this? *Windows*

Is there a network connection? *No*

What capacity will the document feeder support? *20-page capacity* ·

Auto feeder paper size = 8.5 x 14"
without auto feeder supports = 8.5 x 11.7"

Flatbed

By 1993, 58% of the scanners in use worldwide were flatbed scanners. We remember our first HP flatbed scanner fondly from many years ago. It worked beautifully, except that there weren't many compatible programs available for it. We could scan pictures nicely, but just couldn't do a whole lot with the scanned images that resulted. Today, many vendors provide high-quality software solutions that not only capture high-resolution images but permit them to be used in all kinds of interesting ways.

Figure 39.5 shows a typical view of a flatbed scanner. A flatbed scanner works like a copy machine: simply place the work to be scanned face down on the glass surface, and the sensors and lights move just underneath the surface to capture the image from below.

Since there are more moving parts in a flatbed scanner, there are more opportunities for breakdowns. Nevertheless, it's been our experience that flatbed scanners are pretty reliable.

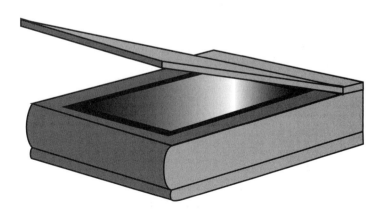

Figure 39.5   *Flatbed scanner.*

The cost range for a flatbed scanners is approximately from $1,500–3,500. We consider such scanners to occupy the middle of the scanner spectrum where cost is concerned. However, the flatbed's lower end price of $1,500 is really attractive if you're looking for a scanner and don't have a bundle of money.

The primary advantage of flatbed scanners is that the paper does not have to be inserted like the sheetfed scanner; another advantage is that the paper is far less likely to move while being scanned. An obvious disadvantage is that most flatbed scanners require you to insert the image face down, making it more difficult to align your image within the scanner's field of vision.

Best Buy:
Let's take a look at four flatbed scanners on the market today. We consider the HP ScanJet IIcx scanner and Epson ES 1200C Pro Scanner to be on the low end of the flatbed spectrum and the other two, Microtek ScanMaker III and Umax Technologies' PS2400SX, to be at the high end of the flatbed scanner spectrum.

HP ScanJet IIcx Flatbed Scanner

List cost: *$1,179*

Resolution: *400 dpi, with interpolation 1600 dpi*

TWAIN compliant? *Yes*

Software bundle: *Yes, by HP and Calera*

- WordScan OCR v3.01 (Colera)
- HP Copier (copier utility—scanner can act as copier)
- HP Deskscan (scanning software)
- PhotoStyler SE Aldus (image editing software)

Does the scanner have support for color? *Yes*

What type of interface does it support?*SCSI*

Does the interface come bundled? *Yes*

What type of PC required to run this? *Windows*

Is a network connection built in? *No*

Document feeder (see Figure 39.6 on page 579 for a view of a typical flatbed scanner with a document feeder.)? *For an additional cost of $559—holds up to 50 pages*

Transparency adapter? *For an additional cost of $759 (scans 35mm film)*

Paper size supported? *8.5 x 14"*

Epson America Inc.'s ES1200C-Pro Flatbed Scanner

List Cost: *$1,499*

Resolution? *600 x 1200 dpi, with interpolation 1200 x 2400 dpi*

TWAIN compliant? *Yes*

Software bundle: *Yes, if you buy the Pro version which includes*

- Adobe Photoshop
- Kai's Power Tools

(If you don't buy the Pro version, you get a scanner and TWAIN driver)

Does the scanner have support for color? *Yes*

What type of interface does it support? *SCSI-2, bidirectional parallel*

Does the interface come bundled? *Yes*

What type of software required to run this? *Windows*

Is a network connection built in? *No*

Document feeder? *For an additional cost of $499—holds up to 30 pages*

Transparency adapter? *For an additional cost of $959 (scans 35mm film)*

Paper size supported? *8.5 x 11.67"*

MicroTek ScanMaker III Flatbed Scanner

List Cost: *$3,499*

Resolution: *600 x 1200 dpi, with interpolation 2400 x 2400 dpi*

TWAIN compliant? *Yes on PC, no on Mac*

Software bundle: *Yes*

- Full version of Adobe Photoshop (image editing software)
- No OCR

Does the scanner have support for color? *Yes*

What type of interface does it support? *SCSI1 (proprietary)*

Does the interface come bundled? *Yes*

What type of software required to run this? *Windows*

Is a network connection built in? *No*

Document feeder? *For an additional cost—holds up to 50 pages*

Transparency adapter? *For an additional cost (scans 35mm films) (8 x 10")*

Paper size supported? *8.5 x 14"*

UMAX Technologies PS2400SX Flatbed Scanner

List Cost: *$3,495*

Resolution: *600 x 1200 with interpolation 9600 x 9600*

TWAIN compliant? *Yes, for PC only*

Software bundle: *Yes, there are two bundles to choose from:*

Pro version includes: *Adobe Photoshop 3.0 and Kai Tools, no OCR*

Limited edition includes scaled down Photoshop and OmniScan Direct (OCR)

Does the scanner have support for color? *Yes (single pass)*

What type of interface does it support? *SCSI-2 (proprietary but should work with Adaptec)*

Does the interface come bundled? *Yes*

What type of software required to run this? *Windows*

Is a network connection built in? *No, but a setup for network software is available.*

Document feeder? None available

Transparency adapter? *Comes with (scans 35mm film) (8.3 x 10")*

Paper size supported? *8.3 x 11.7"*

Drum

We consider drum scanners to be the most expensive type available on the market today. These scanners are designed for heavy duty, high-volume use and for extremely high-quality output (such as an art press or photographic reproduction operation). They are far too expensive ($25,000 and up) for home or office use, unless your office happens to be a professional prepress or publishing operation.

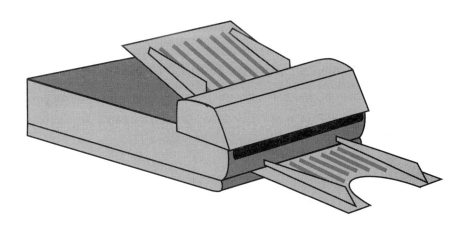

Figure 39.6   *Flatbed scanner with document feeder.*

NETWORKED SCANNERS

Installing a scanner on a network is considered "bleeding edge" technology at present. There isn't much hardware or software support yet in this arena. No scanners come network ready or equipped to meet Microsoft's plug and play specifications.

Not all vendors offer software that is networkable. Caere has a package called PageKeeper 1.1 that qualifies; this program includes a built-in feature that allows it to accept image or text files and then store documents for later retrieval and processing. Additionally, PageKeeper comes with built-in OCR.

Gotcha:
The trick is to remember that, regardless of which scanner and software you select, you're going to need enough bandwidth to handle multiple users moving graphic images over the network. Additionally, storage space may become an issue if you plan on storing these images somewhere else on your network. The higher is your scanner's resolution, the higher these storage requirements will be.

THE SOFTWARE SIDE OF THE SCANNING STORY

Most scanner vendors bundle software with their scanners. Much of what happens on the PC depends on the software that you use with your scanner. When ordering software for your scanner, be sure to tell the vendor or salesperson what operating system you intend to use. Not all software supports multiple platforms. If you have several platforms that you intend to use with your scanner, choose a company like Caere that supports scanner software for multiple platforms.

Best Buy:
Some vendors offer different bundles for you to choose from when purchasing your scanner. For example, they may ask you to choose between full-blown image editing software, or a scaled-down version of the same software for less money. Don't choose the high-end bundle if you plan to do only a few OCR scans per day.

Selecting an Image Type

There are three main image categories that your might want to scan: drawings, halftones, and grayscale images. Before you begin your scan, you must select one of these three types to instruct the software how to interpret what the scanner "sees."

Drawings are images that are scanned in as black and white dots only where the original has no gray or shaded areas. An original drawing might contain color, but will result in a scanned image containing only black and white areas.

Halftones (see Figure 39.7 on page 581) are images used to simulate a continuous scale of gray tones with varying patterns of black dots. This is a useful rendering technique, since printers can produce only same-sized black dots and therefore can't print shades of gray. By using a technique called dithering, the scanner can group several black dots into one area so that portions of the image looks as though it has one larger dot to create the impression of a gray area. Using this dithering technique for the whole image, a scanner can simulate a continuous scale of gray tones. The only real advantage in selecting halftone images when scanning is that halftone files are smaller than grayscale files (see later). One major disadvantage of using halftone imaging when scanning is that you can't edit these images.

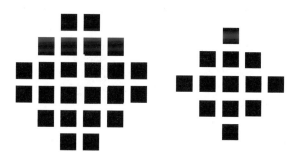

Figure 39.7   *Halftone dots.*

Grayscale or continuous tone images appear to have all the various shades of the gray spectrum ranging from white to black. On most scanners, you'll have the option of scanning in 4-bit (16 levels of gray) or 8-bit images (256 levels of gray) For most scans, 16 levels of gray will suffice; as an added bonus, such image files require less disk space than 8-bit images. Grayscale produces larger file sizes, so if storage space is scarce, you may want to investigate adding more disk space to your system. The biggest advantage of grayscale images over drawings and halftoning images is that grayscale images can be manipulated with image editing software.

Types of Graphic File Formats

You must select a graphics file format before you begin scanning a document. There is a range of file formats to choose, but they can be separated into two categories: raster and vector graphics.

Raster (Bitmapped) Graphics

Raster graphics are composed of bitmapped files, where the file is created by using pixels or dots to create an image. These types of graphics files are used mainly by paint software programs that edit images pixel by pixel. The two most common file formats in this category are PCX and TIFF (tagged image format file) files. If you have a choice, it is better to select TIFF because it is the most prevalent format in use today and is supported by a wide variety of software packages. Be aware that there are three different types of TIFF formats: compressed, uncompressed, and PackBits. Before you buy any software or hardware, ask the vendor which TIFF file formats it supports. Not all software supports all of the TIFF formats. Don't buy anything that doesn't support at least two of the three TIFF formats.

Vector (Outline) Graphics

Vector graphics are comprised of file types composed of lines and objects. You will find that most of sophisticated drawing programs utilize vector graphics files. A good example of a vector graphics file format is EPS (encapsulated PostScript).

Types of Software Packages Available

Image Scanning and Enhancement Software

Image scanning and enhancement software allows you to scan images and then edit them. Items you may wish to edit are size, shape, and color. You must have this type of software to edit your image. Sometimes image scanning and enhancement software will come bundled with the scanner.

Some of the companies that have image scanning and enhancement software on the market today are Aldus, Adobe, and Zsoft Corp. Adobe Photoshop, CorelDRAW, and PhotoFinish are image scanning and enhancement software on the market.

OCR Software

OCR software permits you to convert text printed on paper to an image of text characters. Some companies that specialize in this software are Caere Corp., Calera Recognition Systems, Inc., and OCR Systems, Inc. You may already be familiar with the following popular OCR software: OmniPage, ReadRight, WordScan, or TrueScan.

If you purchase OCR software independently from your scanner, check with the software company to make sure that the software supports that brand and model of scanner.

Desktop Publishing Applications (Ventura, PageMaker)

You may be familiar with Ventura Publisher or Aldus's PageMaker desktop publishing software. Both have been around for at least five years. You may remember installing Ventura Publisher years ago. It was extremely awkward and not very user friendly (or administrator friendly)! Desktop publishing software at that time was reserved only for those who desperately needed the software. Desktop publishing software is not only more user friendly, it's also a lot more scanner friendly!

Utility Software

You may have a need for utility software for your scanner. Some utility software include raster-to-vector conversion, screen capture, and bitmap-to-CAD conversion. Companies preeminent in this arena include Arbor Image Corp., Image Systems Technology, Inc., and ProWorks.

Document Management Software

Once you have scanned in an image and made the proper editing adjustments, you'll need document management software to manage the files you've created. Managing documents is particularly important on a network where more than one user will store and retrieve images from a shared repository.

Some of the document management software permits you to scan an image directly into your fax software. A few companies in the document management software arena include Claris, Keyfile Corp., and Document Storage Systems, Inc. Some software you will find in this category includes Keyfile, Legend, ClarisWorks, and PageKeeper.

INSTALLATION

This section will focus on installing a standalone flatbed scanner.

Preparing to Install a Scanner

✓ Gather all the printer and PC manuals.

✓ Get the scanner and the correct cables (make sure the scanner cable and power cords are long enough to meet your needs).

✓ For serial connections, make sure you have the right cable (do not use a modem cable). Also, make sure you have the right cable for the number of pins in use.

✓ Position the scanner where you want it.

✓ Get image to be scanned ready.

✓ Check the scanner driver. Is it more than 6 months old? If so, call and see if a more recent version is available. Make sure to use the Windows driver for Windows, etc.

✓ Have a piece of paper handy to document the installation, including the scanner's serial number.

✓ Look through manuals for configuration information; resolve any questions that emerge before starting the installation

✓ Have the tech support number of the companies that sold you the PC and the scanner, should you need them.

Installing a Scanner

Hardware

✓ Make sure your PC and scanner are turned off.

✓ Install the interface board (most of the interfaces are SCSI and come bundled with the scanner). For SCSI, make sure to check the device ID on the unit, base address, and IRQ. If this is the first and only SCSI unit you will connect, generally you should not have to mess with these settings.

✓ Hook up the scanner cable from the scanner to the back of the PC.

✓ If your scanner uses a serial connection, you'll have to check for dip switches to set the speed, parity bits, etc. This definitely requires the manual.

✓ Turn on your PC and your scanner (ideally, lights will be a shining).

✓ The last step is to actually scan an image, but we can't do that until we've installed the software.

Software

✓ If you're using a serial cable, you'll have to add the following to your AUTOEXEC.BAT file—MODE COMZ:YYYY,X,W where Z is equal to the COM port you're trying to connect to and YYYY is equal to the speed (i.e., 9600), X is equal to the parity, and W is equal to the number of stop bits.

✓ Which software you got bundled with the scanner or you purchased separately will determine how to install the software. There may be one install program for all of the software or there may be individual installation programs. This part is pretty involved and is really going to depend on the scanner you buy. It's important that you know that there will probably be changes made to your AUTOEXEC.BAT and CONFIG.SYS files. To be on the safe side, always make a backup of them before installing anything. Another thing we always do is make a backup of our Windows INI files. All this only takes a few minutes, but it has saved our bacon more than a few times.

✓ Most scanner software programs include self-installing programs that will do the work for you and reconfigure things, set parameters, etc. The first thing we do with disks we receive is to look for a README.TXT file and then look for an INSTALL.BAT or INSTALL.EXE or SETUP.EXE. Any of those will get you started.

✓ We hate to leave you alone from this point on, but you're going to have to pull out the manual and let them step you through their processes. Good luck!

✓ The test: Go into your application and scan! If you encounter problems, consult the basic Troubleshooting section that follows.

Common Troubleshooting for Scanners

- Are you using the correct software for your operating system? (That is, if you have a Mac, are you using the Mac version of the software?) When you buy the scanner and bundled software, tell the seller what type of PC and OS you plan to use.

- If you're using a SCSI connection, are the devices internally terminated? Are you having a problem in the chain somewhere? Try disconnecting the scanner from the SCSI chain and connect it directly to the PC.

Tip:
You must terminate the SCSI device on faster PCs such as the Pentium and PowerPC.)

- Have you enough memory? Are you trying to scan an image that is too big to fit your present memory profile?

- Is the bulb on the scanner burned out or defective? Even though the light is on, the bulb could be on the blink. Some bulbs live 4–6 months, depending on usage, others can last as long as 1.5 years. Some bulbs can be replaced at the local lighting store.

- Is the glass surface clean or is it smudged with fingerprints? Clean it with whatever your vendor recommends such as Windex).

- If you're using Windows, do you have any temporary files floating around on your hard disk? These temporary files can cause general instability in Windows and you should delete them.

- Check your hard disk more frequently for lost clusters. Some software, when it crashes in the middle of an open scan, can create lost clusters (it's usually quite safe to delete them).

- If your video card is new and the video drivers are brand new (i.e., first set of drivers for this card), your drivers may not have all the bugs worked out. Try calling the vendor to see if later versions are available. If not, try slipping back to straight VGA mode to see if you get better results.

- Some of the applications (like Photoshop) recommend that the virtual memory on the PC be set to half of its actual RAM. Check the hardware/software memory requirements of your device and software to make sure that you are meeting the minimum memory requirements.

WHAT TO BUY

Here are some important questions to ask yourself or your vendor before purchasing a scanner.

Determine Scanning Requirements

- Remember that most scanners are bundled with OCR, image editing and document management software. Knowing both your hardware and software requirements will help mucho.
- Type of images to be scanned?
- Printed?
- Slides?
- Transparencies?
- Amount of scanning to be done (occasional, heavy)
- Amount of work area for scanner (footprint of scanner)?
- Professional use or business presentation use?

Determine Feature Requirements

- How much resolution do you require?
- Is speed important?
- How large will the images scanned be?
- Do you require the scanner to have a 1 or 3 pass rate?
- Do you need the ability to create TWAIN drivers or have the scanner support TWAIN?
- Do you need to scan color or black and white only?
- What graphics formats are supported (TIFF, BMP, etc.)?

Determine OS and System Scanner Will Operate On

- Unix, then you can rule out certain scanners
- Most support Macs and Windows, some support OS/2 and Unix
- Windows NT is supported by a lot of software vendors, but check this carefully before you buy.

Determine Intended Uses for the Scanner

- Will you hook up the scanner to a printer, and if so, what type of printer?
- Will you hook it up to the fax?
- Will it be a networked scanner?

Evaluate the Vendor

- Does the vendor have a BBS?
- Can you call tech support without being put on hold for 1 hour?
- Is the tech support toll free?
- Is the vendor involved in standards bodies?
- Will the vendor sell you the scanner separately if you choose to go that route?
- What is the warranty?

THE TOP FIVE SCANNER VENDORS

Hewlett Packard, Inc.
3000 Hanover St.
Palo Alto, CA 94304-1181
800-752-0900; 800 387-3867 (CD); 415-857-1501
Direct sales: 800-637-7740 (HP Direct)
FAX: 800-333-1917
Tech support: 800-858-8867
Tech support BBS: 415-852-0256
CIS: GO HP

UMAX Technologies, Inc. (subsidiary of UMAX Data Systems, Inc.)
3353 Gateway Blvd.
Fremont, CA 94538
800-562-0311; 510-651-8883
FAX: 510-651-8834
Tech support: 800-468-UMAX
Tech support BBS: 510-651-2550

Fujitsu Computer Products of America, Inc. (subsidiary of Fujitsu America, Inc.)
2904 Orchard Pkwy.
San Jose, CA 95134-2009
800-626-4686; 408-432-6333
FAX: 408-894-1709
Tech support: 408-894-3950
Tech support BBS: 408-944-9899

Microtek Lab, Inc. (subsidiary of Microtek International, Inc.)
3715 Doolittle Dr.
Redondo Beach, CA 90278-1226
800-654-4160; 310-297-5000
FAX: 310-297-5050
Tech support: 310-297-5100

Epson America, Inc.
20770 Madrona Ave.
Torrance, CA 90509-2842
1-800-289-3776 Support: 1-800-922-8911, 9 a.m. to 9 p.m. weekdays
(EST); Faxback service: (310) 782-4214; BBS: (310) 782-4531;
CIS:GO EPSON

SOURCES OF INFO
(ANNOTATED BIBLIOGRAPHY)

Busch, David D. The Complete Scanner Handbook for Desktop Publishing, PC Business
   One Irwin, Homewood, IL.1991-1992. If you're interested in using a scanner for desktop publishing, buy this book! $24.65

Day, Jerry B. Super Scanning Techniques. The Hewlett Packard Guide to Black and White Imaging. New York: Random House. If you've got (or are considering the purchase of) an HP scanner, this book is for you. It also offers a good overview of scanning technologies and techniques. $20.40.

Busch, David D. The Hand Scanner Handbook PC ed. Homewood, IL: Business One Irwin. This book is tightly focused on hand scanners, and nothing else; if you own a hand scanner, this book is a must-have; if you don't, skip it. $24.65.

Fraser, Bruce. "Top-Quality Scanners," MacUser vol. 10, no. 11 (November 1994): 82. An excellent comparison of 12 scanners of all different kinds.

Gilbert, Susan. "Picking up Pixels" Computer Shopper vol. 14, no. 7, (July 1994): 290. An outstanding article on how scanners work.

part

NETWORK MANAGEMENT

V

Once your networking is running, chances are good that you'll want it to stay that way. Although our experience has been that users seldom notice when a network is doing what it's supposed to, they always notice when it's not working all that well. They especially notice when the network stops working altogether!

Here in Part V, you'll learn about the terms and concepts behind network management, the science for keeping your network fit and healthy, which, alas, is still mostly an art. We'll cover the basic concepts and terminology for network management, along with the important protocols and tools you're likely to encounter when keeping your network working is your primary concern (or when fixing a broken one is a matter of life and death).

We begin this Part with an overview of network management and introduce some models for how network operation and control can (or should) be handled. Starting with Chapter 41, we step up the management tour with a discussion of wire-level management tools, like those you'd use to control and configure your organization's hubs and concentrators.

In Chapter 42, we step up to the server, as we investigate tools and techniques for server management. In the following chapter, we visit the other side of the client/server dynamic, focusing on workstation management tools, technologies and standards. Finally, in Chapter 44, we conclude our management discussion with an analysis of those enterprise management consoles like HP's OpenView and IBM's NetView, that can look at the big picture for some very big networks indeed.

In Part V, our goal is to raise your expectations by telling you what network management should be able to do, but we temper those expectations with a realistic assessment of what network management actually can do with the tools and technologies available today. Ideally, you'll come away from this discussion ready to tackle your toughest management issues, somewhat optimistic that technology will help rather than hinder those efforts.

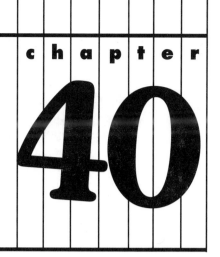

INTRODUCTION TO NETWORK AND SYSTEMS MANAGEMENT

chapter

40

BASIC NETWORK AND SYSTEMS TERMINOLOGY

In this chapter, you'll be introduced to the subject of network and systems management, especially as it pertains to the kinds of tasks that individuals responsible for caring for and feeding networks perform.

The idea is to establish a common vocabulary for these tasks, to help you understand what's required to manage a network and the systems it connects. Then, we'll investigate the state of the current art and science of networking and systems, to explain why management is a critical issue. After that, we'll examine a formal model for how networks and systems should be managed, and explain why the model is only a first step to getting your arms around the entire subject.

To begin with, we'll take a look at what makes up a system, in terms of hardware, software, and behavior. Then, we'll explain what networks are and how they work, to set the stage for discussing their management. We'll conclude the terminology section with a definition of network and systems management, to set the stage for the rest of the book.

UNDERSTANDING SYSTEMS

In the simplest of terms, the network is just a form of plumbing. It exists to link users with services that they might not otherwise be able to get from a standalone computer. From this standpoint, the systems that a network links together are what delivers the services and capabilities that make things happen. This division of capability is not quite as pure in practice as it is in theory, primarily because any system has to have some networking capability to access a network at all, and secondarily because there are some systems whose jobs are entirely or partially focused on performing network functions.

A good example of a network system is a piece of internetworking equipment called a *router*. Basically, a router is a kind of network switch-board. It includes multiple network interfaces, and its job is to examine inbound network traffic to determine where to send it (if at all) for proper delivery. If a packet arrives at the router from Network A that's addressed to Network B, the router may be able to forward the traffic directly, if Network B is also attached to that router. If Network B can be reached only through some other network (perhaps Network C), then the router has to determine if it can reach C or if some other network that can reach C and so on. Routers might also be set up to reject certain traffic, either for security reasons or to limit the amount of information that has to traverse a slow speed link (for instance, it might not make sense to advertise a print server in New York that's located in San Francisco).

Taking care of a router is definitely a network management task, but it involves a considerable amount of systems management as well. *Systems management* refers to managing the hardware, software, and connections of a particular system or computer to make sure that it's running properly and legally. Here's a more concrete laundry list of what systems management involves:

- Initial system hardware installation, configuration, set-up, and testing,
- Initial system software installation, configuration, set-up, and testing,
- Network interface installation, configuration, set-up, and testing (this includes assignment of network address and delivery of access to the system's user or users),
- Software maintenance and upgrades,
- Hardware maintenance and upgrades,

- Periodic system inspection for legal compliance (for instance, making sure no copies of software for which there is no legal license or permission to use are present and running on the system),
- System backup (and restoration, if and when needed),
- Ongoing asset management—purchase and repair records for all systems and related components,
- Systems support services—maintenance and support records for all systems, including problem reports and resolution information, as well as update and maintenance records,
- Configuration data: description of hardware and software configuration, including system, components, operating system, and software (this includes configuration files, network addresses, revision levels on all software, etc.).

As you can see, a lot is involved in managing a system and keeping track of all the different pieces of important information. The more systems there are to manage—and a network automatically dictates that there will be at least a few—the more work there is to do!

EXPLAINING NETWORKS

You're probably familiar with networks already, because you very likely use one in your workplace. Let's start with some basic definitions and move forward from there.

LANs, WANs, MANs, and Internetworks

When a LAN extends outside a building, it becomes a different animal. If it's connected to a special regional type of high speed network, it might be called a *Metropolitan Area Network*, or MAN. MANs are still not very common these days, because they rely on a generally available networking infrastructure whose expense is high enough that only large organizations (like governments or large corporations) can afford to build private ones. Some large cities—like Washington, D.C, or New York City—are considering making WAN technology publicly available, but it's not yet a common form of networking service.

If a LAN is connected by a public or private carrier to another networked site (or a collection of such sites) —typically, by a dedicated line between the two locations—it might be called a *Wide Area Network,* or WAN. It's helpful to think of a WAN as a collection of LANs, communicating with each other by telephone, satellite, or some other non-LAN type of connection. A WAN can extend between two adjacent buildings, across a city, or across the world.

Because MANs and WANs are really groups of networks, they're also sometimes called *internetworks.* In general, an internetwork is a collection of two or more LANs that have been linked together, either by a local or remote link. Thus, a single site could also be an internetwork, if it consists of two or more individual network segments. This distinction is a little subtle for most people, so it's still common to refer to a local internetwork as a LAN, even though this is not absolutely correct, technically speaking.

The most famous internetwork in the world today, and arguably the largest, is the Internet. This is a network of thousands of different networks from all over the world. Some of these networks have only one or two computers, others have thousands. Whatever it is that you have to manage, be grateful it's not as big and complicated as the Internet—but then, no one entity is responsible for managing it, either!

The focus of this book will be on LAN management, so we will not spend lots of time going over issues that are peculiar to either MANs or WANs from now on. But because all three have a lot in common from a management perspective, what you learn will stand you in good stead if you need to venture outside the LAN into either area.

What Needs Managing on a Network?

Because we've already discussed the components of a system that need managing, we can concentrate on nonsystem aspects when talking about network management. Here, the focus is to keep the information flowing between and among systems, so the simple answer to the question is "Everything between systems needs managing."

In practice this boils down to a number of different aspects of the network. If we start with the wires and physical connections that make up the network and work up through the layers of communication and software that make the network do its job, this will guide us through what needs managing from a network perspective:

Gotchas:

- Existing wires and connections need to be kept connected and in good repair; new ones need to be added as needed.

- Network addresses and organization need to be established, assigned, and maintained as things change.

- Networking equipment needs to be used where needed and then maintained.

- Networks always have users, so the user base will have to managed: this includes adding new users, moving around existing ones, and deleting old ones as needed. Users also typically require some care and feeding themselves, when it comes to learning and using networks.

- Network services—like file services, print services, database access, fax services, and much, much more—will have to be established (this crosses over into the systems domain), maintained, and access granted to users.

- Networking software needs to be loaded on systems to let the users access the network and then be maintained and upgraded as needed.

- External connections to other networks (via WAN or MAN) may need to be procured, installed, and maintained; internal internetworks may likewise need to be installed and maintained.

- Network layout and configuration information needs to be recorded and maintained as things change. This includes cabling layouts, address assignments, network server information, network equipment information, and more.

- The health and availability of the overall network needs to be monitored to make sure it's consistently available, and to help anticipate growth and change.

In short, a lot is involved in making up a network, so a lot of things need management as well. Because some of these involve working with systems, as well as with the network, it's important to treat them together.

INTRODUCING NETWORK AND SYSTEMS MANAGEMENT

Since the introduction of PC technology in the early 1980s, the characteristics of the workplace have been forever changed. In a relentless drive to deliver more capability to individual workers, organizations of all kinds have been quick to adopt and adapt their working routines to these ubiquitous machines. In fact, the percentage of workers using computers in their jobs in North America finally surpassed the percentage of those who don't in 1993 (June 1994, IDC Study, "Computers in the Workplace").

Likewise, the push to networking has been even more aggressive in the past decade. While the population of PCs (including workstations, non-Intel machines, and "true PCs") has grown at an annual rate of 20% over the past 10 years, the introduction of networking technology has grown at an annual rate of over 30% in the same time frame (1993, Gartner Group, The Networking Industry Worldwide). Each passing day brings a new infusion of powerful computing technology, ready to help workers do more and communicate better.

Today, the shape of the so-called information superhighway is starting to become clearer, bringing with it more and better ways for individuals and organizations to interact with one another electronically. The number of options for going online and doing business the same way continues to grow at a staggering pace. The availability of information and the opportunities for new business ventures have been greatly expanded, as a truly global information economy is beginning to emerge in the countries of the First World. The future looks incredibly bright, as long as the underlying infrastructure does what it's supposed to do!

But the search for enhanced productivity and interaction hasn't always paid the kinds of dividends that are expected at the outset. While the investment in PC technology and networking has exploded, so too have the costs that go along with it. According to a 1993 study by the Infonetics Research Institute, the costs of running a network of PCs varies from a low of $1,500 per user per year to a high of over $3,000 per user per year, with no end to these costs in sight (February 1993, "The Costs of Network Ownership"). Furthermore, these costs continue to escalate as networking becomes more pervasive, and the tasks that networks are used for become ever more critical to the health and well-being of those organizations.

Today, more than ever, there's a crying need to manage the networks that tie together PCs, and also to manage the individual PCs, printers, fax machines, and other components that are showing up on those networks. Again, that's why this book deals with "Network and Systems Management" instead of simply "Network Management." Taking care of the pieces that link together is at least as important as taking care of the links themselves; but taking care of one without the other quickly turns into an exercise in futility.

THE MIXED BLESSINGS OF CLIENT/SERVER TECHNOLOGY

The rise of the PC and networking has paralleled—some would even argue that it's caused—a decline in the fortunes, usage, and market share for mainframe and minicomputers. Because of the need for centralized information access, even with the increasing amounts of power and capability available on individual users' desktops, the combination of PCs and networking has led to the creation of a new computing paradigm called *client/ server*.

In a client/server environment, information processing tasks are split across the network. An individual user's desktop PC takes on the client role, which involves managing user interaction—especially, supporting the increasingly powerful and demanding graphical user interfaces like Microsoft Windows that are enjoying such widespread use today—including solicitation of requests for all kinds of information and services and presenting the results of such requests to the user as they become available. For obvious reasons, the client role is often referred to as the "front-end" for information processing involving the network.

The server role, on the other hand, can be fulfilled by a number of different kinds of systems. These can range from the mightiest mainframes (as with an airline reservation system), to minicomputers (as with credit checking, tax records, or other large data collections), to a variety of powerful PCs built specifically to take on the server role. The job of any server is to handle requests for information or services from multiple users simultaneously and fulfill those requests as quickly and efficiently as possible. It's not unusual to find organizations using different kinds of servers to service a pool of heterogeneous clients, depending on the nature of the data being processed or services provided, as well as where their prior investments in such technology have been strongest.

In other words, it's often easier to leave the data where it currently resides, even if it's on an expensive mainframe, than to migrate the data to newer, less expensive server hardware. This remains true, notwithstanding the terrific hype you'll find in the computer trade press on the phenomenon known as *downsizing*, where tremendous savings can supposedly be realized by substituting smaller, more powerful computers (with low maintenance and components costs) for big, powerful mainframes (with high maintenance and components costs).

At the same time, powerful networking software has been developed to interconnect clients and servers, so that they can take advantage of the power, capability, and data that resides in centralized and distributed environments. Although companies like IBM and Digital Equipment have labored mightily to make their mainframes and minis easy to network, other companies like Novell, Banyan Systems, and Microsoft have striven to make information equally available from PC-based servers networked to a variety of PC-based clients. In many organizations, this has caused a collision of world views, as departmental users (who grew into computing with PCs and PC-based networks) butt heads with corporate users (who grew up with mainframes and their related network types).

The upside to this computing revolution has been to increase the power and capability of users while at the same time creating collections of information and services that can be shared by growing communities of such users. These benefits are both useful and compelling, but they've arrived with sufficient costs and personnel requirements to make cost differentials nowhere near as compelling an argument for downsizing from larger systems like mainframes or minis to PC-based networks as networking pundits argued in the late 1980s and early 1990s. At the same time, the proliferation of software, machines, and servers has made operating and controlling these environments a major component of the overall costs. In fact, a recent Gartner Group study shows that the full life cycle costs of owning and operating client/server networks are nearly equal to those for minicomputer or mainframe computing environments.

Even though its momentum appears based more on convenience than cost, the client/server phenomenon shows no signs of abating. Even though its costs may not be as low as originally hoped, client/server has delivered more power, capability, and usability to end users than ever before. For those in the mini and mainframe camp that try to argue that a return to centralized computing makes sense, the ultimate rebuttal remains the stubborn refusal of users to give up their PCs and the individual productivity applications that have made that platform such a success in the past decade.

Is Server Management
Network or Systems Management?

Given the popularity and power of the client/server model, the server becomes a pivotal information resource, a system that provides critical network resources and services. In today's networks, servers are responsible for a variety of tasks that range from storing and forwarding electronic mail, to providing access to shared peripherals of all kinds (like printers, fax machines, scanners, and telephone links), to providing access to shared collections of information of all kinds. In many cases, servers also provide the outermost collection of physical links that make networks possible, so it's not unusual to see them acting as network traffic directors and managers, in addition to their other roles.

The need for server management springs from the essential observation that, without an operational server, most networks are useless. As the crown jewels of most networks, organizations readily understand that their care and feeding is unusually important. Other factors that contribute to the need for server management tools can be explained by the way in which most networks are laid out: network professionals tend to be few and far between; the servers they must manage are often widely dispersed and distributed. Then, too, the very importance of these machines to basic functions like printing, file system access, and more means that users will complain very quickly when such functions are impaired or lost altogether. Together, these factors add up to a need for rapid detection and resolution of problems, no matter where an administrator might be nor where a server is physically situated.

But server management extends well beyond mere troubleshooting. As you'll learn throughout this book, observing network and server behavior over time can provide numerous benefits that range from capacity planning, to network design and planning data, to ensuring the right mix of services and resources needed to adequately service any user community. Before delving more deeply into these subjects, let's first examine the status quo for server management, as we explore the prevailing view on what's involved and required to keep a server functioning properly in its pivotal networking role.

The Conventional View

The prevailing view of network management in general and server management in particular is that it exists to supply information about the network itself and not very much more. The most common view of network management data is that it relates to what's moving across the wire at any given time or perhaps over time. In the same vein, server management consists primarily of observing server utilization, dealing with glitches as they occur, and performing routine maintenance on that machine (which usually includes things like hardware and software upgrades when necessary, backups, regular cleaning and checkups). In the same vein, systems management is viewed as an end-user issue and often left in users' hands, except for providing a network connection and limited software support.

This prevailing view also tends to treat components in isolation from one another, often to the point of considering the wire-level aspect of the network as completely separate from the applications or software in use. In many cases, different groups or individuals may even be responsible for those different aspects. But for most environments, the following three topics constitute the total of network and systems management:

- Monitoring, or regularly checking network or server behavior and characteristics. Only when end-user systems cause problems do they receive much notice,

- Troubleshooting, or dealing with problems, faults, failures, or slowdowns in reactive mode, as they're reported by users or observed by server or network managers,

- Maintenance, or performing the kinds of tasks necessary to keep a server or network running smoothly, on a more or less regular basis. End-user systems don't always figure into this viewpoint, and seldom get much maintenance from network or systems management personnel.

In the following subsections, we discuss these topics in a little more detail.

Monitoring

For physicians, checking the patient's pulse has always been a premier diagnostic tool; for networks and servers, keeping track of traffic and usage levels is the analogous tool. Without regular, comprehensive monitoring, it's impossible to understand what "normal" looks like for any given network. Over time, comparisons of monitoring snapshots will illuminate historical trends and help to point out areas of growth, potential bottlenecks, and the most heavily used—and therefore critical—resources.

Troubleshooting

In many organizations, especially smaller ones, troubleshooting is the only management practice that's regularly performed. When this happens, it's a case of taking "if it ain't broke, don't fix it" to its logical extreme: if the only network or systems management that ever occurs is when broken things need fixing, it's almost inevitable that they'll break more often than they might otherwise. Nevertheless, it's still true today that the first thing most people think about when they hear the terms *network management* or *systems management* is "troubleshooting."

Maintenance

As networks and the servers that service them become ever more prevalent, the value of preventive and regular maintenance is beginning to make itself known. For one thing, most software programs and utilities get upgraded by their developers at least yearly, which requires a well thought-out program of testing and incorporation for any network. For another, with the data on most servers growing in importance, the value of regular backups is also becoming more obvious (despite this, less than half of the networks in the United States are backed up on a regular basis, according to Patrick Corrigan's excellent book *Backing up NetWare LANs*). Then, too, hardware upgrades and routine equipment maintenance also require some effort, however intermittent this activity might be. The upshot of all this activity is an increasing awareness that regular, scheduled maintenance is as good for networks and systems as for the mainframes and minicomputers so many of them replace.

Reasons for Network Management

When it comes to tackling the entire scope of network and systems management, a great many more components and elements come into play. The server is only half of the client/server equation; controlling and managing the machines and software on users' desktops is an important concern, not just to keep things working, but also to stay within the confines of the law (particularly as regards software licensing restrictions).

Then, too, the network infrastructure needs care and feeding as well; when such an infrastructure may include numerous pieces of intelligent equipment—ranging from smart hubs to multiprotocol or multitopology routers to telephone switches to satellite links—these items will also require consideration from a management perspective as well. Finally, the human element is involved; not only is it important for the network administrative staff to understand their environment and the tools they have to work with, it's also vital that users understand what a network is and how it behaves and how they can best do their jobs within that environment.

In the following subsections, we'll cover some of the most compelling reasons for taking a proactive and thoughtful stance regarding network and systems management. It should help to explain why management is becoming a buzzword for networking in the 1990s. It should also help underscore the need for management approaches that include more than monitoring, troubleshooting, and maintenance in their underlying motivations.

Gotcha: Proliferation of Networks

As the growth figures for networking over the past decade (over 30% CAGR) should attest, networks are proliferating wildly in the workplace, be they in business, academia, government, or elsewhere. With an increase in the number of networks comes an increased need for control within these various organizations, for reasons that range from ensuring compliance with licensing restrictions, to keeping the number of versions of software under control, to delivering the best return on expensive equipment and personnel investments.

Increasing Distribution and Complexity

Along with the increase in the number of networks worldwide has been an attendant increase in their size and complexity. More and more organizations have passed the initial hurdle of whether to network or not; today, many of them are faced with the need to unite widely dispersed networks, to weld them together into a single cohesive enterprisewide computing environment.

Likewise, the numbers and kinds of devices attached to a network has increased in the past decade as well. In addition to computers that range from the oldest PCs and antique workstations to modern high performance supercomputers or graphical workstations, it's not unusual to find various types of intelligent networking gear attached to a network, including smart hubs, controllers, and routers. It's also relatively commonplace to see printers, fax machines, scanners, and more attached directly to the network, rather than functioning purely as a peripheral device to some other computer attached to the network.

Each type of device brings its own unique configuration, software, and device management requirements. Often, each brand of device requires the use of specialized management tools built solely to control it (and any other identical units on the network) and nothing else. This has led to the proliferation of what some network and systems management experts call *swivel-chair management*, because it requires management staff to switch among so many different management systems to do their jobs.

The more widespread use of networking and the greater variety of devices, services, and resources that networks provide mean that network and systems management must be able to function in a distributed environment, where the manager (or management software) and what's being managed need communicate only over the network between them. It's equally true that network and server management has to be able to deal with a sometimes bewildering array of such devices, services, and resources as well.

Downsizing of Administrative and IS Staff

At the same time that networks have been increasing in size, distribution, and complexity, the staff that manages them has been decreasing. The past decade has seen a tremendous upsurge in allocation of capital to hardware, software and networking, but the investment in head count dedicated to managing or administering these assets has dropped.

Gotcha:
In an era where "lean and mean" is the norm, especially when applied to overhead staff in the information services (IS) department (or in dedicated network or systems administration staff attached to departments or other organizational units), the increase in workload for such staff has been tremendous. Today, there's simply no way for most IS professionals to cope with the systems and networks they must manage without being able to leverage a management toolset to make them more efficient at their jobs.

Emergence of a Mission-Critical Status for LANs

Another aspect of downsizing in the last decade has been directed at systems. Spurred on by a hope that expenses would be lower on networked PCs and by user demand for PCs, many organizations have invested heavily in migrating from their traditional IS platforms and applications. In most cases this has meant moving from minis or mainframes, with mission-critical systems and software and many years of experience working with them, to equivalent client/server applications that take advantage of networked PCs.

Some organizations have built hybrid systems, where user PCs act as intelligent front ends to existing mainframe or minicomputer applications. Others have seized the reengineering opportunity afforded by the change to completely replace their existing implementations with fully rebuilt client/server applications. Not every story has been an unqualified success and costs have not declined as much as hoped, but in every case this kind of change has meant that the organization's local area network has become the glue that ties the enterprise together.

Using a LAN for individual productivity and e-mail is one thing, using it to run one's business is entirely another. Therefore, this aspect of downsizing has focused a great deal of attention on the ability of such networks and systems to function acceptably when running mission-critical applications. A familiar lament that's emerging is: "Why can't I run my client/server environment just like I used to run my mini or mainframe?" This is nothing more than an outright plea for management tools and technologies.

Maximize LAN Effectiveness, Use, and Uptime

Given an increasing shift of investment toward local area networks, PCs, servers, and client/server technologies, organizations want to maximize their returns on such expenditures. Having access to client/server capability may be nice, but it's much more satisfactory to the bean counters if it can be demonstrated to provide increases in productivity, improvements in cash flow, or other tangible returns.

To obtain the kind of information that's necessary to measure such returns, the conventional view of network and systems management has to be addressed, particularly monitoring. Put another way, it's essential to regularly monitor network and service uptime and usage to understand how well those resources are being used within an organization.

Best Buy:

Historical trends in usage and utilization can illuminate patterns of increased resource consumption or adaptations in work behaviors that illustrate how effectively the network and its systems are being used. Network and system management information is key to such measurements and to deciding how to make changes that positively affect the bottom line. This is especially true for network servers, which provide much of rationale for using a network in the first place.

The Bottom Line: Decrease Growing Costs of Ownership

Finally, maximizing the return on network and systems investment has come to mean controlling and limiting the overhead costs that ownership of such technologies entails. Most of the trends we've discussed up to now—proliferation, complexity, distribution, and migration of mission-critical applications, in particular—are also working together to drive up costs of ownership. Left unchecked, they could easily price client/server computing right out of existence.

Therefore, the primary goal of network and systems management has to be to decrease these growing costs, while at the same time helping lean administrative staffs make the most of the human and technology resources they can muster to keep networks, servers, and other systems running as smoothly and effectively as possible.

At this point, we've discussed the prevailing view of network and server management and have tried to explain what motivates the need for such activity and technology. As we move on to discuss some particular approaches and philosophies we believe can prove effective in providing such management, you'll learn more about the state of the art as it's practiced today and the tools and techniques that drive it. You'll also learn more about what my research with actual consumers of such technology has indicated about real need that currently remain unmet.

To begin this remaining discussion, let's examine a standard model for network management, developed by the International Standards Organizations Open Systems Interconnect (ISO/OSI) group. This should help establish a more formal frame of reference, along with some technical terminology. Then, we'll move on to explore what areas this model has apparently overlooked, according to a recent survey of a fairly broad user base of client/server and networking technology.

OSI Network Management Model

Technobabble:

Open Systems Interconnect is an organization devoted to the promulgation of standards for open systems within the International Standards Organization (ISO). OSI originally promised to provide the next generation of networking protocols and services for open systems, but that promise was never realized. Nevertheless, the OSI models and terminology developed for networking and network management have proven to be especially useful for discussing these topics. Here, we'll explore a model developed by the OSI's network management forum, to lay the groundwork for the upcoming categorization of network management requirements and properly contextualize the user management requirements my research helped uncover.

The basic idea that drives the formal concept of network management, as expounded by OSI, is that rather than dedicating personnel solely for network maintenance and troubleshooting, organizations would be much better served if networks could look out for themselves for the most part. An especially important part of this self-management includes an ability to perform routine, scheduled tasks (like backup, mail forwarding, or database replication) at regular intervals, without requiring human intervention once a schedule for such activities is set. Theoretically, this leaves human staff free to handle nonroutine items and plan for future network expansion and growth.

The OSI model also includes a definition of network management, as the process of controlling a complex network to maximize efficiency and productivity. The capabilities of the actual system or systems that administer network management will determine exactly what this means, but such capabilities customarily include data collection, be it manual from explicit human effort or automatic as part of the functioning of the management system. More advanced network management systems will even assist in analyzing such data and present them to a human operator for further action. Most network management systems will at least generate reports based on observed events and activities while such systems are running as well.

According to the OSI model, network management is broken up into five functional areas (each of which is the subject of a subsection that follows this list):

- fault management
- configuration management
- security management
- performance management
- accounting management

Together, these five areas constitute the bulk of activity that surrounds the topic of network management. Let's look at each one in a bit more detail. For the purposes of clarity, we'll call the people who operate networks and interact with network and management systems *network engineers*. Figure 40.1 shows how typical network management tasks might be divided up among these five areas for different aspects of any given network.

Fault Management

Fault management concerns itself with solving problems, or faults, that occur on a network, and typically involves a three-step approach:

1. Identify that a problem exists.
2. Isolate the problem and its causes.
3. Fix the problem if possible, devise a workaround tactic if not.

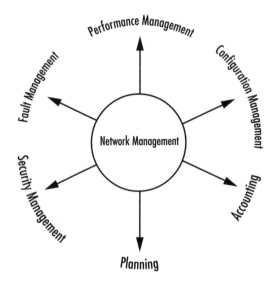

Figure 40.1   *Categorizing management tasks using the OSI Network Management Model.*

Using fault management techniques, a network engineer can handle problems more quickly than he or she might be able to otherwise. Such techniques increase network reliability because they decrease (or eliminate) outright failures and because handling routine problems or faults can be built into network management systems for automatic responses directly from the system (requiring no human involvement in some cases).

Problem identification depends on recognizing that a problem exists (or may be likely to occur). The keys to such recognition include an ability to handle critical network events, which involve failure or impairment of network elements or capabilities, and the ability to query network elements on demand or on a regular basis to monitor their proper operation. Ultimately, any network management system includes an understanding of a range of network events, which may be critical or otherwise, likely or unlikely, and the ability to respond to those events when required. Typically, most network management systems also include an implicit or explicit priority scheme for events, so that a server failure would rank higher and be responded to more quickly than an impairment of an individual workstation, if both occurred at or near the same time. Recognized events will often be called *alerts*, to indicate a condition that requires recognition but may not require immediate action, or *alarms*, to indicate critical network events that often require immediate attention to avoid network impairment or failure.

Problem isolation and diagnosis depends on a variety of elements, many of which can be built into network management systems. Token ring networks, for example, are very well-behaved when it comes to recognizing and dealing with network hardware problems, so that the failure of an individual link simply causes the network to reconfigure itself to bypass the offending element. This process is also the subject of numerous alerts and alarms, so that a management system would include information about the events inherent in recognizing and bypassing the problem. However, there may be network or server pathologies that can't be handled readily without human involvement; to this end, many network management systems include audible alarms from a computer and even the ability to page a designated network engineer.

In most cases, diagnosis leads immediately to cure (as with our token ring example). In some cases, the symptoms documented by various alerts and alarms may have to be inspected and analyzed by the network engineer to be fully understood, and corrective action taken. For most network anomalies, the normal courses of action are as follows:

- Restart and retry problem elements (this will often correct not-so-serious problems).
- Replace or repair failed or impaired elements.
- Bypass failed or impaired elements or reconfigure the network around them (this is a workaround strategy that can buy time for more in-depth diagnosis and a more suitable repair or replace maneuver later on).

Fault management is certainly the most familiar part of network management, as network engineers locate, diagnose, and fix glitches, but there's a lot more to the subject, as the next sections will indicate.

Configuration Management

The configuration of network devices, including servers, very often determines how a network will behave (or why it can't behave in certain ways, desirable or otherwise). Configuration management consists of setting up such devices—creating an initial configuration—and of tracking and maintaining their configuration thereafter.

This sounds deceptively simple, but actually involves keeping detailed records of the software versions and hardware settings on most, if not all, devices on a network. An example should make this clear: assume that all of the users on a network require the installation of a particular program, which requires the 3.11 Windows updates released by Microsoft to bring Windows 3.10 in conformance with their Windows for Workgroups product. The only way short of inspecting each machine to see which version of Windows is installed is to gain access to a configuration management tool that can supply the necessary information for each workstation (or that can query the workstation to supply it on demand).

A configuration management tool should provide descriptive information about all significant information on the network. This could be a list of all servers running a particular version of NetWare, or it might be a list of the version of DOS, Windows, and networking software installed on each PC on the network. Access to this kind of information is critical to planning and executing timely, effective network maintenance.

Security Management

Security management is the process of controlling access to information and resources on the network. Today, much of this functionality is supplied on a per-computer basis by the underlying operating system on each machine, networked or otherwise, or by explicit security controls built into individual applications (like database management systems). But because information needs to be accessed across the network, it's critical to know for a given collection of data (like the payroll database) who's permitted to access any of this sensitive information. It's also important to be able to segregate who gets to see such information from who gets to change it (or you just might be tempted to give yourself a raise!). Most security management systems provide per-user controls over data access for this very reason.

Security management also provides methods for monitoring network access points, for intruder detection and activity logging. This lets organizations provide their employees with remote access capabilities without necessarily exposing them to the prying eyes of unauthorized users. With the increased use of remote access to many networks, this must be a serious concern for those organizations that provide it.

Performance Management

Performance management requires the measurement of utilization, throughput, error rates, and efficiency of network hardware, software, and media. Using the information obtained from such measurements, a network engineer can ensure that adequate capacity is available to support demonstrated demand. More important, following such measurements over time will allow growth requirements to be anticipated and supplied before shortages develop or bottlenecks occur.

Some performance measurements overlap with the kinds of data gathered for fault management purposes. Error rates are a good example: not only does a spike in error rates indicate a potential fault, an upward trend in error rates over time may indicate a network that is nearing its carrying capacity. If this occurs in an environment where demand is likely (or planned) to increase, it's as much a call to add new capacity as it is an indication that problems may occur.

The major distinction between fault management and performance management has to be the use of network characteristics to plan for change, as opposed to the arrival of events that demand immediate response. That is why network characterization—creating a collection of network performance measurements to establish the normal ranges of operation and behavior—is such an important aspect of network management and an important technique for ensuring optimal network performance.

Accounting Management

Accounting management involves tracking consumption of network resources, be it on an individual (per-user) or group (workgroup, department, or other organizational unit) basis. This not only allows a network engineer to determine if users can obtain the quantity and quality of information and services they seek from their network, it can also supply information to charge back for such services if that's how the organization's accounting structures work.

The most important aspect of accounting management, financial concerns aside, is the ability to identify those users and groups that access given network resources (which may be servers, individual applications, printers, routers, or other elements of the network). This lets individual or group patterns of usage be discovered; because such patterns may dictate where the natural "cleavage planes" of a server exist, this information is vital to planning for network growth.

For instance, members of a marketing group may be the only regular users of a particular presentation application, with a large associated clip art library. An analysis of traffic on their current server shows that this group consumes over 50% of the server's CPU cycles, disk space, and network traffic. By splitting this group off onto its own server, you'd not only improve its access to the application and files it needs, you'd also remove a burden from the server that currently supports it and the rest of the marketing department.

Associating who's using which resources and for what purposes winds up being as important to planning for growth and evolution as knowing the overall performance figures for any given network element. That's why accounting management is significant, even in those environment where chargebacks do not apply to the network.

Defining a Network Management System and Its Essential Characteristics

Because the goal of network management is to improve network efficiency and productivity, it's predictable that a network management system would have the same goals. That is, a network management system is a collection of software elements designed to collect network and systems management data and handle routine network and systems management activities and responses, to reduce the involvement of human network engineers, thereby freeing them to deal with more arcane matters and planning for future network development and growth. Network management systems must also be able to gather information about many concurrent events and activities, to communicate about what's being observed on the network, and to respond to events susceptible to automatic handling in a timely manner.

Building a network management system that supplies the necessary functionality to cover the five functional areas in the OSI model is a complex and demanding task. The system's developers must understand the needs of network engineers and their users and must be able to automate as much of the system's operation as is practical and feasible. They must also be able to build and maintain these systems quickly and affordably, to permit them to track the accelerating pace for the introduction of new technologies and management standards and techniques. In order to meet the sometimes contradictory goals of broad coverage versus rapid development and affordability, some interesting characteristics that constrain such systems have emerged in the marketplace:

- *Easy visual recognition and meaningful information displays.* Any worthwhile network management uses a graphical display with overloaded visual cues to faults or problems. For most developers, this means use of a GUI (graphical user interface) like MS Windows, the Macintosh, X-windows, or some reasonable facsimile thereof. It also means heavy use of color, blinking lights, audible alarms, pop-up windows, and other techniques to make important information readily identifiable and easily accessible.

- *Sophisticated data management capabilities.* Given the need to manage simultaneously an ongoing stream of events, performance data, and accounting information, a network management system needs to accommodate large amounts of highly structured information. Add to this the information necessary to represent and categorize large numbers of configuration profiles, user profiles, access lists, and all the other elements needed to control remote and local network access, and you need industrial strength data management capability. This is why most network management systems use a record manager, if not a complete database management system (DBMS), to define, store, update, and access management data. Such tools also include the kinds of sophisticated query and reporting mechanisms that network engineers will want to apply against their management data collections.

- *Information gathering and storage facilities.* Acquiring the data that fills the aforementioned management database is itself no trivial task. The management system will typically include small programs, called *agents*, that run within applications, devices, servers, resource providers, and other important network components to report events as they occur and respond to probes for additional information from time to time. Building all the necessary components requires attention to the instrumentation necessary to support a potentially infinite range of elements that incorporate management agents. In turn, this requires a method of communication between the agents and the management database, along with the capacity to store the information that results.

- *Customizability and adaptability.* The rapid pace of new technology introductions and new management technologies requires that management systems be open ended and extensible; the differences among all the many networks in need of management also demands that management systems be easy to customize to particular implementations and that the database be able to adapt to ongoing changes and reconfigurations. Many management system designers are turning to object oriented technologies as a way to accommodate both a wide-open future and an infinite array of possible implementations, simply because object orientation leaves the door open for savvy systems managers to define (and redefine) their networks and components as needed.

- *Problem tracking and resolution capabilities.* The first step of fault management is to identify problems, but what happens thereafter is typically even more important. Therefore, it's vital for network management systems to include some method for tracking problems that have been identified and for logging the diagnoses, solutions, or workarounds implemented in their wake. In addition to providing an invaluable source of information for future problem solving, keeping such a log demonstrates the value of network management in an inarguable way. Such capabilities are often called *problem tracking,* but may be referred to as *trouble ticketing* or *customer incident reporting.* Whatever it's called, entering a reported problem into a tracking system helps to guarantee resolution, documents administrative activity (and response time), and supplies key information for resolving recurrences.

All these characteristics certainly qualify as desiderata for a network management system, but very few systems incorporate all of the features. Also, it's unlikely that you'll find a single management system that can accommodate every single element in your network. As you'll learn in the next section, most network management occurs through a collection of tools, rather than a single comprehensive be-all end-all system. However, the impetus in this direction is clear in the marketplace, and the future appears to hold significant promise of delivering such capability in a more coherent manner than is the case today.

Current Management Tools and Technologies

Today's management tools reflect the results of many vendors grappling with the need to manage their own products and components together, but not necessarily in concert with one another. Therefore, it's completely normal to find one set of tools for managing hubs from one vendor (with other tools for similar equipment used on a per-vendor basis), another set for managing routers (again with vendor-specific implementations commonplace), another set for managing NetWare servers (with yet other tools for UNIX, Banyan VINES, NT Advanced Server, etc.), and still others for managing shared devices (like printers, or fax servers).

In addition, the focus of management information becomes sharper at lower levels of the protocol stacks in use. The quality of management improves for many networks, the closer management gets to the wire. In English, this means that very good tools exist to manage network wiring, hubs, concentrators, and the like, so this is where a lot of capability and expertise currently resides.

Unfortunately, this also means that management coverage decreases as we climb the stack through the transport layer heading toward applications. This may not sound too bad, given that the lower levels are where most problems occur. Unfortunately, because users run applications more or less exclusively, this leaves them out of the areas that management systems can service effectively. This sometimes makes it difficult for network engineers to relate user complaints or questions to the information that's available to them.

Those network management systems that do offer a more global view of the network and its systems and resources sometimes err by being too global altogether. Some systems will go out and discover every single device on a far-flung Internet, even when the network engineer wants to find just something that's very close to home. Sometimes, establishing a frame of reference can itself be a laborious task: Many management systems depict the networks they control as visual diagrams. This is quite desirable, as our earlier discussion of important characteristics attests, but when the network engineer has to zoom in from a worldwide view, to the country, state, locale, and finally, to the building from which alarms or alerts might be issuing, this can waste valuable time and frustrate impatient administrators. A good interface is an unquestionable benefit, but an interface that makes it possible to get at the source of potential problems quickly and easily is even more valuable.

By far, the biggest real network management problem that network engineers face is what I described earlier as "swivel-chair management." This refers to the many programs that a network engineer must master to manage the individual components that make up a network.

Although many of these components may support a network management standard like the Simple Network Management Protocol (SNMP), it is necessary for network engineers to learn and use their specific management applications. This is because, even though such components may be able to report into a standard management application, their controls and configuration are so specialized that only their applications can provide all the specific details and access needed to run them.

For complex environments, like NetWare or NT Server, a network engineer may have to use more than a dozen utilities just to control the servers for that particular network operating system. By itself, none of these applications is particularly ill-behaved or hard to learn; the issue is that network engineers must learn and many of them simultaneously. In many cases this leads more surely to confusion than to mastery, the more so as the number of applications that must be used increases.

At this point, solutions are easier to describe than to implement. Nevertheless, it's useful to remember that network engineers have to grapple with a wide range of components and applications. It's also important to note that management becomes increasingly difficult as you climb the protocol stack from the wire level, where it's relatively easy and straightforward, to the application level, where it gets harder and harder to relate application errors or symptoms to their underlying network causes. The individuals who manage networks, servers, and other systems have a tough job, but it's not a hopeless one nor is there no relief in sight.

SUMMARY

In this chapter, you've learned the basic elements involved in network and systems management, and have covered the impetus to automate as many related tasks as possible. It's also been demonstrated that the current state of the technology for providing coherent, consistent systems for managing networks, servers and other systems are fragmented, inconsistent, and do not offer complete coverage. Nevertheless, the impetus remains, and much useful work has been done to assist network engineers in their tasks.

In the next chapter, we'll begin our exploration of the current state of the management art, as we investigate wire-level management tools. As we explore the needs for network and systems management further and the capabilities that already exist, the picture should look less bleak than it currently might.

BIBLIOGRAPHY

Black, Uyless: *Network Management Standards*. McGraw-Hill, New York: 1994. An overview of all of the important network management protocols, including SNMPv1 and v2, CMIP, TMN, MIBs, and Object Libraries.

Hegering, Heinz-Gerd, and Sebastian Abeck. *Integrated Network and Systems Management*: Addison Wesley Publishing, Ltd, Wokingham, England: 1994. An excellent overview of network and systems management, with an eye toward practical applications, as well as theoretical frameworks.

Leinwand, Allan, and Karen Fang. *Network Management: A Practical Perspective*. Addison-Wesley Publishing Company, Reading, MA: 1993. Two Cisco employees give their take on network management from the MIB level of SNMP and from the standpoint of practical device, systems, and network control.

Rose, Marshall T. *The Simple Book*, 2nd Ed. Prentice-Hall, Englewood Cliffs, NJ: 1994. A comprehensive overview of SNMP v1 and v2 that compares and contrasts the two, with a wonderfully written overview of MIBs and MIB technology.

Rose, Marshall T., and Keith McCloghrie: *How to Manage Your Network Using SNMP*. Prentice-Hall, Englewood Cliffs, NJ: 1995. A hard and jaundiced look at what's possible by way of network management using SNMP today, with advice about how to do the best with it you can, written by two of the original designers of the protocol.

Sloman, Morris (ed). *Network and Distributed Systems Management*: Addison-Wesley Publishing, Wokingham, England: 1994. A collection of articles and papers from members of the International Federation for Information Processing (IFIP), collected and rewritten for publication as a general network and systems management reference. It includes some very useful chapters on distributed systems, the OSI management model, and SNMP.

Terplan, Kornel. *Communication Networks Management*, 2nd. Ed. Prentice Hall Computer Communications Series, 1992. An excellent, but highly technical overview of network and communications management issues, tools, and trends.

WIRE MANAGEMENT TOOLS

BASIC OVERVIEW

In Chapter 6, we discussed cable testing and diagnostics equipment. That chapter covered tools that test cable lengths, tools that measure noise and signal losses, and a lot more. This chapter focuses on devices used to centralize and manage network wiring.

This chapter differs from the other chapters in Part V of this book. Most of the tools we discuss here are proprietary. They're provided by the vendor that supplies the hub. This is the latest trend in network management. Vendors are beginning to supply management software for the devices they put on the market. Companies like HP are providing platforms that management tools can hook into. This frees a hub manufacturer from having to provide any or all of the following: the hub, the hub tools, and the management platform.

Chapter 25 discusses hubs in detail, and we recommend that you refer to that chapter before reading this one, so that you'll have a good understanding of hub function and performance. In Chapter 25, we talked about management modules that plug into a hub and permit configuration and management of the hub from a remote console. The two main companies in this arena are Bay Networks and Cabletron. We'll take a look at their products: Optiva, and LANView, respectively. We'll also take a look at Network General's distributed management as it has been incorporated into hub management technology.

In addition to some plain vanilla wiring management tools, we'll take a look at the virtual networks beginning to emerge from switching hub technology. In Chapter 25, we mentioned that switched hubs permitted segmentation on a port-to-port basis, allowing two ports to consume the entire bandwidth of a network. This segmentation provides great improvements in network speed. At the same time it offers management for hubs that contain up to 96 ports! That's just for a workgroup hub. Take a look at an enterprise hub, and you'll see how critical this management function has become.

Network Monitors

Before the deployment of intelligent hubs, network administrators used network monitors to monitor traffic on a LAN and to report statistics. Typically, these were standalone hardware devices or some combination of hardware devices and software. Today, intelligent hubs can provide many of those management functions that used to be available only from specialized (and expensive) management consoles.

Intelligent Hubs

We're trying not to repeat material covered in Chapter 25, but there's going to be some inevitable overlap here. Try to bear with us.

Intelligent hubs typically consist of a chassis with several slots for cards or modules. These slots contain modules with workstation ports as well as a management module. The management module typically conforms to SNMP and contains an SNMP agent and MIB. Optionally, software can be purchased from the vendor to allow remote console management of the hub. This software communicates with the hub through the management module or modules. Using such vendor-specific software allows the LAN administrator to remotely configure the hub and gather network statistics.

Most management software is optional. A management card itself has an out-of-band management port that supports a direct terminal connection. Typically, there will also be a management routine stored on the card. When a terminal connection is established, a text-based configuration menu for the hub appears. Connecting to the management card in this fashion is all handled through a text menu. The routine's menu puts the full power of DOS and the extended ASCII character set at your fingertips. (Sigh!)

Unless your organization is completely broke, we recommend that you purchase whatever management software is available from the vendor. This management software provides graphical representations of the hub, its slots, and cards. The vendor's software typically also provides a graphic of the front of the hub with simulated LEDs in various colors that represent ports, status, error conditions, and speeds. We're not kidding when we say that these graphics are tremendous. They provide the same profound enjoyment that you feel when you're sitting in front of the hub—only better!

Because of the specialized information provided by the management module and depicted using the management software, many vendors require additional separate management modules or cards for each data-link protocol like token ring, Ethernet, or FDDI that's running through a hub. Let's take a look at some of the vendor-specific products.

How Does Hub Management Work?

As we mentioned earlier, an organization can manage its hubs by attaching a terminal directly to the hubs or through a remote management console. Initially, you must use a terminal to set the hub's IP address. But it's always preferable to manage all of the installation's hubs from a central location.

Hub vendors typically provide management software support for three types of environments: mainframes, minicomputers, and PCs. The major platforms used for hub management today include HP's OpenView, IBM's NetView, and Sun Microsystem's SunNet Manager. In addition to mainframe and minicomputer platforms, OpenView for Windows is typically supported in the PC arena.

Large organizations employ the PC-based hub management platform at smaller sites. The small sites are linked to a central site running a larger platform like SunNet Manager. The smaller sites perform local traffic analysis for short periods of time and send their information to the central location. The larger platforms used at the central site are designed specifically to collect information from multiple hubs on multiple network segments. Once the site with the larger platform collects information from smaller sites, it can provide trend analysis for the separate smaller sites.

Using small and large platforms in a large organization is common and due in large part to the cost of sophisticated central platforms (PC-based platforms cost substantially less). The hardware investment can be a 386-based processor (although a 486 or Pentium processor is recommended). Crunching enterprise statistics from a large internetwork usually requires a minicomputer platform that costs substantially more. And although experienced PC network hands are almost always at hand, operators for a sophisticated central multi-hub management system aren't. A qualified person, when you find one is going to be highly skilled, highly motivated, and command a high salary.

Once an organization has figured out which network management platform it wants, the right software and hardware can be matched up for hub management.

There's one important thing we should point out here: Up to this point, we've been discussing hub management as if an organization has a homogeneous network. Unfortunately, that is almost never the case. So bear in mind that different management software must be purchased for every different vendor you buy from. Luckily, they can all be rolled up to an Open-View platform, thus negating the need for multiple consoles.

Management Software for a Hub

Before you configure a hub with software, you'll likely have to change some jumper settings on the hub module itself. Once a hub is installed properly and powered up, you have to attach a terminal to the management card through its out-of-band port and assign the card an IP address. Once this is done, the hub can be managed from a management console. This process must be repeated for each hub you install.

Some of the management consoles, like Cabletron's LANView, offer a proprietary NIC card that interfaces with the management console and the network and works in a promiscuous mode. This lets your hub management system track and analyze network traffic and statistics--much like a protocol analyzer does. Using a specialized NIC card ensures that no extra traffic is generated on the network while all this management and analysis is taking place.

Hub management software can provide a lot of useful information. You can set performance and traffic guidelines and get alerts from the system when predetermined thresholds are exceeded. Hub management software typically supports SNMP just like other management software. Network managers are beginning to compile all of their management tools for all the different hardware and software into one big management system. This is the basic paradigm SNMP has created. Once an operator understands SNMP agents, managers, and MIBs, central management of entire internetworks can become a reality.

Real-Time Monitoring

Some hub vendors permit real-time monitoring of port or interface statistics. This can be represented in graphical format. LAN administrators can compare a particular port's activity against a backdrop graph of the rest of the network's activity. This is helpful when determining which ports are generating most of the network traffic. Port traffic can be monitored and the network may be segmented accordingly.

Error Monitoring

Errors can be tracked on a port-by-port basis and displayed in graphical form. In text form, the errors can be broken down by the type of error. Some management software goes so far as to examine the type and number of errors and provide suggestions as to what might be happening. This might sound familiar to users of protocol analyzers with artificial intelligence engines built in.

Alerts

The LAN administrator can preset threshold values for certain events on the network. Once those thresholds have been exceeded, the agent on the hub generates an alert to the management software. These alerts are generally categorized by a preset value. For example, a downed module card on a hub can cause a priority 1 alert. Loss of a crucial module could bring down up to 24 workstations.

RMON

Remote monitoring (RMON) is another hub management routine making inroads into the world of network administration. Network General and Bay Networks united to provided RMON capabilities in Bay Network's hubs. Network General provides RMON agents that monitor multiple network segments from each hub. Prior implementations of RMON required RMON modules on each network segment. With Network General's Distributed Sniffer System (DSS) incorporated into the network management software, this is no longer necessary. DSS in the hubs (actually a subset of the DSS system) permits the management software to analyze all seven layers of the network from the hub down to the port level. Prior to the DSS addition, only the bottom three layers were available for analysis.

TWO MAIN INTELLIGENT HUB VENDORS

Bay Networks

SynOptics and WellFleet joined forces in 1994 to form Bay Networks. Bay Networks provides management for its hubs through the use of management cards and software. Bay Networks supplies different software packages depending on what platform is in use. Table 41.1 lists some of the platforms and products Bay Networks provides.

Product name	Platform	Platforms supported
Lattis View NETMAP	Mainframe	IBM NetView, DEC Polycenter, HP OpenView
Optivity	Mini-UNIX	Sun Microsystems SunNet Manager
Optivity for NetWare	PC-Windows	Novell NetWare Management System
Lattis EZ-View	PC-Windows	Microsoft Windows

Table 41.1 *Platforms and products from Bay Networks.*

Cabletron

Cabletron, like Bay Networks, provides products for the major platforms on minis and PCs, including its own computers. Of particular note is its Spectrum Multivendor Enterprise Management Platform product, which has an advanced modeling engine that runs over multiple processors. In addition to hub management, it incorporates management tools for telephony applications, PBXs, WANs, ATM networks, and more.

On the lighter side of management, Cabletron provides its products: LANView, and Remote LANView. LANView is a Windows PC-based product that works on a Windows OpenView platform. The Remote LANView product permits the LAN administrator to view the console from any workstation that has the Remote LANView software installed.

THE VIRTUAL NETWORK

Our discussion to this point has focused on a hardware-centric network. In this type of network, a particular port on a hub is dedicated to one user at a particular location. That user communicates through that port for all applications, making the configuration of that port static for all applications and uses. The port can be reconfigured, but only from one static assignment to another. This type of view may be fine for older networks, where users need access to resources on just one server for applications like word processing and mainframe terminal emulation, but in modern business change is a constant.

Enterprise information must traverse state and international boundaries seamlessly over networks that have constantly changing topologies and uses. In such an environment, hub maintenance is looked on in a somewhat brighter light. Changes must occur rapidly and dynamically. For example, a node might use a video application that requires a certain bandwidth for a specified time, but not permanently. Another node might use client/server applications that require special bandwidth at times. The network manager has to be aware of these needs and be prepared to adapt the network accordingly.The deployment of switchable hubs in the enterprise brings a whole new outlook to network management. It switches (no pun intended) the focus from a hardware-centric view to a software-centric view. Modern hub management routines let you rearrange the segmentation of the hub by grouping ports into a logical network. The LAN administrator doesn't have to be part mechanic any more (well, not as much at least), physically moving jumper cables on the hub to form segments. Port 1 on Card A could become a part of a network segment with Port 1 on Card B. This could be done by the administrator in a drag-and-drop fashion from management console.

Additionally, many hub vendors now permit the grouping of ports to form logical networks spanning many separate hubs. This functionality is contained in the software management application. As you might imagine, strict adherence to standards comes into play in this type of arrangement. If an organization has a variety of proprietary hubs, logical networking becomes difficult.

And we won't even get into the political nightmare that virtual networking can create in large organizations.

The Top Five Vendors

Bay Networks, Inc.
4401 Great America Pkwy., PO Box 58185
Santa Clara, CA 95054
800-776-6895; 408-988-2400
FAX: 408-988-5525
Tech support: 800-473-4911

Cabletron Systems, Inc.
35 Industrial Way, PO Box 5005
Rochester, NH 03867-0505
800-332-9401; 603-332-9400
FAX: 603-337-2211
Tech support: Use toll-free no.
Tech support BBS: 603-335-3358

Hewlett-Packard Co.
3000 Hanover St.
Palo Alto, CA 94304-1181
800-752-0900; 800 387-3867 (CD); 415-857-1501
Direct sales: 800-637-7740 (HP Direct)
FAX: 800-333-1917
Tech support: 800-858-8867
Tech support BBS: 415-852-0256

Chipcom Corp.
118 Turnpike Rd., Southborough Office Park
Southborough, MA 01772-1886

800-228-9930; 508-460-8900
FAX: 508-490-5696
Tech support: Use main no.

LANNET, Inc. (subsidiary of LANNET, Ltd.)
17942 Cowan Ave.
Irvine, CA 92714
800-5-LANNET; 714-752-6638
FAX: 714-752-6641
Tech support: Use main no.

WIRING MANAGEMENT TOOLS RESOURCES: BIBLIOGRAPHY AND STRATEGIES

For general networking references, please consult Appendix C, "A List of Networking Resources." The magazines and other publications listed there can help you find out lots of information about NICs. The following references are particularly helpful for the information they contain about network interface cards:

Derfler, Frank, Jr., and Les Freed. *How Networks Work.*
Ziff-Davis Press, Emeryville, CA: 1993. An illustration and example-intensive description of how networks actually operate. Includes good discussions of most basic networking components. $24.95.

Terplan, Kornel. *Effective Management of Local Area Networks.*
McGraw-Hill, New York: 1992 An excellent, two-thumbs-up book on every aspect of network management. A good thorough discussion on all the major network management platforms. $40.00.

Steinke, Steve. *Guide to Managing PC Networks.*
Prentice-Hall PTR, Englewood Cliffs, NJ: 1995. An excellent book on managing networks that includes a section on wiring management. $29.95.

Newton, Harry. *Newton's Telecom Dictionary*, 7th ed.
Flatiron Publishing Company, New York: 1994. Harry Newton is a towering field in the telecommunications industry, and his dictionary isn't bad either. Even though it purports to be telecom specific, it's one of the best sources for looking up PC-related acronyms, standards, and other terms that we've ever found anywhere. At $24.95 for 1,200 pages of text, it's a bargain to boot!

Sheldon, Tom. *The LAN Times Encyclopedia of Networking.*
Osborne McGraw Hill, Berkeley, CA: 1994. A general sourcebook for networking terms and technologies. Includes discussions, some lengthy and detailed, about nearly every conceivable networking topic. $39.95.

SERVER MANAGEMENT TOOLS

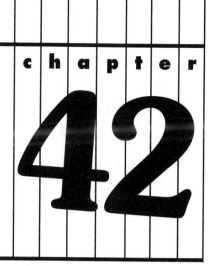

BASIC OVERVIEW

Remember the days when server management tools meant a static wrist guard and a screwdriver? Now, there are so many tools to choose from that it can overwhelm a LAN administrator. As Tim Allen once said "I've got tools that fix tools!"

Tools today come in many different forms. There are tools that correct hardware problems on the server, tools that help the administrator document the file server, tools that help the administrator troubleshoot problems on the LAN, and many more. In this chapter, we'll take a look at some of these different types of tools. Most of these tools are available for Novell's NetWare platform. That makes sense, because most of the servers out there are NetWare servers. However, more products are appearing that support Microsoft's NT-based SMS strategy.

In Chapter 44, we discuss management consoles and applications that can plug into those consoles. We'll take a look at some of the applications that can plug into a network management console and assist in managing servers on an internetwork. We recommend that you glance through that chapter before continuing with this chapter so you'll have a basic idea about what management consoles are and what they can do.

WHY THE NEED FOR TOOLS?

As more and more computers make their way onto desktops and networks, the need to keep them connected and talking grows increasingly more important. If all an organization's applications and files are centralized on a file server, that server had better be running. If the server does go down, users can't do their work; if nothing gets done, nothing gets sold; and the company loses money. And as we've said before, money is good—in this context at least. So the pressure on administrators continues to rise as the number of users and devices on the network continues to grow. The only factor in the equation that isn't increasing steadily is the number of network support personnel. If you can't hire more people, then the logical thing to do is to buy tools that can automate a lot of the network administrator's tasks. For example, it's crucial that a network administrator keep an eye on a file server's hard disk. The administrator has to know when it's time to add additional hard disks. If the administrator doesn't monitor this information, the disk could fill up and cause the network to crash. That's an example of one of the many tasks the network administrator *should* perform on a regular basis but doesn't always have time to do. Tools are available today that can monitor a server's disk capacity and page the administrator when it reaches a preset threshold.

Most LAN administrators carry a cellular phone and a pager. They're always within reach, at least theoretically, should servers or users have problems. It's common for a LAN administrator's pager to beep repeatedly during nonbusiness hours, lunch times, and while commuting. Network administrators live with a feeling in the pit of their stomachs that they forgot to do something that's going to be vital to network operation and performance.

So server management tools that were designed to perform some of these weekly, daily, and hourly tasks for the network administrator. Some tools meter software and can prevent an organization from violating software licensing restrictions. Violations can bring on legal complications and big fines.

Administrators can purchase tools to monitor the server for certain thresholds, like disk capacity, and have those software tools page the administrator when there is a potential for problems. This permits the LAN administrator to take a proactive approach to maintaining a server. So, when the pager goes off, it might not be an upset user. It might be the server saying, "Hey! I'm about to run out of disk space, come and fix me before I break!"

What's Out There?

Just as the physical layer in a network can be critical, so can a file server's hardware. Here, we're not discussing the server's processor speed, we're talking about its stamina, its ability to stay up and running! If the hardware's not working, then the server probably isn't working and the users aren't going to be very productive.

Compaq has been supplying hardware monitoring tools with its file servers for several years now. Compaq continues to supply the most complete management system for its server hardware compared with other vendors. Other server vendors have seen their advantage and have followed suit with similar management tools for their own server hardware platforms. Compaq's Insight Manager, HP's NetServer Assistant, IBM's NetFinity and AST Research's Percepta are only a few examples of file server hardware management tools.

In this section, we're going to go over some general topics that you might want to consider when you're buying and configuring your next server. Do your homework. Check with the vendors. Make sure that you ask them if their management features are provided with the system or if they cost extra. For example, Compaq ships most of its network management items along with the server and included in the cost. Other vendors charge as much as $10,000 extra. Caveat emptor. And watch out, too.

Maybe you've noticed lots of references to features that Compaq Corporation provides for its servers. This is not a paid advertisement for that company. We feel they are the industry leader in the area of server hardware monitoring. Their technology has been around for several years, is tested and solid, and provides a lot of good proactive tools for LAN administrators. Other vendors supply similar products, but today nobody compares with Compaq.

Hardware

Graphical Hardware Component Display

This server management feature lets you pull up a graphical view of your hardware components, components like disk drives and information on installed firmware. Not too long ago, gathering this type of information required powering down the server and bringing up a text-based system configuration for viewing, editing, or changing configurations. Now this information can be obtained from a remote location while the server is up and running! That means administrators can access information about the server's hardware components from a workstation on the network running Windows-based management software.

For example, clicking on an icon for the disk drives might bring up information like manufacturer, make, model, serial number, and capacity, all in a graphical view And, if the server crashes, dialup access to the server is permitted by some vendors. Let's take a look at that next.

Out-of-Band Access

Say you're at home and you get a page from a user telling you that the server isn't working. You can try to dial in to the network through your asynchronous communications server, unless it's down too. Or, you could dial directly into a modem on your file server and attempt to restart it. Compaq sells their Compaq Insight Manager/R (CIM/R) board with an on-board processor, battery backup, and a modem that slides into the server. A LAN administrator can dial directly into that board and perform diagnostics or reboot the server.

Monitoring and Paging

Compaq's Insight Manager (CIM) monitors over 800 operational parameters on its server. If it detects a problem or a pending problem, it can dial out through its CIM/R board and page the LAN administrator. If the manager detects some hardware that looks like its in danger of failing, it pages the LAN administrator. The administrator can correct the problem before the server crashes.

One of these proactive monitoring tools is used to monitor hard disks for potential failures. Compaq, HP, and IBM even go one step further with this notion. If their software monitoring programs detect that a hard disk is about to go bad, Compaq, HP and IBM say they will replace the drives under a special warranty, even if the software has misdiagnosed the problem. So, if you've got Compaq's server and the CIM says that the drive might go bad soon, you get a free one. That's a no-lose situation!

Rack-Mounted Configuration

Most of the vendors are now supplying rack-mountable servers that are easier to get to and maintain. Naturally, rack-mount servers take up less space on the floor. Compaq sells its servers so that you can multiplex the monitor, keyboard, and mouse. Instead of having a monitor for every server, you can have one monitor, one keyboard, and one mouse for many servers. We realize that Rose Electronics has been providing these boxes for some time now, but it's about time that server manufacturers jumped on the same bandwagon.

Not only can you buy Compaq servers and rack mount them, but Compaq supplies a Windows-based program called *Rackbuilder* that helps you graphically design how the racks will look. Simply by clicking on component pieces, you can design your own rack-mounted server configurations easily. Once you've designed the rack, the software prints out a report that lists the necessary components and their part numbers. In addition, the report lists power and cooling requirements for the rack system so you can plan ahead and make sure those items are in place before the server arrives.

Self Correcting Hardware!

That's right. Compaq and other vendors provide memory chips that monitor and alert the administrator when a chip needs replacing! It's called *Error Correcting Code* (ECC). These chips can autocorrect themselves if the error is 4 bits or less. We've seen servers crash and boom because of a memory chip gone bad. And, of course, once you bring the server down and run diagnostics, you can't always find out which module or chip is bad. The ECC memory even tells you which one is the bad guy.

Makes Its Own Recommendations!

Once again, Compaq takes the lead here. Compaq has an enhancement to its CIM called *Version Control*. This is a database that tracks the versions of software and firmware, compares that information to its database, and then makes recommendations on upgrades! Some cynics may say that this is just a way to keep the network administrator buying more equipment but who cares. It's free advice as far as we're concerned. No one says you have to purchase anything!

Fault Tolerance

Although we don't consider fault tolerance a tool, we do feel it's important that a vendor supply choices to the LAN administrator. Why buy a server that can hold only one power supply if you'd prefer to have two? Some of the vendors supply battery backups to the disk controller cache so in the event of a crash, the cache contents can be recovered.

Hardware Summary

So, what we have here are servers that monitor themselves, report on possible failures, and correct some failures automatically. We even have vendors that will replace disks for free under certain circumstances. Wow! We almost feel like saying, "but wait, there's more, if you order now, we'll throw in a free set of Ginsu knives!"

The point here is that with all of the file server hardware fault prevention and detection available to the LAN administrator, we see no reason to consider buying a server that does any less than the preceeding ones. Look for manufacturers and vendors that are making their products easy to support, configure, and maintain. Those same vendors should be working with other vendors to conform to emerging standards like the Desktop Management Interface. Let's shift our focus now to the software on a file server and how it can be managed.

Software

A Self-Installing NOS?

Some file servers come preconfigured for a specified network operating system (NOS). Compaq ships its server with a product called *SmartStart*. It's NOS software that ships on a CD and attempts to install itself on the new server with very little required intervention from the LAN administrator. Unfortunately, sometimes the CD doesn't always work as seamlessly as Compaq purports. The CD version doesn't always match its intended hardware version.

NLM Management (NetWare Only)

If you've ever worked with Novell's NetWare, then you've probably been frustrated at the lack of NLM management capabilities! Even more frustrating is trying to watch the console screen flash by when you bring up the server. If you have a lot of NLMs, they will flash by but they don't write to an error log. Unless, you have a utility called CONLOG.EXE. This captures the serve console as the server is coming up. Everything that flashes on the screen gets written to a log file for later troubleshooting.

A product called NetTune by HawkNet is a great product for NLM management. It provides customized mapping of server memory and statistics in graph form. It tells you where the NLM loads in RAM, graphs statistics, displays memory maps, and shows an NLM's actual code. If you need to track your NLM usage, and actually expose as much of the NLM's role in your server as you can, you'll want to pick up this product or one similar to it. (Where was all this stuff when we were building our first server and banging our heads against the wall!)

Server Documentation

Well, we've covered the NOSs and the NLMs for NetWare, but what about documentation for the server's general configuration. What about startup scripts, system defaults, print server configurations, and the like? Once the server is set up and the administrator takes time to set up all of the print queues, user or group scripts, and system scripts, it's extremely handy to be able to pull that information from the server into a cohesive document. In addition, once the configuration is changed, simply rerunning some reports can immediately provide an update for the documentation notebook. The LAN Support Group's BindView product handles this as neatly as anything we've seen, and better than most!

Software Distribution

This might not sound like a server tool. But it allows an administrator to distribute software to other servers on the internetwork from one central distribution server. Frye's SUDSSRV product does this elegantly. As we all know, automating tasks can sometimes lead to disaster. Because organizations don't always maintain the same hardware for all servers,. updating one driver or application can cause a system to malfunction. This is readily seen in an organization that has at least one NetWare 3.11 1,000 user license. That version is specially designed by Novell, and the administrator is warned not to arbitrarily update any NLMs or System or Public files without calling Novell first. Frye's product anticipates this type of product and permits failed procedures to be reversed automatically.

Software Metering

Keeping track of software license counts on the file server also seems to fall in the LAN administrator's domain of responsibility. Its an irritating fact, but a fact nonetheless, that vendors can't provide proof of licenses in a consistent manner. If there were a standard format across the industry for issuing licenses, life might be a little more simple for the network administrator. Why not just have every company ship a license card with its product and have every vendor follow the same format? Instead, sometimes we receive some licenses in the form of paper, some with serialized diskettes, and some that you can't ever seem to find. Keeping track of up-to-date licensing information puts an undue strain on the heart and career of the network administrator

Now consider the complexity of licensing as it pertains to the suites of software products that are now out! Not all vendors license their suite of products the same way. And can you use software metering tools to monitor suites of products?

Yep, software metering tools are out there. They count the number of users accessing a network software package. If you've purchased 10 concurrent user licenses for a networked application, then the software metering tool would make sure that no more than 10 users at a time access the software. Usually, user 11 would get a message saying that all licenses were in use.

The problem stems from the fact that few application vendors other than Lotus provide a way to monitor the usage of their applications on networks. Companies can purchase a single copy of software and run it from the network. There's no guarantee that the product will always work as expected when it's used this way, but it is definitely a violation of the licensing agreement. Still other companies can purchase a 10 user concurrent license in an attempt to remain legal, only to find out that 11 users, or maybe 110 users, are accessing the software at the same time—also a license violation.

Software metering products were introduced by third party vendors to provide some legal relief to the LAN administrator. These tools have gone a couple of steps beyond their original intent and added features like monitoring suites, daily usage information, and historical reports that can track application usage over a period of time. Based on this type of information, a LAN administrator can look at graphs of these trends (provided by the metering tool) and decide whether or not to purchase more licenses.

Virus Detection and Eradication

We once saw a very large organization lose an entire file server's data to a virus. At that time, no file server virus protection programs were available. There were ways to scan the server, but most organizations had to get hit

with a virus and lose a substantial amount of data before server virus prevention was taken seriously. Unfortunately, servers don't ship with virus
detection. NOSs don't ship with virus detection.

Third-party vendors have been making a lot of money in areas where the
server and NOS vendors fall short. But companies like Intel and McAfee
have finally come out with server-based virus protection programs. A
server without a virus prevention tool is a doomed server.Summary

We've learned that many different software and hardware aspects must
be considered when managing a server. Some of these are legal issues,
some are prevention issues, and some are management issues. We've also
learned that a lot of automated tools are out there to help LAN administrators who have had to manage these tasks on their own.

Using tools to proactively monitor the server frees up more time for a
LAN administrator to perform some more useful tasks, like planning for
the network's future.

We recommend that you call server vendors and ask for any white
papers, faxback numbers, BBSs, URLs or any other kind of documentation
that can provide you with some initial information about their products.
After that, contact the vendors we've listed and ask about their specific
server management tools.

THE TOP FIVE VENDORS

Compaq Computer Corp.
20555 State Hwy. 249
Houston, TX 77070-2698
800-345-1518; 713-374-0484
Direct sales: 800-888-3298 (Compaq DirectPlus)
FAX: 713-374-4583
Tech support: 800-OKCOMPAQ
Tech support BBS: 713-378-1418

Hewlett-Packard Co.
3000 Hanover St.
Palo Alto, CA 94304-1181
800-752-0900; 800 387-3867 (CD); 415-857-1501
Direct sales: 800-637-7740 (HP Direct)
FAX: 800-333-1917

Tech support: 800-858-8867
Tech support BBS: 415-852-0256

Frye Computer Systems, Inc.
19 Temple Place
Boston, MA 02111-9779
800-234-3793; 617-451-5400
FAX: 617-451-6711
Tech support: Use toll-free no.
Tech support BBS: 617-426-1910

Intel Corp.
2200 Mission College Blvd.
Santa Clara, CA 95051
800-548-4725; 408-765-8080
FAX: 408-765-1821
Tech support: 800-628-8686

The LAN Support Group, Inc.
2425 Fountainview Dr., Ste. 390
Houston, TX 77057
800-749-8439; 713-789-0881
Direct sales: 713-789-0882, ext. 508
FAX: 713-977-9111
Tech support: Use toll-free no.
Tech support BBS: 713-789-6776

SERVER MANAGEMENT TOOLS RESOURCES: BIBLIOGRAPHY AND STRATEGIES

For general networking references, please consult Appendix C, "A List of Networking Resources." The magazines and other publications listed there can help you find out lots of information about server management tools. The following references are particularly helpful for the information they contain about server management tools.

Terplan, Kornel. Effective Management of Local Area Networks.
McGraw-Hill, New York: 1992. An excellent 10,000 foot view on network management in general. It includes discussions on layering the approach to managing the entire network, including servers. $40.00.

Steinke, Steve. Guide to Managing PC Networks.
Prentice-Hall PTR, Englewood, NJ: 1995 Another excellent 10,000 foot view book on network management. The book is designed as a "tools and technique" book and covers many aspects of network management, including server management. $29.95.

Newton, Harry. Newton's Telecom Dictionary, 7th ed.
Flatiron Publishing Company, New York: 1994. Harry Newton is a towering field in the telecommunications industry, and his dictionary isn't bad either. Even though it purports to be telecom specific, it's one of the best sources for looking up PC-related acronyms, standards, and other terms that we've ever found anywhere. At $24.95 for 1,200 pages of text, it's a bargain to boot!

Sheldon, Tom. The LAN Times Encyclopedia of Networking.
Osborne McGraw Hill, Berkeley, CA: 1994. A general sourcebook for networking terms and technologies. Includes discussions, some lengthy and detailed, about nearly every conceivable networking topic. If you don't have this book in your library, you should get it today! $39.95.

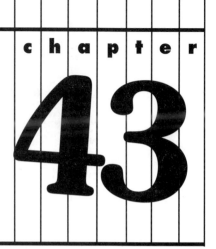

WORKSTATION MANAGEMENT TOOLS

43

EVOLUTION OF WORKSTATION AUDITS

Not too long ago, it was a privilege for a user just to have PC on his or her desktop. A PC was a prized business resource and only really productive users could get their hands on one. When organizations began to realize their importance, it became commonplace to provide every user with a PC. But the awarding of cutting-edge technology to an elite group still goes on. Nowadays, Pentium processors are in demand—so all the PC users in an organization want one.

But these machines are awarded only to the select few. Typically, only the high-powered users in an organization are considered productive enough to merit getting a PC with a Pentium processor. This points out a problem that goes hand in hand with the introduction of new technology. Who gets what? Who's using technology effectively? And how do organizations keep up with all the devices, software, and peripherals it takes to keep the company running? Keeping up with the proliferation of PCs in the workforce—and judging the merits of the diverse software and hardware products for those PCs—has become a major challenge.

With the proliferation of PCs in the workforce today, combined with the diversity of vendors supplying software and hardware products for those PCs, managing those assets has become a master challenge.

Physical Inventory

Trying to keep track of the many variations of software and hardware on PCs was a difficult task for the IS department. As more PCs sprouted up in organizations, keeping up with the types and versions of installed software and internal hardware and peripheral additions became an important and difficult part of the IS department's responsibility. But it was discovered that even if IS maintained an inventory list and performed physical inventory updates from time to time, rapid changes made even the latest inventory lists obsolete. It's just too easy to upgrade and add on to a personal computer. As parts in a PC are replaced or upgraded, the inventory must also be updated. If the installer doesn't update an inventory sheet with each new part's name and serial number immediately after the installation—assuming there is an inventory sheet—the physical inventory is immediately out of date.

Unfortunately, the PC industry did not grow up in as organized and structured a way as the mainframe industry. Many organizations had early XT computers, so that when 286 processors were released, a mixture of XT and 286 processors was created. When the 386 processors came out, the mix of technologies became even more complex, and yet another dimension was added to inventory tracking. Today, 486 and Pentium processors dominate, but some of these older technologies are still in widespread use. Major projects in their beginning stages require complex budget presentations so that higher management can approve the purchase of the required hardware and software. And because client/server applications typically span across WANs, managers are finding out just how nonstandardized many large organizations PC collections have become, not to mention their equally mixed-up LANs, software, and peripherals.

Before any budget can be presented, knowledge of current inventory of processors, memory, and other workstation configurations is necessary. The need for this kind of information has sent IS managers scrambling to get accurate counts. Rapid change and revision has become the hallmark of modern information processing. And in some organizations, this rapid change has brought about chaos. IS departments are always hard-pressed for time and personnel, and it's rare to have spare personnel available to continually monitor hardware and software inventory on PCs.

Luckily, rapidly evolving problems often have rapidly evolving solutions chasing right behind. Companies like The LAN Support Group, Intel, McAfee, Symantec, and Frye have come up with solutions aimed at using the network as a tool to gather and store information about configurations and inventory and to maintain a central database containing that information on the network.

Centralized and Automated Inventory

In 1990, the LAN Support Group company began introducing products designed to assist network administrators in gathering information about a company's file servers and storing that information in a central location on a network. Preliminary releases of the product reported only on servers, but later releases capture information about network workstations as well.

In this chapter, we'll take an in-depth look at the LAN Support Group's BindView NCS product. Network administrators, now charged with automating workstation inventory, need a good understanding of this type of technology.We chose to showcase the BindView product because it won *Network Computing* magazine's Editor's Choice award in June 1995. We showcase this company's product, but you should be aware that many other good products like it are on the market. There's just not enough room in this chapter to provide in-depth coverage of all of them. We do provide the top five vendors' names, addresses, and telephone numbers at the end of this chapter, so that you may evaluate some other vendors' products.

Desktops Futures with DMTF and DMI

In 1992 the Desktop Management Task Force (DMTF) was formed to address the standardization of workstation components reporting for management applications. This task force will have a great impact on the future of inventorying and configuring workstations across the network. We'll take a look at its efforts, indicate the charter members, and list the affiliates. You can see for yourself what's on the horizon of desktop inventory management.The DMTF has already released one standard, called the Desktop Management Interface (DMI), version 1.0. This standard defines the way that companies report certain attributes for their hardware or software. We'll take a look at the standard that's been released and the standards that are still pending.

Today's Desktop Management

Network administrators bless the day that automated workstation inventory across a network became available. Physical inventory of workstations became a thing of the past in some organizations. Current technology permits an administrator to gather workstation information via the network and centralize that data into a database on file server. Items pertaining to the workstation's software, hardware, and configuration files can now be managed from a central location. Today's inventory products rely on lookup tables to identify particular hardware and software components of a PC. When a workstation is inventoried, the inventory product checks it's hardware lookup table for information. The lookup table has a finite number of entries. If a particular hardware component cannot be found in the lookup table, it cannot be identified, and must be *learned*.

This is similar to the way that some workstation virus detection software works. This software can detect only viruses that it knows about. The problem many have found in detecting viruses is when a new strain of a virus is introduced, the current virus lookup table may not be able to identify a new strain. The same holds true when new software or hardware is introduced—at that very point, the workstation inventory program's lookup table must be updated to recognize new components. This typically requires a network administrator to dial into a bulletin board to obtain the latest lookup table.

Although this is one gotcha in workstation inventorying, it certainly is easier to dial into a bulletin board periodically than to perform a physical inventory! Next, we'll look at LAN Support's BindView product from an administrator's point of view, so you can get a good idea of how workstation management works.

BindView's Automated Inventory—The Whole Process

BindView is a modularized product that you can purchase to inventory your server devices, your workstation devices, or both. The server inventory module is called a *SIM* (Server Information Module). The workstation inventory module is called a *WAM* (Workstation Auditing Module). Information about workstations and servers can be gathered across an entire enterprise. Each LAN can maintain such information locally, but enterprisewide queries are also permitted. The information can be rolled up to either Novell's NetWare Management System's platform or the HP Open-View platform discussed in Chapters 41 and 44.

Installation

The administrator installs the BindView product onto a directory on a file server from a workstation logged onto the network. The administrator can then choose which information at the workstation should be inventoried. A good administrator knows what information is valuable about a particular network. Using product defaults makes installation simple but can lead to the capture and storage of lots of extraneous information.

What the User Sees on His or Her Screen

Next the administrator determines what type of interface appears to the user. For example, the administrator might want a user to know that his or her workstation is about to be audited and that this activity may take a certain amount of time to complete. Administrators might also want users to supply information about themselves and their workstations at audit time. BindView provides a set of canned questions and displays an end user screen; the administrator can use this default screen or modify it as needed.

Who and When to Inventory

Once the setup is complete, the administrator determines who will be inventoried and when. Audits can target predefined segments of the network or individual users in any desired combination. It is never recommended to turn on automated inventory for a whole company at once. First, test the product on a small group. Schedule a progression for the automated inventory. Move from one group to the next until the entire inventory is complete. Step-by-step and segment-by-segment inventory capture ensures that only a handful of people are disrupted in the event of an inventory failure.

The Audit

An audit can be set up to kick off when a user logs on to the network. If automatic inventory is set to "active" for a particular user, then that user is presented with a list of questions that have been prepared by the network administrator. After receiving the user's responses, BindView scans the user's PC, checking for items targeted by the administrator for inventory. We've seen detailed inventories take anywhere from 30 seconds to several minutes. The speed of the inventory is determined by the desktop processor and how many files are present on the PC.

Post Audit

On completion of the audit, the network administrator can choose an option called Node Manager from the BindView main menu. Figure 43.1 is a screen shot of what the administrator will see if that option is chosen.

As you can see, Figure 43.1 lists basic information about all of the nodes that have been audited. If the number of workstations audited was 200, then 200 entries would appear. The administrator can drill down further and view all the vital statistics collected about a particular node. To do this, the administrator just selects a node and presses the Enter key.

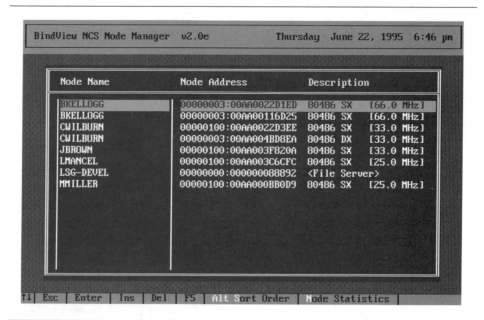

Figure 43.1   *Screen shot of Node Manager.*

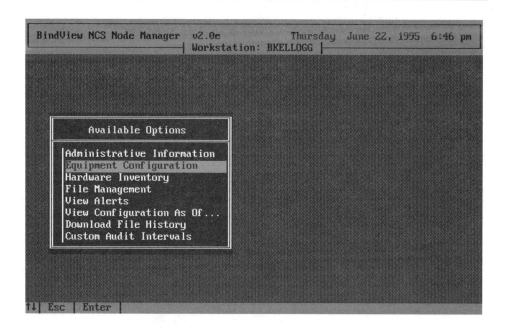

Figure 43.2 *Available options menu screen shot.*

Information About a Particular Node

Figure 43.2 is a screen shot of the menu of available categories presented to an administrator after an audit has been performed. A node has been selected for examination. Let's look at each of these options in a little greater detail. Though this is the BindView product, you will see some similar options in other products. The only differences are the names and the menus.

1. *Administrative information.* This option is used to track and manage information about the node and its user (i.e., name, logon ID, etc.).

2. *Equipment configuration information.* This option allows you to view equipment configuration information like available memory and environment variables. For example, if you're trying to find out how much memory is in each workstation and how that memory is configured, this menu option will allow you to view that information.

To get a complete listing of all workstations and their memory configurations, a report must be generated.

3. *Hardware inventory*. This permits the administrator to view all of the hardware components found in a particular workstation. Asset tracking data, such as information on serial number, warranty expiration date, and recent repairs on a particular piece of hardware can be input via this menu option. This assists an IS department in tracking how many times a particular piece of hardware in a PC has failed or been repaired. A hardware item may be a leased item, and this type of information can also be input at this time.

4. *Software inventory* (not pictured). This option permits the administrator to view all of the "known" software found on a particular workstation. Asset information fields like serial number, manufacturer, purchase date, and purchase price can be filled in to provide software tracking. Any administrator knows that a Software Protection Agency (SPA) agent could enter the premises at any time and ask for license verification for any software in the organization. This method of tracking makes for timely and accurate response to questions about inventory and can create that important warm, fuzzy feeling between the administrator and the SPA.

5. *File management*. Any configuration files like CONFIG.SYS, AUTOEXEC.BAT, or various INI files can be marked for tracking and subsequently viewed, edited, or downloaded back to a workstation. (If you don't want users modifying their own CONFIG.SYS files, for example, you could mark that file to be tracked on every workstation and receive an alert if someone makes a change to that file. Then, you can download the original CONFIG.SYS file to the user's workstation and keep the integrity of the workstation configuration intact.)

6. *View alerts*. Once you've set up the types and the priorities of important alerts, you can view the alerts through this menu option. For example, if you want to know if workstations are nearing 85% disk capacity, you could set this as an alert. Anytime this condition is present during a workstation scan, an alert will be sent to the database for examination.

7. *View configuration as of*. This allows the administrator to view a workstation's configuration at a certain place in time, provided that the workstation was logged in during that time period.

8. *Download file history.* This allows the administrator to look at the history of files downloaded to a particular node.

9. *Custom audit intervals.* Allows an administrator to set a audit time for a particular node or nodes different from any systemwide interval.

Let's drill down through some of these menus, to equipment configuration, seen as a menu choice in Figure 43.2 on page 649. This gives us a look at the equipment information menu shown in Figure 43.3. As you can see from Figure 43.3, an administrator can use this option to gather information on the environment variables in use at a workstation, the device drivers in use, and much more. All of this information may be selected, gathered from each workstation on the local network, and then passed up through the enterprise.

Drilling down even further, Figure 43.4 shows the menu presented when choosing the advanced memory option from Figure 43.3. Being able to find out what version of EMM is in use at a workstation without having to physically go to the workstation was unheard of several years ago!

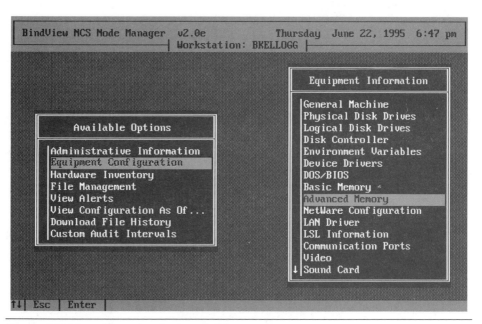

Figure 43.3   *Screen shot of equipment information menu.*

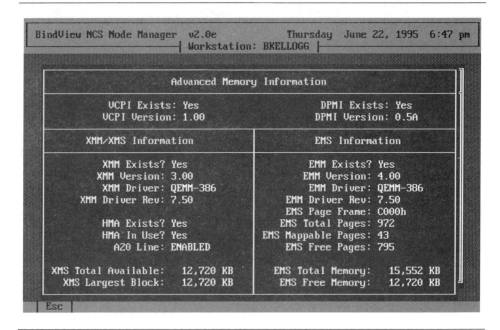

Figure 43.4   *Screen shot of Advanced Memory Information Menu.*

BindView, Technically Speaking

Now that we've gone through one example that takes us from installation to viewing configured memory on a workstation, let's take a look at how the process of inventorying a workstation takes place. Knowing how a hardware and software audit is performed by BindView gives us a look at some of the pitfalls and benefits inherent in this activity.

The Software Side

BindView collects information about software through a lookup table. When the administrator initially receives BindView, he or she also receives a software table. In this table values are stored for different versions of software that are *known* to BindView. For example, the table might have a value for Lotus 1-2-3 for Windows, version 4.0. However, it may not have an entry for Lotus 1-2-3 for Windows 5.0 if this version was released after BindView was shipped. For this reason we urge you to first call the vendor and see if you need to obtain any updated table files before proceeding with the installation. This is one of the pitfalls, but there's no way around it at the present time, for any of the current desktop management and inventory products.

Early releases of inventory software by vendors other than the LAN Support Group provided a program that stored and searched for software by its executable file name. For example, WordPerfect would be identified by searching for WP.EXE on the PC, then cross-referencing captured data in the software lookup table. This soon proved to be a problem when it was discovered that other software used the same file name.

The LAN Support Group, however, took another approach to avoid this problem. They added more search criteria in BindView, including file date and time, directory name, and overlay files. For example, during an audit for software, BindView may find a WP.EXE file.

In early releases of BindView, the program stored and searched for software by the file name executable. For example, WordPerfect would be identified by searching for WP.EXE on the PC, then cross-referencing captured data in the software lookup table. This soon proved to be a problem when it was discovered that other software used the same WP.EXE file name.

It then looks at the date and time stamp of the file as well as the directory where the file resides and compares those values to the values in the BindView lookup table. If there's a match, BindView defines the software and version number. BindView can currently recognize 7,500 different software packages.

Some organizations have their own homegrown applications, or shareware, or other products that BindView does not recognize. When BindView scans each workstation, it provides a list of the *known* software as well as a list of any software it was unable to identify. This list allows the administrator to add product names and versions to the software lookup table so that BindView can learn this software. Future scans will then be able to identify that software.

The Hardware Side

The hardware scan of BindView works in a similar way, but obviously it can't use overlay files and file names as clues. Instead, it scans memory locations as well as other areas like the BIOS for known routines. Because many manufacturers have proprietary methods, BindView has to know all of these different methods and then incorporate them into lookup tables and searches.

Table 43.1 shows a typical list returned from a hardware audit. Within each of these items in the list, further information can be presented once the item is chosen and the Enter key is pressed. For example, highlighting the *Mouse* row and pressing Enter would pull up another screen that provides more detailed information identified in the audit about the mouse. If no manufacturer is determined, the administrator has the option to add that information and update the hardware lookup table.

Hardware product	Manufacturer
3.5" High-Density Floppy Drive	
5.25" High-Density Floppy Drive	
CD ROM	
Clone	American Megatrends, Inc.
Color Monitor	
Hard Disk Drive	
Mouse	Microsoft
Network Card	
Sound Card	
Video Card	

Table 43.1   *List of hardware items found in an audit.*

Configuration Files

Ever get a call from a user saying that he or she has reconfigured something and now the PC doesn't work right? Well, BindView is prepared to handle this because it gives the administrator an option to collect the workstation's INI, AUTOEXEC.BAT, CONFIG.SYS, and NET.CFG files, as well as any other requested configuration files. These configuration files can be gathered centrally, by workstation, on the network. They can be downloaded back to the workstation if necessary. BindView compresses these files at the workstation prior to centrally collecting them on the file server, which cuts down on the network traffic. The files are also stored in a compressed format.

In addition, the administrator can receive alarms that tell when a workstation configuration file has been altered. The administrator can then go back and look at a revision history for that workstation. This means that BindView stores not only the latest configuration, but prior configuration files as well. The administrator can choose which version of a configuration file to restore.

Alerts

The administrator can be "alerted" whenever a change has been made on a workstation. This change can be to the equipment's type, a configuration file change, or something else. Each alert has certain characteristics that can be modified by the administrator. Alerts can be assigned priority values to differentiate the critical changes from the minor ones. Changes in equipment like BIOS information, CD ROM information, disk partition information, logical drive information, and many others can generate an alert to the administrator.

Reporting Capabilities

Once information has been gathered and massaged, extensive reporting capabilities are available to the network administrator. Let's say the IS manager asks for a report on the number of 486 PCs with 4 MB of RAM or greater. This is quite simple since all of the reports are menu driven and selectable. The administrator can use the canned reports that already have most of the requested information defined, or the administrator can design and save his or her own reports.

Type of processor and amount of RAM in a workstation is crucial information to organizations looking to deploy a client/server architecture, or a Windows based network. Having that information readily available can save an administrator's neck!

Asset Management

Along with tracking hardware and software, administrators can keep track of purchase orders, vendors, lease information and more. For example, an administrator can keep track of how many times a particular piece of hardware has been returned for repair. This, of course, assumes that someone inputs that data into the database! In fact, asset management is the one area that requires input at the beginning that can't be automated. However, reports can be generated and assets can be tracked better once the information is on-line.

WAN

BindView permits each local site to perform its own inventory and then allows the enterprise database to query distributed BindView databases to collect information for report generation. This permits the local LANs to perform audits and maintain data locally. However, when an enterprise report is needed or information needs to be viewed, that can be done through BindView in a consistent manner throughout an organization. Many organizations currently maintain inventory sheets in various different formats like spreadsheets and databases. This proves cumbersome when trying to gather inventory assets across the network.

As we mentioned earlier, BindView supports three management platforms: BindView proprietary, HP OpenView and Novell NetWare Management System (NMS). An organization that does not have OpenView, or NMS, they can use BindView's proprietary platform, ships with the product. Organizations already employing the use of either platform can now collectively view workstation information from either of those consoles in GUI form.

As we mentioned earlier, BindView supports two management platforms: HP OpenView and Novell NetWare Management System. Organizations already employing the use of either platform can now collectively view workstation information from either of those consoles in GUI form.

Cost

For an organization with 100 users at one site, monitoring and managing the workstations with BindView would cost an organization approximately $795–1,100, depending on the specific configuration. The cost of comparable systems varies from vendor to vendor, where some charge by the node and some by the server.

Upgrades

Adding software or hardware components that are new, and therefore *unknown* to BindView, means that the administrator must upgrade the lookup tables before the next inventory process. Because not all administrators are notified when new or different equipment is ordered, this can create a coordination problem. Our best advice for dealing with this is to keep your eyes open!

FUTURE DESKTOP MANAGEMENT

BindView and other products provide a more powerful way to inventory desktop PCs than the physical inventory method. But automated desktop management still requires some manual work on the administrator's part in the maintenance and updating of lookup tables. Can workstations be installed in such a way that they tell the management program what they are and what attributes they hold?

That is the wave of the future, but it's a long way off. Let's look at this wave and see what's coming and who's bringing it. In addition, we'll look at the pitfalls that we can expect within the next 10 years.

THE DESKTOP MANAGEMENT TASK FORCE

The DMTF was formed in 1992 to create a protocol-independent, multiplatform interface, or desktop management interface, for workstation and network components. Pioneering charter members include industry giants like Bay Networks (formerly Wellfleet and SynOptics), Digital Equipment Corp., Hewlett-Packard Co., IBM, Intel Corp., Microsoft, Novell, Inc., and Sun Microsystems, Inc.

The DMTF has many subcommittees formed to work on specific interface areas like software and LAN adapters. Members of these subcommittees can include charter members of the DMTF plus additional vendors throughout the industry. Intel Corporation is represented on almost all of the subcommittees as well as being a charter member.

Desktop Management Interface Standard

The Goal

The goal of DMI is to create an open architecture standard for managing workstations, servers, and peripherals. Vendors would implement DMI by providing a component that comes with a standard DMI file, which contains information that can be accessed by a DMI aware management program from a centralized location. For example, HP might provide a laser printer that has a chip with a DMI standard file containing information that allows the management program to know when the printer is off-line, out of paper, and so forth.

Another example could be a software program that provides a DMI file with information like program name and version number. As you should recall from our earlier discussion, products like BindView provide a lookup table with as many software products as the vendor can identify. The DMI approach places the burden of providing product information and attributes on the vendor who provides the software or hardware, not on the administrator.

Hardware Components

The following list is a sample of the hardware that the DMTF is looking to provide an interface for

- graphics cards
- hard disks
- modems
- motherboards
- NICs
- printers
- sound cards

Software Components

Examples of software components being addressed by the DMTF are operating systems, CD-ROM drivers, applications, and virus software.

The Pitfalls—What about Existing Components?

Software can be provided in the form of a TSR at the workstation that can make older products DMI compliant. However, we were told by a DMTF member that the size of that TSR is 33K and can't be modularized so that only necessary portions of the TSR could be loaded.

In fact, even the future implementations of DMI compliant hardware and software will still require a 33K TSR. For DOS-based machines, that will not go over well. Intel is working on a Windows-only version of DMI that will not require the 33K TSR at the workstation.

DMI Architecture

The DMI architecture is composed of three layers: a management interface (MI), a service interface, and a components interface (CI). As shown in Figure 43.5, the service layer is sandwiched in between the CI and the MI layers and provides the interface for those two layers to communicate. Included in the DMI architecture is the management interface file (MIF) that serves as the database repository for the workstation components.

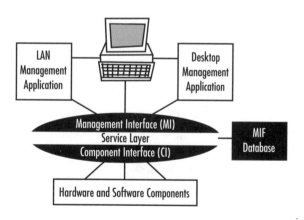

Figure 43.5   *DMI Architecture.*

Management Interface Layer

The MI layer interacts with management applications that are DMI compliant. It does so by requesting information from the service layer and then passing that information up to the management applications. For example, a management application might request information about a printer's serial number. The MI layer queries the service layer, which provides the information to the MI layer. The MI layer then sends the information to the management application.

Service Layer

The service layer manages the workstation database (MIF file), gathers information about components from the component layer, and responds to requests from the management layer.

Components Interface Layer

The CI layer is responsible for gathering information from each of the DMI compliant components and passing that information to the service layer for storage and management. There is much debate over Microsoft's decision not to support the CI layer in their Windows 95 product. The developers of Windows 95 decided that there was a lot of overlap in their plug and play specification, mini-port driver, and Registry configuration store and the DMI's CI layer. Microsoft will use drivers to respond to management applications requests.

Management Interface File

The MIF is an ASCII file that the service layer maintains, and it is considered the DMI database for the workstation. Every DMI compliant component comes with a MIF that is gathered by the CI layer and passed to the service layer to be combined into one MIF. A basic MIF could contain as little as the product's serial number and identifier code.

DMI 1.0 Specification

This specification, released in August 1994, defines how vendors and management application developers should supply products that can be managed.

DMI Software Developer's Kit

This kit was released late in 1994 and provides the information vendors need to provide APIs for their products to be managed. Included in the kit is a MIF-to-MIB tool provided by the DMTF.

Completed and Pending Standards

Product groups are subcommittees composed of a mixture of vendors charged with providing standard MIFs for groups or categories of products. You would typically see LAN adapter companies on the LAN adapter product group, software companies on the software product group, and so on. The following product groups have completed their MIF files:

- LAN adapters
- PC systems
- software

The following product groups have MIF files in progress:

- large mailroom operations
- printers
- servers

The following product groups are expected to develop MIF files in the future:

- modems and fax modems
- PCMCIA products

- NMP agents
- sound cards
- uninterruptible power supplies (UPS)

The completed MIF file format for LAN adapters follows:

Component ID
System Resources Description
System Resources
Network Adapter Port
802 Alternate Address Group
Network Adapter Driver Group
Network Adapter Hardware Group
Operational State
Field Replaceable Unit Group
Boot ROM
Boot ROM Capabilities

Companies Currently Shipping Products DMI Compliant

- HP has been shipping DMI compliant Vectras since December 1, 1994. HP is able to retrofit Vectras built between 1992 and December 1, 1994.
- Intel is shipping LAN adapters that are DMI compliant—TokenExpress and EtherExpress.

Companies Promising to Ship DMI Compliant Management Products

- IBM, NetView
- Intel, all of their products will be DMI compliant by end of 1995
- Microsoft, SMS
- Novell, NetWare Management System

COMPATIBILITY WITH OTHER STANDARDS

SNMP

There has been much debate over integrating DMI MIFs with SNMP MIBs. DMI was introduced because SNMP works at the server level but does not work down to the desktop level. There were no original plans to integrate the two. Now, however, plans are underway by Hewlett-Packard, IBM, and Sun Microsystems to design a mapping layer that will run DMI on the desktop and use SNMP transports to manage the information remotely.

Plug and Play

Plug and play addresses primarily configuration and installation of systems such as boards. The goal of plug and play is to allow systems to configure themselves, without any manual intervention from an administrator. So, the system could configure its own jumpers, dip switches, and so on. Fortunately, the plug and play information can be read and written into the standard MIF.

WHAT DOES ALL THIS MEAN?

It spells out some relief for a LAN administrator in the future but not necessarily in the immediate future. For example, if an organization has a good spread of 486-based processors and has no need to upgrade to a DMI compliant system, it will have to rely on their current vendor to supply it with TSRs to enable its systems with DMI compliance. These TSRs are estimated to take about 33KB of workstation RAM, which is not acceptable in most organizations. Even when a company upgrades, they'll still need to face the 33KB of RAM needed to implement DMI.

The DMTF has paved the way. As more vendors follow suit, like Intel and HP have done, DMI may take a strong hold. Until then, LAN administrators will have to look at the current products on the market to manage the desktop. Companies like the LAN Support Group, which supply a desktop management product that plugs into management platforms like NMS and HP OpenView, provide a very well-rounded solution for now. LAN administrators keep saying, "If they can put a person on the moon ..."

We spoke with Eric Pulaski, president of the LAN Support Group to get his viewpoint on the future of DMI. Eric said, "DMI is very useful for asset management purposes." He mentioned that, with the current standards, a savvy programmer can alter the contents of MIF files or otherwise spoof the DMI service layer, thus altering inventory information.

Workstation Management Tools: Bibliography and Strategies

For general networking references, please consult Appendix C, "A List of Networking Resources." The magazines and other publications listed there can help you find out lots of information about workstation management tools.

Intel has a fabulous faxback system at 1-800-538-3373. The following list of document numbers that we found helpful (although there is a whole lot more than we list here):

Document no.	Document title	No. of pages
5556	Desktop Management Interface (DMI) in Action	7
9009	Node Management Strategy Overview	5
5511	The Cost of Network Management	10

Table 43.2   *Helpful Intel faxback items.*

If you would like to contact the DMTF for more up-to-date information, you can call the DMTF hotline number at 1-503-696-9300. However, we must warn you that we left a message at that number and never received a return call from anyone on the task force.

Ed Arrington of Intel is currently the chair of the DMTF. Stephen P. Balogh is a technical marketing engineer at Intel who is chartered with supporting the DMTF's marketing and technical endeavors. He can be reached by CompuServe e-mail address, 70414,573, or by telephone, 1-503-264-8426.

TOP FIVE WORKSTATION MANAGEMENT TOOLS VENDORS

Frye Computer Systems, Inc.
19 Temple Place
Boston, MA 02111-9779
800-234-3793; 617-451-5400
FAX: 617-451-6711
Tech support: Use toll-free no.
Tech support BBS: 617-426-1910

Intel Corp. (Personal Computer Enhancement Division)
5200 N.E. Elam Young Pkwy.
Hillsboro, OR 97124-6497
800-538-3373; 503-629-7354
FAX: 503-629-7580
Tech support: 503-629-7000
Tech support BBS: 503-645-6275

The LAN Support Group, Inc.
2425 Fountainview Dr., Ste. 390
Houston, TX 77057
800-749-8439; 713-789-0881
Direct sales: 713-789-0882, ext. 508
FAX: 713-977-9111
Tech support: Use toll-free no.
Tech support BBS: 713-789-6776

McAfee Associates, Inc.
2710 Walsh Ave., Ste. 200
Santa Clara, CA 95051
800-866-6585; 408-988-3832
FAX: 408-970-9727
Tech support: 408-988-4181
Tech support BBS: 408-988-4004

Symantec Corp.
10201 Torre Ave.
Cupertino, CA 95014-2132

800-441-7234; 408-253-9600
Direct sales: 800-453-1193
FAX: 408-253-3968
Tech support: 415-892-1424
Tech support BBS: 503-484-6669

MANAGEMENT CONSOLES

EASY AS 1, 2, 3

Don't be afraid of this chapter! Fret no more!

In this chapter, we're going to take you through the very basics and assume you don't know what terms like SNMP and MIB mean. We start off by explaining what a network management system is and then run through some definitions of terms you'll see in this chapter and hear all over the network management world. Once you understand the building blocks, we'll put them all together and talk about common management consoles. That doesn't sound so tough, does it?

In Chapter 41, we discussed network management in general. We discussed the reasons why we need network management, the five areas that the ISO defined, and the ongoing costs associated with management it. In this chapter, we'll focus on the things you can do with a network management system.

Network Management System

A network management system is a collection of hardware and software that enables a network administrator to manage and configure network components. Typically, the administrator works from a *network management console*, which is his or her link to the network being managed.

There are four basic components in any network management system:

1. Management platform
2. Network management software
3. A network management protocol
4. Managed objects

Management Platform

A management platform, such as HP's OpenView, provides basic network management services to network management applications. These services include autodiscovery, event management, graphical mapping, and others. A management platform must specify what network management protocols it will support, such as the Simple Network Management Protocol (SNMP) or the Common Management Interface Protocol (CMIP).

The network platform is designed to be the low level interface. API's are then provided to other vendors to develop programs that will use this platform and its services. So, in its simplest sense, a management platform is a set of routines that perform specific network management functions.

Network Management Software

Network management software is written using the management platform's API functions. Typically, a company provides the management platform and releases APIs to third party network management companies. These companies develop software that uses the platform's basic network management services. This allows companies like Intel Corp. and the LAN Support Group to provide specialized programs without having to know the low level mechanics of the platform. When a network management programmer wants to gather information on an object, he or she merely needs to pass required information, like which object and then invoke a function call to the network management platform software. The network management platform software then handles the low level requests needed to perform the required actions.

Network Management Protocol

Any time two devices wish to communicate, they must choose a common language. In a network management environment, where separate workstations (network management consoles) may be managing many devices on separate network segments, all management stations must use the same protocol. We discussed various networking protocols in Part III of this book. Here we are talking about a protocol that was designed specifically for network management. Several of these network protocols are supported today, the most popular being the SNMP and the CMIP. These are only messaging protocols. SNMP and CMIP both need network layer transport protocols to carry their messages across the network.

In this chapter, we focus on the SNMP protocol. SNMP is supported by most popular network operating systems and has became an industry standard.

Managed Objects

We can't have a management system without having something to manage. Network devices like workstations, routers, bridges, printers, and gateways may all be represented by managed objects. A managed object is a representation of a physical device. We'll discuss managed objects in greater detail later on.

Network Management System Mechanics

Let's take a quick look at the mechanics of network management operation, without worrying about understanding the terminology. In the next section, we'll go into greater detail about each component and the details of its operation. Right now we're taking the 10,000 foot view.

A manager sends a message to a managed object on the network. The object itself is responsible for performing the requested action. The object contains information about itself, its *attributes*; and it contains the procedures for gathering and acting on that information, its *methods*. The manager may be requesting a report on one of the object's attribute values or that the object perform one of its methods. That's all there is to it, at least in our 10,000 foot view. Now let's look at the specifics.

THE BUILDING BLOCKS

Parts of a Network Management Workstation

The Hardware—Network Management Console

A console is a screen where you view information. This screen can be a PC screen or a terminal screen. It can display data in text format or in a "graphical user interface" (GUI) form. For purposes of this chapter, we'll assume that we're working from a PC-based color GUI console.

A management console is similar to a console at an airport that displays information about arriving or departing flights. Airport consoles permit you to view flight status information. The information on the console includes the flight number, the departing city name, expected arrival time, on-time status, arrival gate, and more. This information is available to everybody in view of the console and promotes efficiency. When a plane is boarding, the screen flashes for that particular entry, alerting travelers that it's time to board the plane.

A network management console displays information to a LAN administrator about the network. Network information like router status, node addresses, and bridge traffic can be gathered and displayed at a management console on the network. GUI management applications can display statistics in graph form or display devices like bridges on the network as pictures—similar to icons that you see on your Windows screen. These pictures, or icons, are representations of the objects that make up your network. You can get a report on a printer, a bridge, a LAN segment, or a router by clicking on its related icon. These devices may be configured and manipulated from the management console. The network manager simply makes the necessary changes to the associated managed object.

The Architecture—Network Management Platform

Obviously, flight status information does not just appear on the airport information console by magic. Someone has to key in that information. As a flight's status changes, the information must be updated by the operator. This means that someone either has to call all of the gates periodically and gather the information or the gate personnel must call the data entry person and relay the information. The same is true for a network management console. Network device and status information simply does not just appear on the network management console, it must be gathered before it can be displayed.

A network management platform determines how information is gathered and what form the information is displayed. Windows is a good example of a platform. Windows is an application platform for a PC. Microsoft releases APIs to program developers so that they may write applications that work in conjunction with Windows. For example, the Windows platform defines print tasks for all Windows-based applications. Once you define your print parameters in Windows, Windows permits other Windows-based applications to access that information so each new installation of Windows-based software does not require defining that information over and over.

A network management platform is the underlying software architecture that provides APIs to vendors for developing management applications. Developers writing applications for an application platform, like Microsoft Windows, use APIs to make their applications Windows compliant. The resulting applications can interact with other Windows applications without reconfiguration, because they share the Windows platform in common. A network management platform works the same way. The platform is responsible for managing and making available common services like data management, access to managed objects, and presentation of information. The management applications hook into the platform and share these common services and can also provide additional capabilities of their own. Figure 44.1 depicts this concept.

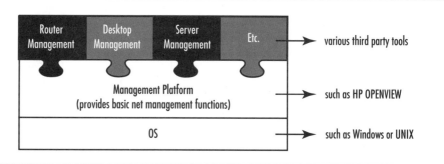

Figure 44.1 *Network Management Platform.*

There are a variety of network management platforms. Hewlett-Pack-ard's platform is OpenView, IBM's platform is NetView, and Sun Micro-system's platform is SunNet Manager. We discuss these platforms in greater detail later in the chapter.

The Simple Network Management Protocol

SNMP is a protocol designed for requesting, packaging, and sending man-agement information over a network. SNMP provides a common set of rules for programmers writing network management programs. A wide variety of devices from assorted vendors and manufacturers may be man-aged on a network as long as they support SNMP. The standards for SNMP are defined in the Internet RFC 1157.

SNMP is popular today in the network management arena. SNMP is controlled by the Internet Activities Board (IAB). Many vendors support SNMP, supplying SNMP-compliant routers, bridges and servers. Figure 44.2 shows an overall view of the components of SNMP which include:

SNMP Manager. The SNMP manager is the network management software that hooks into a network management platform. The SNMP manager component is implemented as software residing on the network manage-ment console station. The SNMP manager uses SNMP commands to talk to agents on a network, which send back information about managed objects. Agents send their MIB information to the SNMP manager which stores all of the MIB information from each of its agents in its own MIB at the man-agement console station. This MIB allows the management software to pro-

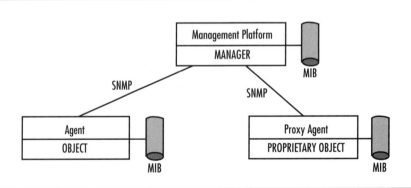

Figure 44.2   *SNMP Components.*

vide services such as trend analysis on the managed objects. Typically, management software vendors supply MIB browsers that allow LAN administrators to see the contents of the manager MIB. The SNMP manager provides a network map of the agents it discovers. The map is displayed in pictorial form at the network management console.

SNMP Agent. An agent is software that resides on a device capable of intelligence, such as a router, hub, or NIC. The agent may be implemented as software residing in memory or as a ROM chip, a PROM chip, or as EE-PROM. The agent serves as the management software's representative at the device itself, furnishing management capability and information about the device. The relationship between SNMP agents and an SNMP managers is called a *community*.

An agent is responsible for monitoring and making changes to its own MIB contents and for providing information about the managed objects to the management application when requested. This communication between manager and agent is handled in the form of messages. The manager sends the agent an SNMP request message (Get Request or Get Next Response) or an action message (Set Request), and the agent sends back an SNMP response message (Get Response).

On a network, it is not uncommon to find agents from different vendors coexisting. For example, a network might contain a Cisco router agent, a Cabletron hub agent, and a server agent. As long as all of those agents support SNMP they can peacefully coexist.

SNMP Proxy Agent. An SNMP proxy agent permits an SNMP management system to converse with non-SNMP agents. The proxy agent can be thought of as a gateway that converts the SNMP protocol to the proprietary protocol.

Some organizations have network management systems that are proprietary and do not support SNMP commands. These systems can communicate very well with the devices they manage but do so in a proprietary manner. Some of these network management systems are in the process of converting to an SNMP-based management system. During the conversion process it may not be possible to replace all of the prior managed devices with SNMP-supported managed devices. An SNMP proxy agent permits the manager to send SNMP commands to the SNMP proxy agent. The proxy agent converts that language to the proprietary command language and passes the commands on to the proprietary agent.

An SNMP proxy agent therefore permits an SNMP management system to converse with non-SNMP agents. The proxy agent can be thought of as a gateway that converts the SNMP protocol to the proprietary protocol.

SNMP Management Information Base. A management information base (MIB) is composed of the set of managed objects in a system. The MIB provides a structure for organizing the kinds of management information that a management system should recognize and store.

A MIB can be implemented as a database, where it would serve as a formal schema, or as a set of data structures within a management application that doesn't use a database management system (DBMS). Generally speaking, the greater the variety of managed objects and the larger the number of objects to manage, the more likely a management application is to use a real live DBMS. Because such systems support interactive queries and all kinds of report writers, this is generally a bonus for network managers.

MIB-2 is the latest definition of the SNMP MIB and is defined in RFC 1213.

Managed Objects

Before we go any further, let's define what we're talking about when we say *managed object*. A managed device can have one or more SNMP managed objects. A managed object is a logical unit that has a five-part formal definition. For a formal list of managed objects, consult your network management software vendor. The following shows the logical breakdown of a managed object:

- *Object.* This is the name of the object (i.e., printer).

- *Syntax.* This follows the standard Abstract Syntax Notation 1 (ASN.1) system (i.e., INTEGER, OCTET, STRING, COUNTER, GAUGE). For example, if the syntax value was COUNTER, it infers that the data type is an INTEGER but that the integer can only increase. So, in our example, we would find the syntax to be COUNTER because the time a printer is off-line can only increase.

- *Definition.* This is the ASCII description of the object (i.e., "how long has it been since this printer was restarted?").

- *Access.* The term defines if the managed object is read-only, write-only, or read-write.

- *Status.* The term defines if the managed object is mandatory or optional.

Object names are registered and publicly available to programmers as supplied by the standard ISO MIB tree. Figure 44.3 displays this MIB tree structure (we've inserted the "how long has this printer been off-line?" object as an example only—it does not represent a standard object.

Looking at Figure 44.3, you see a number in parenthesis. Reading the numbers off of this tree from top to bottom produces a number called an *object identifier* that represents the registered name in numeric format. The object identifier for our printer object is therefore 1.3.6.1.2.1.1.15.

Traps

The SNMP manager gathers information about managed objects by polling the agents and requesting specific information. However, certain conditions may require that the agent alert the SNMP manager that a certain condition has occurred. This alert is called a *trap* in the SNMP world. Traps are generally defined at installation time and can cause alert conditions of different types. The network manager can assign priorities to the alerts and predetermine how the alert will be displayed and logged at the management console.

Consider the following example. A router link on the internetwork fails, isolating a local LAN from accessing its WAN link to the rest of the enterprise. The router link is associated with a managed object and can be viewed on the network management console. The associated agent sends an alert message to the management console, indicating its status. The alert may be simply displayed, or it may be manifested as an audible tone or flashing light. The alert may even trigger a routine that pages the LAN administrator. Alerts that are not mission critical can be sent to a log file for later viewing. It is still up to the manager to then act on the alert and poll the agent to determine the specific status details of the managed object.

Another Common Language: CMIP

CMIP is another protocol used in network management systems. It is defined by the ISO. The two protocols differ in some areas, but also have similarities.

For example, both have the ability to manage objects, and both employ the concept of a MIB. SNMP uses a polling technique where it continually

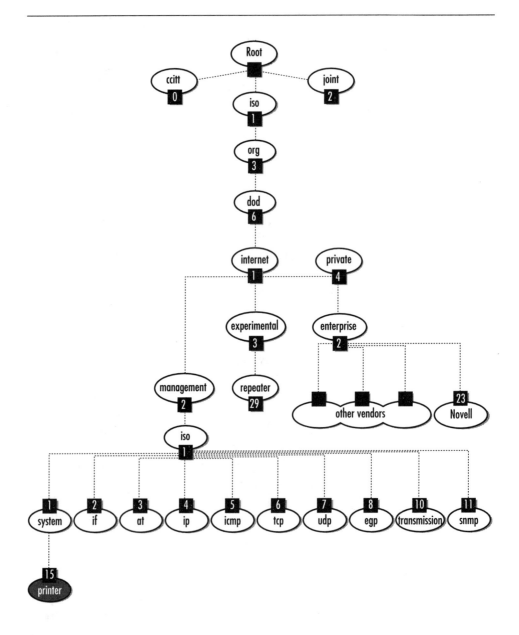

Figure 44.3   *MIB Tree (with fictitious printer).*

polls for the status of objects. CMIP has the objects notify the manager when their status changes.

Both protocols have strong and weak points. Both SNMP and CMIP are commonly used today, and considerable debate has taken place over which one will become the global standard. In the future, one or the other may predominate or the two may somehow be merged.In this chapter, we'll focus on SNMP. Most products today implement SNMP and we feel you should have a good understanding of that protocol. If necessary, you can add another protocol like CMIP to your already established SNMP knowledge base.

PULLING IT ALL TOGETHER

Now that you know the fundamentals of SNMP management the rest of this chapter should be a piece of cake. Now let's take a look at the basic services provided by the most common network management platforms and then at a network management application residing on one of those platforms.

Network Management Console Platforms

Some of the services common to all management platforms follow. Platforms differ mainly in the operating system supported, the protocols supported, and the mechanics of how services are provided.

- *Map presentation.* The platforms provide graphical maps of the physical or logical layout of a network and its discovered managed objects.
- *Event management.* The platforms provide management for events that occur on the network. Events occur when the status of a managed object changes. The platforms allow these events to be given priorities.
- *Object discovery.* This is often called *autodiscovery.* The platforms provide a mechanism in which managed objects can be discovered on a

network and then displayed. Starting autodiscovery during working hours can cause excessive traffic on an enterprise network and must be handled carefully, especially on large internetworks.

- *Management protocol(s) support.* Some provide CMIP, SNMP or both in the form of APIs.

- *Network manager.* No, we don't mean a human being, we mean the platform provides the manager that talks with the agents out on the network.

SunNet Manager

Unless you have a Sun or a Solaris UNIX box, there's no way to use this platform on a LAN-based PC. SunNet Manager is used in large organizations where large databases of objects need to be managed. Typically, the IS communications group manages high level details about the whole enterprise from the SunNet Manager running on a UNIX box while the local sites employ the use of HP OpenView on the local LAN for network management.

Managing Cabletron hubs can be a good example here—local sites don't always have available disk capacity, money, or time to analyze long-term trends. That information can be gathered locally by the network management console and uploaded to the SunNet Manager console for further evaluation and trend determination.

IBM's NetView for AIX

This network management platform was originally designed to run on IBM mainframes and receive alerts and information from SNA networks. It currently runs on an IBM RISC 6000 and can discover nodes down to the LAN level, although it is better suited for the high level topology mappings. NetView is actually based on OpenView's technology and has been licensed to DEC for use with their polycenter network management system as well.

HP OpenView

Hewlett Packard's OpenView was originally designed to run on a UNIX platform but was recently ported so it could also run as a Windows-based product on a PC. HP's OpenView is one of the most prevalent network management platforms available today. Most of the major vendors provide products that snap into OpenView.

Let's take an in-depth look at how OpenView provides its basic network services to a network management application.

Autodiscovery. OpenView can go out onto an IP or IPX internetwork, crossing bridges and routers, and discover manageable objects. To do this, it launches a *discovery manager* that runs as a software process in the background. The scope of this autodiscovery can be limited so that the administrator could define the subnet address or network address of the networks that should be included in the discovery process. The following is a step-by-step process of an IP discovery process.

1. The IP discovery process begins by searching for a default gateway router on the network. The discovery manager looks at the router's next hop table to find additional routers.
2. Once a router is discovered, the discovery manager looks at the router's ARP cache table to identify all of the objects it sees.
3. The discovery manager sends an SNMP request to the discovered objects inquiring about their object ID. The object ID will tell the discovery manager what type of object it is.

The next list depicts what steps the discovery manager goes through to discover IPX devices:

1. The discovery manager first looks for a NetWare server.
2. The discovery manager looks at the next hop table in the NetWare server to discover other servers.
3. As each server is discovered, the discovery manager uses NetWare diagnostic services in each server to determine the IPX objects that are connected.
4. The discovery manager next sends out an SNMP request (same as step 4 in the IP discovery process) to the IPX objects for their object ID so it can identify the objects by type.

Map Presentation. Once OpenView discovers managed objects, it presents them in a graphical view on the management console. The network, therefore, is represented as a collection of icons and connections in a hierarchical map. Submapping capabilities are provided. For example, the top layer of the network map could represent the United States. On the top layer could be an icon for each location across the United States. The network manager can customize these layers by adding bitmap backgrounds for each layer. For example, on the top layer U.S. map, the network manager could add a U.S. bitmap to further clarify this. Selecting a U.S. location icon on the top layer of the map would then open up a sublayer of the map pertinent only to that location.

Event Management. As we mentioned earlier, an event is a notification sent to the OpenView management console that the status of an object has changed and information updates should be made for that object. This is different than the manager polling the agents for information. An event (or alarm) is a notification sent to the manager without a request being issued. The object's agent uses an OpenView API to pass information like object ID, error, or updated status information to OpenView about the event. OpenView receives the alarm and information and then displays the alarm on the management console.

OpenView permits 10 different colors to represent alarm status. Normally the color red indicates high priority alarm status. If an administrator sees a screen full of red icons (representing the managed objects) on the management console, its a sure sign of major problems on the network. However, if the color of only one icon on the management console changed to yellow, it might indicate that a particular object, like a router, might be experiencing a heavy traffic load at that time.

Network Management Protocol Support. OpenView provides LAN administrators and network management applications the ability to communicate with SNMP agents by providing an SNMP manager. The manager is accessible to the network management applications as well as the LAN administrator. Either one can communicate by choosing an object. The manager then searches its MIB to see if it has information on that object. If not, it requests information from the object's agent. Once the manager has the information, it presents the MIB contents to the management software or the LAN administrator. Either can issue GET and SET queries (part of SNMP language) and the manager will perform the appropriate requests.

Network Management System Applications

As we mentioned above, HP OpenView, SunNet Manager, and IBM Net-View are all platforms that provide basic network management functions. They provide icons that represent objects, but they don't provide detailed graphics on these objects. For example, you might see an icon that represents a router. Clicking on that icon may give you information, but you might not be able to pull up a drawing of the actual router itself complete with interface cards and blinking lights.

However, if you purchase a Cisco router network management application that snaps into OpenView, you would be able to see a more meaningful drawing of the object. Next, you might want the same information from your hubs. So, you would go to your hub vendor and see if it has a network management product that supports the OpenView platform. And so on and on you go, building your network control center with management applications that provide you detailed information and configuration options for your most crucial devices.

Until recently, it was possible to recognize a PC on a network, but it was not possible to look at configuration information such as hard disk, BIOS information, software information, and the like. However, companies like Intel and the LAN Support Group have developed workstation management software that hook into OpenView. This provides an end-to-end solution for network managers who would like to manage as much of the network as possible from a single console.

THE TOP THREE MANAGEMENT CONSOLE VENDORS

Hewlett-Packard Co.
3000 Hanover St.
Palo Alto, CA 94304-1181
800-752-0900; 800 387-3867 (CD); 415-857-1501
Direct sales: 800-637-7740 (HP Direct)
FAX: 800-333-1917
Tech support: 800-858-8867
Tech support BBS: 415-852-0256

Sun Microsystems Computer Corp. (unit of Sun Microsystems, Inc.)
2550 Garcia Ave.
Mountain View, CA 94043-1100
800-821-4643; 800-821-4642 (CA); 415-960-1300
FAX: 415-969-9131
Tech support: 800-USA-4SUN

IBM (International Business Machines)
Old Orchard Rd.
Armonk, NY 10504
800-426-3333; 914-765-1900
Direct sales: 800-426-2968 (IBM PC Direct)
Tech support: 800-237-5511
Tech support BBS: 919-517-0001; 800-847-7211 (OS2)

MANAGEMENT CONSOLE RESOURCES:
BIBLIOGRAPHY AND STRATEGIES

For general networking references, please consult Appendix C, "A List of Networking Resources." The magazines and other publications listed there can help you find out lots of information about network management consoles. The following references are particularly helpful for the information they contain about network interface cards.

Rose, Marshall T. The Simple Book, 2nd ed.
  Prentice-Hall, Englewood Cliffs, NJ: 1994. An excellent book on network management and SNMP. Provides both high level models and SNMP language macros.

Terplan, Kornel. *Effective Management of Local Area Networks.*
  McGraw-Hill, New York: 1992. An excellent, two-thumbs-up book on every aspect of network management. A good thorough discussion on all the major network management platforms. $40.00.

Steinke, Steve. *Guide to Managing PC Networks.*
  Prentice-Hall PTR, Englewood Cliffs, NJ: 1995. An excellent book on managing networks that includes a section devoted to SNMP along with a listing of all of the MIB-2 managed objects. $29.95.

"NetWare Management System (NMS) Components and Functionality,"
  Novell Application Notes, (November, 1994): 29-47. Another excellent reference written specifically for NetWare's NetWare Management System that describes the system in a very straightforward method. It includes some good pictures along with an appendix devoted only to SNMP. $150/yr. subscription.

Sheldon, Tom. *The LAN Times Encyclopedia of Networking*.
  Osborne McGraw-Hill, 1994, Berkeley, CA: A general sourcebook for networking terms
  and technologies. It includes discussions, some lengthy and detailed, about nearly every conceivable networking topic. $39.95.

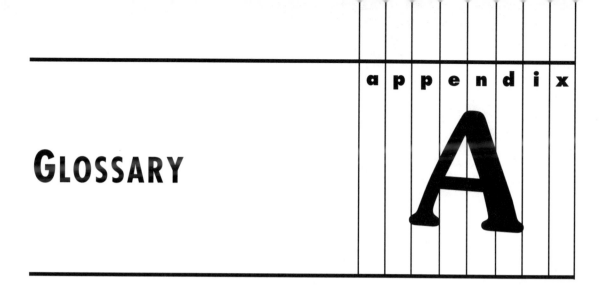

GLOSSARY

10Base2

Also known as *thin Ethernet*. A cabling specification for running Ethernet over thin coax cable.

10Base5

The old way of running Ethernet, over thick coax cable. Also called *thick Ethernet*.

10BaseF

Ethernet over fiber-optic cable.

10BaseT

Ethernet over twisted-pair cable. By far the most prevalent in use.

access method

Messages are communicated across the network by rules called *protocols* and access methods that govern their access to the network cabling. When you think networking, remember that without an access method, you don't have any on-ramps to the network.

access privileges

Definitions of which users have access to files or directories for what purposes.

acronym

An abbreviation formed by taking the first letter of each word of the phrase you want to abbreviate. Because networking terminology is loaded with long wordy phrases, it's also loaded with acronyms. Some networkers talk about TLAs, which stands for three-letter acronyms, as being essential for legitimacy among nerds!

active monitor

Error conditions on a token passing ring are monitored and corrected by a node known as the *active monitor*. The active monitor is elected by the other nodes on the ring when the ring is brought up.

addressing

In the network world, every device needs an identifying number that belongs to that device only. Usually these identifiers are made up of some combination of numbers. For network and internetwork communications to occur, every device needs to have this unique numeric ID or address.

American National Standards Institute (ANSI)

One of the primary standards setting bodies for computer technology in the United States. Composed of manufacturers, users, and computer related companies.

analog signals

A continuous signal, like a sound wave. Telephone transmissions are analog transmission.

API (application programming interface)

Usually, a set of interface subroutines or library calls that define the methods for programs to access external services (i.e., to somebody else's system or program).

AppleTalk

The name of the set of protocols developed by Apple Computer, whose Macintosh was one of the first mass-market computers to offer built-in networking capabilities. In most cases, where there's a Mac, there's also Apple-Talk.

application

any piece of software that you use for your computing tasks, such as a spreadsheet program, electronic mail program, or game

application independent

A format or facility is said to be *application independent* when it works in multiple environments and doesn't depend on a specific application to understand or use its contents.

archival systems

Backup systems that automatically create copies of data every time something changes.

ARCnet

A token-passing type of network technology; inexpensive but rather slow by current standards.

ASCII

Computer acronym for American Standard Code for Information Interchange, an eight-bit code for data transfer that was adopted by ANSI to ensure compatibility among data types.

asynchronous

Literally, "not at the same time," the term refers to computer communications where sender and receiver do not communicate directly with one another but rather through accessing a common pick-up/drop-off point for information.

asynchronous transfer mode (ATM)

A cell switching technology designated as the carrier for broadband ISDN.

ATM

See *asynchronous transfer mode*.

attenuation

The decrease of strength as a signal travels down a network cable.

backbone

A high-speed internetwork connection designed to interconnect multiple networks. A typical backbone connects only routers; normal network nodes occur only seldom if ever on backbones. A link, typically of some high speed medium, between the segments of a network.

backup

A copy of data preserved for purposes of disaster recovery. You can make a backup of a single data file, the contents of your hard drive, or the entire server hard drive (and you should).

bandwidth

The amount of data that can be sent over a given communications circuit. Usually measured in kilobits per second (Kbps) of megabits per second (Mbps).

baseband

An unmultiplexed digital transmission medium.

baseline

The level of network performance against which you judge any changes. You should measure your baseline when you first install your network.

basic rate interface (BRI)

An ISDN interface constituted of two B channels and one D channel. Commonly expressed as 2B+D.

baud

A unit of signaling speed defined as cycles per second. This equals bits per second (bps) only if one bit is transmitted per cycle. Bps is more accurate for rating modem speed, but baud is more commonly used when discussing modems.

bearer service

The method for transporting end user data from one location on the ISDN to another

BBS

See *bulletin board system*.

binary

Literally, this means that a file is formatted as a collection of ones and zeros; actually, this means that a file is formatted to be intelligible only to a certain application, or that it is itself an executable file.

B-ISDN (broadband ISDN)

An ISDN interface that provides up to 600 Mbps and provides services such as high density TV and multimedia applications.

bit

The smallest unit of computer information, a 1 or a 0, as represented in binary (Base 2) form.

bi-tronics cable (bi-directional Centronics)

This is basically a Centronics cable that has bidirectional capabilities. It fits into the Centronics plug in your printer.

BNC connector

The type of connector that attaches to coax cable.

body

The raw data carried by a packet or in many cases, another packet that contains its own header and body.

bps

Computer acronym for "bits per second"; a measure of the number of ones and zeros that a computer or telephone connection can handle in one second.

BRI

See *basic rate interface*.

bridge

A piece of internetworking equipment that operates at layer 2 of the ISO model and forwards packets from one network segment to another without checking address information (see also router).

broadband

A digital transmission medium that may be divided into multiple channels (multiplexed) to support multiple distinct connections.

bulletin board system (BBS)

A synonym for *bulletin board system*, a BBS usually consists of a PC, modem(s), and communications software attached to the end of one or more phone lines. Callers call up the BBS, where they can send and receive messages and download software.

buffer space

NICs contain their own RAM to provide working space for information coming on and off the network. Called *buffer space* because it provides room for incoming and outgoing data to be stored.

bus

A network topology type in which all computers are attached to a single, shared cable. A bus topology is most commonly used for Ethernet networks or other contention based networking schemes.

bus topology

A network wiring layout in which each computer is connected to the two computers on either side of it, except for the ones on the ends.

byte

A set of eight bits. Also called an *octet*. This is, interestingly, about the amount of data it takes to store a single letter (in the Roman alphabet, that is).

cabling

The network media used to connect network nodes. Also called *wiring*, this is just the whole collection of cables, connectors, and hubs that make up your network.

cable connectors

The hardware gadgets that attach to the ends of your cables, which in turn will let you attach those cables to NICs or wall plates.

cable plant

The collection of cables that make up your network connections.

campus

Any collection of buildings that house an organization. Does not necessarily refer to an institute of higher learning.

carrier sense

A feature of Ethernet that indicates that every system on the network is always listening to what's traveling over the wire.

carrier sense multiple access with collision detection (CSMA/CD)

An access method for networking. CSMA/CD allows multiple devices to share a common medium.

CATV

Cable access television.

CCITT

A standards body charged with providing standards for worldwide telephony.

CDDI

Copper distributed data interface, a variant of FDDI that runs over copper wire instead of fiber-optic cable.

CD-ROM

A computer storage medium that works with discs much like the CDs you use on your home stereo but that stores computer data instead of music.

cell

A transmission unit of asynchronous transfer mode technology. ATM technology is based on transmitting of fixed length 53 octet cells.

cellular digital packet data (CDPD)

A transmission protocol for data transfer over cellular communications equipment.

cellular telephones

Telephones that work by transmitting a conversation over radio frequencies instead of wires.

central office (CO)

A local telephone exchange. Telephone customers are attached to the CO by the subscriber loop.

Centronics cable

A parallel cable that fits only in Centronics plugs on printers. If you look on the back of most laser printers, you'll see that big, ugly-looking plug. It is a 36-pin cable on one end, 25-pin connector on the other end.

channel

The voice or data communications pathway connecting two network devices.

circuit

A physical or logical connection between two network devices.

circuit switching

Refers to the setting up of a dedicated path between two nodes on a network or internetwork.

cladding

The insulation layer for fiber-optic cable, which is typically made of fiber-glass or plastic.

client

A PC when it is in the position of requesting a service from a network server.

client/server

A computing paradigm in which processing is divided between a graphical front-end application running on a user's desktop machine, and a back-end server that performs data- or storage-intensive processing tasks in response to client service.

clone

Shorthand for IBM-PC clone. This term refers to any machine that works the same way as an IBM-PC, including running the same software. A clone can do this because it has the same CPU as the IBM.

coating

The outer layer of a cable, typically made of PVC (polyvinyl chloride, a type of plastic), which is the most common type of coating for keyboard, modem, and other types of computer system cables, or Teflon, for use in ceilings and in walls for network cables (as required by most building codes).

coax

Nickname for *coaxial cable*.

coaxial cable

A type of network medium. Coaxial cable is made up of a central solid metal conductor surrounded by an insulator, which is surrounded by a wire mesh shield and an outer cover.

collapsed backbone

A backbone that is a special hub or some other piece of network equipment, rather than a collection of cables.

collision

When two machines send out packets over the network at the same time, you get a collision. A fancy word for error, it might mean your network is getting taxed.

collision detect

A feature of Ethernet. It detects collisions, and if it sees that one has happened, everybody has to wait before resending.

common internetworking topology initiative (CITI)

A networking standard. CITI proposes to provide a common networking topology standard that allows internetworking devices, network design and optimization tools, and network management platforms from different vendors to share configuration data.

communications

The language of a network. The protocol and networking software form the communications portion of a network.

compliant

Conforms to a defined standard of some kind.

concentrator
> A network device that provides a central point for connection of multiple PCs, terminals, or communications devices

connection
> A link opened between two computers for some specific communication.

connectionless
> Communications method in which packets of information are transmitted and left to find the best path to their destination. No circuit or connection is established. Also called *best effort*.

connection oriented
> A communications method in which a connection is established, monitored during the transmission, and released at the end. SPX is a connection oriented protocol.

contention
> In networks, nodes compete for access to the network cable.

CPU
> Central processing unit. The brain of the computer. Everything else, including memory and disk drives, is just gravy.

CPE
> A telephony term meaning customer premises equipment.

crosstalk
> Leaking of a transmission signal from one medium to an adjoining medium.

CSU/DSU (channel service unit/data service unit)
> A device to terminate a digital telephone channel on a customer's premises (commonly used to terminate T1 or higher bandwidth connections).

cyclic redundancy checksum (CRC)
> A frame field that provides some error checking and correction facilities in data link layer transmission.

daisy chain
> A way of installing peripheral devices in which one device is plugged into a PC or workstation and each subsequent device is connected to the one previous.

DARPA (Defense Advanced Research Projects Administration)

The branch of the Department of Defense that funds advanced research, including the initial work that led to the development and deployment of the Internet.

database

A computerized and heavily indexed collection of organized information; common database examples include a library's electronic card catalog, information about an organization's employees, and order and purchase information.

datagram

The smallest independent data unit within the IP layer of the TCP/IP protocol stack. Carries enough information to be routed from the sender to the receiver over the best available route.

data link layer

The layer of the OSI network architectural model that communicates with higher level protocols and formulates frames for transmission over the physical link.

data packet

See *packet*.

data terminal equipment (DTE)

Data communications devices. Computer terminals or PCs with access to a network.

DBMS (database management system)

A complex system of programs and utilities used to define, maintain, and manage access to large collections of on-line data.

decode

The process of translating an encoded signal into the original bit stream.

dedicated connection

Connection established over a link used only for that purpose. A permanent connection.

dedicated server

A PC that is used strictly as a server and is not available as a workstation.

de facto standards

A set of common practices that attains the value of standard through widespread and repeated usage.

desktop, desktop system

See *workstation*.

dial-in connection

Also *dial-up connection*. A method of accessing a network by calling into the network via a modem. A dial-in connection is temporary, as opposed to a dedicated connection.

digital

A transmission signal based on the transmission of binary data.

directory structure

The hierarchical organization of files in a directory tree.

disk duplexing

A form of disk mirroring with not only redundant drives, as in disk mirroring, but also includes redundant disk controllers.

disk mirroring

A process in which you can install duplicate hard drives, one active and one backup, which a network operating system then writes to simultaneously. If a crash or other problem occurs on the active drive, the system automatically begins to use the backup drive and notifies you of the switch.

disk subsystem

A fancy name for some extra storage on your file server.

distributed application

any application that runs partly on one machine and partly on another (often a server) over the network, rather than keeping quietly to itself on a single PC.

distributed computing

A concept of networking that views your PC as a tool that you use to access the network as one computing environment rather than as a collection of unrelated resources.

distributed star

A topology that looks like a cross between a bus and a star. It's used by ARCnet.

DNS (domain name service)

An Internet service that maps symbolic names to IP addresses by distributing queries among the available pool of DNS servers.

DoD (Department of Defense)

The people who brought you the Internet, among other things (see *DARPA*).

domain

A logical collection of devices or objects. In the Internet world, a domain is part of a naming hierarchy. Syntactically, an Internet domain name consists of a sequence of names separated by periods. In the OSI world, a domain is general.

DOS

The most common operating system on IBM-clone PCs.

downstream

On a ring network, the direction in which data is flowing.

dpi

Dots per inch, a measurement of the density of an image. The more dots per unit of measure, the denser it is and the higher its resolution (e.g., resolution is directly proportional to density).

DS-0

A 64 Kbps communications channel. T1 digital lines are composed of 24 DS-0s.

DS-1

A collection of DS-0s analogous to T1.

DS-3

A collection of DS-0s analogous to T3.

e-mail

Messaging application that runs over a network.

encapsulation

The process in which each layer of a protocol suite attaches header information to a network packet.

encode

Transforming a data stream into a transmission format.

end nodes

These are the machines (devices) on a network at which users perform their work. Desktop PCs, printers, and file servers connected to a network are all examples of end nodes.

end to end

The entire pathway used for communications.

enterprise hubs

Incorporate all of the features of intelligent hubs, with the addition of switching and high speed backbone capabilities (see intelligent hubs)

Ethernet

A network access method developed by Digital Equipment Corporation, Intel, and Xerox in the early 1970s. Ethernet is the most widely used local area network technology available today.

Ethernet II (DIX)

This frame format is used for PCs using TCP/IP, AppleTalk Phase I, and networks hooked up to DEC computers.

Ethernet 802.2

This frame type contains both 802.3 and 802.2 fields. NetWare 4.X uses this frame type.

Ethernet 802.3 (IEEE)

Used exclusively by Novell's IPX/SPX protocol in NetWare 3.X and prior versions of NetWare. No other protocols support this frame type.

Ethernet subnetwork access protocol (SNAP)

Derived from the Ethernet 802.2 frame type

electromagnetic interference (EMI)

electromagnetic interference caused by leaking from a network device.

Electronic Industries Association/Telecommunications Industries Association (EIA/TIA)

An electronics industry standards body.

fault tolerance

The resiliency of a system, when faced with component or software failures; measures its degree of fault tolerance. The more fault-tolerant a system, the better it can cope with failure but the more it costs.

fax

A telephonic form of electronic document exchange that allows paper documents to be scanned and transmitted over the phone from sender to receiver. Fax requires sending and receiving equipment to work but is widely used worldwide

fax modem

A device for transmitting and receiving faxes from within an application at the user's desktop.

fiber distributed data interface (FDDI)

The fastest of the major network technologies and also the most expensive. FDDI standards call for implementation of a token passing network over fiber optic cable.

fiber-optic cable

A type of cable containing strands of plastic or glass that transmit information in the form of light pulses (instead of old-fashioned electrical pulses over metal wire).

file server

A server used primarily for data storage.

file transfer

The action of sending a file from one PC on the network to another, over the network.

filtering

Auditing the incoming or outgoing packets in the data stream. Usually done for security, audit, or network management purposes.

font

The look, size, and format of the printed text. Fonts can be built into the printer (internal), plugged into the printer via a cartridge, or generated from software.

frames

Information traveling on network cables is preceded by a bits making up a header and followed by bits making up an end of sequence, thereby *framing* the transmission.

frequency division multiplexing (FDM)

A way to share a communications channel between several users. Channels are subdivided by frequencies which are assigned to specific users.

FTP (file transfer protocol)

An Internet protocol and service that provides network file transfer between any two network nodes for which a user has file access rights (especially a remote host and your local host or desktop machine).

full-motion video

Video that moves quickly enough to seem like natural motion. This requires lots of data and is distinguished from stop-motion video, which is choppy, and stills, which don't move at all.

functional device

CCITT standards for ISDN describe these device types, necessary for the user-network interface to an ISDN.

gamma correction

A process for controlling features such as brightness, resolution and contrast by enhancing the black tones in an image. Some scanners handle gamma correction in the hardware, other scanners rely on software.

gateway

A program or service that knows how to convert input from one type of system to another type of system. A computer in a network that acts as an intelligent router, handling translations between different protocols.

grayscale

The range of gray values pixels can take on in any part of an image.

GUI (graphical user interface)

A generic name for any computer interface that uses graphics, windows, and a pointing device (like a mouse or trackball) instead a purely character-mode interface. Windows, Mac OS, and X11 are all examples of GUI interfaces.

header

The first bytes of a packet or frame. The header carries information such as the source and destination of a packet.

hertz (Hz)

Analog signal measurement. Cycles per second.

hierarchical

A structure where each level is subordinate to the one above it. An essay outline is hierarchical; so is the army.

hop

A node through which a network transmission passes.

hop count

Routers determine the best route for packets through an Internet by learning the distance, or hop count, between communicating nodes.

host
> Synonymous with computer, usually a mainframe or a minicomputer that provides ("host") services for other users on PCs or terminals.

hot swappable
> Parts, such as disk drives, that can be removed and installed without powering down their associated equipment are said to be *hot swappable*.

HTTP (hypertext transfer protocol)
> The TCP/IP-based communications protocol developed for use by WWW, HTTP defines how clients and servers communicate over the Web.

hub
> A device that consolidates and maintains signals in twisted-pair networks.

hypertext
> A form of electronic document in which highlighted words in the text may be used to access other parts of the document or other documents.

IAB (Internet Architecture Board, formerly Internet Activities Board)
> The governing body for the Internet, which manages standards, contracts certain aspects of the network's operation, and handles what little administration there is over the Internet.

IANA (Internet Assigned Numbers Authority)
> The arm of the IAB that assigns new IP address ranges to those who request them (and meet other necessary criteria).

IETF (Internet Engineering Task Force)
> The technical arm of the IAB, responsible for meeting current engineering needs on the Internet, the IETF also has custody of RFC content and related standards status.

impedance
> Measured in ohms, this has to do with how the cable transmits electricity. The effect of the properties of the communications medium.

infrared signals
> Signals carried on light waves making up a portion of the electromagnetic spectrum.

Institute of Electrical and Electronics Engineers (IEEE)
> An organization of technicians who set network standards for the physical and data link layers of the OSI model.

integrated digital network (IDN)

Communications industry standards call for complete replacement of analog telephone equipment with digital equipment. The resulting digital carrier network is known as the IDN.

intelligent hubs

Provide features like fault tolerance, remote management capabilities, SNMP support, and backplanes with multiple buses and multiple media type support.

interactive application

Any application that allows two or more users to interact with each other live; this might mean a video application where the participants can see and hear each other or a text-sharing application where each user can type and see each other's text.

interface

The particular subroutines, parameter passing mechanisms, and data that define the way in which two systems (which may be on the same or different machines) communicate with one another.

international standard

In generic terms, an international standard is one that is honored by more than one country; in practice, this usually refers to a standard controlled or honored by the International Standards Organization (ISO).

International Organization for Standardization (ISO)

A voluntary organization responsible for creating and coordinating international standards in numerous areas, which include communications and computer technology.

International Telegraph and Telephone Consultative Committee (CCITT)

See *CCITT*.

Internet

The name for a worldwide, TCP/IP-based networked computing community with more than 2 million users that links government, business, industry, and education.

internetwork

A network of networks; an internetwork is therefore a collection of individual media segments linked together by special equipment built for that purpose (e.g., bridges and routers are types of internetworking equipment).

interrupt level

> In a PC, an interrupt is a signal that the computer sends to a card. Every card must use a different interrupt; which one it uses is called its *interrupt level*.

I/O (input/output)

> How the computer gets information (input) and arranges for it to be displayed, printed, plotted, and so forth. (output).

IP

> Acronym for Internet Protocol. IP is the connectionless protocol used as a carrier for most TCP/IP transmissions. IP is also used as shorthand for TCP/IP, which is the name of the protocol suite used on the Internet, and consists of a collection of protocols and related networking applications including e-mail.

IP addresses

> IP addresses are unique numerical addresses based on a standard scheme and assigned by a central governing body. They are used to communicate between nodes on an internetwork.

IPX

> NetWare's transport protocol.

IS

> Information services. The department that is, in many organizations, responsible for the organization's data and computing needs.

ISDN (integrated services digital network)

> A high-bandwidth communications service, ISDN combines voice and digital services over a single medium, enabling telephone line to handle both on a single wire. ISDN is a subset of the CCITT broadband ISDN (B-ISDN).

ISDN B channel

> Provides bearer services. Carries voice, data, audio, and video data at a rate of 64 Kbps.

ISDN channels

> Pathways through an ISDN virtual circuit.

ISDN customer premises switching equipment (NT2)

> A digital device at a customer site that switches communications circuits between multiple customer devices and the NT1.

ISDN D channel

Designed to carry signals from users to the network and vice versa. Although it is intended for signal transmissions it may be configured for data transmission.

ISDN local loop terminator (NT1)

An ISDN functional device. Represents the connection between the ISDN service provider and the user network.

ISDN reference point

Interactions between devices and protocols occur at reference points designated for ISDN by the CCITT

ISDN terminal adapter (TA)

Converts a non-ISDN terminal (TE2) into a (TE1) ISDN terminal.

ISDN terminal equipment (TE1)

A terminal that supports digital transmissions over an ISDN. An ISDN functional device.

jitter

Slight changes in frequency that can cause loss of synchronization on a ring network.

kilobits per second

1024 bits per second. Refers to speed or bandwidth of transmission.

light-emitting diode (LED)

A device that converts digital signals to light signals. The light source for multimode fiber-optic transmission.

lobe

The cable running from a token-passing network station to an MAU

local access and transport areas (LATAs)

Telephone service areas.

local area network (LAN)

A network linked together by physical cables or short-haul connections, with a span that is generally less than 1 mile.

local loop

The cable that connects a user site with the local telephone carrier switching office (CO).

MAC layer addresses

Media access control (MAC) addresses are the hardware addresses used by nodes on a network to identify and locate one another. They are used to communicate between nodes on the same wire and are most often built right in to the NIC used for network communication.

map

In the context of the collection of data about your network, including a picture of the building and network layout, a database that contains information about every item in the network.

Mbps

Computer acronym for Megabits per second (mega is a special binary counting prefix for computer terms that means 220 or 1,048,476).

media access control (MAC) layer

In the OSI model, the MAC layer makes up part of the data link layer. The MAC layer deals with the interface between the network and the physical layer.

media interface connectors (MICs)

The connectors used to physically connect a fiber cable.

media network cable

The media is the physical carrier for network signals.

megahertz (MHz)

Hertz is a unit of cycles per second, so megahertz means a thousand cycles per second. This is the unit of speed in which modern CPUs are measured.

message

A piece of information sent between two entities. They might be users or computers on the network.

messaging services

Network services that send messages between computers, as opposed to file information or printing information.

MIS

Management information services.

modem

Stands for modulator/demodulator; a device that translates the digital signals of a computer into analog signals that can run over telephone lines.

modem pool

A method of sharing a limited number of modems between a large number of user's modular connectors. Connectors allow you to plug and unplug them into any jack they fit; you can move network equipment around easily with these.

monitor

Also known as *tube, screen, video display*. The device on which your computer's interactive output is displayed.

multimedia application

An application that presents information using sound, moving video, pictures, text, and other types of data together.

multimode fiber-optic cable

Fiber-optic cable that can carry multiple separate signals Each distinct signal is made by a separate frequency of light

multiple access

A feature of Ethernet, which indicates that more than one client can try to send data on the network at the same time.

multiplexing

Separation of a communications pipeline into multiple separate channels.

multistation access unit (MAU)

A concentrator used particularly on ring networks.

multitasking printer

Some printers can manage their buffer and memory well enough to handle queuing of one print job while printing another. They can print more than just one document at a time.

near-end crosstalk (NEXT)

Interference caused at the termination points of a communications link.

NetBEUI

Stands for NetBIOS Extended User Interface and was designed as a second-generation protocol especially to support NetBIOS-based communications. You can call NetBIOS and NetBEUI a matched set—that's what Microsoft and IBM use for their networking products.

NetBIOS

Stands for Networked Basic Input-Output *System* and was designed by IBM as a networked extension to PC BIOS. NetBIOS is a higher-level protocol that runs on top of lots of lower-level protocols, including IPX and TCP/IP as well as others. Even though NetBIOS is pretty old, it's very easy to program with and consequently is used in lots of different networked applications on a broad range of computers and operating systems.

NetWare

The network operating system software developed by Novell, Inc. NetWare comes in several different flavors targeted at different sizes of installations.

NetWare core protocol (NCP)

NCP is the service protocol for NetWare. Virtually every service that NetWare can provide has an NCP used to let users send requests for that service and start the process of delivering in response to that request. The services provided by the NetWare NCPs range from file transfer to directory services lookups.

NetWare loadable module (NLM)

A program loaded at the file server on a NetWare network. NLMs can be LAN drivers, backup applications, or utilities.

network

Any collection of machines or devices that are connected physically by some type of physical transport medium (i.e., wire). Network devices may all be on the same wire, or they may be connected over a series of wires using bridges, or repeaters.

network address

A unique name by which a particular networked computer is distinguished from all other computers on the same network. The network address is usually a string of numbers, letters, or some combination of numbers and letters.

network administrator

The person responsible for seeing that a network runs smoothly and efficiently and maintaining it and solving problems if they occur.

network analysis tools

Hardware and software that can help you track down problems on your network.

network driver

The piece of software that runs on a PC and provides translation between the network interface card in that PC and the network software running on that PC.

Network device interface standard (NDIS)

An interface specification providing a standard interface at the data link between the device driver and the NIC.

NFS (network filing system)

A distributed file system originated by Sun Microsystems that's in wide use in TCP/IP networking environments today. NFS lets users access remote file systems as if they were an extension of their local hard drives.

network hub

See *hub*.

network interface card

Sometimes abbreviated as NIC, a network interface card provides the link between a computer and the networking technology and topology it wishes to use.

network layer

The layer of the OSI network architectural model. That handles addressing and distribution of packets across internetworks.

network operating system

The software that runs on your network server and moderates the clients' access to the server resources.

network performance

How well the network is doing its job. Usually used to refer to speed of response (after you press Return, does the request happen immediately or do you have time to get coffee while waiting for it?).

network utilization

The amount of network usage, usually expressed as the percentage of bandwidth consumed on the medium for a specific period of time (peak utilization of 80% is no big deal, sustained utilization of 80% usually means it's time to divide and grow your network).

node

An addressable device attached to an internetwork.

non-ISDN terminal equipment (TE2)
> Terminal equipment that does not support ISDN. A TE2 must be attached to an ISDN terminal adapter (TA) to access the ISDN.

OCR (optical character recognition)
> The process of scanning an image, recognizing any text and converting it into an editable binary file.

ODI (open datalink interface)
> A specification for writing LAN drivers that saves vendors from work and gives users a certain comfort level that their ODI drivers will work in a predictable way.

offline
> In an environment where a computer can participate on a network or take part in a telephonic connection, a computer that isn't participating is said to be offline. Offline also means that a device is unavailable (e.g., a printer or other peripheral device can also be offline).

online
> The opposite of offline; that is, online means that a computer or device is participating on a network, part of an active telephone connection, or available to prospective users.

open standard
> The opposite of proprietary standard. Production or protocol standards released to the general community.

operating system (OS)
> The software that runs in your PC, whether you're on a network or not, and manages access to such resources in the PC as your PC's diskettes, hard drive, and memory.

optical disk
> Data storage device that writes to something that looks like a CD.

optical time-domain reflectometry
> In English, this means that, because light is scattered through the fibers in the cable, the signals don't all arrive at once. It's really a technique for using propagation delay to measure cable length.

OS
> See *operating system.*

OSI (open systems interconnect)

A collection of networking and communications standards defined and managed by the International Standards Organization (ISO).

packet

The name for a chunk of data being sent over a network. The size and format of the packet depend on the network protocol over which it's being sent. Information is carried across networks in blocks of information called *packets*. Transmission of uniform packets of information allows for many hosts on a network to communicate simultaneously over the same transport medium. Packets also contain information about themselves that allow for error detection and correction across the network.

patch panel

A collection of modular jacks that let you connect different network devices to each other easily, using a short cable called a *patch cable* rather than rewiring the network.

PC

A computer acronym for personal computer, *PC* usually refers to an IBM-PC or its clone equivalent, even though any microprocessor-based computer that sits on a user's desktop could rightfully be called a personal computer.

peer-to-peer

A method of networking used to share local resources across the network. A server-based network requires all shared resources to reside on a centralized server. A peer-to-peer network gives everyone on the network the opportunity to share his or her local stuff with others on the network.

peripheral

Any device attached to a PC or to the network that is not a PC. Peripherals include printers, scanners, modems, and fax machines.

personal computer

Any computer that is typically used by one person at a time. Might refer to Amiga, Macintosh, IBM-PC or clone, or any other small computer.

phone closet

Often a place where all the phone wiring collects. If your network wiring has a lot in common with the phone system, you'll get to know this room.

physical layer

The layer of the OSI network architectural model that deals with specifications for network cabling and the nature of the electrical signals on the network.

Pixel

Picture element (or PEL). This is the smallest element representing part of an image, usually a dot.

PPP (point-to-point protocol)

A newer, more efficient asynchronous TCP/IP protocol, designed specifically for users who wish to make the most of a dial-in connection to an ISP.

port

Short for transport, usually used as a verb. In computer jargon, *porting code* refers to the effort involved in taking a program written for one system and altering it to run on another system.

port address

In TCP/IP-speak, a port address refers to the socket identifier that a program or a service seeks to address for a specific type of communications. Most TCP/IP protocols have "well-known port addresses" associated to them (e.g., HTTP's is 80), but system configurations allow other port addresses to be used (which can sometimes be a good idea for security reasons).

PostScript

A page description language defined by Adobe Systems, PostScript files usually carry the extension .ps in the UNIX world and are a common format for exchanging nicely formatted print files.

preamble

A frame field. This field flags the beginning of a frame.

presentation layer

The layer of the OSI network architectural model that handles formatting and encryption of data.

PRI

See *primary rate interface*.

primary rate interface (PRI)

An ISDN interface consisting of 23 64kbps B channels and 1 64kbps D channel.

print queue

The mechanism that handles requests for printing from users and that supplies the print image files to the printer in the proper order. See also queue.

print resolution

The quality of a print image. This is usually measured in dots per inch (dpi). It means just that. If you have 300 dpi, your image will be good. If you have 10 dpi, your image will be really bad. Generally, the higher the resolution, the higher the price tag and the more memory your printer will need.

print server

A PC whose main job is to handle print jobs, making sure they don't all print at the same time and notifying users when they are complete.

printer driver

A piece of software installed in applications that translates the application's print request into something understandable by the printer.

printer sharing buffer

A gadget that collects print jobs and doles them out to the printer one at a time, so that if several people send jobs to the printer at once they don't all print on top of each other. Not necessary if you have a full network, because the network software takes care of this for you.

proprietary

Refers to anything developed by a particular company and that works only with that company's other offerings.

proprietary standard

Standards set by an organization and protected as a trade secret.

protocol

A set of rules that define interactions of some type. In networking, stations must share a protocol or they cannot talk to one another.

protocol analysis

performing network analysis functions by examining traffic governed by specific protocols.

protocol analysis software

software that tells you about your network performance. Also called *network monitoring software*.

protocol set

See *protocol suite.*

protocol suite
    A collection of networking protocols that together define a complete set of tools and communications facilities for network access and use (e.g. TCP/IP, OSI, or IPX/SPX).

protocol stack
    See *protocol suite*.

queue
    A line. In computing, a line of print jobs or packets maintained in the order in which they are received.

radio frequency interference (RFI)
    Electronic interference caused by leaking of radiation from a device attached to network cable.

RAM
    Random access memory. High speed data storage in a computer. Usually anything stored in here vanishes when you turn off the computer.

random access memory
    See *RAM*.

raster graphics
    An image represented by dots or a bitmap.

redirector
    A piece of software that runs in a workstation computer to determine whether a command should be handled locally or sent to the network. If it's a network command, the redirector also passes the command on to the network software.

remote-control software
    Software that lets you control one PC from another, over the network.

remote location
    A site or machine elsewhere on the network, remote location also can refer to a machine that is only intermittently connected to a network (usually via a dial-up connection).

repeater
    A network device that takes in signals and retransmits them. Used to make sure that network signals don't get too weak as they travel over long distances.

RFC

A computer acronym for request for comment, a document controlled by the Internet Activities Board (IAB), the governing body for the TCP/IP protocol suite (all TCP/IP protocols, interfaces, and applications are governed by related RFCs).

request for proposal (RFP)

A document that describes everything you need for your network installation or expansion, so that a vendor can give you an estimate on how much it will all cost (that's the proposal).

resistance

A factor of impedance.

ring topology

A network layout in which each PC is connected to the one next to it. Much like a bus topology, except that the ends are connected together to form a circle.

RIP (routing information protocol)

A broadcast protocol (it's addressed to everyone who's listening on a network) that gets used one time per minute by every IPX router on a network to declare what it knows about how to get around on the network. (For Net-Ware 3.11 or higher, any server can be a router.) Routers exchange RIP packets to keep the common knowledge of how a collection of individual networks, called an *internetwork*, is laid out. This information is used to move packets around, which is why the servers that do it are called *routers*.

RJ-45

A type of connector that looks a bit like a modular phone connector.

router

Machines that connect nodes on a network. Routers perform all the functions offered by the network operating system and are responsible for knowing how the network topology is configured and transferring information from one part of the network to another.

scanner

A hardware device that converts printed text or graphics into a binary file format. Scanners use a sensor to detect reflected light from images and convert those images into binary file formats.

SAP (service advertising protocol)

> Advertises the services available on the network. SAP is a broadcast protocol, and each server and sends out its collection of SAPs one time per minute in versions of NetWare before 4.x. In NetWare 4.x, the number of SAPs can be adjusted.

SCSI (small computer system interface)

> An interface standard for PCs and peripheral devices.

segment

> A section of a network. Multiple segments are connected by the network's backbone.

server

> A PC whose function is to provide access to network resources and services.

services

> What networked computers request or provide. The services available depend on the network software and the applications available on a particular network.

session layer

> The layer of the OSI network architectural model that establishes and maintains virtual connections for the duration of network communications.

shielded twisted-pair (STP)

> Twisted-pair cable with an insulating outer sheath added for noise reduction.

Simple Network Management Protocol

> See *SNMP*.

single-mode fiber-optic cable

> Fiber-optic cable that transmits signals of only one frequency of light.

SMTP

> E-mail acronym for Simple Mail Transfer Protocol, SMTP is the basic TCP/IP e-mail application.

SNA (Systems Network Architecture)

> IBM's basic protocol suite. Where there's a mainframe or an AS/400, you also typically find SNA. Because SNA was one of the pioneering protocols, companies that invested heavily in mainframe technology in the 1960s and 1970s also invested in building large-scale SNA networks.

sneakernet

A type of networking involving copying files to disk and walking (in sneakers) to another machine and loading the files. An early form of networking still used to varying degrees in many organizations.

SNMP (simple network management protocol)

A set of rules describing how TCP/IP networks do basic maintenance and system management operations.

socket

A unique identifier for one end of a network connection. The combination of the network address, host address, and port number.

specifications

The collection of data about a piece of equipment that tells how you can expect it to behave. Specifications tell you how far you can run cable, how many ports you can have on a server, etc.

SPX (Sequenced Packet eXchange)

A guaranteed delivery protocol that NetWare occasionally uses.

SQL (structured query language)

A database query language developed at IBM in broad use in DBMS systems worldwide (an ANSI standard version has been defined).

standard

A program, system, protocol, or other computer component that has been declared to be standard may be the subject of an official published standard from some standards setting body, or it may simply have acquired that status through widespread or long-term use. When talking about standards, it's always important to find out if the designation is official or otherwise.

start frame delimiter (SFD)

Part of a frame field. This is the final byte of the preamble of a frame.

star topology

A network layout where every computer is connected to a central hub. See also *ring and bus topologies*.

stored program switches

Early digital telephone carrier switches.

switch box

A box that lets you connect two (or more) peripherals to it and switch between them by turning a knob.

synchronous
> A method of communications wherein all communicating parties interact with one another at the same time.

T1
> A digital transmission link with a capacity of 1.544 Mbps. T1 (also written T-1) is a standard for digital transmission in the United States, Canada, Hong Kong, and Japan.

T3
> A digital transmission link with a capacity of 28 T1 lines (44.746 Mbps).

tandem offices
> The physical termination of multiple telephone communications links.

tandem switch
> Switches telephone circuits.

TCP/IP (transmission control protocol/Internet protocol)
> The basic suite of protocols upon which the Internet runs.

telephony
> Communications technology.

TELNET
> A TCP/IP protocol and service that lets a user on one computer emulate a terminal attached to another computer.

terminal
> A display device for a computer system, usually a cathode-ray terminal (CRT), most often with an attached keyboard, that has little or no local processing power (which is why terminals are often called *dumb terminals*.

thick Ethernet
> See *10Base-5*.

thin Ethernet
> See *10Base-2*.

throughput
> A measure of the speed of a network-access method, typically stated in bps (bits per second).

time domain reflectometer (TDR)
> A device that you can use to measure the length of electrically conductive cables in your network.

token

A piece of data passed around in certain types of networks. It gives whoever holds it the ability to send data.

token ring

Another networking technology, like ARCnet, that works by token passing. Can run much faster than either Ethernet or ARCnet.

topology

The pattern in which you lay out your network wiring. Common topologies are ring, bus, and star.

tractor feed

A method of moving paper through printers. The feeders have little nubs that fit into holes on the sides of the paper; as the nubs advance like the tread on a tractor, the paper advances as well.

traffic levels

Amount of data that travels across your network.

transceiver

Any device which is capable of receiving and transmitting signals. It enables you to connect a network adapter for one type of media to another type of media. Commonly, you use a transceiver in Ethernet to translate from thin Ethernet to unshielded twisted-pair cable. In token ring, a media filter replaces the transceiver.

TWAIN (toolkit without an interesting name)

An industry standard application interface for image capture. For example, if a program is TWAIN-compatible, then you'll be able to use it to edit a scanned image. Such editing may only consist of brightness and contrast controls, but it may save steps by eliminating the need for an image editor.

twisted pair cable

A pair of insulated wires twisted together to reduce electrical interference.

uninterruptable power supply (UPS)

Device that sits between the AC power jack in the wall and your expensive network equipment and protects the latter from spikes or sags in the former.

UNIX

The name of a specific type of computer operating system, originated at Bell Labs in the 1970s. Because it is widely taught in colleges and universities worldwide, UNIX is one of the most familiar OSs in the computing community.

unshielded twisted-pair (UTP)

Twisted-pair wiring without the shielding. Vulnerable to EMI.

upgrade

Adding new software or hardware to an existing network device, so you don't have to replace it.

UPS

See *uninterruptable power supply.*

vector graphic

An image represented by lines instead of dots.

WAIS (wide area information service)

Collection of programs that implement a specific protocol for information retrieval, able to index large-scale collections of data around the Internet. WAIS provides content-oriented query services to WAIS clients and is one of the most powerful Internet search tools available.

wide area network (WAN)

A network that extends over a relatively large area, certainly outside of a single building. Could extend across a city, a continent, or the entire globe.

wireless network

One that works, as you might imagine, without wires. Instead, the data signals are transmitted over broadcast frequencies.

wiring centers

See *hub.*

work group

A collection of individuals who work together and are interconnected via a network of computers.

workstation

A desktop computer, usually a more powerful machine than an ordinary IBM-PC or clone, often with a high speed reduced instruction set computer (RISC) processor, often running UNIX as its OS.

XNS

NetWare's protocols are derived from a similar protocol set developed at Xerox, called the *Xerox Networking System* and abbreviated as XNS. Lots of XNS-derived protocols are out in the networking world, but IPX/SPX is the most prevalent.

VENDOR CONTACT INFORMATION

1Soft Corp.
PO Boxx 1320
Middletown, CA 95461
(707) 987-0256
FAX: (707) 987-3150

3Com Corp.
5400 Bayfront Plaza
Santa Clara, CA 95052-8145
(800) NET-3COM or (408) 764-5000
FAX: (408) 764-5032
Products: Transcend Enterprise Mngr

3rd Planet Software
9911 W. Pico Blvd, Suite 1001
Los Angeles, CA 90034
(310) 553-2808
FAX: (310) 553-1830
Products: Pro Menu v2.02, Network
Assistant Plus v6.58, Exac, iMail v1.0

900 Support Inc.
18277 SW Boones Ferry Road, Bldg. #A,
Second Floor
Portland, OR 97224-7600
(800) 777-9608, ext. 3017
FAX: (503) 639-3946

A Bit Better Software Publishing
1551 Broadway, 6th Floor
Tacoma, WA 98402
(206) 627-6111
FAX: (206) 627-6222

a la mode Inc.
1015 Waterwood Parkway, Bldg F
Edmond, OK 73034
(800) ALAMODE or (405) 359-3346
FAX: (405) 359-8612

A'n D Cable Products Inc.
5100-1B Clayton Road, Suite 302
Concord, CA 94521-3139
(800) 394-3008
FAX: (510) 672-0317

a/Soft Developmont Inc.
One Executive Park Drive
Bedford, NH 03110
(603) 666-6699
FAX: (603) 666-6460

Abelson Communications Inc.
1685 Grand Ave.
Baldwin, NY 11510
(516) 546-2286
FAX: (516) 546-2271

ABL Electronics Corp.
10942 Beaver Dam Road
Hunt Valley, MD 21030
(800) 726-0610
FAX: (410) 584-2790

Abra Software
888 Executive Center Drive West
Suite 300
St. Petersburg, FL 33702
(800) 847-2272 or (813) 579-1111
FAX: (813) 578-2178

AC TECHNOLOGY Inc.
8201 Greensboro Drive, Suite 220
McLean, VA 22102
(800) 228-4365 or (703) 448-5581
FAX: (703) 847-4223

Accelr8 Tochnology Corp.
303 E. 17th Ave, Suite 108
Denver, CO 80203
(800) 582-8898 or (303) 863-8088
FAX: (303) 863-1218

AcCourting Systems Inc.
2950 W. Square Lake Road, Suite 207
Troy, MI 48098
(800) 968-8305 or (810) 641-5150
FAX: (810) 641-5947

Accton Technology Corp.
1962 Zanker Road
San Jose, CA 95112
(800) 926-9288 or (408) 452-8900
FAX: (408) 452-8988

Accu-Tech Corp.
200 Hembree Park Drive
Roswell, GA 30076-3890
(404) 751-9473
FAX: (404) 475-4659

Acculogic Inc.
13715 Alton Parkway
IrvInc. CA 92716
(714) 454-2441 or (800) 234-7811
FAX: (714) 454-8527

Ace/North Hills
7934 Nieman Road
Lenexa, KS 66214
(800) 998-4223 or (913) 888-4999
FAX: (913) 888-4103

ACS Telecom
25825 Eshelman Ave.
Lomita, CA 90717
(310) 325-3055 or (800) 325-0425
FAX: (310) 325-3059

AcuPrim Inc.
5964 La Place Court, Suite 125
Carlsbad, CA 92008
(619) 929-4808

ADC Kentrox
14375 NW Science Park Drive
Portland, OR 97229
(800) 733-5511 or (503) 643-1681
FAX: (503) 641-3341

ADC Legal Systems Inc.
1209 Edgewater Drive, Ste 100
Orlando, FL 32854-0086
(407) 843-8992
FAX: (408) 841-9814

Addtron Technology Co. Ltd.
47968 Fremont Blvd.
Fremont, CA 94538
(800) 998-4638 or (510) 770-0120

Adeptec
691 S. Milpitas Blvd.
Milpitas, CA 95035
(800) 934-2766
FAX: (408) 957-7150

ADTRAN Inc.
901 Explorer Blvd.
Huntsville, AL 35806
(800) 827-0807 or (205) 971-8000
FAX: (205) 971-8699

Advanced Computer Communications
(ACC)
10261 Bubb Road
Cupertino, CA 95014
(800) 444-7854 or (408) 366-9654

Advanced Concepts Inc.
4129 N. Point Washington Ave.
Milwaukee, WI 53210-1029
(800) 222-OPEN or (414) 963-0999
FAX: (414) 963-2090

Advanced Digital Information Corp.
(ADIC)
14737 NE 87th St, PO Box 97057
Redmond, WA 98073-9757
(800) 336-1233 or (206) 881-8004
FAX: (206) 881-2296

Advanced Digital Systems Inc.
135 Second Ave.
Waltham, MA 02154
(617) 990-0330
FAX: (617) 890-0222

Advanced Information Managememt
12940 Harbor Drive
Woodbridge, VA 22192-2921
(703) 643-1002
FAX: (703) 643-2722

Advanced Logic Research Inc.
9401 Jeronimo
IrvInc. CA 92718
(800) 444-4ALR or (714) 581-6770
FAX: (714) 581-9240

Advanced Network Systems Inc.
16257 Monterey Road
Morgan Hill, CA 95037
(408) 779-2209 or (800) 333-6381
FAX: (408) 776-8511

Advanced Relay Communications Inc.
1896 Columbia St.
Eugene, OR 97403
(503) 345-9178
FAX: (503) 484-0216

Advanced Software Technology
5500 Shellmound St, Suite 140
Emeryville, CA 94608
(510) 652-8400
FAX: (510) 652-7054

AEGIS SOFTWARE Inc.
335 Central Ave.
Lawrence, NY 11559
(516) 374-0800
FAX: (516) 374-0846
Products: SyMon, Domain*Manager,
Log*Proxy, Network*State, OS*Proxy,
OS/EYE*NODE, Poll*Proxy, Stat*View

AeroComm Inc.
10563 Lackman Road
Lenexa, KS 66219
(913) 492-2320
FAX: (913) 492-1243

AFIC Technologies Inc.
160 Broadway, Suite 600
New York, NY 10038
(800) 289-1899 or (212) 406-2503
FAX: (212) 406-2415

AGE Logic Inc.
9985 Pacific Heights Blvd.
San Diego, CA 92121-4337
(619) 455-8600
FAX: (619) 597-6030

Aladdin Software Security Inc.
The Empire State Building
350 Fifth Ave. Suite 7204
New York, NY 10118
(800) 223-4277 or (212) 564-5678
FAX: (212) 564-3377

ALANTEC Corp.
70 Plumeria Drive
San Jose, CA 95134
(408) 955-9000 or (800) ALANTEC
FAX: (408) 955-9500

Alcom Corp.
1616 N. Shoreline Blvd.
Mt View, CA 94043
(415) 694-7000
FAX: (415) 694-7070

Aleph Takoma Systems Inc.
7319 Willow Ave.
Takoma Park, MD 20912
(800) 368-5207 or (813) 261-6678
FAX: (813) 261-6549
Products: WinINSTALL

Alexander UN
100 Perimeter Road
Nashua, NH 03063
(603) 880-8800
FAX: (603) 880-8881

Alfa Inc.
325 E. North Ave.
Westfield, NJ 07090
(908) 789-2068
FAX: (908) 789-2403

Alida Inc.
27 McDermott Place
Bergenfield, NJ 07621
(800) 883-GURU or (201) 364-0080
FAX: (201) 384-3382
Products: Gurutape

Alisa Systems Inc.
221 E. Walnut St, Suite 175
Pasadena, CA 91101
(800) 628-3274 or (818) 792-9474
FAX: (818) 792-9474

Allied Telesis Inc.
575 E. Middlefield Road
Mountain View, CA 94043
(800) 424-4284
FAX: (415) 964-8250

Alloy, A Div. of
Impulse Technologies Inc.
25 Porter Road
Lttleton, MA 01460
(508) 486-0001
FAX: (508) 486-4108

Alpha Wire Corp.
711 Lidgervood Ave.
Elizabeth, NJ 07207
(800) 522-5742
FAX: (908) 925-7429

Alphatronix Inc.
PO Box 13978
Research Triangle Park, NC 27709-3978
(800) 849-2611
FAX: (919) 544-4079

Alps Electric (USA) Inc.
3553 N. First St.
San Jose, CA 95134-1898
(800) 825-2577 or (408) 432-6000
FAX: (408) 432-6035

Alsys
10251 Vista Sorrento Parkway
Suite 300
San Diego, CA 92121
(619) 457-2700
FAX: (619) 452-1334

Alta Research Corp.
600 S. Federal Highway
Deerfield Beach, FL 33441
(800) 423-8535 or (305) 428-8535
FAX: (305) 428-8678

Alternative Computer Technology Inc.
7908 Cin-Day Road, Suite WB
Cincinnati, OH 45069
(513) 755-1957
FAX: (513) 755-1958

Always Technology Corp.
31336 Via Colinas, Suite 101
Westlake Village, CA 91362
(818) 597-1400
FAX: (818) 597-1496

Americable
700 Hilltop Drive
Itasca, IL 60143
(800) 533-4418
FAX: (708) 595-3340

American Data Corp.
2662 Holcomb Bridge Road Suite 340
Alpharetta, GA 30202
(800) 783-9799 or (404) 998-5554
FAX: (404) 998-6226
Products: CYBEX AUTOBOOT
COMMANDER

American Hytech Corp.
565 William Pitt Way
Pittsburgh, PA 15238
(412) 826-3333
FAX: (412) 826-3335
Products: NetGuru Mngr, NetGuru
Designer, NetBook

American Power Conversion
132 Fairgrounds Road
West Kingston, RI 02892
(800) 800-4APC

AMP
PO Box 3608
Harrisburg, PA 17105-3608
(800) 522-6752
FAX: (717) 986-7575

Andrew Corp.
10500 W. 153rd St.
Orland Park, IL 60462
(800) 328-2696
FAX: (800) 861-1700

Andyne Computing Limited
552 Princess S1
Kingston, ONT K7L 1C7 Canada
(800) 267-0665 or (613) 548-4355
FAX: (613) 548-3608

Anixter Inc.
4711 Golf Road
Skokie, IL 60076
(708) 677-2600, ext. 2018
FAX: (708) 674-3045

Annexus Date Systems
10559 Lansford Lane
San Diego, CA 92126
(619) 530-0019
FAX: (619) 530-0096

ANS
100 Clearbrook Road
Elmsford NY 10523-1116
(800) 456-8267 or (703) 758-7700
FAX: (703) 758-7717
Products: ANS NOC Outsourcing
Services, TrenData

AP Profossional
525 B St, Suite 1900
San Diego, CA 92101-4495
(800) 3131-APP
FAX: (800) 336-7377 or (407) 345-2525

Apertus Technologies Inc.
7275 Flying Cloud Drive
Eden Prairie, MN 55344
(800) 876-7671 or (612) 828-0300
FAX: (612) 828-0454

Apex PC Solutions Inc.
4580 150th Ave. NE
Redmond, WA 98052
(206) 861-5858
FAX: (206) 861-5757

Apexx Technology Inc.
506 S. 11th St, Suite D
Boise, ID 83702
(800) 767-4858 or (208) 336 9400

Apiary
10201 W. Markham, Suite 101
Little Rock, AR 72205
(501) 221-3699
FAX: (501) 221-7412

Applications Management Corp.
8150 Leesburg Pike, Suite 1100
Vienna, VA 22182
(703) 893-1307
FAX: (703) 827-0716
Products: NS/LANExec, Attache,
Emissary, Envoy

applied computing devices Inc.
100 S. Campus Drive / Aleph Park
Terre Haute, IN 47802
(812) 232-6051
FAX: (812) 231-5280
Products: ACD-SNMP

Applied Educational Systems Inc.
PO Box 2220
Concord, NH 03302
(800) 237-5530 or (603) 225-5511
FAX: (603) 225-2311

Apsylog Inc.
1900 Emabarcadero Road, Suite 209
Palo Alto CA 94303
(800) APSYLOG or (415) 812-7700
FAX: (415) 812-7707
Products: Cabling System Mngr,
APTNet/Mirror Image

APT Communications Inc.
9607 Doctor Perry Road, Suite 107
Ijamsville, MD 21754
(800) 842-0626 or (301) 874-3305
FAX: (301) 874-5255

Arabesque Software Inc.
2340 130th Ave. NE
Bellevue, WA 98005-1754
(800) 457-4243 or (206) 885 4272
FAX: (206) 885-0127

Arcada Software Inc.
37 Skyline Drive, Suite 1101
Lake Mary, FL 32646
(800) 3ARCADA
FAX: (407) 333-7770
Products: Backup Exec for
NetWare v5.01

Archtek America Corp.
18549 Gale Ave.
City of Industry, CA 91748
(818) 912-9800
FAX: (818) 912-9700

Arco Computer Products Inc.
2750 N. 29th St, Suite 318
Hollywood, FL 33020
(800) 458-1666
FAX: (305) 925-2889

Armon Networking Inc.
314 E. Carrillo St., Suite 3
Santa Barbara, CA 93101
(800) 499-RMON or (805) 965-0859
FAX: (805) 965-5689

Armor Systems Inc.
324 N. Orlando Ave.
Maitland, FL 32751
(407) 629-0753
FAX: (407) 629-1401

Arnet Corp.
618 Grassmore Park Drive, Suite 6
Nashville, TN 37211
(800) 366-8844 or (615) 834-8000
FAX: (615) 834-5399

Artisoft Inc.
2202 N. Forbes Blvd.
Tucson, AZ 85745
(800) 233-5564
FAX: (602) 670-7359

Asante Technologies Inc.
821 Fox Lane
San Jose, CA 95131
(800) 662-9686 or (408) 435-8388
FAX: (408) 432-7511
Products: AsanteView

Ascend Communications Inc.
1275 Harbor Bay Parkway
Alameda, CA 94502
(800) 621-9578 or (510) 769-6001
FAX: (510) 814-2300

ASD Software. Inc.
4650 Arrow Highway, Suite E-6
Montclair, CA 91763
(909) 624-2594, ext. 316
FAX: (909) 624-9574

askSam Systems
119 S. Washington St. PO Box 1428
Perry, FL 32347
(904) 584-6590 or (800) 800-1997
FAX: (904) 584-7481

ASP Computer Products Inc.
160 San Gabriel Drive
Sunnyvale, CA 94086
(800) 445-6190 or (408) 746-2965
FAX: (408) 746-2803

AST Research Inc.
16215 Allon Parkway
InvInc. CA 92718
(800) 876-4278
FAX: (800) 926-1278

Async Systems Inc.
203 Middlesex Turnpike
Burlington, MA 01803
(617) 270-3530
FAX: (617) 270-3580

AT&T Advanced Technology Systems
PO Box 20046, Room C3D17
Greensboro, NC 27420
(800) 553-8805 or (910) 279-7829
FAX: (910) 279-6841

AT&T Global Information Solutions
1700 S. Patterson Blvd.
Dayton, OH 45729
(51 3) 445-5000
Products: StarSENTRY

AT&T Secure Communications Systems
PO Box 20046
Greensboro, NC 27420
(800) 243-7883 or (910) 279-3411
FAX: (910) 279-5746

ATG CYGNET Inc.
2560 Junction Ave.
San Jose, CA 95134-1902
(408) 954-1800
FAX: (408) 954-9391

Attachmate Canada Inc.
3739 N. Fraser Way, Unit 101
Burnaby, BC VSJ 5G1 Canada
(800) 663-8702
FAX: (604) 431-0818

Attachmate Corp.
3617 131st Ave. SE
Bellevue, WA 98006
(800) 426-6283 or (206) 644-4010
FAX: (206) 747-9924
Products: ZIP! Console, Backup Exec for
Windows NT v5.01, Storage Exec for
Windows NT Server v2.0

ATTO Technology Inc.
40 Hazelwood Drive, Suite 106
Amherst, NY 14228
(716) 691-1999
FAX: (716) 691-9353

Augmentx
9351 Grant St.
Thornton, CO 80229
(800) 232-4687
FAX: (303) 451-1905

Automated Programming
Technologies Inc.
30100 Telegraph, Suite 402
Bingham Farms, MI 48025
(810) 540-9877
FAX: (810) 540-0403
Products: APTNet/MVS

Automated Systems Methodologies Inc.
16100 Fairchild Drive Boatyard, Suite 105
Clearwater, FL ZIP
(800) 992-0120 or (813) 535-7272
FAX: (813) 531-7510

Avail Systems
4760 Walnut St.
Boulder, CO 80301
(303) 444-4018
FAX: (303) 546-4219

Avalan Technology Inc.
PO Box 6888, 116 Hopping Brook Park
Holliston, MA 01746
(800) 441-2281 or (508) 429-6482
FAX: (508) 429-3179

Avanti Technology Inc.
13492 Research Blvd, Suite l20-271
Austin, TX 78750
(512) 335-1168 or (800) 638-1168
FAX: (512) 335-7838
Products: Nconsole

Axis Communications Inc.
99 Rosewood Drive Suite 170
Danvers, MA 01923
(506) 777-7957
FAX: (508) 777-9905

AXON Networks Inc.
199 Wells Ave.
Newton, MA 02159
(800) 444-AXON or (617) 630-9600

Azure Technologies
63 South Street
Hopkinton, MA 01748-2212
(508) 435-3800, (800) 233-3800
FAX: (508) 435-0448
Products: LANWANPharaoh v5.0

Banyan Systems Inc.
120 Flanders Road
Westboro, MA 01581-5013
(800) 2-BANYAN or (508) 898-1000
FAX: (508) 898-1755

Baranof Software Inc.
479 Washington St.
Brighton, MA 02135
(800) 462-4565 or (617) 783-0080
FAX: (617) 254-1412
Products: MailCheck , LAN Support
Center Network Management Tools

Baseline Data Systems Inc.
3625 Del Amo Blvd., Suite 245
Torrance, CA 90503
(800) 428-5325 or (310) 214-8528
FAX: (310) 214-8529

Baseline Software
PO Box 1219
Sausalito, CA 94966
(800) 829-9955 or (415) 332-7763
FAX: (415) 332-8032

Bay Networks, Inc.
4401 Great America Parkway, PO Box
58185
Santa Clara, CA 95052-8185
(800) PRO-NTWK
FAX: (408) 988-5525

Beame & Whiteside Software
706 Hillsborough St.
Raleigh, NC 27603-1655
(800) INFO-NFS
FAX: (919) 831-8990

Belden Wire & Cable Co.
PO Box 1980
Richmond, IN 47375
(800) BELDEN-4
FAX: (317) 983-5294

Belkin Components
1303 Walnut Park Way
Compton, CA 90220
(800) 223-5546 or (310) 898-1100
FAX: (310) 898-1111

Bellcore Training and Education Center
6200 Route 53
Lisle, IL 60532
(800) TEACH-ME
FAX: (708) 960-6360

Benchmark Publications Inc.
P0 Box 1594
New Canaan, CT 06840
(203) 966-6653 or (203) 659-5830
FAX: (203) 972-7129

BENDATA Inc.
1755 Telstar Drive, Suite 100
Colorado Springs, CO 80920
(800) 778-7889 or (719) 531-5007
FAX: (719) 528-4230
Products: First Level Support

Benedict Computer
220 Felton Drive
Menlo Park, CA 94025
(415) 323-0148
FAX: (415) 323-0158

Berkeley Software Design Inc.
7759 Delmonico Drive
Colorado Springs, CO 80919
(800) 800-4273 or (719) 593-9445
FAX: (719) 598-4238

Berkshire Products
2180 Pleasant Hill Road, Suite A-5185
Duluth, GA 30136
(404) 271-0088
FAX: (404) 932-0082

BESCO Computer Centers
1213 Hwy 45 N, PO Box 1217
Columbus, MS 39701
(800) 844-O860
FAX: (601) 327-2383

Best Power Technology Inc.
PO Box 28O
Necedah, Wl 54646
(800) 356-5794 or (608) 565-7200
FAX: (608) 565-2221

Binar Graphics Inc.
30 Mitchell Blvd.
San Rafael, CA 94903-2034
(415) 491-4182
FAX: (415) 491-1164

Bit Software Inc.
47987 Fremont Blvd.
Fremont, CA 94538
(510) 490-2928
FAX: (510) 490-9490

Blink Inc.
8001 W. Broad St.
Richmond, VA 23294
(804) 747-6700
FAX: (804) 747-4200

Blue Ocean Software Inc.
15310 Amberlv Drive, Suite 250
Tampa, FL 33647
(813) 977-4553
FAX: (813) 979-4447
Products: Track-It!, PC GALAXY

BlueRithm Software
21823 N. Glen Drive
Colbert, WA 99005-9415
(509) 468-1434
FAX: (509) 467-2699
Products: Aeris v3.2

Bluestone
1000 Briggs Road
Mount Laurel, NJ 08054
(609) 727-4600
FAX: (609) 778-8125
Products: Aeris v3.2

Boca Research Inc.
6413 Congress Ave.
Boca Raton, FL 33487
(407) 997-6227
FAX: (407) 997-0918
Products: Aeris v3.2

Bomar Interconnect Products Inc.
1850 Route 46
Ledgewood, NJ 07852
(201) 347-4040
FAX: (201) 347-2111
Products: Aeris v3.2

Brattle Systems Inc.
1100 Massachusetts Ave.
Arlington, MA 02174-4392
(8OO) 597-4597 or (617) 641-1700
FAX: (617) 648-6673
Products: Aeris v3.2

Bravo Communications Inc.
1310 Tully Road, Suite l07
San Jose, CA 95122
(800) 366-0297 or (408) 297-8700
FAX: (408) 297-8701
Products: Aeris v3.2

Bridgeway Software Inc.
5959 W. Loop South, Suite 300
Bellaire, TX 77401
(713) 661-0044
FAX: (713) 661-5120
Products: Aeris v3.2

Bristol Technology Inc,
241 Ethan Allen Highway
Ridgefield, CT 06877
(203) 438-6969
FAX: (203) 438-5013
Products: Aeris v3.2

Brixton Systems Inc.
125 Cambridge Park Drive
Cambridge, MA 02140
(617) 661-6262
FAX: (617) 547-9820
Products: Aeris v3.2

Broadway & Seymour Inc.
128 S. Tryon St.
Charlotte, NC 28202
(800) 274-9287
FAX: (704) 344-3330
Products: Aeris v3.2

Brooktrout Technology Inc.
144 Gould St.
Needham, MA 02194
(617) 449-4100
FAX: (800) 333-5274 or (617) 449-9009
Products: Aeris v3.2

Brownstone Solutions Inc.
295 Madison Ave.
New York, NY 10017
(800) 827-7001 or (212) 370-7160
FAX: (212) 867-2520
Products: Aeris v3.2

Bryant Software
PO Box 102216
Denver, CD 80250
(303) 733-3116
FAX: (303) 777-2876
Products: Aeris v3.2

BST Consultants Inc.
5925 Benjamin Center Drive, Suite 110
Tampa, FL 33634
(813) 886-3300
FAX: (813) 884-8528
Products: Aeris v3.2

Bus-Tech Inc.
129 Middlesex Turnpike
Burlington, MA 01803
(800) 284-3172 or (617) 272-8200
FAX: (617) 272-0342
Products: Aeris v3.2

BusLogic Chantal Group
7220 Trade St, Suite 115
San Diego, CA 92121
(619) 621-2810
FAX: (619) 586-1323
Products: Aeris v3.2

BusLogic Inc.
4151 Bunton Drive
Santa Clara, CA 95054
(408) 492-9090
FAX: (408) 492-1542
Products: Aeris v3.2

BYTEX Corp.
4 Technology Drive
Westborough, MA 01581-1760
(800) 227-1145 or (508) 366-8000
FAX: (508) 366-7970

C-TECH Electronics Inc.
2701 Dow Ave, PO 2098
Tustin, CA 92681
(800) 347 4017
FAX: (714) 757-4533

C. Mer Industries Ltd.
18 Hasatat St.
Holon, 58855 Israel
(212) 594-7871 or +972-3-5572555
FAX: (212) 594-7865 or ()+972-3-5567904

CabiNet Systems Inc.
900 Corporate Drive
Mahwah, NJ 07430
(201) 512-1040
FAX: (201) 512-1650

Cable Management Systems Inc.
3510 S. Susan St.
Santa Ana, CA 92704
(714) 662-0554
FAX: (714) 662-1083

Cables To Go
1501 Websler St.
Dayton, OH 45404
(800) 826-7904
FAX: (800) 331-2841

Cabletron Systems
35 Industrial Wav
Rochester, NH 03867
(603) 332-9400
FAX: (603) 337-2444
Products: SpectroPHONE

Cache Computers Inc.
46600 Landing Parkway
Fremont, CA 94538
(510) 228-9922
FAX: (510) 226-9911

CACI Products Co.
3333 N. Torrey Pines Court
La Jolla, CA 92037
(619) 457-9681
FAX: (819) 457-1184
Products: COMNET III

Cactus Computer Inc.
1120 Metrocrest Drive, Suite 103
Carrollton, TX 75006
(214) 416-0525

CalCom Products
181 Orangethorpe, Suite A
Placentia, CA 92870
(714) 961-1888
FAX: (714) 981-1994

Calculus Inc.
1761 W. Hillsboro Blvd.
Deerfield Beach, FL 33442-1530
(305) 481-2334
FAX: (305) 481-1866

California Software Inc,
2121 E. Pacific Coast Highway
Suite 120C
Corona del Mar, CA 92625
(714) 729-4224
FAX: (714) 644-6277

Cameo Communications Inc.
71 Spitbrook Road
Nashua, NH 03060
(800) 438-4827 or (603) 888-8869
FAX: (603) 888-8906

Campbell Services Inc.
21700 Northwestern Highway
10th Floor
Southfield, MI 48075
(800) 345-8747 or (810) 559-5955
FAX: (810) 559-1034

Canary Communications Inc.
1851 Zanker Rood
San Jose, CA 95112-4213
(800) 883-9201 or (408) 453-9201
FAX: (408) 453-0940

Canoga Perkins Corp.
21012 Lassen St.
Chatsworth, CA 91311
(818) 718-6300
FAX: (818) 718-6312

Caravelle Networks Corp.
301 Moodie Drive, Suite 306
Nepean, ONT K2H 9C4 Canada
(800) 383-5292 or (813) 596-2802
FAX: (613) 596-9659
Products: NetWORKS

Cardff Software Inc.
531 Stevens Ave, Building B
Solana Beach, CA 92075
(800) 659-8755 or (619) 259-6450
FAX: (619) 259-6435

Cascade Communications Corp.
5 Carlisle Road
Westford, MA 01886
(508) 692-2600, ext. 257
FAX: (508) 692-5052

Castelle Inc.
3255-3 Scott Blvd.
Santa Clara, CA 95054
(800) 289-7555 or (408) 496-0474
FAX: (408) 492-1964

Castle Rock Computing Inc,
20863 Stevens Creek Blvd, Suite 530
Cupertino, CA 95014
(408) 366-6540
FAX: (408) 252-2379

Cayman Systems Inc.
400 Unicorn Park Drive
Woburn, MA 01801
(800) 473-4778 or (817) 932-1100
FAX: (617) 932-3861

CD Masters
7495 Hwy 53
Toney, AL 35773
(205) 652-7577

CE Software Inc.
1801 Industrial Circle,
PO Box 65580
West Des Moines, IA 50265
(800) 523-7638
FAX: (515) 221-1806

CEC Corp.
208 E. 51, Suite 400
New York, NY 10022
(800) 477-0791

Cemral Data Corp.
1602 Newton Drive
Champaign, IL 61821
(800) 482-0315 or (217) 359-8010
FAX: (217) 359-6904

Centennial Computer Services Inc.
3299 Northcrest Road, Suite 200
Atlanta, GA 30340
(404) 491-1221
FAX: (404) 934-7571

Century Computer Marketing
4755 Alla Road
Marina Del Rev, CA 90292-6378
(310) 827-0999, ext. 316
FAX: (310) 578-2160

CGI Systems Inc.
1180 W. Swedesford Road, Suite 350
Berwyn, PA 19312
(800) CGI-EDUC
FAX: (919) 847-2457

CGS Research Inc.
46560 Fremont Blvd, Suite 119
Fremont, CA 94538
(800) 875-3224 or (510) 226-5776
FAX: (510) 226-5775

Chase Research
545 Marriott Drive, Suite 100
Nashville, TN 37214
(800) 242-7387
FAX: (615) 872-0771

Chatsworth Products Inc.
9541 Mason Ave.
Chatsworth, CA 91311
(818) 882-8595
FAX: (818) 718-0473

Cheyenne Software Inc.
3 Expressway Plaza
Roslyn Heights, NY 11577
(800) 243-9462 or (516) 484 5110
FAX: (516) 484-3446

CHI/COR Information
Management Inc.
300 S. Wacker Drive
Chicago, IL 60606
(312) 322-0150 or (800) 448-8777
FAX: (312) 322-0161
Products: CRMS

Chinon America Inc.
615 Hawaii Ave.
Torrance, CA 90503
(800) 441-0222
FAX: (310) 533-1727

Chipcom Corp.
118 Turnpike Road
Southborough, MA 01772
(800) 228-9930 or (508) 460-8900
FAX: (508) 460-8950

CIE America Inc.
2701 Dow Ave, PO Box 2096
Tustin, CA 92681-2096
(800) 877-1421, ext. 4494
FAX: (714) 757-4488

Cimage Corp.
3885 Research Park Drive
Ann Arbor, MI 48108
(313) 761-6511
FAX: (313) 761-6551

Cincinnati Microwave Inc.
One Microwave Plaza
Cincinnati, OH 95249
(513) 489-5400
FAX: (513) 489-8036

Ciprico Inc.
2800 Campus Drive
Plymouth, MN 55441
(612) 551-4000 or (800) 727-4669
FAX: (612) 551-4002

Circuit Masters Software Inc.
10014 Kent Town Lane
Sugar Land, TX 77478
(713) 242-9353
FAX: (713) 242-4632
Products: Z-Menu

Cisco Systems Inc.
930 E. Arquez Ave.
Sunnyvale, CA 94086
(800) 238-2334 or (408) 526-4000
FAX: (408) 526-8401
Products: CiscoWorks

Citrix Systems Inc.
210 Universitv Drive, Suite 700
Cora Springs, FL 33071
(800) 437-7503
FAX: (305) 341-8880

CLARiiON
4400 Computer Drive
Westboro, MA 01580
(800) 67-ARRAY
FAX: (508) 898-7501

Clary Corp.
1960 S. Walker Ave.
Monrovia, CA 91016
(800) 442-5279
FAX: (818) 305-0254
Products: UPS

CLEO Communications
3796 Plaza Drive
Ann Arbor, MI 48108
(800) 233-2536
FAX: (313) 682-1965

Clinical Resource Systems Inc.
3701 N. Lamar Blvd, Suite 207
Austin, TX 78705
(512) 452-7261
FAX: (512) 452-2390

Clover/Plexus Networking Education
41290 Vincenti Court
Novi, MI 48375-1925
(810) 471-3850
FAX: (810) 471-4460

Clovis Inc.
25 Ponter Road
Littleton, MA 01460
(508) 486-0005
FAX: (508) 486-3755

CMD Technology Inc.
1 Vanderbilt
IrvInc. CA 92718
(800) 426-3832 or (714) 454-0800
FAX: (714) 455-1656

CNet Technology Corp.
2199 Zanker Road
San Jose, CA 95131
(408) 954-8000
FAX: (408) 954-8866

Codenoll Technology Corp,
1086 N. Broadway
Yonkers, NY 10701
(914) 965-6300
FAX: (914) 965-9811

Cogent Data Technologies Inc.
175 West St., PO Box 926
Friday Harbor, WA 98250
(800) 426-4368 or (208) 378-2929
FAX: (206) 378-2882

Collabra Software Inc.
1091 N. Shoreline Blvd.
Mountain View, CA 94043
(800) 474-7427
FAX: (415) 940-6440

Colorado Memory Systems
800 S. Past Ave.
Loveland, CO 80537
(800) 845-7905 or (303) 669-6500
FAX: (303) 667-0997

Colorgraphic Communications Corp.
5980 Peachtree Road
Atlanta, GA 30341
(404) 455-3921
FAX: (404) 458-0616

COM&DIA, L.L.C.
3000 Highwoods Blvd, Suite 100
Raleigh, NC 27604-1012
(800) 383-6986 or (919) 878-6503
FAX: (919) 878-0875

Coman Data Communications Ltd.
PO Box 3781
Jerusalem, 91035 Israel
(315) 637-0247
FAX: (315) 637-0247

Comm One Inc.
8170 S. Highland Drive, Suite ElA
Sandy, UT 84093
(801) 943-5010
FAX: (801) 943-4413
Products: LAN Inventory
Management System

Command Line Corp.
1090 King Georges Post Road, Suite 802
Edison, NJ 08837
(908) 738-6500

Command Software Systems
1061 E. Indiantown Road, Suite 500
Jupiter, FL 33477
(800) 423-9147 or (407) 575-3200
FAX: (407) 575-3026

CommVision Corp.
510 Logue Ave.
Mountain View, CA 94043
(800) TEAM LAN
FAX: (415) 254-9320

Compaq Computer Corp.
PO Box 692000
Houston, TX 77269-2000
(800) 345-1518
Products: Insight Mngr, Disk Optm,
Network Management Tools

Compatible Systems Corp.
4730 Walnut St, Suite 102, PO Box 17220
Boulder, CD 80801
(303) 444-9532 or (800) 356-0283
FAX: (303) 444-9595

Compex Inc.
4051 E. La Palma
Anaheim, CA 92807
(800) 279-8891, pin# 1071 or (714) 830
7302
FAX: (714) 630-6521

Complementary Solutions Inc. (CSI)
4250 Perimeter Park South, Suite 200
Atlanta, GA 30341
(404) 936-3700
FAX: (404) 936-3710

CompLink Ltd.
175 Community Drive
Great Neck, NY 11021
(516) 829-1883, (212) 626-6731, or
(708) 382-9191
FAX: (516) 829-5001 or (708) 382-9190

Compu-Link Cable Assemblies Inc.
13100 56th Court, Suite 705
Cleanwater, FL 34620
(800) 231-6685
FAX: (813) 573-5321

CompuLAN Technology Inc,
1630 Oakland Road, Suite A111
San Jose, CA 95131
(408) 432-8899
FAX: (408) 432-8699

Compulink Management Center
370 S. Crenshaw Blvd, Suite E-106
Torrance, CA 90503
(310) 212-5465
FAX: (310) 212-5217

CompuServe Network Services
5000 Arlington Centre Blvd.
Columbus, OH 43220
(800) 433-0389 or (614) 798-3354
FAX: (814) 791-9298

Computer Assistance Inc.
82277 Weiss Road
Creswell, OR 97428
(503) 895-3347
FAX: (503) 895-3999

Computer Associates International Inc.
One Computer Associates Plaza
Islandia, NY 11788-7000
(800) CALL-CAI
FAX: (516) 342-5734

Computer Conversions Inc.
9580 Black Mountain Road, Suite J
San Diego, CA 92126
(619) 693-1697
FAX: (619) 693-6003

Computer Economics Inc.
5841 Edison Place
Carlsbad, CA 92008
(800) 326-8100 or (819) 438-8100
FAX: (619) 431-1126

Computer Knacks Inc.
621 Shrewsbury Ave.
Shrewsbury, NJ 07702
(800) 551-1433 or (908) 530-0262
FAX: (908) 741-0972
Products: Habitat for NetWare, iniScript

Computer Law Systems Inc.
11000 W. 78th St.
Eden Prairie, MN 55344
(800) 328-1913, ext. 773
FAX: (612) 942-3450

Computer Library
One Park Ave.
New York, NY 10016
(800) 827-7889
FAX: (212) 503-4414

Computer Mail Services Inc.
20300 Civic Center Drive, Suite 300
Southfield, MI 48076
(810) 352-6700 or (800) 883-2674
FAX: (810) 352-8387

Computer Modules Inc.
2350 Walsh Ave.
Santa Clara, CA 95051
(408) 496-1881
FAX: (408) 496-1886

Computer Peripherals Inc.
667 Rancho Conejo Blvd.
Newbury Park, CA 91320
(805) 499-5751 or (800) 854-7600
FAX: (805) 498-8306

Computer Power Inc.
124 W. Main St.
High Bridge, NJ 08829
(800) 526-5088, ext. 153, or
(908) 638-8000, ext. 153
FAX: (908) 638-4931

Computer Resources Inc,
PO Box 60, 94 Route 125
Barrington, NH 03825
(603) 664-5811
FAX: (603) 664-5864

Computer Security Institute
600 Harrison St.
San Francisco, CA 94107
(415) 905-2378
FAX: (415) 905-2218

Computer System Products Inc, (CSP)
14305 N. 21st Ave.
Plymouth. MN 55447
(612) 476-6866 or (800) 4-CABLES
FAX: (612) 475-8457
Products: StackUP series hubs,
concentrators, & bridges

Computers Plus Information
Services Inc,
5775 SW Jean Road, Suite 203
Lake Oswego, OR 97035
(503) 635-7645
FAX: (503) 635-1438

Computone Corp.
1100 Northmeadow Parkway
Roswell, GA 30076
(404) 475-2725, ext. 230
FAX: (404) 664-1510

CompuTrend Systems Inc.
1306 John Reed Court
Industry, CA 91745
(800) 677-6477
FAX: (818)369-6803

COMWEB Technology Group Inc.
579 Route 23
Cedar Grove, NJ 07009
(800) 382-4384 or (201) 857-8770
FAX: (201) 857-7303

Concentric Data Systems Inc.
110 Turnpike Road
Westboro, MA 01581
(508) 366-1122 or (800) 325-9035
FAX: (508) 366-2954

Concord Communications Inc.
753 Forest St.
Marlboro, MA 01752
(508) 460-4643
FAX: (508) 481-9772

Concurrent Controls Inc.
880 Dubuque Ave.
South San Francisco, CA 94080
(800) 437-2243 or (415) 873-6240
FAX: (451) 873-6091

Conextions Inc.
1545 Osgood St, Suite 108
North Andover, MA 01845
(508) 689-3570
FAX: (508) 689-2450

Connect-Air International Inc.
50-37th St. NE
Auburn, WA 98002
(800) 247-1978
FAX: (206) 939-4880

Conner Peripherals Inc.
3081 Zanker Road
San Jose, CA 95134
(800) 426-6637
FAX: (408) 456-4501

Conner Storage Systems
36 Skyline Drive
Lake Mary, FL 32746
(800) 5-CONNER
FAX: (407) 263-3555
Products: HSM Software

Conner Tape Products Group
1640 Sunflower Ave.
Costa Mesa, CA 92626
(800) 6-Conner or (714) 641-1230
FAX: (714) 641-2590

CONNEXPERTS
13355 Noel Road, Suite 1600
Dallas, TX 75075
(800) 433-5373 or (214) 233-8800
FAX: (214) 239-6490

Contact East Inc.
335 Willow St.
North Andover, MA 01845
(508) 682-2000
FAX: (508) 688-7829

Contemporary Control Systems Inc.
2512 Wisconsin Ave.
Downers Grove, IL 60515
(708) 963-7070
FAX: (708) 963-O109

Contemporary Cybernetics Group
Rock Landing Corporate Center
346 Rock Landing
Newport News, VA 23606
(804) 873-9000
FAX: (804) 873-8836

Contingency Strategies Associates Inc.
111 Simsbury Road
Avon, CT 06001
(800) CSA-5678 or (203) 674-1855
FAX: (203) 677-5947

ContrAcct Systems Corp.
208 N. Washington St.
Naperville, IL 60540
(800) JOB-COST or (708) 355-8188
FAX: (708) 355-8675

Controlled Power Co.
1955 Stephenson Hwy
Troy, MI 48083
(800) 521-4792
FAX: (800) 642-9625

Conway Engineering Inc.
8393 Capwell Drive
Oakland, CA 94621-2113
(800) 626-6929 or (510) 568-4028
FAX: (510) 568-1397

Copia International Ltd.
1342 Avalon Court
Wheaton, IL 60187
(708) 682-8898
FAX: (708) 665-9841

Cordant Inc.
11400 Commerce Park Drive
Reston, VA 22091
(800) 843-1132
FAX: (703) 758-7320

CORE International
7171 N. Federal Hwy
Boca Raton, FL 33487
(407) 997-6044
FAX: (407) 997-6009

Corel Corp.
1600 Carling Ave.
Ottawa, ONT K1Z 8R7 Canada
(800) 772-6735 or (613) 728-3733
FAX: (613) 761-9176

Corning Inc.
35 W. Market St., MP-RO-02
Corning, NY 14831
(800) 525-2524
FAX: (607) 974-7522

Corollary Inc.
2802 Kelvin
IrvInc. CA 92714
(714) 250-4040
FAX: (714) 250-4043

COS Inc.
9 Huron way
Lawrenceville, NJ 08643
(609) 771-6705
FAX: (609) 530-0898

Courtland Group Inc.
10480 Little Patuxent Parkway
Columbia, MD 21044
(410) 730-7668
FAX: (410) 730-8271

Cray Communications
9020 Junction Drive
Annapolis Junction, MD 20701
(800) FOR-CRAY or (301) 317-7710
FAX: (301) 317-7220

Crisis Computor Corp.
2298 Quimby Road
San Jose, CA 95122
(800) 726-0726 or (408) 270-1100
FAX: (408) 270-1170

Cross International Corp.
854 Walnut St, Suite B
Boulder, CO 80302
(800) 288-2887 or (303) 440-7313
FAX: (303) 442-2616

CrossWind Technologies Inc.
6630 Hwy 9, Suite 201
Felton, CA 95018
(408) 335-5450
FAX: (408) 335-1086

Crosswire Corp.
105 Locust St, Suite 301
Santa Cruse, CA 95060
(800) 747-9060 or (408) 459-9060
FAX: (408) 426-3859

Crystal Group Inc.
1165 Industrial Ave.
Hiawatha, IA 52233-1120
(800) 378-1636
FAX: (319) 393-2338

Crystal Point Inc.
22232 17th Ave. SE, Suite 301
Bothell, WA 98021
(800) 982-0628 or (206) 487-3656
FAX: (206) 487-3773

Crystalogic Inc.
2525 Perimeter Place Drive, Suite 121
Nashville, TN 37214
(615) 391-9100
FAX: (615) 391-5292

CUBIX Corp.
2800 Lockheed Way
Carson City, NV 89706
(800) 829-0552
FAX: (702) 882-2407

CyberCorp Inc.
PO Drawer 1988
Kennesaw, GA 30144
(404) 424-6240
FAX: (404) 424-8995

Cyclades Corp.
44140 Old Warm Springs Blvd.
Fremont, CA 94538
(800) 347-6601 or (510) 770-9727
FAX: (510) 770-0355

Cygnus Support
1937 Landings Drive
Mountain View, CA 94043
(800) Cygnus-1 or (415) 903-1400
FAX: (415) 903-0122

Cylink Corp.
310 N. Mary Ave.
Sunnyvale, CA 94086
(800) 533-3958 or (408) 735-5800
FAX: (408) 735-6643

CYMA Systems Inc.
1400 E. Southern Ave.
Tempe, AZ 85282
(800) 282-2962 or (602) 831-2607
FAX: (602) 345-5703

CypherTech Inc.
250 Caribbean Drive
Sunnyvale, CA 94088
(408) 734-8765
FAX: (408) 734-8763

D & G Infosystems Inc.
148 Patterson Ave.
Long Island, NY 11550
(800) 430-4583 or (516) 538-1240
FAX: (516) 538-1240
Products: LANWatchMan

D-link Systems Inc.
5 Musick
IrvInc. CA 92718
(800) 326-1688 or (714) 455-1688
FAX: (714) 455-2521

DacEasy Inc.
17950 Preston Road, Suite 800
Dallas, TX 75252
(800) 322-3279 or (214) 248-0305
FAX: (214) 713-6331

Dallas Semiconductor
4401 S. Beltwood Parkway
Dallas, TX 75244-3292
(800) 258-5061
FAX: (214) 450-3869

DANPEX Corp.
1342 Ridder Park Drive
San Jose, CA 95131
(800) 452-1551 or (408) 437-7557
FAX: (408) 437-7559

Data Access Corp.
14000 SW 119 Ave.
Miami, FL 33186-6017
(800) 451-3539 or (305) 238-0012
FAX: (305) 238-0017

Data Interface Systems Corp.
11130 Jollyville Road, Suite 300
Austin, TX 78759
(800) 351-4244 or (512) 346-5641
FAX: (512) 346-4035

Data Race
11559 IH 10 West, Suite 395
San Antonio, TX 78230-9974
Products: Mach DS+

Data Technical Research Inc.
2960 Hartley Road
Jacksonville, FL 32257
(800) 822-4387 or (904) 292-4387
FAX: (904) 292-4807

Data Technology Corp.
1515 Centre Pointe Drive
Milpitas, CA 85035
(408) 942-4081

Data Transmission Network
9110 W. Dodge Road, Suite 200
Omaha, NE 68114
(800) 369-2345
FAX: (402) 255-3688

Data Trek Inc.
5838 Edison Place
Carlsbad, CA 92008-6596
(800) 876-5484 or (619) 431-8400
FAX: (619) 431-8448

Datacom Technologies
11001 31st Place West
Everen, WA 98204
(800) 468-5557 or (206) 355-0590
FAX: (206) 290-1600

Dataflex Corp.
3920 Park Ave.
Edison, NJ 08820
(800) 700-TRAIN
FAX: (908) 321-6590
Products: Software Training & Systems
Integration

Datalight Inc.
307 N. Olympic Ave., Suite 201
Arlington, WA 98223
(206) 435-8086 or (800) 221-6630
FAX: (206) 435-0253
Products: PCMCIA Mem Card File Mngr

Datamedia Corp.
20 Trafalgar Square
Nashua, NH 03063
(603) 886-1570
FAX: (603) 598-8268

DataModes Inc.
4200 Perimeter Center. Suite 202
Oklahoma City, OK 73112
(405) 947-3887
FAX: (405) 947-5948

Dataview Imaging &
Information Systems
321 Fifth Ave.
New York, NY 10016-5015
(212) 684-4141
FAX: (212) 684-3658

Datawatch Corp.
PO Box 13984
Research Triangle Park, NC 27709-3984
(919) 549-0711
FAX: (919) 549-0065

DAVID Systems Inc.
615 Tasman Drive
Sunnyvale, CA 94088-3718
(800) 762-7848 or (408) 541-6000
FAX: (408) 541-8985

DaVinci Systems Corp.
4200 Six Forks Road
Raleigh, NC 27608
(919) 881-4320 or (800) 328-4624
FAX: (919) 787-3550

Dayna Communications Inc.
Sorenson Research Park,
849 W. Levoy Drive
Salt Lake City, UT 84123
(801) 269-7200
FAX: (801) 269-7363
Products: ProFiles v1.0.1

DCA
1000 Alderman Drive
Alpharetta, GA 30202
(800) 348-3221
FAX: (404) 442-4366

DCE Corp.
1275 Summer St.
Stamford, CT 06905
(800) 326-3821
FAX: (203) 358-3944

Deltec Electronics Corp.
2727 Kurtz St.
San Diego, CA 92110
(800) 854-2658 or (619) 291-4211
FAX: (619) 291-2973

Denmac Systems Inc.
1945 Techny Road
Northbrook, IL 60062
(708) 291-7760
FAX: (708) 291-7763
Products: ALERTPAGE, TrenData,
HTFS

Develcon
856 51st St. East
Saskatoon, SK S7K 5C7 Canada
(800) 667-9333 or (306) 933-3300
Europe: (352) 30-71-35
FAX: (306) 931-1370
Europe: FAX: (352) 30-53-64

Devont Software Inc.
1300 S. Frazier, Suite 111
Conroe, TX 77301
(409) 788-1881
FAX: (409) 788-2181

DFI
135 Main Ave.
Sacramento, CA 95838
(918) 568-1234
FAX: (916) 568-1233

Dharma Systems Inc.
15 Trafalgar Square
Nashua, NH 03063
(603) 886-1400
FAX: (603) 883-6904

Diamond Micro Solutions
1615 Alvarado St.
San Leandro, CA 94577
(510) 351-4700
FAX: (510) 352-1089

Digi-Data Corp.
8580 Dorsey Run Road
Jessup, MD 20794
(301) 498-0200
FAX: (301) 498-0771

DigiBoard
6400 Flying Cloud Dnve
Eden Prairie, MN 55344
(612) 943-9020 or (800) 344-4273
FAX: (612) 943-5398

Digicom Systems Inc.
188 Topaz St.
Milpitas, CA 95035
(408) 262-1277
FAX: (408) 262-1390

Digilog
900 Business Center Drive
Horsham, PA 19044
(800) DIGILOG
FAX: (215) 956-0108

Digital Analysis Corp.
1889 Preston White Drive
Reston, VA 22091
(703) 476-5900
FAX: (703) 476-1918
Products: Acct*Proxy

Digital Communications
Associates Inc. (DCA)
8230 Montgomery Road
Cincinnati, OH 45236
(513) 745-0500
FAX: (513) 745-0327
Products: NetWizard

Digital Directory Assistance (DDA)
6931 Arlington Road, Suite 405
Bethesda, MD 20814-5231
(800) 284-8353
FAX: (617) 639-2980

Digital Equipment Corp.
550 King St, LKGl -3/J17
Littleton, MA 01460
(800) DIGITAL or (508) 486-6963
FAX: (508) 486-6311
Products: DECagent 90

Digital Equipment Corp.,
OEM Storage Business
333 South St, SHRt-4/A16
Shrewsbury, MA 01545
(508) 841-6330
FAX: (508) 841-5078

Digital Equipment Corp.: PCBU
100 Nagog Park
Acton, MA 01720
(800) 256-9257, Priority Code JCA
FAX: (800) 388-3228

Digital Link Corp.
217 Humboldt Court
Sunnyvale, CA 94089
(408) 745-6200
FAX: (408) 745-6250

Digital Pathways
201 Ravendale Drive
Mountain View, CA 94043
(415) 964-0707, ext. 621
FAX: (415) 961-7487

Digital Products
411 Waverley Oaks Road
Waltham, MA 02154
(800) 243-2333
FAX: (617) 647-4474

Digitech Industries Inc.
55 Kenosia Ave.
Danbury, CT 06813
(203) 797-2676
FAX: (203) 797-2682

Distinct Corp.
12901 Saratoga Ave.
Saratoga, CA 95070
(408) 366-8933
FAX: (408) 366-0153

Distributed Systems International Inc.
531 W. Roosevelt Road, Suite 2
Wheaton, IL 60187-5057
(...)
FAX: (708) 665 4706

Diverse Logistics Inc.
2862 McGaw Ave.
IrvInc. CA 92714
(800) 345-6432
FAX: (714) 476-0633

Diversified Computer Systems Inc.
3775 Iris Ave., Suite 1
Boulder, CO 80301
(303) 447-9251
FAX: (303) 447-1406

DURACOM Computer Systems
1425 Greenway Drive
Irving, TX 75038
(800) 551-9000 or (214) 518-1200
FAX: (214) 518-1090

E Ware
145 W. 28th St., 12th Floor
New York, NY 10001-6114
(800) 743-8645 or (212) 564-7781
FAX: (212) 564-7499

E-COMMS Inc.
5720 144th St. NW
Gig Harbor, WA 98332
(206) 857-3399 or (800) 247-1431
FAX: (206) 857-3444

Eagle Technology, A Business Unit of
Artisoft Inc.
2202 N. Forbes Blvd.
Tucson, AZ 85745
(800) 233-5564
FAX: (602) 670-7359

Easel Corp.
25 Corporate Drive
Burlington, MA 01803
(617) 221-3000
FAX: (617) 221-6899

eccs Inc.
One Sheila Drive
Tinton Falls, NJ 07724
(800) 322-7462 or (908) 747-6995
FAX: (908) 747-6542

Eden Systems Corp.
9302 N. Meridian St. Suite 350
Indianapolis, IN 46260
(800) 779-6338
FAX: (317) 843-2271

Edinburgh Portable Compilers
20 Victor Square
Scotts Valley, CA 95066
(408) 438-1851
FAX: (408) 438-3510

Edutec Computer Education
Institute Inc.
321 Fifth Ave.
New York, NY 10016-5015
(212) 684-4141
FAX: (212) 684-3658

Edutrends Inc.
25 Clifton Road
Milton, NJ 07438
(800) 252-8736 or (201) 687-7638

EFA Corp.
3040 Oakmead Village Drive
Santa Clara, CA 95051
(408) 987-5400
FAX: (408) 987-5415

EFC Systems
1964 W. Gray, Suite 214
Houston, TX 77019
(800) 799-3337
FAX: (713) 522-2642

EFI Electronics
2415 S. 2300 W,
Salt Lake City, UT 84119
(800) 877-1174
FAX: (801) 977-0200

Eicon Technology
2196 - 32nd Ave. (Lachine)
Montreal, QUE H8T 3H7 Canada
(800) 80-EICON
FAX: (214) 239-3304

ELAN Software Corp.
17383 Sunset Blvd, Suite 101
Pacific Palisades, CA 90272
(800) 654-3526
FAX: (310) 454-4848

Electronic Technology Group Inc.
9333 Penn Ave. South
Bloomington, MN 55431-2330
(800) 480-4384 or (612) 948-3100
FAX: (612) 948-3106

EliaShim Microcomputers Inc.
4005 Wedgemere Drive
Tampa, FL 33610
(800) 477-5177
FAX: (813) 744-5197

Elisa Technology Inc.
4368 Enterprise St.
Fremont, CA 94538
(510) 651-5817
FAX: (510) 651-4834

ElseWare Corp.
101 Stewart St, Suite 700
Seattle, WA 98101
(800) ELSEWARE or (206) 448-9600
FAX: (206) 448-7220

Emerald Systems Corp.
15175 Innovation Drive
San Diego, CA 92128
(800) 787-2587 or (619) 673-2161
FAX: (619) 673-2288

EMPACT Software, A Div. of Boole &
Babbage
2375 Wall St.
Conyers, GA 30208
(404) 483-8852
FAX: (404) 388-9453

Emprise Technologies
South Pittsburgh Technology Park, 3117
Washington Pike
Bridgeville, PA 15017-1496
(800) 727-9060 or (41 2) 257-9060
FAX: (412) 257-9012
Products: Intersend v3.1, Stage 3 v2.1

EMS Professional Shareware
4505 Buckhurst Ct
Olney, MD 20832
(301) 924-3594
FAX: (301) 963-2708

Emulex Corp.
3545 Harbor Blvd.
Costa Mesa, CA 92628
(800) 854-7112 or (714) 662-5600
FAX: (714) 513-8266

Enable Software Inc.
313 Ushers Road
Ballston Lake, NY 12019-1591
(800) 888-0684
FAX: (518) 877-3337

Enterprise Solutions Ltd.
32603 Bowman Knoll Drive
Westlake Village, CA 91361
(818) 597-8943
FAX: (818) 597-9621

EPE Technologies Inc.,
a subsidiary of Square D
1660 Scenic Ave.
Costa Mesa, CA 92626
(800) 344-0570
FAX: (714) 435-1445

Epilogue Technology Corp.
11116 Desen Classic Lane
Albuquerque, NM 87111
(505) 271-9933
FAX: (505) 271-9798
Products: Ambassador

EPSON
20770 Madrona Ave.
Torrance, CA 90503
(800) 289-3776
FAX: (310) 782-4248

Ergotron Inc.
3450 Yankee Drive, Suite 100
Eagan, MN 55121
(800) 888-8458 or (612) 452-8135
FAX: (612) 452-8346

ESKER Inc.
1181 Chess Drive, Suite C
Foster City, CA 94404
(415) 341-9065
FAX: (415) 341-6412

ETR Computer Group Inc.
1030 St. Georges Ave., Suite 305
Avenel, NJ 07001
(908) 750-8855
FAX: (908) 636-7466

ETS Inc.
1394 Willow Road
Menlo Park, CA 94025
(800) 752-8208 or (415) 324-4949
FAX: (415) 324-1608

Events Management International Inc.
737 Webster St.
Marshfield, MA 02050
(617) 834-4703
FAX: (617) 834-4578

Evergreen Systems Inc.
120 Landing Court, Suite A
Novato, CA 94945
(415) 897-8888
FAX: (415) 897-6158

Exabyte Corp.
1685 38th St.
Boulder, CO 80301
(800) EXATAPE
FAX: (303) 447-7170

EXFO Electro-Optical Engineering
465 Godin Ave.
Vanier, QUE G1M 3G7 Canada
(418) 683-0211
FAX: (418) 683-2170

Express Systems
2101 4th Ave, Suite 303
Seattle, WA 98121-2314
(206) 728-8300
FAX: (206) 728-8301
Products: Windows Express

Extended Systems Inc.
7 E. Beall
Bozeman, MT 59715
(800) 235-7576 or (208) 322-7575
FAX: (208) 377-1906

Extension Technology Corp.
30 Hollis St.
Framingham, MA 01701
(800) 856-2672 or (508) 872-7748
FAX: (508) 872-7533

F3 Software Corp.
Cypress Plaza
6365 NW 6th Way, Suite 320
Fort Lauderdale, FL 33309
(800) 477-2562
FAX: (305) 489-3220

Farallon Computing Inc.
2470 Mariner Square Loop
Alameda, CA 94501-1010
(510) 814-5000
FAX: (510) 814-5023

FEL Computing
10 Main St, P0 Box 72
Williamsville, VT 05362
(800) 639-4110 or (802) 348-7171
FAX: (802) 348-7124

Ferris Networks
353 Sacramento St., Suite 600
San Francisco, CA 94111
(415) 986-1414
FAX: (415) 986-5994

Fiber Instrument Sales Inc.
161 Clear Road
oriskany, NY 13424
(315) 736-2206
FAX: (315) 736-2285

FiberCom Inc.
3353 Orange Ave, NE
Roanoke, VA 24012
(800) 537-6801
FAX: (703) 342-5961

Fibermux Corp.
21415 Plummer St.
Chatsworth, CA 91311
(800) 800-4624
FAX: (818) 709-1556
Products: LightWatch/Open

Fibronics International Inc.
33 Riverside Drive
Pembroke, MA 02359
(617) 826-0099
FAX: (617) 826-7745

FireFox Inc.
2841 Junction Ave., Suite 103
San Jose, CA 95134
(408) 321-8344 or (800) 230-6090
FAX: (408) 321-8311

First Floor Inc.
444 Castro St, Suite 200
Mountain View, CA 94041
(415) 968-1101
FAX: (415) 968-1193
Products: Network Central, NLMAuto,
NLMerlin, NLM Auto Professional,
FileAuditor, File Wizard, File Wizard,
File Auditor, NLMerlin, NLMAuto Prof.

Fischer International Systems Corp.
4073 Mercantile Ave.
Naples, FL 33942
(813) 643-1500 or (800) 237-4510
FAX: (813) 643-3772

Fluke Corp.
PO Box 9090
Everett, WA 98206
(800) 44-FLUKE
FAX: (206) 356-5116

Forms Management Data Systems
PO Box 11155
Reno, NV 89510
(800) 328-7604
FAX: (702) 852-2408

Fotec Inc.
529 Main St, PO Box 246
Boston, MA 02129
(800) 537-8254 or (617) 241-7810
FAX: (617) 241-8616

Four Seasons Software
2025 Lincoln Highway
Edison, NJ 08817
(908) 248-6667
FAX: (908) 248-6675

Fourth Shift Corp.
7900 International Drive
Minneapolis, MN 55425
(800) 342-5675
FAX: (612) 851-1560

Fourth Wave Software Inc.
560 Kirts Blvd, Suite 105
Troy, MI 48084
(810) 362-2288
FAX: (810) 362-2295

Frontier Software Development Inc.
1501 Main St.
Tewksbury, MA 01876
(508) 851-5700 or (800) 357-RMON
FAX: (508) 851-6956

Frontier Technologies Corp.
10201 N. Port Washington Road
Mequon, WI 53092
(414) 241-4555
FAX: (414) 241-7084

Frye Computer Systems Inc.
19 Temple Place
Boston, MA 02111
(617) 451-5400
FAX: (617) 451-6711
Products: SUDS v1.5, HEAT

FTP Software Inc.
2 High St.
North Andover, MA 01645
(800) 282-4FTP or (508) 685-3300
FAX: (508) 794 4477

Fujitsu Computer Products
of America Inc.
2904 Orchard Parkway
San Jose, CA 95134
(408) 432-6333
FAX: (408) 894-1709

Funk Software Inc.
222 Third St.
Cambridge, MA 02142
(800) 828-4146 or (617) 497-6339
FAX: (617) 547-1031
Products: Proxy AppMeter, WanderLink

Future Domain Corp.
2801 McGaw Ave.
IrvInc. CA 92714
(714) 253-0400
FAX: (714) 253-0913

FutureSoft
12012 Wickshester Lane, Suite 600
Houston, TX 77079
(713) 496-9400 or (800) 989-8908
FAX: (713) 496-1090

Futurus Corp.
211 Perimeter Center Parkway. NE
Suite 910
Atlanta, GA 30346
(800) 327-8296
FAX: (404) 392-9313

Galacticomm Inc.
4101 SW. 47th Ave., Suite 101
Fort Lauderdale, FL 33314
(800) 328-1128 or (305) 321-2404
FAX: (305) 583-7846

Galaxy Networks Inc.
9348 De Soto Ave.
Chatsworth, CA 91311
(818) 998-7851
FAX: (818) 998-1758
Products: SNMP Network Mngt,
WireScope 100 v3.0

Galcom Inc.
211 Perry Parkway, Suite 4
Gaithersburg, MD 20877
(800) 966-4444 or (301) 990-7100
FAX: (301) 963-6383

Gambit Computer Communications Ltd.
PO Box 9697
Yokneam, 20692 Israel
()+972-4-890140
FAX: ()+972-4-890189

Gandalf Technologies Inc.
Cherry Hill Industrial Center - 9
Cherry Hill, NJ 08003-1688
(800) GANDALF
FAX: (613) 226-1717

Garrett Communications Inc.
48531 Warm Springs Blvd.
Fremont, CA 94539
(510) 438-9071
FAX: (510) 438-9072

Gateway Systems Corp.
4660 S. Hagadorn Road, Suite 110
East Lansing, MI 48823-5353
(800) 333-9366 or (517) 337-8960
FAX: (517) 337-2868

General DataComm Inc.
1579 Straits Turnpike
Middlebury, CT 06762-1299
(203) 574-1118
FAX: (203) 758-9468

General Software Inc.
PO Box 2571
Redmond, WA 98073
(206) 391-4285
FAX: (206) 557-0736

General Technology Inc.
415 Pineda Court
Melbourne, FL 32940
(800) 274-2733 or (407) 242-2733
FAX: (407) 254-1407

Genicom Corp.
14800 Conference Center Drive, Suite 400
Chantilly, VA 22021-3806
(800) 443-6426 or (703) 949-1708
FAX: (703) 949-1392

Gilbert & Associates Inc.
705 Second Ave, Suite 710
Seattle, WA 98104
(206) 223-7740
FAX: (206) 223-7713

Gimpel Software
3207 Hogarth Lane
Collegeville. PA 19426
(610) 584-4261
FAX: (610) 584-4266

Glenco Engineering Inc.
270 Lexington Drive
Buffalo Grove, IL 60089
(800) 562-2543 or (708) 808-0300
FAX: (708) 808-0313

GlobalWare Inc.
10474 Santa Monica Blvd, Suite 304
Los Angeles, CA 90025
(310) 441-1024
FAX: (310) 441-0824

GN Navtel Inc.
6611 Bay Circle, Suite 190
Norcross, GA 30071-9878
(404) 446-2665 or (905) 479-8090
FAX: (404) 446-2730 or (905) 475-6524

Gold Key Electronics Inc.
18 Lamy Drive
Goffstown, NH 03045
(603) 625-8518
FAX: (603) 625-4881

Golden Pacific Electronics
560 S. Melrose St.
Placentia, CA 92670
(714) 993-6970
FAX: (714) 993-6023

Grand Junction Networks Inc.
47281 Bayside Parkway
Fremont, CA 94538
(510) 252-0726
FAX: (510) 252-0915

Great Plains Software
1701 38th St. Southwest
Fargo, ND 58103
(800) 456-0025
FAX: (701) 281-3700

Greenware Technologies
32545 B. Golden Lantern, Suite 424
Dana Point, CA 92629
(714) 489-2299 or (800) 839-5000
FAX: (714) 489-7799

Group 1 Software Inc.
4200 Parliament Place, Suite 600
Lanham, MD 20706-1844
(800) 368-5806 or (301) 731-2300
FAX: (301) 731-0360

GSI Inc.
17951-H Skypark Circle
IrvInc. CA 92714-6343
(800) 486-7800 or (714) 261-7949
FAX: (714) 757-1778

GTSI
4100 Lafayette Center Drive
Chantilly, VA 22021
(301) 564-0047
FAX: (301) 564-3606

Gupta Corp.
1060 Marsh Road
Menlo Park, CA 94025
(800) 876-3267 or (415) 321-9500
FAX: (415) 321-5471

GVC Technologies Inc.
376 Lafayette Road
Sparta, NJ 07871
(201) 579-3630
FAX: (201) 579-2702

H T I Networks
532 Weddell Drive, Suite 1
Sunnyvale, CA 94089
(408) 745-0100
FAX: (408) 745-7711

Hadax Electronics Inc.
310 Phillips Ave.
South Hackensack, NJ 07606
(201) 807-1155
FAX: (201) 807-1782

Hammersly Technology Partners Inc.
909 Montgomery St., Suite 202
San Francisco, CA 94133
(800) 786-4778
FAX: (617) 575-0666
Products: Utopia Help Desk, Resolve,
Inventory & Training

Handley Computer Corp.
P0 Box 3039
Boulder, CO 80307-3039
(303) 494-6035
FAX: (303) 494-1050

Hauppauge Computer Works
91 Cabot Court
Hauppauge, NY 11788
(516) 434-1600
FAX: (516) 434-3198

HawkNet Inc.
5950 La Place Court, Building 101
Carlsbad, CA 92008
(800) 729-5638 or (619) 929-9966
FAX: (619) 929-9969
Products: NetTune 2.0

Hayes Microcomputer Products Inc.
5835 Peachtree Corners East
Norcross, GA 30092
(404) 441-1617
FAX: (404) 449-0087

Haystack Laboratories Inc.
8920 Business Park Drive
Austin, TX 78759-7405
(512) 343-2552
FAX: (512) 794-9997

Helix Software Co.
47-09 30th St. Third Floor
Long Island City, NY 11101
(800) 451-0551 or (718) 392-3100
FAX: (718) 392-4212

Help Desk Technology Corp.
835 Silver Birch Trail
Mississauga, ONT L5J 4C8 Canada
(800) 563-4357 or (905) 855-0000
FAX: (905) 823-7156
Products: HelpSTAR, iniScript

Hergo Ergonomic Support Systems Inc.
321 Fifth Ave.
New York, NY 10016-5015
(212) 684-4666
FAX: (212) 684-3658

Hertz Computer Corp.
325 Fifth Ave.
New York, NY 10016-5012
(212) 684-4141 or (800) 232-8737
FAX: (212) 684-3658

Hewlett-Packard Co, Network Test Div.
1 Tara Blvd.
Nashua, NH 03062
(603) 888-7000
FAX: (603) 888-7700
Products: HP OpenView

Hewlett-Packard Co.
3000 Hanover St.
Palo Alto, CA 94303-0890
(800) 826-4111
FAX: (800) 333-1917
Products: HP OpenView

Hewlett-Packard Co.
5070 Centennial Blvd.
Colorado Springs, CO 80919
(800) 452-4844
FAX: (719) 531-4526
Products: HP OpenView

Hewlett-Packard Co., Direct Marketing
Organization
Building 51, PO Box 58059
Santa Clara, CA 95051-8059
(800) 826-4111
Products: HP OpenView

Hewlett-Packard Co., Roseville
Networks Div.
8000 Foolhills Blvd.
Roseville, CA 95747
(800) 533-1333
FAX: (800) 333-1917
Products: HP OpenView, HP OpenView

HIARC
3 Corporate Park, Suite 250
IrvInc. CA 92714
(714) 253-6990
FAX: (714) 253-6995
Products: SPARCUS, HIARC v2.x

HICOMP AMERICA
P0 Box 22758
Houston, TX 77227-2758
(800) 232-8863
FAX: (713) 626-3654

High Caliber Systems Inc.
171 Madison Ave. - 8th Floor
New York, NY 10016
(212) 684-5553
FAX: (212) 532-2362

Highland Technologies Inc.
7701 Greenbelt Road, Suite 505
Greenbelt, MO 20770
(301) 345-8200
FAX: (301) 345-8201

Hilgraeve Inc.
111 Conant Ave., Suite A
Monroe, MI 68121
(313) 243-0576
FAX: (313) 243-0645

Hill Associates Inc.
17 Roosevell Highway
Colchester, VT 05446
(802) 655-0940
FAX: (802) 655-7974

Hitachi Computer Products
(America) Inc.
3101 Tasman Drive
Santa Clara, CA 95054
(408) 986-9770
FAX: (408) 980-9616

Hitachi Home Electronics (America) Inc.
401 W. Artesia Blvd.
Compton, CA 90220
(310) 537-8383 or (800) 537-8383
FAX: (310) 515-6223

HiTecSoft Corp.
3370 N. Hayden Road, Suite 123-175
Scottsdale, AZ 85251
(602) 970-1025
FAX: (602) 970-6323
Products: ManageWare

HiTek Solutions Inc.
2361 Campus Drive, Suite 107
IrvInc. CA 92715
(714) 474-8270
FAX: (714) 474-8272

Hooleon Corp.
260 Justin Drive
Cononwood, AZ 86326
(800) 937-1337 or (602) 634-7515
FAX: (602) 634-4620
Products: Custom Key Imprinting
Software

Horizons Technology Inc.
3990 Ruffin Road
San Diego, CA 92123
(800) 28-3808
FAX: (619) 565-1175
Products: LANauditor, InfoPump

HT Communications
4480 Shopping Lane
Simi Valley, CA 93063-3451
(805) 579-1700
FAX: (805) 522 5295

HT Research Inc.
1342 Bell Ave, Unit 3E
Tustin, CA 92680
(714) 566-9100
FAX: (714) 566-9109

Hubbell Premise Wiring Inc.
14 Lord's Hill Road, PO Box 901
Stonington, CT 06378-0901
(800) 626-0005 or (203) 535-8326
FAX: (203) 535-8328

Hummingbird Communications Ltd.
2900 John St.
Markham, ONT L3R 5G3 Canada
(905) 470-1203
FAX: (905) 470-1207

I, Levy & Associates Inc.
1633 Des Peres Road, Suite 300
St. Louis, MO 63131
(314) 822-0810
FAX: (314) 822-0309

I/O Concepts Inc.
2125 112th Ave. NE, Suite 303
Bellevue, WA 98004
(206) 450 0650
FAX: (206) 622-0058

Ibex Technologies
550 Main St, Suite G
Placerville, CA 95667
(916) 621-4342
FAX: (916) 621-2004

IBM Corp.
PO Box 12195, Department CO9/B060
Research Triangle Park, NC 27709
(800) IBM-CALL or (800) IBM-CARY
FAX: (800) 2-IBMor (800) IBM-4
Products: Network Door/2

IBM Corp.
Old Orchard Road
Armonk, NY 10504
(800) IBM-CALL or (800) IBM-CARY
FAX: (800) 2-IBMor (800) IBM-4
Products: Network Door/2, CATS v3.2

IBM Corp., DatagLANce Network
Analyzer Development
Dept E67, Bld. 660, PO Box 12195
Research Triangle Park, NC 27709
(919) 254-1364
FAX: (800) IBM-4
Products: Network Door/2

IBM Personal Computer Co.
Route 100
Somers, NY 10589
(914) 766-1900
FAX: (914) 766-0116
Products: Network Door/2

IBM, Software Solutions Div.
Route 100, Bldg 1, M.D. 1335
Somers, NY 10589
(8OO) IBM-CALL or (800) IBM-CARY
FAX: (800) 2-IBMor (800) IBM-4
Products: Network Door/2

ICON Resources Inc.
1050 N. State St., Suite 210
Chicago, IL 60172
(312) 573-0142
FAX: (312) 573-0143

ICOT Corp.
3801 Zanker Road
San Jose, CA 95134
(800) SNA-3270 or (408) 432-3138
FAX: (408) 433-9466

IDAS Corp.
1936 E. Deere Ave.
Santa Ana, CA 92705
(714) 553-1904
FAX: (714) 553-1935

IDEA
29 Dunham Road
Billerica, MA 01821
(800) 251-5027 or (508) 663-6878
FAX: (508) 663-8851

IDOC Inc.
10474 Santa Monica Blvd, Suite 404
Los Angeles, CA 90025
(800) 336-9898
FAX: (310) 446-4661

IEM Inc.
14329 Blue Spruce Drive
Ft. Collins, CO 80524
(800) 321-4671 or (303) 221-3005
FAX: (303) 221-1909

IGEL, LLC
3375 Scott Blvd, Suite 420
Santa Clara, CA 95054
(800) 988-4435 or (408) 988-4883
FAX: (408) 988-0834

Illustra Information Technologies Inc.
1111 Broadway, Suite 2000
Oakland, CA 94607
(510) 652-8000
FAX: (510) 869-6350

Imatek Inc.
1029 Pecten Courtt
Milpitas, CA 95035
(510) 683-8888 or (510) 226-4774
FAX: (510) 683-0777

IMC Networks
16931 Millikan Ave.
IrvInc. CA 92714
(714) 724-1070
FAX: (714) 724-1020

INCOM Integrated Computer Systems
9735 Valley View Road, Suite 115
Macedonia, OH 44056
(800) 41-INCOM or (216) 467-5222
FAX: (216) 467-6521
Products: CSuper NLM

Incotel Inc.
5 Penn Plaza, 17 Floor
New York, NY 10001
(212) 594-8340
FAX: (212) 695-5889

Independence Technologies Inc.
42705 Lawrence Place
Fremont, CA 94538
(800) 605-9010
FAX: (510) 438-2034
Products: iVIEW

Infinite Technologies
11433 Cronridge Drive
Owings Mills, MD 21117
(800) 678-1097 or (410) 363-1097
FAX: (410) 363-0846

Information Builders Inc.
1250 Broadway
New York, NY 10001
(800) 969-INFO or (212) 736-4433
FAX: (212) 629-8819

Information Management Research
5660 Greenwood Plaza, Suite 210
Englewood, CO 80111
(303) 689-0022
FAX: (303) 689-0055

Information Resource Engineering Inc.
8029 Corporate Drive
Baltimore, MD 21236
(410) 931-7500
FAX: (410) 931-7524

Informative Graphics Corp.
706 E. Bell Road, Suite 207
Phoenix, AZ 85022
(802) 971-6061
FAX: (602) 971-1714

Informer Data Security
12833 Monarch St.
Garden Grove, CA 92641
(800) 860-lNFO or (714) 379-4480
FAX: (714) 379-4490

Informix Software Inc.
4100 Bohannon Dnve
Menlo Park, CA 94025
(800) 331-1763
FAX: (415) 926-6593

Infosys International Inc.
6080 Jericho Turnpike, Suite 202
Commack, NY 11725
(516) 462-6474

InfraLAN Wireless Communications
360 Massachusetts Ave.
Acton, MA 01720
(800) 266-1505 or (508) 266-1500
FAX: (508) 635-0806

Innosoft International Inc.
1050 E. Garvey Ave. South
West Covina, CA 91790
(800) 552-5444 or (818) 919-3600
FAX: (818) 919-3614

Instant Information Inc.
7618 SW Mohawk St.
Tualatin, OR 97062
(503) 692-9711
FAX: (503) 691-1948

Intech
28346 Pueblo Drive
Trabuco Canyon, CA 92679
(800) 850-5267 or (714) 539-0164
FAX: (714) 589-0999

Integral Poripherals Inc.
5775 Flatiron Parkway, Suite 100
Boulder, CO 80301
(303) 449-8009
FAX: (303) 449-8089

Integrated Marketing Corp.
1038 B Kiel Court
Sunnyvale, CA 94089
(800) 537-5999

Intel Corp.
5200 NE Elam Young Parkway
Hillsboro, OR 97124
(800) 538-3373
FAX: (800) 525-3019
Products: LANDesk Response LANDesk
Manager, LANrecord

Intellicom Inc.
20415 Nordhoff St.
Chatsworth, CA 91311
(818) 407-3900
FAX: (818) 882-2404

IntelliPower Inc.
10-A Thomas St.
IrvInc. CA 92718
(714) 587-0155
FAX: (714) 587-0230

Intellisoft Inc.
2114 W. Mayfield Road
Arlington, TX 76015-2841
(800) 933-4889
FAX: (817) 467-7133

IntelliSys Corp.
762 Nuttal Oak Ct.
Sunnyvale, CA 94086
(408) 253-5164
FAX: (408) 253-5164

InterActive Inc.
204 N. Main
Humboldt, SD 57035
(800) 292-2112
FAX: (605) 363-5102

InterCon Systems Corp.
950 Herndon Pkwy.
Herndon, VA 22070
(703) 709-5555
Products: WatchTower

InterConnections Inc.
14711 NE 29th Place
Bellevue, WA 98007
(800) 950-5773 or (206) 881-4023
FAX: (206) 867-5022
Products: Leverage Host Services

Interface Solutions
6390 Johnson Road
Bozeman, MT 59715
(406) 586-1673
FAX: (406) 585-0753

Interlink Computer Sciences Inc.
47370 Fremont Blvd.
Fremont, CA 94538
(800) 422-3711
FAX: (510) 659-6381
Products: SNS/TCPaccess v2.1

International Connectivity Consortium
(ICC)
3872 Grove Ave.
Palo Alto, CA 94303
(415) 494-3706
FAX: (415) 949-9170

International Connectors and Cable
Corp.
16918 Edwards Road
Cerrilos, CA 90701
(800) 333-7776 or (310) 926-0734
FAX: (310) 926-5290

International Data Sciences Inc.
301 Jefferson Blvd.
Warwick, RI 02806-1317
(401) 737-9900 or (800) 437-3282
FAX: (401) 737-9911

International Power Machines
2975 Miller Park North
Garland, TX 75042
(800) 527-1208
FAX: (214) 494-2690

International Transware Inc.
1503 Grant Road, Suite 155
Mounlain View, CA 94040
(800) 999-NETS or (415) 903-2300
FAX: (415) 903-9544

Interphase Corp.
13800 Senlac
Dallas, TX 75234-8823
(800) FASTNET or (214) 919-9111

INTERSOLV
1700 NW 167th Place
Beaverton, OR 97006
(800) 547-7827
FAX: (503) 645-4576

INTRAK Inc.
9999 Business Park Ave., Suite B
San Diego, CA 92131
(800) 233-7494
FAX: (619) 271-4989
Products: ServerTrak, ServerTrak for
Windows, TrendTrak

Iomega Corp.
1821 W. 4000 S.
Roy, UT 84067
(800) 777-6654 or (801) 778-3460
FAX: (801) 778-5763

Iomega Tape Products
15110 Ave of Science, Suite 100
San Diego, CA 92128
(619) 673-5500
FAX: (619) 673-3942

Ipswitch Inc.
669 Main street
Wakefield, MA 01880
(617) 246-1150
FAX: (617) 245-2975
Products: Acadia VxD, Network
Management Tools, Piper/IP, Coax/
Twinax Analyzer

IQ Technologies
13625 NE 126th Place, Suite 400
Kirkland, WA 98034
(800) 227-2817
FAX: (206) 821-3961

IRI Software
200 Fifth Ave.
Waltham, MA 02154
(800) 765-7227 or (617) 890-1100
FAX: (617) 672-4600

ISICAD Inc.
1920 W. Corporate Way
Anaheim, CA 92803
(714) 533-8910 or (800) 634-1223
FAX: (714) 533-8642
Products: COMMAND HelpDesk
COMMAND, CNM

ITV Communications Inc.
6800 Owensmouth Ave.
Canoga Park, CA 91303
(813) 975-0564
FAX: (813) 972-5587

J&L Information Systems
9600 Topanga Canyon Blvd.
Chatsworth, CA 91311
(818) 709-1778
FAX: (818) 882-9134

James River Group Inc.
125 N. First St.
Minneapolis, MN 55401
(612) 339-2521

JetFAX (nc.
1376 Willow Road
Menlo Park, CA 94025
(800) 753-8329 or (415) 324-0600
FAX: (415) 326-6003

JOLT
PO Box 53354
Jerusalem, 91533 Israel
+972-2-710445 or (415) 964-7173
FAX: ()+972-2-710448

JSB Corp
Products: MultiView Mascot

JSG Corp.
108 Whispering Pines Drive, Suite 115
Scotts Valley, CA 95066
(800) 359-3408 or (408) 438-8300
FAX: (408) 438-8360

JSI FundRaising Systems Inc.
210 Lincoln St.
Boston, MA 02111
(800) 521-0132
FAX: (617) 482-0617

JYACC Inc.
116 John St.
New York City, NY 10038
(212) 267-7722
FAX: (212) 608-6753

Kalpana Inc.
1154 E. Arques Ave.
Sunnyvale, CA 94086-4602
(800) 488-0775 or (408) 749-1600
FAX: (408) 749-1690

Kaseworks Inc.
1 Meca Way, Suite 150
Norcross, GA 30093
(800) 888-4335
FAX: (404) 564-5679

Katron Technologies Inc.
7400 Harwin Drive, Suite 120
Houston, TX 77036
(713) 266-3891
FAX: (713) 266-3893

Kedwell Software Inc.
75 Congress St.
Portsmouth, NH 03801
(603) 433-4777
FAX: (603) 433-4222
Products: ManualWriter

Keyfile Corp.
22 Cotton Road
Nashua, NH 03063
(603) 883-3800 or (800) 4-KEYFILE
FAX: (603) 889-9259

KeyLogic Inc.
Independence Place, PO Box 278
Goffstown, NH 03045
(603) 472-4006
FAX: (603) 497-3785
Products: LANBatch

Keyword Office Technologies Ltd.
2816, 11 St. NE
Calgary, ALB T2E 7S7 Canada
(800) 866-6539 or (403) 250-1770
FAX: (403) 250-1964

Kingston Technology Corp.
17600 Newhope St.
Fountain Valley, CA 92708
(800) 435-2620 or (714) 435-2600
FAX: (714) 435-2699

KL Group Inc.
260 King St. E. Third Floor
Toronto, ONT M5A 1K3 Canada
(416) 594-1026 or (800) 663-4723
FAX: (416) 594-1919

Klever Computers Inc.
1028 W. Maude Ave.
Sunnyvale, CA 94086
(800) 745-4660
FAX: (408) 735-7723

Klos Technologies Inc.
604 Daniel Webster Highway
Merrimack, NH 03054
(603) 424-8300
FAX: (603) 424-9300

KnowledgeWare Inc.
3340 Peachtree Road, NE
Atlanta, GA 30326
(800) 444-8575
FAX: (404) 365-0246

Knozall Systems Inc., A Division of
Tangram Enterprise Solutions, Inc.
375 E. Elliot Road, Suite 10
Chandler, AZ 85225-1130
(800) 333-8698 or (602) 545-0006
FAX: (602) 545-0008
Products: FileWizard

KofAX Image Products
3 Jenner St.
IrvInc. CA 92718-3807
(714) 727-1733
FAX: (714) 727-3144

L-Com Inc.
1755 Osgood St.
North Andover, MA 01845
(508) 682-6936
FAX: (508) 689-9484

Lago Systems Inc., A StorageTek Co.
151 Albright Way
Los Gatos, CA 95030
(800) 866-LAGO
FAX: (408) 374-2330

Lan Performance Labs
4901 Morena Blvd., Suite 805
San Diego, CA 92117
(800) 726-8101 or (619) 273-1442
FAX: (619) 273-2706

LAN Scope Inc.
18 W. Langhorne Ave.
Havertown, PA 19083
(800) 879-5330 or (610) 359-3573
FAX: (610) 446-2663

LAN Surveyors
371 Ariel Drive
Harvest. AL 35749
(205) 837-9718

LAN-ACES Inc.
12777 Jones Road, Suite 461
Houston, TX 77070
(800) LAN-ACES or (713) 890-9787
FAX: (713) 890-9731

LAN-hopper Systems Inc.
3180 Presidential Drive, Suite K
Atlanla, GA 30340
(800) 350-5540 or (404) 458-1044
FAX: (404) 451-9843

LAN-Link Corp.
1724 Clarkson Road
Chesterfield, MO 63017
(314) 537-9800
FAX: (314) 394-6659

LAN\mind
2000 N. RacInc. Suite 4600
Chicago, IL 60614
(800) 325-5267 or (312) 935-9900
FAX: (312) 935-0238

LANart Corp.
145 Rosemary St.
Needham, MA 02194
(800) 292-1994 or (617) 444-1994
FAX: (617) 444-3692

LANCAST
10 Northern Blvd Unit 5
Amherst, NH 03031
(800) 752-2768
FAX: (603) 881-9888

LANcity Corp.
100 Brickstone Square
Andover, MA 01810
(800) LANcity or (508) 475-4050
FAX: (508) 475-4050

LANDCADD International Inc.
7366 S. Revere Parkway, Building 900
Englewood, CO 80112-3942
(303) 799-3600
FAX: (303) 799-3696 or 3697

Landings Technology Corp.
Merrill Block, Unit A2, 163 Water St,
Exeter, NH 03833
(800) 222-3734 or (603) 772-4500
FAX: (603) 772-0141
Products: adapters hubs switch cards
repeaters concentrators

LANNET Inc.
17942 Cowan Ave.
IrvInc. CA 92714
(800) 522-6638
FAX: (714) 752-6641

LANovation
1313 Fifth St. SE
Minneapolis, MN 55414
(800) 747-4487 or (61 2) 379-3805
FAX: (612) 378-3818
Products: LAN Escort

LANQuest
2225 Qume Drive
San Jose, CA 95131
(800) 487-7779 or (408) 894-1000
FAX: (408) 894-1001
Products: Frame Thrower 3.2

LANshark Systems Inc.
6502 E. Main St.
Reynoldsburg, OH 43068
(614) 866-5553
FAX: (614) 866-4877
Products: Network Management Tools

LANSource Technologies Inc.
221 Dufferin St., Suite 310A
Toronlo, ONT M6K 3J2 Canada
(800) 677-2727 or (416) 535-3555
FAX: (416) 535-6225

Lantech of America Inc.
4401 Vineland Road
Orlando, FL 32811
(317) 251-7975
FAX: (317) 254-3305

LANTELL
16250 Ventura Blvd, Suite 202
Encino, CA 91436
(800) 526-8355 or (818) 905-1262
FAX: (818) 905-1292

Lantronix
15353 Barranca Parkway
IrvInc. CA 92718
(800) 422-7055 or (714) 453-3990
FAX: (714) 453-3995

Lanworks Technologies Inc.
2425 Skymark Ave.
Mississauga, ONT L4W 4Y6 Canada
(800) 808-3000 or (905) 238-5528
FAX: (714) 367-0895 or (905) 238-9407
Products: BootWare Mngr, Notework v3,
DaVinci eMail, AuditTrack NLM,
SofTrack Network Management Tools

Larscom Incorporated
4600 Patrick Henry Drive
Santa Clara, CA 95054
(408) 988-6600
FAX: (408) 986-9690
Products: Network Management Tools

Laser Communications Inc.
PO Box 10066, 1886 Charter Lane, Suite F
Lancaster, PA 17605-0066
(717) 394-8634
FAX: (717) 396-9831

LaserData Inc.
300 Vesper Park
Tyngsboro, MA 01879
(800) 527-9773 or (508) 649-4600
FAX: (508) 649-4436

LaserMaster Corp.
6900 Shady Oak Road
Eden Praire, MN 55344
(800) 365-4646 or (612) 944-9330
FAX: (612) 944-9519

Learning Tree International
1805 Library St.
Reston, VA 22090
(800) 843-8733
FAX: (703) 709-6405

LeeMah DataCom Security Corp.
3948 Trust Way
Hayward, CA 94545
(510) 786-0790 or (800) 992-0020
FAX: (510) 786-1123

Legacy Storage Systems Inc.
25 South St.
Hopkinton, MA 01748
(508) 435-4700
FAX: (508) 435-3080

Legent Corp.
375 Herndon Parkway
Herndon, VA 22070
(800) 676-LGNT
Products: Network Management Tools

Legeto Systems Inc.
3145 Porter Drive
Palo Alto, CA 94304
(415) 812-6000
FAX: (415) 812-6032

Levi, Ray & Shoup Inc.
2401 W. Monroe St.
Springfield, IL 62704
(217) 793-3800
FAX: (217) 787-0979

Leviton Manufacturing Co. Inc.
59-25 Little Neck Pkwy
Liltle Neck, NY 11363
(800) 323-8920
FAX: (800) 832-9538

Leviton Tolcom
2222 - 222nd St. SE
Bothell, WA 98021-4422
(800) 722-2082
FAX: (206) 483-5270

Lexmark International Inc.
740 New Circle Road NW
Lexington, KY 40511
(800) 358-5835
FAX: (306) 232-2380

Liant Software Corp.
8911 Capital Of Texas Highway North
Austin, TX 78759
(512) 43-1010 or (800) 762-6265
FAX: (512) 343-9487
Products: RM/InfoExpress, NodeInfo,
TaskMaster

Libra Corp.
1954 E. 7000 S
Salt Lake City, UT 84121-3094
(800) 453-3827 or (801) 943-2084
FAX: (801) 944-7210

Liebert Corp.
1050 Dearborn Drive
Columbus, OH 43229-9479
(800) 877-9222
FAX: (614) 841-6973
Products: UPStation S

Lightstream Corp.
1100 Technology Park Drive
Billerica, MA 01821
(508) 262-1000
FAX: (508) 262-1072

LinkPro
PO Box 6044
Irvine. CA 92716-6044
(800) 449-7962
FAX: (714) 833-3301
Products: PowerSync v1.11

Linksys
16811A Millikan Ave.
IrvInc. CA 92714
(800) 546-5797
FAX: (714) 261-8868

LINQ Systems
PO Box 11040
Tucson, AZ 85734
(800) 870-3185 or (602) 741-8420
FAX: (602) 741-6489

LION America Inc.
1900 S. Proforma Ave, Suite F-1
Ontario, CA 91761
(909) 923-5700
FAX: (909) 923-5708

Locus Computing Corp.
9800 La Cienega Blvd.
Inglewood, CA 90301-4440
(310) 670-6500
FAX: (310) 670-2980

Logic Works
106 Route 206
Princeton, NJ 08540
(800) 78-ERWIN or (609) 252-1177
FAX: (609) 252-1175

Logical Engineering LC
5364 Ehrlich Road, Suite 250
Tampa, FL 33625
(813) 264-5236
FAX: (813) 264-5140

Logical Operations
595 Blossom Road
Rochester, NY 14610
(800) 456-4677
FAX: (716) 288-7411

Logicode Technology Inc.
1380 Flynn Road
Camarillo, CA 93012
(800) 735-6442
FAX: (805) 388-8991

Logicraft
22 Cotton Road
Nashua, NH 03063
(800) 880-5644 or (603) 880-0300
FAX: (603) 880-7229

LOOK Software
PO Box 78072, Cityview
Nepean, ONT K2G 5W2 Canada
(613) 837-2151
FAX: (613) 837-5572

Lotus Development Corp.
55 Cambridge Parkway
Cambridge, MA 02142
(800) 343-5414 or (617) 577-8500; Canada
(800) 465-6887
FAX: (617) 253-9150

Luxcom Inc.
3249 Laurelview Court
Fremont, CA 94538
(800) 322-5000 or (510) 770-3300
FAX: (510) 770-3399

Macola Software
333 E. Center St.
Marion, OH 43302
(800) 468-0834 or (614) 382-5999,ext 650
FAX: (614) 382-0239

Madge Networks Inc.
2310 N. First St.
San Jose, CA 95131
(800) 876-2343 or (408) 955-0700
FAX: (408) 955-0970

Magee Enterprises Inc.
2909 Langford Road, Suite A-600
Norcross, GA 30071
(800) 662-4330 or (404) 446-661 1
FAX: (404) 368-0719
Products: Network H.Q., Automenu for
Networks

Magic Software Enterprises
1200 Main St.
IrvInc. CA 92714
(800) 345-6244
FAX: (714) 250-7404
Products: SupportMagic

MAGIC Solutions Inc.
180 Franklin Turnpike
Mahwah, NJ 07430
(201) 529-5533
FAX: (201) 529-2955

MagicRam Inc.
1850 Beverly Blvd.
Los Angeles, CA 90057
(213) 413-9999
FAX: (213) 413-0828

Main Strike Telecommunications Inc.
485-18 S. Broadway
Hicksville, NY 11801
(800) 735-5631 or (516) 933-2005
FAX: (516) 933-2004

Make Systems Inc.
201 San Antonio Circle
Mountain View, CA 94040
(800) 545-MAKE or (415) 941-9800
FAX: (415) 941-5856
Products: NetMaker XA

Mannesmann Tally Corp.
PO Box 97018
Kent, WA 98064-9718
(800) 843-1347 or (206) 251-5524
FAX: (206) 251-5520

Marine Management
Systems (MMS) Inc.
102 Hamilton Ave.
Stamford, CT 06902
(203) 327-6404
FAX: (203) 967-2927

Markham Computer Corp.
One South Ocean Blvd., Suite 301
Boca Raton, FL 33432-5111
(800) 262-7542 or (407) 394-3994
FAX: (407) 394-3844
Products: NetOp Dial v4.1, NetOp v4.30,
NetOpPM v4.30

Marpet Technical Services
PO Box 2275
Fremont, CA 94536
(510) 792-9204, ext. 2
FAX: (510) 797-5053

Marvic International Inc.
768 E. 93rd St.
Brooklyn, NY 11236
(718) 346-7822
FAX: (718) 346-0438

Mass Memory Systems Inc.
1414 Gay Drive
Winter Park, FL 32789
(407) 629-1081
FAX: (407) 628-3862

Master Software Corp.
5975 Castle Creek Parkway N Drive
Suite 300
Indianapolis,IN 46250
(800) 950-2999, ext. 4104
FAX: (317) 849-5280

Mastersoft Inc.
8737 E. Via de Commercio
Sconsdale, AZ 85258
(800) 624-6017 or (602) 949-4388
FAX: (602) 948-8261

Matrox Electronic Systems
1055 St. Regis Blvd.
Dorval, QUE H9P 2T4 Canada
(800) 361-4903
FAX: (514) 685-7030

Maxell Corp of America
22-08 Route 208
Fair Lawn, NJ 07410
(201) 794-5900
FAX: (201) 796-8790

Maximum Strategy Inc.
801 Buckeye Courtt
Milpitas, CA 95035
(800) 352-1600 or (408) 383-1600
FAX: (408) 383-1616

McAfee
2710 Walsh Ave.
Santa Clara,CA 95051-0963
(408) 988-3832
FAX: (408) 970-9727
Products: BrightWorks, VirusScan, LAN
Inventory, Site Meter

MDI —A Sybase Co.
3035 Center Green Drive
Boulder, C0 80301
(800) 221-3634 or (303) 443-2706
FAX: (303) 443-2797

Media Integration Inc.
3949 Research Park Court, Suite 190
Soquel, CA 95073
(800) 824-7385 or (408) 475-9400
FAX: (408) 475-0110

MediaSoft Telecom Inc.
2380 Notre-Dame West, Suite 300
Montreal, QUE H3J 1N4 Canada
(514) 939-3838
FAX: (514) 939-7292

Medical Office Software Inc.
2280 SW 70th Ave, Suite 9
Davie, FL 33317
(800) 486-1667
FAX: (305) 476-5616

Mega Drive Systems Inc.
489 S. Robertson Blvd.
Beverly Hills, CA 90211
(800) 404-MEGA
FAX: (310) 247-8118

Megaherz Corp.
605 N. 5600 W., PO Box 16020
Salt Lake City, UT 84116
(800) LAPTOPS
FAX: (801) 320-6022

Memorex Telex
Texas Commerce Tower
545 E. John Carpenter Freeway
Irving, TX 75062
(214) 444-3500
FAX: (214) 444-3501

Mercurv Interactive Corp.
3333 Octavius Drive
Santa Clara, CA 95054
(408) 987-0100
FAX: (408) 982-0149

Mergent International Inc.
70 Inwood Road
Rocky Hill, CT 08067
(800) 688-1105 or (203) 257-4223

Meridian Data Inc.
5615 Scotts Valley Drive
Scotts Valley, CA 95066
(800) 767-2537 or (408) 438-3100
FAX: (408) 438-6816

Meridian Technology Corp.
11 McBride Corporate Center Drive
Suite 250
Chesterfield, MO 63005-1406
(314) 532-7708
FAX: (314) 532-3242

Merlin Gerin
1660 Scenic Ave.
Costa Mesa,CA 92626
(800) 344-0570
FAX: (714) 434-7652

MetaCard Corp.
4710 Shoup Place
Boulder, CO 80303
(303) 447-3936
FAX: (303) 499-9855

Metacomp Inc.
10989 Via Frontera
San Diego, CA 92127
(619) 674-5000
FAX: (619) 674-5005

MetaWare Inc.
2161 Delaware Ave
Santa Cruz, CA 95060-5706
(408) 429-6382
FAX: (408) 429-9273

METZ Software Inc.
PO Box 6699
Bellevue, WA 98008
(800) 447-1712 or (206) 641-4525
FAX: (206) 644-6026

Micah Development Corp.
955 Massachusetts Ave., Suite 365
Cambridge, MA 02139
(800) 853-1783 or (617) 641-1500
FAX: (617) 641-1973

MICOM Communications Corp.
4100 Los Angeles Ave.
Simi Vallev, CA 93063
(800) 642-6687 or (805) 583-8600
FAX: (805) 583-1997

Micro Computer Systems Inc.
2300 Valley View, Suite 800
Irving, TX 75062
(214) 659-1514
FAX: (214) 659-1624

Micro Data Base Systems Inc. (MDBS)
1305 Cumberland Ave, P0 Box 2438
West Lafayette, IN 47906
(800) 445-6327 or (317) 463-7200
FAX: (317) 463-1234

Micro Design International Inc.
6985 University Blvd.
Winter Park, FL 32792
(800) 228-0891 or (407) 677-8333
FAX: (407) 677-8365

Micro Focus
509 Seaport Court
Redwood City, CA 94063
(415) 856-4161
FAX: (415) 496-7362

Micro Pulse Inc.
409 Calle San Pablo
Camarillo, CA 93012
(805) 389-3448
FAX: (805) 389-3448

Micro-Integration Corp.
One Science Park
Frostburg, MD 21532
(800) 832-4526
FAX: (301) 689-0808

Microcom Inc.
500 River Ridge Drive
Norwood, MA 02062
(800) 822-8224
FAX: (617) 551-1021

Microdyne Corp.
3601 Eisenhower Ave.
Alexandria, VA 22304
(800) 255-3967
FAX: (703) 683-8924

MicroNet Technology Inc.
80 Technology
IrvInc. CA 92718
(714) 453-6100
FAX: (714) 453-6101

Microplex Systems Ltd.
8525 Commerce Court
Burnaby, BC V5A 4N3 Canada
(800) 665-7798 or (604) 444-4232
FAX: (604) 444-4239

Micropolis Corp.
21211 Nordhoff St.
Chatsworth, CA 91311
(800) 395-3748
FAX: (818) 718-5312

Microrim Inc.
15395 SE 30th Place
Bellevue, WA 98007
(800) 628-6990 or (206) 649-9500
FAX: (206) 649-2785

Microsott Corp.
One Microsoft Way
Redmond, WA 98052-6399
(800) 227-4679

MicroSpec Inc.
1809 Ave. K
Plano, TX 75074-5907
(800) 451-3383
FAX: (214) 881-1809

Microsystems Engineering Co.
2500 Highland Ave, Suite 350
Lombard, IL 60148
(800) SYS-DRAW
FAX: (708) 261-9520
Products: Sysdraw v7.1

Microtest Inc.
4747 N. 22nd St.
Phoenix, AZ 85016-4708
(800) 526-9675
FAX: (802) 952-6401
Products: Network Management Tools

Microwave Bypass Systems
72 Sharp St, Build C8
Hingham, MA 02043
(617) 337-2005
FAX: (617) 337-0544

Microwork Inc.
47 W. St. Andrews Lane
DeerField, IL 60015
(708) 940-8979
FAX: (708) 940-8979
Products: Job Scheduling Server

MiLAN Technology Corp.
894 Ross Drive, Suite t0t
Sunnyvale, CA 94089-1443
(800) G0-MiLAN or (408) 752-2770
FAX: (408) 752-2790

MilesTek Inc.
1 Lake Trail Drive
Argyle, TX 76226
(800) 524-7444 or (817) 455-7444
FAX: (817) 455-2111

Millidyne Inc.
3645 Trust Drive
Raleigh, NC 27604
(919) 876-6413
FAX: (919) 876-6492

Minolta Corp.
101 Williams Drive
Ramsey, NJ 07446
(800) 9-MINOLTA
FAX: (201) 818-3240

MINUTEMAN
1455 LeMay Drive
Carrollton, TX 75007
(800) 238-7272
FAX: (214) 446-9011

MIS Training Institute
498 Concord
Framingham, MA 01701
(508) 879-7999
FAX: (508) 872-1153

Mitron Computer Inc.
2220 S. Bascom Ave.
Campbell, CA 95008
(800) 713-6888 or (408) 371-8166

MOD-TAP
PD Box 706
Harvard, MA 01451
(508) 772-5630
FAX: (508) 772-2011

Modatech Systems Inc.
1681 Chestnut St.
Vancouver, BC V6J 4M8 Canada
(800) 804-MAXX
FAX: (214) 929-5177

Modular Industrial Solutions Inc.
1729 Little Orchard St.
San Jose, CA 95125-1039
(408) 971-0910
FAX: (408) 971-0763

Montrose/CDT
28 Sword St.
Auburn, MA 01501
(800) 318-8828 or (508) 791-3161
FAX: (508) 793-9862

Moses Computers
15466 Los Gatos Blvd Suite 201
Los Gatos, CA 95032
(408) 358-1550 or (800) 30-MOSES
FAX: (408) 356-9049

Mountain Network Solutions Inc.
360 El Pueblo Road
Scotts Valley, CA 95066
(800) 458-0300 or (408) 438-6650
FAX: (408) 461-3047

MTI
4905 E. La Palma Ave.
Anaheim, CA 92807
(714) 970-0300
FAX: (714) 693-2256

Multi-Tech Systems Inc.
2205 Woodale Drive
Mounds View, MN 55112
(612) 785-3500 or (800) 328-9717
FAX: (612) 785-9874

Multima Corp.
One Rosewood Court
East Greenwich, RI 02818-1543
(800) 532-4862 or (401) 885-1916
FAX: (401) 885-2605
Products: NETKEEPER HELP DESK
PRO, NetKeeper Express,

MUST Software International
101 Merritt 7
Norwalk, CT 06856
(800) 441-MUST
FAX: (203) 845-5252

Mustang Software Inc.
6200 Lake Ming Road
Bakersfield, CA 93306
(800) 999-9619 or (605) 873-2500
FAX: (805) 873-2599

National Business Consultants
1009 Wilshire Blvd, Suite 221
Santa Monica, CA 90401
(310) 392-5127
FAX: (310) 395-9284

National Computer Security Association
10 S. Courthouse Ave.
Carlisle, PA 17013
(717) 258-1816
FAX: (717) 243-8642

National Data Conversion Institute
5 E. 16th St.
New York, NY 10003
(212) 463-7511
FAX: (212) 645-9327

National Instrumemts
6504 Bridge Point Parkway
Austin, TX 78730-5039
(51 2) 794-0100 or (800) 433-3488
FAX: (512) 794-8411

National Management Systems
1945 01d Gallows Road, Suite 206
Vienna, VA 22182
(703) 827-0797
FAX: (703) 790-1965

National Semiconductor
2900 Semiconductor Drive
Santa Clara, CA 95052-8090
(800) 227-1817

National Semiconductor Corp.
M/S D3-615, PO Box 58090, 2900
Semiconductor Drive
Santa Clara, CA 95052-8090
(800) 227-1817, ext. 100
FAX: (408) 721-7662

NDP
2145 Calumet St.
Clearwater, FL 34625
(813) 989-5500 ext 7
FAX: (813) 562-2244

NEC America Inc, Data
Communications Systems Div.
1525 W. Walnut Hill Lane
Irving, TX 75038-3797
(800) 222-4NEC or (214) 518-4480
FAX: (214) 518-5572

NEKOTech
9272 Jeronimo Road, Suite 115
IrvInc. CA 92718
(714) 580-0055
FAX: (714) 580-0060

Neon Software
3685 Mt. Diablo Blvd, Suite 203
Lafayene, CA 94549
(510) 283-9771
FAX: (510) 283-6507
Products: Network Management Tools

Nestor Inc.
One Richmond Square
Providence; RI 02906
(404) 331-9640
FAX: (401) 331-7319

Net Manage
10725 North De Anza Blvd
Cupertino, CA 95014
(408) 973-7171
FAX: (408) 257-6405
Products: NEWTtrace, NEWTWatch

Net+Effects
6475 Dwyer Court
San Jose, CA 95120-2845
(408) 739-0557 or (408) 997- 1915
FAX: (408) 997-1915

NET-CON LTD.
454 Las Gallinas Ave, Suite 279
San Rafael, CA 94903-3618
(415) 472-7145
FAX: (415) 507-1553

Net-X-Terminator Inc.
956 S. Bartlett Road, Suite 161
Bartlett, IL 60103
(800) 700-NETX or (708) 830-8199
FAX: (708) 830-7689

NetEdge Systems Inc.
GE Aircraft Building #3
3701 S. Miami Blvd.
Raleigh, NC 27703
(919) 361-9000 or (800) NET-EDGE
FAX: (919) 361-9060

NetFRAME Systems Inc.
1545 Barber Lane
Milpitas, CA 95035
(800) 852-3726 or (408) 944-0600
FAX: (800) 852-3726 or (408) 434-4190

NetGuard Systems Inc.
3020 Old Ranch Parkway, Suite 300
Seal Beach, CA 90740-2751
(800) 670-0003
FAX: (310) 799-5590

NETInc.
20218 Bridgedale Lane
Humble, TX 77338
(800) 365-6384 or (713) 446-2154
FAX: (713) 540-3045
Products: Netsentry, NetMenu LAN
Toolkit v5.0

Netix Communications Inc.
15375 Barranca Pkwy Suite G-107
IrvInc. CA 92718
(714) 727-9335
FAX: (714) 727-3922

NetLabs Inc.
4920 El Camino Real
Los Allos, CA 94022
(800) 525-4565
FAX: (415) 961-4300
Products: Network Management Tools

NETLAN Inc.
29 W. 38th St.
NewYork, NY 10018
(212) 768-2273
FAX: (212) 768-2301

Netlink Inc.
3214 Sprint Forest Road
Raleigh, NC 27604
(919) 878-8612
FAX: (919) 872-2132

Netmagic Systems Inc.
2393 Maple Ave.
Peekskill, NY 10566
(914) 739-4579, ext 14
FAX: (914) 739-4616

NetManage Inc.
10725 N. De Anza Blvd
Cupenino, CA 95014
(408) 973-7171
FAX: (408) 257-6405

NetPlus Software Inc.
47 Wake Robin Road
Sudbury, MA 01776-1771
(508) 443-6043
FAX: (508) 443-0638
Products: OnQueue

Netrix Corp.
13595 Dulles Technology Drive
Herndon, VA 22071
(703) 742-6000
FAX: (703) 742-4048

NetSoft
39 Argonaut
Laguna Hills, CA 92656
(800) 352-3270 or (714) 768-4013
FAX: (714) 768-5049
Products: Ns/Transfer

NetSource Corp.
8470 Tyco Road
Vienna, VA 22182
(703) 827-8585
FAX: (703) 893-1911

nett Information Products
8522 National Blvd, Suite 106
Culver City, CA 90232
(310) 836-5225 or (800) THE-NETT
FAX: (310) 836-5226

Network Application Technology Inc.
16886 Dell Ave.
Campbell, CA 95008
(800) 474-7888 or (408) 370- 4300
FAX: (408) 776-8448

Network Compatibility Group Inc.
130 E. Wilson Bridge Road, Suite 100
Columbus, OH 43085
(614) 436-2962
FAX: (614) 436-0116
Products: Network Management Tools

Network Computing Devices Inc
PC-X Div
9590 SW Gemini Drive
Beaverton, OR 97005
(503) 671-2200
FAX: (503) 643-8642

Network Computing Inc.
100 N. Winchester Blvd. #262
Santa Clara, CA 95050-6566
(800) 736-3012 or (408) 296-8080
FAX: (408) 296-8329
Products: LANControl, LANAlert for
NetWare, LANChart, LANChart

Network Dimensions Inc.
1620 Saratoga Ave. #1281
San Jose, CA 95129
(408) 446-9598
FAX: (408) 255-4576
Products: GrafBASE

Network Equipment Technologies Inc
(NET)
800 Saginaw Drive
Redwood City, CA 94063-4740
(415) 366-4400
FAX: (415) 780-5160

Network Genural Corp.
4200 Bohannon St.
Menlo Park, CA 94025
(415) 473-2000

Network Performance Corp.
11811 Cedarwood Drive
Dunkirk, MD 20754
(301) 855-4600
FAX: (301) 855-4600 or (410) 257-1932

Network Peripherals Inc.
1371 McCarthy Blvd.
Milpitas, CA 95035
(800) NPI-8855
FAX: (408) 321-9218

Network Products Corp.
1440 W. Colorado Blvd.
Pasadena, CA 91105
(800) 838-7785 or (818) 441-6504
FAX: (818) 441-6894

Network Resources Corp.
61 E. Daggett Drive
San Jose, CA 95134
(408) 383-9300

Network Specialists Inc (NSI)
1099 Wall St. West, Unit 2, Suite 354
Lyndhurst, NJ 07071
(201) 804-8400 or (800) 775-4674
FAX: (201) 804 2799
Products: Network Management Tools

Network Systems Corp.
7600 Boone Ave. North
Minneapolis, MN 55428
(612) 424-4888
FAX: (612) 424-2853

Network Technologies Inc.
1275 Danner Drive
Aurora, OH 44202
(800) 742-8324 or (216) 562-7070
FAX: (216) 562-1999

Network-1 Software & Technology Inc.
PO Box 8370
Long Island City, NY 11101
(800) NETWRK1
FAX: (800) NET1

Networks Northwest Inc.
3633 138th Pl. SE., Suite 100
Bellevue, WA 98006
(800) 835-9462 or (206) 641-8779
FAX: (206) 641-8909

NetWorth
8404 Esters Blvd.
Irving, TX 75063
(800) 544-5255 or (2t4) 929-1700
FAX: (214) 929-1720

New England Software Inc.
411 W. Putnam Ave. Suite 280
Greenwich, CT 06831
(203) 625-0062
FAX: (203) 625-0718

New Horizons Computer
Learning Center
1231 E. Dyer Road, Suite 140
Santa Ana, CA 92705-5605
(714) 556-1220
FAX: (714) 556-4612

New Media Corp.
One Technology, Building A
IrvInc. CA 92718
(714) 453-0100 or (800) CARDS-4-U
FAX: (714) 453-0114

Newbridge Networks Inc.
594 Herndon Parkway
Herndon, VA 22070
(800) DO-VIVID or (703) 834-3600
FAX: (703) 708-5959

Newport Canyon Associates
2082 Business Center Drive, Suite 150
IrvInc. CA 927t5
(714) 833-0333
FAX: (714) 833-2350

Newport Systems Solutions Inc.
4019 Westerly Place
Newport Beach, CA 92660
(714) 752-1511 or (800) 368-6533
FAX: (714) 752-8389

NHC Communications
5450 Cote de Liesse
Mount Royal, QUE H4P lA5 Canada
(800) 361-1965 or (514) 735-2741
FAX: (514) 735-8057
Products: Network Management Tools,
NLM-Profile

Niwot Networks Inc.
2200 Central Ave, Suite B
Boulder, CO 80301
(303) 444-7785
FAX: (303) 444-7767
Products: Direct File Transfer, Direct File
Transfer for Macintosh

No Hands Software
1301 Shoreway Road, Suite 220
Belmont, CA 94002
(800) 598-3821 or (415) 802-5800
FAX: (415) 593-6868

Nomadic Systems Inc.
300 Ferguson Drive, Suite 200
Mountain View, CA 94043
(800) 641-5902 or (415) 335-4310
FAX: (415) 968-8300

Nonstop Networks Ltd.
20 Waterside
New York, NY 10010
(212) 481-8488
FAX: (212) 779-2956

Northern Telecom Inc.
6201 W. Oakton St.
Morton Grove, IL 60053-2756
(800) 262-9334
FAX: (800) 262-9334

NovaStor Corp.
30961 Agoura Road, Suite 109
Westlake Village, CA 91361
(818) 707-9900
FAX: (818) 707-9902

Novell Inc.
122 E. 1700 S
Provo, UT 84606
(800) NETWARE or (801) 429-5588
Products: File Management Tools,
UnixWare

Novell Inc.
1340 Treat Blvd. Suite 300
Walnut Creek, CA 94596
(800) NETWARE

Novell Inc.
2180 Fortune Drive
San Jose, CA 95131
(800) NETWARE
FAX: (801) 429-2700 or (408) 577-5668

Noyes Fiber Systems
PO Box 398
Laconia, NH 03247
(800) 321-5298 or (603) 528-7780
FAX: (603) 528-2025

NU-Mega Technologies Inc.
PO Box 7780
Nashua, NH 03060
(603) 889-2386
FAX: (603) 889-1135
Products: NET-Check

Numidia Press
P0 Box 2281
Fremont, CA 94536
(510) 790-1199
FAX: (510) 791-5053

Nuntius Corp.
5025 Panison Road
St Louis, MO 63110
(314) 776-7660 or (314) 776-7076
FAX: (314) 776-2070

OAZ Communications
44920 Osgood Road
Fremont, CA 94539
(800) 638-3293 or (510) 226-0171
FAX: (510) 226-7079

Ocean Information Systems Inc.
688 Arrow Grand Circle
Covina, CA 91722
(818) 339-8888 or (800) 325-2496
FAX: (818) 859-7668

Ocean Isle Software
1201 19th Place
Vero Beach, FL 32960
(800) 677-6232 or (407) 770-4777
FAX: (407) 770-4779

Ocean Microsystems Inc.
11235 Knott Ave., Suite A
Cypress, CA 90630
(800) 944-8232 or (714) 898-1340
FAX: (714) 891-8484

Ocean Network Corp.
21221 Commerce Pointe Drive
Walnut, CA 91789-3056
(909) 535-3499
FAX: (909) 595-9683

Odyssey Development Inc.
650 S. Cherry St, Suite 430
Denver, CO 80222
(303) 394-0091
FAX: (303) 394-0096

Olicom USA Inc.
900 W. Park Blvd, Suite 180
Plano, TX 75074
(800) 2-OLICOM
FAX: (214) 423-7261

Olympus Image Systems Inc.
15271 Barranca Parkway
IrvInc. CA 92718
(800) 347-4027 or (714) 753-5935
FAX: (714) 453-4425

On Demand Software & Services Inc.
1100 Fifth Ave. South, Suite 208
Naples, FL 33940
(800) 368-5207 or (813) 261-6678
FAX: (813) 261-6549
Products: WinINSTALL, LAN Printer
Switch

ON Technology Corp.
One Cambridge Center, Sixth Floor
Cambridge, MA 02142
(617) 374-1400
FAX: (617) 374-1433
Products: Meeting Maker XP

Online Computer Systems Inc.
20251 Century Blvd.
Frederick, MD 20874-1196
(800) 922-9204 or (301) 428-3700
FAX: (301) 601-2450

Ontrack Computer Systems
6321 Bury Drive
Eden Prairie, MN 55346
(612) 937-1107 or (800) 752-1333
FAX: (812) 937-5815
Products: Ontrack Data Recovery for
NetWare

Ontrack Data Recovery
6321 Bury Drive
Eden Prairie, MN 55346
(612) 937-5161 or (800) 872-2599
FAX: (612) 937-5750
Products: Network Management Tools

OnWord Press
2530 Camino Entrada
Santa Fe, NM 87505-4835
(800) 223-6397
FAX: (505) 471-4424

OpenConnect Systems Inc.
2711 LBJ Freeway, Suite 800
Dallas, TX 75234
(214) 484-5200
FAX: (214) 588-0688

Operation Technology Inc.
17870 Skypark Circle, Suite 102
IrvInc. CA 92714
(800) 476-ETAP or (714) 476-8117
FAX: (714) 476-8814

Optical Cable Corp.
PO Box 11967
Roanoke, VA 24022-1967
(800) 622-7711 or (703) 265-0690
FAX: (703) 265-0724

Optimum Educational Software
Ron Office Center, 142 Ahuza St.
Raanana, 43300 Israel
()+972-9-910882
FAX: ()+972-9-449867

Optiquest Inc.
20490 E. Business Parkway
Walnut, CA 91789
(800) THE-OPTI
FAX: (909) 468-3770

Optus Software
100 Davidson Ave.
Somerset, NJ 08873
(908) 271-9568
FAX: (908) 271-9572

Orchestra MultiSystems Inc.
12200 Industry St.
Garden Grove, CA 92641
(800) 237-7733
FAX: (714) 379-5595

Orevox USA Corp.
248 N. Puente Ave, P0 Box 2655
City of Industry, CA 91746
(818) 333-6803
FAX: (818) 336-3748

Ornet Data Communication
Technologies
P0 Box 323
Carmiel, 20100 Israel
()+44-672-516060
FAX: ()+44-672-616125

Ornetix Network Products
1249 Innsbruck Drive
Sunnyvale, CA 94089
(800) 965-6650 or (408) 744-9095
FAX: (408) 744-1068
Products: CD-View

Ornetix Technologies Ltd.
77 Orlov St.
Petach-Tikva, 49342 Israel
(408) 744-9095: (49) 89-324-8980, or (972)
3-934-2764
FAX: (408) 744-1068: FAX: (49) 89-324-
69877: or (972) 3-934-2932

Osborne/McGraw-Hill
2800 Tenth St.
Berkeley, CA 94710
(800) 227-0900 or (510) 549-6600
FAX: (510) 549-6603

OSIware
#210 - 4400 Dominion St.
Burnaby, BC V5G 4G3 Canada
(604) 436-2922

OST Inc.
14225 Sullyfield Circle
Chantilly, VA 22021
(703) 817-0400
FAX: (703) 817-0402

Overland Data Inc.
8975 Balboa Ave.
San Diego, CA 92123-1599
(800) 729-3725
FAX: (619) 571-0982

Overtime Software Inc.
7413 Six Forks Road, Suite 111
Raleigh, NC 27615
(800) 467-0493 or (919) 847-9466
FAX: (919) 847-7138

Pacer Software Inc.
1900 W. Park Drive,, Suite 280
Westborough, MA 01581
(508) 898-3300 or (800) 722-3702
FAX: (508) 366-1356

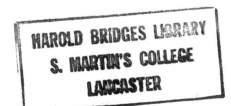

Pacific Communication Sciences Inc.
(PCSI)
9645 Scranton Road
San Diego, CA 92121
(619) 535-9500
FAX: (619) 535-0106
Products: Clarity Series
Access+Integrated AccessMultiplexer

Pacific Data Products
9125 Rehco Road
San Diego, CA 92121
(619) 525-3663
FAX: (619) 552-0889

Pacific Micro Data Inc.
3002 Dow Ave, Bldg 140
Tustin, CA 92680
(800) 933-7575
FAX: (714) 838-9787

Palindrome Corp.
600 E. Diehl Road
Naperville, IL 60563
(708) 505-3300
FAX: (708) 505-7917

Panamax
150 Mitchell Blvd.
San Rafael, CA 94903
(800) 472-5555 or (415) 499-3900
FAX: (415) 472-5540

PaperClip Imaging Software Inc.
Continental Plaza One
401 Hackensack Ave,
Hackensack, NJ 07601
(800) 929-3503 or (201) 487-3503
FAX: (201) 487-3503

PaperView Inc.
141 E. 5600 S., Suite 300
Salt Lake City, UT 84107
(801) 261-8850
FAX: (801) 261-8842

Parallax Graphics Inc.
2500 Condensa St.
Santa Clara, CA 95051
(408) 727-2220
FAX: (408) 980-5139

Parallel Storage Solutions
116 S. Central Ave.
Elmsford, NY 10523
(800) 998-7839 or (914) 347-7044
FAX: (914) 347-4646

Parker Systems Inc.
7200 Hwy 50 E, PO Box 1728
Carson City, NV 89702
(800) 458-1049 or (702) 885-0488
FAX: (702) 885-1946

Passport Communications Inc.
1101 S. Capital of Texas Hwy
Suite 250-F
Austin, TX 78746
(512) 328-9830
FAX: (512) 328-3847

Patapsco Designs Inc.
5350 Partners Court
Frederick, MD 21701
(301) 694-8744
FAX: (301) 694-5152

Patton Electronics Co.
7622 Rickenbacker Drive
Gaithersburg, MD 20879
(301) 975-1000
FAX: (301) 869-9293

PC Age
420 Route 46 East, Suite 10
Fairfield, NJ 07004
(800) PCAGE-60 or (201) 882-5370
FAX: (201) 882-4955

PC DOCS Inc.
124 Marriott Drive
Tallahassee, FL 32301
(904) 942-3627
FAX: (904) 656-5559

PCR Personal Computer Rentals
2557 Route 130
Cranbury, NJ 09512
(800) 922-8646
FAX: (609) 395-7049

PDC
Continental Plaza, 1002 W. 9th Ave.
King of Prussia, PA 19406
(800) 654-4PDC
FAX: (610) 265-2165
Products: Bud Tool, Bud Tool Live, Bud
Tubo, Disk Info

PEER Networks Inc.
3375 Scott Blvd., Suite 100
Santa Clara, CA 95054
(408) 727-4111
FAX: (408) 727-4410
Products: The Encapsulator, Multi-MIB
SNMP Agent

Pennant Systems
The IBM Printing Systems Co.
501 Merritt 7
Norwalk, CT 06856
(800) PENNANT

Penril Datability Networks
Corporate Headquarters
1300 Quince Orchard Blvd.
Gaithersburg, MD 20878
(800) 4-PENRIL or (301) 921-8600
FAX: (301) 921-8376
Products: Series 6000 Network Mgmt
Software

Perceptive Solutions Inc.
2700 Flora St.
Dallas, TX 75201
(214) 954-1774 or (800) 486-3278
FAX: (214) 953-1774

Peregrine Systems Inc.
1959 Palomar Oaks Way
Carlsbad, CA 92009
(619) 431-2400
FAX: (619) 431-0696
Products: PNMS Network Management
Tools

Performance Computer,
A Performance Technologies Co.
315 Science Parkway
Rochester, NY 14620
(716) 256-0200
FAX: (716) 256-0791

PerifiTech Inc.
1265 Ridge Road
Hinckley, OH 44233
(216) 278-2070
FAX: (216) 278-2309

Perisol Technology
1148 Sonora Court
Sunnyvale, CA 94086
(800) 447-8226 or (408) 738-1311
FAX: (408) 738-0698

Persoft Inc.
465 Science Drive
Madison, WI 53711
(800) EMULATE
FAX: (608) 273-8227

Personal Computer Card Corp.
5151 S. Lakeland Drive, Suite 16
Lakeland, FL 33813
(800) 992-1079 or (813) 644-5026
FAX: (813) 644-1933

Philips LMS
4425 ArrowsWest Drive
Colorado Springs, CO 80907
(800) 777-5674 or (719) 593-7900
FAX: (719) 593-4597

Phylon Inc.
4027 Clipper Court
Fremont, CA 94538
(510) 656-2606
FAX: (510) 656-0902

Pilot Network Services Inc.
1000 Marina Village Parkway
Alameda, CA 94501
(510) 748-1850
FAX: (510) 748-1849

Pilot Systems Inc.
P0 Box 222042
Anchorage, AK 99522-2042
(800) 770-6368 or (907) 349-3260
FAX: (907) 349-1550
Products: AutoPilot Menu Systems v1.2

Pinnacle Micro
19 Technology
IrvInc. CA 92718
(800) 553-7070 or (714) 727-3300
FAX: (714) 727-1913

Pinnacle Publishing Inc.
18000 72nd Ave. South, Suite 217
Kent, WA 98032
(800) 231-1293 or (206) 251-1900
FAX: (206) 251-5057

PinPoint Software Corp.
6531 Crown Blvd, Suite 3A
San Jose, CA 95120
(800) 599-3200
FAX: (800) 308-3777
Products: Network Management Tools

Pioneer New Media Technologies Inc.
2265 E. 220th street
Long Beach, CA 90810
(800) 444-OPTI

Pixelworks Inc.
7 Park Ave.
Hudson, NH 03051
(800) 247-2476 or (603) 880-1322
FAX: (603) 880-6558

Plaintree Systems
70 Walnut St.
Wellesley, MA 02181
(800) 370-2724
FAX: (617) 239-7570

Plexcom Inc.
2255 Agate Court
Simi Valley, CA 93065
(805) 522-3333
FAX: (805) 583-4764

Plustek USA Inc.
1362 Bordeau Drive
Sunnyvale, CA 94089
(408) 745-7111
FAX: (408) 745-7562

POC-IT Management Services Inc.
429 Santa Monica Blvd., Suite 460
Santa Monica, CA 90036
(310) 393-4552
FAX: (310) 451-2888

Polywell Computers Inc.
1481 San Mateo Ave.
So. San Francisco, CA 94080
(800) 999-1278 or (415) 533-7222
FAX: (415) 583-7222

Popkin Software & Systems Inc.
11 Park Place, 15th Floor
New York, NY 10007
(212) 571-3434
FAX: (212) 571-3436

Portfolio Technologies Inc.
5600 Mowry School Road, Suite 100
Newark, CA 94560
(510) 226-5600
FAX: (510) 226-8182

Positive Support Review Inc.
2500 Broadway St., Suite 320
Santa Monica, CA 90404-3061
(310) 453-5100, ext 120
FAX: (310) 453-6253

Postalsoft Inc.
4439 Mormon Coules Road
La Crosse, WI 54601-8231
(800) 831-6245 or (608) 788-8700
FAX: (608) 788-1188

Powercom
1812 State St.
Santa Barbara, CA 93101
(800) 288-9807
FAX: (805) 962-0104

Powersoft Corp.
561 Virginia Road
Concord, MA 01742
(800) 395-3525 or (508) 287-1500
FAX: (508) 369-5071

PowerTronics
PD Box 735, 145 Raymond Road
Candia, NH 03034
(603) 483-5876
FAX: (603) 483-5938

Pranicom
3275 1st St., Suite 1
Saint-Hubent, QUE J3Y 8Y6 Canada
(514) 443-2909
FAX: (514) 443-2878

Preferred Systems Inc.
250 Caplain Thomas Blvd.
West Haven, CT 06516
(203) 937-3000 or (800) 222-7638
FAX: (203) 937-3032
Products: Network Management Tools

Premenos
1000 Burnett Ave, Second Floor
Concord, CA 94520
(800) 426-3836 or (510) 602-2000
FAX: (510) 602-2024

Premier Metal Products Co.
361 Canal Place
Bronx, NY 10451
(718) 993-9200
FAX: (718) 993-9211

Prentice Hall Professional Software
2400 Lake Park Drive
Smyrna, GA 30080
(800) 241-3306 or (404) 432-1996
FAX: (404) 435-5036

Primavera Systems Inc.
Two Bala Plaza
Bala Cynwyd, PA 19004
(800) 423-0245 or (610) 667-8600
FAX: (610) 667-7894

Primax Electronics
254 E. Hacienda Ave.
Campbell, CA 95008
(800) PRIMAX-1
FAX: (408) 370-2009

Principia Products
1508 McDaniel Drive
Wesl Chester, PA 19380
(800) 858-0860 or (610) 429-1359
FAX: (610) 430-3316

Printronix
17500 Cartwright Road
IrvInc. CA 92713
(800) 826-3874
FAX: (714) 660-8682

PRISMAOFFICE Corp.
29 W. Anapamu St., Suite 405
Santa Barbara, CA 93101
(800) 774-7821 or (805) 962-0993
FAX: (805) 966-4211

Process Software Corp.
959 Concord St.
Framingham, MA 01701
(800) 722-7770
FAX: (508) 879-0042

Procom Technology Inc.
2181 Dupont Drive
IrvInc. CA 92715
(800) 800-8600 or (714) 852-1000
FAX: (714) 852-1221

Procomp USA Inc.
6777 Engle Road, Suite L
Cleveland, OH 44130
(216) 234-6387
FAX: (216) 234-2233

Professional Computer
Development Corp. (PCDC)
401 Tomahawk
Maumee, OH 43537
(800) 322-PCDC or (419) 891-9700
FAX: (419) 891-9702

Profidex Corp.
80 Park Ave.
Hoboken, NJ 07030
(800) 229-8353 or (201) 420-7700
FAX: (201) 420-9013
Products: SCAMP v2.9

Programmed Logic Corp.
200 Cottontail Lane
Somerset, NJ 08873
(800) 967-0050 or (908) 302-0090
FAX: (908) 302-1903
Products: DTFS, HTFS, DEFS

Progress Software Corp.
14 Oak Park
Bedford, MA 01730
(617) 280-4700
FAX: (617) 280-4095

Progressive Computer Services Inc.
PO Box 7638
Metairie, LA 70010-7638
(800) 628-1131 or (504) 831-9717
FAX: (504) 834-2160
Products: EZ-MENU v6.0

Promise Technology Inc.
1460 Koll Cir.
San Jose, CA 95112
(800) 888-0245
FAX: (408) 452-1534

ProSoft Corp.
14800 Quorum Drive, Suite 530
Dallas, TX 75240-6745
(800) 477-6763 or (214) 386-7769
FAX: (214) 386-4491

Protec Microsystems Inc.
297 Labrosse
Pointe-Claire, QC H9R 1A3 Canada
(800) 363-8156
FAX: (514) 694-6973

Proteon Inc.
9 Technology Drive
Westborough, MA 01581
(415) 960-1630
FAX: (415) 964-5181

PSI Direct, a Div. of Supra Corp.
501 SE Columbia Shores Blvd., Suite 700
Vancouver, WA 98661
(800) 622-1722
FAX: (206) 905-1401

Pulizzi Engineering Inc.
3260 S Susan St.
Santa Ana, CA 92704-6865
(714) 540-4229
FAX: (714) 641-9062

Qlogic Corp.
3545 Harbor Blvd., PO Box 5001
Costa Mesa, CA 92628-5001
(800) TCP-SCSI or (714) 438-2200
FAX: (714) 668-5008

QMS Inc.
One Magnum Pass, PO Box 81205
Mobile, AL 36689-1250
(205) 633-4300 or (800) 523-2696
FAX: (205) 636-0013

QNX Software Systems Ltd.
175 Terence Matthews Cresent
Kanata, ONT K2M 1W8 Canada
(800) 363-9001 or (613) 591-0931
FAX: (613) 591-3579

Qstar Technologies Inc.
600 E Jefferson St.
Rockville, MD 20852
(800) 568-2578 or (301) 762-9800
FAX: (301) 762-9800

Quabbin Wire & Cable Co. Inc.
10 Maple St.
Ware, MA 01082
(800) 368-3311 or (413) 967-6281
FAX: (413) 967-7564

Quadbase Systems Inc.
790 Lucerne Drive, Suite 51
Sunnyvale, CA 94086
(408) 738-6989
FAX: (408) 738-6980

Quadron Service Corp.
209 E. Victoria St.
Santa Barbara, CA 93101
(805) 966-6424
FAX: (805) 966-7630

Qualitas Inc.
7101 Wisconsin Ave., Suite 1024
Bethesda, MD 20814
(800) 733-1377
FAX: (301) 718-6060

QuantumNet Inc.
2255 Agate Court
Simi Valley, 93065
(805) 527-7775
FAX: (805) 522-2919

Quaterdeck Office Systems
150 Pico Blvd.
Santa Monica, CA 90405
(310) 392-9851
FAX: (310) 314-3219

Quyen Systems Inc.
1300 Piccard Drive, Suite 108
Rockville, MD 20850 4303
(800) 827-1856
FAX: (301) 258-5088
Products: netViz

Racal InterLan Inc.
155 Swanson Road
Boxborough, MA 01719
(800) LAN-TALK
FAX: (508) 263-8655

Racore Computer Products Inc.
170 Knowles Drive, Suite 204
Los Gatos, CA 95030
(800) 635-1274 or (408) 374-8290
FAX: (408) 374-8290

RAD Data Communications
900 Corporate Drive
Mahwah, NJ 07430
(201) 529-1100
FAX: (201) 529-5777

Rad Network Devices Inc. (RND)
3505 Cadillac Ave. Suite G5
Costa Mesa, CA 92626
(714) 436-9700
FAX: (714) 436-1941
Products: Network Management Tools

RADCOM Equipment Inc.
900 Corporate Drive
Mahwah, NJ 07430
(201) 529-1100
FAX: (201) 529-5777

RADCOM Equipment Inc.
8 Hanechoshet St.
Tel-Aviv, 69710 Israel
(201) 529-1100
FAX: (201) 529-5777

Radlinx Ltd.
7 Arad St.
Tel-Aviv, 69710 Israel
(201) 529-1100
FAX: (201) 529-5777

RADLINX Ltd.
900 Corporate Drive
Mahwah, NJ 07430
(201) 529-1100
FAX: (201) 529-5777

Raidtec Corp.
105-C Elembree Park Drive
Roswell GA 30076
(404) 664-6066
FAX: (404) 664-6166

Raima Corp.
1605 NW Sammamish Road, Suite 200
Issaouah, WA 98027
(800) dbRaima or (208) 557-0200
FAX: (206) 557-5200

Rainbow Technologies Inc.
9292 Jeronimo Road
Irvine. CA 92718
(71 4) 454-2100 or (800) 852-8569
FAX: (714) 454-8557

Raindrop Software Corp.
833 E. Arapaho Road, Suite 104
Richardson, TX 75081
(214) 234-2311
FAX: (214) 234-2674

Rancho Technology Inc.
10783 Bell Court
Rancho Cucamonga, CA 91730
(909) 987-3966
FAX: (909) 989-2365

Raritan Computer Inc. (RCI)
10-1 Ilene Court
Belle Mead. NJ 08502
(908) 874-4072
FAX: (908) 874-5274
Products: MasterConsole, PC Reach,
Video Share

Rasmussen Software
10260 SW Nimbus. Suite M2A
Portland, OR 97223
(503) 624-0360
FAX: (503) 624-0760

Rational Data Systems Inc.
11 Pimentel Court
Novato, CA 94949
(800) 743-3054 or (415) 382-8400
FAX: (415) 382-8441

RDC Communications Ltd.
11 Beit Hadfus St.
Jerusalem, 95483 Israel
()+972-2-519311
FAX: ()+972-2-519314

Reach Software Corp.
872 Hermosa Drive
Sunnyvale, CA 94040
(408) 733-8685
FAX: (408) 733-9265

Realsoft
PO Box 1198
Belhesda, MD 20827
(800) USA-2140, 2150 or
(301) 564-3600, 3601
FAX: (301) 564-3603

RealWorld Corp.
282 Loudon Road, PO Box 2051
Concord, NH 03302-2051
(800) 678-6336 or (603) 224-2200
FAX: (603) 224-1955

Redish Communications Systems Inc.
5744 Central Ave., PO Box 20220
Boulder, CO 80308-3220
(303) 443-2237
FAX: (303) 443-1659

Reflex Inc.
2100 196th St. SW. Suite 124A
Lynnwood, WA 98036
(800) 673-3539 or (206) 776-2524
FAX: (313) 741-9528

Relay Technology Inc.
1106 Spring Hill Road
Vienna, VA 22182-7409
(800) 795-8674 or (703) 506-0500
FAX: (703) 506-0510

Relevant Business Systems
3130 Crow Canyon Place, Suite 300
San Ramon, CA 94583
(510) 867-3830
FAX: (510) 867-3840

Relia Technologies Inc.
761 University Ave, Suite B
Los Gatos, CA 95030
(408) 399-4350
FAX: (408) 354-2545

Relisys
320 S. Milpitas Blvd.
Milpitas, CA 35131
(408) 945-9000
FAX: (408) 945-0587

Remedy Corp.
1965 Landings Drive
Mountain View, CA 94043
(415) 903-5200
FAX: (415) 903-9001
Products: Action Request System
Network Management Tools

Rememory Corp.
3186 Airway Ave, Building E
Cosla Mesa, CA 92626
(800) 644-2300 or (414) 708-0990
FAX: (714) 708-0993

Renex Corp.
Lakepoint 1, 2750 Killarney Drive
Woodbrldge, VA 22192
(703) 878-2400
FAX: (703) 878-4625

Retix
2401 Colorado Ave.
Santa Monica, CA 90404-3563
(800) 255-2333 or (310) 828-3400
FAX: (310) 828-2255

Revelation Technologies Inc.
181 Harbor Drive
Stamford, CT 06902
(800) 262-4747 or (203) 973-1000
FAX: (203) 975-8755
Products: Network Management Tools

Rexon Software
2750 N. Clovis Ave.
Fresno, CA 93727
(800) 228-9236
FAX: (209) 292-8908

RG Software Systems Inc.
6900 E. Camelback Road, Suite 630
Sconsdale, AZ 85251
(602) 423-8000
FAX: (602) 423-8389

Rhetorex Inc.
200 E. Hacienda Ave.
Campbell, CA 95008
(408) 370-0881, ext. 1
FAX: (408) 370-1171

Rhimek Inc.
8835 Columbia 100 Parkway
Columbia, MD 21045
(410) 730-2575 or (800) 234-4546
FAX: (410) 730-5960

Ricoh Corp.
Five Dedrick Place
West Caldwell, NJ 07006
(800) 83-RICOH

RightFAX
4400 E. Broadway, Suite 312
Tucson, AZ 85711
(602) 327-1357
FAX: (602) 321-7456

Rimage Corp.
7725 Washington Ave. South
Minneapolis, MN 55439
(800) 445-8288
FAX: (612) 944-7808

Riser-Bond Instruments
5101 N. 57th St.
Lincoln, NE 68507-3141
(402) 466-0933
FAX: (402) 466-0967

RIT Technologies Inc.
900 Corporate Drive
Mahwah, NJ 07430
(201) 529-1100, ext. 202
FAX: (201) 529-5777

RiverComm Technelogy
2957 Glen Alden Ct.
San Jose, CA 95148
(408) 238-4764

Rockwell Network Systems
7402 Hollister Ave.
Santa Barbara, CA 93117
(800) 262-8023
FAX: (805) 968-6478

Rose Electronics
10850 Wilcrest, 900
Houston, TX 77092
(800) 333-9343 or (713) 933-7673
FAX: (713) 933-0044

Rosetta Technologies
9417 Princess Palm Ave.
Tampa, FL 33619
(800) 937-4224 or (813) 623-6205
FAX: (813) 620-1107

RoseWare
PO Box 8564
Asheville, NC 28814-8564
(800) 767-3887 or (704) 258-9166
FAX: (704) 258-9374

Roth Publishing Inc.
185 Greal Neck Road
Great Neck, NY 11021
(800) 899-7684 or (516) 466-3676
FAX: (516) 829-7746

RSA Data Security Inc.
100 Marine Parkway, Suite 500
Redwood City, CA 94065
(415) 595-8782
FAX: (415) 595-1873

Rupp Technology Corp.
3228 E. Indian School Road
Phoenix, AZ 85018
(602) 224-9922

Russell Information Sciences
115 Columbia, Suite 100
Laguna Hills, CA 92656
(714) 362-4000
FAX: (714) 362-4040

S. I. TECH
PO Box 609
Geneva, IL 60134
(708) 232-8640
FAX: (708) 232-8677

Saber Software Corp.
5944 Luther Lane, Suite 1007
Dallas TX 75225
(800) 338-8754 or (214) 361-8086
FAX: (214) 361-1882
Products: Network Management Tools

SABRE Training Systems & Solutions
PO Box 619285—MD 4382
DFW Airport, TX 75261-9285
(800) 842-3693 or (817) 963-3526
FAX: (817) 963-3853

Safesupplies Inc.
4 Elmwood Hill Lane
Rochesler, NY 14610-3446
(800) 445-3309 or (716) 385-9007
FAX: (718) 385-8739

Safetynet Inc.
55 Bleeker St.
Millburn, NJ 07041-1414
(800) 851-0188 or (201) 467-1024
FAX: (201) 467-1611
Products: LANSD Drive-in LAN

Sales/Tech Int'l
2000 Linwood Ave, Suite 23E
Fort Lee, NJ 07024
(201) 461 -0932

SalesKit Software Corp.
10845 0live Blvd, Suite 190
St Louis, MO 63141
(800) 779-7205
FAX: (314) 567-0439

Salix Systems
9345 Byron St.
Schiller Park, IL 60176
(800) 725-4948
FAX: (708) 678-7676

Sanyo Icon
18301 Von Karman, Seventh Floor
Irvine. CA 92715
(800) 487-2696 or (714) 263-3777
FAX: (714) 263-3758

Saros Corp.
10900 NE 8th St, 700 Plaza Center
Building
Bellevue, WA 98004
(800) 82-SAROS

SAS Institute Inc.
SAS Campus Drive
Cary, NC 27513
(919) 677-8000 or (919) 677-7000
FAX: (919) 677-8123

SBS Corp.
2084 Valleydale Road
Birmingham, AL 35244
(800) 788-1785

SBT Accounting Systems
1401 Los Gamos Drive
San Rafael, CA 94903
(800) 944-1000
FAX: (415) 444-9901

SCALA USA Inc.
427 Whooping Loop, Suite 1825
Altamonte Springs, FL 32701
(407) 331-7493
FAX: (407) 830-1498
Products: SCALA business and
accounting software

Scope Communications Inc.
100 Otis St.
Northboro, MA 01532
(508) 393-1236
FAX: (508) 393-2213
Products: FrameScope 802 v214

Seabreeze Engineering Assoc. Inc.
119 Commerce Way, Suite E
Sanford, FL 32771
(407) 321-2096
FAX: (407) 321-2059

Sealevel Systems Inc.
PO Box 830, 102 W. Main St.
Libeny, SC 29657
(803) 843-4343
FAX: (803) 843-3067

Secure Design
PO Box 475
Corvallis, OR 97339
(503) 752-5988
FAX: (503) 752-5990 E-mail:
Support@sdesign.com
Products: Network Management Tools

Security Dynamics
One Alewife Center
Cambridge, MA 02140
(617) 547-7820
FAX: (617) 354-8836

SEEK Systems Inc.
SEEK Office Park, 11014 120th Ave. NE
Kirkland, WA 98033
(206) 822-7400
FAX: (206) 822-3898

Semaphore Communications Corp.
2040 Martin Ave.
Santa Clara, CA 95050
(408) 980-7750
FAX: (408) 980-7769

Sentinel Systems Inc., A Helionetics Co.
161 Gibraltar Road
Horsham, PA 19044
(215) 957-1900
FAX: (215) 957-1903

Sequoia Data Corp.
433 Airport Blvd., Suite 414
Burlingame, CA 94010
(408) 739-0557 or (408) 997-1915
FAX: (408) 997-1915

Servantis Systems Inc. (SSI)
4411 E. Jones Bridge Road
Norcross, GA 30092
(404) 441-3387 or (404) 840-1614
FAX: (404) 840-1530

Service Systems International Ltd.
8717 W. 110th St, Suite 600
Overland Park, KS 66210
(800) 826-4351 or (913) 661-0190
FAX: (913) 661-0220

SFA DataComm Inc.
7450 New Technology Way
Frederick, MD 21701
(800) 270-CONX or (301) 662-5926
FAX: (301) 694-6279

Shaffstall Corp.
7901 E. 88th St.
Indianapolis, IN 46256
(800) 243-3475
FAX: (317) 842 2077

Shany Inc.
1101 San Antonio Road
Mountain View, CA 94043
(415) 694-7410 or +972-9-851166
FAX: (415) 694-4728 or ()+972-9-851177
Products: Network Management Tools,
Vantage/IP, Catapult TCP/IP Gateway

Shaxon Industries Inc.
4950 E. Hunter Ave.
Anaheim CA 92807
(800) 345-8295
FAX: (800) 345-5106

Sheridan Software Systems Inc.
35 Pinelawn Road, Suite 206E
Melville, NY 11747
(516) 753-0985 or (800) VB-DIRECT
FAX: (516) 753-3661

SHIP STAR Associates Inc.
36 Woodhill Drive, Suite 19
Newark, DE 19711
(302) 738-7782
FAX: (302) 738-0855
Products: Network Management Tools

Shiva Corp.
Northwest Park, 63 Third Ave.
Burlington, MA 01803
(800) 458-3550 or (508) 788-3061
FAX: (508) 788-1301

ShopPro Software Inc.
7265 Kenwood Road, Suite 368
Cincinnati, OH 45236
(513) 891-8344
FAX: (513) 891-2519

ShowCase Corp.
4909 Hwy 52 N
Rochester. MN 55901-3144
(507) 288-5922
FAX: (507) 287-2803

Siecor Corp.
PO Box 489
Hickory, NC 28603-0489
(704) 327-5000
FAX: (704) 327-5973

Siemens Nixdorf Printing Systems
5500 Broken Sound Blvd.
Boca Raton, FL 33487
(800) 523-5444; (407) 997-3126; or
(407) 997-3128
FAX: (407) 997-9160

Sierra Software Innovations
923 Tahoe Blvd., Suite 102
Incline Village, NV 89451
(702) 832-0300
FAX: (702) 832-7753

Sigma Data Inc.
17 Newport Road, PO Box 1790
New London, NH 03257
(800) 446-4525 or (603) 526-6909
FAX: (603) 526-6915

Sigma Designs Imaging Systems Inc.
46515 Landing Parkway
Fremont, CA 95438
(800) 437-6424 or (510) 770-2900
FAX: (510) 770-2993

SilCom Manufacturing Technology Inc.
4854 Old National Highway, Suite 110
Atlanta, GA 30337
(800) 388-3807 or (404) 767-0706
FAX: (404) 767-0709

Silicom Connectivity Solutions Inc.
15311 NE 90th St.
Redmond, WA 98052
(800) 474-5426 or (206) 882-7995
FAX: (206) 882-4775

Sim Ware
32235 Industrial Road
Livonia, MI 48150
(313) 422-5470
FAX: (313) 422-5940
Products: Smart Panel

Simpact Inc.
9210 SkyPark Court
San Diego, CA 92123
(800) 746-7228 or (619) 565-1865
FAX: (619) 292-8015

Simplify Development Corp.
20 Induslrial Park Drive
Nashua, NH 03062
(603) 881-4450
FAX: (603) 595-0387

Simware Inc.
2 Gurdwara Road
Ottawa, ONT K2E lA2 Canada
(613) 727-1779
FAX: (613) 727-3533

Sinper Corp.
31 Mountain Blvd. Bldg. N
Warren, NJ 07059
(800) 822-1596 or (908) 755-9880
FAX: (908) 755-9230

Sirius Systems Technology Inc. (SST)
4344 Young St.
Pasadena, TX 77504
(800) 424-0724 or (713) 946-0724
FAX: (713) 946-5451

Skopos Corp.
4966 El Camino Real, Suite 216
Los Allos, CA 94022
(415) 962-8590
FAX: (415) 962-8692

Smith Micro Software Inc.
51 Columbia
Aliso Viejo, CA 92656
(800) 964-SMSI or (714) 362-2345

Snow Software Distributing
2360 Congress Ave.
Clearnwatler, FL 34623
(813) 784-8899
FAX: (813) 787-1904

SofNet Inc.
1110 Nonhchase Parkway, Suite 150
Mariena, GA 30067
(800) FAXWORKS or (404) 984-8088
FAX: (404) 984-9956

SoftArc Inc.
100 Allstate Parkway
Markham, ONT L3R 6H3 Canada
(905) 415-7000 or (416) 609-2250
FAX: (905) 415-7151

Softblox Inc.
1201 W. Peachtree St, NE
Atlanta, GA 30309
(800) 434-0202 or (404) 892-0202

Softbridge Inc.
125 Cambridge Park Drive
Cambridge, MA 02140
(800) 955-9190 or (817) 576-2257
FAX: (617) 864-7747

SoftKlone Distributing Corp.
327 Office Plaza Drive, Suite 100
Tallahassee, FL 32301
(800) 634-8670 or (904) 878-8564
FAX: (904) 877-9763

SoftLaw Corp.
317 Court St. NE
Salem, OR 97301
(800) SOFTLAW or (503) 588-3222
FAX: (503) 581-2260

SoftLogic Solutions Inc.
One Perimeter Road
Manchester, NH 03103
(800) 272-9900 or (803) 627-9900
FAX: (603) 627-9610
Products: Cubit

SoftSolutions Technology Corp., A Div of
WordPerfect
625 S. State St.
Orem, UT 84058
(801) 226-6000
FAX: (801) 224-0920

Software AG
11190 Sunrise Valley Drive
Reston, VA 22091
(800) 423-2227 or (703) 860-5050
FAX: (703) 391-8200

Software Artistry Inc.
9449 Priority Way W. Dr.
Indianapolis, IN 46240
(800) 795-1993 or (317) 843-7477
FAX: (317) 574-5867
Products: Expert Advisor v2.1

Software Corp. of America
100 Prospect St.
Stamford, CT 06901
(800) 966-7722 or (203) 359-2773
FAX: (203) 359-3198

Software Engineering of America
1230 Hempstead Turnpike
Franklin Square, NY 11010
(516) 328-7000
FAX: (516) 354-4015
Products: KEYS/PC

Software Marketing Group Inc.
108 3rd St.
Des Moines. IA 50125
(800) 395-0209 or (515) 284-0209
FAX: (515) 284-5147
Products: Support Express

Software of the Future Inc., d.b.a.
MarketForce
PO Box 531650
Grand Prairie, TX 75053-1650
(800) 766-7355 or (21 4) 264-2626
FAX: (214) 262-7338

Software Partners/32 Inc.
447 Old Boston Road
Topsfield, MA 01983
(508) 887-6409
FAX: (508) 887-3680

Software Security Inc.
6 Thorndal Circle
Darien, CA 06820
(203) 656-3000
FAX: (203) 656-3932

Software Store Products Inc.
PO Box 562
Oakdale, NY 11769-0562
(516) 244-6927
FAX: (516) 567-5563

Softwarehouse Corp.
326 State St.
Los Allos, CA 94022
(415) 949-0203
FAX: (415) 949-0208

Solid Technologies
1762 Westwood Blvd., Suite 420
Los Angeles, CA 90024
(310) 474-5383
FAX: (310) 474-7794

Soloctek Corp.
6370 Nancy Ridge Drive, Suite 109
San Diego, CA 92121-3212
(800) 437-1518
FAX: (619) 457-2681

Solomon Software
1218 Commerce Pkwy, PO Box 414
Findlay, OH 45839
(800) 879-0444 or (419) 424-0422
FAX: (419) 424-3400

Soratoga Systems Inc.
1550 S. Bascom, Suite 200
Campbel1, CA 95008
(408) 371-9330
FAX: (408) 371-9376

SourceMate Information Systems Inc.
20 Sunnyside Ave.
Mill Valley, CA 94941
(800) 877-8896 or (415) 381-1011
FAX: (415) 381-6902

Southern Computer Systems Inc.
2732 7th Ave. South
Birmingham, AL 35233
(800) 533-6879 or (205) 251 -2985
FAX: (205) 322-4851

Southern Data Comm Inc.
19345 U S. Hwy 19 North, Suite 200
Clearwater, FL 34624
(813) 539-1800
FAX: (813) 535-7971

SouthWare Innovations Inc.
PO Box 3040
Auburn, AL 36831-3040
(205) 821-1108
FAX: (205) 821-1146
Products: SouthWare Excellence Series
v5.2

Southwest Network Service
9130 Jollyville Road, Suite 200
Austin, TX 78759
(800) 999-2864 or (512) 795-3000
FAX: (512) 795-3008

Specialix Inc.
745 Camden Ave, Suite A
Campbell, CA 95008
(800) 423-5364 or (408) 378-7919
FAX: (408) 378-0786

Specialized Systems Inc.
234 33rd St. Drive SE
Cedar Rapids, IA 52403
(319) 366-0208
FAX: (319) 366-8545

Spectra-Com
PO Box 610068
San Jose, CA 95161
(800) 475-8329 or (408) 270-8070
FAX: (408) 270-0698

Spider Island Software
4790 Irvine Blvd, Suite 105-347
IrvInc. CA 92720
(714) 669-9260
FAX: (714) 669-1383

Sprague Magnetics Inc.
15720 Stagg St.
Van Nuys, CA 91406
(818) 994-6602 or (800) 553-8712
FAX: (818) 994-2153

Spry Inc.
316 Occidental Ave. S, Suite 200
Seattle, WA 98104
(800) 777-9638 or (208) 447-0300
FAX: (208) 447-9008
Products: Network Management Tools

SPSS Inc.
444 N. Michigan Ave.
Chicago, IL 60611
(800) 543-2185
FAX: (312) 329-3668

St Paul Software
754 Transfer Road
St. Paul, MN 55114
(612) 641-0963
FAX: (612) 641-0609

Stairway Software
913 First Colonial Road, Suite 102
Virginia Beach, VA 23454
(804) 437-7000
FAX: (804) 437-7077

Stalker Software Inc.
15 Skylark Drive, Suite 21
Larkspur, CA 94939
(800) 262-4722
FAX: (415) 927-1026

Stallion Technologies
60 Penny Lane
Watsonville, CA 95076
(800) 347-7979
FAX: (408) 761-3288
Products: Crocodile

Stampede Technologies Inc.
78 Marco Lane
Dayton, OH 45458
(800) 763-3423 or (513) 291-5035
FAX: (513) 291-5040

Standard Microsystems Corp.
80 Arkay Drive
Hauppauge, NY 11788
(800) SMC-4-YOU or (516) 435-6900
FAX: (516) 273-1803
Products: Network Management Tools

Starlight Networks Inc.
325 E. Middlefield Road
Mountain View, CA 94043
(415) 967-2774
FAX: (415) 967-0686

StarNine Technologies Inc,
2550 Ninth St, Suite 112
Berkeley, CA 94710
(510) 649-4949
FAX: (510) 548-0393

Sterling Software, Storage Management
Div.
11050 White Rock Road
Rancho Cordova, CA 95670
(916) 635-5535
FAX: (916) 635-5604

StonyBrook Software
630 Johnson Ave, Suite 4
Bohemia, NY 11716
(516) 567-6060
FAX: (516) 567-6648
Products: TroubleTrax, Router Manager,
TrendTalk

Storage Computer Corp.
11 Riverside St.
Nashua, NH 03062
(603) 880-3005
FAX: (803) 889-7232

Storage Concepts Inc.
2652 McGaw Ave.
IrvInc. CA 92714
(714) 852-8511
FAX: (714) 557-5064

Storage Dimensions
1656 McCarthy Blvd.
Milpitas, CA 95035
(800) 765-7895, ext. 1000

Storage Solutions Inc.
550 West Ave.
Stamford, CT 06902
(203) 325-0035
FAX: (203) 327-4675

Strategic Business Systems Inc.
300 B Lake St.
Ramsey, NJ 07446
(201) 327-8746, ext 154 or (800) 727-7260,
ext. 154
FAX: (201) 934-5684

Structured Software Solutions Inc.
4031 W. Plano Parkway, Suite 205
Plano, TX 75093
(214) 985-9501
FAX: (214) 612-2035
Products: FacetTerm v3

Sumitomo Electric U.S.A. Inc.
3235 Kifer Road Suite 150
Santa Clara, CA 95051
(408) 737-8517
FAX: (408) 737-0134

Sun Microsystems Computer Corp.
2550 Garcia Ave.
Mountain View, CA 94043
(800) 821-4643

Sunbelt Computer Systems Inc.
1517 WSW Loop 323
Tyler, TX 75701
(800) 359-5907 or (903) 561-6005
FAX: (903) 561-6007
Products: Compiler Product, TRENDnet
VIEW Network Management Tools

Sunnyside Software
236 Queensbury Ave.
Queensbury, NY 12804
(800) 225-9539 or (518) 798-6081
FAX: (518) 798-1103
Products: Mountain Menus v3.1

Superior Electric
383 Middle
Bristol, CT 06010
(203) 585-4500
FAX: (203) 582-3784

SuperOffice Corp.
130 Great Road
Bedford, MA 01730
(800) 328-8888 or (617) 275-2140
FAX: (617) 275-6921

SuperSolutions Corp.
722 N. First St, Suite 143
Minneapolis, MN 55401
(612) 340-9212
FAX: (612) 332-8411
Products: Network Management Tools

Sutton Designs Inc.
215 N. Cayuga St.
Ithaca, NY 14850
(800) 326-8119
FAX: (607) 277-6983

SVEC Computer Corp.
2691 Richter Ave. Suite 130
IrvInc. CA 92714
(714) 756-2233
FAX: (714) 756-1340

SYBEX Inc.
2021 Challenger Drive
Alameda, CA 94501
(800) 227-2346
FAX: (510) 523-8233

Symantec Corp.
10201 Torre Ave.
Cupertino, CA 95014
(800) 441-7234 or (408) 253-9600
FAX: (408) 252-4694
Products: Network Management Tools

Symbiotics Inc.
725 Concord Ave.
Cambridge, MA 02138
(800) 989-9174
FAX: (617) 876-0157

Symplex Communications Corp.
5 Research Drive
Ann Arbor, MI 48103
(313) 995-1555
FAX: (313) 995-1564

Synapsis Corp. Ltd.
5460 White Oak Ave., Suite A336
Encino, CA 91316-2407
(800) 796-2774 or (818) 906-1596
FAX: (818) 906-2070

Synaptec Software Inc.
4251 Kipling St, Suite 390
Denver, CO 80033
(800) 569-3377 or (303) 422-2893
FAX: (303) 422-4156

Synaptic Micro Solutions Cooperative
1075 S. Van Dyke Road
Appleton, WI 54915
(800) 526-6547 or (414) 734-6535

Synergistic Technologies Business
Systems Inc.
2715 Nevada Ave. North
Minneapolis, MN 55427
(612) 545-0072
FAX: (612) 545-2858

Synergy Software
2457 Perkiomen Ave.
Reading, PA 19606
(610) 779-0522
FAX: (610) 370-0548

Synergy Solutions Inc.
2150 S. Country Club Drive, Suite 1
Mesa, AZ 85210
(602) 545-9797
FAX: (602) 545-9827

Synergystex International Inc.
3065 Nationwide Parkway
Brunswick, OH 44212-2361
(216) 225-3112
FAX: (216) 225-0419

Syntax Inc.
840 S. 333rd St.
Federal Way, WA 98003
(206) 838-2626
FAX: (206) 838-9836

SysKonnect Inc.
1922 Zanker Road
San Jose, CA 95112
(800) SK2-FDDI or (408) 725-4650
FAX: (408) 725-4654

Syspro Corp.
PO Box 243
Orinda, CA 94563
(510) 254-9755
FAX: (510) 254-4377
Products: Customer Response System

Systems Enhancement Coop.
174 Chesterfield Industrial Blvd.
Chesterfield, MO 63005
(314) 532-2855
FAX: (314) 532-2037

Systems Software Resource Inc.
11-A S. Meridian
Kalispell, MT 59901
(406) 752-9696 or (609) 895-1309
FAX: (406) 756-1110 or (609) 844-0590

SYSTRAN Corp.
4126 Linden Ave.
Dayton, OH 45432-3068
(800) 252-5601 or (513) 252-5601
FAX: (513) 258-2729

Systron
400 Oser Plaza, Suite 150
Hauppauge, NY 11788
(516) 231-8600
FAX: (516) 231-8981

Sytron Corp.
134 Flanders Road. PO Box 5025
Westboro, MA 01581-5025
(800) 877-0016 or (508) 898-0100
FAX: (508) 898-2677

Syzygy Communications Inc.
269 Mt Hermon Road
Scotts Valley, CA 95066
(408) 438-6838
FAX: (408) 438-5115

T3plus Networking Inc.
3393 Octavius Drive
Santa Clara, CA 95054
(408) 727-5151 or (800) 477-7585
FAX: (408) 727-5151
Products: Network Management Tools

TAC Systems Inc.
1031 Putman Drive Suite A
Huntsville, AL 35816-2271
(205) 721-1976
FAX: (205) 721-0242

Tadpole Technology Inc.
12012 Technology Blvd.
Austin, TX 78727
(512) 219-2200
FAX: (512) 219-2222

Tally Systems Corp.
PO Box 70
Hanover, NH 03755
(603) 643-1300 or (800) 262-3877
FAX: (603) 643-9366
Products: NetCensus & CentaMeter

Tandberg Data Inc.
2685 Park Center Drive
Simi Valley, CA 93065
(800) 258-8285
FAX: (805) 579-2555

Targent Computer Inc.
197 Airport Blvd.
Burlingame, CA 94010
(800) 800-5550 or (415) 342-9388
FAX: (415) 342-9380

Target Systems Corp.
33 Boston Post Road West
Marlboro, MA 01752
(800) 233-3493 or (508) 480-9206
FAX: (508) 481-9187
Products: TARGET->HOTLINE, Target
Enterprise

TCE Technology Group
1977 O'Toole Ave, Suite B202
San Jose, CA 95131
(408) 321-7600
FAX: (408) 321-7601
Products: Banscan II, Banscan II for
Vines, NetWare Management v2.0, LAN
Directory v1.5, SMART v1.5, NetWare
Console Commander v1.0, Node Tracker
v2.0

TCL Inc.
41829 Albrae St.
Fremont, CA 94538
(510) 657-3800
FAX: (510) 490-5814

TD Systems Inc.
24 Payton St.
Lowell, MA 01852-5127
(508) 937-9465
FAX: (508) 458-1820

TDX Peripherals Inc.
80 Davids Drive
Hauppauge, NY 11788-2003
(800) 842-0708 or (516) 273-5900
FAX: (516) 273-6476

TEAM Software Inc.
5858 Westheimer, Suite 405
Houston, TX 77057
(800) 785-1112 or (713) 784-4480
FAX: (713) 784-4498

Technical Communications Corp.
100 Domino Drive
Concord, MA 01742
(617) 862-6035
FAX: (508) 371-1280

Technology Development Systems
800 S. Northwest Highway, Suite 200
Barrington, IL 60010
(708) 382-9191
FAX: (708) 382-9190

Technology Managers Forum
International
160 Riverside Drive, Suite 4E
New York, NY 10024
(212) 787-1122
FAX: (212) 580-1976

Technology Works Inc.
4030 Braker Lane West, Suite 350
Austin, TX 78759
(800) 688-7466 or (512) 794-8533
FAX: (512) 794-8520
Products: Network Management Tools

TEKELEC
26580 W. Agoura Road
Calabasas, CA 91302
(800) TEKELEC, ext. 6338, or
(818) 878-6338
FAX: (818) 880-6993

Tektronix Graphics Printing and
Imaging Div.
26600 SW Parkway, PO Box 1000
Wilsonville, OR 97070
(800) 835-6100
FAX: (503) 682-7450

Telco Systems Inc.
Magnalink Communications Div.
83 Nahatan St.
Norwood, MA 02082
(617) 255-9400
FAX: (617) 255-5885

Telebit Corp.
1315 Chesapeake Terrace
Sunnyvale, CA 94089
(800) TELEBIT
FAX: (408) 745-3310

TeleMagic Inc.
5928 Pascal Court
Carlsbad, CA 92008
(800) 835-MAGIC or (619) 431-4000
FAX: (619) 431-4055

Telenex Corp.
13000 Midlantic Drive
Mount Laurel, NJ 08054
(800) 222-0187
FAX: (809) 778-8700
Products: 2700 LAN/WAN Switch

TELEPOWER
6451 Independence Ave.
Woodland Hills, CA 91367
(818) 587-5540
FAX: (818) 587-5546

TeLeVell Inc.
1629 S. Main St.
Milpitas, CA 95035-6261
(408) 956-0511
FAX: (408) 956-0202
Products: TeleSell Modules

Tempustech Inc.
295 Airpont Road North
Naples, FL 33942-3522
(800) 634-0701 or (813) 643-2424
FAX: (813) 643-4981

Ten X Technology Inc.
13091 Pond Springs Road, Suite 200
Austin, TX 78729
(800) 922-9050 or (512) 918-9182
FAX: (512) 918-9495

Tenon Intersystems
1123 Chapala St.
Santa Barbara, CA 93101
(800) 662-2410 or (805) 963-6983
FAX: (805) 962-8202

Teubner & Associates Inc.
PO Box 1994
Stillwater, OK 74076
(800) 343-7070
FAX: (405) 624-3010
Products: Expert Support Program

Texas Instruments
PO Box 202230
Austin, TX 78720-2230
(800) TI-TEXAS
FAX: (512) 250-7329

Texas Microsystems Inc.
5959 Corporate Drive, PO Box 42963
Houston, TX 77242-2963
(800) 950-9199
FAX: (713) 541-8232

TextWare Corp.
PO Box 3267
Park City, UT 84060
(801) 845-9600
FAX: (801) 645-9610

TGV Inc.
101 Cooper St.
Santa Cruz, CA 95060
(408) 457-5200
FAX: (408) 457-5205

Tharo Systems Inc.
2967 Nationwide Parkway #5
PO Box 798
Brunswick, OH 44212-0798
(216) 273-4408
FAX: (216) 225-0099

The ADM Group
477 Madison Ave
New York, NY 10022
(212) 371-4900
FAX: (212) 750-7419
Products: QuickFlash

The AG Group Inc.
2540 Camino Diablo, Suite 200
Walnut Creek. CA 94596
(800) 466-AGGP or (510) 937-7900
FAX: (510) 937-2479
Products: EtherPeek, LocalPeek,
NetWatcman, Silver Cloud

The Diverse Business Group
8573 109 "B" St.
Delta, BC V4C 4H4 Canada
(604) 596-6088
FAX: (604) 596-7684

The ForeFront Group
1360 Post Oak Blvd., Suite 1660
Houston, TX 77055
(713) 961-1101
FAX: (713) 961-1149

The LAN Support Group Inc.
2425 FounlainView, Suite 390
Houston, TX 77057
(800) 749-8439 or (713) 789-0881
FAX: (713) 977-9111
Products: BindView NCS Network
Management Tools

The Learning Network
a Div of Vanstar Corp.
76 Progress Drive, 2nd floor
Stamford, CT 06902
(800) LESSONS
FAX: (203) 325-5880

The Light Brigade Inc.
7639 S. 180th St.
Kent, WA 98032
(206) 251-1240
FAX: (208) 251-1245

The Network Connection
1324 Union Hill Road
Alpharetta, GA 30201
(800) 327-4853 or (404) 751-0889
FAX: (404) 751-1884

The Periscope Co. Inc.
1475 Peachtree St, Suite 100
Atlanta, GA 30309
(800) 722-7006 or (404) 888-5335
FAX: (404) 888-5520

The Santa Cruz Operation Inc. (SCO)
400 Encinal St., PO Box 1900
Santa Cruz, CA 95061-1900
(800) SCO-UNIX or (408) 425-7222
FAX: (408) 458-4227

The Siemon Co.
76 Westbury Park Road
Watertown, CT 06795-0400
(203) 274-2523
FAX: (203) 945-4225

The Software Lifeline Inc.
Executive Court One, 2295 Corporate
Blvd, Suite 110
Boca Raton, FL 33487
(407) 994-4466
FAX: (407) 994-6304

The Unipalm Group
216 Science Park, Milton Road
Cambridge, Cambridgeshire CB1 3AD,
England
+44 223 250 114
FAX: ()+44 223 250 101

The Wiremold Co.
60 Woodlawn Str, PO Box 332500
West Hartford, CT 06133-2500
(800) 621-0049
FAX: (203) 233-2062

THEOS Software Corp.
1777 Botelho Drive, Suite 110
Walnut Creek, CA 94596
(800) 600-5660 or (510) 935-1118
FAX: (510) 938-4367

Thomas-Conrad Corp.
1908-R Kramer Lane
Austin, TX 78758
(800) 332-8683
Products: Network Management Tools

Thompson Network Software
15 Hamby Road
Marietta, GA 30067
(800) 521-8849 or (404) 971-8900
FAX: (404) 971-8828

TIMC Tirer International
Marketing & Consulting Ltd.
95 Hachashmonaim St.
Tel-Aviv, 87133 Isreal
()+972-375-11567
FAX: ()+972-375-21110

Token Technology Inc.
1265 Montecito Ave., Suite 101
Mtn. View, CA 94043
(415) 965-8607
FAX: (415) 965-8658

Top Microsystems Corp.
3320 Victor Court
Santa Clara, CA 95054
(800) 827-8721 or (408) 980-9813
FAX: (408) 980-8626

Total Concept Sales
501 W Glenoaks Blvd., Suite 343
Glendale, CA 91202-2896
(818) 547-9476

Touchstone Software Corp.
2130 Main St., Suite 250
Huntington Beach, CA 92648
(800) 531-0540 or (714) 969-7746
FAX: (714) 960-1886

Traffic Software Inc.
2300 Corporate Blvd., Ste. 241
Boca Raton, FL 33431
(407) 995-5282
FAX: (407) 990-5272
Products: Object Fax Object Fax
Advanced ObjectFax Lite 3.01

TransFax Corp.
6133 Bristol Parkway, Suite 275
Culver City, CA 90230
(310) 641-0439
FAX: (310) 641-4076

Transition Engineering Inc.
7090 Shady Oak Road
Eden Prairie, MN 55344
(800) 267-4908
FAX: (612) 941-2322

Transitional Technology Inc.
5401 E. La Palma Ave.
Anaheim, CA 92807
(714) 693-1133
FAX: (714) 693-0225

Traveling Software
18702 N. Creek Parkway
Bothell, WA 98011
(800) 343-8080
FAX: (206) 487-1284
Products: LapLink, Commworks,
Transcend NETBuilder Mngr

Trax Softworks Inc.
5840 Uplander Way
Culver City, CA 90230-6620
(800) 367-8729 or (310) 649-5800
FAX: (310) 649-6200

Trellis
225 Turnpike Road
Southborough, MA 01772
(800) 793-3390 or (508) 485-7200
FAX: (508) 485-3044
Products: Trellis Help Desk, StreetMap,
Network Management Tools

Trellis Communications Corp.
592 Harvey Road
Manchester, NH 03103-3320
(603) 668-1213
FAX: (603) 668-9211

Trend Micro Devices Inc.
2421 W. 205th Street, Suite D-100
Torrance, CA 90501
(310) 782-8190
FAX: (310) 328-5892
Products: PCopy

TRENDware International Inc.
2421 W. 205th St, D-102
Torrance, CA 90501
(310) 328-7795
FAX: (310) 328-7798
Products: SNMP Hub

Tricord Systems
3750 Annapolis Lane
Plymouth, MN 55447
(800) TRICORD or (612) 557-9005
FAX: (612) 557-8403

Trimm Industries
11949 Sherman Road
North Hollywood, CA 91605-3717
(800) 854-2658 or (619) 291-421 1
FAX: (619) 291-2973

Trinzic Corp.
101 University Ave
Palo Alto, CA 94301
(800) 952-8779 or (603) 427-0444
FAX: (603) 427-0385
Products: InfoHub, PowerAlert Plus

Trio Information Systems Inc.
8601 Six Forks Road, Suite 105
Raleigh, NC 27615
(800) 880-4400 or (919) 846-4990
FAX: (919) 846-4997

Tripp Lite
500 N. Orleans St.
Chicago, IL 60610-4188
(312) 755-5401
FAX: (312) 644-6505
Products: UPS

Triticom
PO Box 444180
Eden Prairie, MN 55344
(612) 937-0772
FAX: (612) 937-1998
Products: Assortment of network
management tools

Triton Technologies Inc.
200 Middlesex Turnpike
Iselin, NJ 08830
(800) 322-9440
FAX: (908) 855-9608

TRS Technologies Inc.
4547 SW 96th Ave.
Beaverton, OR 97005-3329
(503) 626-7841
FAX: (503) 646-8928

TSI Power Inc.
2836 Peterson Place
Norcross, GA 30071
(800) 874-3160 or (404) 263-6063
FAX: (404) 263-0638

TTC (Telecommunications
Techniques Corp.)
20410 Observation Drive
Germantown, MD 20876
(301) 353-1550
FAX: (301) 353-0734

Turnaround Computing Inc.
1721 W. Plano Parkway, Suite 101
Plano, TX 75075-8633
(800) ITS-TURN or (214) 424-TURN
FAX: (214) 578-2500

TxPORT
127 Jetplex Circle
Madison, AL 35758
(800) 926-0085 or (205) 772-3770
FAX: (205) 772-3388

TyLink Corp.
10 Commerce Way
Norton, MA 02766
(800) 828-2785 or (508) 285-0033
FAX: (508) 285-2738
Products: Network Management Tools

U.S. Design Corp.
9075 Guilford Road
Columbia, MD 21046
(800) 622-USDC or (410) 381-3000
FAX: (410) 381-3235

U.S. Robotics Inc.
8100 N. McCormick Blvd.
Skokie, IL 60076
(800) 877-2677 or (708) 982-5001
FAX: (708) 933-5800

UconX Corp.
4669 Murphy Canyon Road
San Diego, CA 92123
(619) 627-1700
FAX: (619) 627-1710

UNICOM Electric Inc.
11980 Telegraph Road, Suite 103
Santa Fe Springs, CA 90670
(800) 346-6668 or (310) 946-9650
FAX: (310) 946-9167

Unidata Inc.
1099 18th St., Suite 2500
Denver, CO 80202
(303) 294-0800
FAX: (303) 293-8880

Unified Communications Inc.
2051 Killebrew Drive, Suite 300
Minneapolis, MN 55425
(800) 272-1710
FAX: (612) 851-1716

Uninet Global Networking
2625 Butterfield Road
Oak Brook, IL 60521
(800) 447-0707 or (708) 573-0050
FAX: (708) 573-0172

UniPress Software Inc.
2025 Lincoln Highway
Edison, NJ 08817
(908) 287-2100 or (800) 222-0550
FAX: (908) 287-4929

Unisys Corp.
2700 N. 1st St.
San Jose. CA 95134-2028
(800) 448-1424 or (408) 434-2185
FAX: (408) 434-2122

United Barcode Industries Inc.
12240 Indian Creek Court
Beltsville, MD 20705-1242
(301) 210-3000
FAX: (301) 210-5498

United Software Associates Inc.
21155 Woodfield Road
Gaithersburg, MD 20882
(301) 840-9733
FAX: (301) 869-5636

Unitrac Software Corp.
229 E. Michigan Ave.
Kalamazoo, MI 49007-6402
(800) 456-TRAC or (616) 344-0220
FAX: (616) 344-2027

Unitrol Data Protection Systems
1177 W. Hastings St, Suite 2108
Vancouver, BC V6E 2K3 Canada
(800) 665-2212 or (604) 681-3611
FAX: (604) 681-3615

Unlimited Systems Corp. Inc.
8586 Miramar Place
San Diego, CA 92121
(800) 275-6354 or (619) 622-1400
FAX: (619) 550-7330

UPSONIC Inc.
29 Journey
Aliso Viejo, CA 92656
(800) UPSONIC or (714) 448-9500
FAX: (714) 448-9555

UPTRENDS Management Services Inc.
10555 Old Placerville Road
Sacramento, CA 95827
(800) 800-4465
FAX: (916) 368-4490

ValCom - Professional Computer Center
Inc.
1433 Hamilton Parkway
Itasca, IL 60143
(708) 285-6893
FAX: (708) 285-0044

Van Nostrand Reinhold
115 5th Ave.
New York, NY 10003
(800) 842-3636 or (800) 544-0550
FAX: (606) 525-7778

Ventana Press
110 E. Main St.
Carrboro, NC 27510
(919) 942-0220
FAX: (919) 942-1140

VenturCom Inc.
215 First St.
Cambridge, MA 02142
(617) 661-1230
FAX: (617) 577-1607

Verbatim Corp.
1200 W.T. Harris Blvd.
Charlotte, NC 28262
(704) 547-6500
FAX: (704) 547-6609

Verilink Corp.
145 Baytech Drive
San Jose, CA 95134
(800) VERILINK or (408) 945-1199
FAX: (408) 962-6260

Verity Inc.
1550 Plymouth St.
Mountain View, CA 94043
(800) 424-3682 or (415) 960-7600
FAX: (415) 960-7698

VESCO Inc.
5614 Royalton
Houston, TX 77081
(800) 366-6939 or (713) 432-0403
FAX: (713) 432-0418

Videotex Systems Inc.
11880 Greenville Ave., Suite 100
Dallas, TX 75243
(800) 88-VIDEO

ViewStar Corp.
1101 MarinaVillage Parkway
Alameda, CA 94501
(510) 337-2000
FAX: (510) 337-2222

Visioneer
2860 W. Bayshore Road
Palo Alto, CA 94303
(800) 787-7007 or (415) 493-9599
FAX: (415) 855-9750

Visionware
4500 Bohannon Drive, Suite 280
Menlo Park, CA 94025-1029
(800) 949-8474 or (415) 325-2113
FAX: (415) 325-8710

VisiSoft Inc.
2700 NE Expresswav, Suite B-700
Atlanta, GA 30345
(800) VISINET or (404) 320-0077
FAX: (404) 320-0450
Products: VisiNet

VMark Software Inc.
30 Speen St.
Framingham, MA 01701
(800) 966-9876 or (800) 370-2791
FAX: (800) 486-2613 or (617) 279-4009

VMIC
12090 S. Memorial Parkway
Huntsville, AL 35803
(800) 322-3616 or (205) 880-0444
FAX: (205) 882-0859

VTEL Corp.
108 Wild Basin Road
Austin, TX 78746
(800) 856-VTEL
FAX: (512) 314-2792

VYCOR Corp.
5411 Berwyn Road
College Park, MD 20740
(800) 888-9267
FAX: (301) 220-0727
Products: DP Umbrella SQL

Walker, Richer & Quinn Inc.
1500 Dexter Ave. N
Seattle, WA 98109
(800) 872-2829 or (206) 217-7100
FAX: (206) 217-0293
Products: Desk Direct, Reflection, NS
Connection, Express Meter

Wandel & Goltermann Technologies Inc.
1030 Swabia Court
Research Triangle Park, NC 27709
(800) 277-7404
FAX: (919) 481-4372

Wang Laboratories Inc.
One Industrial Ave.
Lowell, MA 01851
(800) 639-9264
FAX: (508) 967-0828
Products: Help Desk

Wavetek Corp.
9145 Balboa Ave.
San Diego, CA 92123
(800) 854-2708 or (61 9) 279-2200
FAX: (619) 450-0325

Webster Computer Corp.
2109 O'Toole Ave, Suite J
San Jose, CA 95131-1338
(800) 457-0903 or (408) 954-8054
FAX: (408) 954-1832

Wellfleet Communications Inc.
8 Federal St.
Billerica, MA 01821
(508) 670-8888
FAX: (508) 436-3658

Westbrook Technologies Inc.
22 Pequot Road, PO Box 10
Westbrook, CT 06498-0910
(800) WHY-FILE or (203) 399-7111
FAX: (203) 399-7137

Westek Data Storage Products Inc.
48521 Warm Springs Blvd., Suite 308
Fremont, CA 94539
(510) 770-1191
FAX: (510) 770-1722

Western Datacom Co. Inc.
959-B Bassett Road
Westlake, OH 44145
(800) 262-3311 or (216) 835-1510
FAX: (216) 835-9146

Western Telematic Inc.
5 Sterling
Irvine, CA 92718
(800) 854-7226
FAX: (714) 583-9514
Products: Network Hardware (Switches)

WestShore Data Inc.
1328 Linda St., Suite 8
Cleveland, OH 44116
(216) 356-6363 or (800) 328-2894

White Pine Software Inc.
40 Simon St.
Nashua, NH 03060
(800) 241-PINE
FAX: (803) 886-9051

Wi-LAN Inc.
308 - 809 Manning Road NE
Calgary, ALB T2E 7M9 Canada
(403) 273-9133
FAX: (403) 273-5100

WildSoft Inc.
10 Northern Blvd., Suite 1
Amherst, NH 03031
(603) 598-4477
FAX: (603) 598-3505

Winchester Systems Inc.
400 W. Cummings Park
Woburn, MA 01801
(800) 325-3700 or (617) 933-8500
FAX: (617) 933-6174

Windata Inc.
543 Great Road
Littleton, MA 01460-1208
(508) 952-0170
FAX: (508) 952-0168

Windsor Technologies Inc.
130 Alto St.
San Rafael, CA 94901
(415) 456-2200
FAX: (415) 456-2244

Wingra Technologies Inc.
450 Science Drive, One West
Madison, WI 53711-1169
(800) 544-5465
FAX: (608) 238-8986

WITC Information Systems
1420 4th St.
Lanham, MD 20706
(301) 341-1099
FAX: (301) 341-3528

Wollongong Group Inc.
1129 San Antonio Road
Palo Alto, CA 94086
(415) 962-7000
FAX: (415) 962 0286
Products: Pathway Series Network
Management Tools, STAyUP, Upgrade
Express

WordPerfect, the Novell Applications
Group
1555 N. Technology Way
Orem, UT 84058-2399
(800) 451-5151 or (801) 225-2000
FAX: (801) 222-5077

WorkGroup Solutions
PO Box 480190
Aurora, CD 80046-0190
(303) 699-7470
FAX: (303) 699-2793

Workstation Solutions
One Overlook Drive
Amherst, NH 03031-2800
(603) 880-0080
FAX: (803) 880-0696

Worldtalk Corp.
475 Alberto Wav
Los Gatos, CA 95032-5418
(408) 399-4072 or (408) 399-4022
FAX: (408) 399-4013

Wright Line Inc.
160 Gold Star Blvd.
Worcester, MA 01606
(800) 225-7348
FAX: (508) 853-8904

Wyse Technology Inc.
3471 N. First St.
San Jose, CA 95134-1803
(800) GET-WYSE or (408) 473-1200
FAX: (408) 473-1222

XCd Inc.
2172 Dupont Drive, Suite 10
Irvine, CA 92715
(714) 476-7855
FAX: (714) 752-0609

XcelleNet Inc.
5 Concourse Parkway, Suite 200
Atlanta, GA 30328
(800) 322-3366 or (404) 804-8100
FAX: (404) 804-8102

XDB Systems Inc.
14700 Sweitzer Lane
Laurel, MD 20707
(800) 488-4948
FAX: (301) 317-7701

Xerox Engineering Systems - DocuPlex
607 Herndon Parkway, Suite 301
Herndon, VA 22070
(800) XES-TALK, ext. 8295, or (703) 787-
2110
FAX: (703) 787-2110

Xinet
2560 9th St., Suite 312
Berkeley, CA 94710
(510) 845-0555
FAX: (510) 644-2680

Xinetron Inc.
2302 Walsh Ave.
Santa Clara, CA 95051
(800) 345-4415 or (408) 727-5509
FAX: (408) 727-6499

Xircom
26025 Mureau Road
Calabasas, CA 91302
(800) 874-7875 or (818) 878-7600
FAX: (818) 878-7830 or (818) 878-7175

Xitel Inc.
615 Mt View Road
Benwyn, PA 19312
(610) 647-2866
FAX: (610) 993-9127

XNET Technology Inc.
426 S. Hillview Drive
Milpilas, CA 95035-5464
(800) 788-0148 or (408) 263-6888
FAX: (408) 263-8898

Xpoint Corp.
3100 Medlock Bridge Road, Suite 370
Norcross, GA 30071
(404) 246-4493
FAX: (404) 446-6129

XSoft, A Div. of Xerox Corp.
3400 Hillview Ave.
Palo Allo, CA 94303
(800) 428-2995 or (415) 813-6920
FAX: (415) 813-7499
Products: TabWorks

Xylogics Inc.
53 Third Ave.
Burlington, MA 01803
(800) 89-ANNEX
FAX: (617) 273-5392

Xyplex Inc.
295 Foster St.
Littleton, MA 01460
(800) 338-5316
FAX: (508) 952-4702

Z/Max Computer Solutions Inc.
Radisson Woods Office Park,
8287 Loop Road
Baldwinsville, NY 13027
(315) 635-1882 or (909) 694-5343
FAX: (315) 635-1908

Zenith Electronics Corp.
1000 Milwaukee Ave.
Glenview, IL 60025
(800) 788-7244 or (708) 391-8000
FAX: (708) 391-8919

Zephyr Development Corp.
Summit Tower, 11 Greenway Plaza
Suite 1610
Houston, TX 77046-1104
(800) 986-3270 or (713) 623-0089
FAX: (713) 623-0091

ZERO ONE NetWorking
4920 E. La Palma Ave.
Anaheim, CA 92807
(714) 693-0804
FAX: (714) 693-0705

ZNYX ASD Inc.
48501 Warm Springs Blvd, Suite 107
Fremont, CA 94539
(510) 249-0800
FAX: (510) 656-2460

ZyLAB
100 Lexington Drive
Buffalo Grove, IL 80089
(800) 544-6339
FAX: (708) 459-8054

Zypcom Inc.
2301 Industrial Parkway West, Bldg 7
Hayward, CA 94545
(510) 783-2501
FAX: (510) 783-2414

ZyXEL
4920 E. La Palma Ave.
Anaheim, CA 92807
(714) 693-0808
FAX: (714) 693-0705

APPENDIX

A LIST OF NETWORKING RESOURCES

There are a great many more networking- and computer-focused magazines available than those listed here. If we've overlooked one that you particularly like, forgive us (and drop us a line to let us know). These are the ones we read regularly and that seem to provide the most balanced network-related news and information. Most of them are free to qualified subscribers, so nothing should stop you from getting them. Just be sure to indicate that you have technical and budget responsibility for a network on the qualification forms, and you'll get what you deserve from these publications!

Computer Shopper is published 12 times a year by Coastal Associates, a division of Ziff Communications Company. The address is One Park Avenue, New York, NY, 10016, and its subscription department can be reached at 800-274-6384 (inside US) or at 303-447-9330 (outside US). The magazine costs $29.97 inside the United States, and an additional $39 for postage outside the United States. *Computer Shopper* is primarily a PC-focused advertising supplement -- a normal issue looks like an oversized phone book -- but it includes ads and contact information for hundreds of mail-order dealers who carry networking equipment and software. It's a great place to shop around and to establish the floor for pricing on any items you might need to purchase.

Computerworld is published 53 times a year by IDG Publications, P.O. Box 9171, 375 Cochituate Road, Framingham, MA, 01701-9171, and can be reached at 800-669-1002 for subscriptions, 508-879-0700 for editorial information. The magazine costs $48 inside the United States, and between $95 and $295 outside the country, depending on exact location. *Computerworld* covers the computer industry in general, but gives networking issues good coverage as well. It's a good counterpoint to the Ziff-Davis *PC Week*, in that its focus includes coverage of non-PC systems as well.

Infoworld is published 51 times a year by InfoWorld Publishing Company, a subsidiary of IDG, at 155 Bovet Road, San Mateo, CA, 94402, and can be reached at 415-572-7341. The magazine is free to qualified subscribers, but otherwise costs $130 inside the United States, and $145 in Canada (other subscription costs available upon request). *InfoWorld* covers the computer industry in general, but gives networking issues good coverage as well. It also publishes Rich Tennant's cartoons in every issue (our personal favorite nerdy form of entertainment).

LAN: The Network Solutions Magazine is published monthly by Miller Freeman, 600 Harrison Street, San Francisco, CA, 94107, who can be reached at 415-905-2200. An annual subscription costs $19.97. This magazine provides coverage on a broad range of networking topics, including technology overviews, user tutorials, and product reviews. For an excellent source of network product and vendor information, be sure to check out its annual *Buyers Guide* (published in September of each year).

LAN Times is published 25 times a year by McGraw-Hill, Inc., 1221 Avenue of the Americas, New York, NY, 10020, who can be reached at 415-513-6800. The magazine is free to qualified subscribers. *LAN Times* also provides coverage on a broad range of networking topics, including technology overviews, network industry news, product reviews, and includes editorials from networking industry leaders and personalities. For an excellent source of network product and vendor information, be sure to check out its annual *Buyers Directory* (published in August of each year).

Networking Management is published 12 times a year by PenWell Publishing Company, 1421 South Sheridan, Tulsa, OK, 74112, who can be reached at 918-831-9424 (subscriptions) or 508-692-0700 (editorial inquiries). The magazine is free to qualified subscribers, and costs $42 inside the United States, and $65 outside the country, for nonqualified subscribers. *Networking Management* provides coverage on a broad range of network management topics, including technology overviews, network industry news, and standards information.

Network World is published 51 times a year by IDG Publications, 161 Worcester Road, Framingham, MA, 01701-9172, and can be reached at 508-875-6400. The magazine is free to qualified subscribers, and costs $95 inside the United States, and between $95 and $245 outside the country, depending on exact location, for nonqualified subscribers. *Network World* provides weekly coverage on a broad range of network management topics, including technology overviews, network industry news, and offers special departments for enterprise internets, local networks, global services, and client-server applications.

Open Systems Today is published 28 times a year by CMP Publications, Inc., 600 Community Drive, Manhasset, NY, 11030-3875, 708-647-6834 (subscription). The magazine is free to qualified subscribers, and costs $79 inside the United States and Canada, and between $179 and $200 outside the country, depending on exact location, for non-qualified subscribers, per year. *OST* provides semi-monthly coverage on a broad range of computer industry topics, including technology overviews, and industry news, and offers special departments on networking, that is primarily focused at the open systems side of the computer industry, with a strong emphasis on UNIX. It offers a valuable complement to most of the other magazines mentioned here, which devote most of their networking coverage to PC-related topics.

PC Week is published 51 times a year by Ziff-Davis Publishing Company, a division of Ziff Communications Company, One Park Avenue, New York, NY, 10016, 609-786-8230 (subscriptions). The magazine is free to qualified subscribers, and costs $160 inside the United States, and between $200 and $350 outside the country, depending on exact location, for non-qualified subscribers, per year. *PC Week* provides weekly coverage on a broad range of computer industry topics, including technology overviews, industry news, and offers special departments on networking. It also publishes a weekly network-focused supplement, called *PC Week Netweek*, that will be shipped to readers who express interest in networking.

ACCESSING NETWORKING INFORMATION ONLINE

Our goal in providing this appendix is not to tell you how to use an online information service or the Internet in general, or CompuServe or the World Wide Web in particular. Rather, we just want to tell you what information is available on CompuServe and the Internet, what it's made up of, and why you might find it interesting.

This appendix focuses, therefore, on what's up on CompuServe and the Internet, how best to interact with it, and what kinds of things you can and cannot find there. It tells you how to be effective when you work with CompuServe or the Internet, from the standpoint of knowing what to look for, which kinds of questions you can ask, and the answers you're likely to get. It also helps you to understand just what kind of help you can expect to get from the online community and what to do if you can't get the help you need.

By now, you've probably noticed that we've mentioned only CompuServe and the Internet as sources of online information. "What about the others?" you might ask. Yes, we know there's also America Online, Prodigy, GEnie, and a bunch of other lesser contenders in this field. But none of them has staked a presence in the area of technical information and support online like CompuServe, nor does any of them have the breadth and reach of the Internet (which can't yet compare with CompuServe's depth of offerings, but is quickly catching up).

That's why we focus the bulk of our discussion in this appendix to these two information sources, even though there are more to choose from. In the next-to-last section, entitled "Other online Resources," we'll try to give you some ideas about other places worth looking, but this will be a set of cursory suggestions, rather than an in-depth investigation.

What Does *Online* Really Mean?

In the context of our discussion, *online* means that you have to log in to somebody else's network (frequently using a modem) to access their information collection rather than your own network. Even though this may sound inconvenient—and it sometimes is—the benefits invariably outweigh any inconvenience, costs, and effort the might be involved.

For the record, these benefits include

- Free access to technical support operations for questions and answers via forums (CompuServe) or newsgroups and mailing lists (the Internet). Even if you never ask a question yourself, reading other people's questions (and the answers that go with them) can be enormously informative.

- Access to online sources for software patches and solutions for a broad range of products. Rather than waiting for the vendor to send you a disk or paying long-distance charges to access their private bulletin board, you can get the latest versions of software (or the tools to turn your software into the latest version) with a local phone call and a (sometimes lengthy) download.

- Access to shareware and freeware that can extend your network's capabilities or increase your personal productivity. Much of the software this book's authors use for things like screen shots, graphics, file compression, and more originated on the Internet or CompuServe. A little prospecting can work wonders in this area!

- The biggest benefit by far, is the opportunity to meet and interact with your peers and colleagues in the networking profession and to learn from other people's experiences and mistakes. You'll also have the occasional chance to learn from the wisdom of real experts, including the developers of the software or hardware you're using, or world-renowned gurus from a variety of fields.

All in all, a lot can be gained from going online to look for information on just about any subject, but especially for technical and computer-related subjects. Because that's where networking fits pretty neatly, these resources are excellent (some would argue, indispensable) sources for information on the whole gamut of networking topics, products, technologies, and issues.

Now that we've gotten you all excited about the possibilities inherent in online information access, let's talk about the costs. Whether you join up with CompuServe, get onto the Internet, or—like this book's authors—do both; you can't join up without incurring some costs.

For CompuServe, this involves a series of account options, with associated monthly fees and additional charges for online time (usually above a certain number of "free" monthly hours). A light user shouldn't have to spend more than $10–15 a month for the service, but if you make regular downloads or spend significant amounts of time online, it's easy to spend $50-100 a month or more.

For the Internet, you'll have to arrange for a connection with an Internet service provider (ISP) and select one of the many options available for an Internet connection. For individuals or small businesses, we recommend using a V.34 modem with a PPP connection. Prices vary from location to location, but you should expect to pay between $25 and $50 a month for dial-up service with this kind of a connection. This usually entitles you to 10–20 hours per month of "free" online time, after which an hourly fee will be charged for additional hours.

Lots of other Internet account options are available from most ISPs, which can vary from dial on demand to dedicated accounts or according to the bandwidth of the connection involved (modem, ISDN, T1, T3, etc.). If you're interested in attaching your network to the Internet or need more bandwidth than a modem connection can provide, talk to your local ISPs or to national ISPs that offer service in your area. If you shop carefully for the best combination of price and service, you should be able to find something you can live with!

As with any other service, whether it's CompuServe the Internet or both, you'll want to do your best to learn how to use these information conduits effectively, to get the best bang for your bucks. Please consult the Bibliography at the end of this appendix for a list of resources that can help you learn what it takes to get the best use of either or both of these services.

CIS: THE COMPUSERVE INFORMATION SERVICE

The CompuServe Information Service (CIS) is an electronic information service that offers a selection of thousands of topics for your perusal.

CompuServe, a for-a-fee service, requires an individual account (called a *membership number*) with an accompanying password to be accessed. There are many ways to obtain trial access at no charge, but if you want to play on CompuServe, sooner or later you have to pay for the privilege. CompuServe charges a monthly membership fee, in addition to a fee for connection time. Some of the services available on CompuServe have additional charges as well. Be warned! It's easy to spend time—and money—on CompuServe.

Forums for Conversation and Investigation

When you access CompuServe, it's necessary to select an area of interest to focus your exploration of the information treasures available. On CompuServe, information is organized into forums. A forum is an area dedicated to a particular subject or a collection of related subjects, and each forum contains one or more of the following:

- *Message board*: This features electronic conversations organized by specific subjects into sections related to particular topics (Ethernet issues, for instance, is a topic, as is token ring issues; in the Ethernet section, you would expect to find discussions of frame types, drivers for particular NICs, and the like). A given sequence of messages, chained together by a common subject or by replies to an original message, is called a *thread*. It's important to notice that threads may read like conversations but that messages in a thread can be separated from one another by hours or days. Following threads is a favorite pastime for those who spend time on CompuServe.

- *Conference room*: An electronic analog to the real thing, it brings individuals together to exchange ideas and information in real time. It's much like a conference telephone call except that, rather than talk to each other, the participants communicate by typing on their keyboards. Conference rooms are not for the faint of heart, and they can be frustrating for those with limited touch-typing skills.

- *File library*: This is a collection of files organized by subject that can be copied (*downloaded* is the CompuServe term) for further perusal and use. Examples of file types found in CompuServe libraries include archived collections of interesting threads, documents of all kinds, and a variety of software ranging from patches and solutions for programs to entire programs.

In all, many, many worlds of information are available on CompuServe, any of which can by themselves be a completely absorbing source of information, gossip, software, and activity. With all its elements taken together, CompuServe is a perfect example of what might be called an *electronic information warehouse.*

Getting a CompuServe Membership

You can obtain an account over the telephone or by writing to CompuServe and requesting a membership. For telephone inquiries, ask for Representative 200. Here are the numbers to use:

- Within the United States (except Ohio), including Alaska, Hawaii, Puerto Rico, and the American Virgin Islands, call toll free at 800-848-8199.

- Outside the United States, in Canada, and in Ohio, call 614-457-8650. Telephone hours are from 8 a.m. to 10 p.m. Eastern time Monday through Friday, and from noon to 5 p.m. on Saturday. Written inquiries for a CompuServe account should be directed to:

  CompuServe, Inc.
  Attn: Customer Service
  P.O. Box 20212
  5000 Arlington Centre Boulevard
  Columbus, OH 43220

Accessing CompuServe

To get access to CompuServe, you must equip your computer with a modem and attach that modem to a telephone line. You also need some kind of communications program, to let your computer "talk" to CompuServe by using the modem and to help you find your way around its online universe. Finally, you have to obtain a telephone number for CompuServe—most of them are local numbers, especially in the U.S.—that's appropriate for the type and speed of modem you're using.

Connection-time charges are based on how fast your modem is—faster modems cost more—but the higher charges are typically offset by even faster transfer speeds. If your CompuServe bill is $30 a month or higher, most high speed modems will pay for themselves in six months or less based on the reductions in fees you realize by using one.

After you are connected to CompuServe, you enter your membership number and your password. First-time users should follow the instructions provided by your CompuServe representative or in the *CompuServe Starter Kit* that's available from CompuServe (for an additional fee).

After you're logged in, getting to Novell's online forums, NetWire, is easy. When you simply type GO NETWIRE from the CompuServe prompt, you are presented with a menu of additional choices for Novell and Net-Ware information. Otherwise, if you're interested in some other vendor's information, use the FIND command with the vendor's name or the product's name that you're after. This will normally produce a list of forums that you can visit, to further explore your search for information.

What Is NetWire?

NetWire is a collection of CompuServe forums, all dedicated to networking topics and all focused on Novell products or related information. NetWire is a great alternative to using Novell's telephone hotline for technical support. With over 90,000 users, NetWire is the busiest collection of forums on CompuServe, With the wide range of Novell products and related topics, Novell uses (at the time this overview was written) 18 CompuServe forums, and the number is are growing all the time.

The Benefits of Using NetWire

The benefits of using NetWire are hard to overstate but easy to understand. First, there's the help that's available: NetWire is staffed by volunteer system operators (SysOps), most of whom are not Novell employees but all of whom are extremely knowledgeable about Novell and NetWare topics. The busiest SysOp has set a record of near to a thousand messages answered in one week; and most SysOps average at least four hours a day of connect time, when they upload and download information to their colleagues and to you—the curious and, sometimes, the desperate.

Together with other power users, the SysOps and their colleagues are an invaluable source of information, help, and advice about networking topics. As a bonus, almost all questions are answered within 24 hours of being posted. You will want to log in at least once a day, in fact, when you are waiting for replies to questions. The *scroll rate,* the speed at which messages age and get deleted from the NetWire forums, is about two days, depending on message volume.

When technical problems cannot be solved by the SysOps or other power users on NetWire, SysOps can escalate these thornier issues directly to the Novell engineers responsible for dealing with those topics in Novell's Services and Support. This process uses the same channels that services Novell's hotline but does not incur the typical fees. Calling the hotline directly can cost upward of $100 per incident or $20 for a Novell DOS incident, unless you are covered by some other preexisting arrangement. (Get out your credit cards, please!)

NetWire is also the place to go for the latest and greatest patches and solutions for NetWare and other Novell products. The libraries that contain the files available for downloading are uploaded daily and documented extensively in catalogs of information available online. These files include the most recent patches, fixes, drivers, and tips for tuning your NetWare server for maximum effect. Lots of third party applications and utilities are available for your perusal, as well as a collection of *shareware* (software that can be downloaded for free and used for a trial period, but that must be paid for to be legitimately used).

NetWire is also the place where NetWare users of the world congregate. It puts you in touch with thousands of other users, most of whom are eager to share what they have learned—and the mistakes they have made—with others. Messages are posted in public forums so that all who access NetWire can see and add to the growing collection of information. As a side effect, NetWire is also the premier source of contacts for consulting, sales, and business opportunities for the NetWare community. If you need something that's NetWare related, there's no better place to start looking than on NetWire.

The Other Guys

Of course, if you're interested in something outside the NetWare umbrella, there are plenty of other vendors and networking communities represented on CompuServe. You'll find a rich selection of Microsoft-related forums and libraries, for everything from vanilla Windows, to Windows for Workgroups, Windows95, and Windows NT Advanced Server (use GO MI-

CROSOFT to get to the root of the Microsoft forums; don't skip the Microsoft Knowledge Base at GO MSKB, either). You'll also find plenty of IBM-related forums (GO IBM) or OS/2-related information (GO OS/2). Don't forget to use the FIND command to locate other vendors and products, either.

THE INTERNET

The Internet, as a wag might put it, is a "whole 'nother story." More riches are to be found on the Internet than you could shake a stick at. This won't stop us from pointing you at a few good stops along the way, but it will effectively prevent us from covering all the possible bases. Rather than trying to tell you where all the goodies are, we're going to explain how to search for the information you seek.

Our primary approach to the Internet requires that you have access to the World Wide Web (WWW), usually known as *the Web*. The Web is a worldwide collection of hypertext information servers that is made easy to navigate through the use of hypertext links, that let you jump effortlessly from document to document (or within a document) simply by activating a link on a document you're examining (and for most users, this requires no more effort than double-clicking a word or graphic on your display). Secondarily, access to electronic mail or USENET newsgroups will be quite helpful as well.

Searching for Satisfaction

In much the same way that the FIND command on CompuServe lets you ask for information by company or product name, the Web sports a number of database front ends called *search engines*, which will let you enter a keyword (or several, in fact) for a search. These programs will return a collection of hypertext links to sites that match your keywords to various locations on the Web, ready for you to double-click on them and investigate further.

The name used to attach to a Web resources is called a *URL* (an acronym for uniform resource locator, a way of designating sites and information accessible through the Web). Here are the URLs for a handful of popular—and useful—Web search engines. If you simply point your Web browser at one of these, you'll then be able to get pointers to the information you're looking for.

Sometimes, using the right tools can make using the World Wide Web for research much simpler. A class of software tools, called *search engines*, can examine huge amounts of information to help you locate Web sites of potential interest. Here's how most of them work:

- Somewhere in the background, laboring in patient anonymity, you'll find automated Web-traversing programs, often called *robots* or *spiders*, that do nothing but follow link after link around the Web ad infinitum. Each time they get to a new Web document, they peruse and catalog its contents, storing the information up for transmission to a database elsewhere on the Web.

- At regular intervals, these automated information gatherers will transmit their recent acquisitions to their parent database, where the information is sifted, categorized, and stored.

- When you run a search engine, you're actually searching the database that's been compiled and managed through the initial efforts of the robots and spiders, but that is handled by a fully functional database management system that communicates with a customized program for your search form.

- Using the keywords or search terms, you provide to the form, the database locates "hits" (exact matches) and also "nearhits" (matches with less than the full set of terms supplied or based on educated guesses about what you're *really* trying to locate).

- The hits are returned to the background search program by the database, where they are transformed into a Web document to return the results of the search for your perusal.

If you're lucky, all this activity will produce references to some materials that you can actually use!

The Search Engines of (Our) Choice

We'd like to share some pointers to our favorite search engines with you, which you'll find in Table AD.1. This is not an exhaustive catalog of such tools, but all of them will produce interesting results if you use "CGI" or "CGI scripts" as search input.

Search engine name & info	URL:
EINet Galaxy MCI spinoff EINet's engine	http://www.einet.net
Lycos Carnegie-Mellon engine	http://lycos.cs.cmu.edu
W3 Org Virtual Library W3 Org outsourced project	http://www.stars.com
Wandex MIT spinoff's engine	http://www.netgen.com/cgi/wandex
WebCrawler University of Washington engine	http://webcrawler.cs.washington.edu/WebCrawler/ WebQuery.html
World Wide Web Worm (WWWW) University of Colorado engine	http://www.cs.colorado.edu:80/home/mcbryan/ WWWW.html
Yahoo	http://www.yahoo.com

Table D.1   *These Web Search Engines Can Make Looking for CGI-Related Materials Much Less Taxing*

When you're using these search tools, the most important thing to remember is that the more specific you can make your search request, the more directly related the results will be to what your looking for. Therefore, if you're looking for information about NetWare management, you might try using *NetWare management* or *NetWare management software* as your search terms instead of simply using *NetWare*. Although you may get plenty of nothing when using search terms that are too specific, that's better than looking through a plenitude of irrelevant materials when nothing is all that's in there!

The Web has to be experienced to be believed. Since the author's initial exposure to it about two years ago, it's completely changed the way we approach research of any kind. We hope you'll find it to be useful, but we must warn you—it's also completely addicting!

Other Ways to Get Internet Satisfaction

When it comes to classifying the kinds of information you'll encounter on the Internet in any search for networking information, specifications, and examples, here's what you're most likely to find.

Focused Newsgroups

Focused newsgroups are basically congregations of interested individuals, who congregate around a specific topic on USENET, BITNET, or one of the other regular message exchange areas on the Internet.

Where networking is concerned, this involves a handful of primarily USENET newsgroups with varying levels of interest in (and coverage of) networking- or vendor-specific or related topics, like NetWare, LAN Server, or NTAS, networking protocols or products, related technologies like Ethernet, token ring, or FDDI, and other related areas.

To begin with, you'll want to obtain a list of the newsgroups that your Internet service provider carries. Normally, you will already have access to this list through whatever newsreader you're using, but you can usually get a plain-text version of this list just by asking for it.

Then, take this plain-text file and open it with your favorite editor or word processor that contains a search command. By entering the name of the company, technology, or product that you're interested in, you can see if any newsgroups are devoted to its coverage (a recent check on our part discovered numerous hits for terms like *windows.nt, netware, ethernet, token-ring,* and so forth.

The only way to tell if a newsgroup can do you any good is to drop in for a while and read its traffic. You should be able to tell, in a day or two, if the topics and coverage are interesting and informative. If they are, you should consider subscribing to the newsgroup or at least dropping in from time to time to read the traffic. Remember, too, that these newsgroups are a great source of technical information and that often vendor technical support employees are assigned to read them, ready to answer technical questions on your behalf.

Focused Mailing Lists

Focused mailing lists originate from targeted mail servers that collect message traffic from active correspondents and then broadcast the accumulated traffic to anyone who signs up for the mailing list.

Entering and leaving a mailing list takes a little more effort than subscribing to or leaving a USENET newsgroup, but otherwise, these two categories provide the same kind of information: daily message traffic—sometimes quite voluminous—focused on networking or related topics.

Locating mailing lists can sometimes be tricky. Although you often learn about them only by reading message traffic on newsgroups, you can sometimes find them mentioned in search engine output or by asking a users group or a technical support person focused on a particular topic or area. Even so, they can be incredibly useful.

Information Collections from "Interested Parties"

Sometimes individuals with special interests in a particular area, like networking, will collect information about their area of concern and publish it in a variety of forms that can range from Web pages to file archives available on private or public servers.

Such collections can often be eclectic and idiosyncratic, but the best of them can offer outstanding "jumping-off points" for investigating any particular topic. This is as true for networking as it is for other topics.

Like mailing lists, finding these gems can be a matter of hit or miss. By watching the message traffic on newsgroups or mailing lists, you'll figure out who are the gurus or forward-looking individuals. By looking in their messages for pointers to Web pages or other resources (which you'll often find in the .sig, or signature files, at the end of their messages), you can sometimes get pointers to great sources of information.

In the same vein, if you see that a particular individual is a consistent and reliable source of good information on a particular topic, send him or her an e-mail message and ask to share the person's list of recommended online resources. You may not always get a response (some of these people are very busy), but it never hurts to ask, and the occasional answer can provide a real treasure trove of information pointers!

Information from Special Interest Groups

Special interest groups cover a multitude of approaches to their topics: they can be trade or industry organizations, research or standards groups, or even companies involved in particular activities.

Often, the groups with vested interests in a technology will provide information on that technology, along with pointers to other sources as well. This is as true for networking as it is for other topics, but because these groups are nonpareils of Web and Internet presence, they are often among the best places to start looking.

It's often been said that "It's not *what* you know, it's *who* you know, that counts." When it comes to locating Internet resources, this may sometimes seem more like *"where* you know," but the principle remains pretty much the same. So, for particular topics, you shouldn't point your search engine only at company, product, or technology names; try pointing them at the names of such groups as well. Here again, these can be incredible sources of useful information.

OTHER ONLINE RESOURCES

Many companies too small, too poor, or otherwise disinclined to participate on CompuServe or the Internet will maintain their own private Bulletin Board Systems (BBSs), which you can dial up and investigate. These are always free, but they're also almost always long-distance calls, so what you save in connect time costs to a service provider you'll probably end up paying to your long-distance company instead.

Nevertheless, when other avenues fail to turn up what you're looking for, it's a good idea to call the vendor and ask if it offers a BBS. This kind of setup often gives the opportunity to communicate with technical support via e-mail, instead of enduring "eternal hold" while waiting to speak to a real human being, and can often provide direct access to software patches, solutions, upgrades, FAQs, and other kinds of useful documentation.

In the same vein, many companies offer faxback services that can ship paper-based documentation, order forms, and other goodies to your fax machine. This has the advantage of costing you only as much long-distance time as it takes you to request the information you're after; after that, the transmission costs are usually born by the vendor.

Digging for information is an endeavor where persistence usually pays off. If you're bound to get the facts, figures, or help you need, you'll eventually be able to get it. Just be sure to leave no resource uninvestigated, no possible avenue untraveled, and no stone unturned!

Noncomputerized Resources Worth Investigating

Even though they may not be as dynamic and interactive as online resources, don't overlook the information you can glean from more conventional paper-based publications. (We know you've got to be somewhat open-minded in this regard, because you're reading this book!) Nevertheless, we'll do our best to acquaint you with some books, magazines, and publishers to check out in your quest for the latest and greatest networking information. You should find this information in the bibliographies at the end of each chapter in this book, and in Appendix C, "A List of Networking Resources."

SUMMARY

In this appendix, we've tried to point you at the best and brightest of online (and other) information resources. Over the years, we've learned that both CompuServe and the Internet are essential to our research, but you will probably be able to get by with only one or the other. Whatever your choice of online information, however, we're sure you'll become dependent on it in no time (if you aren't already). It's definitely one of those things that, as soon as it becomes familiar, you wonder how you ever managed without it! In the Bibliography that follows, we try to provide some tools to bring you up to speed quickly enough to make the investment pay off right away.

BIBLIOGRAPHIES AND RESOURCES

General

Bernard Aboba. *The online User's Encyclopedia*: Addison-Wesley Publishing Co, Reading, MA: 1993. A general book that covers online topics from A-Z, this tome defies description but is incredibly useful.

CompuServe

Chappell, Laura. *Using Novell's NetWire.* Know, Inc., Provo, UT: 1992 A dated but useful overview of NetWire's composition and uses.

Tidrow, Rob, Jim Ness, Bob Retelle, and Chen Robinson. *New Riders' Official CompuServe Yellow Pages.* New Riders Publishing, Indianapolis, IN: 1994. A directory to CompuServe resources organized like the Bell Yellow Pages, with great sections on vendors and networking (warning; be sure to get a current edition, as this information goes stale quickly).

Wagner, Richard: *Inside CompuServe*, 2nd Ed. New Riders Publishing, Indianapolis: 1994. A useful overview of how CompuServe behaves, what kinds of access software is worth considering, and what sorts of resources it contains.

Wiggins, Robert, and Ed Tittel. *The Trail Guide to CompuServe.* Addison Wesley Publishing Company, Reading, MA: 1994. A quick overview of the CompuServe Information Manager (CIM) software for Windows and Macintosh, and a quick, but useful, guide to resources online. It includes a chapter on network-related forums and topics.

Wang, Wallace. *CompuServe for Dummies.* IDG Books Worldwide, Indianapolis: 1994. One of the best all-round resources on CompuServe available, this book covers software, organization, and effective "surfing" techniques.

Internet

Angell, David and Brent Heslop: *Mosaic for Dummies*, Windows Ed. IDG Books Worldwide, Indianapolis: 1995. Excellent coverage of the Mosaic Web browser and Web-based online resources.

December, John and Neil Randall. *The World Wide Web Unleashed.* SAMS Publishing, Indianapolis: 1994. The best of the general WWW reference books, this one covers all the topics, including one of the most comprehensive guides to online resources we've ever seen anywhere.

Dern, Daniel: *The Internet Guide for New Users.* McGraw-Hill, Inc., New York: 1994. One of the three best all-around Internet books, this one covers a little bit of everything, including programs to use and places to look for information.

Hahn, Harley and Rick Stout. *The Internet Complete Reference.* Osborne/McGraw-Hill, Berkeley, CA: 19xx. Another of the three best all-around Internet books, this one is aimed more at intermediate to advanced users, but covers a lot of ground anyway.

Krol, Ed. *The Whole Internet User's Guide*, 2nd. Ed. O'Reilly & Associates, Sebastopol, CA: 19xx. The third of the three best Internet books around, this was the earliest and is still a personal favorite.

Levine, John R. and Carol Baroudi. *The Internet For Dummies*, 2nd Ed. IDG Books Worldwide, Indianapolis: 1994. An excellent overview of the Internet's many protocols, programs, and capabilities.

Levine, John R. and Margaret Levine. Young: *More Internet for Dummies.* IDG Books Worldwide, Indianapolis: 1994. A continuation of the coverage in the first book, this volume provides a good introduction to the World Wide Web and how to use it.

Tittel, Ed, and Margaret Robbins. *Internet Access Essentials.* Academic Press Professional, Boston: 1994. The fourth of the three best all-around Internet books, this one was cowritten by the author, which means he thinks it's pretty darned good indeed!

Locating Vendors and Product Information

Our goal in providing this appendix is to tie together several of the tools and resources in this book, to help you locate the information that you need from vendors, about products, technologies, technical support, and other concerns you might have.

This appendix focuses, therefore, on how to use the references that we've made to vendors throughout this book, as well as the various tools and information sources we've also mentioned from time to time. We'd like to start with an idea of what things in addition to products you can get from vendors, what methods there are of learning about products, and finally, our recommended approach should you ever need to get in touch with a vendor.

What Else Is Available from Vendors?

In addition to being the ultimate source for products, vendors can also be great sources for information, including educational materials, documentation, technical support information, and more. The key to understanding what's available is to learn how to ask for the following things:

Buyer's Guides

Many vendors offer comprehensive listings of their product lines in the form of a paper- or CD-ROM-based buyer's guide. The publication frequency on these things typically ranges from quarterly to annually, but however often they're published, these documents can furnish much more than product information, which they normally do in abundance. The other things you'll find in these documents that be can of significant interest include contact phone numbers for many groups within the company; lists of publications, documents, and other things you can then request; and addresses and phone number for sales offices, around the country and around the world.

- *White papers*. Often, vendors will commission or create a special kind of document when introducing a new product, technology, or something else they think is significant (e.g., a new set of development tools). White papers are part sales tools, but they're primarily educational, and their aim is to explain and justify the vendor's wonderful new idea, widget, or whatever. Even though such documents need to be read with healthy sense of skepticism, they can be quite informative and educational (we used many of them to research this book).

- *"Free" (or low-cost) seminars*. Vendor seminars are free in the same sense that Salvation Army suppers are; except that instead of having to sing for your supper, you have to listen to the vendor sing to you! Nevertheless, they can often provide lots of useful information about current or planned products. This is true both in a general sense about the state of the technology or market that's being discussed and in a specific sense about the vendor's take on that technology and market and about its particular product features, functions, and perceived benefits.

- *For-a-fee educational services and classes*. Many of the larger networking vendors, including the network operating system companies, router manufacturers, and management system mavens offer for-a-fee classes to the technical staff of the organizations who sell, service, support, and own their systems and software.

  If your organization has a serious commitment to one of these companies, or its products, the vendor's training can be invaluable. Also, shop around for training from third party training companies that cover the same topics and areas. Expect to spend $250-400 a day for such training, so be choosy about from whom who buy your training, and demand a money-back guarantee (or credit to retake the class from another instructor) if not satisfied.

Some vendors even have programs to certify technical staff at various levels of training (e.g., Novell's Enterprise Certified NetWare Engineer, Certified NetWare Engineer, Certified NetWare Technician, Certified NetWare Administrator programs) and to certify individuals to be instructors for such training. Both sets of credentials can be useful for individuals seeking to advance their careers in the networking field, as can similar credentials from Microsoft, IBM, Banyan, and others.

- *User groups*. Some vendors sponsor user groups that focus on their products outright; others, simply encourage such groups in whatever ways they can (invariably with free product, access to inside information, etc.). Joining a user group can be a great way to network in the old-fashioned sense, too, because it will bring you together with other people in your area who share similar interests and concerns. It's been our experience that the best technical support comes from knowledgeable friends and colleagues who are only a local phone call away. User groups are a great place to meet and make such friends (or become one yourself).

- *"Nondisclosure" information*. Once you become a vendor's customer, especially if your business is large in volume, prestige, or special interest, you can often request private meetings with a vendor under the terms of a legal NDA (nondisclosure agreement). This will give you a chance to ask questions about the vendor's future plans and current research activity, and it gives them an opportunity to answer in as much detail as you can stand, without worrying about the information winding up in a competitor's hands (or on the front page of a computer trade magazine). If you're willing to negotiate and abide by the terms of such an agreement, you'd be amazed what vendors are willing to share under such circumstances!

Otherwise, if you're ever in search of information about topics or resources that we didn't cover in this section, remember that it never hurts to ask the vendor for more information.

One last note: if a vendor operates a local or regional sales office in your part of the world, cultivating a relationship with a salesperson can be a terrific way to cut through the bureaucracy and get the information you need. Such a relationship gives you access to someone who's on the inside of the company who understands the unofficial ways to get things done, as well as the official ones. If no salespeople ever pass your way, you'll have no choice but to go in the front door, and that's what we explain in the next section!

Doing the Contact Thing

The most important goal to keep in mind when contacting a vendor is to have a clear sense of what you want, or what questions you need answered. It can be quite helpful, in fact, to write this down beforehand, and glance at it from time to time while you're trying to locate the information you need. It's easy to get lost in the maze that seems to operate just beyond the metaphorical doors into many organizations, so it's helpful to keep your ultimate goals in mind.

One of the most important things to establish before contacting a vendor is to figure out what kind of information you're after. Even though you may think this doesn't matter, you may be amazed to learn that, given the nature of your questions or requests for information, you may end up talking to separate fiefdoms within a company (that may even have little or no knowledge of what other departments are up to within their own organization).

Here's what we mean.

- If you have a technical question, you'll probably end up talking to someone in a technical support operation. If it's a really small company, you may ultimately end up talking to a product engineer (somebody who builds products, instead of answering questions about them). If it's a large company, you'll seldom get to an engineer and, if you do, it normally costs dearly.

  These days, paying for technical support calls is becoming the norm, so if you can stand to wait for an answer, we'd recommend e-mailing or faxing your questions to technical support, and then waiting as patiently as you can for an answer. It may take (a lot) longer, but it won't cost anywhere near as much. Otherwise, expect to spend around $1 a minute for telephone time with technical support operations (if you're lucky, they won't charge you for the time you spend on hold).

- If you have a product question about shipping products, you'll probably end up talking to someone in the sales department. Larger companies will have telephone sales staffs that include "presales technical support;" if your product questions are technical, you'll probably end up talking to them. If they're price, delivery, or availability related (or the company doesn't have a presales technical support operations), then you'll end up talking to a telesales person. Just remember, if you can't get the information you need, remain polite, and ask to speak to a supervisor. If you're polite but persistent, you can almost always get the information you need, even if it's just a promise to let you know as soon as the information is available.

- If you have a question about products that may have been announced but aren't shipping yet or even about unannounced products, you'll probably end up talking to someone in the marketing department. They're responsible for future and ongoing development directions and work closely with engineering groups to build these products. In most cases, you won't get much information about futures without a nondisclosure agreement, except when a senior executive has already disclosed significant futures information to the press.

Knowing the organizational layout of a company can indeed be very helpful, so we'd always recommend that you learn as much as you can before getting too far along in telling your story or asking your questions. Otherwise, you'll end up telling and retelling your story to a bunch of people before you get to someone who can really help you.

That's why we recommend that when you have to call a vendor "cold"-- that is, without knowing who to ask for or which department to talk to--tell the operator or receptionist something like, "I have a technical sales question about your Quack product. Can you please help me find someone to talk to about this?" rather than launching into your invoicing problems with him or her. That way, you can get a pointer to the next person in line without taking up too much of anybody's time (especially yours). Keep this up until you feel like you're getting somewhere; then you can launch into the details (and even then, don't be surprised if you get cut off somewhere down the line with "Oh, you need to talk to Joe Blow. He's the one who handles all these kinds of questions; let me transfer you . . .").

This brings us to our next (and probably most important point): whenever you call a vendor for any kind of business purpose, keep a log of your phone call. Note the time you called, and keep track of how much time you spend on hold. Also ask for (and write down) the name of each person you talk to and take notes on what was discussed. If you happen to stumble across someone who seems to be unusually helpful, perceptive, or informative, ask for that person's direct phone number. You might be able to cultivate an "inside relationship" with someone, and take advantage of this contact in the future!

THE CONTACT HIERARCHY

We have a "short list" of preferred methods for dealing with vendors that can also save you lots of time and energy (not to mention money, if this strategy will let you avoid making lots of long-distance phone calls). Here goes.

1. Always try e-mail first, especially if you can get pointers about how to contact individuals at an organization using e-mail. It's fast, cheap, reliable, and includes a built-in "paper trail" of the information exchanged.

2. If you're looking for technical information and e-mail isn't doing the trick, find out if the vendor has a "faxback service." In many cases, vendors publish large libraries of technical information (often based on the most frequently asked questions in technical support) as a service to their customers. All you have to do to use such a service is make a call to a voice menu system, pick the document you want, and give the faxback server your phone number. It will do the rest (we've found this to be an invaluable source of technical information, especially during tricky or fouled-up installations or upgrades).

3. If you need to call a vendor, always try a vendor's toll-free number first, if it has one published, no matter what you're calling about. Even if the number says "orders only" or "sales only" it's still worth a try. You'd be surprised how many vendors are willing to pay for your calls, if you only try this approach.

4. Don't be afraid of voice mail; if you can't get someone live, leave a brief message (less than 30 seconds is best, stating the basic facts:

"Hello, my name is Mary Muir; I am having a problem with your Quack product's installation. Please call me at 512-555-1314 as soon as possible."). If you do get voice mail, and have a real emergency, don't be afraid to press 0 on your phone to see if you can get the operator back. Otherwise, call back and ask to speak to someone else (if necessary explain that it's an emergency and you've already tried "Fred Boggs").

5. Use "snail mail" only as last resort. Letters have an uncanny way of getting lost inside large companies, especially if they're not addressed to someone in particular. If you must use the mail, reread our "department breakdown" from the preceding section and address your correspondence to the "Marketing Department" (if that's appropriate) rather than simply to "Company X." Be sure to provide a phone number or e-mail address in your correspondence; if you do get an answer, it'll come back much faster through either one of these channels than through regular mail.

Getting the information you need from a vendor can sometimes be an exercise in frustration. But if you're persistent, polite, and try as many avenues of approach as possible, ultimately you'll get what you need. If you follow some of our tips, we sincerely hope it will help to speed up your quests!

SUMMARY

In this appendix, we've tried to provide some pointers for contacting vendors, and some reasons why they may be worth the effort. If you use the vendor list information from Appendix B, the list of networking resources in Appendix C, and the on-line resources and approaches mentioned in Appendix D, it's our fond hope that you'll never even have to pick up the telephone. But if you do, it's nice to know what to do, and what to ask for!

INDEX